BLOOD
AND
OIL

ALSO BY MANUCHER FARMANFARMAIAN

Considerations on the Problems of Oil
Travels to Persia

BLOOD
AND
OIL

A Prince's Memoir of Iran,
from the Shah to the Ayatollah

MANUCHER FARMANFARMAIAN
AND
ROXANE FARMANFARMAIAN

RANDOM HOUSE TRADE PAPERBACKS
NEW YORK

2005 Random House Trade Paperback Edition

Copyright © 1997 by Manucher Farmanfarmaian and Roxane Farmanfarmaian
Introduction copyright © 2005 by Roxane Farmanfarmaian
Map copyright © 1997 by Anita Karl and Jim Kemp

Published in the United States by Random House Trade Paperbacks,
an imprint of The Random House Publishing Group,
a division of Random House, Inc., New York.

RANDOM HOUSE TRADE PAPERBACKS and colophon
are trademarks of Random House, Inc.

Originally published in hardcover in the United States by Random House,
an imprint of The Random House Publishing Group,
a division of Random House, Inc., in 1997, and subsequently in paperback by Modern Library,
an imprint of The Random House Publishing Group, a division of Random House, Inc.,
in 1999 in slightly different form.

All photographs reprinted herein are from the authors' personal collection.

Library of Congress Cataloging-in-Publication data
Farmānfarmā 'iyān, Manūchihr.
[Az Tihrān tā Kārākās. English]
Blood and oil: a prince's memoir of Iran, from the Shah to the Ayatollah /
Manucher Farmanfarmaian and Roxane Farmanfarmaian.
p.   cm.
Originally published: New York: Random House, 1997.
Includes index.
ISBN: 0-8129-7508-1
1. Farmānfarmā 'iyān, Manūchihr.   2. Statesmen—Iran-Biography.
3. Iran—Politics and government—1925–1979.   4. Petroleum industry
and trade—Iran—History—20th century.   I. Farmanfarmaian, Roxane.
II. Title.
DS316.9.F377A313   1999
955.05'092—dc21   98-55537

Printed in the United States of America

www.atrandom.com

246897531

Book design by Jo Anne Metsch

To my mother and father,
and to my three children,
Roxane, Alexander, and Teymour
— MANUCHER FARMANFARMAIAN

To my mother and father, my son, Kian,
and the Farmanfarmaian family
— ROXANE FARMANFARMAIAN

You have only to endure to conquer.
You have only to persevere to save yourselves.
—Sir Winston Churchill.

And other spirits there are standing apart
Upon the forehead of the age to come;
These, these will give the world another heart,
And other pulses. Hear ye not the hum
Of mighty workings in a distant mart?
Listen awhile, ye nations, and be dumb
—John Keats

CONTENTS

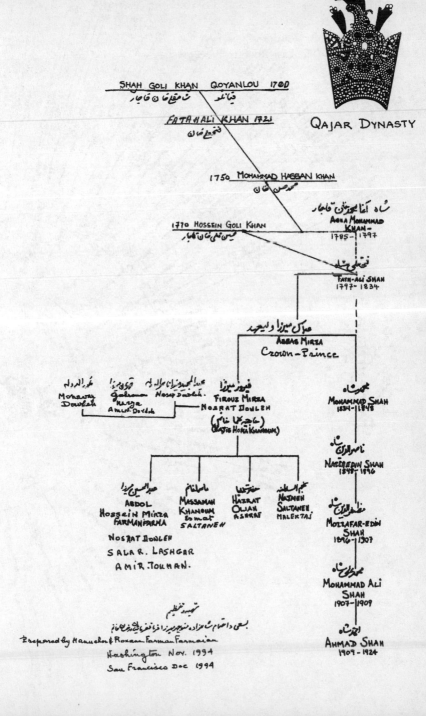

QAJAR DYNASTY

SHAH GOLI KHAN QOYANLOU 1700
قیانلو   شاه‌قلی‌خان ۵ قاجار

FATH ALI KHAN 1721
فتح‌علی‌خان

1750 MOHAMMAD HASSAN KHAN
محمد حسن خان

1770 HOSSEIN GOLI KHAN
حسین قلی‌خان قاجار

شاه آغا محمد خان قاجار
AGHA MOHAMMAD KHAN
1785 - 1797

فتح‌علی‌شاه
FATH-ALI SHAH
1797 - 1834

عباس میرزا ولیعهد
ABBAS MIRZA
Crown-Prince

غیور میرزا   FIROUZ MIRZA
NOSRAT DOWLEH
(حاجیه‌نیا خانم)
(HADJIE HODA KHANOUM)

خیرالدوله   ملک‌زاده‌میرزا   عبدالمجید‌میرزا‌حاج‌علی...   غیور میرزا
MOHAVAR   Galirousa   Nosr Dowleh   Hadja
DOWLEH   Narya   Amir-Dowleh
           Amir-Dowlch

عبدالحسین میرزا   ماه‌سلطان   حضرت‌علیا   نجم‌السلطنه
ABDOL   MASSAMEH   HAZRAT   NAJMEH
HOSSEIN MIRZA   KHANOUM   OLIAH   SALTANEH
FARMANFARMA   Esmat   ASHRAF   MALEKTAJ
              SALTANEH

NOSRAT DOWLEH
SALA R. LASHGAR
AMIR TOUMAN.

محمد شاه
MOHAMMAD SHAH
1834 - 1848

ناصرالدین‌شاه
NASSEREDIN SHAH
1848 - 1896

مظفرالدین‌شاه
MOZZAFAR-EDIN
SHAH
1896 - 1907

محمد علی‌شاه
MOHAMMAD ALI
SHAH
1907 - 1909

احمدشاه
AHMAD SHAH
1909 - 1924

تهیه و تنظیم
بسعی و اهتمام شاهزاده منوچهر میرزا و خانم رکسانه فرمانفرما خانم
Prepared by Manuchor & Roxane Farman Farmaian
Washington Nov. 1994
San Francisco Dec 1994

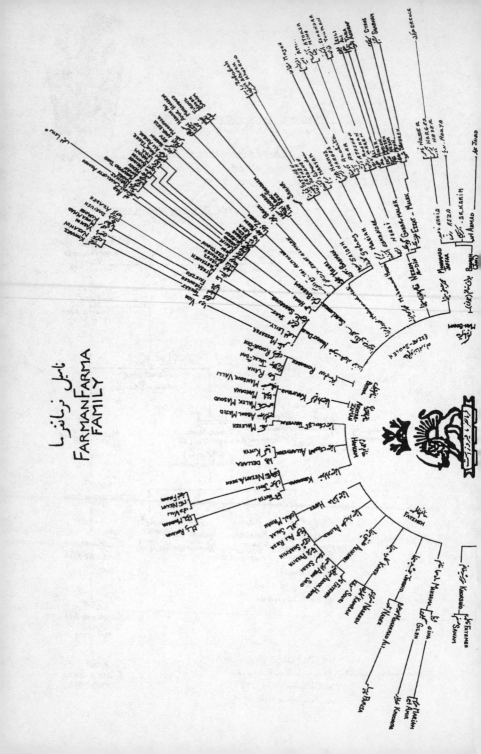

FarmanFarma
FAMILY

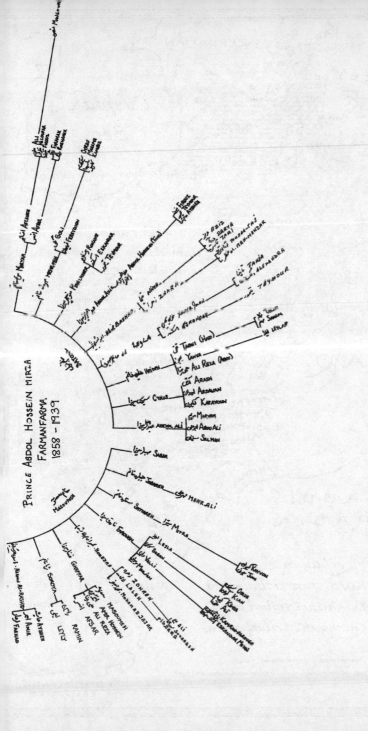

Prince Abdol Hossein Mirza
FARMANFARMA
1858 - 1939

Prepared by Manucher & Roxane Farman Farmaian
Washington Nov. 1994
San Francisco Dec 1994

TURKEY

ARMENIA

AZERBAIJAN

AZERB.

Van

Caspian
Sea

Tabriz

Rezaiyeh

Mianeh

SYRIA

Rasht

ZAGROS

ELBORZ MTS.

Tehran

Tigris R.

Hamadan

Kermanshah

Qom

Euphrates R.

Arak

Kashan

Baghdad

MTS.

IRAQ

Masjed
Soleyman
(oil field)

Isfahan

Yazd

Shatt-
al-Arab

Ahwaz

Persepolis
(ruins)

Basra

Khorramshahr

Abadan

Shiraz

KUWAIT

KHARG I.

Bushir

SAUDI
ARABIA

Persian
Gulf

Azerbaijan

Kurdistan tribal area

Bakhtiari tribal area

Qashgahi tribal area

BAHRAIN

KISH I.

Kms. ───────── 300

QATAR

Miles 0 ───────── 300

UNITED ARAB
EMIRATES

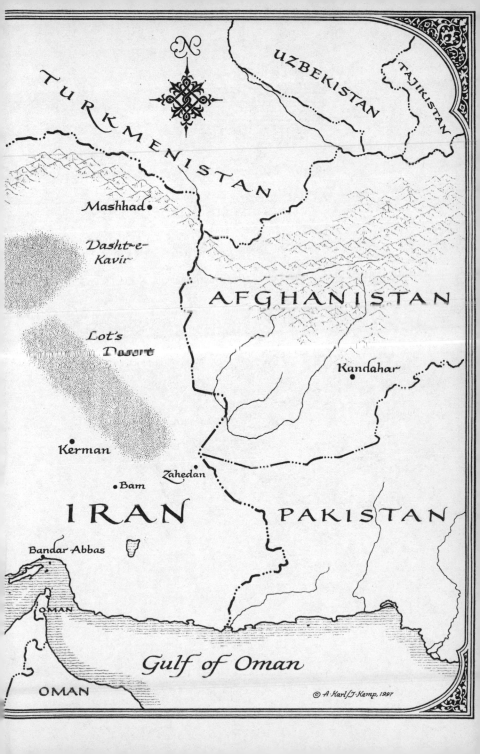

INTRODUCTION

ROXANE FARMANFARMAIAN

Cambridge 2005

The "I" in this book is my father's. He lived just long enough to witness the events of 9/11 and to hear President George W. Bush pronounce Iran a member of the Axis of Evil in February 2002. He took a long view of these developments in what would turn out to be the last year of his life. He'd witnessed too many wars and coups and other cataclysms of human artifice to be easily impressed. We walked around his garden terrace in Caracas as he snipped the dead blooms off the bougainvillea in the fall of that year. He was eighty-five. Having spent his life as a political actor and commentator, he admitted he must at last be getting old, for nothing surprised him anymore. The long, lurid drama between the United States and Iran, a tango between two old lovers who now only knew how to face each other with knives in their teeth, had been going on for almost twenty-five years. As in any good play—he particularly liked those by Shakespeare—there were kings and fools, whether they wore crowns or turbans or gave presidential speeches; moments of comic relief (as when England played in the World Cup football finals in Tehran in 2001) and moments of chivalry (such as the citywide silence in Tehran for the victims of 9/11); and too few women on the set for his taste (he died before Shirin Ebadi won the Nobel Prize), but lots of intrigue to make up for it. He considered this drama a tragedy, undoubtedly as much a personal one as one taking place on the international stage. He never looked back on Iran once he left. He simply turned and strode the other way.

My father never expected the Ayatollahs' grip to loosen quickly. The revolution brought a great gift to Iranians: the awareness that as people they had power, which for the first time gave them a sense of citizenship. The Shah never did that. This fact should not be taken lightly; it acts as the tipping point of public support for the Ayatollaen regime, even in the face of the arbitrary exercise of internal power. It rallies Iranians around their country, right or wrong; it feeds the spirit of patriotism. This is something Americans feel instinctively, too. It's what connected Democrats to Republicans in the U.S. Congress when they decided to attack Afghanistan after 9/11. It's what unites Reformists with Conservatives in the Iranian parliament (Majles) when it comes to developing a nuclear bomb. The different Iranian parties disagree on the specifics, of course—how to reveal the bomb, and when, and to whom? Yet the fact that there is discussion within the system is appreciated by the public. Little of substance was ever debated in the Shah's Majles.

Iranians have always considered theirs a special country. It's not just a matter of having an old culture; it's more about an innate approach to the world. They feel themselves unique, but also enviable; they feel that they have power over those around them, but that they are also benevolent. Once again, this is something that Americans feel in a similar way. Today, surrounded by American troops, with tumult in Iraq to the west and tribal standoff in Afghanistan to the east, it is Iran that has taken in the refugees from both sides—one million since 1985. Iran does not attack its neighbors. It hasn't sent an army out as an invasionary force since 1847. The fighting it gets involved with for the most part takes place on its own land; this is something Iranians have seen many times, and for millennia. At the center of the Silk Road, they were overrun by Alexander the Great's army, attacked by the Roman Legions, occupied by the Mongol Hordes, invaded by Islamic warriors from Mecca and Medina—and each time, Iranians were like a hollow log in the middle of the stream, always holding their shape while the waters flowed through. Iran was at the pivot of "The Great Game" between Queen Victoria's Britain, czarist Russia, and the crumbling Ottoman Empire—and it played the game with such consummate skill that the Qajar Dynasty was described by all three as corrupt and deceiving, a reputation that has lasted to this day. Now, once again, Iran is considered a source of evil, this time by the West, a menace within the War on Terror. For Iranians this is déjà vu. They know what to do; they've done it before. They will rally around their own leaders when they're threatened from the outside—whether they like them or not.

Besides, it's an issue of pride. Iranians are proud to be a people that chooses its own government. They've never accepted change from the outside, as neither would Americans, of course. Hell of one's own making is infinitely preferable to the promise of heaven dangled from outside. And, as these pages unfold, the record in Iran shamefully reveals that the heavens imposed by those in offices thousands of miles away never congeal into local halcyons. The 1956 coup that overthrew Mohammad Mossadeq, my father's cousin and a complicated, controversial man but nonetheless the first democratically elected prime minister, is still part of Iranians' long collective memory. To have a democracy snatched away and replaced by an absolute monarchy becomes the stuff of legend—a variation on David and Goliath that is told and retold to children as they go to bed at night. This is why Iranians remember. It is not just a question of saving face; it is a question of holding their ground.

It's a pity that political participation is not more trusted by the clerical leadership. Their fear eclipses what successes have taken place in Iran: the rise in women's literacy from 24 percent at the time of the revolution to 85 percent today; the average age for girls to marry rising to eighteen, despite the law that allows marriage at nine; the building of the metro; the paving over of the potholes that so disfigured the towns; the development of homegrown industries in the vacuum left by U.S. economic sanctions; the flourishing of an economy that has diversified away from oil. In part, these positive changes occurred because of Iran's long drawn-out war with Iraq—the First Gulf War, in essence—and, more to the point, the first war to usher in the post—Cold War era. Saddam Hussein was Iran's enemy long before he became a Hitler to Americans. It is a shame that the Persian press is not allowed to flourish, for Iranians love to talk, play with words, tell tales, gossip through poetry, and dress up political views in jokes. It is also a shame that Americans do not read the Iranian press, for even in its reduced form they would come to understand a lot about a place they distrust so much. It is censorship from within and without, and it makes for murky politics. Yet would greater clarity reveal a way through the torturous byways when it is the similarities between Iranians and Americans that cause as much conflict as those aspects that are different? In the evening of his life, my father would have seen Baudelaire's *"mon semblable, mon frère"* (from *Les Fleurs du Mal*) as grounds for optimism, rather than interpreting it as the irony of resemblance. I, on the other hand, am not so sure. I am more prone to take on board the first two words of that famous line, *"hypocrite lecteur,"* as I always wonder whether what we *want* to read or see doesn't often trump reality.

THE TALE OF A FATHER AND DAUGHTER

I am much less cheerful than my father was about how the tangled skeins of politics and religion, of oil and water, of power, and of land, will unknot themselves in the region of Iran. My father was a perennial optimist about the way of the world in general, and the United States in particular. For him, the United States, for all its missteps, embodied Hope, continually reinventing itself as an engineering miracle, a thrumming motor that naturally drove the world. It was one of the issues that divided us as we wrote this book together, as each evening in the tropical dusk we discussed the day's pages coming off my computer. We both found it strange that I, the younger generation and half American, would represent a view so generally pessimistic, while he—and he always claimed he typified his friends who were his age—would always imagine a reprieve, and further flowering. Our search was for common ground, and that ground was Iran. In the process we discovered ourselves to be engagingly alike—and disconcertingly unalike. For a long time we fought about many things brought up by the book, and his life, and mine. Iran became a testing ground for who we were and who we had become.

When we began this project we were not friends. I was an ambitious Western journalist living the independent New York high life; he was the Eastern patriarch holding court of sorts in Caracas, with (what I considered) contradictory views toward women and a heavy-handed approach to parenting daughters. When I first came down to Caracas to begin writing the memoirs, we circled around each other like cats, wary and suspicious. We spoke in stilted tones; there were long silences at dinner; he didn't understand why I pursued such details as the color of people's hair, the meaning of royal titles, the exact dates that events really took place. His view was that this was to be purely a personal recounting, a diary of a life. And at first it was. I considered this book his, and my attitudes and goals to have nothing to do with it. I was just the scribe, and would write my own book on Iran later. Only slowly did I come to realize that here was a chance to capture a many-tiered world that no longer existed, a complex world that only he had access to through memory. This world was my past as well as his, and the past of my brothers and cousins, and of my son and my son's sons and daughters to come, a past that was not on the public record, that was not part of institutional memory. And so my father and I passed on to the next stage—from standoff to battle.

We argued most about the Shah. Today it has become more commonplace to view the Pahlavi era as troubled, maladroit, wasteful, arrogant— but not then, when the wounds of Mohammad Reza Shah's friendless roaming about the globe before his death added great pathos to the revolution's memory. For my father, who embodied the deep Persian aristocratic belief in honor and respect for the symbolism of power, the Shah might indeed have been someone ill-suited for the job, but as long as he was on the throne he was the sovereign, the emblem of the nation, and hence worthy of deference and esteem. Besides, my father, as an ambassador, had not only represented Iran but had personally represented the

Shah. He had hosted him in Caracas; at times, he had even been his friend. There was a special connection in that.

I, on the other hand, judged the Shah through no such lens, but simply on his merits. To me, as a woman educated in the 1970s in the United States, his performance was poor: Tehran was filled with palaces and slums; the press was vacuous under the heavy hand of censorship; the oil wealth had been squandered on advanced F-16s and heavy Cobra tanks designed for swamps, not deserts. The towns were in ruins; the streets, even the one in front of our posh apartment block, were deeply rutted; the central squares were dry wastelands where children played in the dust. Out in the countryside the villagers still farmed with donkeys and used rope to keep their trousers up because they had no belts. My father and I battled because each of us was a witness, and each of us was responsible for the record we were setting down. Even recalling the same memory, we saw different things: for example, he would picture a street filled with cars, many of which were being produced in Iran itself and running on gas that was being refined near the southern oil fields. He felt a sense of achievement, something he shared with all the rest of the Iranians on that street, content behind the wheels of their locally made Peykans and Renaults. Meanwhile, I would remember the same street as packed with cars that were dented and decrepit, drivers running red lights because there was no policeman maintaining the law, a beggar hunched against one of the walls, pedestrians picking their way through the broken sidewalks—and I would feel dismayed, and filled with a sense of failure.

It took us some time to accept that neither of our views was completely true. It was only in listening, at times painfully, to each other, and often stomping off to take a breather, since all of this was proving much more emotionally wearing than either of us wanted to admit, that we gradually came to paint a picture that was more rounded, that we could both live with. At last, we ended up with a portrait of the Shah that was neither too heroic nor too bumbling, a rendering of a human being who was inexorably driven by love of his country. Khomeini, too, became a man, neither messianic nor diabolic, a man who had a wife and sons, and who also, to the risk of all else, loved his country deeply. Strangely, for both of us, it was our beloved country that proved so elusive. As my father and I wrote about Iran we lived outside it. We speak and write of Iranians as "they," as well as "us." It is the curse of the emigrant.

Sometime in the midst of this, my father and I began to laugh together. The book acted as a catharsis for us both: his life, his soul, my soul, my pen. Sometime in the midst of this, we became friends. And his story—and all its vast world—passed into mine.

PROLOGUE

Caracas 1995

In the afternoon I come home from the factory and sit on the terrace. I putter among my plants with their large tropical leaves and am at peace. There is always a small breeze. In the dusk Caracas takes on the reflection of paradise.

I take great pride in my factory. I have always loved machines. After supervising the great oil refineries of Iran for so many years, I developed a hankering for my own operation. Now I produce potato chips. The banging and whooshing of the machines sounds as beautiful to me as the symphonies of Mozart or Beethoven. My chips come off the belt like gold coins. The bags are all over Venezuela now. On the front is my emblem, a laughing Persian lion holding up a sword. The sun peeks from behind his mane. It is my salute to the old country. It is also my talisman for creating a successful life in this one.

Coming back to Caracas after being an ambassador to Venezuela was not easy. As a Greek colleague, now the ambassador to the United States, once said, "Your glittering parties were famous." (He had heard of them only secondhand.) "Twelve years later people still remember your flamboyance. Even so you come back and realize most of the people you thought were friends were just shadows at your door. It is that way everywhere." He is right. Coming back meant returning as a has-been. Even more painful, I was an Iranian returning after Ayatollah Khomeini's violent revolution, and that meant seeing dismay in the eyes of even my best friends. The worst were those who thought I might beg them for some favor. "How are

you, Manucher?" they'd ask with no interest, hoping to get through the interview without having to write me a check. I could see the fear in their
faces. "Better off than you," I'd say, winking at their secretaries and turning for the door.

Yet every time I get off the plane at the Caracas airport I bend to kiss
the ground. This country has been good to me. It gave me a new life. One
of my most loyal friends during the halcyon days was the president, Rafael
Caldera. Right after I arrived he was voted out of office. Still, I invited him
to visit Iran, and I told him if the state did not pay, I would. "It is strange,"
he said. "No one has come to see me since I left the presidency. Now, Ambassador, not only do you come, but you invite me to your country." In Iran
he met the Shah and saw the beauties of Shiraz and Isfahan. He visited the
oil refinery in Abadan. It was a favor Caldera did not forget. When I was
without a nation, stripped of my properties, a refugee fleeing from Ayatollah Khomeini, Caldera offered to help get me citizenship. What a gift. The
announcement of new Venezuelan nationals always comes out in the paper
in rigid alphabetical order. That day my name was tacked on at the end
under the Z's.

I arrived in my new country in August 1981. Although Venezuela is
lush and new, while Iran is arid and ancient, the two are uncannily similar.
The smell of the dust after the rain sometimes makes me draw my breath,
for it is the smell of the spring streets of Tehran. There are hallways here
that have their twins back there, the hallways of middle-class apartment
buildings built after the oil boom, with the same sandy-colored tiles
flecked with bits of stone.

It's not only nostalgia that makes me notice such things. The two countries are both oil meccas and have gone through the same rapid development. Their capital cities are filled with smog and snarled traffic and ugly
high-rise buildings. Nothing is adequately planned, and money is wasted.
Venezuela, despite being a democracy, a free-market capitalist state, and a
friend and neighbor of the United States, is as deaf as Iran to the thrum of
the future. In Caracas as in Tehran there are water shortages, the telephone
system is fragile, and there is no mail service to speak of. The people complain but do not really mind. Most have never known a system that
worked. It is the classic third-world problem: They live badly on what they
have.

Yet proximity to the United States and its own vast natural resources
have helped Venezuela to walk more readily along the path of the world.
It is not burdened by the pride of history. I find this refreshing. Everyone
plunders the country and sends the profits abroad. When foreign companies do the same, the people do not feel cheated. The collective aspiration

is to get rich and move to Miami. You may laugh, but as a third-world goal it is much more attainable than the Shah's delusions of becoming the fifth most developed power in the world.

Even so, Venezuela does not escape suspicion. Down the street the United States has constructed a new embassy. The entire top of a hill has been leveled. The building sprawls across it like a fortress of liver-colored stone, the land dividing it from its far-off neighbors stripped and cemented. Every time I see it my heart quails. To me it bodes ill to see this lone and barricaded building rising from the slopes of this small, democratic, neighborly nation. Why build a fortress on the land of one's friends? The Venezuelans are amazed at the amount of money that's been spent. They feel America does not trust them. They feel pushed around. It makes me question whether the United States learned anything from the fiasco in Iran.

A few days ago I was invited to dinner at the Finnish Embassy. The house was one I once owned. It lies just up the road from the embassy residence I lived in when I represented the Shah and my country. I bought the house on a whim. Thank God! It was one of the few assets left to me when I walked out of Iran in 1980 across the Turkish border with nothing but a suitcase. On the way to dinner I passed the old residence I'd spent five such happy years in. I'd named it Persepolis. Now it's called Omat, the Arabic word for "people." Each time I see it I am affronted. At the very least, could not a Persian word have been found for the one building that represents the country in this foreign land? At the ambassador's yearly reception on February 12 marking the birth of the Islamic Republic, the women are consigned to a separate floor upstairs. No alcohol is served. The atmosphere is tense. Not surprisingly, few of the diplomatic community go. But I have made a point these many years of attending. The place has gone to seed. Much of it now is office space. The dining room is a dorm. The ambassadors are always young and speak no foreign language. They think they have a religious mission here. We greet each other warily. Like everyone else, I am a stranger in their house.

Over drinks at the Finnish Embassy I find myself being eyed by a tall, predatory woman. She turns out to be the wife of the Romanian ambassador.

"Everyone had such hopes for the new government," she says, referring to Rafael Caldera's recent surprise presidential victory after twenty years of being out of office. "But," and she looks disappointed, "Venezuela seems only to be getting worse."

I am not interested in talking politics. I think Caldera will stumble through, but he is too old, like me, for such a job. I am more taken by the way her dress falls into the curve of her bosom. I want to make advances, find out what terrain I'm in. I catch myself. "Every country gets the government it deserves," I say.

She purses her lips.

"Venezuela is not civilized," I add. "It's the jungle. What did you expect?"

"Not civilized," she echoes. "Unlike Iran," she says seductively. I damn her persistence. "Now *that* was a civilized country—under the Shah."

"Civilized?" I mock her. "Iran was never civilized. You make a mistake. It's got culture, of course. But it is not civilized. It's backward. And it was backward under the Shah. It too got what it deserved."

By the way her eyes widen I can tell I've shocked her. I am pleased. I like shocking people. It makes for better conversation. The ambassadress gathers herself together with admirable speed. "What about you then?" she asks. "What about you and all the rest of the elite, the poets, the artists . . ."

"They're gone," I say curtly. "And even they weren't civilized." I venture to put my hand on her elbow. "Watching television, wearing blue jeans, drinking Coca-Cola—that's being modern, not civilized. Few read books or collected art. We were not patrons. Our European educations went only skin deep. Their gloss washed off the minute we returned to Iran. We did not bring discipline or order to our country. We allowed ourselves to live surrounded by ignorance. We were decadent, like the lords of the ancien régime. But instead of Napoleon we got Khomeini."

"Why?" she asks. "What went wrong?"

Even as she asks the question, the host takes her arm and squires her in to dinner. She casts a long glance over her bare shoulder. There was a time I would have signaled the waiter to bring me a scotch and belted it down before facing her at dinner. But those days are gone. I am seventy-seven. I don't have the energy anymore. I've turned my back on Iran. I've finally left her to her wounds.

What went wrong? I have been asked that ever since I left Iran. For years I evaded the question. I knew I would only sound bitter. What's more, the eagerness in people's eyes turned my stomach. They did not want to know what really happened. If I spoke of the mistakes made by their own countries in Iran, they turned a deaf ear. They wanted to hear horror stories, exotic gossip to pass on about the frightening face of Islamic fanaticism. They wanted to hear condemnations—and condemnations only.

I refused. Pride held my tongue. And shame. I needed to regroup, send down new roots before I could speak of Iran. Many dear friends were killed in the bloodbath of the revolution. For eight years after the revolution two of my brothers wallowed in Khomeini's prisons, and I rationalized silence as imperative to their protection. By the time they were released, events had overtaken even my own experience in Iran: Its new martyrs were acting as minesweepers in the war with Iraq, Iran-Contra was in full swing, Salman Rushdie was a hunted man. At every turn Iran amazed and traumatized the world. And yet unlike Iraq it never invaded its neighbors. Unlike Syria it holds elections for its president and Parliament. Unlike Saudi Arabia it allows women to work and drive. No matter. Over the years its partiality for assassinations in Paris and its funding of the Hezbollah in Lebanon have further blackened its image. Outstripping Cuba and Libya, it has become the pariah of the world.

Each new revelation of Iran's excesses sickens me. But I do not blame Iran alone. I also blame England and the United States. This is not a case of isolated lunacy. Even now I see the same festering anger growing in easygoing Venezuela, in the violent outbursts in Somalia and Egypt, in the attitude of the well-heeled Asian nations that balked at what they called the imposition of Western norms at the Human Rights Conference in Vienna in 1993. Call it what you will: the malady of third-world servility, the David and Goliath syndrome, the maddening inability of those with power to learn from their mistakes.

Today Iran tops the list of Washington's "rogue nations." But the superpowers did much to mold it into what it has become. Iran is where the double standard of international politics finally came home to roost. It is not a simple story.

I have watched Iran for more than fifty years as it has reeled and stumbled from one cataclysm to the next. The first shah to fall under British pressure was my second cousin, the last of the Qajar line, which had ruled Persia for 140 years. He wanted to be a constitutional monarch. The failing British empire wanted a dictator. Its ministers considered it easier to deal with one man than an independent parliament—a policy they followed throughout the Middle East. It was just after World War I. The candidate they chose was Reza Shah, the first of the short-lived Pahlavi dynasty, a soldier who had worked for my father.

From then on my family was perpetually in and out of power and a constant discomfort to the throne. We formed a clan—blue-blooded, educated, the wellspring of a harem. Even in Iran we were unusual. There was not a major event that took place in the span of this century where one of us was not prominent on the scene. Seven of my siblings or close cousins served at one time or another in the cabinet. My brother Khodadad headed the Central Bank for a while. One of my sisters founded the School of Social Work and introduced family planning into Iran. Another married the head of the Communist Party. Four of my brothers started banks, among them the Bank of Tehran, the largest private bank in the country. Two were generals in the army. My brother Aziz founded the largest architectural firm in the Middle East; he built the airport and the Shah's own Niavaran Palace. There were so many of us that at parties visiting foreign dignitaries would hear our name repeated so often that they would mistakenly think it a form of salutory address and start saying Farmanfarmaian themselves as they made their introductions and shook hands.

We thought it amusing. We were used to the Farmanfarmaian name being magic. Once while traveling in Pakistan I was offered a good deal on a number of Greco-Buddhist statuettes. I was a thousand miles and a country away from the border of Iran. The man wanted cash. I couldn't pay. He asked me my name. When I told him he grinned. "I know that name," he said. "I'll give you credit." He lent me $5,000 that day.

Although there were times when we were genuinely close to the royal family, our relationship with the Pahlavis was always charged. For good reason they never stopped being suspicious. Three times we were credited with threatening the throne, and each time they held on to it only through foreign intervention. We represented a side of Iran they could never tap— the gossamer web of loyalty between landlord and peasant, and between landlord and tribe.

Why do I understand the actions of Iran today? Because I know her underbelly. I can tell you why her xenophobia toward the West exceeds that of any other country in the world. I have seen it grow like wheat in my own fields. I have seen the men who sowed it: smart English colonels with whips and colonial mentalities just off the boat from India; fresh-faced Americans from the Point Four Program who had never worked the land but who, with the best of intentions, counseled the peasants to change what had worked for a thousand years and instead store their grain the way they did in Iowa. When the villagers were beaten like oxen and their grain rotted, when they saw British and American troops impound their bread and march across their land to protect them from the threat of communism—is it any wonder that they felt cheated and used and wrote "Yankee go home" on their mud village walls?

Democracy, human rights. To the common Iranian these words just mean more famine, poverty, and corruption. To the intellectuals they mean two-faced political intrusion. Why did President Jimmy Carter tell the Shah to improve his human rights record, they ask, when he never uttered a word to England about getting out of Gibraltar? Why has the United States still never told Saudi Arabia to free its women? Unlike the simple appeal of communism, which told the poor to kill the rich and take the land, democracy could never muster grassroots enthusiasm in places like

Iran. In all my life I have yet to see a spontaneous popular demonstration for democracy. It's too complicated a creed. It requires professional politicians and organized media.

What's happening now in Iran has all happened before. I've seen it two, three times—the violent separation from a superpower, the shudder to live up to its own sense of sovereignty, the shattering disappointment. When Mohammad Mossadeq, my cousin, ran the Shah out of Iran in the 1950s and nationalized oil, his actions were as ill-conceived and as regressive as any of Ayatollah Khomeini's. Iran was as isolated then as it is now. Opposition was silenced by threat of assassination or, worse, public accusation of collusion with the British government. Many in London and Washington thought Mossadeq was a madman. He wasn't. He tried to do good by Iran. He was loved by the people. He evinced a simple honesty the Shah never attained. He permanently evicted the British from the oil fields. But in all else he failed.

In Iran the wounds are still open. In a country that rebuffed the Romans in the third century and took the emperor Valerian prisoner, a country that redefined the Arabs' Islam and made it its own, nothing is done halfheartedly. Yet in Washington, London, and the United Nations, the slate has been cleaned by collective amnesia. Events have moved on. To most Americans the Khomeini era is so bizarre it's inexplicable. They don't care that it's the most recent chapter of a long history. Some don't even know the difference between Persia and Peru. "You're from Persia?" said the man next to me on a plane not long ago. "That's next to Colombia, right?" Yes, I nodded, and left it at that.

Am I saying that Iranians are not responsible for their actions? I would never say that. We are our own greatest victims. It is a question of perspective. Westerners have never heard it from the Iranian point of view. Quotes from the Iranian papers never make it into the New York or London *Times*. You would understand more if they did. You would know, for instance, that there is more to the story of oil. For us it is as much a curse as a treasure. You would know that tons and tons of it were stolen, wasted, fought over, that people died mysteriously, that millions of dollars disappeared. The accounts were all in my files at the Ministry of Finance when I was director of concessions. Later, when I was on the board of the National Iranian Oil Company, I showed our numbers to other oil-producing nations. They were appalled. That is why my signature was at the top of the protocol that created OPEC, the Organization of Petroleum Exporting Countries. This is a matter of public record. The notes and numbers are in the British national archives, typed in carbon on dusty onionskin. Today the only ones who read them are angry Iranian students—and people digging up the past, like me.

Every once in a while my children ask me what properties we still have back in Iran. They hope to return sometime and reclaim what is rightfully theirs. I know they've had their heritage cut off at the knees. They feel a rootlessness, a gap in their lives that Venezuela has filled for me but not for them. Nonetheless I cannot bring myself to sit down and make them a list. It all seems so pointless. My elder brother still lives in Tehran in my father's old summer house. It has been his home for fifty years. He does not dare leave even on a short vacation. If he does, the revolutionary guards have warned him they will move in.

But a country is like a woman—no matter how ugly, it always has its lovely angles. That is why I am finally telling the story. "Persians don't write memoirs," said one of my earliest mentors many years ago in London. "They are not like the British, whose adventurers and ambassadors have written whole libraries for their countrymen to read." From that moment on I decided to leave behind a record. All my life I collected files. When these were abruptly lost during the revolution, I was left with only my recollections. At the time they seemed woefully thin. I am an engineer. I'm used to backing up my statements. That's my Western side, drilled into me by my very English education. My Eastern side pushes me to spin the tale. As the sun sets over the terrace I go inside and begin to talk to my daughter. Together we find the right words. That too has been a revelation. It is not in my nature to talk so to a woman. I am a man who lives alone and thinks alone. Nevertheless, as the story of my country has unfolded night after night, we have become friends. If I cannot give her the earth of her country, at least I've been able to share with her the lost world in my mind.

She asks me to warn you of one thing. The tales are all true, but they are like kaleidoscopes: Turn them a different way, and you see a different set of images.

I will tell you a story. It is about a friend of mine, a landlord with property just over the hill from our place in the western district of Kermanshah. It was winter and he sat chilled and lonely in front of his fire. Toward evening his servant announced that a traveling poet was at the door.

"Show him in," said the landlord, suddenly cheered at the thought of company. He ordered sweets and hot tea, and when the visitor appeared, he motioned him to a cushion next to his own.

The evening passed quickly after that, for the poet was entertaining and adept with his rhymes. When at last the evening wore down, the poet got to his feet and, bowing, spoke a final ode to the landlord, complimenting him lavishly for his wisdom and grace and praising him beyond all others for his generosity.

The landlord was moved. "How sweet are your words," he said. "For that I will grant you a hectare's worth of spring wheat in gold when it is harvested from my fields."

Now it was the poet's turn to be moved. He fell to his knees and kissed the landlord's robe. Each parted that evening with a bright glow in his heart.

In late July the poet returned to the estate. He walked down the road with a strut, for he knew he would soon be a rich man. At the castle gate he demanded loudly to see the landlord.

"I've come to collect my hectare's worth of wheat in gold," he announced, throwing himself to the ground when the landlord appeared. "You do remember that cold night when we shared a few hours of poetry together?"

The landlord looked at him blankly. Then his brow cleared. "Of course I remember," he said. "And what a cold night that was. But why did you say you've come back?"

"To collect the gold, sir, which you promised me that night," answered the poet.

"Ah," said the landlord. "But that was winter and now it's spring. Get up and be off with you, dear poet. You said something to please me that night, and I said something nice to please you. Though you did not really believe all those glowing things you said to me, I went to bed feeling good indeed. I felt so fine, in fact, I wanted you to feel good too. And so, because I'm a landlord not a poet, I promised you a harvest of wheat, hoping the thought of all that gold would give you pleasant dreams."

BLOOD
AND
OIL

ESCAPE FROM THE
AYATOLLAH

Dark night, fearful of the waves and whirlpools, such a fragile craft. What do they know of what we feel, those easy travelers on the shore!

—HAFEZ

Tehran 1979

The house already looked abandoned. Behind the high garden walls the upstairs windows were shuttered. The striped awning over the balcony's arched colonnades had been rolled up, revealing a patch of whiter paint where the house had been protected from the sun. I waited a long time at the gate after honking, not daring to honk again. At last the doors swung open. The old gardener stepped out suddenly with a little bow. I searched his face to see if he was one of the loyal ones, or if he had turned coat. His weak smile gave nothing away. I nodded as I drove past, but he was already scuttling into the back to give the alert that I had arrived.

My brother Khodadad answered the door himself. He looked worn and peered at me through red eyes. The grayness of sleepless nights creased his face. As we hugged I noticed his palms were sweating, despite the cool weather. Khodadad had always been the emotional one in the family; everything in his heart was written on his face. His hair had turned iron gray, but his smile still drew women like honey. He'd aged during his short stint in prison when the Pasdaran, Khomeini's revolutionary guards, had seized him as the ex-governor of the Central Bank.

Khodi's career had been electric: chairman of the Central Bank, then head of the Plan Organization, where he crafted Iran's economic plans. He was always the one people had heard of in the West—the jovial Persian with doe eyes that they'd met at a conference at Princeton or whose long name they'd seen in academic journals or Ford Foundation reports. It rankled my own sense of pride. But now here he was, humbled, his hands shaking, anxious to leave the nightmare of Iran behind.

He spoke softly as though there were ears behind the sumptuous wallpaper of the vast hall. White sheets covered the gilt and velvet furniture, making the place look like a morgue. His American wife, Joanna, had left months before for London. Now he lived like a bachelor in only two or three rooms. I looked out the window of the library. It was Friday morning, and a quietness hung about the neighborhood. Not a car horn, not a single motorcycle, not even the voice of a child. The people were all downtown praying with the mad-voiced Ayatollah Montazeri, who led the Friday prayers from his pulpit at the university.

I didn't stay long. Khodadad fiddled with his hands. Although he didn't say anything specific, I knew it was farewell. I didn't begrudge him his silence. You didn't escape alive by telling everyone your plans. Later, when I heard he'd left that same day, it came as no surprise.

I was also thinking of leaving. Already I'd had a couple of close calls. The noose around the family was tightening. The regime was closing in, picking us off one at a time. Alinaghi and Eskandar were already languishing behind bars, poor devils. Alinaghi had practiced the anti-Islamic art of banking—charging people interest on their money. Eskandar had served the Shah as minister of the environment. How long would it be before it was my turn as an ex-director of the National Iranian Oil Company or, worse, an ambassador, a personal representative of His Imperial Majesty? Already my minister of foreign affairs, Abbas Ali Khalatbari, a gentle man who had filled the post for twelve years, had been executed.

In the months right after the revolution, Khomeini had published a list of traitors to the state. Ministers, generals, prominent members of the great families, tribal leaders, and a few big businessmen were all specified by name. Not so the Farmanfarmaians. There were too many of us. Rather than enumerate us one by one, the list referred to us simply—and devastatingly—as "the family of." In one sweep of the pen all of us, born or unborn, were damned, our bank accounts flagged for seizure, our properties claimed in perpetuity by the revolution. Barred from appearing before a notary public or appealing to a judge, we could neither sell a car nor register a marriage. Any baby born into the family would come into the world without birth certificate or right to property.

But the threatened confiscation took time to carry out. And who was pegged for arrest we did not know. Until the Pasdaran closed in we moved about easily, imagining that we could still twist fate in our favor, that the new contacts we hastened to secure might help, that somehow all of this would pass. As we sat over tea through the empty afternoons waiting for news, waiting for *something,* someone would always look up and say, "*Az een sotoon beh ahn sotoon farajeh.*" The saying comes from an old Persian story about a minister who is tied to a pillar, waiting to be executed by the caliph's soldiers. Asked if he has a last wish, he requests to be moved to the next pillar. Just as he is being untied, news arrives that the caliph has been assassinated, and instead of having his throat slashed the minister is freed. "From this pillar to the next, there can always be respite."

How blinding is the power of hope! Perhaps more than the rest of my brothers and sisters I misjudged the danger. I had been abroad for the past five years and had not witnessed the final dissipation of the Shah's regime. There simply were no more pillars.

As things got worse I tried to justify escape as a temporary solution. I could no more imagine losing my country than losing a limb. My blood was in Iran's earth, my family's name printed on pages of its history, and the results of my work poured from the wells that paid for the rings on the Shah's fingers and the turbans on the ayatollah's head. For centuries my ancestors had been buried in its ground, their bones fixed with its clay. Unlike the oil boom's new rich, who had bought flats and yachts abroad, I believed in my homeland, had invested in it, trusted it. I could not afford to renounce Iran.

Yet the fact was Khodi had just disappeared. The Pasdaran would be even more vigilant. I was an ordinary man; I did not want to be a martyr.

THE TALE OF THE PICASSO

A week later I knew the time had come. It was late October 1979 and I was visiting my brother Rashid on his estate outside town, as I had every Friday since well before the revolution nine months earlier. We rode as usual into the desert, the horses steaming in the crisp air. On the surface nothing seemed changed. Smoke curled from the village houses, the fields were neat, back at the house white-gloved servants greeted us with hot tea as we dismounted. We sat long over lunch, saying little, for Rashid was not a talkative man. As the dessert plates were being cleared we saw two men in combat garb steal across the lawn.

"You'd better go," Rashid said. "The Pasdaran came through this morning. They threatened to come back." We saw two more men emerge from the bushes, clearly having just scaled the walls.

"I can't leave you here," I said. "This is a trap. They're going to take you away."

"If that is so, I won't be able to escape now," he said dryly. "But you can. Go on. Get out of here. There's no point in their netting you too." His voice was level. In sharp contrast to Khodadad, Rashid rarely showed his feelings. Even now his movements were measured as he rose and waited for my response.

With a heavy heart I grabbed my things and headed to the car. As usual I'd parked nose out, so all I had to do was slip behind the wheel. As I hit the road an army of Pasdaran converged on the driveway and shouted at me to stop. I watched through the rearview mirror as they swarmed into the house. There was nothing I could do. Rashid was finished.

That night I heard a commotion in the hallway of my flat. By chance Rashid and I had bought apartments on the same floor in the downtown twin towers of Saman on Boulevard Elizabeth. Now, through the peephole in my door, I saw him in the hall surrounded by his captors, pushed and shoved toward his flat with the butt ends of their guns. He opened the door with resignation, his expression unspeakably sad. Leaving one gun-toting hoodlum at the door, the rest disappeared inside.

Within seconds they came pouring out again. I saw Rashid sign a paper shoved before him by one of the guards. Then, dragging him behind them, they piled into the elevator and were gone.

A wave of sickness swept over me. But though my knees shook, I could not tear myself from the peephole. Suddenly I thought of the Picasso— "my most precious possession," Rashid had said as we'd sat drinking tea in his salon just twenty-four hours before. I knew it was preposterous, but at that moment I knew I had to get it. I hurried to get my copy of Rashid's key. Again I surveyed the scene from the peephole. The hall, tiny in the reverse magnitude of the glass, was empty.

I took a deep breath and eased open the door. Expanded to its normal amplitude, the hall jumped out in front of me. The overhead light gleamed eerily. I told myself sharply that my fear was absurd and tried to shrink it down to size. But it was useless; the ringing in my ears would not go away. Twitching with the guilt of a criminal, I quickly crossed the short passage to Rashid's door. With a shaking hand I slipped the key into the lock and quickly stepped inside.

On the wall in front of me, glowing softly in the cool quiet of the flat, was the Picasso. It was a beautiful gouache whose vivid turquoises and pinks outlined a lyric Greek temple, with graceful columns hung about by nymphs. The familiarity of the apartment was heartbreaking; Rashid's voice, his smell, his step were still so present.

Shaking, I lifted the painting from its hook. If nothing else, at least I could save this for him. I would pass it to one of our sisters, those masters at spiriting our most cherished belongings out of the country.

The Picasso came almost to my waist and was unbelievably heavy. I grasped the ungainly three-by-four-foot frame and clicked the lock open with my elbow. The frame slipped through my hands and I panicked, banging a corner against the wall as I pulled the door closed with my foot. I ran down the hall, the painting jabbing painfully into my legs.

At my own door the lock jammed. I could hear the elevator begin to climb up the shaft. My fingers had turned wooden. At last the key turned. I flung open the door and kicked the painting in front of me across the threshold.

In the blessed stillness of my own apartment I leaned weakly against the door. This was the end. Such fear I could not live with.

THE TALE OF THE KURDS

My brother Cyrus was experienced in the business of escape. He'd driven Khodadad all the way to the Kurdish frontier with Turkey, a rash thing to do, typical of the madcap risks Cyrus was prone to taking—and miraculously surviving. He agreed to put me in touch with intermediaries—Kurdish "mafia"—who lived along the frontier and knew all the border posts by day and night. We could trust them, he assured me, because our mother was Kurdish, and so they trusted us. The price was 300,000 toman—$43,000—to be paid up front in cash. When I protested he explained that it was already discounted since there was the prospect of other "customers" from the family. "Group rate," he said, smiling. With a small flourish of his hand, he indicated that he too might be following soon. The price included all expenses as far as Istanbul, plus a first-class air ticket from Istanbul to Paris. There would be a Turkish-speaking guide throughout.

A few months before the clampdown I'd sold some land on the Caspian coast, anticipating that I might need a large amount of ready cash. Now I would write a few checks in the name of some trusted friends, which they would cash and then hand me the money.

A few days later two Kurds came to my office. They were tall but otherwise very ordinary. We agreed it would be wiser to fly to Rezaiyeh, a large town in western Kurdistan, rather than to drive to the border. The risk of being spotted on such a long road journey had become too great—worse even than when Khodi had gone just two weeks before. Admittedly I ran a risk of being recognized at the Tehran airport, but though I was well known on the international side, I had not taken a domestic trip for some time. I would travel under a false name.

"Pack lightly," they said, even though I was paying for luggage transport. "You will be walking part of the way across the border." I was to have no more than $2,000 in U.S. currency on me. A false passport would be handed over to me after I'd crossed the Kurdish frontier into Turkey.

I gave the men a photograph for the passport and handed them the money, wrapped in newspaper and string. It came to thirty bundles of old, worn bills, though now an elaborate religious motif had been stamped over the Shah's face. I'd stowed the money the night before in the trunk of my car. It seemed as safe a place as any.

A week later one of the Kurds came to my office and introduced himself as Mehdi. "I'll be accompanying you tomorrow on the plane," he said. "Here's a two-way ticket. Your name is given as Farman. Tell anyone who asks that you are going to see Sheikh Shamzin in Rezaiyeh to shoot wild duck on the lake. Sheikh Shamzin will be your new identity once you cross the border. To avoid suspicion you are booked to return to Tehran next week."

I went home and packed, numbed by a sense of unreality and certain that I would soon be back. I chose two small suitcases and filled them with clothing. Nothing else in the apartment seemed worth taking, except for a gold watch and a few gold coins, which I dropped into the bottom of my coat hem. My only indulgence was my camera, which I stuffed in at the last minute. I hadn't been told what to wear and had forgotten to check with Cyrus. I chose a sheepskin coat to protect me from the cold at the border, regular pants, an extra sweater, and high lace-up American boots. My closet door clicked closed on the rest of my belongings: suits, riding crop, silver-headed shoehorn. It all meant nothing. I'd already lost so much.

A whole shipment weighing a full English ton had gone down on the high seas when I'd moved back to Tehran from Caracas two years before. The cargo had included a valuable collection of pre-Columbian sculptures, priceless Persian pottery, Peruvian paintings, French clocks, carpets, and a pair of seventeenth-century European tapestries. I lost interest in things after that. Only my carefully gathered collection of old books, histories of Iran by European travelers, was precious to me—and I could not take that. What were a few more ties, socks, and shoes?

I spent my last night in Tehran with old friends, taking the precaution of keeping my bags in the car to avoid arousing the servants' suspicion. I'd visited their house often ever since I was a child. It was the property of

Sarameh-Doleh, best friend of my eldest brother, both of whom were long dead. His daughter, Victoria, lived there now.

The trees were tall in the large park surrounding the stately old Qajar palace. Much of it was overgrown, neglected. Still it carried familiar ghosts—of garden parties when I was in my twenties and thirties, of women in tight skirts and pinch-waisted jackets lounging on the terrace, of men in animated clumps ambling toward the lake with the island in its center, waving their long cigars as they argued about the war and later the nationalization of oil. Those were times almost as unsettled as these, when the country rallied around its newest prophet, Dr. Mohammad Mossadeq, who proclaimed that Iranian oil was for the Iranians and sent the Shah packing. I'd had to flee then too, since Mossadeq, in spite of being my cousin—the son of my father's sister—hadn't appreciated my speaking out against his heroic visions.

The next morning I drove to the rendezvous, a quiet street with trees in a downtown residential neighborhood. Mehdi was already waiting in another car. As soon as I stopped he came over. He took my keys and threw my luggage into the trunk of his car. In less than a minute we were off.

Earlier, something about the setup had made me suspicious. After turning it over in my mind I realized that the Kurds planned to return later and make off with my luxury car—an extra bonus not in the contract. So I decided to pull a trick of my own. Shirkhan, my servant and driver, followed me to the rendezvous. He parked a few hundred yards away and checked that I was met as planned. Then, with his own set of keys, he took the car as a parting gift, coming back later for his own.

At the airport Mehdi took my cases. "It's safer if they're registered in my name," he said. "Go and board. Do not speak to anybody. Sleep the whole way. I'll be sitting right behind you."

We boarded the plane and were soon airborne. I closed my eyes, barely looking out the window as Tehran fell away. I did not need to see all that I was losing. My beautiful house in the green suburb of Farmanieh grew smaller and smaller in my mind's eye. I'd built that house, and two others, when not a single tree had grown on the rocky hills. Where only dust and weeds had languished, I had laid out formal gardens, bringing bulbs in from Holland, facing the pools with old Persian tiles, marching cypresses down the graveled walks. Later I'd planted another garden in the desert of Vardavard across the valley from Rashid's place. For years I'd nurtured it like a child, cajoling from its hard, dry clay sprays of flowers that now fell from oriental cherry trees, from bowers of wisteria around the entrance gate, from beds of hyacinth and pansy, and, lower down, where the lawn fell out of sight as though over the lip of the earth, from the water lilies of the blue-tiled wading pool. I missed it already, for today would have been my day of pilgrimage to this secret spot away from the smog of the city.

As the plane rose I also pictured the Tehran Refinery soon coming into view. On that too I had lavished the care of a father, laying out its tanks, compressors, and chimneys with the same concern I had given to the rose-bushes in my gardens. The refinery stretched like a mammoth computer chip across the desert, built by Persian hands, a testament to my country-men's hard-earned industrial skill. Oil had been my life for forty years; to no other mistress had I given so much.

Exile. I thought of my father's own flight many years before. He had been accused of gathering too much power and of threatening his father-in-law's throne. When he was finally invited back, he was welcomed with open arms. Just as I had been after my cousin Mossadeq fell. For both of us the years following exile were benificent. My father was made prime min-ister and began to enjoy his harem. I put my signature to the foundation of OPEC and basked in the ensuing oil boom. In our own ways we each felt heroic. Who would have believed it would come to such a crashing end? Who would have imagined that in old age we would each be shorn of our heritage, damned for the work we'd done and the lives we'd led? My father at least was allowed to keep his country and his lands and remain on, a ves-tige of old tradition as Iran changed dynasties and jolted into the twenti-eth century. But I was once again escaping for my life, expelled by the country that at my birth had anointed me a favored son. So much for the loyalties of history.

And so I lay back and feigned sleep.

After an hour we touched down in Rezaiyeh. It was a gray city of about sixty thousand people, huddled against the mountains. Just to land here seemed like madness. A full-scale war was going on. The notoriously vengeful mollah at the head of the city's commanding revolutionary com-mittee frequently made the newspapers as he put his own firing squad to work meting out instant justice in the streets. The Kurds, eager for au-tonomy, had fought this war many times—against the Turks, against the Arabs, against the Persians. It was a merciless battle. Khomeini had sent helicopters to strafe the fields and villages. Some of the worst atrocities of the revolution had taken place here. Pictures of men lined up against a wall, all shot, of men hanging in lines from rafters, their necks broken, had been made into posters and pasted on the buildings of Tehran. But the Kurds were masters of guerrilla warfare. They were unresigned. The cities, like Rezaiyeh, might be government held, but the countryside was theirs.

As I had no luggage to claim, I walked out slowly. I looked around for the person who was to meet us. We made eye contact in seconds. He waited until I'd ambled over before greeting me. He said there were three jeeps standing outside and told me to sit in the middle one and wait. A young woman sat in the front seat, breast-feeding her child. I climbed into the back. Mehdi and the other man arrived a few minutes later with my luggage.

No sooner had we hit the highway than we noticed a car following close behind us. Our driver slowed to let it pass, but it slowed as well. There was a sudden hush in the car. No one dared look back, afraid of raising suspicion. I strained to stay calm, staring fixedly at the driver's neck, watching it turn rigid as a little vein started to knot under his ear.

Making a quick decision, I told the driver to pull over and stop. If we had to negotiate or make a dash for it, better to do so while we were still outside of town.

He swerved over and hit the brakes. The other car continued on at the same slow speed. We watched, hardly breathing, as it melted in with the traffic ahead. We waited a few minutes more before pulling out onto the highway—long, cold minutes in which every car seemed to slow as it approached and every face bore the squinty-eyed look of a spy.

We came to a road leading off to the right toward the Turkish frontier and turned, leaving Rezaiyeh behind. Revolutionary guards were everywhere, and traffic had thinned. I felt very exposed. This was country I had never seen: My family's properties in Kurdistan lay much farther to the south. The hills were dry and treeless. A dusting of snow had erased all line and color.

Thirty miles later we pulled up in front of a windowless shack. A woman in rags wearing a dusty black turban, her face worn and wrinkled, came out carrying two Russian-made automatic rifles. Mehdi took one, positioning himself on the right of the car, and gave me the other, indicating that I should sit on the left.

"We're on our own now," the driver said. "If anybody approaches the jeep, there's to be no waiting, no pity, no humanity. It's kill or be killed."

I grasped the gun. I was more afraid of dying alone in that forlorn terrain than of staining my hands with another man's blood. I had not held an automatic weapon since the 1940s, when Iran had seemed about to split in two as clashes between the Russians in the north and the British in the south brought the country to the verge of civil war. Now the gun felt good in my hands, and I almost hoped that I would get a chance to use it.

It began to grow dark, and we approached a crossroads with a number of people milling about. As we got closer I saw hundreds of guns set up along the side of the road. This was one of the gun markets we'd heard so much about in Tehran, where Kurds gathered from miles around to sell,

buy, or exchange arms. I could see old collector's items propped like lounging cowboys against the fence. There were piles of used rifles, new German
G3s stolen from the Shah's disintegrated army, and Russian Kalashnikovs
smuggled through the porous Iraqi border not far to the north. Business
was brisk. The crowd, dressed in billowy pants with tassels on their cummerbunds, haggled and gossiped in easy voices.

A number of the dealers, recognizing Mehdi, called greetings. But
night was falling and we had to move on.

About ten more miles down the road we came to Mehdi's village, turned
through a big gate, and entered a courtyard. Mehdi's house was the biggest
in the village. Two rooms in the back were occupied by Mehdi's first wife
and her two children. His second wife lived in the front with three more
children. Mehdi used a large room in between, furnished with just a carpet and some fifty guns lined against the walls. Among his trophies was a
rare French World War I rifle called a *canne à pêche,* or "fishing rod"; he also
had a curious old shotgun with two barrels. A mattress and bedcover were
laid in this room for me.

We sat down immediately to supper. The meat and rice looked greasy
and gray, and I didn't eat much. Mehdi informed me that the guns were
loaded and ready, although, Allah be praised, there had never been an attack on *his* house.

We slept in the same room, each with a window to defend, but our only
antagonist that night was the cold. I woke up shivering in the early dawn
and scrambled around in the dark looking for my greatcoat, terrified that
I would inadvertently set off one of the guns and get shot by Mehdi in the
process.

In the morning Mehdi announced that he was going into Rezaiyeh and
that we would spend at least two more days in the village. Another fugitive was on his way, and he would take us both over the frontier.

I protested at the delay. But Mehdi just laughed. He said some people
would be coming to test the guns while he was away and that if they spoke
to me I should tell them I'd come from Kermanshah in the south for an
arms deal. "Your mother was from there. You know the people," he said,
punching me good-naturedly in the arm. "You can talk about old times—
and find out the news." I was not appeased by his joviality, and I watched
with consternation as he drove away. To pass the hours I went out and
walked around the courtyard, where I snapped a few pictures of Mehdi's
second wife and her children. Like all Kurdish women, she wore no veil.
But her clothes were ragged and dirty. The barefoot children played in the
snow.

Soon I went inside to read, but arms dealers came and went all day, testing the guns and destroying my concentration. To my relief the guns weren't loaded, for the dealers swung them about recklessly, pretending to take aim and pulling the triggers like boys playing cowboys and Indians. They laughed uproariously whenever they shot an imaginary Khomeini soldier, slapping each other on the back for sending one more martyr to God.

It was a noisy way to spend a quiet afternoon, but when the last dealer rode away the silence was oppressive. I got up to check for Mehdi's arrival, but the road beyond the courtyard stretched emptily across the crusted foothills toward the mountain. The village, five or six windowless houses huddled around Mehdi's courtyard, looked sinister in the hard winter glare.

Finally, after dark, Mehdi reappeared, accompanied by a short, insignificant-looking fellow named Sa'id. I had assumed that everybody trying to flee Khomeini's Iran were men like me—landowners, government officials, industrialists. But this man was just a small-time businessman from the bazaar. He had no luggage, not even a toothbrush.

I tried to be courteous and talk with him. But he spoke only a little, preferring to sit alone in a corner of the room and smoke.

Yet suddenly, the following afternoon he decided to talk. "You, sir, Sheikh Shamzin?" He laughed mockingly. "You're a strange one. You don't look like a sheikh and you don't look like a Shamzin either. But," he said, tipping his head with a self-deprecating wrinkle of his forehead, "if you say so, I'll believe it."

Sa'id was short and husky like a bulldog. His cropped black hair and flat nose added to the boxiness of his head, which dropped squarely into his shoulders without passing through any kind of a neck. He wore a shabby striped suit that bagged at the knees and probably hadn't been cleaned once since the day he'd bought it. He was amused by my consternation and smiled as I warily tried to figure out what to answer.

"I'm the last person to give you away," he finally said, relenting. "You act like an aristocrat. Look at the way you're dressed. Look at the way your hair is cut. Look at the way you talk! Who do you think you're fooling?"

"Yes, well . . . ," I said lamely. "I'm, ah, that is, my name is . . ." I stopped and took a deep breath. "My name is Manucher Farmanfarmaian."

"I knew it," he said gleefully, his face breaking into a wide grin. "I'm so pleased to meet you finally." He bowed. "We meet in strange circumstances. I know your family—such a famous family, the real royal family. You are the son of the great Prince Abdol Hossein Farman Farma." He paused to see how I was taking this. "I have been on your properties often in Hamadan and Kurdistan," he said, waving his arm about. "I have eaten

in the houses of your *kadkhodahah,* your village headmen, the most gracious, the most generous. I have slept under their roofs, *Inshallah,* God
have mercy on them."

He bowed again, this time very low and with his hand open in supplication across his heart. "I am honored, *hazrat-valah*—Your Highness," he
said, suddenly gruff. "Truly honored. *Gorboneh-shomah*—I am your slave."

"And who are you?" I asked, flabbergasted by this extraordinary performance.

The smile disappeared from his face. "Just a small businessman," he said
evasively. "I'm on my way to Germany with my two hands and nothing
else."

I figured he must have run afoul of the authorities, but he clearly didn't
want to elaborate. We settled back into silence.

Night came and my impatience to get going grew unbearable. Every
few minutes I found myself looking up from my book, staring into space
or having to take a quick turn around the room.

Dinner was boiled meat and rice again. Although I was very hungry, I
could not eat it. I smiled at Mehdi's wife and covered my bowl with my
hands. Instead, I ate some bread moistened with water, but the bread was
old and I couldn't even get much of that down.

Finally, at half past eight, the door opened and a man burst in. It was
our new contact, Ahmad. He cut a striking figure: He was about thirty,
nattily dressed in a blue-gray suit and tie, his clipped mustache and dark
felt homburg giving the impression that he'd stepped right out of a 1930s
detective film. He greeted us warmly and said everything was set to go. I
hurriedly collected my shirt, which Mehdi's wife had washed for me that
morning. Otherwise my luggage was ready.

There were five of us in the car, including the driver and Mehdi. It was
very dark outside, and snow was coming down thick and hard. We drove
only about ten minutes before the driver pulled over and told us to get out.
We had come to a bridge. "On the other side is Turkey," Ahmad said,
pointing. I could barely see the tip of his finger in the swirling snow.
"There's a Turkish frontier post where no Iranian guards have been since
Khomeini came to power." He looked around at the others. "OK? Let's go!"

He and the driver each grabbed some of my luggage and we started to
run. But how far can one run in the snow in the dark? I gasped for breath,
trying to keep up with my guides. They had obviously done this run hundreds of times. Finally we crossed the bridge.

How easy it would be, I thought, for a single man with a shotgun to kill
us in this godforsaken place, take our possessions, and vanish into the
night. But when I mentioned this to Ahmad he laughed.

"Never," he said. "Everyone knows that if such a crime were committed, our men would find out who did it, track him down, and destroy his family, down to his smallest child. We each have our own business here—we know who the thieves are, who the bandits are, who does the smuggling—and we do not interfere in each other's affairs.

"As for the Turks, they check the bridge routinely every two or three hours, and we are in between two such inspections."

We came to the end of the bridge, but I saw no border post and we did not stop. Sometimes running, sometimes walking, we trudged on for a good forty minutes more. The one time I dared look back, I saw our footsteps covered by snow almost as quickly as we imprinted them. If they had killed us on that dark road, we would have disappeared without a trace until the spring thaw.

At last I saw a light ahead. It was the Turkish frontier post. We were out of Iran. I felt a momentary release of the spirit and wondered where my leaden boots had passed over the border.

Mehdi and Ahmad told us to dry out in the waiting room while they went in to fix up our entry visas. Exhausted, Sa'id and I settled onto a long wooden bench and watched in silence as puddles of melted snow gradually gathered at our feet. The Turkish guards were obviously friends of Mehdi's, and they talked and joked for almost an hour. By the time we were told to go to the car parked outside, it was nearly midnight.

At last our guides joined us and we started to move. A Turkish guard car, its lights off, followed close behind. We drove in silence until we reached a Turkish village a little way down the road. We stopped at the home of the village headman, or *kadkhodah,* a friend of Ahmad's. The house was well furnished and carpeted. I had never seen such luxury in a Persian village. It seemed the Turks, despite their lack of natural resources, had achieved a level of prosperity we hadn't dreamed of in Iran.

A number of men were gathered at the house, clearly the village social spot. They sat cross-legged with their backs against the walls, talking quietly. Some were already curled up, fast asleep. Sa'id moved to a corner and pulled out a cigarette. After our one odd conversation he'd refused any further communication. All he would say was "Yes, sir" or "No, sir," behaving more like a servant than an equal.

Ahmad and Mehdi settled down for some serious business with the frontier guards and a couple of the other men in the room. Money was passed, and for the first time, my luggage was searched. The entire eastern section of Turkey was under martial law as a result of the upheavals in Iran, and every village had both military and civilian police watching and checking on the movements of the population. Were they to find an escaping Ira-

nian, they were to send him back over the border immediately—a direc-
tive that applied even as far as Istanbul. But the guards hardly looked at
my weakest point—the passport. They were more interested in taking
things out of my bags: a pair of gloves, socks, shirts, everything they could
put their hands on. Henceforth I packed my right shoes in one case, my left
in the other, hoping to reduce the chance of theft.

A QUICK-AND-DIRTY PASSPORT TALE

According to my new passport, which Ahmad handed to me the next
morning, my name was Taher Mir Mohammad Sheikh Shamzin. The passport had been issued by Khomeini's authorities in Rezaiyeh, and my photograph replaced that of the original owner.

Sa'id was also handed a passport, though I realized it must be his own
to which they'd simply affixed a new Turkish visa. It was torn and tattered
and looked at least twenty years old.

"*Een olaghah*—these donkeys," he muttered, leaving me to guess
whether he was referring to the Turks, whom the Persians always call donkeys, or the Kurds. "These guys never check anything." He jabbed his finger with contempt into the page with his picture. "Look. It's expired and
they never even noticed!" I leaned over, but Sa'id had already dropped the
passport and was tapping his pockets for a pen. Then, to my utter amazement, he said, "But here, let me renew it," and with eyebrows cocked, he
looked at me intently. "Costs money to get a renewal, you know. I always
do it myself . . . have for twenty years."

I stared at him nonplussed, but he'd already found his pen and, uncap-
ping it, started to scribble in the passport.

After a moment he looked up, his mouth still pursed with the effort of
writing. "I've put, 'This passport is renewed for three years.' But I'm going
to Germany, and they won't understand the Farsi. So if you please, Your
Highness, you write in French the same thing." He handed me the pen.
His expression dared me to challenge him, but his voice was so pleasant he
could have been offering me a cup of tea.

What the devil! I thought, feeling begrudging admiration. After putting
on my glasses, I reached for the pen and, despite the thumping in my chest,
wrote in my most formal French that the passport had been validated for another three years.

I handed the passport back. Without even a nod, Sa'id took out a number of ordinary postage stamps from his wallet and began to stick them on

the page so it looked exactly like the countless renewals I'd gotten in my own passport over the years in Tehran. I watched him out of the corner of my eye, not wanting to show too much curiosity but barely able to believe what I was seeing. Finally, with a knowing smile, he pulled a regular CANCELED seal from his pocket and embossed the page. Unless someone held the passport carefully up to the light at just the right angle, it was impossible to tell it wasn't the real thing.

This was not an ordinary fugitive, I suddenly realized. This man could be dangerous. Slipping through the fingers of the authorities was child's play to him. Here, I thought, was a gangster. I still didn't know what contraband he was dealing in—arms? carpets? drugs? government secrets? This last didn't seem likely, but whatever it was, it was no small-time business. Nonetheless, though he'd raised my guard, Sa'id might be a useful person to have about.

Sa'id, meanwhile, had nonchalantly put his passport into his pocket and, with an air that said, "Don't worry; this is all very routine," asked, "Would you like me to recite some poetry? I've written some of my own. It is not the best, but it's amusing."

Midway through the first verse, however, he said he'd forgotten the rest. And when he tried another, he ended up biting his lip, saying that had slipped his mind too. Yet he'd succeeded in clearing the air, for his absurd verses had me laughing, and after some prodding I quoted him a stanza of Hafez.

We left early that morning after only two or three hours of sleep. I was surprised when Mehdi said he was going back and we would now be in Ahmad's care. Although I had known him only a few days, I felt sick at heart as we said good-bye. He was my last link to Iran.

Snow choked the roads, and I began to fear we would be late reaching Van, the first large town across the border, where a plane to Istanbul was scheduled to take off at about two o'clock. But the journey proved shorter than I'd expected, and we reached Van about lunchtime, only to find that the plane had been canceled due to snow.

A TALE OF TWO SPIES

I was desperately hungry, and we decided to pick up some lunch. We found a restaurant, a popular neighborhood place with long tables set in rows across the room like an English boarding school refectory. Van was crawling with Turkish and Khomeini informers, and we ordered our food quickly, knowing we had to be on the alert. In my sheepskin coat and American boots I looked, if not like an outright fugitive, at least like a conspicuous stranger.

My tongue was wet with anticipation of my first real meal in three days. But as I returned to our table from the washroom, I saw from Ahmad's face that something was wrong. "There are two spies in the restaurant, big guys right behind you, and they're looking very curiously at us," he whispered when I sat down. "We've got to clear out. The others are already in the street. The driver and I will get the car and wait for you up the road. Join us as quickly as you can."

I glanced at the spies as I followed Ahmad out, worried that we were making ourselves even more obvious by leaving our uneaten meals on the table. Their dark tailored suits made them stand out like a pair of cornstalks in a hay field. One held a strange-looking stick that could have been a camouflaged gun. Both looked as if they could kill a man with one pop of their powerful fists.

In the street we separated. Sa'id, who was waiting just outside, fell into step with me, while Ahmad turned left toward the car. "Let's cross," I said under my breath. "Continue to walk away from the restaurant."

The street was crowded and a light snow was falling. Keeping my head down, I shrugged off my long furry coat and thrust it into Sa'id's arms. I pulled my trouser legs out of my socks and shook them out over my boots. Then I threw my cap into the gutter and put on my reading glasses. Within seconds I had completely changed my appearance. We were now about 150 feet from the restaurant. Casting a quick glance over my shoulder, I saw the two spies standing outside the door. They towered head and shoulders above the crowd and stood back-to-back peering down the street, trying to locate us.

Do the least expected thing, I thought quickly. Disappear right in front of their eyes.

"Come on," I whispered to Sa'id. "Let's cross and walk back toward the restaurant. They will look right over us, thinking we've sprinted down the street." He nodded, and we doubled back resolutely.

Clearly not seeing us, the spies suddenly began to walk toward us, their big square shoulders carving a path through the crowd. They moved fast, and it was only a matter of seconds before we were almost face-to-face. As we got nearer and nearer I grew deathly calm. I could see the unshaven hair on their chins and their eager eyes darting around. Sa'id and I pretended to be in heavy conversation. We looked down at our toes and mumbled so that they would not recognize our Farsi. We passed within inches of them. They looked right over our heads and didn't notice us.

At the crossroads I saw our car idling around the corner. The Kurds had not deserted us. Our hearts pounding, we threw ourselves into the backseat. It was the most awful moment yet of the trip.

We decided to leave Van and drive to Diyarbakir, the closest town with an airport. It was a three-hundred-mile trip. By five o'clock I doubted whether either we or the car would make it. We were in mountainous terrain. The road was under construction and often narrowed to a single lane. At times the nose of the car cleared the cliff walls with only inches to spare; at other times the wheels swung wide and we listed precariously toward the yawning abyss below. Visibility was getting worse, and darkness was closing in.

It was well past midnight when at last we pulled up to a little hotel in Diyarbakir. We stumbled out of the car, stiff and bleary-eyed. My head ached. I'd been in the same clothes for three days. The hotel—a small building lost in the fog of swirling snow—was owned by friends of Ahmad's, and the rooms had showers. I marveled at the rush of gratitude I felt upon learning I could have a wash before bed. Before turning in for the night we checked on planes to Istanbul and were assured there would be one the next morning about eleven.

I was up early. It was still snowing. The travel agent said the plane would not arrive.

Although we had succeeded so far in eluding the political forces from which we were fleeing, it seemed that nature itself was against our escape. It was turning into a long, long road to Istanbul.

At midday Sa'id knocked on the door and suggested we get something to eat and then go for a walk. After lunch in the hotel we headed for the outskirts of town, where we came upon a beautiful park and an ancient Greek temple. It was strange, in the mad rush of escape, to suddenly be transformed into a tourist. We stepped into a pastry shop filled with the sweet smell of honey, and like the Turks we ate our baklava from a little plate while standing up.

Sa'id told me he was on his way to Hamburg. Choosing my words carefully I asked if he was in carpets. "No, Shahzdeh," he said, wagging his head back and forth. "There's no money in carpets. Besides, they're too bulky. No point in doing that kind of donkey work when there are easier ways to make money." At that he stuffed a huge piece of baklava into his mouth and wouldn't say another word.

The snow was still falling when I rose the next day and looked outside. It was useless to hope that the plane might be on time. It was still dark, my room was cold, and I was dejected as never before. Time usually rushes by me in the early morning, but now it dragged its feet. As I lay tossing on the bed, haunting images played across my mind—of smoky laughter, sequined dresses, the wink of a platinum blonde beckoning with full lips. I wondered wistfully whether I would ever reach the West and linger again at nightclubs until morning.

I sat up in a cold sweat. I was running away from my own shadow. I never went to nightclubs. I can't keep my eyes open after midnight. Miserable and cold, I was dreaming of lives I'd never led.

That morning we decided to forget Diyarbakir and the plane. We said good-bye to the driver and bought tickets on the midday bus to Ankara, about six hundred miles away. When the bus arrived—a maddening hour late—my heart dropped. It was a Turkish contrivance built with no consideration for the passengers. The seats were hard and small and had no armrests. It was not even a proper bus, just a chassis on wheels with the body bolted on. At its maximum speed of twenty miles an hour it rattled and shook like a tormented soul.

In Malatya the bus developed engine trouble and had to be towed to a garage. We had hardly gone 250 miles from Diyarbakir, and it was already morning. At this rate it would take four days to reach Istanbul.

Despite my anxiety, I had to smile at Sa'id's efforts to overcome the situation. The minute we alighted, he took himself off to the garage to make friends with the drivers, drink tea, and pump them for information. But no matter how hard he tried, they could not conjure up another bus. He came back empty-handed but cheerful and suggested a walk around town. Ahmad agreed, but I didn't have the heart.

Six hours later they were still not back. What could they be doing? I wondered fearfully as the day dragged on.

"We had to sleep somewhere," said Sa'id when they finally returned. "So we went to the brothel. There were no customers at that time of the morning, so we went to bed with a couple of girls and got in a few hours of sleep as well." He scratched his nose. "We didn't pay any more than for a hotel room, you know, and we had good fun, a hot Turkish bath, and a wash."

I was chagrined. As though reading my mind, Sa'id added, "You, of course, Shahzdeh, are a prince, and so such places are not for you." His impish expression made me laugh in spite of myself. Sa'id was a scoundrel; but though simple and unschooled, he read people with disconcerting accuracy and was always wily in his handling of them.

The bus was finally repaired, and we were on our way by midday. The road was winding and full of potholes. Ahead of us loomed snowcapped mountains. Though the sun was shining, the world glinted hard and painfully cold. Reaching the small town of Gurun, the driver stopped and announced he would go no farther. If more snow fell before morning, he added, he would not go the next day either.

THE GREAT MOUNTAIN

My patience snapped. I was not going to stay in Gurun. I didn't want to stop anywhere anymore. I'd had enough. I wanted to get going and keep going until I reached Istanbul.

Were there any buses going to Ankara from behind that mountain over there? I demanded.

Ahmad, rather crumpled now and, like the rest of us, wearing the shadow of a three-day beard, scurried to find out. "Yes," he said when he came back. "There's a village on the other side with regular bus service that connects to Ankara and Istanbul."

But how to get across that mountain? "It will take us over eight hours on foot," I pointed out to Sa'id, "and there's my luggage too. What are the chances we can do it on horseback? Or even by mule?"

"I didn't realize you could ride!" he exclaimed as he slapped his hands around his shoulders to ward off the cold. "I thought your kind of horse was a Mercedes-Benz. Well, sir, I can tell you, it won't be my first time through these mountains in such weather. Your estates in Hamadan are much colder, and I've gone through them a hundred times in winter."

As far as I knew, the only people who would even attempt to travel through the snowbound mountains of Hamadan in winter were opium smugglers. So that was it, I surmised. He really was from the underworld.

But Sa'id did not realize he might have given away his game. Happy to have a new project he turned about, singing a little ditty in his deep baritone, and hurried off. An hour later he reappeared with four horses in tow and a mule for the luggage. The owner of the horses came too, as our guide.

Ahmad turned out to be a good rider, but Sa'id was the best rider I'd ever seen. Taking up the reins, he became our leader, and all traces of servility disappeared. He moved to and fro, seemingly everywhere at once, observing where our horses placed their hooves, pointing out the path, and riding on ahead to protect us from unseen dangers.

We set off as the sun went down over the horizon, four miserable horsemen and a mule. On my properties in Hamadan the falling of the light had meant it was time to go back to the warmth of the hearth, drink hot tea, and snuggle into a chair for the evening. Now, instead, I was heading *out* to cross a mountain.

The first hour dragged. A strong head wind beat at our faces, making my eyes water so that I could barely see and freezing my fingers into useless stubs of ice. Every five minutes I asked how far we had gone. As we rode I marveled that this had been one of the tracks of the famed Silk Road between West and East. Flying over this terrain by jet, I had refashioned the long, arduous trip into a whimsical, magical journey. Now that I was crossing the lonely, wind-whipped road myself, I was humbled by the courage of the men who had plied this route for eight hundred years and by how little things had changed.

After the second hour Sa'id called a stop for a brief rest. He gave me some bread and cheese that he'd secreted away in his pocket, wetting the bread with snow. But, he warned, there would be no more until we'd crossed to the other side of the mountain.

Yet another couple of hours. We climbed and climbed. Half awake, half in reverie, I remembered being thrown from my horse as a child while riding with my father. He was a strong horseman and had often ridden hundreds of miles across Iran. He considered it a duty to ride well and felt more comfortable on horseback than in a car. He shouted with uncontrolled rage when I fell, taking it as a personal affront that his son should be so inept on horseback. He waved his crop and circled about me on his horse, forcing me back onto my mount. I scrambled back up, more afraid of him than of the steed that had thrown me to the ground. Now, once again I was barely hanging on. But this time Sa'id was at my side, encouraging me with quiet words, coaxing me through the nightmare of that long, dark ascent.

The owner of the horses, seeing our plight, said he knew a shepherd's house near the summit. "If anybody's there, we can stop for a short rest, perhaps even some tea," he said.

It was midnight when we reached the hut. A man opened the door after some spirited knocking and shouting on the part of our guide. A long discussion ensued, and at last he invited us in. After taking our horses into a small stable to feed them, he returned to serve us tea. Miraculously Sa'id produced more bread.

I never thought I could be so hungry, so cold, and so dispirited. I could not feel my feet or my fingers. I had never been very keen on tea—especially with sugar—but that night I drank it like a hot elixir.

We all dozed for about two hours. Sa'id roused me from my slumber, shaking me softly. A last cup of tea was served and my horse was brought to me. As I clambered astride, I thought grimly how often I had swung onto a horse for pleasure, never imagining that someday I would have to ride in such pain for my life. The wind whipped loudly through the trees.

The saddle was icy, and I had no gloves—one of those damn Turkish guards had stolen them.

At last we reached the summit. It was close to two o'clock in the morning, and the moon had risen.

"How fortunate it is not snowing or raining," Sa'id said brightly. His high spirits buoyed me as we headed into the second half of our journey. Toward the bottom I glimpsed the lights of a far-off village twinkling on the plain. I became frenzied with hope, feeling as the shipwrecked must when espying land after days at sea. What had seemed unachievable was finally ours: We were down at the foot of that terrible mountain.

The village, no more than a hamlet seemingly forgotten in the deep passes of the mountains, was just stirring as we arrived. My eyes were so chapped that I couldn't see the dogs that ran through the streets, and their barking frightened me. At the bus depot Sa'id almost had to lift me from the saddle.

The bus was not due to leave for another two hours, but we agreed it was too dangerous to wait in case the gendarmes should ask how we had gotten to the village. Even Sa'id was nervous. He suggested we buy tickets for all the seats and then tell the driver to start off immediately. I agreed, and in less than half an hour we and half a dozen Turks were under way.

The scenery was extremely beautiful and the road good, and I began to feel better. My natural optimism started to reassert itself. We arrived in Keyseri by lunchtime and there caught a big, comfortable Mercedes bus to Istanbul.

It wasn't as cold as we headed west, and there were fewer, less stringent military inspections. Soon we were passing through towns with names I recognized. Yet as the landscape became more familiar, the atmosphere within our little group became more tense. Sa'id retreated into his shell. Now, however, I could no longer bear his "Yes, sirs" and "No, sirs."

Istanbul, wrapped in a late-afternoon drizzle, did not look particularly inviting when we arrived. For Ahmad it was the end of the road. He flagged a taxi to take us to a special hotel that supposedly protected fugitives, his last task before heading back to Kurdistan. The first-class air ticket Mehdi had arranged was useless now after our delay, he explained matter-of-factly. Perhaps I could travel with Sa'id part of the way to Paris. He looked away, knowing he'd let me down.

The taxi wound through a maze of dilapidated streets before pulling up to a third-rate hotel on a narrow alley downtown. Ahmad told the driver to wait while he escorted us in and introduced us to the proprietor. Then, after hugging us briefly, he left.

A TALE OF THIEVERY

I looked around the dreary entrance. It was just a hallway really, the check-in desk a scuffed wooden table topped by a lamp. Paint peeled along the walls, and a bare 25-watt bulb hung from the ceiling, throwing out such shadowy light that we could barely make out the proprietor. If the lobby is this dirty, what must the rooms be like? I wondered. The proprietor, a young man in a dirty white shirt, was jittery and ill-humored. It was obvious that he hated his work and blamed his customers. He spoke a little French, though Sa'id, who could stumble through Turkish, did most of the talking.

After some discussion the proprietor agreed to show us a room before we signed in. The room was ghastly. The sheets were rumpled and dirty. When I asked that they be changed, the proprietor began to whine. His maid had left, he said, and he didn't have the facilities to honor every small request of his many guests.

The more we talked, the more I could see him weighing whether he could get more money by extracting it from us or by turning us over to the police. Next to me I could feel Sa'id twitching with nerves.

As we walked back down to the lobby the proprietor pulled us up sharply. "This hotel protects people like you," he said nastily. Then he winked, leering, as though we were coconspirators. "But you can count on us being most helpful."

"Shahzdeh, this is a dangerous place for me," Sa'id suddenly said in Persian. "I can't stay here. I have felt the grease of such lard before, and it bodes ill. You can come with me if you like. But I'm getting out of here."

"OK, let's go," I agreed. This was his milieu; he knew much better than I the rules of the game.

Nodding my head politely toward the proprietor, I said we preferred another hotel. He began to shout. Refusing to call us a taxi, he insinuated that if we didn't stay and pay up, he was going to call the police.

Sa'id snatched up my bags. "Come on!" he said through clenched teeth. I grabbed my briefcase, and we ran out into the rain. Glancing over my shoulder, I saw the proprietor already reaching for the phone.

We crisscrossed a maze of streets and alleys until finally I stumbled to a halt. Sa'id continued on, and I wondered at his energy. At the corner he paused and took a look around. When he came back an odd smile played over his face.

"I suppose you know how to drive, sir," he said, more a statement than a question. "Well, you're about to get some practice."

I felt my body shiver. I knew him well enough to know he wasn't planning on renting a car from the local Hertz office. Was I now to become a car thief? I looked away to avoid his eager eyes, but I was unable to think of an alternative. At last I nodded.

Before I could change my mind he dropped my bags on the pavement and disappeared into a shop across the street. He emerged with a length of electric wire and a triumphant look on his face. Next he began scouting around for an old car—"because," he explained, "the steering wheels of new cars can only be started with a key." Spotting an old Vauxhall, he sprang the door and started busying himself under the hood. I piled in the luggage, seeing in every passerby the threat of discovery and arrest.

Sa'id came around and pulled the starter. The engine jumped into action on the first try.

We were off, but I was shaking with mortification and had no idea where to go. Suddenly I saw a policeman and went cold. Sa'id just smiled his lousy smile and wriggled in his seat. "How about my telling him what a good ride we're having," he said, mocking me. I was too nervous to respond. My hands shook on the wheel, and it was all I could do just to negotiate the strange streets. Rounding a corner, we saw a taxi, and I threw on the brake. Sa'id understood. He unloaded my luggage and waited as I parked our stolen car. Since I was unable to shut it off I abandoned it, still running, in the street.

I didn't want to risk going to a luxury hotel, since Khomeini fanatics were rumored to haunt such places for the purpose of nabbing people like me. Instead we went to a medium-class establishment, where we registered under our false passports. I had not had a shower for a week. Above all I needed a shave and a change of clothes.

I gave Sa'id a pair of pants, a shirt, and some clean socks, and he looked like a changed man when I met him downstairs later in the evening. Feeling refreshed, we went out to find a restaurant. The meat and rice we ordered seemed like a gift from heaven.

Until that moment we'd had no time to succumb to physical exhaustion. Now I was overwhelmed. Midway through the meal I fainted dead away. I have no idea how Sa'id got me back to the hotel. In the morning I awoke lying across my bed, with my shoes and clothes still on and the door to my room unlocked.

Refreshed but apprehensive, we went for a walk and tried to plan our next move. We had three choices. First, we could fly out, but I was worried that I'd be recognized by the group of young revolutionaries who, with great fanfare, had left Iran to scout out fugitives at the Istanbul airport. What's more, since the Kurds had not arranged for visas, I considered it unlikely that we'd be allowed on a plane. Our second option was to go by boat, but once again, we were liable to be turned back. Finally, there was the train—the famous Orient Express across Bulgaria, Yugoslavia, and Italy, where Sa'id could change at Milan for Hamburg. It was difficult for Iranians to get visas from the French or German authorities, but we knew that once at the frontier we could probably convince them to let us in. I was sure that if I reached the French border, I could call my relatives in France or, if worse came to worst, appeal to François-Poncet, the minister of foreign affairs, who had once been a counselor at the French Embassy in Tehran and whom I knew quite well.

Only afterward did I find out that I actually had a fourth option. The papal representative to Tehran, Monsignor Asta, a good friend of mine, had just been posted to Istanbul. He would gladly have given me a place to stay and arranged for a visa. As the saying goes in Farsi, when there is water in the pitcher, we still run thirsty beside it.

It was, therefore, to the train station that we headed the next day after breakfast. But the train was full, and we had to book first-class seats on the next day's passage. I was relieved by the delay: It meant an extra day to relax and a chance to see a bit of the city.

We stopped first at the Mosque of Hagia Sophia, where a guide at the door tried to interest us in buying women. "*Sigheh*—wives for an hour," he called, offering us different prices for brunettes and blondes. According to the Koran, a man can marry a sigheh, or concubine, for any amount of time they both agree on—an hour, a day, a lifetime. Sa'id was game, but I refused, and he would not go alone. I felt a pang at keeping him from his desires, but buying prostitutes at the mosque door was not for me. How different our lives were, I thought as we set out to view some of the city's other mosques. To him national boundaries meant nothing. He crossed the corridors of the underworld with impunity while choosing his women among prostitutes and taking his showers in the morning across the brothel hall. Sa'id had opened a door on a way of life I could never have imagined.

Sa'id prayed and recited everything he knew from the Koran at each successive stop. As I inspected the art on the walls, he bent down to the ground, bringing his hands to his face and crying crocodile tears of supplication. By the time we had gone in and out of two or three more mosques and I'd seen him repeat his performance with greater and greater flamboyance, I'd had enough. "You're a thief and a cheating scoundrel, an unscrupulous individual with no morals," I said disdainfully, "and now you come to the mosque and cry and search the dust from the shrine to put in your eye. You're not repentant. This is just another one of your shows."

"How dare you!" he shouted back. "That night on the mountain I could have killed you and stolen your money. What have I done that I should feel guilty? You think you're above it all? I've dealt with your people; they're smugglers and cheaters and thieves just like everyone else. Look at you! You're running away like a thief in the night with a dishonorable villain who is useful when you need him but now, in your eyes, nothing more than a vulgar gangster."

I felt ashamed. He had saved my life and helped me more than I could repay him. Whatever I thought about his lifestyle, his loyalty had been un-wavering. I'd hurt him deeply by not taking him for a true Moslem. I should have realized that, like many believers, he was convinced that be-cause he recited his prayers and performed his ablutions, whatever else he did was forgiven.

It was my turn to understand and protect. I put my arm around his shoulders, and we walked slowly back to the hotel. The city was gold in the growing sunset—Constantinople in all her old glory. In that mass of humanity—trucks, cars, bazaars, street vendors of corn, beets, and brown boiled beans—of danger and escape, Sa'id was my only friend. We had be-come like brothers.

I went up to my room immediately after dinner to pack. I had never wanted to leave a place so much. How soulless it felt to be a fugitive, how lost one feels without a country to call one's own. In Istanbul I was a trai-tor. In two days France would protect me, and I'd be back on solid ground. Just two more days, and it would all be over.

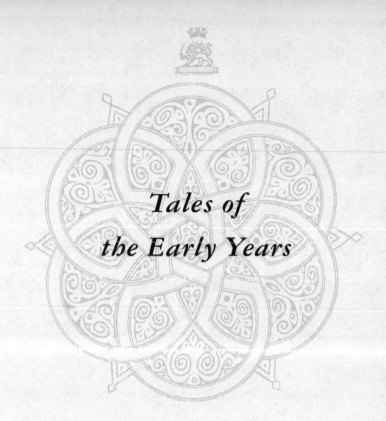

*Tales of
the Early Years*

CHAPTER
1

INSIDE THE WALLS OF
THE HAREM

Let the tears flow while you are sad;
Have patience, and the bird of destiny may pluck you up.

— HAFIZ

Tehran 1925

I was born in 1917 on the steps of the shaking Peacock Throne. Five years later it would be toppled by one of my father's own guards. I came into the world a prince of the ruling Qajar dynasty. It was May, and the plane trees were heavy with flowers. The snow-covered peaks of the Elborz Mountains, pierced by the volcanic cone of Mount Damavand, floated across the blue spring sky, their high valleys carpeted with wild tulips and hyacinths.

Tehran, a mere town inside medieval walls, was a sanctuary of fresh gardens, and that day I was born into its largest and most beautiful one. As news of my birth spread from the mouths of the nurses to the ears of the tutors and the chamberlains, across the drive to the chauffeurs and the stable hands, and on into the kitchens and the guardhouses, each of the seven hundred members of my father's household fell in turn to the ground before Allah to give thanks, imploring him to shield me from the evil eye.

Persians love fire, and Batoul Khanoum, my mother, commanded her maid to light a plate of *esfand,* the aromatic seed of the desert, so that its pungent smoke would fill her room when my father came in to see us. Rapping with his cane upon the bolted door that separated his house from hers, he strode in, catching me up with a look of such extreme wonder that one might have imagined I was his very first child. In fact I was his thirteenth, and his eighth son. Yet as my mother used to say, whenever a child was born, it was as though a new river of love opened up in his heart.

As children, however, we never felt that love. My father, Prince Abdol Hossein Mirza Farman Farma, was fifty-eight when I was born. As the husband of eight wives and, by the time he died at the age of eighty-one, the father of thirty-six children, he ran his harem with an iron hand. To maintain order and harmony I suppose he had to. The servants jumped at his slightest gesture, his wives and children bowed whenever he appeared, and the endless string of tutors, secretaries, village headmen, and others in his employ who streamed daily through our gates quaked and shuffled in his presence. By the time I got to know him he was white-haired and plagued with gout. He walked with a cane, which he shook at people when he wanted something—which was all the time. But it was his eyes that stopped everyone cold. They were piercing, steel-blue eyes that never smiled. They hooked you, cutting right to the soul, and then held you dangling until he finally looked away. Even in the pictures of him as a young man the cold fire in his eyes burns through the black and white of the photographs.

Long before I could begin to fathom the man behind that icy façade I, like all my elder brothers before me, was packed off to school in Europe. Unlike them, however, I returned to Iran only after he'd died. By then he was already being turned into a legend. The family was scattered, each of the wives living in her own house, and the one overarching bond among them was his memory. His political savoir faire, his prodigious ability for progeneration, and the exploits of his long and tumultuous career became the yardsticks against which we, his children, measured our own lives. "When you are alive, fire should come out of your mouth," he used to say. "When you are dead, fire should come out of your grave." It was not just that he became our model. He became our conscience.

When I was thirteen and away at school in France, I read a line of Voltaire that hit me like a revelation: *dur pour lui-même comme pour les autres*—as hard on himself as on others. That was my father. I never saw him take any of my brothers or sisters into his arms. He never cuddled me or displayed any of the paternal affection we saw other fathers express toward their children. He kept his emotions so in check that only anger was ever allowed to show—and even that only very rarely. Tenderness, warmth, mirth—never. Any fatherly kindness was kept tightly sheathed behind his mask of princely authority.

THE TALE OF THE CHOCOLATE

I remember standing in his room one afternoon—we always had to stand in his presence and were never supposed to turn our backs to him—when his woman slave, Delroba, "Seducer of the Heart," brought him a bar of chocolate on a silver tray. We had a number of black slaves, including eunuchs, whom my father had acquired in Egypt on his way back from a pilgrimage to Mecca. In Persia slaves were highly prized and enjoyed special privileges in the household, usually being entrusted with the personal care of both the master and the family's valuables. As Delroba withdrew, my father opened the chocolate's silver wrapper and, breaking the bar into pieces, began to eat it. Chocolate was a rare treat, imported from Europe, and I absolutely loved it. But he didn't offer me any. He didn't even look at me. Instead he stared off into the middle distance.

I watched his hand go up and down from the tray to his mouth, looking on in anguish as the chocolate gradually disappeared. Then, hardly believing my ears, I heard a piece, just a corner, drop with the slightest ring into the salver. Saliva sprang into my mouth. Mine, I thought impatiently. After he's gone, I'll run over and grab it. The anticipation of putting the chocolate into my mouth and tasting its smooth, sweet creaminess made me so excited my knees began to wobble, and I could barely stand.

Finally he put the last piece of chocolate into his mouth.

I looked at him expectantly. I knew he would get up now. But to my horror his hand went back to the tray. Ever so slowly his fingers closed on that last little piece. He popped it into his mouth and swallowed. Then he rose and left.

Such was my father's rigor. It was not that he didn't like children. Rather his remorseless code of discipline allowed for no bridge. I hated him for it. He made me feel so small, so insignificant. The only picture ever taken of the two of us alone together says it all. We both wear cylindrical felt hats, which my father had made fashionable and which therefore were called *kolah farmanfarma'i*. I must be about six. He sits like a pasha, his arms closed rigidly over his cane, tilting slightly away from me, scowling. I huddle against his knee, my head just about even with his elbow, wearing a piteous expression of complete despair.

My father never raised his voice to obtain obedience. The fear he commanded was weapon enough. Every week we presented ourselves before him to perform gymnastics at a barre. He would sit with his lips set in a hard line, as though watching a slightly contemptible play rather than the newest athletic exploits of his own children. Inevitably, somewhere in the routine, one of us would make some misstep. With a simple gesture of irritation he would get up, a frown thickening over his face, and walk out, destroying us with infinitely greater force than if he'd raved or shouted.

On those rare occasions when he did speak to me or any of my brothers and sisters, it was always to berate us about our studies or our objectives in life. Suddenly the world would darken, and he would be towering over us, the buttons of his coat barely closing over his large stomach, and in a refrain I was to hear over and over until it echoed in my ears, he'd blame us for being weak and lacking initiative. It was not enough for us to have ambition; to navigate the treacherous waters of Persia's dynastic politics we needed drive. He had dreamed of becoming minister of war, he told us, and had succeeded. In fact he had even become prime minister. Obviously we too were to aspire to heights beyond our dreams.

Yet there were moments when, completely unexpectedly, Farman Farma would reveal fatherly love. When I was seven he presented me with one of the first bicycles to arrive in the city. It was so wonderful I practically wouldn't go to sleep without having it next to my bed. It meant I could whiz around all over the property at will and even ride into town occasionally on my own, under the watchful eye of my tutor.

This combination of irascibility and generosity made for a character that was revered for its traditional Persian nobility. His servants venerated him and took pride in being part of his establishment, even though every last one of them quivered in his presence. With him they felt secure, for he knew better than anyone that saving face and sustaining a clearly structured pecking order were the two pillars upon which any well-oiled Persian establishment invariably rested. His household was like a mobile so perfectly strung that although the pieces twisted and turned, they never fell out of harmony. It was a lesson I learned young. One day, coming home early from school, I saw Old Youssef Khan, my father's favorite chamberlain, slumped on a couch in the receiving lounge catching a nap. Old Youssef Khan was an odious man, unctuous in front of my father but prone to take liberties behind his back. Sudden rage at his laziness filled my young heart, and bounding across the room, I slapped him on the face. He jumped to his feet, and without making any of the gestures of respect that house etiquette required, he ran to my father's office to complain.

"I've been in your service for thirty years," I heard him blather, the sound muffled by the carpet into which he was clearly pressing his face. "Your son is beyond control. Your Highness must intervene." I waited, trembling at the thought of my father appearing like a storm in the doorway. To my amazement his voice was calm when he finally answered. "He's a tempestuous boy," he said. "And I can't punish him every day, or he'll stop respecting me too."

After some further talk Old Youssef Khan returned to the lounge. "Your father is a great man!" he cried, trying to hug me as tears sprang from his wrinkly eyes. "He has given me a gold coin and promised to pay for my son's studies. You are his beloved son. Just as the spirit of Allah is eternal, so I am forever your devoted servant."

Only once did I ever see my father punish anyone by force. It happened to Young Youssef, our second chauffeur, whose duties included washing the car. Young Youssef was as lazy as he was ingenious and washed only one side of it, the side my father used to get in. It was spring, and the whole compound was in a flurry of cleaning and repairing after the winter snows. The pool had cracked, and my father, followed by a herd of masons and retainers—and me as I ran around the bushes—walked to the end of the garden to inspect the work, all the while giving orders and gesticulating with his stick. When he turned to walk back he happened to see the car reflected in the pool and noticed that only one side glimmered in the sun. Suddenly he gave a terrible shout. In seconds, with his retinue cowering behind him, he was standing in front of the dirty part of the car, the blood drained from his face in rage. Young Youssef was prostrated on the ground at his feet. Everyone else who happened to be passing by stopped in their tracks, and an awful silence settled over the courtyard.

My father gestured to the *farash,* the palace guards, to come over. These were big, mustachioed men who stood at attention at the gates and doorways of the palace and who wore special tunics clasped in the middle by six-inch leather belts. One farash grabbed Young Youssef and hoisted him onto his back. Another slipped the belt from his waist and, removing the square copper buckle that held it in place, began to flog the unfortunate driver. It was the only time I ever saw a servant beaten.

To me, as a rebellious young boy scampering about the harem, my father was a dictator, and I gave him wide berth. Luckily, in a household as vast as the one I grew up in, it wasn't hard to disappear. The property itself stretched for hundreds of acres past the military academy in what was then northern Tehran. To the east lay the huge British and Russian Embassy complexes, walled emblems of the enormous power both countries had exercised for hundreds of years in Iran. Each had their own soldiers guarding their doors, and almost every day mounted troops, a contingent of British Cavalry or Russian Cossacks, trotted up the unpaved roads, passing our gardens in a great show of plumage and clinking harness.

To the south lay the bazaar, a maze of shops, public baths, and caravanserais that looped and spread under one undulating roof across several square miles. Whenever my tutor had to go there to buy ink or paper, I begged him to take me along. We caught the horse-drawn trolley that

passed by our gate and rode it down the length of Avenue Sepah, jumping
out at the bazaar's soaring mosaic portal. Camel caravans from Baghdad
and Damascus stood tethered along the walls of the Sabze Maydan, the
main square. Though he never wanted to, I always dragged my tutor over
to look at the animals in their worn tasseled velvets, their humpy backs
crowned with great Persian carpet cushions that served as saddles. The
camels spat and blinked their long lashes, and when they moved, huge
bells attached to their saddlecloths tinkled through the air.

There was nothing so exciting and scary as being downtown. Hawkers
sat cross-legged next to pyramids of oranges, eggs, watermelons, and
onions, calling out their wares, promising to put their children in the
poorhouse to give their clients a good price. Packs of yellow dogs curled
near the pool at the Maydan's center or sniffed about among the stalls.

It was here that our eunuch Agha Hossein said he dumped the stray cats
that would inevitably collect in our gardens. Every month he'd hunt them
down with the help of the gardener, sticking them in a big bag, where the
cats meowed and spat and jumped around, their claws piercing the burlap.
When he couldn't find any more, he'd hoist the bag over his shoulder and
set off through the gate to the bazaar. My mother said she was sure he let
them go the minute he rounded the corner, however, for the cats were always back before he was.

Although the bazaar was covered, holes in the brick-domed ceilings fil-
tered a heavenly light into the shops and passageways. In summer it was
cool. In winter round charcoal stoves provided heat, and the merchants did
their bargaining sitting under *korsis,* low tables that were covered with
blankets and had a burning brazier in the center. Throughout the bazaar
grizzled men in striped pajama pants slipped from shop to shop with trays
on their heads bearing thimble-glasses of tea. At the tailor shops men sat
in clumps smoking their water pipes and had their shoulders measured.

Once when I was seven or eight my father took me to his favorite tailor
to have a suit made. It was like walking into a club. Men wearing turbans
or domed felt hats talked, sipped tea, and made an afternoon of it. When
a mollah walked by, everyone looked solemn and raised their hands in
greeting. The minute my father walked in he checked for dangerous loi-
terers by beating all the curtains with his stick, a precaution he took in
every room he entered, even at home.

Most of Tehran's 250,000 people lived in small mud houses clustered in
the crooked streets near the bazaar. It was a world unto itself, impregnable
to the army, which could not easily enter its labyrinthine alleys. The leaders of the bazaar were weighty men, often tightly allied with the mollahs,
and they could start riots or shut down the bazaar to instant political effect.

The turquoise domes and double minarets of the city's two great mosques, the Masjed Shah and the bazaar's Sepah Salar, rose high above the skyline. So did the inlaid mosaic arches of Golestan Palace, the home of the Shah, just a few blocks from our house. Sixty years before, the old city ramparts had been razed and the moat filled in to form Tehran's first avenues. These had been planted with trees, and even the houses of the poorest inhabitants were now blessed by their shade. The city had expanded, and to the north of our compound lay open fields, grazing land for sheep and goats. Beyond ran the heavy octagonal fortifications that defined the city's new perimeter, the walls pierced by twelve towered gates and surrounded by a moat.

Inside its walls our compound was like a pulsing city. It was a fairyland of pools and garden hideaways, with its own bakery house, which we called the Factory, and its own woodworking and metallurgy shop. Generators supplied the compound with electricity, lighting it like a beacon while the rest of Tehran relied on candles and oil lamps. We also had our own water system that piped fresh water into all the houses. It was not until twenty years later, when I returned to Iran after my studies abroad, that I realized how unusual that was, remembering it with nostalgia as for the first time, like the rest of Tehran, I drew my household water from the open streams, or *joob*, in the street.

As children we moved about the gardens and buildings of the complex with impunity. We played together heedless of whose mother was whom and formed bonds with other brothers and sisters of our own age that were often as strong as those with siblings born of the same mother. Though we lived with our own mothers, we grew to know, respect, and love the other mothers almost as our own. We ate in their houses, hid in their hedges, and played tricks on their servants, oblivious to where the domain of one began and the other's ended. As a little boy, I barely even noticed the dividing walls between the women's quarters, or *andarooni,* and the public spaces, or *birooni.* Only my father's house, the central palace, was off-limits unless we were specifically commanded to go see him.

Farman Farma's palace was one of the most impressive buildings in the capital. White colonnades marched across the front. On the left were the offices of the estate, on the right a huge, windowed receiving gallery and my father's private chambers. A broad outdoor staircase descended into the garden past the tea kitchens, or *qaveh khaneh,* where every afternoon the henna-haired man who was both my father's steward and the palace's official "boss" gathered with his cronies and played *aas bazi,* a type of poker using figured tiles. At the base of the staircase lay a big, round reflecting pool with fountains at its center.

The palace was at the apex of a large oval drive divided in the middle by a band of bamboos and faced at the other end by an enormous entry gate guarded by elms. The drive, like a main street, was always in motion—drivers washing cars, servants carrying produce from the market, endless visitors arriving or taking their leave, petitioners gossiping in the shade of the plane trees, horse-drawn carriages idling on the way to the stables as the grooms stepped in for tea and a few puffs off the *qalyan* (water pipe), gardeners and carpenters with wheelbarrows, and children playing underfoot. Flanking both sides and set primly back behind their andaroon walls like handmaidens to the sire were the residences of Farman Farma's wives.

My father's wives lived together peaceably. As a child I never noticed any jealousy among them, despite their differences in station and age—which were vast. His first wife, Princess Ezzat-Doleh, was only some fifteen years younger than my father and of the purest royal blood. The eighth and last wife, whom he married just before he died, was close to sixty-five years his junior and was a nurse. Yet my father was careful to observe the Koranic rule of seeing each wife with the same eye, and, outwardly anyway, he always accorded them the same respect and standard of living. Early on, having himself had the benefit of a better education than most of his peers, my father took upon himself the unorthodox task of personally teaching each of his wives how to read. He began with Princess Ezzat-Doleh, who, though she was the daughter of a shah, had like most girls been brought up under the benighted view that literacy was wasted on women. Only my mother escaped the stifling limitations of this traditional view and enjoyed a religious education as a child. By the time I was born all Farman Farma's wives were literate, and one of my father's great pleasures was to listen to them read in the evening when he visited them each in turn during the week.

My mother, Batoul Khanoum, was by far the best educated of the wives, and also the most vivacious. She and my father were married in the western province of Kermanshah while he was governor there, responsible for quelling an uprising by his cousin. She was fourteen years old; he was fifty-three. She came from a family of provincial Kurdish nobility. She was a striking woman with milk-white skin and raven hair, which she tied into a knot at the back of her neck. Often she would gather me and my two older sisters, Maryam and Mehri, around the korsi and read us translations from the great works of European literature. She also loved poetry, and she set herself the task, as was the custom among well-educated Persians, of copying out the complete works of her favorite poet, Saadi, the light-hearted sage of Shiraz, whose wisdom she frequently used to admonish us or enlighten us in the ways of the world. " 'Would that God had given us two lives,' " she'd quote when we were testing her patience. " 'One to gain experience, the other to use it.' "

Like my father, my mother was open-minded about the modern influences seeping into Persia from the West. Compared to his other wives, she was also less religiously doctrinaire. She gave my sisters much freer rein to run about than the other girls in the harem had. And she made them light, frilly dresses, which, to her private amusement, shocked the piety of the other wives.

Batoul Khanoum often held gatherings for her friends and relatives from her hometown of Kermanshah, and the house would fill with the lilting sounds of their Kurdish accents, the original form of the Persian language. My favorite visitor was her youngest brother, Ali Reza Etezad-Soltan, a dashing army officer who came by whenever he was in the capital. It seemed to me then that he was the only man who really loved us. Unlike my father, he listened to our stories, played games with us, tossed us in the air, and never gave us lectures.

Our house was right next to my father's and was the only one to connect directly to his quarters. Delroba, my father's private slave, actually lived with us, although her primary duties were to take care of his laundry and clean his chambers. She was also the keeper of his supply of goods from Europe, which were piled in cases in her room. There were large bottles of eau de cologne, as well as whiskey, rum, and cognac, which he would give as gifts to friends. Delroba guarded them closely, telling us they contained evil spirits. She was a short, hearty, meddlesome woman who would natter at my father in the familiar *tu* form, chiding him in a way no one else dared and complaining to him that he was out of handkerchiefs because he kept losing them at his friends' houses. She also felt it perfectly within her rights to chime in whenever my mother was chastising us, crying, "What's going on here?" as she'd run up to look my mother straight in the face. "These are the prince's sons," she'd say. "Leave them alone and they'll grow up to be great men."

Every morning Delroba presented my father with a tray piled with paper rolls of ten silver coins, called *dolmeh,* like the rice wrapped in grape leaves. Farman Farma would select a few and put them in his pockets, later giving them out to beggars, the children of friends, or anyone else to whom he wanted to give a small gift. I never saw my father actually touch the metal of money, just as I never saw him carry anything significant in his own hands. Yet I never saw him ignore a beggar either. In a country without state-regulated social services, the poor were taken care of by the rich in strict accordance with one of Islam's five tenets, and my father, though he never made a show of it, always handed out the dolmeh whenever he saw the need.

As a military man and a highly disciplined thinker, my father ran his domain at times more like a regiment than a household. In no way was this more obvious than in the matter of our clothes. The compound had a permanent tailor who worked year-round to keep everyone attired. His sense of style, however, was at best utilitarian. He would fashion one pattern at a time that would then be adapted by his battery of assistants to the various sizes of everyone in the family. As a result we all looked alike, as though in uniform. Whenever the seasons changed, summer into fall or winter into spring, a striking transformation took place throughout the compound as everyone simultaneously switched attire.

Nonetheless, all the girls had to wear the head-to-foot veil, or chador, over their clothes, whenever they were out playing. And although my mother herself often wore stylish dresses of imported fabric and design, like all the other wives she covered herself with a light chador even in the house, in deference to Islamic custom.

Within the compound we paid rigid attention to religious matters. Prayers were said five times a day, according to the Moslem ritual, but because I was at school I only regularly attended the ones at sundown. At the twilight hour, when the lights were lit and supper was almost ready, the call to prayer floated over our walls from the mosques around the city, signaling that the day's work had come to an end.

One of my mother's servants prepared the scene every evening, placing a Koran on a small prayer carpet, opening up a Kashmir shawl for us to kneel on, and setting a small baked earthen tablet, taken from the land near the holy shrine of Karbala, beside the Koran. My mother would appear enveloped in a chador, her face partially revealed, reciting verses from the Koran. Stepping to the carpet, she faced Mecca. As she pronounced the holy words *Allah-o-Akbar* (God is great), a hush fell over the room. Not a sound could be heard as everyone recited their prayers, each alone with God.

My formidable father would stand facing Mecca. He bowed to the familiar unknown and, in reverent humility, scraped the dust with his face. Allah alone could make him bend down with respect and devotion. That was indeed power. God, I decided, must truly be great.

NOSRAT-DOLEH

Because he more or less lived at our house, we saw my father frequently. Not only was he there every morning, but on those rare occasions when he entertained in the evening, he would invite the guest around to my mother's house to sit under her korsi. Our living room, therefore, served as the setting for many of my father's encounters with his four eldest sons, the children of Princess Ezzat-Doleh, who were all considerably older than the rest of us. The most resplendent was Nosrat-Doleh, the eldest, who, like the next in line, Salar-Lashkar, had obtained his title from my father.* In his late thirties at the time, Nosrat-Doleh was erudite, vastly wealthy, and, despite his diminutive size, a commanding presence. He was a passionate student of the law, and his interpretations of French jurisprudence formed the basis of Iran's modern legal system, which still stands today—in tandem with Islamic law—largely unchanged. Until then Iran, like Saudi Arabia, operated on the dogma of the Koran: an eye for an eye, without trials or assumption of innocence.

When he was thirty-five Nosrat-Doleh became minister of foreign affairs under the last Qajar monarch, Ahmad Shah. It was in this capacity that he authored, along with his best friend, Sarameh-Doleh, then minister of finance, and Vosugh-Doleh, prime minister, the infamous Anglo-Persian Agreement of 1919. Although it obtained for Persia a much-needed loan of £2 million, it gave in exchange complete control of Persia's army (what there was of it) and treasury (which was empty) to Great Britain. The agreement was never ratified, but the British were so taken with Nosrat-Doleh that at one point they tapped him as their candidate to take over the throne. When the throne passed instead to General Reza Pahlavi after a military coup, Nosrat-Doleh nimbly transferred his allegiances, and in 1927 he was back in the political saddle as Reza Shah's minister of finance.

Nosrat-Doleh lived life on a grand scale. He owned one of the two Rolls-Royces in the city (Sarameh-Doleh had the other), entertained more lav-

*Titles in Persia were awarded by the Shah. Some were hereditary, though even those passed from father to son had to be confirmed by the Shah. Others were awarded for special service or favor and used the person's given name. There were several general title forms: Doleh, meaning "of the state"; Saltaneh or Soltan, meaning "of the Crown"; Salar or Sardar, meaning "head of the army"; Amir, from the Arabic, meaning "chief"; Mirza, roughly meaning "descendant of the Shah"; Malek, meaning "of the Shah," used primarily for women; and Banou, meaning "lady." Nosrat-Doleh was a hereditary man's title meaning "victory of the government"; Ezzat-Saltaneh, a hereditary woman's title, meant "cherished of the Crown." Matine-Doleh, however, who was head of my father's office and received his title at my father's instigation, simply had the word "Doleh" added to his given name, "Matine," to form the title. Farman Farma, meaning "commander of commanders," was an unusual title. Drawn from the word *farman,* meaning "order," it was the only title with a repeating pattern, aside from the monarch's, Shahanshah, meaning "Shah of Shahs."

Haji, though not a title per se, is added to the name of those who have made a pilgrimage (*haj*) to Mecca (the woman's form is Hajieh). Finally, the suffix "Khan" was often added to a name out of respect and roughly meant "sir," as does the prefix "Agha."

ishly than my father, and maintained an active correspondence with friends from the French literary group Le Boeuf sur le Toit, whom he'd met while a student in Paris. His friend the avant-garde filmmaker Jean Cocteau called him "the prince with the mind of Montesquieu and the heart of the Uzbek." To us little ones Nosrat-Doleh was the scion of the family, the hope upon which our future greatness rested.

Nosrat-Doleh often invited me up to his home in the hills of Farmanieh, even though his son Mozzafar was away at school in England. Those were days spent in heaven, for they meant freedom from my father's suffocating yoke. I inspected with fascination the framed newspaper clippings from France in his office, written in letters I could not read but with pictures of him lounging on tasseled couches in the midst of exotic balls and parties.

Nosrat-Doleh had lived like a true oriental prince in Paris as a student at the Sorbonne at the turn of the century. His address was a suite at the fashionable Hôtel Lutécia. A butler kept him in pressed suits and polished spats. The duke of York, the future George VI of England, was one of his friends. So were Picasso, Diaghilev, Stravinsky, Massine, and the author Raymond Radiguet, whose book *Le Bal du Comte d'Orgel,* published in 1924, was inspired by a fancy dress party he attended with Cocteau and Nosrat-Doleh.

Not too long before I was born my father deeded over a large part of his estate to his four eldest sons so that they would not worry that their heritage was being undercut by the new brood growing up in the harem. But Nosrat-Doleh lived well beyond his means, and so he sent his best friend, Prince Sarameh-Doleh, to approach Farman Farma for funds on his behalf. I was there on one of these occasions, standing mute as usual in the corner. Sarameh-Doleh, a striking figure in an impeccable suit and cravat, bowed humbly and, after giving the news of his daughter, Victoria, and the welfare of his own estates, asked Farman Farma to grant Nosrat-Doleh the favor of an advance.

My father, sitting like a mountain in his chair, glowered. "No!" he declared. "I have given him enough." He pointed a long arm at me. "Now I have him and the others to think of. Let him sell his properties if he cannot live on his income." This is exactly what Nosrat-Doleh eventually did.*

---

*Nosrat-Doleh first rented his magnificent mansion in Farmanieh to the French Embassy; later it was sold to the Italian Embassy as a summer residence. Many of his other properties also were sold to pay off his debts. In 1990 the Italian government published a book on its two embassy residences in Tehran; the winter one in town was built by my grandfather Firouz Mirza, the second in Farmanieh was Nosrat-Doleti's summer residence.

Only once did I perceive any tension in our household over Nosrat-Doleh's political affairs. It was late afternoon. I must have been about seven. Running past the living room, I glanced through the half-open curtain at its doorway and saw my father sitting under the hot korsi with his old friend Seyyed Hassan Modaress, a highly respected and controversial mollah who was a member of the Majles (parliament). My father was feeling sick as a result of his gout and was running a fever. His face looked red against the white cloth of the korsi. On top of the korsi at one of the corners sat Nosrat-Doleh, a glittering diamond pin in his silken tie.

I crouched in the curtain and watched. Seyyed Hassan Modaress was pointing at Nosrat-Doleh. "It was your fault," he shouted, his face purple with rage. "Were it not for what you did, the country would not be where it is today."

I was too frightened to hear more and, shivering, ran away, not understanding anything of what was being said. I did not know Nosrat-Doleh had been a candidate to be shah. Or that he had been a cabinet minister under the Qajars, serving as Iran's point man on oil. Neither did I know that he had switched loyalties and that he was well ensconced in the new Pahlavi regime, still negotiating the terms of oil, still riding high. He was just my brother—an important man, of course, but everyone in my father's household was important.

I had no notion of who my father was—and, therefore, of who I was. Under Reza Shah the schools taught us nothing of the immediate and dangerous past. The Qajars were never mentioned. Just as today the Islamic regime has wiped out every vestige of the Pahlavis, so the Pahlavis destroyed the history of the Qajars. Vaguely I knew that important affairs took place under our roof. But how important they were, I did not know. To me my father was just a ponderous old nobleman with gout. I still had much to learn.

THE BLOOD OF
THE QAJARS

What happened to the Kings Kavoos and Kay?
Who would have imagined that the Kingdom of Persia would be
thrown to the wind?

—HAFEZ

Tehran 1925

My father was born Prince Abdol Hossein Mirza Firouz. Over the span of
his long life he acquired the titles of Salar-Lashkar (head of the army),
Nosrat-Doleh (victory of the state), Amir Tuman (chief of a thousand [sol-
diers]), and finally, the most illustrious of all, Farman Farma (commander
of commanders). At the age of thirty-four he also received the Knight
Grand Cross of the Order of St. Michael and St. George from the British
government, but although he sometimes wore the medal, it was beneath
his dignity to use the foreign title "Sir."

Farman Farma was born in 1858 at a high point in his family's history.
His cousin, the visionary Nasser-edin Shah, sat on the Peacock Throne, and
Persia was enjoying a period of extended prosperity. The Qajars had already
been ruling for seventy-three years, and the dark legacy of the founding
Qajar shah, the vengeful eunuch Agha Mohammad Khan, had already all
but faded from memory.

The Qajars were an old tribe, with a recorded lineage that extended as
far back as 1501, though when it suited them the family could point to ref-
erences dating to the Mongol era of the twelfth century. They were nobles,

or khans, from the windswept plains of Turkmenistan in what was later southern Russia. Fair-skinned, with large, pointed noses and quick wits, they filled a number of diplomatic missions and governorships in the sixteenth and early seventeenth centuries for the Safavid shahs—the builders of the exquisite blue-domed mosques in the oasis capital of Isfahan. For the next two hundred years the Qajars intermarried with each successive dynasty of shahs—and fought them for dominion. Finally, in 1785, just as the Americans and the French were fighting their own revolutions on the other side of the world, Agha Mohammad Khan, the Qajars' ruthless chief, emerged victorious in a civil war that had wracked the country for thirty years. After an extended campaign he unified Persia and moved its capital closer to his tribal seat, choosing the little town of Tehran at the base of the Elborz Mountains—where it has remained ever since.

Agha Mohammad Khan's was a reign of unalloyed terror built on revenge. As a child he'd been captured by the shah before him and castrated. Mortified, in a country of bearded, hairy men, to have a chin as clear as a baby's and speak with the voice of a woman, he showed his manhood in acts of vicious cruelty and dominance in war. By the time he was assassinated in 1797, the deserts of Persia were soaked in blood: skulls piled in mounds stood outside the citadels to deter the inhabitants from revolt, and every last man in Kerman, a town he felt had betrayed him, was either dead or blinded.

During his two years as shah, Agha Mohammad Khan instituted a number of reforms, anticipating the spirit of democratization that was beginning to percolate around the world. Most important, like Peter the Great in Russia earlier in the eighteenth century, he separated the institutions of the monarchy and the state. Among other measures, he collected the crown jewels, which had become scattered during the wars that preceded his rule, and gave them to the government. The bulk of the jewels had originally been captured by Nader Shah fifty years before in the invasion of India. During the anarchy that followed his death, some of the most valuable jewels, including the Kuh-e-Noor (Mountain of Light) diamond, were seized by an Afghan khan. Its sister, the Darya-Noor (Ocean of Light), the biggest unflawed diamond in the world, remained in Persia and was duly passed to the state. In 1892, when Nasser-edin Shah (Agha Mohammad Khan's great-grandnephew) visited England on his third trip to Europe, Queen Victoria proudly showed him the Kuh-e-Noor, which had just come into her possession through the East India Company. Nasser-edin apparently refrained from tarnishing the queen's joy by informing her that the gem she was wearing had been stolen from Persia a century before. He also did not tell her that his great-granduncle Agha Mohammad Khan had given all his jewels to the state and instituted a strict accounting procedure for their use by the shahs during their reign (an issue the British Crown has still not addressed).

In one of life's ironic twists, Agha Mohammad Khan was killed for the Darya-Noor, which his murderers stole along with a number of gem-studded swords, bracelets, and the Crown of the Moon, another of the world's great diamonds. The villains were eventually forced to return the booty, and to this day the jewels remain the property of the state and are displayed to the public in the vaults of Tehran's Central Bank.

Agha Mohammad Khan died in 1797. An astrologer, asked on the preceding New Year's Day what he foresaw in the upcoming year, is said to have replied, "Prosperity for the country and peace for the inhabitants." Hearing this, Agha Mohammad Khan turned to his nephew Fath-Ali Khan and reportedly remarked, "The astrologer is announcing the death of your uncle, for as long as he lives, nobody will enjoy peace."

Prosperity and peace did settle over Persia after Fath-Ali Shah, my father's great-grandfather, inherited the throne. (Agha Mohammad Khan, being a eunuch, had no children to pass it on to.) Fath-Ali Shah ruled, like all of Persia's thirty-one dynasties of shahs before him, as an absolute monarch. During his thirty-seven years on the throne the country flowered. Its richly woven carpets appeared in salons and palaces all over the world. Pearls and horses were traded with India. Silk and cotton were shipped to Europe. And the arts flourished.

It was under Fath-Ali Shah, however, that two Great Powers, England and Russia, began the menacing pas de deux over Persian territory that would eventually draw the country into World War I. England, proud as a new mother with her recently acquired prize of India, considered southern Persia and the Persian Gulf a critical bridge in the expanding empire that, under Queen Victoria, defied the setting of the sun. Russia, ever anxious to obtain warm-water ports, viewed northern Persia and the Caspian Sea as an obvious extension of its own southern provinces. Fath-Ali Shah, and later his grandson Mohammad Shah, tried to play one off against the other, which only tightened the noose. After much hounding (and, in the case of Russia, after a war that won vast tracts of land in the northwest for the czar), both countries negotiated favorable trading terms with Persia. Soon Persia came to owe both powers money. It incurred a balance-of-trade debt, and it started borrowing heavily to modernize.

Like his contemporary Napoleon, Fath-Ali Shah gathered a resplendent court around him and was rather a dandy. The iron engravings in Western travelogues depict him with a beard so long and flowing that it wraps around his face like a chador, connected eyebrows that hang gracefully above his eyes like a bird in flight, and a narrow waist (in which he took much pride) girdled with sumptuous jewels. Fath-Ali Shah was also renowned for his large and beauteous harem. Some accounts credit him with having more than one hundred wives. By the age of twelve he'd sired five sons (and perhaps as many daughters, though girls, good only for giving away, were not recorded with the same attention).

Yet despite his huge retinue, Fath-Ali Shah was constantly on the move, preferring, as the British envoy William Ouseley remarks in his *Travels in the East,* a nomadic to a settled life, a village to a city, a tent to a palace. It was a characteristic of many Qajars, not least among them my father, whose propensity for relocation drove us all to distraction. During the summers, when we moved to our cool garden estate of Rezvanieh (Paradise) in the green foothills above Tehran, my father would insist on staying in a tent. And every few days, just like the nomads, he'd want to move to a new site, causing enormous commotion and disarray. First everything in the tent had to be taken out—the carpets, the bed, his armoire and reading lamp, and all the rest of his personal belongings. Then, while he shouted and waved his stick, more than fifty men swarmed together to raise the huge central pillar that held the tent aloft. Invariably, every few days Farman Farma wanted to try a new place, pointing out that the sun now moved across it or that the shade was wrong, and once again the laborious transfer of the tent would begin.

Fath-Ali Shah died in October 1834, leaving the succession in turmoil. His son Crown Prince Abbas Mirza, my great-grandfather, had died a year earlier at age twenty-eight. In his place Fath-Ali Shah chose Abbas Mirza's eldest son, Mohammad, who as the new crown prince duly moved to the rich northern province of Azerbaijan to become governor. But when Fath-Ali Shah died, his eldest surviving son, Prince Hossein Ali Mirza, who bore the title of Farman Farma, contended the succession.

To counter his uncle's claim, Mohammad Shah dispatched his younger brother, Firouz Mirza, to Fars, where Farman Farma was governor. Though only seventeen at the time, Firouz Mirza routed his uncle's forces, settling once and for all Mohammad Shah's claim to the throne. Firouz Mirza was my grandfather. Forty years later, Nasser-edin Shah, his nephew, would bequeath him the coveted title of Farman Farma in honor of his role in the succession.

THE AGHA KHAN

Hardly had Mohammad Shah settled onto the Peacock Throne (which was in fact a copy, since the original had been destroyed as Nader Shah carried it from Delhi to Persia) when he encountered new opposition on his south-eastern flank. Agha Khan Mahalati, the leader of the Ismaili sect, was on the warpath in Kerman.

The Ismailis were a branch of the notorious guerrilla warriors known as the Assassins, who in the eleventh century crossed swords with the Crusaders. The "Old Man of the Mountain," Hassan Sabbah, the sect's leader, would have his recruits (called Ashashin) drugged with hashish and then brought into his beautiful garden high up in the Elborz Mountains. There they would awaken surrounded by damsels, and, convinced that there truly was a paradise, they would thereafter carry out any deed of valor or conquest to recapture the garden of heaven.

In Persia the sect had been active since the ninth century, claiming descent from the Prophet Mohammad's daughter, Fatima.* Their base covered a swath of territory in the southeast, where they had lived more or less peacefully for nine hundred years. In 1838, however, Agha Khan I rose up in rebellion, taking over the towered fortress of Bam on the lip of the much-dreaded Dasht-e-Lut, or Lot's Desert. Mohammad Shah once again dispatched my grandfather Firouz Mirza to the rescue. Though still under the age of twenty, he mounted a siege and prevailed, sending the Agha Khan fleeing to Tehran.

There, as the leader of an important religious community, the Ismaeli was received, after a few months of comfortable incarceration, with friendly pomp in the chambers of the Shah. Mohammad Shah, as enamored of ornament as his grandfather, wore heavy diamond-encrusted epaulets for the occasion. The two sat under tiers of mirrored mosaics that scattered the light like dancing water into every corner of the hall. After much pouring and sipping of tea, the Shah offered the Agha Khan a royal pardon on the condition that he retire to his estates in the eastern province of Kashan and not bother the Qajar throne again.

The Agha Khan scurried directly to Kashan, where he sat quietly for a few years on his barren lands. All the while, however, he entertained British emissaries, who watched with growing consternation the waxing friendship between Mohammad Shah and the Russians. Offering the Agha Khan both money and arms, they fueled his ambitions, and once again he collected a force and marched from Kashan. The Agha Khan was inept in the field, however, and though he talked big, his successes were small. This time he was forced to escape to Sind in India, where the British knighted him Sir Mohammad Shah and then bestowed upon him the title prince.

Relations between the two families were not severed for long, however,

---

*Another offshoot of the sect is the Alawi—a heritage claimed by both the current leader of Syria, Hafez al-Assad, and the current president of Argentina, Carlos Menem.

and soon it was arranged that Prince Agha Khan II would marry a cousin of my stepmother, Princess Ezzat-Doleh. When I was eight Lady Ali Shah visited Tehran on her way to Europe from India. She stayed at Ezzat-Doleh's house, causing a great sensation at the palace compound. Overnight Farman Farma's domain was transformed into a point of pilgrimage for thousands of her Ismaili followers. Daily deliveries of sweets and food poured through the gates to feed her visitors, who lined up along the road in a long queue leading to her door. We were ordered to get dressed up and go and kiss her hand. She was an old woman, with skin like soft, lined tissue paper, and every time she moved, the whole room rustled with the exotic sound of her Indian silks.

Years later, in 1950, her son the great Agha Khan III visited my mother's house on the occasion of Mohammad Reza Shah Pahlavi's marriage to Soraya. He was a ponderous man of wide girth, surrounded by the scent of pomade. In an odd way he reminded me of my father. A few years back the Shah had awarded him Iranian nationality, which the family had lost when it moved to India, and though he chose his words carefully, the Agha Khan spoke passable Persian. His eldest son, Ali, who married Rita Hayworth, was already dead, and his grandson Karim would become Agha Khan IV.

A WESTERN VOYAGE

Mohammad Shah died in 1848, leaving his throne to his seventeen-year-old son, Nasser-edin Shah. Nasser-edin ruled for almost half a century, and under his hand Persia changed radically. Regular mail carriers started crisscrossing the country, the first daily newspapers were published, and a railroad was laid going east.

In 1873 Nasser-edin made history by becoming the first shah to travel to Europe—and the first Persian monarch ever to visit a foreign land without the intent of conquering it. My grandfather went along as part of the suite. An engaging man who enjoyed wine and played the *kamancheh,* a wide-bodied, violin-like instrument, Firouz Mirza had been minister of war and was a member of the High Council of State. After the trip he published a world geography and a vocabulary in both Persian and English.*

Nasser-edin Shah set out for Europe with a pair of horses and one of his

*Nasser-edin Shah, for his part, had a large floor-standing globe made of loose stones from the crown jewels. The equator is a line of diamonds, the seas are of sapphires, and the continents are composed of rubies and emeralds, making it one of the most extraordinary pieces in the collection.

wives, although she was immediately sent home once the Shah realized that he could not keep her invisible during the trip. To the Europeans, the tall, forty-two-year-old Shah, with his flashing black eyes and handlebar mustache, was the epitome of their *1001 Nights* vision of an oriental king. His wide-skirted coat was studded in massive jewels, and he wore a high domed hat adorned with a waving egret's feather.

The British public was captivated. The newspapers were filled with illustrations of the Shah's jaunty figure astride a prancing horse as he visited the industries, mines, and armories of London. "Have you seen the Shah?" became the question of the day and was soon turned into a song and then a play. Throngs lined the streets as he rode to and from his quarters at Buckingham Palace. "A surprising turmoil," he wrote in his diary. "I saluted incessantly with head and hands."[1]

THE TALE OF THE GARTER

At Windsor Castle Queen Victoria, nervous and shy, presented Nasser-edin Shah with the Order of the Garter. My grandfather Firouz Mirza stood with the other courtiers in the sun-filled room watching with interest as the queen wrapped the cornflower-blue sash diagonally across the Shah's chest and, as Nasser-edin delicately noted in his diary afterward, "saluted his cheek." Out of decorum she did not approach his leg, as was the custom, to fasten to it the bejeweled Garter.* Instead his grand vizier took the glittering diamond-star broach from its silver box and pinned it to the Shah's chest. Then Nasser-edin Shah presented the queen with Persia's Sovereign's Order, which had never before been awarded to a woman.

Seventy years later, rummaging around an old shop in Tehran's downtown antique district, I came upon a badly tarnished silver box with an odd slot in its side and the marvelous phrase *"Honi soit qui mal y pense"* engraved on its lid. After some bargaining I bought it for 120 toman, about $14. It

---

*The Most Noble Order of the Garter, Britain's highest honor, was first awarded by Edward III about 1348. As the story goes, he apparently picked up a garter dropped accidentally by the countess of Salisbury in a crowded assembly hall and, upon seeing smirks on the faces of his courtiers, snuffed out their humor by saying in French, the language of the court, *"Honi soit qui mal y pense"* (Shame to him who thinks evil of it). Pleased with the phrase—and the trophy—he contrived to create from them a new order. England in the fourteenth century was still engaged in the Crusades, and the Order of the Garter was considered a purely Christian honor. Nasser-edin Shah was only the second non-Christian to receive it, the sultan of Turkey having collected it the year before. All told only five non-Christian monarchs have ever received it: two Persian shahs, two Turkish sultans, and one Japanese emperor.

was the perfect size for holding tie tacks, cuff links, and studs, and after some polishing it looked very nice on my bedroom shelf.

One evening in 1964 I was on the point of going out for dinner when I noticed I'd broken a cuff link. Calling to my servant Shirkhan, I asked him to bring the box down to the hall so that I could put in new ones. Just then my friend Hossein-Ali Khan Garagozlu drove up with a British visitor, and not being in a terrible rush, I invited them in for a drink. As we talked the Englishman's eyes returned over and over to the box, which I had set before me on the coffee table. At last, leaning over, he asked if he could take a look at it.

"Next time you go to London, take this to an expert," he advised, turning it over a few times and looking at the crest.

The next time I traveled to London, I duly brought the lid along with me. The woman at the Silver Vault looked at it with interest. The silver mark, she said, indicated that it had been cast in London in 1873. The crest was that of the House of Windsor. She offered me £400 for it. I told her it was not for sale.

Next I showed it to the resident art historian at British Petroleum, who confirmed that it was a Garter box. "They are extremely valuable," he said, showing me how the notch in the side allowed the ribbon to pass through it. "Normally, when the holder of the order dies, the British government reappropriates the medal so that it cannot be falsely claimed by someone else." He sniffed at the offer I'd received for £400 and said I could probably get more like £1,000.

I shook my head. I had no idea how the box had become separated from the medal, but it was clearly the one given to Nasser-edin by Queen Victoria. By chance after the revolution my daughter, with no knowledge of the story behind the box, carried it out of the country with her, and so it is one of the few pieces from my collection that I still own today.

In 1858, during Nasser-edin Shah's tenth year on the throne, my father, Abdol Hossein Mirza, was born to Firouz Mirza and his green-eyed second wife, Hajieh Homa Khanoum. She was a granddaughter of Fath-Ali Shah. Her mother was from the Caucasus, the high mountain wall that divides the Black and Caspian Seas, and she bequeathed to my father his light steely eyes. Of her four daughters, one was to marry Nasser-edin's son Mozzafar-edin Shah and bear the crown prince Mohammad-Ali Shah; another was to become the mother of Mohammad Mossadeq, the powerful prime minister who nationalized oil in the 1950s.

By the time my father was born, Persia was deeply enmeshed in what came to be called "The Great Game," nineteenth-century colonial Europe's ill-fated play for world control. For almost a century the English flag had flown from Gibraltar across the Horn of Africa to the distant shores of Ceylon; in the north all belonged to Russia; the rest of the Middle East was Ottoman. Only Persia in this vast expanse of colonial enterprise was independent. Foreigners poured into the country to build trade and infrastructure, and the fight between the British and the Russians was played out over every concession and every smile bestowed by the Shah upon the emissaries of one or the other. To the Shah's dismay the benefits of westernization often accrued in much greater measure to the concessionaires than to the Persian people, and frequently he canceled agreements that he perceived as being no better than sanctioned looting.

To be fair, the Persians' own judgment on what to import was not always well considered. Infatuated on his trip to France by the tutus worn by ballerinas onstage, Nasser-edin Shah insisted that the ladies of his court incorporate them into their dress. A picture taken during that era shows my father's sister Hazrat-Oliah (who later married Mozzafar-edin Shah) all dolled up for a summer's day. Her face is tightly pinned in a chador with a flower at its crown, and her legs are bare under the broad flounce of a miniskirt.

The clash of cultures, the imposition of the modern over the traditional, was accelerating in the Persia of my father's youth. But under the Qajar shahs the threat of "progress" was held in check. Though often accused by Western chroniclers of being weak, vain, and despotic and of failing to invigorate the antiquated economy or systemize the administration, the Qajars succeeded, until their fall in the 1920s, in retaining a balance between old and new. Suspicion of the infidel was kept at bay, and the country went forward without going back. Ruling on the cusp of change while the huge forces of Britain and Russia scrabbled over their land, the Qajars preserved the personal link, the sense of family, with their people. Their twice-yearly levees, called Salaams, at which any citizen, rich or poor, could present his case directly to the monarch and expect redress, provided a direct contact between shah and people that was critical for Persian identity and a sense of national pride. As the British diplomat and chronicler Sir Harold Nicolson was to point out after the last Qajar fell and the first Pahlavi assumed the throne, "The old Persia was a loose-knit pyramid resting on its base. The new Persia is a pyramid almost equally loose, but resting on its apex; hence, it is much easier to overthrow."[2]

The turmoil of overwesternization was still far off as my father grew into a young man, and he was inspired by the foreign habits and ideas that flowed with greater and greater force into the country. As he had a bent for mechanics, he was particularly intrigued by the inventions of the industrial age. He was among the first to have a car in Tehran. By the 1920s, though there were still fewer than a thousand cars in all of Persia, he owned four or five—Fords, Dodges, and a specially made Mercedes-Benz, a big limousine that had a divider between the front seats and the interior compartment so that communication with the driver had to be by phone. A German chauffeur drove it all the way through Russia to deliver it and arrived, to everyone's amazement, wearing a bow tie, the first such neck gear any of us had ever seen.

Although he was fascinated by machinery and motors, my father's notion of speed was that "a car should not go faster than a good horse." Even on long trips, such as when he traveled to the holy city of Qom on his yearly pilgrimage at No Rooz, the Persian New Year, he would ride at no more than twenty-five miles an hour, though the car could easily have done seventy.

My father also had the first private typewriters ever seen in Persia—one for Farsi correspondence, one for English—which his secretaries brought back from their studies in Beirut. Although his secretaries were respected men of affairs, such as Ali Ashgar Khan-e Sadr, whom we called "Monsieur" because he spoke French and acted as my father's intermediary with the grandees of the time, they took great pride in their typewriters and wouldn't let anyone else come near them. Yet, though my father encouraged the use of new inventions, he rarely touched them himself. And he never spoke on the telephone. Instead he had a telephonist, Mansur Khan, who in turn knew all his secrets—which Farman Farma much preferred to the indignity of picking up the receiver himself.

Privately my father appreciated the unflappable pride of the English, even when the actions of their government were humiliating, and in characteristically Persian fashion, he found their cunning and eccentricities admirable. The Russians he disliked heartily. Nonetheless he felt both powers should be kept at bay, a view that earned him a major brush with the court at the age of forty.

THE TALE OF BAGHDAD

Nasser-edin Shah had died at the hand of an assassin's bullet in 1896, and his son Mozzafar-edin Shah, a prosaic man without his father's talents or vision, succeeded him to throne.* Under his unsteady hand the court

*Mozzafar-edin Shah was an odd character, and many tales circulated about his foibles. One concerned a concert that he attended while on a trip to Paris. When his hosts asked which of the five pieces in the program he'd enjoyed most, he enthusiastically answered, "The first. But there were six pieces, not five." The tuning of the orchestra, it turned out, had appealed to him more than the symphonies and fugues of Mozart, Bach, and Beethoven.

turned into a kaleidoscope of shifting allegiances. At the time my father
was serving as governor of the rich province of Kerman, as well as governor of Tehran. Since Nasser-edin Shah's assassin was from Kerman, it fell
to Farman Farma to chair the interrogations and organize the trial. The assassin was a Baha'i, the follower of a new sect that had sprung up in Shiraz
in the nineteenth century and was not only widely viewed as heretical by
the larger Persian population but generally suspected of being sponsored
by the British government. Baha'is had attempted to assassinate Nasser-
edin Shah three times to protest the widespread persecution of their community, and at last they had succeeded.

Once the trial was over, the Shah appointed my father minister of war.
Dashing, well-educated, ambitious, and married to Ezzat-Doleh, the
Shah's own daughter, Farman Farma interpreted the appointment as a go-
ahead to set up a standing Persian army. Until then each tribe and family
had commanded its own militias. It was time, Farman Farma felt, for Persia to counter the constant military threat from Russia and Britain with a
central command of its own.

Mozzafar-edin Shah, though he had by this time taken into his harem
my father's sister, which made him brother-in-law, father-in-law, and second cousin to my father all at the same time, became suspicious and sought
to block the idea. Farman Farma tried to force the Shah's hand by mounting a military parade and marching with great fanfare through the capital
at the head of his newly formed, 12,000-man army. But this only made the
Shah more frightened, and after decorating my father with a big medal, he
banished him as a danger to the throne.

Adversity was a constant in my father's life, just as it would be in mine.
Yet not until Khomeini's revolution in 1979 did I fully appreciate his determination to keep moving forward without glancing back. First sent to
the southern province of Fars as governor general in 1899, he continued his
exile in Baghdad, where he cooled his heels in luxury, buying properties
and acquiring two factories that produced the city's ice. Immediately he
became one of the most sought-after members of society, for when summer
came to the shimmering desert along the Tigris, ice was more precious
than gold.

Four years after his arrival, in 1903, the House of Nobles of Baghdad
asked my father to lead its movement to evict the Ottoman Turks and
reestablish Iraqi independence. The British, appalled that Persia and Iraq
might come under the same dynasty if by some turn of fate my father was
then chosen king, quickly intervened and facilitated his return to Persia.

Tehran was then in the throes of a constitutional revolution. In 1906 the
dying Mozzafar-edin Shah accepted an elected parliament (Majles) and re-

strictions on his power. Farman Farma supported the movement and, upon his return to the capital, was appointed minister of justice in the first cabinet of the constitutional government. When Mohammad-Ali Shah acceded to the throne in 1907, however, he rejected these measures and, dissolving the First Majles, reclaimed absolute power.

The next year, however, the constitutionalists rose up again, this time forcing Mohammad-Ali Shah from the throne. Mounted Bakhtiari tribes from the south, backed by the British, moved into Tehran in July 1909 and took over the city. Three days later, Mohammad-Ali Shah abdicated. In his place his twelve-year-old son, Ahmad, was anointed Shah.

A TALE OF TREASON

This was not the end of Mohammad-Ali Shah. With the help of the Russians he conspired with his brother Salar-Doleh to mount a counterattack. As Salar-Doleh occupied the western provinces of Kurdistan and Luristan bordering on Turkey, my father was sent to neighboring Kermanshah with his own militia to defuse the uprising. Among his personal guard was a tall, broad-shouldered giant of a soldier named Reza Khan, who carried the contingent's Maxim gun, a massive new piece of field weaponry.

My father successfully deterred Salar-Doleh from his treasonous campaign, though not before a tense exchange of letters took place between the two. Salar-Doleh pleaded with Farman Farma to join his campaign, proposing to share the spoils and offering him control over half the nation. "My dearest cousin, chief of the Qajar clan," he wrote in one missive. "Why are you digging the grave of this family? Get down from the devil's donkey. After me, the Qajars will disappear, *Besmellah*—in God's name."[3]

Salar-Doleh's words were to prove prophetic. To my father, however, he was a traitor. Relying on his own army's superiority, Farman Farma refused him any quarter, insisting that the feeble Ahmad was the only legitimate Shah. Little did he know that among his own troops, Reza Khan, whom he'd promoted to field commander for his bravery in the encounter, would ten years later mount his own successful coup, toppling the Qajars and crowning himself the first shah of the Pahlavi dynasty.

In a picture taken in Kermanshah of my brother Mohammadvali Mirza, who had just returned from his studies in Paris and was aiding my father on the battlefield, the future shah gazes out from the back next to the servants, one of three military officers in the picture. Reza Khan's curved sword is proudly strapped across his belly, and he wears a youthful grin—perhaps the last time he was ever photographed with a smile. Mohammadvali Mirza, by contrast, stands dressed in civilian clothes with a far-away look on his fine-boned face. And so it was as the dynasties rolled one into the other: the old guard in front, viewing Persia as an administrative duty; the new in back, eager for conquest.

THE FIRST TALE OF OIL

While governor of Kermanshah Farman Farma made an expedition to a desolate British camp on the mountainous border of Persia and Iraq. Traveling two hundred miles across open, trackless territory and spending the bitter nights in a tent, he reached the shallow plateau of Chiah Sorgh after five days' trek. There he saw a wooden obelisk-like structure rising forty feet into the air. The contraption was an oil derrick, and George Reynolds, the chief engineer, was a proud man as he showed it off to my father.

Oil had been struck in January 1904 after fourteen months of drilling. It was the first oil to be found in the Middle East. Wells in Iraq would not be sunk for another ten years. Geological surveys flatly stated that there was no oil at all in Saudi Arabia or Kuwait—and none would be found there until the 1930s. Reynolds was quite sure, however, that there was more to be tapped in Iran some two hundred miles away, where it shimmered in rainbows on the rocks of a vast plateau called Masjed Soleyman. Two years later he would start drilling there and discover one of the greatest oil fields in the world.

Farman Farma was not ignorant of the new international passion for oil. A concession granted by the Persian government in 1889 to Baron Julius von Reuter, the founder of the worldwide wire service, had included land owned by my family. Farman Farma had bought shares in the concession and had visited Reuter's camp, but nothing came of it before the concession expired. Reynolds was working under a new concession, this one granted to Sir William Knox D'Arcy, and had clearly been more successful.

Although Farman Farma was fascinated with the mechanics of the well site, he was more concerned with the administrative difficulties it posed: the need to strike an amicable arrangement with the Bakhtiari tribes, who not only shared the land with a powerful, semi-independent Arab named Sheikh Khazal, but whose leaders were still powerful in Tehran. As he persuaded and cajoled the Bakhtiaris and the British into working together through the rest of his tenure in Kermanshah, he set the stage for what would become an ongoing family enterprise. Nosrat-Doleh, as minister of foreign affairs and then minister of finance, would renegotiate the concession's terms under both Ahmad Shah and Reza Shah. In 1941, upon my return to Iran, I would take up the banner, representing the government until oil was nationalized by my cousin Dr. Mohammad Mossadeq in 1951.

After serving as minister of justice, Farman Farma achieved at last a lifelong goal: to be appointed premier. It was not a post he would hold for long. Russia and Britain, after haggling for years over Persia, had in 1907 divided the country into spheres of influence, with Russia taking the north and Britain a corner in the southeast next to India. A neutral zone occupied by British forces and the oil wells of the Anglo-Persian Oil Company was left untagged in the middle. Now, in 1915, the British were renegotiating to formalize their control over this neutral area. Seeing his country cut up like a colony in broad black pen strokes, Farman Farma refused to sign the agreement. Emissaries of the two Great Powers informed him that he had no choice.

That night Farman Farma paid a visit to the most powerful merchant in the bazaar, Haji Amin-o Zarb Mahdavi, the head of the state mint. "I have been handed an ultimatum," he told Haji Amin-o Zarb, "that divides our country into pieces. As the grandson of Abbas Mirza I cannot sell my country into slavery. Here is my share of the money you'll require—100,000 toman in silver coins. Organize a riot in the streets tomorrow rejecting the agreement and have the people demand my resignation. In the name of Allah, do this for the good of our country."

The next morning uprisings wracked the bazaar, and my father tendered his resignation. The agreement went into effect with the signature of his successor.

A TALE OF TRIBES AND TRIANGLES

In 1920, three years after I was born, Ahmad Shah asked my father to go to the province of Fars in the south as governor. Its capital, Shiraz, the city of poets and roses, lying near the ruins of Persepolis, was suffering a disastrous famine. It was the last official post my father was to hold.

The assignment was tricky. Shiraz was a focal point of political tension, and the famine was as much due to manipulation as to drought. On the one side were the British, whose dominating military presence, the South Persia Rifles, was under the direction of Sir Percy Sykes. On the other side of the conflict were the Qashgahis, a bellicose tribe of some 100,000 nomads. Their leader, Solat-Doleh, was a headstrong, ambitious man who considered the province of Fars as rightfully his and had made a financial deal with the Germans to help them wage a war of attrition and banditry against the British.

In between these two was the government of Persia. The country had been invaded by the forces of Britain, Turkey, and Russia during World War I, and now the government's treasury was empty and its hold over its people tenuous. The prime minister, Vosough-Doleh, had just resigned along with the rest of his pro-British cabinet—including my brother Nosrat-Doleh. The Majles was divided in a bitter struggle between monarchists and anti-British constitutionalists, further hampering the exercise of central authority.

Several factors recommended my father for the job. As the patriarch of the Qajar family he had become a mentor to the young Ahmad Shah. He was a strong believer in a unified, centrally organized Persia, as his performance in Kermanshah had proved, and he was a staunch royalist. He was also an old acquaintance of Solat-Doleh's. My family had served as governors in the south for years, and we owned vast tracts of land there. Finally Farman Farma knew Sir Percy Sykes. The two had met twenty years before when my father was governor of the western province of Kerman and Sir Percy, a young officer, was traveling across Persia with the typically intrepid wanderlust of the English. They had become instant friends, and my father had taught Sir Percy how to shoot gazelles from the back of a galloping horse. A sepia photo, washed out at the edges by the desert sun, shows them sitting in camp chairs one afternoon—Sir Percy in a broad-brimmed cavalry hat and holding a silver-headed cane; his sister, Ella Sykes, fitted out in a riding habit; my father in tall boots—all looking rather dusty before the camera. "The Prince rode a horse with a gold collar," remarks Ella Sykes in her memoirs, *Through Persia on a Side-Saddle,* "and His Highness ordered our servants around freely . . . in Persia . . . a sign of particular friendship."[4]

My father set off for Shiraz with a personal militia and a huge retinue, including his two youngest wives—my mother, Batoul Khanoum, and Masumeh Khanoum, whom he had married the year before he went to Kermanshah.

Holding Solat-Doleh at gunpoint out in the desert, Farman Farma struck a deal that allowed the Qashgahis to retain title to the land as long as they stopped cozying up to the Germans and respected the rights of the British. To Sir Percy Sykes he gave a tough warning: The South Persia Rifles must be kept in check, and the British were to leave Persia alone to work out its own domestic troubles.

The three signed an agreement in a dusty little village outside Shiraz. My father required a guarantee from Solat-Doleh, and so it was arranged that his son Mansur be sent to our house as a hostage. He lived as a special "guest" throughout our stay, and being about the same age as I, he and I struck up a lifelong friendship.

"The position of His Highness was one of the utmost difficulty, caught between the Cabinet at Tehran and our demands on the spot, and perhaps he alone could have made it tenable," Sykes recalls in his memoirs, *A History of Persia*.[5]*

Shiraz, meanwhile, was not calm. None of Persia was. It was 1920, and World War I had just ended. The weak and by then corpulent Ahmad Shah was ill-equipped by either training or temperament to provide strong leadership at a time when Persia was groping for direction. He dreamed of being a constitutional monarch well before democracy was possible.[6] The country, pummeled and clawed over by the Great Powers, was on its knees. The Ottoman Turks, thoroughly vanquished, were withdrawing not only from Persia but from neighboring Iraq as well. Before the year was out Ataturk would take over Constantinople and bring massive reforms. To the north the Russians were well in the midst of their own revolution, which had toppled Nicholas II and ushered in first the Mensheviks and then the Bolsheviks. Abruptly withdrawing all their troops to the homeland, they left a military and political power vacuum in Persia that was readily filled by the British.

CHANGING DYNASTIES

Seeing opportunity in the mayhem, Reza Khan, who by then had left my father's employ and risen through the ranks to command the Persian Cossack Brigade, began to move rapidly into political prominence. In 1921 he joined a British-supported government coup to become minister of war and commander in chief.

My father, sensing something amiss, set out from Shiraz for the capital just before the coup. He arrived in time to be thrown into jail along with my two oldest brothers, Nosrat-Doleh and Salar-Lashkar, and some thirty other grandees of the state. All were condemned to death.

---

*Some years later, under Reza Shah, Farman Farma was accused of accepting bribes from the British amounting to a monthly allowance of 6,000 toman (£2,000). When Farman Farma presented his accounts to the government for audit, it was revealed that the British Foreign Office's Eastern Committee had paid the money directly to the South Persia Rifles for their upkeep but had falsely labeled the receipts with Farman Farma's name to make it appear that the regiment was a Persian, not an occupying, force. Farman Farma was cleared of any wrongdoing.

We were not to learn of this until later. My mother and her huge household had set out for Tehran soon after Farman Farma's departure and were still on the road. That was the first trip I remember taking. We rode in cars and covered carriages. It was a journey of five hundred miles on bad roads and in choking dust. We moved like a massive flotilla, more than a hundred of us—wives, children, cooks, servants, horsemen, maids—fanned out across the plain. We covered only a few miles a day, surrounded by hordes of guards to protect us from bandits. Posted as sentries in a far-flung ring, they galloped over the hills on reconnaissance, circled in a plume of dust at the rear, or trotted smartly alongside the carriages, where I could see their long guns and water canteens slapping against their thighs.

Toward afternoon attendants ventured on ahead to pitch tents for us to stay in at night. Or we slept in caravanserais scattered at intervals along the road. These had been built mainly in the sixteenth century and were usually two stories high, with rooms connected by archways surrounding a central courtyard.

Upon arrival in Isfahan, about midway between Shiraz and Tehran, we were greeted with the bad news of my father's arrest. Not only were my father and brothers in jail, but so was Prince Sarameh-Doleh, Nosrat-Doleh's close friend, in whose palace we were staying. What had been planned as a short visit to this most beautiful city of Persia, with its intricate mosaics and old palaces, turned into a weary sojourn of four months. Every movement we made was watched. Soldiers from the new government in Tehran came down to spy on us. Informers were posted at the doorways and at the gates across the street.

At last news arrived that Tehran was settling down. The friendship between my father and Reza Khan had paid off. They had met in my father's cell at the old Qasr Qajar in downtown Tehran.

"We're all going to be killed," my father had said without preamble once the two were alone.

"What do you expect me to do?" Reza Khan retorted. "I'm not the prime minister."

"The head of the prison reports to you, not the prime minister," Farman Farma rejoined. "Tell him not to deliver us in the morning when he receives his orders to bring us before the firing squad. I promise I will make it worth your while."

Reza Khan knew my father was a rich man, and the price he extracted was steep: five acres of land along the Avenue Sepah, a swath that cut deep into our property. In addition he received 20,000 toman in cash (equivalent to about $1 million today).

The transaction was an odd turning point in both men's careers. In one fell swoop Reza Khan had acquired a private domain in the most elegant section of Tehran—and the means to maintain it. My father and two brothers were henceforth forever indebted to him for their lives.

Two days after the prison cell meeting the prime minister, a journalist and political outsider named Seyyed Zia Tabatabai, was toppled, and my father and all the other grandees were released.

Hearing the news in Isfahan, we set off once again, this time in open carriages and rough, horse-drawn carts. It was a hard time to travel, and children remember hard things. Though I was only four, I clearly remember the heat, the shifting desert sand, and the look of strain on my mother's face.

Back in Tehran my father abruptly retired, declining an offer by Ahmad Shah to become prime minister. Nosrat-Doleh, however, returned to public office, serving as a member of Parliament and becoming a staunch supporter of Reza Khan.

It took Reza Khan four years to solidify his power. In 1925, after forcing Ahmad Shah to take an extended vacation abroad, he had the Majles pronounce him shah, with the secret backing of the British government. Crowning himself with pomp, he deposed the 140-year-old Qajar dynasty and inaugurated the Pahlavi period, which was to last until 1979, only a short half century.

From one day to the next we went through a reversal of fortune. Although Reza Khan had prospered under my father's command, he was suspicious of anyone from the dynasty he'd just deposed and made sure they would serve, rather than command. Like Ataturk he wanted to westernize his country and gradually brought in new blood to do the job. Although Nosrat-Doleh served as his minister of finance through 1929, it became clear that our family was being eclipsed. The power we had was no longer honorable but dangerous.

The historical changes taking place beyond our garden walls were shrinking our world and turning it upside down. On the surface, however, life in the harem proceeded unruffled. My father continued to consort with the powerful and the titled, though now they talked of political tensions and personal incertitude. We still went to school every day and, being young, did not know that what we were learning had changed. Prayer was still called five times a day, and the typewriters in my father's offices still clattered with the business of running his estates.

If there was any change, it was that Farman Farma became even more exacting with our studies. Coming from a class that believed in its own preservation, he saw education as the key to his family's future. As a young lord he had supplemented the traditional exercises of swordsmanship,

hunting, and court etiquette with a few years of training at the Austrian
and French military academies in Tehran. Knowing some French, he recognized the benefit of speaking more than one language and of learning the
customs of other countries. Education, contacts, and wealth—in that
order—were his legacy, and he insisted that every one of his children, including all the girls, be thoroughly educated. Before he died, he sent his
nine eldest sons to study abroad, establishing a precedent for the rest of my
brothers and sisters, who went on to get degrees from universities throughout Europe and the United States after his death. In this he anticipated history. As the nature of authority changed in Iran, we were able to restore our
family prestige because we were uniquely well equipped to serve our country.

Farman Farma scrutinized every one of our grades, and if any of us did
badly, he would raise an awful fuss at the school. The same was true of our
tutor, Mirza Jafar Khan, who was renowned for being a very tough
taskmaster. Every day after school he took my brothers and me on a two-
hour walk, forcing us through threats and exhortations to memorize lines
and lines of poetry. Every time we made a mistake he rapped our hands
with his stick. Many days he hit me so many times I could barely hold my
pen the next morning.

My mother, aghast at seeing my hands in such a state, helped me wash
them in hot and cold water, since we had no medicines then—only quinine
for fevers and sulfates for indigestion—and no one dared to get sick or
complain about pain. But there was nothing she could say, for my father
allowed for no discussion.

THE TALE OF THE
PATRIARCH'S LUNCHEONS

When I was eight, to my great dismay, my father ordered me to attend the
luncheons he gave every day for his friends. Though I did not understand
it then, it was a critical step in fulfilling the second of his legacies: presenting me to his vast network of acquaintances so that links would be
forged that would serve me for the rest of my life.

From then on I headed directly to my father's palace after school. In the
large receiving gallery, separated from the main dining room by closed
double doors, I had to act as host, getting up as each guest walked in, addressing the new arrival by name, and conducting a conversation until the
next guest appeared. Gradually the room filled with prominent men of the
day: members of Parliament, provincial governors, well-known poets and

writers, ministers, merchants from the bazaar, and foreign emissaries. The only person besides Nosrat-Doleh whom I ever saw go into my father's study rather than waiting in the lounge was the well-known cleric Seyyed Hassan Modaress. He was the symbol of humility and modesty, and would appear in the garden barefoot. His black turban, which only the descendants of the Prophet Mohammad are allowed to wear, would be dusty from his walk through the streets, and the hems of his robes would be caked with mud. Making his way to the reflecting pool in front of the palace steps, he would wash his feet before pulling a pair of sandals from under his arm and slipping them on. Thus properly shod he headed directly in to see my father.

At midday sharp the servants threw open all three sets of doors to the dining room, which easily sat sixty people at its long table. My father already stood behind his chair at the center, having come through a passage from his private chambers. The guests inclined their heads to him as they filed in one at a time. No one spoke except Farman Farma, who with inscrutable politeness might murmur, "It is good of you to come. Welcome," or, to someone of whom my father was particularly fond, "This is your house. The honor is mine that you are here."

I was always struck by the deference and warmth in his voice, which was in such stark contrast to how he addressed his own offspring. He might even embrace someone he'd not seen for a long time and with genuine chagrin say, "Why do you come so rarely? You know my deep feeling of friendship for you and your family." He also at times greeted younger men, newly arrived at his table, with venerable kindness. "Your father never neglected me," he'd say. "Consider me now your father."

The guest of honor always sat to my father's right; the rest scattered themselves around the table without concern for protocol. I always sat at the far end, a lone child among my father's friends, for Sabbar, the only brother immediately older than I, was already away at school in Europe and all my younger brothers were still too little to attend. The conversation usually focused on politics. Although my father was retired, many decisions of national import were made across that table or later, in private, in his office.

The setting was dazzling. The silver was English from Mapin and Webb. Crockery marked with the Farman Farma seal had been made specially in Germany in sets of 250. My favorite was a set of Cantonese plates in green splashed with bright-eyed birds, bearing his name and titles in Persian script at the center. Many years later I came across a few of these dishes stacked in a corner of an old shop in Tehran—plates that had probably carried gifts of fruit to friends and never been returned or that had been stolen or had somehow disappeared. I bought them with a pang, adding them to the six place settings that were left to me after my father split the huge collection among his many children.

I ate in silence as the white-jacketed steward behind my chair occasionally leaned over to wipe away the crumbs. I watched the guests around me, comparing the parasites, who showed up every day to eat a gargantuan meal, to the men of stature, such as Seyyed Hassan Modaress, who ate sparingly while speaking words that everyone listened to.

Back in the kitchen the cooks were divided by specialty. Since alcohol was never served, the *sharbat-saz,* or mixer of fruit drinks—an especially honored cook—concocted syrups of sour cherry, cucumber, pomegranate, and lettuce. The rice and *khoresht* cooks were also important figures, since their jeweled pilafs and rich stews, called khoreshts, were the staples on which a Persian's table was judged.

My father also served canned foods, jams, sweets, chocolate, and French biscuits, ordered as a special treat from Paris. No foods forbidden by the Moslem religion, such as pork or shellfish, were ever served, although caviar was brought out in vast quantities. My father ate his caviar with rice, the only person I ever saw eat it that way. I thought of rice as something to accompany khoresht and found the blackness of the caviar against the bright white of the rice ugly and distasteful. The image left such a lasting impression that I have never willingly eaten caviar since.

Lunch lasted a long time, though I usually left early to get back to school. I would go and stand near my father's chair, seeking his leave to depart. His face was hard and indifferent behind his walrus mustache, and without a glance he'd flick his head to indicate that I could go. At times, however, he asked me to recite some poetry. By then I had learned hundreds of lines of verse, since recitation of the great poets was a sign of erudition and culture. Confident as only a boy of eight can be in front of powerful men, I spoke out in a loud voice. Conversation ceased, and smiles would light the faces of the guests. No one spoke, except my father, who occasionally murmured, "How beautiful, how marvelous, repeat those lines again." And of course I did.

One day before lunch Old Youssef Khan appeared with the news that I was to report to my father's private suite. This did not bode well, especially as Farman Farma was alone. At the entrance to his office I bowed apprehensively. Maps of the world lined the walls. On his desk were a set of pens, some papers, and a bell. He made me wait a long time in the dusky silence while he finished reading some letters. At last he looked up, and his steel-blue eyes glinted even more sharply than usual. He got up in front of me like a giant, his arms locked behind his back, his thick brows plunging together over his nose.

"You think that I have not noticed you sizing up my guests at lunch when they are served?" he said in a terrible voice. "You should never look at someone else's plate or observe how they eat. It's rude! And who are you to judge how often they come or how much they eat? Is there not enough for you?" He banged his cane against the floor. "If I catch you glancing about once more, there will be no end to your punishment," he warned. "This is my house, and you have no right to pass judgment on my friends. Now, out of my sight!"

Shaking under his anger, I backed out of the room.

My father's formidable capacity to invent his own destiny was something I only vaguely understood as a child. I rebelled and rebelled, suffocated by his rigidity. To me his sense of purpose was only pointless routine, his lectures catechisms, his determination authoritarianism, and his punctiliousness unbearable.

Summers were the only real release. For two months, while the city baked and cracked and gradually sank under the desert's encroaching sand, we lived at Rezvanieh, our blue-green estate next to the village of Shemiran. As in town, each mother had her own house and garden. My father rarely stayed the night, coming to the gardens only toward evening for dinner and then returning to town after dark. There his luncheons continued as usual, moving to large cellars located under the houses of the compound, where he and his guests were cooled by a huge fan that servants pulled back and forth with ropes in another room. I, luckily, was allowed to stay in Rezvanieh, where I turned into an untethered urchin far away from his stern glance.

It was during the summers that I was taught to ride. At first we were thrown on donkeys, which were more of a handful than one might expect. Not trainable like horses, they would suddenly start running and throw us off. At last we graduated to mules. We were taught to keep our legs back and our bodies forward, just like American cowboys—a comfortable, easy position suited to long-distance riding. I enjoyed the sport enormously and, despite the fractiousness of the mules, went out every day with my master. Horses had been in Iran for more than three millennia, and the style and tradition of riding were old. Back in the time before Christ, when the Greeks and Romans rode around in togas, the Persians were already wearing trousers. Frescoes and carvings in Persia, Turkey, and Greece show the Persians in pants, with the Western emperors on their knees in togas. Wearing pants meant they could ride more easily. In addition their invention of the stirrup—the greatest invention of the time—provided them balance while leaving their hands free to fight.

A TALE OF LOVE

Throughout my early childhood I thought life began and ended in the harem. Yet every few years my father had sent my older brothers to France and England to study. Now it was my turn. I was nine years old. One evening in Ramadan, the month of religious fasting, I was summoned to my father's office and given notice to prepare to leave for Europe within three days. I was thrilled. I had thought my turn would never come. Not to see my father anymore—to get out of that prison—would be heaven.

I was to be accompanied by my cousins from Kermanshah, as well as an official from the Foreign Ministry. We would go via the port of Bandar-e Pahlavi on the Caspian Sea, where we would take a boat and then a train to Europe.

On the appointed morning I went to look at my bicycle for the last time. "It's yours," I told my brother Aziz, kicking it a little to show him I didn't really care that I was leaving it behind.

From there I went to say good-bye to my mother. She was distraught and trembled as she walked me to the door, clutching my hand as she pulled on her chador. She hugged me, and tears ran down her cheeks. Holding a Koran over my head in the Persian tradition of sending the word of God behind the traveler, she said, *"Safar bekheyr. Dast-e Khodah ham rah*—May you have a safe trip. The hand of God be on your road." I kissed the Koran and ducked under it as she threw drops of water—a sign of prosperity—and rose petals over the ground behind me.

As I went for the last time to my father's palace, there was a silence among the entourage of servants who gathered behind me in the protocol of departure. Our eunuch, Agha Hossein, walked beside me; two farash, their buckles catching the sun, followed behind. I could hear my mother sobbing, but though my throat was tight and I was dizzy with emotion, I didn't dare cry.

At my mother's suggestion I climbed up the steps to my father to kiss his hand in farewell. For the first time I noticed how big and fat his hands were—the emblem of a man who for twenty years had taken nothing but a pen into his fingers. His eyes, behind his bright silver spectacles, froze me in their gaze. Only his cane quivered, rising an inch or two from the ground before settling down again. I took his hand and kissed it. He said nothing. I turned to go.

Toward the bottom of the steps I looked back and saw him standing there motionless, stick in hand. He looked so stalwart, his head straight, determined to reveal no pain. Was he thinking of his first son, or his second, who had gone off so many years ago and were now members of Parliament, mature men? Was he seeing me already grown like them? Was he wondering whether he would ever see me again? I looked up at him one last time. He gazed out at the throng around me, totally alone.

The servants, cooks, secretaries, and gardeners stood at a distance, watching us. Then they rushed to the main gate to say farewell, as if I were departing for a new planet. All of them were there, and despite my father's presence they began making a loud hullabaloo.

The car approached slowly down the wide avenue lined with plane trees, its engine roaring, my luggage strapped to the back. The driver, Young Youssef, got out of the car and bowed. "I have the honor of driving Your Highness," he said, addressing me for the first time in the same respectful tone he used with my father.

At the main gate the crowd surged forward to embrace and kiss me. All the guards, masons, cooks, and secretaries—even Old Youssef Khan, who pushed past everyone to give me a hug—were crying, and I was crying too. They displayed such genuine affection that I thought I probably loved them more than my own parents. In a household where paternal severity had ruled, I had thought no love existed. But that day the tree of love shed its flowers so heavily I felt enclosed by its embrace.

CHAPTER
III

ON THE WAVES
OF WAR

Shipwrecks we are, sped on the breeze
Perhaps, again, I shall see my beloved at ease.
                                        —HAFEZ

The Shatt-al-Arab 1941
Fourteen years passed before I saw Iran again. My first glimpse was of the
barren south from the window of a small, twin-engine seaplane. I was terribly disappointed. Everything was black—a burnt wasteland of mountain
and stone. There wasn't a tree to be seen, only oxidized rock shifting and
pulsing in a mesmerizing play of heat waves.

We flew close to the ground, cruising at one hundred miles an hour,
which seemed an extraordinary speed as I sat hunched at the window
watching the shadow of the plane scuttling along the rocks like a racing
beetle. Soon after my arrival in Europe my brother Sabbar had taken me for
a five-shilling ride in an open World War I fighter plane—five minutes up,
five minutes down, the pilot and Sabbar and I sitting one behind the other
in a line, all wearing goggles, the propeller whirring in our ears. I hadn't
been in a plane since then. This was only the second commercial flight I
had ever taken. The first had been the day before, when I had flown from
Bombay to Karachi.

My mother's voice had echoed in my ears as I'd boarded, quoting Saadi's
thirteenth-century poetic prophecy: "You with shackled feet have watched
enviously the flight of the bird / On with you across the threshold! until

you see the flight of mankind." We were on the veranda; I was about seven, and a German Junkers plane rose slowly into the thundering air and flew past our house. It was our first introduction to the miracle of flight, and as the plane passed my mother quoted those lines.

Now I was on my way to Basra, the last leg of my trip home from England. In my bag was my degree in petroleum engineering from the University of Birmingham. It was the most important thing in the world to me, as it reflected not only the hours I'd spent in the mines of Sheffield or scribbling equations in the lecture hall but also my anger and frustration at the deception among men and the relationship between nations—between Iran the oil producer and England the colonizer, and between Germany and the Allies as they locked themselves into war.

I'd landed on petroleum engineering purely by chance. The summer after I graduated with my *baccalauréat* from my French high school, I visited England and promptly fell in love with the country. I had planned to study architecture in France, but I abruptly changed course. When the University of London did not accept my French degree on such short notice, I appealed to our ambassador in London, Hossein Ala, for help. He was a friend of my father's, a small, delicate man with an enormous intellect and a commanding feel for language. He suggested Birmingham as more likely to accept my French credentials. It also offered a specialty in petroleum engineering, unique in Europe, which, he advised, might provide a compelling argument to my father for studying in England.

I applied immediately. Birmingham accepted me, and the die was cast. Henceforth I would become versed in chemistry and physics, mechanics, mathematics, and drilling. I didn't mind. I was in England, a country that gave me an identity card right away—unlike France, which for ten years had promised me a *carte d'identité* that never arrived. Instead of going to the post office to call abroad, I could dial directly from the street; instead of going to a special bank to cash a foreign check, any bank would do. England was fifty years ahead of France. Its empire had forced it to modernize. What I studied was irrelevant to me then; it was the place that was important.

My father telegrammed his approval, ordering me to study hard and report regularly to the ambassador.

Ironically, therefore, it was my infatuation with England that threw me into oil, my country's one great industry and the source of its political destiny. Oil *was* Iran's economy. For better or worse it would define the country's future. Oil was not just a commodity for Iran. It was the blood of its earth and the means to catapult its people into the twentieth century. It was a weapon and a lure, and most important it was money.

By deciding to study oil I was also following in the footsteps of Nosrat-Doleh, who for ten years had served as Iran's premier negotiator against the British-held Anglo-Persian (and later, Anglo-Iranian) Oil Company (APOC).*

The questions he grappled with were still outstanding in 1941. Filled with the zeal of the recent graduate, I wanted to continue his work. Equally important I wanted to exonerate his name.

At Birmingham I was taught by the successors of the very men who had sent George Reynolds wildcatting for oil in Chiah Sorgh and Masjed So-leyman at the turn of the century and who, after his stunning strike, had created Anglo-Persian. Sir John Cadman, the redoubtable second chairman of APOC, had founded the petroleum engineering department at Bir-mingham. Ironically it was the Iranians who most appreciated the degree. In Iran anything "Made in England" was still considered peerless. When I was a child, British gold sovereigns were so highly sought after that I was sure all the gold in the world was mined in England. Had I not been from Iran, I would have thought the same for oil. And so it was England, not Iran, that offered the scholar the secrets of our black gold.

A TALE OF RICHES AND RAGS

At the very last moment, the degree for which I'd worked for more than four years almost slipped from my fingers. A letter announcing my father's death arrived six months before I was to graduate. Abruptly my allowance was cut, and I had no means to pay for my last courses, let alone my room and board. World War II had erupted just three months before in Septem-ber 1939 when Germany invaded Poland. Communication with Iran had broken down; I was on my own.

My experiences in Europe never approached the magical, opulent es-capades of my glamorous brother Nosrat-Doleh. My elementary schooling in Belgium and France was passed in rigid, drafty institutions. The bread we ate was stale, and our baths were cold. My father had to send a special order all the way from Iran demanding that I be allowed to take a bath once a week rather than the usual once a month. For months I went hungry, and at night the pangs in my stomach kept me awake. I never had any money,

*In 1935, the government of Reza Shah changed the name of Persia to Iran. The com-pany followed suit and, at a cost of $1 million (to change its logo, stationery, and the like), henceforth became the Anglo-Iranian Oil Company (AIOC). In 1949, the government stated it would no longer insist on the use of Iran, and today the two names are used, often interchangeably.

and once, when my grades were particularly bad, my meager allowance was severed for nine months, robbing me of the chocolate I used to buy on the sly to quiet the growls in my belly.

In England my lot marginally improved. Every month I received £25 by draft from Lloyds Bank in London. I picked up the first installment in person. The manager came down especially to say hello, and after settling me into a plush red leather chair, he explained that although he had as yet not had the honor of meeting my father, the prince, he had met Nosrat-Doleh when the latter had passed through London fifteen years earlier as minister of foreign affairs. Then he showed me the records of Farman Farma's account. I noticed an exceptionally large draft that had been debited in 1921, probably the ransom money paid by Farman Farma to Reza Shah.

It didn't take me long to discover that even in 1936, £25 didn't stretch very far. It was the same sum that the Iranian government gave its scholarship students in England, and my father typically made a point of treating us children no better than people without our means. At Birmingham my richer Persian friends often needled me about my small purse. Though room and board ran just over £10 a month, clothes, books, dinner dates, and my prized motorcycle ate into the remaining £15 at top speed. When my father died I had barely any savings at all.

I was living at the time with a young couple, Derek and Winnie Philips. I'd met Derek during my second year when my motorcycle broke down in the street. It was pouring rain, and I was struggling to get the engine restarted when a small car stopped and a man of about thirty jumped out. Pulling a couple of wrenches from his raincoat, he took out a spark plug and gave it a deft swipe with a cloth. When the motorcycle started at first kick, he introduced himself. He was a mechanic at the behemoth Birmingham Austin Motorworks and lived right around the corner from my digs.

Over the following weeks we saw each other often. One night he and his wife, Winnie, who played the piano like an angel and had a bubbly sense of humor, suggested I rent the spare room in their house. The following year I did so, bringing my girlfriends over for dinner—which they always encouraged, though they counseled me from time to time not to change companions quite so often—and accompanying them on weekend drives to cathedrals and castles in the countryside.

The next summer, in 1938, I visited my brother Sabbar in Geneva, where he was finishing up his last year of training in medicine. Geneva was then home to the League of Nations, and there was much going on that summer in the international sphere. The Soviet Union had just applied for membership, and rioting had erupted in the streets as voting took place inside the building. A couple of months earlier Italy had invaded Abyssinia.

Meanwhile Germany had entered the Ruhr. The French prime minister Edouard Daladier and Britain's Neville Chamberlain went to Munich like beggars on their knees, enjoining Hitler not to go to war. Hitler insulted Daladier and then marched on Austria, carrying out in record time what became known as the Anschluss, or annexation of Austria. I watched and reveled in being so close to it all, happily motoring about the Alps in Sabbar's car as the winds of war gradually gathered force throughout Europe.

In September I returned to England very short of money. Thinking that I could save more if my allowance were bigger, I resolved to ask my father for a raise. I knew he would not recognize my need unless it was compelling. So in my most respectful tone I wrote that I intended to marry an English girl.

The answer came sooner than I expected. His secretary Agha-ye Sadr (the formidable "Monsieur") had as usual written the letter, but in signing it my father had added a few words of his own. "I have looked forward to seeing one of my sons marry a foreign girl," he wrote. "None of your five elder brothers has done so. You have my congratulations and blessing. I am sure you must have thought seriously of the arrival of children and the consequences. It is not for me to anticipate your problems, so you will receive your usual allowance of £25 a month until the end of your studies." The note ended with a final flourish: "Find out if your fiancée has a sister. If so, send her to Tehran to me."

I had to laugh. My father was no fool. Nonetheless I decided to try one more salvo. Earlier in the spring I had come down with appendicitis and spent a couple of weeks in the hospital. I wrote an impassioned plea to Agha-ye Sadr imploring him to tell Farman Farma that I was still sick and needed to see a specialist. Specialists were expensive. This was a question of life and death. Could he please plead my case to my father and ask him to send funds for treatment, even if it was just £50?

I waited two or three weeks for an answer. When it finally came, it was terse. "Your letter has been read to His Highness, who is extremely annoyed and concerned," wrote Agha-ye Sadr. "He is well aware that all students are insured. Should your insurance prove insufficient, you should refer the matter to our ambassador in London, who will settle with the doctors directly. If you are still very sick, it shows you have taken up bad living habits and raises doubts about a definite cure. Should anything untoward occur, orders have been given for your burial in England. His Highness, having many sons, wishes you good health."

Thoroughly vanquished, I shot off a disrespectful letter to Agha-ye Sadr saying I had expected better from him, then put the matter out of my mind. That year I saved less than the last.

After I took my exams in June 1939, my sister Mehri invited me to Bucharest, where her husband, Mohsen Khan Raiis, had just been appointed ambassador from a previous posting in Germany. My brother Aziz, a student of architecture in Paris, decided to come too, and I hopped across the Channel to spend a few days with him before heading to Romania. Aziz was only two years younger than I, and we looked so similar that people often mixed us up. But whereas I favored British tweeds and corduroys and wore a double-breasted blue university blazer with the school's coat of arms, Aziz preferred the streamlined pose of the fashionable French *étudiant:* tight pants and a jacket with no lapels.

The last time I'd passed through Paris I'd met a dark-eyed Spanish beauty named Solange. Together with Aziz and his belle, we did our best on a diminished budget to emulate the dazzling exploits of Nosrat-Doleh when he'd been in Paris thirty years before. Whereas he had arrived at the Hôtel Lutécia in a chauffeur-driven car and had occupied a whole suite, we showed up on foot, rain-soaked, and could only gaze longingly through the windows. Nonetheless we tasted the life, and though we did not think of it as a homage, it was, for Nosrat-Doleh was dead.

At last we set out for Bucharest, traveling through Vienna, whose blue Danube I found disappointingly muddy, and then crossed into the Balkans. There we entered another world, downtrodden and grim. Barefoot women in rags, bent double over spades and shovels, shifted gravel on the railways. One morning we sat gaping through the train window as a colonel climbed from his car and snatched a newspaper from the hands of a destitute newsboy without paying for it. In the towns and villages people walked without shoes along the roads, a third-world sight that rekindled discomfiting memories of Iran.

In Bucharest Mehri picked us up at the station in a splendid Buick, and for a month we were shielded from the indignities of the countryside. Romania, thanks to its oil, was enjoying a wave of prosperity. As Hitler geared up his war machine, the country had benefited greatly from the industrial bonanza taking place across its borders.

Left to our own devices during the day, we explored the tortuous backstreets of Bucharest, walked its grand boulevards, and enjoyed the unreal hush that marked Europe's last days of peace. At night Mehri and Mohsen Khan brought us to the theater or to the casino on the hill, where princes, dukes, and counts—as well as a smattering of German generals—gathered in profusion to gamble.

Mehri, two years older than I, had become strikingly beautiful. She spoke good French, drilled into her by her acid-tongued governess in Tehran, Mademoiselle Dupuiche, and had a flair for the pillbox hats then coming into fashion. Her marriage to Mohsen Khan had been arranged, as all my older sisters' marriages were. In Mehri's case, however, the ceremony took place without the husband-to-be; he had already been posted to Germany by the time they were engaged. After the festivities, during which Mohsen Khan's name was affixed to the necessary documents by proxy, Mehri, with no idea what type of person her husband would turn out to be and having never traveled beyond the borders of Iran, packed her bags and joined him in Berlin. Luckily the match was a success. Though well endowed with the iron will typical of all my mother's daughters, Mehri had been brought up to expect a marriage of convenience and counted her blessings that Mohsen Khan was a gentle, dedicated man, neither philanderer nor louse, whose career was brilliant and whose intellect would challenge her for the length of their lives.

At the beginning of September Mohsen Khan called us into his highceilinged study and told us that the situation in Europe was deteriorating fast. A short, taciturn man with a round face and the distinction of being the youngest ambassador in the Iranian diplomatic corps, he listened avidly to the radio every night—first the BBC, then the German news, and finally the French—culling information about the impending war. Dallying in Bucharest would be unwise, he said. His contacts in Berlin had confirmed that time was running out.

Aziz and I caught a train the next morning to Constantsa on the Black Sea. There we boarded a boat that stopped for a few hours in Istanbul and then headed on to Athens. In Istanbul we presented our passports to the immigration official, eager after so many years to catch a glimpse of the Middle East. But he told us that anyone with an *-ian* at the end of their name was Armenian, and Armenians were not allowed to leave the ship. We protested, falling over ourselves to recite passages from the Koran in the vain hope of convincing him we were not Christians, as Armenians typically are, but Persian Moslems. He would not be swayed, and we passed the day on the boat, cursing.

In Greece we learned that Hitler's powerful foreign minister, Joachim von Ribbentrop, had signed a nonaggression treaty with Moscow. It was a *coup de foudre,* for up until then Hitler had adamantly refused to speak with Stalin. The Allies had been trying for months to convince the Russians to join their side. Now, in one masterstroke, Hitler had outmaneuvered the English and the French.

The next day, as we chugged through the hills of Greece and old Macedonia, Germany invaded Poland. Within twenty-four hours England retaliated, declaring war as we crossed into Italy and giving the Germans until morning to pull back their forces. As dawn broke and the train turned north from Milan toward Paris, the deadline passed. France declared war as we crossed the frontier onto French soil. World War II had begun.

The journey from the border to Paris, which normally took ten hours, lasted three days. We stopped overnight in the Alpine village of St. Nicolas, where I had passed many summers while a student in France. There I saw the mayor with a French flag wrapped around his waist. Everyone was crying. I didn't understand. Surely an accommodation would be reached. Besides, war was a heroic adventure. Why the tears?

When we finally reached Paris, we found the city in chaos. There was nobody at the Gare de Lyon to collect our tickets. The metro and buses had stopped running, and already there were electricity and water outages. Within twenty-four hours France ground to a halt. People began packing up and leaving the country without a thought of patriotism. Whereas only a few years earlier the Spanish had fled north to escape civil war, now the French poured south into Franco's Spain and Mussolini's Italy. It seemed to me that France had already lost the war.

England, by contrast, was bustling and orderly as I stepped off the boat train a few days later. Public services and businesses were working as usual. Only the dimmed lights of cars at night indicated that all was not normal. Once back in Birmingham, however, I realized that precautionary measures were already widely in force. Little by little rationing became part of our lives. As the autumn wore on and Germany invaded Norway, occupied Denmark, and overran the Low Countries, a ten o'clock curfew was instituted. Police notification was required for travel by all foreigners. The petrol pumps were all painted dark green, and gas, meted out at a few gallons a month per person, was sold under the single brand name of Pool. At the age of twenty-two I viewed these developments as part of a grand caper and hardly considered them the precursor of approaching holocaust. Besides the restrictions had the pleasant side effect of making life more affordable.

Nonetheless, on December 15, 1939, when I received a letter from Tehran telling me in my mother's flowing hand that my father had died, I knew I had not saved enough to get me through. I read the letter on the bus as I headed to the university for my first exams of the term. I felt no sorrow or pain. The violent demise of Nosrat-Doleh two years before had made me callous. I took the exam without a second thought.

Only later did I experience a sense of loss. I suppose since childhood I'd been expecting my father's death. He'd been an old man for so very long. Having to stand by helplessly as his eldest son was ignominiously slain had no doubt dealt a mortal blow to Farman Farma's spirit.

My father's death threw into sharp relief my own sense of family responsibility. So many of my siblings were still underage; my youngest brother, Abdol Ali, was only five. I had no idea whether they were safe or adequately provided for. Yet there was nothing I could do.

As for me, I was in a quandary. My allowance, which had arrived like clockwork for four years, had suddenly stopped. No doubt chaos was reigning in Tehran, and no one had thought to send a letter to the bank authorizing my remittance in my father's stead. Mehri and Mohsen Khan had been unreachable since the outbreak of war, and Ambassador Hossein Ala, my mentor, had left London some time before. I looked back on my moneyed days with a certain remorse and sheepishly approached Derek to tell him that my father's death had, for the moment, severed my income and that I had not saved enough to continue my studies. In fact, I told him, I would probably have to move.

Derek would hear none of it. The room was mine, and as for tuition and basic living expenses, he would pay. I was overwhelmed. Derek and Winnie were not rich, and she was eight months pregnant with their first child. They were offering me their life savings in the midst of war. Such faith in friendship was rare, and I clasped him to me, moved beyond words.

Their generosity was all the more poignant because in England at the time racism was rampant. At university foreign students were shunned. We were not allowed to hold student office, and the college deans, at a meeting held at the beginning of each year, went so far as to warn girls to stay away from us, insinuating that we were from base cultures. At one point I became so incensed that I complained bitterly to Ambassador Ala. He promised to approach Lord Cadman, the chairman of the Anglo-Iranian Oil Company and a trustee of the university. But the barrier of discrimination did not recede. It was not just the university but British society in general that held such views, from the foreman at the garage where I worked one summer to the rich lady with the Daimler who had her butler repeat everything I said because it was below her dignity to converse with me directly. All the more extraordinary, then, were the Philipses' confidence and goodwill.

A TALE OF BOMBINGS

I passed my exams in June of 1940. The German blitzkrieg had advanced rapidly over Europe and had now reached England. The industrial centers of Manchester, Sheffield, and Birmingham were suffering massive attack. One night the Germans sent three hundred planes over Birmingham, two every four minutes, to keep us awake.

After my exams I helped Derek dig a shelter in the garden. At night when the bombardments began, Derek, Winnie, and their new baby girl, Trudi, would repair there for safety. I would join them for a while but would soon get restless and claustrophobic, and after listening to the BBC news at ten, I would return to my comfortable bed in the house.

The first week of July a solitary German plane was dropping incendiary bombs on the horizon as I walked from the London train station to AIOC's Sunbury Laboratories, hoping the company could arrange a passage home for me to Iran. Miraculously a letter had arrived from my father's secretary—a freak delivery across battle lines—that listed the properties I had inherited. They turned out to be varied and considerable. In the same mail I received the first letter from my mother since her news of my father's death. She enclosed, to my enormous relief, £250. I paid the Philipses back a small portion of the £300 I owed them and kept the rest to cover the expenses of my return.

AIOC regularly sent five or six Iranian students a year to Birmingham to study and then hired them to work at the refinery in Abadan. The company also shuttled employees back and forth from Iran to England for home leave. Commanding, as it did, the clout of the British government, it seemed the most likely organization to arrange for my return in the midst of war. Charles Myles, the head of students, agreed to book my passage on *The Merchant of Venice,* which was to sail around the southern tip of Africa and land in Bombay. From there I would double back to Basra in Iraq and then take a boat to Abadan.

I returned to Birmingham stunned by the destruction in London. The bombing had left thousands of people homeless. The underground stations were jammed as whole families with children huddled all along the platform. There was barely a yard of space left to stand in as I waited for the train. Outside I walked around with a thick book over my head to protect myself from antiaircraft shrapnel—pieces of steel about the length of a finger—that fell like rain from the skies. One of my friends in London gathered a whole collection of these lethal metal shards. I pocketed a few as well, displaying them for years in my library in Tehran.

A WAR CRUISE

The Merchant of Venice was scheduled to depart from Liverpool at the beginning of December 1940. I arrived a few days early and checked into a modest little hotel near the docks, reserved and already paid for by AIOC. The cashier there was a stunning girl named Eileen Howard, who agreed to show me the town. Every night German bombs showered down on the city, and I would look at her beautiful profile in the half light and wonder whether I was again falling in love. Eileen accompanied me to the boat to see me off. We hardly spoke a word. She didn't cry. What future was there to hope for anyway? Neither of us knew whether we were even going to be alive the next day.

The Merchant of Venice didn't set sail for another three days. Well in sight of Liverpool we waited at anchor as thirteen more ships gradually joined us to form a giant convoy. Every night bombs tore up the water, and we would awake to the news that ships to our left and right had been sunk during the air raids.

It was late afternoon when we finally set off. Soon after the ship weighed anchor, the sirens began to wail and all the passengers were called into the main lounge. Asking for a show of hands by those who knew how to row, the captain explained that the lifeboats were ready in case we were torpedoed and assigned each of us to one.

Most of the passengers were British officers going to Bombay; a half dozen were AIOC staff returning to Abadan from home leave. There were only about twenty women aboard, and almost everyone was under the age of thirty. Right from the beginning we became friends. At sea the real world fades away, and the universe shrinks to fit within the guardrails of the ship. With the knowledge that the passengers might all go down together, a recklessness takes hold, barriers of etiquette and class fade into irrelevance, and friendships flourish with incredible speed.

I spent the first four days confined to my cabin, desperately sick from the pitch and roll of the boat. On the fifth day, feeling suddenly better, I went up on deck. The weather was raw, and the swells so tossed the vessel that one could only venture along the sides, holding on to the guard ropes. I looked out over the convoy, noting that six or seven more ships had joined us. Ours was the only passenger ship, though even it had a small cannon in its prow. We were at the convoy's center, with an escort of three gunboats, all sailing very close together. None carried running lights, and I marveled that we hadn't yet collided in the dark.

I breathed in the salty sea air and started talking with an officer standing near me. Just as he was inviting me to join a game of bridge that evening, we saw a ship to our starboard rock violently, split in half, and begin to sink. Within seconds two more ships were hit, their severed hulls slanting crazily into the water. The gunboats veered to the starboard, dropping depth charges to destroy the submarine that had apparently sneaked into our midst.

I dashed for the lifeboat to which I'd been assigned. But even before I got there, I saw a group of people running toward me, heading for the aft of the ship. Alarmed, I turned and ran back with them. Before we had gone thirty feet, another group hurtled toward us yelling, "Watch out, the Jerries [Germans] are shooting, the Jerries are shooting!" Thinking that firing was taking place at the back end of the craft, we turned in confusion and stumbled forward. Running and stopping and turning in total panic, I found myself next to the ring of my lifeboat once again and stopped short, deciding in the blur that the best place to be was right here, where I could cut the boat loose should the ship go down.

Within an hour the convoy had dispersed and we were alone, uprooted and unprotected. It had all been so sudden; I was overcome by our vulnerability as we floated blindly across the battle zone. I had swaggered on deck as though this were a country cruise, thinking we'd left the war behind in Liverpool. Instead it was all around us.

Dinner was served an hour late that night. The long table that normally sat twenty-five stretched emptily across the dining room, most of the passengers feeling too queasy to face a meal. Only the first mate was there, and a plucky family who had already been rescued once from a ship shot out of the water.

Over soup I asked the first mate why we'd taken off on our own, exposing ourselves to German attack. He cheerfully explained that in addition to the submarines, a German pocket battleship had been sighted in the vicinity, one of the fastest, most dangerous warships of the day.* We'd had no choice but to bolt. At a capacity of fourteen knots, we could never have escaped were it to attack the convoy. Better to be out on our own.

The sea remained choppy, but the dangers of nature seemed infinitely less frightening than the threat of our enemies. As time passed, however, even that fear eased, and by the eighth day, having seen nothing but whitecaps on the water, we settled down to a routine of deck games in the afternoon and dressing for dinner.

Early one evening I stopped at the bar and ran into the ship's doctor, who had a much greater affinity for the bar than the sick bay. We chatted a little as I ordered my drink. Before the waiter could hand me my beer, however, the ship gave a huge lurch and began to heave upward. I watched, fascinated, as it rose and rose and the entire room began to slide past me, the ice bucket tipping over and cascading ice cubes to the floor, the olives and pearl onions rolling around like marbles, the chandelier teetering against the ceiling. Then, with an awful shudder, the ship pitched forward

---

*As there was no radar in those days, the BBC would send out secret signals through its regular broadcasts to alert ships at sea of enemy movements. It was through a BBC signal that *The Merchant of Venice* had learned a pocket battleship was in the vicinity.

and plunged to the other side. A bottle of soda fell from the bar and exploded. A steward went down with a chunk of glass in his eye. Someone broke a leg. I dove under the bar to avoid the tumblers and ashtrays that skidded across the counter and rained from the shelves. Another torpedo strike, I thought grimly. We were done for. The Jerries had hit us, and we were going down.

But it was not a torpedo. It was a hurricane, which had scored a direct hit on the boat and was bashing it from side to side.

The storm lashed the ship for four days and four nights. It seemed more like Noah's forty. We passed the days sitting on the floor, though even then we were rolled over. We played bridge continuously, the ship's service providing us with sandwiches, which the waiters brought in bags hung about their necks.

When the storm finally wore down, the sea suddenly became so calm that it was hard to imagine we had lived through such a nightmare. In the middle of the night I awoke to the sudden stillness, strangely missing the thunderous torment. I threw on some clothes and headed for the deck, where I emerged under a firmament of stars. The water, flat as glass, here and there sparkled with flashes of phosphorescence. It was a moment of supreme beauty.

We reached Cape Town after five weeks on the water. The harbor pulsed with activity. The *Queen Mary,* the pride of the British merchant fleet, was at anchor, transformed into a troop carrier, and thousands of British soldiers were all over town. I joined three officers from *The Merchant of Venice* and went ashore. In those days Cape Town was not large, and girls were scarce. After stopping in a few bars and nightclubs, we resolved to leave ship and go by car to Johannesburg to see if things were any better there. The ship was scheduled to dock a week later in Mombasa, where we would reboard it before setting sail for India.

In Johannesburg the weather was warm, the hotel was stuffy, and the girls had gone to Cape Town. We missed the pleasure of being by the sea and left Johannesburg after a few idle days, sorry to have abandoned ship.

When we arrived in Mombasa *The Merchant of Venice* was not there. Seeing the port authority office, we pounded through the door, desperately shouting that it was only two o'clock and the ship was not due to leave until five. The man behind the desk explained that because of the shortage of port facilities, *The Merchant of Venice* was anchored offshore. We could get to it by motor launch, easily hired right at the dock.

I thought I would burst with joy when we finally caught sight of our dear ship. But then I realized that boarding was going to be a nightmare.

A forty-foot rope ladder had been thrown from the deck and swung free from the point on the hull that bulged out over the water. To get aboard we had to hoist ourselves straight up without hope of using the ship's side for leverage.

Two pairs of strong hands grabbed my shoulders and mercifully pulled me over the rail when I reached the top. But in place of a welcome they dragged me to the pool and threw me headlong into the water. Two of my companions were already there, and the last soon joined us. Our fellow passengers surrounded the pool and, as punishment for being late, gleefully tramped on our fingers and threw us back in every time we tried to get out. Dragged down by my clothes, tired out, and sick with the stench of salt water, I finally sank to the bottom.

Hours later I woke up in my cabin still wearing my wet clothes, my waterlogged shoes hanging from my feet. I had no recollection of how I'd gotten there. I lay in my berth happy to be alive. All was silent save for the sound of the waves against the hull. We were well on our way to India.

A TALE OF COLONIAL SHOCK

Bombay was the dirtiest, busiest, most chaotic city I had ever seen. Everywhere I turned it provoked buried instincts, calling forth emotions I did not recognize and invoking a familiarity at once strange and comfortable. I was not home, but I was getting there. In India I recognized the forgotten scent of desert dust in the rain, the shape of burlap bags spilling forth seeds and nuts, and the sight of beggars with cataracts.

But India was not Iran. It teemed with people, while Iran was empty. Over the centuries Iran had conquered India many times, on each occasion carrying off its treasures, including its famous Peacock Throne. Though in England Persians were looked upon as darkies from an inferior race and religion, here we were regarded as esteemed guests—of England of course, not India. We were invited to stay in the toniest hotels, and the doors of every chic restaurant were open as long as we wore dinner jackets or tails (which we invariably did)—though an Indian would be thrashed were he to venture so much as a look inside. At the opening of Laurence Olivier's *Wuthering Heights,* an affair attended by all the pomp of the Opéra in Paris, we were escorted with the rest of British society to the theater balcony where no Indian was allowed, except for those bearing trays to serve the dinner that followed. And just like the British to my left and right, who got to their feet when their anthem, "God Save the King," was played through the movie hall speakers, I looked down at the rabble below and was genuinely dismayed when three or four refused to listen and made a ruckus as they hurried away.

Prejudice came easily in India. The Indians didn't have the stubborn toughness that had helped the Persians throughout history retain their independence and identity. "Anyone can beat an Indian," observed Sir Arnold Wilson when as a young British Cavalry officer he was transferred from duty in India to protect the oil wells in Iran. "But if you must punish a Persian, be sure to have him beaten by one of his own; otherwise you risk severe retaliation." We Persians traditionally prided ourselves on our social resilience and our tolerance for the displaced—the Armenians, Assyrians, and Jews—who had taken up residence in Iran as a haven from religious persecution. Yet in actual fact we considered ourselves superior to everyone else. We were Aryans, with a rich and ancient culture. Once we had masterminded a huge empire. Since Alexander the Great no one had succeeded in colonizing us. Full of compunction, I too disdained the Indians. It was all a question of place: In England we were the ones who were despised. In Iran the British and Persians were equals—and enemies. In India we were friends and similarly supercilious.

Just before we'd disembarked from *The Merchant of Venice,* a man had come aboard selling clubs and whips of beautifully worked leather. Finding them decorative and a bargain, I'd chosen two or three, but the man had shaken his head and allowed me to buy only one. It hadn't occurred to me that they were anything but ornaments to hang on the wall. But as I walked down the street with my English companions, I saw them using the clubs to clear the people from their path. It was barbarous but efficient, and soon I too was using my club to beat back the swarms.

Bombay was packed with people with nowhere to go and nothing to do. One afternoon we saw a crowd gathering as an old Rolls-Royce rolled down the street. An ancient woman wrapped in a luxuriant sari sat in the back, scattering handfuls of coins out the window. A maidservant next to her held up a gilded bowl from which she plucked the coppers; an attendant in front beat back the beggars who approached too closely. People strained to catch the coins in midair or scrounged like rats along the sidewalk as the money fell to the ground. The woman dispensing her charity from the Rolls was the "grand old lady" of the Tata family, whose empire included industry, textiles, and airlines.

The inhumanity of this display outraged me. It reminded me of the earl of Dudley, who owned half of Birmingham and every election year sent his Rolls to bring voters—including my first landlady—to the balloting booths. My landlady, who never lost an opportunity to point out how superior the English race was to mine, was infuriated when I suggested that the earl's Rolls might be affecting her political judgment.

I suppose my father's power and birth made him no different from the Indian maharajas and British lords. Nonetheless, as he had in his lifetime so ably demonstrated, wealthy families had to change with the times and cease beating back the crowds with whips of title and prestige.

Yet in India nothing is simple. It struck me as appropriate that the Hindu gods have a hundred arms and myriad shapes. Every heartfelt resolution I made as I observed the life in the streets was immediately mocked by the temptations all about and repudiated by the rites of India's history and caste system. And every revelation I came upon as I walked the teeming alleyways was immediately outwitted by a new one.

My two weeks in Bombay passed like lightning. Before I knew it I was boarding a Tata plane for Karachi. There I stayed in a guest house and, with no regrets, set off for Basra the next day.

THE TALE OF THE SHATT-AL-ARAB

Karachi and Basra are separated by six hundred miles as the crow flies—a couple of hours' flight by today's measure, but it took us ten. After the parched and acrid view of Iran's southern littoral, the scene improved as we flew over the deep blue waist of the Persian Gulf and up the golden Arabian coast, stopping several times to refuel before finally crossing into Iraq.

We landed on the wide waters of the Shatt-al-Arab, the swampy delta where the Tigris and Euphrates Rivers join to divide the lands of Iran and Iraq. Neither country had ever recognized the other's sovereignty over this precious waterway, and for centuries battles had spilled blood across its marshes. At the time it belonged to Iraq, thanks to the British, who had taken it over from the Ottoman Turks and created the Basra Port Authority, which held a monopoly over all shipping in and out of the Shatt-al-Arab. Because of a war the Persians had lost to the Turks almost one hundred years before, Iran could claim only a few yards of the water off its coastline and was forced to use Iraq's tugs now that oil shipping had suddenly enlivened its Gulf seafront. Thirty years later the Shah would strike a deal to have the waterway split more evenly. Ten years beyond that the Shatt-al-Arab would spark the bloody, decade-long Iran-Iraq War in which Saddam Hussein would reclaim it all and then, during the Gulf War, spontaneously return Iran's share in hopes of gaining an ally in his ill-fated play for Kuwait.

The morning broke clear and clean; a thin mist hung over the lapping water, and it felt more like a spring day than the first week of February 1941. The Shatt-al-Arab glimmered under the sun, and the launch sliced soundlessly through its still, green water.

I looked anxiously at the far bank, anticipating the view of Abadan, its smokestacks and electrical pylons the technological minarets of its mammoth refinery. Abadan was the culmination of everything I had studied over the past four years. Yet having gone halfway around the world to get here, I was once again about to disembark onto a slice of Britain. Abadan was on Iranian soil, but it was English to the core. Even in my own country Abadan would make me second class. I felt apprehensive. Charmed as I was by England's eccentricities and inspired as I was by its industrial vision, I was sickened by its political chauvinism and xenophobia. I'd emerged from my years at the University of Birmingham caught between love and hate for all that England was and wasn't vis-à-vis Iran. Now political sentiment would play as essential a part in my future as any of the courses I'd taken in drilling, refining, and physical chemistry. I set my jaw, wondering what this quasi-British homecoming would be like.

"They're not so different. They're really just like us," two pretty English girls had whispered in wonder to each other one evening on a date with my friend Saifollah Moazemi and me. The Anglo-Iranian Oil Company, I eventually came to realize, would never make such a discovery in Abadan.

CHAPTER
IV

THE DANGEROUS
GAME OF OIL

Do not complain of hardship in your quest of knowledge;
No success can be complete without the suffering of pain.
—HAFEZ

Iran 1941

Maheen Taba held out a plate of saffron cookies and asked if I wanted more
tea.

"*Dast-shoma dard nakoneh*—May your hands never suffer pain," I said,
shaking my head. I had never met Maheen before, but she'd made me a special homecoming lunch of *shirin polo,* a pilaf with slivers of oranges and al-
monds, always served at celebrations. I had done it justice. Dr. Abdol
Hossein Taba chuckled, as though his X-ray eyes could see my straining
stomach muscles. He lit his pipe. The room was cool. The only air condi-
tioner in all of Bawardeh rumbled in the corner.

"You'll find Tehran much changed," Maheen said. "Don't expect any of
the privileges you once had when you get there."

"Privileges?" I asked.

"You think that having left at the age of nine you have forgotten all that
you took for granted? You will see." Maheen crossed her lovely legs and
looked away. She was the youngest daughter of Vosugh-Doleh, the prime
minister who with my brother Nosrat-Doleh had signed the ill-fated
Anglo-Persian Agreement of 1919. By chance she was here in Abadan,
married to Dr. Taba, whom I'd met briefly in Birmingham, where he had

studied medicine. She came down the path to greet me when I arrived, a vision of dark eyes and Middle Eastern tentativeness, a stark contrast to the Western women I was used to. I did not know many Persian women and was struck by how beautiful she was. I felt shy and pleased. I had not imagined a Persian woman to be so chic, so smart, so educated—so very different from British descriptions of Iranians. In place of my natural loquaciousness I found myself tongue-tied.

I looked out the window at the flat expanse of one-story houses set in neat rows that composed the exclusively Persian residential section of Bawardeh. To the right were the prim brick houses of Braim, the British section. From here Braim looked as if it had been sliced right out of Birmingham and dropped into Abadan: The flower boxes, postboxes, apron gardenettes, and whitewashed stoops and shutters were all so perfectly English. Even the cars and buses—all English makes—drove on the left. This was a company town from top to bottom. Everything here was stamped AIOC.

"Our family is in better political standing than yours," Maheen was saying. "And yet my father's brother Qavam-Saltaneh is under house arrest." A languid sadness hung about her. I wondered whether she begrudged her life in the forgotten wasteland of Abadan or whether I'd find this sadness in all the families ground down by Reza Shah.

"My father stopped sending me the newspapers so I wouldn't get any ideas about going into politics," I said quickly. "But wasn't Reza Shah in Qavam-Saltaneh's cabinet when he was prime minister?"

"As the Persian saying goes: Cover your eyes with a curtain. It is not your business to try and understand the why and how of it." She did not meet my eyes.

Dr. Taba rose irritably. "Maheen, you're depressing him. He's just arrived. Let him contemplate the wonders of the refinery without worrying about politics in Tehran." He strode to the door. "Come on. I'll drive you to your tour."

Maheen gave me a wistful look as I took my leave. Dr. Taba was a good doctor, but he was out of place bringing a daughter of Vosugh-Doleh down here to live with no friends of her rank and no society. There were hardly any women here—the British mostly came without their wives, and the Iranians were either from the villages or newly graduated and unmarried. The Abadan hospital couldn't even keep a full contingent of nurses, they married so rapidly after stepping off the boat from England. Even when the company made a point of hiring ugly ones it was to no avail.

I felt lucky at being assigned to stay with the Tabas. It was my first experience in Iran of the rewards of aristocratic privilege. The other students who'd traveled to Abadan had been assigned to dorms. Not only had I been offered a luxurious bed in one of the only two-story houses in Abadan, but the Tabas were my people. I felt pained by their sadness. It would not turn out to be a happy marriage. They would eventually have a daughter—and eventually divorce.

I stayed a week in Abadan. The Anglo-Iranian Oil Company had arranged everything: tours of the refinery, the labs, the plants; dinner with other Persian graduates of Birmingham; drinks at the Persian Club—all in an effort to woo me into taking a job.

The refinery was awe inspiring. It was the biggest in the world and was shipping 300,000 barrels a day. Laid out in a huge set of interlocking grids along the coast, it sprang from the earth in a plethora of smokestacks and piping. Gas burned off in towering flames like torches to Zoroaster. I breathed in the heavy smell of sulfur and kerosene and felt transported. The great holding tanks looked like bastion towers plucked from the walls of citadels and placed into perfect rows along the quay. The heat from their metallic sides shivered the air, turning the whole vast, smoking, spitting complex into a wavering mirage.

Our little party of new recruits wound along the baking paths like a string of ants, inspecting details of the maze stretching above us in steel and brick as we shaded our eyes from the white sun. Escaping steam whistled and sputtered from the coiling pipes. A huge electric plant hummed along one side of the refinery. We wove through piles of barrels stacked into pyramids and watched as they were rolled down gangplanks into the tankers and flatboats docked on the water's edge. The heat was so intense that the asphalt on the docks was as soft as marshmallow. If it was this hot in February, what would it be like in July? As it was, the water pipes became so hot under the morning sun that we poured our baths hours before we planned to wash so that the water could cool down.

Abadan employed 30,000 workers. Most were hired locally, although there were still 3,000 imported Palestinian and Indian laborers working there when I arrived. Only 16 Iranians with British degrees had been inducted into middle management. Abadan's upper administration was all British: 2,000 expatriates filling jobs that later on I would discover only required about 150. Had so many come to Abadan to escape the war?

The division between the British and the rest of us was black and white. My first lesson in total segregation came as I waited to catch the bus back from the refinery to the Tabas' house that evening. As the bus approached I flashed the pass I'd been given at the driver. "Not this bus, mate," he

shouted. "Mine's a British bus. No Persians allowed." Even though I was a
VIP visitor, I had to wait. He shut the door in my face and moved on.
What a bitter insult—and in my own country.

Abadan was like that: parallel worlds side by side on a salty, inhospitable
island of barely over ten square miles. One world was closed off by law
from the other; one rarely breached the other out of prejudice. Just as in
India a British mercantile enterprise had developed into a colonial system
so rigid and severe that no conquest of arms could ever match it.

THE TALE OF PERSIA'S
BRITISH OIL

It had started out as a partnership between equals, a concession granted by
the Shah in 1901 to a small private company owned by William Knox
D'Arcy in England. The contract had been a tour de force, guaranteeing
Persia 16 percent of all company revenues while safeguarding D'Arcy's investment.

That was before World War I, when oil was still a minor commodity.
First drilled in Pennsylvania in 1859, oil was primarily a lighting and
heating fluid until Henry Ford produced his first assembly-line Model Ts
and the horseless carriage went mass-market. Oil was originally an American phenomenon. As Lord Cadman started lecturing his first course in petroleum engineering at Birmingham, John D. Rockefeller's Standard Oil
monopoly was being broken up under the Sherman Antitrust Act in Washington, D.C. Its offspring, born in 1911, would turn into many of the gi-
ants we know today: Exxon (originally Standard Oil of New Jersey), Mobil
(Standard Oil of New York), Chevron (Standard Oil of California), and
Amoco (Standard Oil of Indiana).

At the turn of the century Russia joined the oil race and, under the competing aegis of the powerful Rothschilds and Nobels, started pumping oil
from its Caspian port of Baku. In 1892 the first oil tanker passed through
the Suez Canal, bearing Russian kerosene to the Far East. Then oil was
found in Romania, the only known source in Europe, making it a prime
target in both upcoming world wars. Oil was also discovered in the steamy
jungles of the Dutch East Indies. There two companies, British-based Shell
and Royal Dutch, at first competed and then, in 1901, joined forces in the
first-ever oil merger.

William Knox D'Arcy, a big, hearty man newly wealthy from an Aus-
tralian gold-mining venture, decided that an oil concession in Persia was a
good bet. Thoroughly underestimating the degree of financial commit-

ment involved, he signed the deal with Mozzafar-edin Shah and sent George Reynolds over to start the drilling. Within the year he knew he was in over his head. Oil, unlike gold, was costly to find and slippery to market, and soon he was spending sleepless nights wondering whether he was going to go under.

THE TALE OF A HEIST

The United States, the largest producer in the world, felt smug about its resources and was unperturbed by its increasing dependence on oil. Not so England, where the notion of switching its venerable navy out of coal was hotly debated. "Oil," as Admiral J. Fisher pointed out, "don't grow in England," while coal was in abundance.[1] Oil-powered ships, however, were faster and didn't require manpower to stoke the engines. To the Royal Navy, used to ruling the waves, this was significant as it anxiously watched the growing prowess of Germany's navy.

In 1912 Winston Churchill, first lord of the Admiralty and a strong supporter of converting to oil, hit on a solution. A small outfit called the Anglo-Persian Oil Company (APOC), he told the House of Commons, had just discovered oil in Persia. It was an all-British company, operating on a concession to William Knox D'Arcy that ran until 1961. Although the oil strike was significant, the company needed funds: It was building a refinery in Abadan, required a transportation fleet, and lacked adequate distribution in England. His voice rising to a fever pitch, Churchill called on those seated about him to see how perfect the match could be: APOC would sell the Admiralty all the oil it needed at a reduced price for twenty years, guaranteeing its fuel needs as surely as if the oil were located right there in England. In return the government would buy 51 percent of the shares, infusing the company with capital while ensuring that it would remain under tight British control.

The House of Commons voted with Churchill. From then on Persia would deal not just with a private company but with "a sovereign state masquerading as a tradesman," as a report delivered on my desk in 1948 and written by an anonymous Englishman so aptly put it. The Persian government was never consulted, though the concession it had granted was specifically and exclusively to D'Arcy, a private individual. Instead it was delivered a fait accompli. APOC, it was informed, was now controlled by the British government. And to ensure that the company was governed as much by British national interests as entrepreneurial judgment, Whitehall placed a director with veto power on the board.

To Persia this was a crushing blow. The Admiralty agreement alone meant it would suffer huge losses in profits. But Britain was the early twentieth century's superpower. Its empire towered over both sides of Persia's eastern and western flanks. Its Admiralty commanded the biggest fleet in the world. To cry foul to a partner that was the British government was very different from accusing a private individual of concessionary violations. The Persian government no longer enjoyed the luxury of terminating the arrangement as a business deal; to threaten cancellation would now be to risk a losing war.

For Britain World War I confirmed Churchill's prescience in buying the oil company. Oil became a critical commodity not only on the high seas but also on land and in the air. At the beginning of the war England had only 250 planes, mostly for reconnaissance, its pilots leaning out the windows to shoot down enemies with a rifle. By 1918 it had constructed a staggering 55,000 planes. All told, both sides built more than 200,000 planes in four years as aviation took its place as a critical new weapon.[2] On land troops moved around with much greater precision in gas-powered trucks than in steam-engine trains, and in 1916, when the British developed tanks, soldiers started bulldozing their way across enemy lines, turning trench warfare into a mockery. On the oceans not only were oil-powered ships found to be vastly superior to coal-driven ones, but for the first time boats were constructed that traveled incognito underwater, providing a whole new dimension to naval warfare.

Oil changed the rules of combat, just as it changed the peace that ensued. Having a stash they could call their own was a boon for the British, even if it did need to be shipped three thousand miles around the world. Across the Atlantic in the United States, demand for oil in 1917 for the first time outstripped supply, leaving Americans ever after with a deep-seated fear of shortages. The U.S. military's thirst for oil had turned prodigious as the number of cars skyrocketed from 1.8 million in 1914 to a whopping 9.2 million by 1920.

Midway through World War I Lord Cadman departed Birmingham to head up the British government's Petroleum Executive. The department he left behind attracted such luminaries in my time as Dr. Niels Bohr, the Danish physicist renowned for his work on electrons, and Professor Norman Haworth, who won the Nobel Prize for chemistry while I was there in 1937. Cadman, for his part, moved on to the Anglo-Persian Oil Company and in 1927, as the government's candidate, became its chairman.

In the course of World War I APOC boomed. With government help the company developed a tanker fleet, set up a research laboratory in Sunbury, and bought a marketing and distribution company (conveniently named British Petroleum).

The Persian wells, it turned out, were not like any others in the world. The average well in the United States produced just 4½ barrels a day. In Masjed Soleyman one well alone gushed 9,100 barrels a day. And unlike in the United States, Romania, Russia, or the Dutch East Indies, the flow did not dwindle for years on end.* This rendered the costly process of pumping unnecessary.

The ease of the situation at the wells, however, contrasted starkly with the difficulties encountered in the building of the refinery at Abadan. An island of mudflats and palm trees in the Shatt-al-Arab 138 miles from the oil fields, Abadan, though in Iran, was part of a semi-independent Arab fiefdom controlled by Sheikh Khazal (who also held claim to Basra and all of Kuwait). Narrow-faced and shrewd, the tall, black-robed sheikh drove a hard bargain with the British oilmen who came to lease his land in 1909. He was concerned that on the one hand a huge, foreign industrial complex would alienate and inflame the area's Moslem tribesmen more used to camels than distillators, and that on the other the central government in Tehran, noticing the commercial activity taking place on its southwestern flank, would rouse itself from its somnolence and interfere. Both fears were to prove well-founded. But a deal was struck, and 600 acres were leased to APOC in 1910, rising by 1918, after much haggling, to 2,400.

Abadan was a desolate spot, and every last screw, pump, rail, canister of fresh water, and plate of food had to be imported. A thousand laborers were hired from the surrounding villages, and a thousand more were imported from India, all administered by a handpicked staff of fifty-three Europeans. The big problem that soon surfaced was how to refine Masjed Soleyman's "sour," or sulfur-soaked, oil. For the first three years, until 1913, Abadan turned out such smelly, low-grade fuels that the company could not meet its contracts, plunging it into the dire financial straits that made D'Arcy so amenable to Churchill's deal. By the outbreak of the war, however, the quality of Abadan's production had improved, and over the next few years the refinery expanded rapidly.

AN ONGOING TALE OF DISAGREEMENT

APOC was turning out to be a success. But its very achievements gave rise to conflicts that would plague the relationship between the Persian government and the company until Iran finally nationalized oil in 1951.

---

*In Masjed Soleyman one well gushed 2,000 barrels a day for thirty years.

D'Arcy's concession, to the growing dismay of Sir Charles Greenway, the company's first chairman, stated that the Persian government authorized "the Concessionaire to found one or several companies for the working of the concession" and that it was to receive "16 percent of the annual profits of any company or companies formed." At first this seemed innocuous enough. But as the company acquired subsidiaries in Brunei, Kuwait, and Bahrain, as well as 51 percent of a syndicate that held what was expected to become a valuable concession in Mesopotamia (later Iraq), Greenway and his colleagues began to backpedal. What right, they reasoned, did the Persian government have to collect a share of profits on business that had nothing to do with Persian oil? Better to pay a royalty on each barrel, they decided—forgetting that the profits of the mother company had paid for all the subsidiaries. This they proposed to the Persian government in 1917.

The proposition was rejected out of hand, even though at first it would have dropped an extra £40,000 a year into the Persian treasury. The official selected to explain just how outraged the Persian government was at such cupidity was the minister of foreign affairs, my brother Nosrat-Doleh. APOC was nothing without Persian oil, he argued, and its other projects were flourishing only because it was siphoning company profits their way.

In 1919, after the close of the war, the young Ahmad Shah, accompanied by Nosrat-Doleh, made a state visit to Europe, his last as sovereign of Persia. Initially they'd hoped to attend the Paris Peace Conference, where the Europeans and Americans were redrawing the map of the Middle East in the wake of the Ottoman Empire's collapse. But like thousands of others who came to appeal for war reparations, they did not succeed.

The American delegation, filled with the lofty ideals of President Woodrow Wilson's Fourteen Points embodied in the League of Nations, encouraged the Persian appeal. It was the British, in the person of Lord George Nathaniel Curzon, newly appointed foreign secretary from his post as viceroy of India, who blocked it. Persia, he felt, was a key link in the British Empire, a "bulwark for peace" without which India could slip from England's grasp. To this end he opened negotiations with Nosrat-Doleh in April, bullying him into dropping Persia's appeal for an audience in Paris in favor of a bilateral agreement for funds with Britain.

The resulting Anglo-Persian Agreement, signed and fêted in London on August 9, 1919, in effect turned Persia into a British protectorate by giving Britain control over both the treasury and the military (an agreement, incidentally, never accepted by Ahmad Shah). International public response was withering. "The independence of Persia was surrendered and control of the nation transferred to British hands," blustered *The Washing-*

ton Post a few months later on October 5. "The change will greatly benefit Persia from a material point of view—[but] that is not the point."

To the three Persian signatories—Vosugh-Doleh, the prime minister; Sarameh-Doleh, the finance minister; and Nosrat-Doleh, together commonly called the Triumvirate—that *was* the point. Agreement or no agreement Britain exercised supreme control over the area, especially once Russia withdrew because of its own revolution. (A strangely similar situation prevails today, with the United States, rather than Britain, commanding center stage.) By becoming party to the 1919 agreement, Nosrat-Doleh and the rest of the cabinet hoped that at the very least they would be formalizing Persia's rights and obtaining a needed loan.

Yet, it was a payoff that even they were not at peace with. Before signing, the Triumvirate extracted two very unusual concessions from Curzon: (1) a 400,000-toman (about $200,000) advance as a public relations budget to help smooth the agreement's passage through the Majles, and (2) a written affidavit promising British protection and asylum for each of them personally in the event of serious political deterioration.

The 1919 agreement never saw the light of day. With the Russian bear withdrawn to its lair, the Persian people felt suddenly free and saw no reason to pander to Britain. Immediately scuttled by the Majles, it was not one of Nosrat-Doleh's finer achievements—and one he would pay dearly for later on. His work on the other task before him, however—clarification and renegotiation of the D'Arcy Concession—was.

Claims and counterclaims were being made on both sides. The British accused Persia of reneging on the concession by failing to adequately protect the installations at Abadan. In 1915 the pipelines had suffered damage as a result of tribal unrest—exactly what Sheikh Khazal had feared. For two years the company blocked the payment of royalties against a claim of damages amounting to £614,489. Nosrat-Doleh argued that the company had made a private security arrangement with the Bakhtiari khans and could not now come complaining to the Persian government. He also insisted that Persia had every right to its 16 percent of the company's profits, no matter where they came from, because it clearly stated such in the contract. What's more, Persian oil was virtually subsidizing the British Admiralty. Were the company not selling to the Royal Navy at a tenth of the going rate (10 shillings versus £5 a ton), its overall profits would be higher and the Persian government would be considerably richer.

APOC had become so withdrawn, in fact, that when a new issue of shares was planned in the winter of 1919, Nosrat-Doleh had to appeal directly to Curzon to allow the Persian government to buy some. On December 6 heavy skies and a misty drizzle gathered beyond the tall windows

of Curzon's office. Nosrat-Doleh had been away from Persia for almost a
year. Turning to Curzon, he pointed out with more than a slight hint of
exasperation "that it would be deeply appreciated in Tehran if His
Majesty's government were to offer the Persian government some of their
new shares in view of the fact they were not procurable by any other
means."[3]

The man he was addressing could not have been more his opposite. Lord
Curzon was a massive individual, with a broad, proud face and an ego to
match. A popular jingle going around Oxford and Cambridge in those
days ended with the words "Lord George Nathaniel Curzon is a Very Important Person"—the basis for what became in common English parlance
"VIP." It was a subject of public ridicule that the book he wrote on Persia
before being posted to India used the word *I* so often that the printer's
stock of letters was depleted before the book was fully set. Nosrat-Doleh,
tight-featured and fastidious, barely came to his shoulder. The two perfectly embodied the roles of England and Persia as one asked the other for
the right to buy a piece of his own business. With a flourish of superiority
Curzon was to note afterward, "I believe it would be desirable on political
grounds to give the Persian government a further financial interest in
APOC."[4] A nominal number of shares did change hands.

Upon his return to Persia Nosrat-Doleh, in accordance with a stipula-
tion in the 1919 agreement (which had still not reached the Majles), hired
a British treasury official to serve as financial adviser to the Persian government. The first job confronting Sydney Armitage-Smith was to resolve
once and for all the conflicting interpretations of the D'Arcy Concession.

Armitage-Smith's report turned out to be a bombshell. First it disclosed
that the £614,489 claimed by the company for the pipeline damages was
a complete fabrication, the actual cost being only £20,000. Furthermore it
revealed that the company had already been charging £10,000 a year for
these damages and then disguised them as operating expenses, which reduced its profit margin and, hence, the amount it paid in royalties to the
Persian government. Gimmicks, in fact, riddled the accounts, resulting in
gross underpayment to the Persian government for the past five years.[5]

Equally important, the report clearly confirmed that the government
was entitled to its 16 percent regardless of whether the subsidiaries were
operating inside or outside Persia.

APOC chairman Greenway was at first unmollified. Yet over the next
few weeks an agreement was finally struck between APOC and the Persian
government. Known as the Armitage-Smith Agreement of 1920, it was in
large part a triumph for Persia. It reiterated that the Persian government
was entitled to 16 percent of all operations directly associated with Persian

oil. British reparation claims were dropped. In addition £1 million was to be transferred to Persia to settle its unpaid royalties.*

It was a victory, but for Nosrat-Doleh it was short-lived. Soon after, the government of Vosugh-Doleh fell when the 1919 Anglo-Persian Agreement was rejected by the Majles. Internal politics took center stage, and little thought was given to APOC and its operations in far-off Abadan. Within the year Reza Khan, whose appointment as head of the Cossacks Nosrat-Doleh had helped to arrange, rose to become minister of war, while Nosrat-Doleh and my father were briefly jailed. The British government, still hoping to get the 1919 agreement ratified, abruptly switched tactics. Withdrawing its support from Ahmad Shah, it decided instead to back Reza Khan, seeing him as a strongman who could subdue the cauldron of Persian politics and safeguard their oil interests.

Right off as minister of war Reza Khan assured APOC that it could count on his support if in turn it would back him against the tribes. The stage was set. In September 1923, a month before becoming prime minister in a move that eventually sent Ahmad Shah into exile, Reza Khan dispatched troops to the strategically located town of Shushtar, midway between the oil fields of Masjed Soleyman and the Abadan Refinery. From there he crushed the local Bakhtiari tribes and in 1925 arrested Sheikh Khazal,† whom he transferred under cover of night to Tehran and eventually put to death. To strengthen his position he appointed one of his most able officers, General Fazlollah Zahedi, governor of the province. Zahedi immediately posted police and military guards at the plant.

By 1922 Nosrat-Doleh's feelings for the British had soured. Despite the British government's written guarantee to ensure the Triumvirate's safety, it had not lifted a finger when the three ministers had been thrown into jail, and had refused even to answer Nosrat-Doleh's letters. Afterward it had demanded a return of the public relations funds advanced for the agreement's passage, money that had already been spent and now had to come from the ministers' own purses.

---

*Sydney Armitage-Smith went on to reorganize Persia's finances, again as stipulated under Curzon's still unratified 1919 Anglo-Persian Agreement. But when the agreement was scuttled, he came under sharp criticism for having acted out of turn. Because British government and APOC interests were so closely intertwined, the Shah's ministers, including Nosrat-Doleh, henceforth questioned Armitage-Smith's objectivity in drafting the 1920 oil agreement and refused to recognize its terms. This was unfortunate because its terms were far better than any Persia would subsequently obtain.

†My father, a friend of Sheikh Khazal's, anticipated the danger of his position, and some years before wrote him a letter warning him to watch out. Then, on a lighter note, he added, "I have married a Shirazi girl [my stepmother Fatemeh Khanoum] and find her so appealing I have a mind to marry another."

The strong nationalist flavor of Reza Shah's message, backed by his propensity for immediate action, offered an inspiring alternative to British dependence, and Nosrat-Doleh rallied to his cause. In 1925, when Reza Shah formed his first cabinet after his coronation, Nosrat-Doleh was named finance minister.

Just prior to his nomination I remember my aunt making a shocking comment to Nosrat-Doleh about the flurry of negative press he'd unloosed by changing camps. Najmeh-Saltaneh, whose own son Mohammad Mossadeq would twenty-five years later cause more upheaval in Iran than any other leader in the twentieth century besides Khomeini, was a salty old bird—tough, imperious, and acid-tongued. Older than my father and his only living sister, she bossed him around like no one else. Though well into her eighties, she would snap at him if he so much as asked her how she was feeling. "Stop fussing over me, Abdol Hossein," she'd say. "Sit down over there and mind your own health."

That particular afternoon we were visiting her on her estate outside of town when Nosrat-Doleh drove up in a big new Hudson (he'd given the Rolls to Reza Shah, though his British driver was still at the wheel). He stepped out, resplendent, bowed, and gave Najmeh-Saltaneh a peck on both cheeks. He called her "my dear aunt," which I thought extraordinary, since I couldn't imagine calling her anything but her title. Najmeh-Saltaneh surveyed her nephew with her head cocked a little to one side, then said crisply, "I'd prefer to be sexually abused than to be fucked like you have been by the papers."

She said it right in front of me, right in front of my father, just like that. We all stood around stunned, although as usual I didn't have a clue as to what was going on.

When we left, Najmeh-Saltaneh put a five-crown piece into my hand. She also gave one to Nosrat-Doleh.

"Really, Aunt," he said, his eyes twinkling, "don't I deserve a little more?"

"Absolutely not," she retorted. "In my eyes this child and you are both the same. Now good-bye!"

A TALE OF BLOOD FOR OIL

As Nosrat-Doleh took up the reins at the Finance Ministry, Greenway was stepping down from APOC and Lord Cadman was emerging from the wings. Yet the old lines of antagonism remained intact. The company, implacable, insisted that its new businesses in Kuwait, Iraq, and Bahrain were beyond Iran's scope and not negotiable.

Meanwhile revenues paid to the Iranian government were dropping, even though output had risen fourfold. Royalties, at a high of 11.9 shillings per ton in 1919 when the Armitage-Smith Agreement was being negotiated, were down to a mere 3.1 shillings in 1925. The company blamed this on the market. Iran was dubious.

Over the next five years Abdol Hossein Teymourtash, Reza Shah's powerful minister of court, traveled back and forth to Europe, a trip that still took weeks and more often months, trying to find some middle ground. Part of the standoff was thanks to Reza Shah, whose interest in affairs of state was subservient to his need to consolidate control over the country. During his first years of power he paid only capricious heed to administrative questions and focused instead on harnessing the tribes and bringing the widespread net of religious leadership under his yoke. Among his targets was my father's old antagonist Solat-Doleh, chief of the Qashgahi tribe, who after a pitched battle outside Shiraz was crushed by Reza Shah's superior forces. Another victim was the ascetic mollah Seyyed Hassan Modaress, who had shaken his finger at Nosrat-Doleh over my mother's travel for supporting Reza Shah. Although he always backed Nosrat-Doleh in public, he used his seat in the Majles to unleash a barrage of criticism against the new regime, which the monarch eventually found tiresome. Both Solat-Doleh and Modaress, like so many others during this period, suffered death as a result.

Initially Reza Shah considered Anglo-Persian interesting only as a cash cow and left most of the business to his impresario Teymourtash.

To Teymourtash the answer lay in exerting more Iranian control. That August he presented Cadman with his demands: a 25 percent share in the company, a guaranteed minimum annual revenue, a royalty of 2 shillings per ton, payment of taxes and duties (from which the company had until then been exempted), and a reduction of the concession to a quarter of the area currently covered. And, he added sharply, "If this had been a new concession instead of an exchange or extension of the present D'Arcy Concession, the Persian Government would have insisted not on 25 percent but on a 50/50 basis."[6] (Teymourtash's 50/50 threat was a stroke of genius, anticipating by fifteen years what would become the accepted revenue split between the major international companies and producer nations such as Venezuela, Saudi Arabia, and Kuwait.)

Cadman was a big man with a penchant for spats whose affability often veiled his unshakable commitment to British government interests. Yet as the year progressed, the two sides began to approach an agreement—perhaps the closest they ever came over their years of haggling.

Then, in the autumn of 1929, Reza Shah struck. Suspicious of the growing clout of his counselors, angered by the inadequacy of his revenues, and never one to be upstaged, Reza Shah arrested Nosrat-Doleh and relieved Teymourtash of his post. The accusations against Nosrat-Doleh were vague: communicating with the deposed shah and encouraging tribal unrest in Fars, where his best friend and cousin Sarameh-Doleh was serving as governor. (Sarameh-Doleh was also arrested and was to remain in exile outside Isfahan until 1940.)

Teymourtash fared better and was reinstated as minister of court in March of 1930. But the noose had permanently tightened. The Shah had emerged from his military chrysalis to take a strong hand in the functioning of his government.

Nosrat-Doleh was replaced as finance minister by Seyyed Hassan Taqizadeh, an old friend of my father's. (Later, when Taqizadeh was assigned to Germany as ambassador, he acted as guardian to my younger brother Kaveh, whom he took with him and placed in school in Berlin.) Taqizadeh, like Teymourtash, found little room for maneuver as the talks hobbled through the following year. The world oil market, thanks to the collapse of the New York Stock Exchange in 1929, was in the doldrums, and in May of 1932, when the royalty figures were released, Iranian government income from the now renamed Anglo-Iranian Oil Company (AIOC) had dropped by two thirds, from £1.2 million to a little over £400,000.

The Shah was livid. After making a quick tour of the company in October 1932 (inexplicably accompanied by Farman Farma—whose signature I saw many years later in the company books), he returned to Tehran and had Teymourtash arrested. On November 26 he canceled the concession.

This time Teymourtash did not escape. Within the year he was tried and put to death by strangulation.

The British government, publicly outraged by the concession's cancellation, was in fact neither surprised nor unhinged. Reza Shah, whose play for the throne it had strongly supported, was an ally and a pawn. As AIOC's largest shareholder, the British government did not want any further dickering over terms. Concerned about the rising nationalism in such countries as Turkey, Mexico, and India, it did not want Iran to flare up and irreparably compromise the critical link between Iranian oil and Britain's defense. Rumblings of discontent at AIOC's "imperialism" had already appeared in the press, supported by such diverse factions as the left and the clergy.

By canceling the concession Reza Shah took the matter out of public hands. Britain offered a deal designed to quell the wolves of nationalism— a deal recognizing that Iran's fortunes were handcuffed to its oil and that for both company and government to survive, more money had to flow from the coffers of the former into the treasury of the latter.

Cadman was immediately dispatched to Tehran, and in 1933 a new agreement was signed. It guaranteed Iran 4 shillings per ton in royalties (regardless of fluctuations in the price of oil), a minimum annual payment of £750,000, and a percentage of the global profits—all of which was to be backdated to 1931. The concession was extended to 1993, while the area it covered was reduced by three quarters to roughly 100,000 square miles. In addition employment of Iranian nationals would be rapidly accelerated. Said Cadman ruefully after the settlement, "I felt we had been pretty well plucked,"[7] though whether he was blaming his own government or Iran's he never specified.

The 1933 agreement, though not perfect—and later, in the 1940s, vilified as a travesty by a bloodthirsty Majles—was nonetheless an important test of Iran's grit. The interests of a country would never coincide with the interests of a company, particularly one owned by another nation. Oil is a business, not a political platform, despite temptations to treat it otherwise. Yet this agreement, signed by Hassan Taqizadeh, would have been a good one—had it ever been honored and honestly carried out by the British.

For the moment peace was secured. Anglo-Iranian, its legitimacy restored, resumed operations in a status quo that was to last for twenty years. Back in Tehran, relieved to have the British monkey off his back, Reza Shah held festivities to mark the signing. Nosrat-Doleh, after eleven months of house arrest, was brought before a criminal court and condemned for bribery. He served four months in jail.

At fifty-two Nosrat-Doleh's political career seemed over. In prison he started a treatise on jurisprudence and began a translation of *De Profundis,* Oscar Wilde's moving epistle written during his own incarceration in 1895–1897. He continued these projects after his release and, for the next few years, adopted a quieter lifestyle than had previously been his wont.

Nevertheless he misjudged the personal nature of the Shah's animosity toward him, thinking it instead a product of exigency. As a result he did little to temper a public image that gnawed dangerously at the Shah's pride. Too often his name was in the papers. Too often his political clout, international contacts, and skills as a lawyer were brought to the Shah's attention. Even the Oxford historian E. G. Brown unwittingly added fuel to the fire when he refused a court invitation to travel to Iran to write up a new set of civil laws, saying that with a scholar such as Prince Firouz

Nosrat-Doleh in the Shah's dominion, he saw no reason to come. The last straw came when the French newspapers began a smear campaign against the Shah's new policies.

Nosrat-Doleh, who for some time had been waging a libel suit against Reuters, had just won his case and was enjoying a good deal of favorable press in France, particularly in the newspaper *Le Figaro*. He had also gotten into the habit of riding on horseback with the wife of the French chargé d'affaires across the steppe above his domain in Farmanieh. Being a suspicious man, the Shah suspected treachery.

This was in 1936 while I was in my second year at Birmingham. Mehri, newly arrived in Germany to join Mohsen Khan, had invited me to Berlin for Christmas. Hitler was already in power. Men in uniform were everywhere, and it was obvious that Germany was preparing for war. Also ubiquitous were JUDEN VERBOTEN signs forbidding Jews to enter restaurants, shops, and public gardens. One afternoon while I was drinking a beer in a café near the embassy in Tiergartenstrasse, two SS officers stormed in and threw out all the Jews—including me, thinking I looked Jewish.

On New Year's Eve we went to a dinner at the Aiglon Hotel, studded with Germany's glitterati. Among the guests were Joseph Goebbels, Hitler's notorious minister of propaganda, and Leni Riefenstahl, a buxom blonde and famous filmmaker, rumored to be Hitler's ideal Aryan woman. The French ambassador, François-Poncet, was also there. (I would later meet his son in Tehran.)

A few days later we received the frightening news that Nosrat-Doleh had again been arrested and this time sent under guard to the small desert town of Semnan, more than one hundred miles from Tehran. Agha-ye Sadr ("Monsieur") had just arrived in Berlin with orders from Farman Farma to visit each of his sons and report on our studies and living habits. The news of Nosrat-Doleh's arrest, however, abruptly halted these plans, and Agha-ye Sadr hurried back to Tehran in answer to my father's summons.

A feeling of dread settled over the embassy. Mehri, wan and anxious, became highly agitated, not only for the safety of her brother but for the political ramifications that association with our family might have on Mohsen Khan. In fact, Mohsen Khan's career never did suffer from the taint of our family. From Berlin he went on to serve as ambassador in Bucharest, Baghdad, London, Paris, and eventually The Hague. Just three months after the incident with Nosrat-Doleh, the speaker of the Majles, Mohtesham Saltaneh Esfandiari, passed through Berlin on his way to London to attend King George VI's coronation and paid Hitler a call, taking Mohsen Khan along. A picture shows them sitting in Hitler's plush receiving chamber, Mohsen Khan sporting a short, square mustache, Esfandiari wearing dark spectacles, and Adolf Hitler smiling in his uniform with the swastika prominently displayed on his armband. Many years later Mohsen Khan told me that after delivering the Shah's messages of goodwill, Esfandiari mentioned to Hitler that he'd served at the Persian Embassy in Berlin during the last years of Bismarck. Hitler was fascinated, for not only was he an admirer of Bismarck but he'd met few people who had actually known him. Plying Esfandiari with questions he signaled that a Czechoslovakian delegation in the parlor would have to wait. "We didn't know it then," Mohsen Khan recalled, "but of course he dismissed the Czechs because he was planning to overrun their country the following year."

No further news of Nosrat-Doleh arrived while I was in Berlin, and I returned to Birmingham apprehensive and distraught. Letters kept coming from my mother, and I opened each one with shaking hands. But for two months they mentioned nothing. Then one morning I heard the tread of my landlady bringing up my letters, and I felt a shiver go up my spine. Rigid in front of the window, I tore open my mother's letter. Nosrat-Doleh had died, it said, of "food poisoning." That was all. Not a word of consolation. No explanation.

I sank to my bed, tears filled my eyes, and I wept as I'd never done before. I don't know how long I sat there, alone, bereft, feeling betrayed and devastated. The scion of the family had been destroyed. Nosrat-Doleh had given me my name—Manucher—and my father had accepted. Everything had centered on him. He was the one who had both the capacity and the merit to lead the family forward as Farman Farma's successor. We believed in him. With his death the trunk of the family had been felled.

At last the tears ceased and I stared sightlessly out the window. I did not even think of going to the university.

About midday the doorbell rang. Painfully I dragged myself to the door. Standing there was Saifollah Moazemi, a fellow Persian and one of the engineering students at Birmingham under the auspices of AIOC. He was four or five years older than I and of a good family—someone I looked up to and respected. I didn't know he even knew where I lived.

"I know what's happened," he said. "Please let me in."

Holding my face in my hands, I returned to the bed and started weeping again. He left me to my grief and, to hide his own emotion, covered his eyes with his hand. At last, when my tears were spent, he told me his family had written him the news a few days before. When I did not appear in the lecture hall, he knew I too had heard.

He made me a cup of tea, and we sat together awhile in silence. Finally he began speaking to me softly, his voice monotonous and soothing.

"You're afraid to face your friends and compatriots. Don't be. Don't worry about other people rejoicing over your unhappiness. This type of thing has happened to famous families throughout history, and now it is your turn in Iran."

I shook my head, uncomprehending.

"Grief makes one feel beaten and lost," he went on. "I know. I remember when my father died. Though he passed away naturally, I too was confused and could not face other people. *'Mard anbashad keh dar keshah keshe dahr, Sang zireene asia bashad*—A man becomes a man when under the push and pull of the world, he is as resistant as the lower stone of the mill wheel.' " It was an old Persian poem, and I looked at him through more tears.

"Come," he said. "Be brave. Don't let people pity you. Let's go to the university for lunch and together we will face them."

I realized he was right. The tragedy of my brother's assassination was not for others to judge.

His arm about my shoulders, steadying me, we went to the student union for lunch. In the afternoon I went on to the physics laboratory. My grief was already turning to anger. My world would never be the same.

Later I heard that the authorities had not even allowed a funeral ceremony. My family had been violated in silence.

Nosrat-Doleh's death hardened me, and for the first time it made me personally despise the British government. I understood now how critical Lord Curzon's written guarantee to protect Nosrat-Doleh had been, and how by ignoring it under the political circumstances existing then in Iran the British government had abetted his murder.

In 1941, as I stood at the bus stop in Abadan, anger boiling through my veins, I vowed to bring this all to an end. One day, I promised myself, we would run this refinery. One day Persians would work in Abadan and know it was theirs.

At the end of the week I told the manager that I would probably not want to work for Anglo-Iranian. "Ever heard of the Farsi word *zamharir*?" I asked him.

He shook his head.

"It means 'ice hell.' "

His face began to twitch.

"Abadan's got no women," I said solemnly. "Would you wish that on any young buck?" He broke into a grin, visibly relieved.

"There are other compensating factors . . . ," he began.

I held up my hand. "I know. You pay ten times as much as any job going in Tehran. I could soon become a foreman. I'll think about it. I'll give my final decision to your representative in Tehran. But if I decide no, you'll know why." I winked. "Perhaps in a few years, when the gas torches have fed enough flames to Zoroaster, I'll find this zamharir a little warmer."

That night I had dinner with the Shaws, friends from *The Merchant of Venice.* He was the head geologist in Abadan; she sang wonderful songs at the piano. At their house I saw something I'd never seen before: Their servants, Persians like me, were not allowed to wear shoes or socks. I recalled the servants in India, decked out in sumptuous uniform but with naked feet—a potent reminder of their servile position. Every time the steward approached the table the soft padding of his feet on the floor made me break out into a sweat. I began to strain my ears for the sound. By the end of the evening I could feel every movement of those feet upon my skin.

Maheen and Dr. Taba saw me off at the station at the end of the week. They waved wildly as the train gradually pulled away, Maheen's noble brown eyes sad in the purple twilight.

I looked out at the rocky expanse all around me and felt elated. This was it. I was on my way to Tehran.

UNDER THE HAND OF
REZA SHAH

As our destiny was forged without our presence,
If it does not live up to expectations, do not complain.
                                                    —HAFEZ

Tehran 1941

The train ride took twenty-four hours. We rumbled north, cutting across the dry spears and valleys of the Zagros Mountains and into the heart of ancient Media. Four thousand years ago, the fierce Elamites lived here, building the great templed city of Susa thirty-five miles west of where the train tracks now lay. Through the window I saw only vast emptiness. Forsaken villages crouched against the heavy slopes; horsemen and mule drivers appeared in twos and threes, their mounts so voluminously laden they looked like lumpy pillows on stilts; a far-off flock of sheep with bright hennaed grease sacks in place of tails clambered across the rocky mountain faces. Otherwise all was stone and open sky.

Yet here the concert of history had created empires. The armies of Cyrus and Darius had tramped through these valleys; the divisions of Alexander the Great had toiled east along these rivers; the Mongol hordes had massed and struck here on their Chinese horses.

The real stories locked in the stones of these slopes had long since been forgotten. Graves had been robbed, the inscriptioned gold and silver melted down and the broken pottery thrown away. Old rock walls had been plundered to build new forts, sometimes by invaders, sometimes by the Persians themselves. There were of course exceptions—monuments that remained a source of pride—such as the graves of the great shahs Cyrus and Darius, set high in the rock of a mountain just outside Shiraz, or the monumental palace of Persepolis a few miles beyond. But for the most part history had been refashioned into poetry, and the facts behind these ancient wonders had grown as rose-colored as the epics so close to the Persian heart.

That was until Professor Roman Ghirshman, archaeologist and explorer, arrived in Iran in 1931 and began to dig up the past. What he found was layer upon layer of civilization, all recorded in proto-Elamite, Akkadian, Assyrian cuneiform, Aramaic, and Pahlavi.[1] His findings, backed up by the records of Herodotus, gave new meaning to the mammoth slabs of carved rock scattered over the Zagros Mountains. Even as I headed north Ghirshman was working a site at Shahpur in the far south. Though I had heard of his work, I would not meet him for another three years.

Many of the ancient sites were the very places where oil was now being found. Masjed Soleyman, or Solomon's Temple, where George Reynolds had hit his first gusher in 1908, was a wide terrace hewn from the rock where a holy fire had burned for thousands of years. It was one of the things that made oil prospecting easy in Iran: Wherever there was a fire temple, it indicated the presence of escaping gas and, often, a pool of oil below ground. Ghirshman told me that a tribe of Jews from Egypt, which had settled in the area during Shah Darius's reign in the fifth century B.C., called the black liquid that poured in a fountain nearby *radia-nasay.* The name is the oldest on record for what we today call petroleum. The thick, unctuous liquid easily caught fire but couldn't be burned inside because it gave off such smoke and fumes that it killed anyone who remained close by. The seepages were hard to work with—the oil was black and sticky, and once it got on the skin it was impossible to wash off. After it hardened into bitumen, however, it could be fashioned into statues and also served well as caulking for boats.

For the ancients the spontaneous ignition of the gases into fire was clearly the work of God, and they saw in its constant movement the sign of life. At the time no one knew how to make fire, so the Zoroastrians kept a flame stoked by tallow in every house, a symbol of the Almighty both practical and divine. In the Persian language fire never just goes out, it is killed or dies, like the soul. Today the source of the Zoroastrian flame has become a new god—the precious blood of industry and development. Now we know how to transport and refine it, how to distill the combustible commodities of gasoline and kerosene out of the heavy asphalt. But oil is still revered, and in that little has changed over twenty-five hundred years. Like many deities it exacts homage, and in the twentieth century it has become the cause of death and war, and of insidious manipulation. "The people in the place of debauchery cherish me," wrote Hafez, "Because the fire that never dies burns always in my heart."

By the time we awoke in the morning there was snow on the ground. The holy city of Qom already lay behind us, the blue-domed Shrine of Fatima fading into the white of the plain. We were crossing the northern fringe of the Dasht-e-Kavir, the vast salt-soaked desert that is all that remains of the sea that once covered Iran.

Ahead of us, rising like a wall into the blanched sky, towered the snow-clad Elborz Mountains. I looked for the singular cone of Mount Damavand, 19,000 feet up, but it was gone, veiled in clouds. The homage of Malek Sho'arah Bahar flashed through my mind: *"Ey kuh-e sefid pa-ye darband, ey gonbad-e giti ey Damavand."* It was difficult poetry, even for those of us who were used to memorizing such things: "O White mountain peak with fettered feet, O Dome of the world, O Damavand." Malek Sho'arah, who was married to one of my mother's cousins, was considered the most lyrical poet alive in Iran. His title meant "King of Poets" and had been bestowed on him by the Shah.

I had slept well. The train was brand-new, the tracks had just been completed the year before, and we were riding first class in a sleeper car. The *couchettes* had been made up with fresh linen, and every hour a man came around with a tray of tea, served from a samovar that steamed all night at the end of the corridor. Dinner had also been served, and before we left the south fresh lettuce had been brought aboard as a special delicacy. There was no refrigerated freight then; in Tehran I wouldn't see lettuce for another couple of months.

By chance I had encountered a friend of my brother-in-law Mohsen Khan's at the train station in Ahwaz. His name was Fazlollah Nabil, and he had been chargé d'affaires at the embassy in London. With him were a couple named Farkhou, who told me they lived near my mother's house in the new neighborhood of Kakh. This came as a certain relief, for there had been only one phone line in Abadan, and I had not been able to reach my mother to alert her of my arrival.

We arrived in Tehran suddenly, the normal urban effluence that heralds the outskirts of Western cities being all contained within its walls, leaving the surrounding countryside free of any hint that massed humanity teemed nearby. The train station, newly built by the Germans, was topped by a swastika (an ancient Persian symbol, it was pointed out) rendered with Middle Eastern flourishes. (The emblem is still there, sunk into the massive cornice of a building otherwise unadorned.)

The platforms were full. People and bundles poured from the windows and doors of the third- and second-class cars. Cats, chickens, and children ran underfoot, while women with babies at their breasts cried out for alms. With difficulty we pressed through the tumult, squeezed and buffeted until, like balls popped from the roaring mouth of a cannon, we were tossed onto the street and, miraculously, into Nabil's waiting car.

I looked out the window bewildered. It all looked so dirty and old-fashioned. Even Bombay had appeared more advanced. Horse-drawn carts filled with goods clattered to and fro across the square. Open carriages called droshkies far outnumbered cars. The people were strange, and I could feel the poverty despite the improvements in their dress. The population had increased rapidly as a result of health care advances under Reza Shah, and the fight against smallpox had saved many children from early death. But, I thought grimly, what a life—condemned to the gutter, to lice and ringworm, and no doubt to hunger too.

From the train station in the extreme south of the city we headed toward the mountains. At the Farkhous' I tried again to reach my mother, but getting no answer, and having no operator service to turn to, I told them I would be back and strode out to the street. I had no idea where to go, since my mother had moved while I'd been away, and I had no idea where she now lived. Nonetheless, seeing a droshky trot by, I jumped in, thinking to return to the old palace and ask the neighbors for directions.

THE TALE OF THE LOST HOUSE

We backtracked south through newly laid avenues, all built while I'd been away. I felt lonely in the back of the droshky and glumly watched the broad back of the driver as he lounged leisurely up on his bench, the reins loose in his hand. The droshky smelled heavily of horse. The black leather seats crumbled at the edges. Above me the top of the carriage had been folded back, baring me to a crisp breeze. Even here in the upper section of town there was none of the orderliness I was used to seeing in an English city. Mounds of sand and brick dropped at random interrupted foot traffic along the sidewalks, while construction workers squatted unconcernedly against the walls sipping tea. Where Kakh Street crossed the grand avenues of Shah Reza and Shah, shops filled the ground floors of the houses. Their grates were up, and I could see the shopkeepers amidst their wares, tubes of neon shedding an unearthly blue glow into the back of their workrooms. The water in the open gutter, or joob, gurgled as it headed downtown, sometimes catching on a broken branch to flood into the street, then disappearing entirely as refuse split the stream into tiny rivulets. All was untidy and haphazard, except the plane tree saplings, planted in strict rows along the joob so their roots could absorb the water untended.

At first there wasn't much traffic. Farther south it got busier. Donkeys appeared in the street, and cyclists wove crazily between the ruts. Here no shrubs or bushes interrupted the patternless flow of people from sidewalk to road as they balanced trays of cakes or earthenware jugs on their heads. We trotted past a line of people waiting at a bakery for bread, the head of the queue bunched as people shoved and shouted to get served. I glimpsed the fire burning in the pit and the silhouette of the baker lifting the sheaves from the glowing rocks with a flat-faced shovel. *Sangak*—bread baked on stones. The taste of it suddenly came back to me, hot and crusty, and I remembered it as the best bread in the world. The aroma followed me down the road, and I felt a stab of hunger.

When the droshky finally stopped at a corner, I sharply accused the driver of having mistaken the address. Nothing looked familiar. Streets cut through where the old garden had been. Princess Ezzat-Doleh's house, unrecognizable now, had been transformed into the Shah's new Marble Palace. The pools and fountains had disappeared. Even the trees were gone—the towering elms by the entrance gate, the stand of bamboos.

I must have stood there several seconds before I could shake myself from the reverie of what was clearly gone. Vaguely I remembered my mother having written that Reza Shah had seized the land of the compound and literally thrown the family into the street. They'd been informed of the move by the construction workers who had shown up to break a road through Masumeh Khanoum's living room. I recalled that the Shah had taken our property of Doulab too, where the train station now stood.

In England none of this had meant much to me; too many years, too many miles, had separated me from it all. Now it registered with a bruising shock. A storm of emotions swept through me: blind outrage, followed by a deep, wrenching sorrow, and then a horrible sense of foreboding. My chest constricted, and with heavy tread I headed for the first door to ask for directions.

But the people who answered had only recently moved in and knew nothing. Later I found out I'd even knocked at my cousin Dr. Mohammad Mossadeq's house, but he'd been exiled to the countryside and his butler had been scared of answering my questions. Many of the servants slammed the door in my face, the name "Farman Farma" causing their eyes instantly to harden in fear.

Finally I crossed the street and knocked at an older house. This time, instead of abruptly raising his chin and clicking a backward *t* sound with his tongue in the typical Persian fashion of expressing a negative, the servant turned and called to his master. An elderly gentleman with a luxurious mustache came running to the door, and in turn he called to his wife, saying, "Look who's here—it's a son of Prince Farman Farma, and imagine, he cannot find his own house!"

With sudden emotion he clasped me to him as though I were his own son, and when he presented me to his wife, she had tears in her eyes. The old gentleman introduced himself as Heshmat-Doleh, the head of the Diba family, whose grandniece, many years later, would become Empress Farah. He had been a close friend of my father's, whose sharp-tongued sister Najmeh-Saltaneh had been the second wife of Heshmat-Doleh's father. Farman Farma had even named one of the streets on our property after him.

Heshmat-Doleh called for tea and refreshments and motioned me into a chair. His affable face became serious. "You are not without a home," he said. "But pay heed. None of us have been spared. We too have had our victims. The new Shah has taken your house and killed your brother. Never talk of that. Do not become excitable. Do not mention your brother, ever."

He passed his hand over his eyes and then, after a quiet moment, smiled. "I don't know where your mother lives," he said. "But stay here, have some tea, and I will find out."

When he came back he was almost jovial, hurrying me through my tea and bundling me into his car. He called for his hat, which, to my surprise, he put on with a grimace, grumbling that he hated Western hats but that the Shah insisted they be worn. Then we headed north, farther even than the Farkhous', which I had not considered possible, since it had all been empty fields and desert when I was a child. The road was not paved, just dirt and mud and full of stones. We reached the end of Kakh. Only a few hundred yards beyond lay the bed of the Karaj River. Below it there was water. Above it not a drop until the mountain springs of Shemiran. He gestured to a majestic white villa with tall second-story windows, bounded by a high apron wall. It was the last house on the road.

I got out and rang the bell. My heart pounded as I waited at the blue metal gate. One of the old servants from my father's household opened the door. He recognized me immediately and started such a hullabaloo—crying out that everyone thought I was dead, but here I was, *Mashallah*— Allah be praised—a legend come to life—that my mother came running out, closely followed by my eldest sister, Maryam. When she saw the cause of the servant's outburst, my mother threw herself into my arms, crying and praising God for having delivered me safely into her care. Soon the whole household had congregated in the courtyard, and everyone was making such a noise that the neighbors, including Qavam-Saltaneh, Maheen Taba's uncle, who lived next door, had come over to see why there was such a commotion.

I had not seen my mother since I was nine. She had changed from the willowy young woman with four children I remembered to a middle-aged lady with nine. Her hair was iron gray, and crow's-feet fanned from her sparkling eyes. My five younger brothers and sisters all still lived at home, the youngest, Ali, being only six. Aziz had returned from Paris right after our father's death. Maryam, I learned over lunch, was getting a divorce and had just moved back in too, bringing along her two baby daughters, Afsaneh and Afsar. Now I had returned. Although the house had eight bedrooms, it was packed.

My mother had saved the master bedroom for me as the oldest son. During the months that had passed without news of my whereabouts, it had come to enshrine her hopes of my return. Dusting it, she said, had made her feel closer to me.

From the moment I walked through the gate, it was clear that I was now head of the household. My mother led me to the head of the long lunch table. The delicate design of the walnut, hewn from trees that had grown on my father's properties, brought back memories of when the table had stood in Farman Farma's private dining room and he had sat at its head. My mother took the chair to my right, and my brothers and sisters lined both sides of the table, boisterous and gay and all talking at once. I experienced an unfamiliar tenderness and the sharp desire to watch over them, guide them in their studies, and set an example they could admire and respect. As I looked at each of them in turn, my spirit soared. I was home.

Over the course of the afternoon, news spread of my arrival. By teatime other siblings—the sons and daughters of Masumeh Khanoum, Fatemeh Khanoum, Hamdam Khanoum, and Farman Farma's other wives—were beginning to drop by, as were friends of the family and more distant relatives. It was a ritual that was to continue morning and afternoon for a fortnight. We sat over tea in the salon, a large sunny room with French doors leading out to the back garden. It smelled of rose water. Against the wall stood an upright piano with gold fold-out candleholders. We perched uncomfortably on the edge of the overstuffed chairs, talking of the war, the British, our oil, and Birmingham girls. Homemade sweets and baklava were passed back and forth, and vast quantities of tea were consumed.

After the two weeks of visitations it was time to reverse the process. My mother and I had already paid our respects to several people within the first twenty-four hours of my arrival: Mohammadvali Mirza, the family patriarch; his mother, Princess Ezzat-Doleh; and Heshmat-Doleh, who had slipped away during the commotion of my homecoming before my mother and I could adequately thank him. I was fed up with the endless ceremony but had to admit it was an excellent method of social reintegration. Everyone was a stranger after so many years. I didn't even know most of my own brothers and sisters. The Iranian friends I'd made in Birmingham had, for the most part, stayed in Abadan. I came to realize that this age-old ritual of house calls was the very fuel of our social engine, a genteel, stylized liaising that included both sexes and all generations and far outpaced its Western successor—the network—in establishing lines of trust as well as credit. In a couple of months I'd met everybody and the ice was broken. Being an eligible bachelor, I was invited often for lunch and dinner, and though I would not marry for another ten years, I was soon adopted by the mothers of many of the prettiest girls in town.

Iran's customs still reflected a society unused to telephones or easy transportation. When I arrived the phone numbers had only four digits, which meant there were fewer than ten thousand phones in Tehran. People used them—if and when they worked—to exchange news but never as a substitute for social interaction. Houses were constantly prepared for entertaining guests, and everyone dropped in on each other at teatime without calling in advance. Lunches were open houses at which the guests often stayed into the evening, sometimes even spending the night. No one went to restaurants, which were primarily the purview of men and usually shy on clean linen and mannered service. Instead everyone had their weekly salons. My mother gave a lunch every Friday, after which people played backgammon or a Russian card game called *pasour*, took a siesta, did their ablutions and prayers in the upper rooms, or gossiped endlessly over the korsi.

THE NEW PATRIARCH

Every month the family gathered for a meeting of the board my father had set up to run the businesses and estates he'd left behind. Presiding was Mohtesham Saltaneh Esfandiari, the speaker of the Majles, whom I'd met in London after his visit with Hitler. He was the father of Maryam's estranged husband and, after Farman Farma's death, had stepped in to become a father to us all.

Officially representing the family was Mohammadvali Mirza, Ezzat-Doleh's third son, whose levelheadedness and wisdom had rapidly earned him the position of new patriarch. He filled the role with dignity and power until he died fifty-five years later at the age of ninety-two. When Nosrat-Doleh and my father were imprisoned during the 1921 coup, Mohammadvali Mirza escaped to Baghdad. Afterward he returned to live in virtual seclusion under Reza Shah.

Mohammadvali Mirza was as different as could be from Nosrat-Doleh. He spent much of his life in Azerbaijan, where he owned considerable estates, and the Turkish dialect was his language of choice. At twenty-six he earned himself a prominent position in Parliament as the delegate from Tabriz. He was an extremely modest man who, in stark contrast to his older brother, counted every cent that passed through his hands. At the tail end of World War I, when the Russian Communists seized many properties in Azerbaijan, Mohammadvali Mirza traveled to Moscow to settle accounts. Disguised as a beggar, he crossed the mountain passes of Turkey on his way north but was captured by a Venezuelan general named Rafael de Nogales, who was fighting on the German side and almost shot him as a spy. Mohammadvali Mirza escaped only because at the last minute he spoke to Nogales in French, prompting the general to realize, as Nogales wrote in his memoirs, "that he was a prince of the lineage of Farman Farma." Afterward the two became friends, and Mohammadvali Mirza later bestowed a medal on Nogales in gratitude.[2]

Mohammadvali Mirza was a man of few words. He preferred the quiet surroundings of his fields and knew every peasant personally on his estates. He lived in a small, unpretentious house that gave no inkling he was one of the biggest landholders in the country. Ironically, in a family that strutted and preened and fairly bristled with bright plumage, Mohammadvali Mirza was almost colorless—a genuinely humble man. His one foible was a deep-seated conviction that he was constantly ailing, a concern that did not impede him from living past ninety.

Mohammadvali Mirza did not look like a patriarch. He was too thin and wispy. His face was barely more than a profile, and he could not have weighed more than eighty-five pounds. When I was in boarding school in France, he'd invite me to dinner in Paris whenever he passed through, and he would look at me enviously as I wolfed down my food—and his—saying peevishly that he wished *he* could eat that way. But though frail, he had my father's burning eyes and the mind of a sage. He had the gift of being able to judge situations from other people's points of view, to observe what others missed, and, greatest of all, to pursue a neutral course that never entangled him in others' motives. His mere presence was a catalyst for mediation, and his suggestions were always followed without question.

Yet the family was a vast and ungainly horde. Had Nosrat-Doleh lived, he might have harnessed its sprawling numbers into a cohesive entity, forcing us to fulfill our enormous potential for power in Iran. To live up to such promise, however, we needed strong leadership, for we were not naturally a cooperative bunch. As it was, Mohammadvali Mirza provided an axis. Yet soon after Farman Farma's death hairline divisions began to form as the family separated into each mother's household, beginning the unraveling that our final diaspora at the time of Khomeini would only confirm.

Our family fortune was significant. When my father died he bequeathed us vast lands in the rich provinces of Hamadan and Kermanshah, orchards spanning the mountain villages of Poonak and Shemiran outside Tehran, a house for each child in the capital, land in Baghdad and other parts of Iraq, as well as estates, town properties, and gardens dotting the rest of Iran. To each of his wives' oldest sons he also gave one extra property; mine was in Assadabad, a beautiful, well-watered mountain slope in Hamadan. The girls inherited smaller properties, but they were the easiest to manage and among the most lovely in all of Iran.

Although my properties were valuable, I was ambitious and wanted a job. At the time a man gained stature only by holding a position in government. Soon after the No Rooz festivities—and the inevitable visits that followed—I began my search. It proved to be much more difficult than I imagined.

The Iran of 1941 was a very different place from the one I had left fourteen years before. The military dictatorship of Reza Shah was absolute. Through sheer force of will he had imposed a crushing program of modernization on the country. The three Russian and four British battalions that had occupied Iran since World War I (despite Iran's neutrality) were sent home; the Anglo-Russian hammerlock on banking and customs collection was prized free.* This left the army and the financial system independent of foreign influence and fully under Reza Shah's control. With the former he centralized the country, defining its borders, disarming the tribes, and breaking the power of the ulema, or religious establishment. Heads had rolled, tribal leaders had been brought to Tehran while the nomads' annual migrations were partially stopped. House arrest became a common occupation of the nobility. The military, and its new handmaiden the secret service, were modernized and equipped with funds that poured in from the oil wells.

With the strings of the financial system all leading into his palm, Reza

---

*Anxious to break the British stranglehold on the country, Reza Shah set up Iran's first national bank, Bank Melli, which henceforth issued the country's currency. Up until then the British-controlled Imperial Bank had printed all the nation's money. As the only banking institution in Persia, the Imperial Bank had operated for twenty years both as Persia's central and commercial bank and, in an obvious conflict of interest, as the financial arm of the British government. It underwrote APOC's loans and investments and processed its royalty payments into Persia's treasury. Not wanting to lose control over Iran's money supply, the Imperial Bank balked at the Shah's order to stop printing money. To facilitate the transfer to Bank Melli he changed Iran's currency from the crown to the rial.

Shah embarked on an ambitious program of construction. A tax on tea and sugar financed the Trans-Iranian Railway, which, besides the southern leg that had carried me from Khorramshahr to Tehran, connected the capital to the Caspian Sea at the eastern port of Bandar-e Shah. Money spun off from a system of levies paved new roads between all the major cities, opening the country for the first time to travel by motor vehicle. Until then roads had been under *Moluk-e tavayefi* (the rule of the tribes). Brigandage, thievery, and contest for dominion had made them dangerous, and travelers were often relieved of their belongings and even their clothes in the course of passage. Goods had been transported over the ancient dirt trails by camel, mule, or *gari,* open-load carriages drawn by four horses. Now trucks hauled produce across the land, and a woman could travel alone safely from one end of the country to the other. Camels were banned from the cities, whose central neighborhoods were ripped out and laid with wide avenues and open squares. Ports were built on the Caspian Sea and the Persian Gulf. With German technical aid paper, cement, and sugar factories had sprung up in Kerman, Tehran, and Isfahan.

REZA SHAH

The man at the helm of all this change stood six foot four in his stocking feet and had an education so rudimentary he could barely read or write. He always dressed in uniform with a square, visored cap and simple leather baldric, refusing to bedeck himself in the false prestige of gold braid or a spray of meaningless medals. He was never seen in his crown after the day of his coronation. The English writer Vita Sackville-West, who attended his coronation, called him "in appearance an alarming man . . . with grizzled hair and a brutal jowl."[3] He cursed a great deal, using the low, bawdy epithets of the army. In his palace, built on my father's property, he housed a harem of three wives and eleven children. By the time he left the throne he had seized by some counts a quarter of the land of Iran—entire provinces of rich farmland on the Caspian coast, millions of acres around Tehran, and untold stretches of tribal property.

Reza Khan was born in 1878 in the small, northern village of Alasht. His mother was apparently a Caucasian, and through her he learned to speak fluent Turkish. His father, who died young, was a soldier, and it seemed natural for the young Reza to follow in his footsteps. At age fifteen, already tall and beginning to exhibit the brash courage that was to characterize his life, he joined the Russian-officered Persian Cossack Brigade as a stable boy. Big-shouldered and shrewd, Reza was too ambitious to shovel straw and was soon out of the stable and moving up the ranks. One of his assignments was to Kermanshah, where, as my father's aide, he engaged in the skirmish against Salar-Doleh. "Whenever an expedition was sent to any part of the country to round up brigands or quell a disturbance," wrote a British diplomatic biographer in 1937, "he seems to have taken part in it."[4] During this period Reza Khan observed firsthand the anarchy and wretchedness of the countryside, the insecurity of the roads, and the independent power bases of the tribes. He also witnessed the extraordinary degree of control exercised by his own Russian superiors, as well as the British establishment, over the direction of his country.

Reza Khan gradually rose to become a colonel and then a general. At nineteen he married a cousin, who died bearing him a daughter, whom he later called Hamdam-e-Saltaneh. While still a child she contracted smallpox, which left her face deeply pitted. Reza Khan then married another country woman, Taj-o-Molouk, the sister of a fellow Cossack, who bore him four children: a daughter named Shams, twins—a boy named Mohammad Reza and a girl named Ashraf—and a son named Ali Reza, who suffered from a mild mental handicap. As his career took off and he began to move through the circles of higher society, Reza Khan took a third wife, a daughter of the Amir Soleimani family. Although she was pretty and soon bore him a son named Gholam Reza, the marriage ended in divorce. Undeterred, Reza Khan fastened his eye on another society lady, Esmat Khanoum, from the Dowlatshahi family of Kermanshah, who like my mother was related to the Qajars through Fath-Ali Shah. Reza Khan developed a grand passion for Esmat Khanoum, and she gave him five more children. She was a true oriental beauty, with a moon-shaped face, almond eyes, a small nose, and an alluringly rounded figure. Her lips were full— to the point of looking swollen—and it was said that Reza Shah loved her so much that he constantly bit them. Ironically Nosrat-Doleh's oldest son, Mozzafar, was to marry a cousin of Esmat Khanoum's, relating him by blood to his father's old rival.

Reza Khan's lot would have been much like any other loyal soldier's if a confluence of events had not changed his life, and that of the country, the year he turned forty-three. In the summer of 1920 it finally became clear to the British government that the Anglo-Persian Agreement of 1919 would not be ratified. Concerned that the country would slip from its grasp, it decided on a new scheme: to bring the Russian-officered, but partially British-funded, Persian Cossack Brigade under British control. The British minister in Tehran, Herman Norman, in his cable to Lord Curzon explained, "Expulsion of Starosselski and his Russian officers and virtual control by British officers . . . would make us practically independent of the vagaries of Persian internal politics and . . . ensure gradual execution of the Agreement."[5] For this purpose they singled out Seyyed Zia Tabatabai, a pro-British journalist, to lead a coup and subsequently become prime minister. To back him up militarily they chose Reza Khan. That Reza Khan wasn't particularly pro-British was balanced by the fact that he was anti-Russian, depended on the British financially, and could count on the loyalty of his fellow soldiers. To further ensure that all went smoothly, they obtained the backing of the major mollahs, offering them both bribes and promises, who guaranteed that there would be no countermovement in the bazaar.

On February 21, 1921, Reza Khan marched into Tehran at the head of his Cossack Brigade and rapidly took control of the army, clearing the way for Seyyed Zia to oust the government and take over the reins of power. The streets remained quiet, and Ahmad Shah remained unharmed on his throne. Such was Britain's power in Persia at the time that it could topple a premier and shift the allegiance of the army, all with barely a whisper from the populace. The whole operation went so smoothly, in fact, that it seemed like nothing more than a political reshuffling at the top. Yet it was the harbinger of serious political upheaval, which ultimately would cause the downfall of the ruling dynasty and its replacement by another.

Seyyed Zia, in whom the British had high hopes, lasted only three months as premier. He was succeeded by Qavam-Saltaneh, who promoted Reza Khan to minister of war.

This was Reza Khan's chance to bring the country under a single command. He promptly terminated the contracts of the British officers who had just replaced the Russians and transferred control into Persian hands. This proved quite suitable to the British, since they could ill afford their military operations in Persia and were anxious to hand over the government to a strongman they felt they could rely on.

Over the next five years Reza Khan consolidated his power, moved into the premiership, and sent Ahmad Shah packing. In 1925, he crowned himself Shah.

In 1941, sixteen years after his takeover, his star was still rising. His unwavering belief in his country's strength, which had enabled him to throw off the British and Russian shackles, had earned him respect. His ability to command, to make decisions, and to get things done had galvanized the viscous Persian bureaucracy, and the country had begun to move. In ten years Reza Shah built twenty-five hundred schools and increased the number of teachers colleges from one to thirty-six. The first buildings of the new University of Tehran were going up on Takhte Jamshid, just beyond my mother's house. The entire system of justice was revamped, transferring the law from the hands of the mollahs to a civil bureaucracy.

Reza Shah, unlike his son, was not one to ask for advice. He was first and always a general, who extended his command to the unwieldy entirety of Iran—a nation unruly, uneducated, and cynical of any form of authority. He suffered no political debate and was suspicious of everyone around him. Notoriously sensitive to insult—real or imagined—his anger would shake the ramparts of the palace, and his retribution was immediate. What happened once on a trip to Kermanshah was typical. The governor, Amirkol A'zam Zanganeh, a wealthy landowner whose family had long been close to mine, was presenting the Shah to the gathered nobles of the town. Stopping in front of one of them, the Shah seemed to recognize him and asked, "Haven't I seen you before?"

"Yes," answered the man a trifle too eagerly. "We knew each other when you were here, under the command of Prince Farman Farma." The Shah's eyes narrowed, and without another word he turned on his heel.

That night after Amirkol was in bed, he received a call summoning him to the royal quarters. When he was ushered into the Shah's presence, he was greeted with a stream of invectives the likes of which, he told me afterward, he'd never heard. The Shah paced, throwing about his arms, his riding boots glinting dully in the half light. "*Pedar sag, madar gabeh*—you son of a dog, you son of a prostitute!" he yelled. At last the Shah told Amirkol to get out, his voice leaving no question that the governor had been relieved of his job.

Many considered Reza Shah ruthless. To get what he got done in Iran, he had to be. It was not a time when popularity was a requisite for good leadership. That he was a man who lacked charm and humor and who ruled by fear and respect more than love had no bearing in a country that was over 90 percent illiterate when he came to power. Iran was wracked by famines; its people were without adequate clothing or potable water and often subject to the arbitrary exactions of warring tribes. Popular leaders are a luxury of prosperous nations, not the indigent, where the living is so impoverished that improvement involves by definition further sacrifice.

Most of Iran's 16 million people lived on unleavened bread and goat cheese. Only rarely could they afford meat and rice. The vast majority worked the land, trying to eke out enough to pay for the next season's water, seed, and rent to the landlord. A smattering of the town inhabitants worked in cottage industries—carpets, textiles, metalwork—the workshops often no bigger than a single room, poorly lit and ventilated, where child labor was common and twelve-hour workdays the norm. The only employer worthy of the label was the government, which ran the mines, ports, and army. Consumerism, and the accompanying rancor in the face of deprivation, was unknown.

Looking to Turkey, where Ataturk's massive modernization programs were at work, Reza Shah was encouraged in his view that the only way to haul a country such as his into the twentieth century was to wipe out the old and overlay it with the new. The traditional vaulted architecture of Persia, with its pointed arches and inlaid mosaics, was replaced by the heavy block forms of Europe's Art Deco. Titles were abolished, and each man, for the first time in Persia's history, had to choose and register a last name. When I arrived in Belgium at the age of nine, I was registered as Manucher Firouz, taking as was customary my grandfather's first name. A few years later I was abruptly informed that our last name was now Farmanfarmaian, my father having chosen a version of his title as our new surname.* The records of the school were changed, and I suddenly had a new identity, as did millions of people throughout Iran, who took the name of their villages or occupations as their own in perpetuity. Two of my older brothers, Nosrat-Doleh and General Mohammad Hossein Mirza, had borne the name Firouz too long to want to change it, so their children carried a different name than I and the rest of my siblings. The Shah took the name of Pahlavi, after the ancient Persian language spoken by the Sassanians. Even the name of the country was changed, the word "Iran" connoting an older history than "Persia."

Though largely unfettered by public opinion, Reza Shah instituted social reforms that struck hard at the traditional fabric of the country and caused much resentment. The ulema, or clergy, felt particularly betrayed. Stripped of their role as the legal conscience of the people, they were also losing their hold on the ethical and moral education of their flock. Reza Shah had little patience for the old religious establishment, seeing it not only as a threat to his power but, worse, as a drag on Iran's development. Not a very religious man himself, he banished the mollahs with little grace or compunction to their mosques and robbed them almost entirely of their day-to-day functions in society. He also labeled any mollah who did not hold a diploma from a *madreseh* (religious school) a fraud and allowed only those who did to wear the distinguishing long tunic and turban, a mea-

---

*At first my father had wanted to register his title unaltered as our family name, but this was forbidden by Reza Shah. He then tried to register the name "Farmanfarma'i" but, to his astonishment, found the name had already been taken, as had a number of other variations. Later he found out that an agent of the Shah's had falsely registered the names to deter my father from devising any way of projecting the title into the future. But the name "Farmanfarmaian" had been overlooked—sounding perhaps too Armenian—and so my father chose that.

sure that swept many claiming divine purpose out of the inner courtyards.

For the most part all this caused little reaction on the part of the populace. That is, until the Shah tried to change the way people dressed.

THE TALE OF THE VEIL

Reza Shah felt that if his people were to be modern, they must look it. First he banned the *sardari,* the men's traditional wide-skirted frock coat, and accompanying untasseled fez (kolah), requiring instead suits with trousers and a vest and a peaked kepi called the Pahlavi hat. Then, in 1935, he forced the adoption of the European brimmed fedora.

Revolts broke out in Mashhad, the capital city of the northeastern province of Khorassan and, as the resting place of the Imam Reza, the eighth Imam of Shiite Islam, the holiest city in Iran. Crowds poured into the shrine in protest. Ordering his army into the mosque, Reza Shah commanded them to drive the crowds out with machine guns. Then he hurried to Mashhad to face the people himself. There he accused the governor of being unable to maintain order and had him shot by firing squad.

When the next year the Shah abolished the women's chador, or veil, few dared to raise a murmur. A British diplomat, H. M. Knatchbull-Hugessen, witnessed the scene on January 8, 1936, when the unveiling of women became official. In his dispatch to Anthony Eden, then foreign secretary of Britain, he describes what he saw:

> The 8th of January was . . . an historic day. The Shah drove to open the new Ecole Normal Primaire, accompanied by the Queen and Princesses. The Royal ladies were unveiled for the first time. The route was sparsely lined with police, and it was to be noticed that any veiled woman who made an appearance was promptly hustled behind a door or into a side street. According to the *Journal de Teheran,* "hundreds and hundreds of women confirmed their joy and their profound respect for the Sovereign whose powerful, enlightened spirit has granted them the right to live in equality." I remember however, that . . . similar remarks were made when the Pahlavi hat was first made universal and the old "Kulah" with no brim abolished. Nor did my personal observation of the crowd make it easy for me to acquit the *Journal de Teheran* of a certain amount of exaggeration.[6]

Enacted in the name of women's liberation, the banning of the chador caused profound shock and pain in Iran's Moslem society. Women felt naked and profane without it. To go about without the chador was blas-phemy, turning one into a "hypocrite"—odious in the eyes of Allah.

In my own family the decree was received with widely varying emo-tions. My mother was thrilled and spoke of it as the greatest achievement since Islam. She promptly went out and bought a hat and then had a pic-ture taken of herself, in the hat, with my father. She even made him wear a tie for the occasion. Masumeh Khanoum, more devout and traditional, at first refused to leave her house, and when she did, she covered her head in a large shawl and kept her eyes cast down in the street.

From a practical perspective shedding the chador was not an easy mat-ter. The chador made owning a coat unnecessary and hid all manner of po-tentially embarrassing traits, from ragged clothes to ugliness to pregnancy. Many of the most devout had worn a handkerchief-size piece of gauze over their eyes in addition to the swirling, semicircular chador wrapped like a tent around their body, and their faces had almost never seen the light of day. Not only were they terrified of showing their emotions in front of strange men, but they had no skills in makeup, coiffure, or fashion with which to present themselves once they dared appear in public. To help them out women's magazines hurriedly began to give Emily Post–like ad-vice on how to comport themselves without their safety blankets. "Women on entering public meetings must on no account remove their hats," wrote *Setareh-ye Jehan* (Star of the World) on January 20. "But to take fruit or sweets with gloves on is forbidden."[7]

With ladies of the upper class leading the way, the veil was gradually cast aside. People didn't have much choice, no matter how angered a man felt at seeing his wives and daughters walking about exposed or how em-barrassed the women were at being openly stared at. The police had been told to clear veiled ladies from the main streets and to forbid them to sit in cafés or attend movies.*

The banning of the chador was Reza Shah's most revolutionary act. Rid-ing through the streets with his own wife and daughters unveiled was his-

---

*After Reza Shah fell in 1941, his son Mohammad Reza Shah loosened the strictures against wearing the chador and allowed men to wear any kind of hat they chose. Many of the poorer sectors reverted to wearing the chador, though the gauze facepiece was never readopted. Only later did militant Islamic groups transform the chador and the wide, shoulder-length scarf called the *roussari* into a political symbol. Unfortunately Reza Shah's decrees on dress had the effect of wiping out many of the traditional fashions of Persia, fashions that had been developed over the centuries to withstand the extremes of climate and the demands of the terrain. The long cloaks or caftans, the summer bolero-type jack-ets, and the wrapped cummerbunds disappeared, to be replaced by European pants, often tied with a string, and mismatched suit jackets worn day in and day out into a state of un-recognizable shabbiness.

toric, the first time the faces of the royal harem had ever been seen by the public. Though the instigator of reform, Reza Shah was in fact quite a traditional man, and even for him it couldn't have been easy.

Removing the veil was not just about lifting folds of cloth from women's eyes. It exposed the norms of society as well. With one sweep the entire moral fabric of Iran was exposed. For the old it was a nightmare. In the young it inspired hope. In our household the woman on the cusp was my sister Maryam. Hers was the first generation of women to step from the andarooni, the harem's inner quarters, into the open crosswinds of liberty. It was a heady feeling, but the road was not easy. There were no role models, no ethical guidelines, only prejudice and dismay in a society that for the most part deeply resented the enforced changes and was flabbergasted by their consequences.

In 1941 Maryam was a magnetic, strong-willed woman of twenty-eight, whose voice cut like silk cord through a crowd. She had been my father's favorite and was used to having her way. Very soon I realized that she had as forceful a say in the household's affairs as my mother, and frequently we clashed.

I was stiff and had strict English views about how the house and the family should be run. I considered it important to preserve the sanctity of my mother's home. Yet Maryam invited friends over all the time—virtual strangers to the rest of us—who moved in and out of the house constantly, making demands on the kitchen, the telephone, and the servants.

Maryam's strident laugh across a crowded room made me shrink. It bothered me how boldly she talked to men. She jousted with them as though she were in Paris. But this was not Paris; this was Tehran, where the interaction between the sexes was uneasy and restrained. There was still no such thing as dating. If a man took an unmarried girl out once, he married her. Courting—if one could call it that—took place in the home, under the watchful eyes of siblings and relatives. If a man wasn't interested in marriage, he kept his distance.

What I did not understand was that Maryam was caught between the moving plates of a social upheaval. She had had the best education a woman in Iran of her time could aspire to: a high school degree from the French Jeanne d'Arc School. Unlike my younger sisters Haideh and Leila, who would go on to universities abroad thanks to softening views about sending women overseas for their education, Maryam, ten years older, did not have access to advanced instruction. She was bundled into an arranged marriage and neatly transferred from the sequestered world of Farman Farma's domain to that of her husband.

She was an angry young woman, intellectually smothered and resentful of her shackles. When the slash-and-burn development program of Reza Shah swept the country, Maryam broke out like a bronco in a rodeo ring, free of the fetters, not caring much where she was going. For the new Iranian women striking out for self-definition, it was a battle of wits against the long tongues of gossip. Maryam's reaction was to seek educated company—which meant the company of men—and the friends she gathered around her were in fact the intelligentsia of the day: poets, musicians, and political thinkers. Maryam—petite, high-strung, and increasingly eccentric in her tastes and views—became obsessive in her need to gain a foothold in the domain of scholarship, art, and, particularly, politics. She jumped wildly from one political concept to the next, one day extremely fond of someone whose theories she admired, the next their staunchest enemy as she fastened on to someone else to revere.

Often, after a night out together, my brother Aziz and I would come in to find the hallway full of coats and umbrellas and the living room jammed. We would join in, seeing only one or two women among the otherwise all-male gathering. I would grow gradually more tense as I watched Maryam acting like the queen among her courtiers. She was gregarious and flamboyant, arguing with the best, seeking out controversy, a powerful woman bursting from the bud. But it was too much for me.

When one of the musicians took up his lute, or *tar*, and a hush fell upon the company, it was my cue to escape. Persian music is in any case a nightmare to my ears. Whenever I hear it, I think of Professor Shakespeare, who taught physics at Birmingham and started his first lecture by saying, "Science is science because it is written down." Since Persian music has never been scored, it is deadly static and subject to the caprices of its performers. Already uncomfortable in that setting, I did not want to suffer further torture by listening to a round of its endless, primitive droning.

A TALE OF AN INTERVIEW

As I searched for a job I was impressed by how anxious my father's friends were to help me—and how helpless they were to do so. Under Reza Shah their wings were clipped. Mohammad Mossadeq had been imprisoned and then exiled. Qavam-Saltaneh and Heshmat-Doleh were both under house arrest. Taqizadeh, the minister of finance who had signed the 1933 Oil Concession and was sent to Berlin as ambassador, had escaped from there to London. My elder brother General Mohammad Hossein Mirza had left for Paris. For those who stayed, such as Mohammadvali Mirza, it was survival of the quietest.

In fact Reza Shah could have been a lot harsher, and no one would have said a word. If he'd wanted to kill everyone at the top and seize their lands, he could have, just as Ferdinand Marcos did later in the Philippines and the Bolsheviks had done in Russia. But he didn't. He killed my brother Nosrat-Doleh and a number of other top officials to establish his own dominion. Had they been allowed to live, they would undoubtedly have jeopardized the future of his dynasty. But he did not kill the rest of us. He allowed us to keep a good portion of our properties and, in many cases, to live as other citizens—under the thumb of the police state but free—provided we did not interfere in government affairs.

Nonetheless being a Farmanfarmaian was not an easy matter. At home our meals were served by Lali, a deaf-mute, so that when we talked he could report nothing. The Shah's police were everywhere. Servants and chauffeurs were encouraged to inform. One day two men appeared on bicycles and posted themselves openly at our door, introducing a virtual state of siege to the household. Every evening we sent them out trays of food, hoping to soften their daily reports. A few days later they disappeared as inexplicably as they had come.

Since my father's friends could not help me get a job, it was with my father's secretary, the indomitable Agha-ye Sadr ("Monsieur"), that I went to the Ministry of Industry, where he introduced me to the director general. He also took me to the Ministry of Finance, as well as a number of other government offices. But none gave me any encouragement. Sometimes we were virtually thrown out minutes after I announced my name. Having a Farmanfarmaian about was just too risky. No one was going to endanger their job to hire me.

Yet I had made up my mind I was not going back to Abadan to work at the refinery. I said as much to the Tehran representative, Mostafa Fateh—politely of course—when I went to visit him at AIOC headquarters on Avenue Sepah. He was the highest Iranian official in any foreign company operating in Iran and the head of internal distribution. The only other Iranian holding a job of similar account was Mosharaf Nafici, a lawyer in AIOC's legal department.

Fateh was fattish, with a round face and shiny brilliantined hair, and he dropped a lot of names. He was from Isfahan, whose citizens are known in Iran for being astute, intelligent, and cunning. He told me to sit down in one of his plush leather chairs, said a few kind things about my family, and then mentioned Nosrat-Doleh, whom he said he'd worked with during the oil negotiations in the 1920s, claiming, quite preposterously, that he'd often offered him counsel.

The preamble over, Fateh wrinkled his eyebrows. "There are no jobs here in Tehran," he said. "Though this is the head office, the only employment for Persians is in Abadan."

I nodded. Even Fateh's distribution job was a small operation. There were only six gasoline pumps in all of Tehran at the time, serving just seven hundred cars. The majority of the gasoline sold in the country was distributed in five-gallon cans, which people put in the back of their cars whenever they headed out of town. In the provinces there were no pumps at all. AIOC wasn't interested in internal distribution; it saw no profit in it and refused to invest in Iran.

As I walked out I thought how strange it was that though Fateh was not someone I would naturally have taken to, I'd found him simpatico despite myself. He exuded goodwill in much the same manner as a fatherly headmaster, a role he had taken upon himself at AIOC by organizing bridge games and staff social events and by keeping people like me on a list of invitees. I looked up enviously at the windows of his office on the second floor, little knowing that in ten years I'd be moving into that very same office as a director of the newly nationalized National Iranian Oil Company.

A PRISON TALE

A few days later I decided to take a break from the frustrations of job hunting and drive up to the old summer residence of Rezvanieh with my mother and sisters. Little had changed. My mother had planted a swath of cherry trees in the garden, and they were all in bloom, filling the air with a quiet rain of petals. We spent the afternoon walking the property, for under the influence of her green thumb I had become fascinated with the propagation of plants.

In the late afternoon we drove back to town. The sun sat on the horizon like an enormous orange, inflaming the sky with bands of gold. I was filled with a sense of peace, imagining the gardens I would start soon on my own property in Assadabad.

But peace was not to be mine that night. Just outside our gate a police motorcycle with a sidecar suddenly swerved in front of my car and came to a screeching halt. A policeman jumped in beside me and ordered me to drive to the main police station downtown. When we arrived my mother and sisters were brusquely told to leave. My mother cried out, panicked by the memory of Nosrat-Doleh, and begged me not to say good-bye. I could do nothing but stand there, surrounded by police.

Inside a lieutenant with stars on his epaulets sat at a table. He asked me my name, my address, and where I had been at midday. I told him I'd been at home. A secretary took down all I said.

The lieutenant told me to wait. All police stations are wretched places, and I sat miserably in the poorly lit hallway, hungry and anxious, turning over in my head what I could possibly have done to land in this situation. Finally, escorted by two slovenly policemen and an officer, I was taken to the central jail. Forms were filled out. They took away my belt and the contents of my pockets and gave me a receipt.

The prison was a circular building surrounded by a large yard. Armed guards patrolled a catwalk above us. More guards with guns were posted at four points on every landing. A man was sleeping on the floor of the cell that was apparently mine. Brutally waking him with the butt of a rifle, one of the guards threw him into the adjacent cell, where other prisoners dozed against the walls.

"You will be alone," the officer sneered as he turned the key in the lock, a hollow, grating sound against the thick walls. "Your case is very important. We call this the aristocracy's cell. It was used by your late brother, Prince Firouz, among others." He gave me a sickly grin and turned away.

I was left alone in the semidarkness. There was a filthy mat on the floor. A small, dirty lightbulb hung from the ceiling, far from reach. A grated window with a sloped sill was sunk deep into the wall, cutting out a tiny square of black sky. I was famished and terribly tired. I eyed the mat and, with resignation, huddled into a corner and wrapped it around me. But I was too keyed up to sleep. I relived every incident of the day, trying to pinpoint a cause for my predicament. I jumped farther back, browsing through the preceding days, the train ride, Abadan. Then I thought of Birmingham, trying to remember whom I'd talked to, where I'd gone. Could it have been something I had said at the cafeteria? Or was it the socialist club meetings I had attended?

This last thought gave me a chill. I had always gone as a joke, acting as devil's advocate. There would be towering arguments, my friends and I agreeing only that we were all anticolonialist, to which we'd drink a round of stout and clap each other on the back. Had I misjudged? There were always jealousies. I was a clear-cut blue blood, reason enough for resentment.

Straining to remember through the fog of weariness, I began to doubt my friends. Maybe they'd taken our political disputes personally. Maybe they'd despised me, thinking how easy it was for me to sit and declaim so loudly when I had everything. In my anxiety, I began to turn my head from one side to the other against the hard floor. Maybe one of them had written a report. Maybe I would be stuck here forever.

The next morning a guard brought me tea and bread and deposited some bedding sent by my mother. He left the door open, warning me that I would be visited by other prisoners. I'd be well advised to make friends, he told me, as I would be inside for some time.

He seemed more approachable than the night guard, and I asked him if he knew why I had been arrested.

"Yes, sir," he said matter-of-factly. "You have committed a terrible crime, and you will be punished. At midday your car overtook and passed that of the crown prince. Your registration number was taken . . ."

I looked at him dumbfounded. I had been home at midday, waiting for Aziz to get back with the car so that I could go up to Rezvanieh. Suddenly I felt like laughing. There had been a mistake! I thanked God that it was me, and not my brother, who had been arrested for such a ridiculous crime. Yet the very absurdity of the offense was shocking. No matter how accustomed one becomes to the rigors of dictatorship, its arbitrariness is horrifying.

Prisoners walked to and fro in the corridor as I sat in a daze on the floor of my cell. I commanded myself not to feel bitter or afraid. I thought of my beloved brother Nosrat-Doleh, as I had so often over these past couple of years, imagining him now in this very cell as he wrote his last letters to our father, warning him that he was about to be killed. I often wondered if I would have the same courage and dignity under such circumstances. Now I was being forced to confront myself: Was it strength I would find in the inner recesses—or weakness? Did I have the nerve to act with detachment and bravery?

I told myself contemptuously that my offense was nothing. I smiled thinly to myself. I would force myself to be optimistic.

As I sat there a fellow prisoner popped his head around the door and offered me a cup of tea. I looked up slowly and met his eyes. He smiled, gesturing down the corridor. "Come on," he said. "In my cell."

I got up apprehensively. Outside, prisoners in rags milled about, talking in groups, leaning languidly against the walls. When we reached his cell I stopped cold. The cell had everything: cutlery, crockery, clothes, washing utensils, chairs, even beds. His two cell mates sat at a table playing chess, the pieces little sculptures made from the doughy part of bread and then dried. I shuddered. These people had been here for a long time.

They offered me tea and motioned for me to sit down for a game. I had given up chess after years of being addicted to it. Nonetheless this was prison, and as they were so eager, I made an exception and sat down. All at once I was transported back to the times I'd bent over the chessboards at the Café Régence in Paris. One of the tables had had a label on it saying

NAPOLEON BONAPARTE PLAYED HERE. Professionals gathered there to play for money, and occasionally even world champions stopped by to play a round. I would catch the twelve-thirty train from school right after lunch on Sundays and arrive at the Gare Saint-Lazare in Paris by one. Half an hour later I'd walk into the café. To a boy of fifteen it was an amazing place, filled with the smells of tobacco and coffee and the heady buzz of serious competition.

Games cost 20 francs, but as I got only 35 francs a week for spending money, the men made an exception and allowed me to play for 15. By two o'clock I'd lost my two games, paid my 30 francs, and was back out on the sidewalk. There was a famous chocolate shop next door called Madame de Récamier, and with my hands sunk deep in my empty pockets I'd look longingly through the window at the rows of bonbons. Then, head down, I'd shuffle past the Comédie Française and up the Avenue de l'Opéra, feeling too destitute even to window-shop. Still I dragged my feet as slowly as I could, since on Sunday afternoons there was no one at school and once back I'd have just myself for company. On the train I replayed the games in my mind to see where I had failed and began the long wait until I could return to the Café Régence the following week.

That summer, when I arrived at my tutor's house in St. Nicolas, he informed me that there was a professional chess player in town and if I liked he'd set up a game. Monsieur Roustan was himself good at chess and had taught me to play. He even offered to put up the money for two rounds—though he said he could not risk losing more than that.

Monsieur Naoun came by the next day. He recognized me from the café, revealing the secret of my Sunday jaunts to my tutor, who looked at me severely, having no idea that I'd been spending my time that way.

Right from the start I could tell Naoun had written me off. I started with the whites and, hoping to shock him, made a queen opening. It took him by surprise, but he didn't really care. He played fast, smiling through his spectacles to his friends in a manner that casually implied he knew all the tricks, gambits, and endgames infinitely better than I. As the game progressed he tried to catch me in a series of traps, but I wriggled out of them, having played enough with professionals to know at least what to avoid. After a struggle he beat me, but not devastatingly.

We turned around the board. Now he played the queen opening, remarking haughtily, "It's good for a young man to be adventurous, but now you have to learn to respond to your own opening." His face wore a bored expression, and he barely bothered looking at my responses. By underestimating my concept of strategy he overestimated the strength of his own. It led him to make a mistake—and one mistake was enough. Tense as a wound-up clock, I made my move. Suddenly, to everyone's surprise, the game was over, and I had won.

In fact, I could really not beat him. He was a much better player than I was. With every move I could feel his professional touch. It was his mood that made him lose. After five hours we'd played twelve games, of which I won eight, lost three, and drew one.

At the end Naoun got up with a scowl. He made no gesture to pay, and etiquette forbade me to ask.

A year later I met Naoun again at the Café Régence. Thereafter he was kind enough to play a game with me whenever we met. He never lost a game to me again. And he never asked me to pay. He was a gentleman as it turned out. He even invited me once to see a championship game of Emanuel Lasker's, who had won the world title more than thirty times. Afterward he introduced me to Lasker, saying, "This young man won against me. He may have a future in this."

Lasker just grunted. "Don't put your future in chess," he said. "Study and learn to earn your living. There is no money in chess." Lasker did not know that one day the world would pay Bobby Fischer $1 million for winning as grand master. How could he? Lasker didn't see that kind of money in all of his years of winning at chess.

I had ambitions. I thought of chess as a Persian game and, being Persian, assumed I would become a champion. At Birmingham I immediately joined the chess team, lining up that first day with all the new boys to receive our thrashing from the old. I licked all of them and, despite being a Persian, became the youngest captain of the team the next year. But Lasker was right. Unless I set aside my studies, set aside everything in fact, for chess, I could not become a champion. And what was the point if you didn't reach for the top? The next year I gave it up.

Now it seemed oddly appropriate to be playing in prison. I warmed to the men, feeling a kinship as we sat together across the makeshift board and with care placed the little bread pieces on the side to make sure they didn't crack.

> Come down from your horse, put the rook on the floor
> Look underneath the feet of the elephant [the bishop]
> The King Nohman has been check-mated.

In this passage of Persian poetry, the bard, Khaghani, plays chess with the words. It is really untranslatable, for in Farsi the words jump in squares and diagonals and all have double meanings.

The men told me there were no political prisoners on the fifth floor, which is why we were allowed out of our cells during the day. The state wasn't worried about us brewing counterrevolution. They wore stubbly beards, saying they didn't see much reason to shave every day. Their hair was very short, clipped every week by the wardens.

Two of the men in the cell were train drivers who had caused an accident and then accused each other of the crime. Both claimed they were innocent; after hearing their stories I began to wonder whether anyone in jail was guilty. Maybe they were all liars. According to that reasoning I probably was one too.

One of the men told me to get used to the place, since nobody had any hope of getting out. I told them I had done nothing. They guffawed. "Do you see those trees, sir?" one asked. "When they dumped us here, we thought the same thing. But the leaves on those trees have dropped three or four times since." He laughed bitterly at my look of dismay. From the little cutout window I could just see the branches and noticed they were poplars. The leaves were the delicate yellow-green of spring.

The man picked up a dog-eared volume of Hafez and flipped through it lovingly. As with the Bible one traditionally opens Hafez at random to read one's luck. *Lesan ol qeib* "the tongue of the hidden." He chuckled softly, saying, "We have opened it up so many times there's probably not a page we haven't read. But no matter what we think we see in the words, we have still not been freed."

I trudged back to my cell and sat down dejectedly on the floor. I was completely disheartened. Prisoners trooped in to look at me, whispering and eyeing me like a monkey in the zoo. In a place where nothing happened day in and day out, a new prisoner was a novelty.

About midday there was a commotion, and a large tray with a hot lunch was brought in from my mother. I was soon surrounded by prisoners, and having little appetite myself, I told them to dig in. One of my friends from the chess game approached and began to whisper in my ear. "You should eat your lunch," he said. "You will soon be forced to accept prison soup and stale bread. Your family will forget you." His voice was wistful. "Our families used to send us all sorts of delicacies at first. But gradually they forgot us. My wife wants a divorce, for what use is a husband in prison? What use is an absent father to his children? We are as good as dead now to our relatives. Tomorrow eat your lunch. You will not have it to enjoy much longer."

The following day my mother sent a few more things from home, and I wore pajamas that night to sleep. But there was no news of release.

On the third day, in the afternoon, a group of officers and a policeman noisily entered my cell. A colonel saluted me with ill-disguised contempt.

"You are free to go," he said, his lip curling as he glanced around the cell. "What do you want to do with your bedding and belongings?"

I looked at him in disbelief. "N-nothing. Give them to anyone here who wants them," I answered hesitatingly, not trusting my ears.

My mother, I found out later, had appealed to Agha Esfandiari, who was still the speaker of the Majles. He had gone through channels, appealing to the prime minister, even visiting the crown prince. It had taken three days, but at last the order of release had been signed.

The colonel turned on his heel and stalked out. I followed, passing a number of prisoners who had gathered to watch me leave. Their faces were miserable as they witnessed a man of the privileged class being allowed to go. I felt self-conscious and ashamed, knowing that the laws of justice in my country were not fair and that the next spring these men would still be watching the poplars bloom through the grates of their little cutout windows.

I was taken to the main desk, where the contents of my pockets were handed back—with one little difference. Instead of the single five-hundred-rial note I'd turned in originally, there were five separate one hundreds.

"Don't forget our tip . . . Your Highness," said the clerk, winking at me cheekily. I dully handed him a note. The remaining bills I gave to the four wardens who opened the door. On the other side stood my mother, with our driver and the car. The rest of the family had been too frightened to come. A policeman hurried to the car and opened the door with a flourish. He held out a hand for a tip, but I had nothing left.

THE OCCUPATION

Excuse those who fought the wars of the seventy-two nations
As they never saw the truth, they only made a tale of it.
—HAFEZ

Tehran 1941

I finally joined the army three months before the Allies invaded Iran. It was my cousin General Nasser-e-Doleh's idea. Word had gotten about that I was having an affair with a woman I liked to call Femme Fatale. She was from a prominent Shirazi family and had become famous for her elegant half-moon hats, which she wore so that the brim dropped tantalizingly over one eye. She was the wife of a general who was apparently out for my blood.

My cousin dropped me at the barracks downtown in his Cadillac with orders not to let me off the premises until the end of the month. My head was shaved, and I was put in uniform, then sent off to join the cleaning detail. It was hard work—fifteen hours at a stretch scrubbing toilets and scouring kitchen floors. They paid us 3 rials a day—10 cents. At night I collapsed into my bunk with the other recruits. The washing facilities were so minimal they made my French boarding school seem like a first-class hotel.

On June 22, 1941, Germany invaded Russia. Tehran was jubilant. The Soviet Union's expansion into the Baltics and its invasion of Poland in 1939 had caused consternation in Iran, and there was real fear that we might be next.

The German invasion balanced the scales somewhat. It wasn't that the Iranians were pro-German; it was that they were anti-British and anti-Russian, and hence by definition supported any country that could give those two a licking. At the movies, if a British ship sank, everyone applauded; if the film showed British resistance getting the upper hand, everyone booed. Meanwhile, Nazi propaganda played on the two nations' common Aryan heritage, and local agents even went so far as to tell unsuspecting villagers that Hitler's name was actually Mohammad and that he was a closet Moslem.

During the years between the two world wars Iran had actively sought Western expertise to jump-start its industrialization program. The United States and France had not responded with much interest. Germany had, and by the outbreak of World War II more than six hundred German experts were employed in a variety of projects from mining to building an armaments factory. They were also building two sulfur plants for AIOC at Masjed Soleyman in exchange for a million barrels of oil. After World War I and the Treaty of Versailles, Germany was more or less frozen out of the international oil market; this was one of the few big deliveries it was able to secure. Hitler's need for oil was one of the reasons he went to war.

When Germany invaded Poland, Iran declared itself neutral and Reza Shah focused on building up his military machine to keep aggressors at bay. In an effort to stay firmly on the fence he appointed a pro-German to the premiership and then signed a credit agreement with Britain for £5 million specifically for war matériel, incurring the first foreign debt since his coronation.

The British soon reneged on the agreement, deciding they needed all the matériel themselves for the war. In a further blow the AIOC contributed its tankers to the British war effort. As a result, or so AIOC's new chairman, Sir William Fraser, claimed, AIOC's trade was reduced, and the Iranian government's revenues would be cut.[1] Iran's revenues, at a high of £3.7 million in 1937, were to fall below £2 million by 1940, even though AIOC paid almost £3 million in taxes that year to the British government and its own profits were more than £2.8 million.

The Shah, incensed, informed the company that it was "unthinkable that because the company happens to be under the control of the government of a country at war, he should . . . receive payments below the level he [had] a right to expect."[2] The British, considering the Iranians "unreliable"[3] and the Shah quite capable of again canceling the concession, first made sure they could protect Abadan using airpower based in Basra before offering the troublesome monarch—who was after all acting as a buffer against the Soviet Union—a guaranteed minimum of £4 million a year until actual oil revenues exceeded that amount.

Sir Reader Bullard, the British ambassador to Tehran, delivered the first check by hand a few months after war was declared. At a time when relations between the two countries were so critical, it was astonishing that the British placed a representative in Iran who so openly despised its people and culture—and as a result was so disliked in return. Bullard, aptly named, was a bully. He was probably the most powerful man in Iran at the time and became notorious for the vainglorious scorn with which he addressed the Persians. His delivery of that first oil check to the minister of finance was no exception. Without preamble he threw it down on the table and, curling his lip, remarked, "This is a dagger you have sunk into our backs."[4]

Despite the millions Reza Shah poured into his military, the army I joined in the spring of 1941 was ill-equipped and badly paid. A standing army was a new concept in Iran, which for centuries had relied on private and tribal militias to maintain order and fight foreign wars. To gain power, Reza Shah had centralized the country's administration along the British colonial model, making all areas of the nation dependent on the sovereign and his army. More appropriate for Iran, with its deeply rooted tradition of tribes and semiautonomous provinces, would have been a structure based on the American model of self-governing states.

Nonetheless, under Reza Shah's leadership the army had gradually tightened up, and an uneasy truce was maintained between the capital and the provinces. Although the uniform commanded respect in the streets, the majority who wore it were forced recruits who had joined after a draft law in 1931 required all men over twenty-one to serve for two years. Discipline was haphazard and corruption rampant. Within the first week, thanks to the maneuvers of Femme Fatale, I was allowed off camp for weekends. After the first month she arranged a vacation so that I could go up to Hamadan and inspect my properties. A little wangling on my own part got me transferred to the army supply division as a chemist. The major in charge, hearing my name, promptly suggested I spend nights at home and report to him in the mornings.

The trip to Hamadan was a welcome break from the war frenzy in the capital. I traveled up with another Hamadani landowner in a rented car, as the roads were so bad and the price of tires so high that it wasn't worth taking one of our own.

After dropping off my friend I headed toward the family seat of Janatabad, about twenty miles west of Hamadan. On the right I passed the

tomb of Esther, whom we Persians call Hadassah. It sits on the crest of a
hill, its double domes—the smaller one pointed, the bigger one a round
inverted bowl—white against the rocky slope. "So when the king Artax-
erxes's order was proclaimed," it says in the Bible, "and when many maid-
ens were gathered in Susa, Esther also was taken into the king's palace. And
the maiden pleased him and won his favor."⁵ A few pilgrims were gathered
at the tomb's door; a few more were already winding their way down the
hillside. In Iran Esther was a queen, and she is therefore as important to us
as she is to the Jews. Her shrine, just outside the great capital of the Medes,
was neat and well maintained and had remained an active point of pilgrimage for more than two thousand years.

I pulled up to Janatabad after the sun had set and the air had turned
agreeably cool. It was the first time I'd been there, and I was amazed. The
castle took shape suddenly out of the darkness, huge and impregnable,
with thick walls and sturdy medieval watchtowers at each of its four corners. The stables could easily have quartered two hundred horses, and there
was a well in its front courtyard.

A throng from the surrounding villages had gathered at its massive gate
to welcome me. My brother Abol Bashar, looking scholarly behind his
clipped mustache and wire-rimmed glasses, had taken his place at its head
next to the kadkhodah, or village headman. As I got out of the car, the
crowd swarmed to greet me, and I was suddenly surrounded by the hub-
bub of excited chatter.

Inside there was little furniture, but carpets covered every inch of the
floor and a huge fire blazed in the hearth. Several of the estate managers followed me inside. According to custom, a sheep had been slaughtered and
preparations had been made for a feast. After washing off the worst of the
grime from my journey in one of the rooms—there were enough, I noticed,
to house a legion, with storerooms and kitchens leading off a maze of corridors and inner courtyards filled with trees and pools—I rejoined the
company downstairs in the main hall.

Like them I sat on my haunches to eat my dinner. Soon a group of *ko'oli,*
or gypsies, trooped in for a rousing dance. The women performed first in
an array of colorful skirts that whirled in rainbows across the floor. Then
came the men, mustachioed and fierce, stamping and shouting in unison
as their billowing pants caught the wind like cavorting bellows and the
gold coins strung around their necks tinkled and reflected the light. At the
time I thought I'd never see these wayfarers again, but after the war they
returned. The gold coins were gone, sold one by one to stave off starvation.
In their place they wore strings of Coca-Cola bottle caps.

The next morning a dozen horses were readied to take us to the villages on the rolling green plains. The air was clear, and snow glittered on the mountains that hung like a Hollywood set against the horizon. We were accompanied by two wizened Bakhtiaris who had been Farman Farma's *jelodar,* or front riders, and at each successive village they galloped ahead to announce our arrival. They were polite and acute, well versed in horses and expert in the geography and weather patterns of the region. As we rode that day and the days that followed, I began to understand the spirit of the people of Iran and the special status that landowners such as my father had held.

After visiting some of our villages in the Hamadan district, we turned west to Kurdistan, where my father had left us more than thirty large properties, the most beautiful and productive in the region. Water flowed in rivers from the foot of the mountains, and the valleys were arrayed in fields of soft green wheat, flowering orchards, and the geometry of vineyards. The woods held wild boars and bears. At every village the peasants lined up and bowed as we passed through. Some handed me letters, while others waited to make their requests in person. Abol Bashar and I would dismount, take tea sitting on the ground, and listen to their plaints.

Though we were young, they turned to us for judgment, for ours was the final word that everyone instinctively obeyed. The gendarmes, on the other hand, were dreaded because they would take disputing parties to court, sometimes miles away and for as long as ten or fifteen days. If it was at harvest or planting time, the peasants' absence could be ruinous. Landlords would sometimes get involved and have to bribe officials to engineer a release. We would never shirk our duty, for the relationship between landlord and peasant was interdependent: In times of need we called on the peasants to help defend us and our property. Often my father had called on local villagers to fight wars, and the guards around Janatabad were vestiges of that past force.

Whom did the fruit belong to, asked one man, from a tree planted on his land that dropped its entire harvest over the wall onto his neighbor's land?

"My husband beats me unmercifully," sobbed a woman, covering her face tightly with her chador. "Surely Your Highness can make him stop. And perhaps give up his mistress in the next village as well."

One young man told us he had been engaged for more than two years but was unable to marry his intended because he still could not afford the dowry. Now, to his despair, the girl's father was threatening to marry her off to someone else. He stood limply in front of us, his pants tied at the waist with a piece of rope, his woven cloth shoes worn through at the toes. "What should I do?" he asked, his eyes glued to the ground.

Suddenly a man broke from the crowd and announced that he was the girl's father. "Your Highness," he said, flicking his eyes from one to another of the elder peasants for approval, "my daughter is very beautiful. Let me bring her to you. Surely you will decide to take her." There was a murmur among the crowd.

"Marry her to whomever she wants and do it quickly," I said, hurriedly getting to my feet and striding to my horse before I could be accused of having looked lecherously at a peasant girl. I did not want to leave the countryside a married man, tricked into wedlock with one of my villagers.

In the evening the kadkhodah came by to pay his respects and show me the accounts. He was fortyish with a cunning face and skin like weathered mahogany. The literal meaning of kadkhodah is "god of his realm," and he alone was exempt from paying taxes to the landlord. Nonetheless he bowed and remained standing during our talks, for it would have been unthinkable for me to ask him to sit down. As was customary he'd left his shoes at the door and stood before me in his bare feet, though he kept his brown brimless hat on the entire time. The kadkhodah sounded prosperous and satisfied, and after we exchanged a few pleasantries he told me openly of his role in the opium business. The poppies flowered in the early spring, and the plot of each peasant could produce about half a pound of dried sap. The harvest was supposed to be delivered to the government, but the peasants kept a portion for themselves to sell privately.

Luckily for him, the kadkhodah explained, Janatabad was at the junction of the domestic opium trade. Horsemen traveling under cover of night would arrive with five or six pounds strapped to their saddles. The kadkhodah paid them cash and put them up until morning. The next evening another set of armed horsemen would arrive from the north or from the eastern areas around Tehran to carry the opium to their home regions.

It was a very profitable business, and the kadkhodah had so much cash that he eventually became my banker. He kept his money in his pillow and slept on it every night. It would never have occurred to him to spend it on a bigger house, a horse, a new pair of pants, or any of the other trappings that constitute prosperity in the West. His money was in his voice and the air with which he conducted his business. When I jokingly threatened to have him publicly flogged for moneylending and trading illegally in opium, he put on a pained look. "Your Highness, I am offering the money to you as a gift," he replied, "without any receipt. All I ask in return is that you repay it with eighteen percent extra for my trouble, rather than the twenty-four percent asked by the banks. As for the opium, I'm not doing anything worse than the government. It forces us to sell the opium at a cheap price under the pretext of stopping its use, when in fact we all know the government resells it for export as medicine, or for the addicts abroad, at ten times what it buys it for."

With each sentence he leaned over dutifully and almost touched the ground with his head. In truth he was right—the government's policies and its agents were our biggest headache, and when at last our land was taken from us and distributed, the kadkhodah lost as much as we did. As landowners we had more than thirty thousand peasants in our care and were responsible for building roads and keeping the *qanat* (water system) in good repair. The government bought wheat—our main crop—at a fixed rate that bore no relation to the actual market value. This meant our income was fixed, even though our costs weren't. The peasants rightly complained that we did not pay them enough, much as we complained to the government that it did not pay us enough. *Har sag-i yek ostokhun mikhad*—each dog wants its own bone.

Janatabad had been bequeathed to a number of us brothers, and we shared its burdens—as well as its wonders. The area was inhabited by tribes that in the past had used its valleys in summer but now, forced to become sedentary, had settled there permanently. They lacked housing and employment, and as the government was not expending adequate funds for the purpose, we filled the breach. That autumn Abol Bashar decided to take up residence at Janatabad and became the Il-Khan of the Zuleh tribe. Although he planned to stay indefinitely, he found that to make money he had to be harsh with the people, tax them and drive them, and not being an exploiter by nature he finally gave up after a couple of years.

The night before I left I walked across the plain and up a knoll behind the castle to watch the sun set over the valley. The dusk dropped first into the folds of the river, then, running like lava across the valley floor, jumped into the copses of trees and finally up the slopes, leaving only the top ramparts of the fortress flaming in the sun's last breath. I gazed around with a heavy heart. Only half an hour before, the kadkhodah had brought me the last accounts and I had noticed that all the year's reserves had been spent on my visit. Everyone had made a claim it seemed, and all had been compensated. It made me feel a little desperate. The Russians called us "feudalists," the Americans "absentee landlords." They accused us of oppressing the peasants when we stayed on our properties and neglecting them when we didn't. What about ranchers? I wondered. Did their estate managers have any option but to execute the orders of their employers? And weren't their employers often gone?

Besides, for years Reza Shah had stopped us from visiting our properties, concerned that the old nobility would set their local armies against him. New laws required special permits to travel to the countryside. Only now that Reza Shah felt completely secure was it becoming easier to reestablish the old relationships with our villagers. As for my father, he'd died having not seen Janatabad for almost twenty years.

I didn't want to leave the old fortress. I wanted to move the world there. These people needed health facilities, schools, roads, baths, tractors, and much more.

A chill wind wrapped itself around me, and I took one last look across the valley. Then sinking my hands deep into my coat pockets, I turned down the hill.

THE BBC

Back in Tehran I found the city embroiled in a radio war. At seven o'clock sharp the rich, sonorous voice of Bahram Sharogh would announce the news on shortwave from the capital of the Third Reich. Not only was Sharogh, the chief commentator for Radio Berlin, Farsi Service, a gifted orator, but the news he was reporting was compelling stuff. The Axis powers were racking up the victories, the Allies were falling back, and General Erwin Rommel was in North Africa threatening the British in Egypt—perhaps even threatening the Suez Canal. Whenever he had a chance, Sharogh took a stab at the British, accusing them of playing fast and loose with politics in the Middle East.* He also reported the rise of Germany's share of Iranian trade from 27 percent in 1937 to more than 40 percent in 1941 and the success of the factories and mines being developed with German expertise.

In May the British government, disturbed by the effect of Radio Berlin on Iranian public opinion, began BBC broadcasts in Farsi every other day. "The Shah . . . should be presented as an energetic, modern-minded ruler," explained the Foreign Office in a memorandum to "British officials only and . . . not to be shown or communicated to any Persian." Most important, "care should be taken not to suggest that His Majesty's Government has any influence whatever over Iranian policy."[6]

Then came the German invasion of the Soviet Union. Hitler, starved for fuel and thinking Russia would crumble as easily as France had, made no secret that he was heading straight to the oil fields of Baku to fill up and

---

*Sharogh was later discredited in Berlin when the Nazis discovered that he was a British double agent. He returned to Iran toward the end of the war and, to everyone's amazement, became the director of news and propaganda, supporting the British from his new soapbox at Radio Tehran.

that he would attend to Moscow later. As Stalin observed a few months later to Averell Harriman, President Franklin D. Roosevelt's special envoy to Moscow, this was a war of motors.[7]

Misjudging the Russian campaign was to prove one of Hitler's greatest strategic blunders. With Moscow standing, the Soviet Union would not fall. Nazi troops never reached Baku. By the time they were routed in the critical Battle of Stalingrad in February 1943, they had only twenty miles' worth of fuel left; safety behind their own lines lay more than thirty miles away.[8] At the time, however, the Allies knew only an undefeated Hitler and hurriedly moved to shore up the Russian bear despite Stalin's on-the-fence stance until his borders were breached. Thanks to the Nazi-Soviet Nonaggression Pact of 1939, engineered by Joachim von Ribbentrop, the Soviet Union had even been providing Germany with a third of its oil until then.

Now the Russians were frantic. And the British were petrified, thinking that the Germans, once in control of Baku, would move across the Caucasus into Iran, cut the Admiralty from its oil source, and then move on to India.

By July 10, 1941, a British counterplan had been devised. "It is essential to the defense of India," wrote General Archibald Wavell, commander in chief of India, to the War Office, "that Germans should be cleared out of Iran now. . . . If the present Government is not willing to facilitate this, it must be made to give way to one which will."[9]

Already the British had quashed a Nazi-inspired coup in Iraq in April; now they felt little compunction in putting the screws on a shah they viewed as belligerent and pro-German.

At 4:45 A.M. on August 25, 1941, the Allies invaded Iran. Russian troops took over the north; British forces occupied the west and south. Fighter planes crisscrossed Tehran: The Russians dropped a few bombs; the British rained down leaflets exhorting the population to stay calm and defending the Allied occupation as a necessary protection against German spies and terrorists. British warships bombarded the Gulf coast and occupied Khorramshahr, killing Admiral Gholam Ali Bayandor, the valiant commander of the Iranian fleet. Fighting erupted that first day in the mountain passes beyond Kermanshah, and a few British soldiers were captured. But within hours Iranian troops were overwhelmed and resistance crumbled.

In Tehran the streets were deserted. Despair gripped the shuttered city; once again foreigners had come to invade our country—this time because of a few Germans. And we knew the British: Hard times lay ahead.

I walked down Avenue Kakh toward the Shah's palace, passing only a few people, silent as shadows in front of the grated shops. It was hot, and the sun found passage around every leaf and balcony to bake the empty sidewalk. I came to the gate of the Foroughis' house and decided to stop in and see my friend Masoud. We had passed the *baccalauréat* together in France and, because our initials were the same, had sat next to each other during the exam. Masoud told me that at eight that morning the Shah had come to see his father, who had served as premier some years before.

"The prime minister, Ali Mansur, is going to resign," he told me. "The Shah wants my father to step in and won't listen to his excuses that he's too old and too ill for the job."

That afternoon I saw the first British trucks roll past Tehran. The next day Mohammad Ali Foroughi was appointed prime minister, and martial law was announced under the direction of a tough Cossack known as the Butcher of Kurdistan.

The quiet of the previous day was gone. Pandemonium and panic had taken hold. The chaos was such that *sag sahabesh-ra nemishnakht*—even a dog could not have found his master. Rumors circulated that the minister of defense had been arrested and shot. A pronouncement was made that the military would offer no more resistance, throwing the ranks into turmoil. Generals deserted the troops and escaped to their country houses. Soldiers grabbed their guns and headed to the villages. The roads were jammed with trucks and cars.

At army headquarters I was sent on a wild-goose chase to deliver bread to a regiment I was never able to find. The army's trucks had all disappeared, and after signing for the bread I had to commandeer one in the street. With only vague directions we drove for hours along a dusty road past Karaj well on toward the city of Qazvin. But as night fell we were forced to turn back, afraid of encountering armed stragglers from the Iranian army or advancing Russians.

In Tehran we found the barracks deserted. My footsteps echoed among the buildings as I ventured out while a soldier in the truck covered me with his gun. The whole day was a waste. Even the bread was inedible. The truck I had grabbed was a coal transport, and the sheaves of bread scattered about its bed after the day's bumpy ride were covered in black dust.

The Allies' arrival had appeared to be a coordinated effort. Yet right away it became clear that the soldiers were operating under no single command. The Russians and British distrusted each other thoroughly and immediately began a tug-of-war over Iranian territory, ignoring the local population to devastating effect.

The Red Army had a list of Persians and Soviet immigrants who had cooperated with the White Russians during and after World War I. They

were hunted down and shot. Fearing for their lives in the face of the occupying Russian army, droves of people began heading south from the
Caspian coast. One of my brothers-in-law, General Nosratollah Motazedi,
the governor of Gorgan province, disappeared for two weeks as he escaped
across the mountains disguised as a peasant. Our friend Jafar Jafari, who
had worked in Baku under the White Russians, bundled up his family and
headed straight for Baghdad. These two got away; others did not. The
owners of Cinema Tehran, responding to a knock on their door, were
greeted by a phalanx of Russian rifles. They were killed on the spot.

The overthrow of local officials by the Russians, however, was just a
sideshow to the increasingly obvious intent of the British to overthrow the
central government. With each passing day the BBC upped its barrage of
insults against the Shah. In increasingly incendiary language it accused
him of being a *sabzi-feroush* (streetside vegetable monger) who had turned
into a vicious tyrant. In shock we heard the same voices that less than a
month earlier had described him as visionary and strong now blast him as
a peasant, small-minded, crude, greedy, and dishonest. It was a disgusting
performance, and we grew to despise the BBC for it.

Within days of the occupation Britain insisted on a devaluation of the
rial. Incomes were almost halved, and the Shah, concerned that the people
would go hungry, immediately reduced the price of bread.

The BBC blasted the action, taking its cue directly from Ambassador
Bullard, whose telegram to London began, "Raw material for Persian
broadcast. Reduction in price of bread good thing in principle, but by
what constitutional right does the Shah give such orders? Is he paying the
difference in price himself? Not at all, apparently poor bakers pay it."[10]

Wheat was a state monopoly, and the government, not "poor bakers,"
paid for the shortfall, a fact Bullard knew perfectly well. Furthermore the
Shah's domestic policies had, until less than thirty days previously, never
concerned the British.

On September 15, 1941, Bullard met with the Shah's top ministers to
suggest that the monarch step down. Pressured on all sides, with the occupying armies on his land and the airwaves filled with their rhetoric, Reza
Shah had no choice. The next day he abdicated in favor of the crown prince,
Mohammad Reza. Bullard's telegram to London indicated that he was still
unsatisfied. "The Crown Prince must be ruled out on account of his well-
known pro-German sympathies. . . . Possible alternatives would be one of
the younger Pahlavis or a Qajar restoration."[11]

That same night Bullard and Smirnof, the Soviet ambassador, traveled
to Isfahan and, waking Sarameh-Doleh (Nosrat-Doleh's old friend), offered
him the crown. Sarameh-Doleh, who at first thought they had come to ar-

rest him, refused. Thereafter Bullard approached him many times to become prime minister, which he always turned down. As he told me later he henceforth avoided coming to Tehran "because people might think I was coming finally to take up the premiership."

Reza Shah, hollow about the eyes, his name besmirched and his uniform laid aside for the first suit of civilian clothes anyone had ever seen him wear, was conducted unceremoniously south, where a British boat transferred him first to Mauritius and then into exile in Johannesburg.* He died there in obscurity in 1944, though his son later had him designated with the title of "Great" and erected many statues of him around the country.

Reza Shah's ouster was greeted with relief: no more police state, no more arbitrary self-aggrandizement on the part of the Crown. We celebrated his fall, quickly forgetting that the most important human right is to live under a government strong enough to maintain law and order—and that he had delivered such a government. Even the worst tyranny is better than no government at all, since nothing causes human beings so much misery as anarchy. Yet anarchy is what we were in the midst of as we hailed the new king, enthroned by the Great Powers as they squatted on our land, while turning our faces from the man who had brought a modicum of cohesion to our country and relief from outside predators. As Hafez observed so wisely: "I tell you again, Hafez is not alone; within the cauldron of this world, many others have drowned in this dirty pool."

We had great hopes for the new twenty-two-year-old Shah. He had been educated for a few years in Switzerland—the first Iranian monarch to have studied abroad—and we dared to imagine that the experience had left him with a greater respect for constitutional monarchy than his father had had. He was suave and charming and embodied a future that promised to be fairer and free. Right off Mohammad Reza Shah was popular.

I was driving down Avenue Sepah when Mohammad Reza Shah's cavalcade swept by after he'd taken his oath before the Parliament to honor the

---

*On his way south Reza Shah stopped in Isfahan, where Sarameh-Doleh went to see him. Reza Shah had acted almost as harshly toward Sarameh-Doleh as he had toward Nosrat-Doleh and, though he had allowed him to live, had relieved him of his post as govenor of Shiraz and exiled him. (In Shiraz the Qashgahis would line his passage into the desert with hundreds of carpets—a tradition leading to the English phrase "red-carpet treatment.") Nonetheless, hearing that the fallen monarch was passing through, Sarameh-Doleh left his desert fortress for the first time in twelve years to pay his respects to the sovereign. The Shah was the Shah; although he had been banished, he had still been king, and Sarameh-Doleh considered it only proper to pay him homage. As Sarameh-Doleh told me afterward, Reza Shah looked at him sadly during the visit and said, "Saram, look what the British have done to me too." Sarameh-Doleh nodded. Sadly, he said, "We, the old Qajar aristocracy, were always your most obediant servants. But you never understood."

Constitution. With some resentment I pulled to the right to let it pass, for I had just been made a second lieutenant and he, two years younger than I, had just been made Shah.

The British, for lack of any other compelling candidate, decided to let Mohammad Reza stay, though within the complicated politics of the day he was largely ignored. The grand vizier calling the shots behind the curtain was really the stocky, unsmiling Bullard. The British Embassy assumed the aura of a colonial government seat—appearing much as it must have a hundred years before. In a gesture of perfectly honed humiliation, high-turbaned Indian soldiers were posted as guards in front of the compound on Ferdowsi Avenue with orders to hit any passing Iranian with their batons. Invitations bearing the emblem of the British Crown began to pour out, and though we Persians despised Bullard, we considered it a novelty to go, since under Reza Shah we'd been strictly forbidden to mingle with foreigners. I remember walking through the fortress gates to that first reception quite beside myself at the prospect of once again meeting and taking out a foreign girl.

With the departure of our gruff sovereign, the mood in Tehran changed abruptly. The Germans were rounded up and sent away, and the Axis embassies all shut down. The press, suddenly freed, erupted with a plethora of new publications. The tribes, loosed from government control, regrouped and became more belligerent in their efforts to gain independence from Tehran. A general amnesty released hundreds of prisoners back into the political fray, including "heads of tribes, princes of the Qajar family, servants of Farman Farma, subversive lovers of liberty, labor strikers, landowners who had refused to sell their land to the Shah, and one or two actors who had poked fun at the marriage of the Crown Prince."[12]*

General Fazlollah Zahedi, who had quashed Sheikh Khazal before he was himself promoted into semiretirement, surfaced and was made governor of Isfahan. Nasser Qashgahi, the Il-Khan of the Qashgahi tribe, who had spent the last few years under house arrest near Tehran, rejoined his people in the south. My brother General Mohammad Hossein Mirza flew back from exile in Europe and was appointed governor of Shiraz. A by-election in Azerbaijan returned our patriarch Mohammadvali Mirza to Parliament. Dr. Mohammad Mossadeq reappeared in town. Our family was back in the political arena, though we were by no means the only ones.

*Crown Prince Mohammad Reza had married Princess Fawzieh, sister of Egypt's King Farouk, in 1938. By law monarchs were supposed to marry Persian women (during Qajar times the law required them to marry Qajar women). To get around this problem Reza Shah had a law passed stating that Fawzieh sprang from ancient Persian ancestry, igniting much scorn and ridicule among the population.

A TALE OF COMMUNISM

Where there had been political silence, a tumult of activity broke out. Aided by the Russians, fifty-two Communists who had been imprisoned by Reza Shah in 1937 became the core of an active left-wing movement that took shape with record speed. The Irano-Soviet Society for Cultural Relations became a hot spot for social gatherings and anti-imperialist rhetoric. Among the intellectual elite communism became fashionable, and for no one more so than my eldest sister, Maryam.

Like so many children of privilege, she fell hook, line, and sinker for the theories of Weber, Marx, Lenin, and Engels, seeing in them salvation from the imperialist powers. We argued all the time, and whenever I called Stalin a despot (rather than a democrat, as she claimed he was), she'd accuse me of being decadent—and pro-British to boot, having just come home from Birmingham. It caused my mother much unhappiness.

Maryam did not change her mind easily once she finally made it up, and she was to pay dearly for the strength of her convictions. But those were still days of promise. The Soviet Union was young, its plans for world hegemony still unrevealed—or pointedly ignored by the war-weary West. McCarthyism in America was twelve years away, and being labeled "pink" bore none of the connotations of political double-talk and connivance that its witch-hunts would leave in their wake.

Maryam's friends were all members of the Tudeh ("Masses") Party, the Communist Party in Iran, a stubborn, honest group that earnestly believed in their political opinions. Their dedication and spirit of sacrifice won them much admiration among the people. I quarreled with them not because they were Communists but because they were so unreasonably pro-Russian. Every step the Russians took they considered right, even if it was to the detriment of Iran. When the Soviet Union endorsed the Kurdish and Azerbaijani autonomy movements, I was sure Maryam would recant and see the move for what it was: the first step by our northern neighbor to once again try to partition Iran. Instead, to my shock, I saw my sister marching around the streets with her friends, waving a red flag.

Maryam's activities, which included founding the women's section of the Party, made me worry that we would have trouble with the government. My concern intensified when one of her friends, a tall, spare architect whom she'd hired to design her house in Shemiran, became her constant companion.

Noureddin Kianouri was from a family of sheikhs with a history of fanatical thinking. His sister was married to one of the heads of the Party, and Kia, as he was called, was one of the hard-liners. When Maryam and he went off to get married in Moscow, we were disturbed by the effect it would have on the family name and deeply concerned for Maryam's welfare.

Little did we imagine that Kia, with his coughlike laugh and rumpled suits, would one day become head of the Tudeh Party or that he and Maryam would spend twenty-five years in drab exile in East Germany. And it was all for naught: Though pockets of Communist sympathy budded at times in the north under Russian influence or in the oil fields when labor movements were ignored and crushed, its philosophy of shared property held little appeal for most Iranians, who were by nature ill-disposed to give anything away without a good haggling. This unfailing bazaar attitude, labeled by some as corrupt, was to Iranians the essence of life on earth, just as Allah is the essence of the soul, and any political ideology not including both had little chance for a lasting place in their hearts.

RETRIBUTION

At the dawn of political release that followed Mohammad Reza Shah's accession, Mozzafar Firouz, Nosrat-Doleh's oldest son, brought a case of murder against the government. Mozzafar looked at the world through big, thick glasses and saw the Pahlavis sitting on the throne, a sight that so enraged him that he dedicated his life to bringing them down. He could not have been from better lineage for such a task. Not only was he Nosrat-Doleh's son, but his mother was Daftar ol-Moluk, Dr. Mossadeq's sister. Over the course of their lives Nosrat-Doleh, Mossadeq, and Mozzafar threatened the Pahlavi throne more than any other figures in the country, Mossadeq coming closest to success when he ran the Shah out of Iran in 1953.

Mozzafar was, like his father, small-boned and highly refined, though his face was more angular, a study of squares and triangles like a Picasso painting. His wife, Maheen, was piquant and very beautiful. The cousin of Reza Shah's last wife, she was also the niece of General Ali Razmara, who was a close confidant of Reza Shah's.

Mozzafar had studied at the Harrow School in England and then at Cambridge, where he'd read political economics and become a doctor of law. Back in Tehran he'd made a name for himself in the 1930s when he'd taken on the case of Kurt Lindenblatt, a German adviser to the Bank Melli accused of committing forgery. With singular courage Mozzafar had shown that it was as much the government as his client that was at fault. The case had caused a scandal, and Mozzafar had been relieved of his license.

Upon Reza Shah's fall Mozzafar brought a civil suit for plotting the assassination of his father against the much-feared ex–chief of police, Sarpas Mokhtari, a Himmleresque character who played the violin whenever he wasn't out murdering someone. There were other defendants too, including one Abbas Shish-Angushti (Abbas the Six-Fingered), whom Mozzafar accused of murdering his father.

The courtroom was packed during the trial, and the papers were full of the affair. Sarpas Mokhtari was sentenced to ten years in jail.* Abbas Shish-Angushti was condemned to death and hanged. Mozzafar walked from the courtroom in triumph. It was the only case ever brought against Reza Shah's government for political assassination.

Although we did not see it that way then, it was a victory that would condemn our family. The Shah took it as a sign that we had the means and the self-confidence to battle the monarchy, and it was an insult he would not forget. Our formidable education—which none of the other big families enjoyed—and our sense of domain intimidated the relatively timorous Mohammad Reza Shah. Other members of the old nobility effaced themselves with good behavior, but we fought with the stubborn arrogance of our inherited ambitions and suffered the consequences.

THE FIFTH COLUMN

As winter settled over Iran and the bleak year of 1942 unfolded, the atmosphere grew more tense under the desperate measures of war. On January 29, 1942, Iran signed the Tripartite Treaty of Alliance with Russia and Britain, giving the Allies the unrestricted right to transport troops and supplies through Iran. The treaty further guaranteed the withdrawal of Allied forces no later than six months after the termination of hostilities.

Meanwhile British and Soviet forces arrested more than two hundred Iranian politicians, merchants, journalists, lawyers, clergymen, and landowners in their respective zones over the five years they occupied Iran. A detention camp was set up in the arid wasteland of Arak, where political prisoners were sent and forgotten during the course of the war. Early in 1942 General Zahedi was spirited out of Isfahan and into exile in Beirut on British suspicions that he was fomenting fifth-column activities with the Germans. My brother General Mohammad Hossein Mirza was relieved of his governorship in Shiraz on similar rumors.

---

*He was later pardoned by Mohammad Reza Shah, who made a policy throughout his reign of protecting his father's subordinates, and appointed to head the office of the Shah's eldest sister, Princess Shams.

The Allies had reason to be nervous. With Reza Shah's abdication the Qashgahi tribe immediately resumed contact with the Germans, continuing the relationship of mutual interest against the British that predated World War I. Khosrow Qashgahi stopped by my mother's house to say good-bye the very night it was announced that Reza Shah had stepped down. He was a good friend of my brother Aziz's, and he did not mince words when he told us he was going back to his tribe to fight the Shah.

Khosrow's brothers Hossein and my childhood friend Mansur had chosen Berlin as their haven of exile when they'd escaped Iran after the murder of their father, Solat-Doleh. While there they encountered a young businessman named Hassan Goreshi who spoke fluent German and was well acquainted with a number of top Nazi officials. The meeting was to have serious ramifications for ensuing German-Iranian relations.

Hossein Qashgahi introduced me to Goreshi some ten years later, and we became fast friends. He was a thoroughly amiable man. He'd grown up in Germany, and the role he played with the Nazis had fallen into his lap rather than springing from any deep-seated ideological beliefs or political ambition. His real goal was to lead the good life, which he pursued with singular aplomb. He always drove snappy BMWs, Ferraris, or convertible Mercedes-Benzes and lived in gaudily grand apartments with black onyx bathrooms and gold plumbing fixtures. Goreshi, despite his small size and unprepossessing features, had a way with women. His money talked of course, but there was a genuine goodness about him. He pampered all his friends: He was always running them to the airport or arranging a meeting with a useful contact, and it was through him that the Qashgahi brothers met Graf von Schulenburg, the Nazi chief of Near East undercover operations, right after the Allies invaded Iran.

When the Allies began their purge of Germans in Tehran, a number of pro-Nazi spies had escaped south and found protection with the tribe's Il-Khan Nasser Qashgahi. Now von Schulenburg proposed that an independent Iranian government be set up in Berlin to support the German cause. A month later Hitler gave his stamp of approval, and a seven-member government-in-exile, which included the two Qashgahi brothers (Hossein and Mansur) and Goreshi, was formally recognized by the Nazis. The Germans pledged to help the group financially, provide arms and ammunition to the tribe, and funnel commercial and industrial business their way.

The deal worked out well for both parties. The Germans were able to fly planes all the way from the Crimea to the south of Iran, where they airdropped arms and money to their agents ensconced in the safe haven of the Qashgahis' territory. The Qashgahis, for their part, regained much of their lost power and accumulated vast wealth. Forming a federation of tribes that numbered more than 300,000 people, they developed a luxuriously equipped, well-trained corps of 20,000 cavalry soldiers that constituted a significant threat to the British and American installations in the area. Nasser Qashgahi, the head of this vast federation, became one of the richest men in Iran and an important player in the political intrigues in Tehran.

Unsettled by the tenacious pro-German maneuverings in the country, the Allies dealt ruthlessly with pro-German suspects in a purge that reached a frenzy right before Roosevelt, Churchill, and Stalin arrived in Tehran for the "Big Three" summit in late 1943. The Allies also increased their pressure on the Shah, who at last capitulated to their demands and three months before the summit formally declared war on Germany.

A TALE OF STARVATION

Great Power interests were transforming Tehran into a mecca of espionage and undercover intrigue. But what most frightened us were the increasingly obvious signs that the occupying forces were literally starving our country. Right from the beginning the Soviets had sealed off 250,000 square miles in the grain-rich north and started shipping Azerbaijani wheat across the border into Russia. In the meantime, all transport lines and vehicles had been taken over by the Allies for the shipment of goods to Russia to bolster its war effort, leaving none to carry food to the provinces for local consumption. The Trans-Iranian Railway was completely co-opted, and not a single chicken or bag of rice was allowed passage on its freight cars to provision the Iranian villages through which it passed.

With more than 150,000 foreign troops to feed and reserves of wheat streaming north, food quickly grew scarce throughout the country. What food there was went first to the occupying forces. Then in March of 1942 Bullard forced the treasury to print 700 million more rials—a stopgap measure that continued throughout the war. Prices doubled and then tripled, and breadlines collected in the streets. But the shops were almost empty, and what bread there was was black with stones and dirt. Famine began to spread its long, bony fingers across the country.

To make matters worse, in June the Soviets, at Roosevelt's suggestion, started routing thousands of Polish prisoners from Siberia to a camp on the outskirts of Tehran. Women and children, ragged and hungry, arrived by the boatload across the Caspian Sea. Haggard, stumbling men poured across the border on foot.

The occupying powers, having pledged to feed the sixty thousand Poles who eventually took up residence behind the camp's barbed wire fences, delivered huge baskets of bread to the gate every morning—right under the noses of the starving Iranians. At last rioting broke out. The baskets were seized, and the Iranians fell upon the loaves, tearing them apart and eating them ravenously right there in the desert.

I have never seen such desperation. The devaluation of the rial meant that we were in effect paying for Britain's and Russia's war expenditures. Meanwhile, our own people were dying of hunger.

AN AMERICAN TALE

The attack on Pearl Harbor in December 1941 finally and formally brought the Americans into the war. The following July they arrived in Iran. Thanks to a deal struck between Averell Harriman and British prime minister Winston Churchill, their primary task was to double the capacity of the railroad. The Persian Gulf Service Command—thirty thousand non-combat troops—began to arrive under the direction of General Donald Connolly. Prime Minister Foroughi, when asked in Parliament why the Americans had shown up, answered ironically, *"Miayand o miravand. Be kasi kari nadarand*—They just come and go and have nothing to do with anyone." The Iranians had not been consulted.

Unlike the British and Russians, however, the Americans were welcomed in Iran as representatives of a nation without ulterior motives. Their camps, set up outside Hamadan, Khorramshahr, and Tehran, became famous for their cinemas, cafés, restaurants, and shops. It soon became common to see U.S. soldiers in their fatigues hawking such luxuries as razor blades, toothbrushes, and cigarettes (which they bought for 10 cents a carton and resold for 10 cents a pack) among the beet sellers and kabob stands on the avenues. Yet the Americans were unruly and were feared for their alcoholism and sexual abuse. In a telegram to Washington the U.S. ambassador, Louis Goethe Dreyfus, lamented, "There is no doubt that the numerous accidents and incidents due to drunkenness and debauchery are having a deplorable effect on American prestige in Iran."[13]

The Americans had an electrifying effect on the transport system that over the next four years funneled more than five million tons of war supplies through Iran into the Soviet Union. By May of 1943, three months after the crushing defeat of the Germans in Stalingrad, they had more than doubled the daily capacity of the railroad to fifteen thousand tons.

In addition every day thousands of Dodge and Studebaker trucks could be seen filing north in long caravans past Tehran and across the mountains. The trucks and their cargo were left on the other side of the border while their drivers caught the train back to the Gulf to repeat the process all over again. Clouds of Hurricane fighter planes also flew regularly across Tehran and over the Elborz Mountains, their pilots handing the keys to the Russians before heading back south to pick up the next set of deliveries.

Stalin didn't want foreign troops on his land. All he wanted was goods: 4,000 tons of barbed wire and 1,000 tons of armor-plated steel a month, 5,000 jeeps, 20,000 trucks, and as many planes, tanks, and rations of food as the Allies could spare. He got it all free on Roosevelt's Lend-Lease program. And the Iranians, thanks to the generosity of AIOC, paid the shipping costs by providing all the fuel gratis, even though in many of the coldest parts of the country there was not enough kerosene to warm people's homes.

Getting the transport system in shape was by far the biggest task for the Americans, but it was not their only one. Anxious to bring in American expertise as a balance against the other Great Powers, the Majles, at the instigation of my brother Mohammadvali Mirza, invited American advisers to help reform the military, the rural security system, or gendarmerie, and the public financial sector.

General Clarence Ridley arrived in Tehran in mid-1942 to strengthen the Iranian armed forces. Soon after, Colonel Norman Schwarzkopf, father of the Gulf War hero, flew in to revamp the gendarmerie. Schwarzkopf was already world famous for his attempted rescue of Charles and Anne Lindbergh's kidnapped baby in 1932. A former chief of the New Jersey police, he set about recruiting and training a competent Iranian force in consultation with my brother General Mohammad Hossein Mirza, who had been appointed chief of the gendarmerie. Schwarzkopf's mission was renewed three times, and by the end of the decade he was still dealing with Iran, going on to play a role in the coup that followed the nationalization of oil in the 1950s.

The third U.S. adviser to Tehran was Dr. Arthur Millspaugh from the Department of the Treasury, who arrived during the first snowy weeks of January 1943. Just days before he stepped onto Iranian soil I was finally discharged from the military. By then I'd almost forgotten that I'd once been a student of oil engineering. What I had not forgotten was my English, and it was a most valuable asset at a time when few Iranians knew

English well. An opportunity for employment opened up immediately at Millspaugh's new mission.

Millspaugh had served successfully as financial adviser to Iran for two years in the 1920s and had written a book titled *The American Task in Persia*. Now he was back with sweeping powers to hire and fire bank directors and Ministry of Finance officials and to reorganize Iran's treasury and financial system. Unlike the other missions, however, his was not as a representative of the U.S. government but as an independent adviser hired by the Majles.

Millspaugh brought with him a motley crew of some fifty aides, many of whom didn't have the first clue about applied economic strategy, let alone how it related to a war-torn, starving, third-world country. Their lack of knowledge, combined with a liberal salting of arrogance, would be the downfall of the mission, which left Iran a few years later under a cloud.

My interview was with William Berges, the aide Millspaugh had assigned to Kermanshah. He was younger than I, about twenty-three years old, and, though clever, unversed in the situation of the provinces. No doubt that is why I was assigned to his office as his counterpart.

AN ELECTION TALE

Working in Kermanshah seemed like a good idea for many reasons: I would live in my mother's hometown, look after our properties, and be able to exercise political influence. Elections for the Fourteenth Majles were coming up,* and my nephew Mozzafar Firouz was running from Kermanshah.

I also had other motives. Right before Reza Shah abdicated, the family had received a nasty scare. A man from Kermanshah had appeared one day with a document written thirty years before indicating that my father, when he was governor there, had borrowed 30,000 English gold sovereigns, pledging to repay the sum at an annualized rate of 20 percent upon presentation of the document. The transaction was signed by witnesses and bore some well-known seals. The debt, said the man, had never been repaid.

The sums involved would have ruined my family. Thirty thousand English gold sovereigns with thirty years of interest at 20 percent meant a debt of more than $9 million! The family board convened to discuss the

*The parliaments were numbered in succession, the first dating back to 1906 when the Constitution was signed into law by Mozzafar-edin Shah.

matter. Besides the president of the Majles, Agha Esfandiari and Moham-madvali Mirza, Mohammad Ali Farzin, the director of Bank Melli (whose daughter later married my brother Jamshid), was present as an adviser.

Esfandiari suspected the document was specious. The witnesses, he pointed out, were all dead. Even more singular was a signature that was missing—that of Seyyed Ali, a famous mollah who had been the leader (*mojtahed*) of the Friday prayers during Farman Farma's tenure in Kerman-shah. My father would never have borrowed so much without having Seyyed Ali as a witness.

Persian ink was—and still is—made using a fourteenth-century Chi-nese recipe based on soot and water. Even copies of the Koran are written with this ink, despite the fact that a brush dipped in clean water can wash it away.* My father's signature was genuine, but the document to which it had originally been affixed had been washed and doctored.

Finding the forger was the most efficacious way to reject the claim and was not difficult in a town the size of Kermanshah. Not long after, Abol Bashar, who was still living at Janatabad and traveled frequently to Ker-manshah, was informed that the forger, who was also a shop owner and dealer in wheat, was spending the night on our properties. Abol sent around his guards, who caught the man and threw him into the stables to pass the night with the cows and bull—a bad punishment indeed, called *tavileh.* The next day they sat him backward on a donkey and marched him into town, where all of Kermanshah bore witness to his crime before he was handed over to the police. The case was dropped, and we never saw the claimant with his document again.

Since that incident I had not been back to Kermanshah, though it was important for me, as a property owner, to maintain a presence, particularly in view of the upcoming elections. I stayed at my uncle Etezad-Soltan's, my mother's wonderful brother, where I occupied a suite of rooms on the second floor and entertained frequently in its spacious salons.

Kermanshah was supposed to be under the control of the local governor but was in fact entirely in the hands of a British political adviser named Colonel W. Fletcher. His assistant, Captain Eric Shipton, dropped by to nose around the very same day that Berges and I moved into our offices. He asked a lot of questions without answering any of ours and puffed con-stantly on his pipe as his sunken eyes roamed restlessly about the room.

---

*Ella Sykes, sister of Sir Percy Sykes, was stunned by this discovery and thus describes a scribe at work in Farman Farma's household: "He held the writing close to his eyes . . . and went on to erase another word with his tongue, making me think that the forging of documents must be an easy matter in Persia" (*Through Persia on a Side-Saddle,* page 160).

Thereafter I encountered Shipton often, always poking about the bazaar, checking on prices, watching people's movements. He was Fletcher's eyes and ears, and nothing in town escaped his notice. He was a strange character, at once sullen and astute. His great passion was mountaineering, and later we heard that he was on the first expedition to climb Mount Everest.

Not long after my arrival Amirkol Zanganeh, who had been reinstated as governor after his tongue-lashing by Reza Shah, suggested I go see Colonel Fletcher myself. The British controlled all the food distribution in the province, and his policies would affect my properties.

It was with a wary heart that I went to see Fletcher. He used to ride through the town every day on horseback, accompanied by his Indian guard of Gurkhas. The shopkeepers and hungry onlookers, paralyzed by fear, saluted him with trembling hands, while the few cars on the road pulled over and stopped so as not to raise any dust. Like a conqueror crossing a field of enemy dead, Fletcher looked neither right nor left, but sat ramrod straight upon his steed, impervious to the misery around him. Then suddenly he would stop and, lashing his long whip into the air, let it fall randomly upon anyone so ill-advised as to have remained close by.

You could tell by the way he sat on his mount and by the jut of his chin that Colonel Fletcher, like so many British officers in the Middle East at the time, saw himself as another Lawrence of Arabia. He was the envoy of the empire, the ray of civilization sent to bring order to the natives. He radiated contempt before the empty bread shops. On a visit to Kurdistan he had one of the Il-Khans of a small tribe shot on the spot for impertinence. It was said he had served in India, which had nurtured his condescension. To him we were little better than the animals in our stables.

Fletcher received me upstairs in his study. He was tall and powerfully built. His face was unsettling, an injury of some kind having deformed his mouth so that whenever he spoke or was angry it sloped to one side in a twisted grimace. His voice was insolent as he told me he was going to visit the tribal chiefs in the region and needed sugar, tea, and cloth for gifts. He looked at me expectantly.

My portfolio under Berges was to regulate the sale and flow of these commodities and ration them among the population. Tea, sugar, and cloth were like gold—better even, since everyone needed them and there was almost none to be had once the British sent their quota to the troops. The tribal khans would be able to sell such gifts at an enormous profit. Sugar, valued at 50 cents a pound, fetched $8 on the black market. The tribes could then spend the money on arms and support the British cause. It was blatant exploitation of Iran's precious staple resources, and it made me highly indignant.

"Such goods are scarce," I said, trying to keep my voice flat. "Surely it is the responsibility of the government, and not mine, to provide you with such valuable commodities."

His eyes whitened at the edges, and red spots appeared on his cheeks.

"Anyway, they're not at my disposal," I said quickly. "We must give an account to Tehran, and permission can be given only by Dr. Millspaugh."

Fletcher sprang to his feet and threw open the door. "Such a rare display of public spiritedness!" he hissed sarcastically. "Now that you are such a prominent public servant, you had better watch out. When the government collector comes around for his wheat, he'll know exactly what you've got. Don't try to weasel out of it. Cross me"—he was shouting now—"and I'll send you to the concentration camp in Arak."

Fletcher had insinuated that in my new capacity as Berges's aide I would unfairly influence the collection of wheat to the benefit of my family. His was a wicked warning, and I left very worried. The Iranian government, pushed by the British government, had again dropped the price of wheat and was paying landowners only a quarter to a fifth of its actual worth. The inspectors routinely overestimated the levels of production, forcing us to bribe them to state the truth. If we did not, our own villagers would go hungry. As it was, the government did not allocate sufficient sugar or tea for the villagers, and they simply went without.

The situation in our area was very different from that in the north, where rice was grown. The Russians did not manipulate the market like the British, and during the war the price of rice shot up ten times. The landowners there—including our cousins the Aminis—became fabulously wealthy, while we suffered a continuous erosion of our incomes.

Like all the British provincial commanders, Fletcher was running his own candidates for Parliament and doing all he could to publicly discredit us. The following week he upped the ante when he visited Kangavar, home of some of our most prosperous estates. Kangavar is one of the oldest towns in Iran, having been inhabited continuously for four thousand years. Spread all over it are the remains of a huge fire temple dedicated to the earth goddess Anahita. The village's houses and stables are built between and among the white carved stones.

When Fletcher came he insulted the village kadkhodah, which was as good as insulting us, and then had him arrested. Before he left, his bodyguard of turbaned Indian soldiers turned on the bystanders and beat some of them up.

The next day we moved to have the kadkhodah released, but we had no recourse against Fletcher. His senseless disdain was beyond me. I have met only a few men like him in my life, and they rattle my soul. They are frightening—people without boundaries—and you can never anticipate the turn of their minds or the extent of their greed. They are in fact criminals uncaught by society.

Fletcher was the product of all that was awry in the British colonial system and the ultimate example of its propensity for abuse. But his darkness was more than that—it came from within, a deeper rot that made him transgress the rules of his own system as much as ours. He must have known as well as we that he would never be a Lawrence. He must have thought Kermanshah was hell. In such a place, far away from one's own kin and culture, a man comes face to face with all the frightening secrets within.

There was no point in refuting all his false accusations. *Een shotor dar-eh manzelemun khabideh*—the camel had lain down on our doorstep—and if we were to go about our lives, we simply had to find a way around him.

My uncle's house had been transformed into an election headquarters by then, and because I was too young to run (candidates had to be thirty, and I was only twenty-six), I threw all my efforts behind Mozzafar. Dozens of people came for lunch and dinner every day, and there were constant meetings among the more powerful landowners to select a roster of candidates.

It was by no stretch of the imagination a democratic process. The villagers, most of them illiterate, with no access to newspapers, radio, or any other means to inform themselves, depended exclusively on us to tell them whom to vote for. In Iran every man had a right to vote from the first parliamentary election in 1906, but it meant little—just as in many democracies of the world—since we lacked the infrastructure for such an advanced political process to function. In Kermanshah that year votes were cast for four candidates on a single piece of paper. It was a routine matter for us to write down the candidates' names and hand the ballot to the peasants to drop into the voting box.

Mozzafar was running as an independent candidate, though he was generally against the British and of course very anti-Shah. Over the past year he had started to write political commentary for a number of newspapers, and his opinions had enjoyed considerable coverage. He had also taken a well-publicized trip to Palestine, where he had met with Seyyed Zia Tabatabai, the journalist who'd briefly served as prime minister during the coup in 1921.

Although Seyyed Zia was an ardent Anglophile and in turn the Iranian politician most beloved by the British, Mozzafar came back from Palestine insisting Seyyed Zia was as anti-Shah as he. Seyyed Zia had lived in exile since Reza Shah took power, but was now planning to return and was running for Parliament as the British-backed candidate from the city of Yazd. He would probably be the next prime minister, Mozzafar said, since he epitomized the people's hopes for change. His big nose wagging delightedly, Mozzafar confided that he'd asked Seyyed Zia to pass through Kermanshah during the election to celebrate his triumphal homecoming to Iran.

It was mid-November and clear the day that Seyyed Zia arrived. That morning two brothers named Nasrollah and Assadollah Rashidian appeared at our door so heavily laden with gold watches, pomade, and the plush air of new wartime wealth that they looked like a pair of peacocks. They stepped from a pair of Chrysler Imperials, each worth $60,000 in that time of want. Assadollah was broad, fat-faced, and jovial; Nasrollah was a heroin addict, thin to the extreme, with yellow eyes. Their father had been a spy for the British Embassy, and they made no secret of the fact they too worked for the British. In that capacity they were backing Seyyed Zia financially, they said, and had come to provide cars to escort him into town.

We started for the outskirts of town, for it is an old Persian tradition for hosts to travel out to meet their guest on the road. Twenty miles out toward the mountains we pulled up at a village where half a dozen parked cars filled the square and a knot of men stood beside the road. They were the grandees of Kermanshah, weathering the winter wind for a proper welcome. Not too much later we saw a black dot on the horizon, and soon Mozzafar and Seyyed Zia pulled up.

They stepped out jubilantly. Seyyed Zia wore a pointed Turkish fur cap from which a crop of unusually long hair sprouted in all directions. He made a short speech that clearly indicated he considered this but a prelude to becoming prime minister, and after everybody clapped and shook his hand we climbed back into our cars and headed to my uncle's house.

At dinner that night I found Seyyed Zia to be extremely amusing and such a compelling speaker that we all found ourselves hanging on his every word, despite the fact that he spoke with a pronounced stutter. He suggested replacing the veil with a hooded British cloak with a button at the neck. He said he was publishing a pamphlet of new Farsi words to modernize our tongue. He insisted that the best food on earth was alfalfa, not the sprouts but the grass. Later he became famous in Tehran for serving it to his guests.

Yet as I listened to him I became disillusioned, for he was a lightweight, albeit a flamboyant one. He did not live up to his reputation of being the next political star. Yet, Mozzafar was completely in his thrall and in Tehran became somewhat of a laughingstock for eating Seyyed Zia's alfalfa.

We were still sitting at the dinner table when a knock came at the door. A servant was ushered in bearing a telegram with news of the election that had taken place that day in Yazd. Though Seyyed Zia had not set foot in his hometown for more than twenty years—had not even been in the country—the election results were so favorable that he had come in first place. Such was the way the British respected our democracy.

Mozzafar was not so lucky. After the Kermanshah election, which took place a few days later, not a single vote was found bearing our candidates' names. Fletcher's candidates won unanimously. It brought to mind my father's friend Seyyed Hassan Modaress, the ascetic mollah, who had remarked after a rigged election right after Reza Shah came to power, "What happened to my vote? I could have sworn I voted for myself."

A STRANGER IN HIS OWN LAND

I was not around to witness the debacle. The day before the election Colonel Fletcher made it known that he wanted to see me. Once again I went to his study. This time he did not even gesture to a chair but stood behind his desk.

"It seems you are slinging mud at everybody," he said with ill-disguised pique.

"At whom?" I asked.

"At my candidates," he said.

"That's quite within my rights," I answered calmly.

"No!" he shouted. "Because you are also splashing me."

"Why then are you standing where we are throwing mud?" I asked.

I thought of Zill-e-Soltan, Sarameh-Doleh's father, who had dominated the south during Mozzafar-edin Shah's reign. One day he was approached by the mollah of Isfahan, who angrily accused him of stepping on his tail. "Oh?" replied Zill-e-Soltan, "is there a place in this city where your tail is not to be found?"

"Your candidate isn't even from Kermanshah," I continued heatedly. "We do not even know him. This is supposed to be a democratic election among the people of this province. And yet you, who are not even of this country, are interfering in the campaign."

That afternoon I was informed by an Iranian inspector in Fletcher's pay that I had been taken off Berges's staff. When I got home a command jeep was waiting in front of the house. A British officer presented me with an official order to leave the city within two hours. I was to be taken by escort to Hamadan.

I sat in the middle, between an Indian chauffeur and the officer. Snow was banked on both sides of the road, which had turned icy. We passed the three-hour journey in silence.

Hamadan is located six thousand feet in the mountains and is windy and bitterly cold in the winter. It was late when we arrived, and the city was dark and deserted. The jeep pulled up at the corner in front of the house of Salar Lalejini, an old family friend. The officer signaled for the driver to get out, obliging me to slide across the seat past the steering wheel to alight. As I stepped down, the officer swung his leg up and kicked me in the back, sending me sprawling onto the pavement.

I hit the ground hard—the wind knocked out of me, the sharp grit of dirt and ice in my mouth. Surely he would now open fire and kill me, I thought.

For a moment I must have lost consciousness. I didn't hear the driver climb back into the jeep, but I did hear the crunch of the tires as they screeched past my head and drove off.

I listened to the engine die away before I dared to move. In the crystalline silence that followed, my ragged breath thundered against the road. All of a sudden the noise of the engine returned. I scrambled to my feet, panicked that they were coming back to finish me off. A narrow lane led off to my right, and I jumped toward it, ducking into the shadows. My trousers were torn at the knees, and I could feel blood on my leg. I shook uncontrollably, and my breath was beginning to congeal on my mustache in tiny, needlelike droplets. But all I cared about was the car, its headlights swinging down the road.

Yet the car did not slow down and, in an explosion of sound, passed by.

Galvanized by fear, I stumbled as fast as I could to my friend's door and began beating on it like a wild man. Although I kicked and yelled and pounded, nobody stirred. The wind howled, and I wondered dimly whether my frantic knocks were being swallowed by its ghostly song. The lines of Saadi rattled in my head: "What bastards they are. The stones are set with ice, and the dogs are after me."

Just as I was about to give up hope a neighbor opened his door and looked out. "I am trying to reach Salar," I called in desperation, my teeth chattering. He motioned for me to wait, and I could see him crossing the back courtyard to wake the household. Finally, surrounded by lamps and servants, Salar opened the door.

I stumbled in, delirious with exhaustion and cold.

Salar was an old man, and though he was astonished to see me alone at his doorstep in such a state, he refrained from asking any questions until he'd settled me under the korsi and given me a hot dinner. Even then I was in too severe a state to talk much. I was traumatized at having been thrown out of my own hometown, parted from my estates, and left for dead on an icy road. It was a sad, sad night, I told Salar, to be exiled by a foreigner in my own land.

BEARS AND LIONS AT
THE DOOR

You, amorous nightingale, should trill for time;
To see at last the garden green, and the breaking of the dawn.
—HAFEZ

Tehran 1944

I met Dr. Hossein Pirnia at a funeral. Women wailed in the room next door, shedding pent-up tears. The body had already been sent to the morgue, wrapped in a white *caffan,* or holy cloth blessed in Mecca. We were not there to mourn the body; we were mourning the baffling passage of a soul.

The Pirnias were an old and important family, famous for their honesty, and counted among their luminaries two powerful prime ministers and the wife of Reza Shah. We were there to represent Mohsen Khan Raiis, whose uncle had passed away.

Dr. Pirnia was tall and pear-shaped. When he heard I'd studied oil at Birmingham, he smiled. "I am the director general for oil and mining concessions at the Ministry of Finance," he said. "Why don't you come to my office tomorrow? I need an assistant. It's not a well-paid job, but then one serves the government for honor, not for money."

It was a surprise that someone so young—he couldn't have been more than thirty—occupied such an important position. But over the years I discovered there was nothing ordinary about Dr. Pirnia. He was among the very few Persians to have attended the Polytechnic Institute in Paris and was gifted with a true mathematical mind. At a time when the 1933 Concession with the British was once again being questioned, he brought to the table a talent for reading between the lines. To the dismay of both his superiors and the officials at AIOC, he posed questions about the execution of the law that no one had conceived of before. Yet for all the sophistication of his thinking, his heart often failed him at the crucial moment, and he was unable to present his ideas with the forcefulness they deserved. As a result, though he entertained ambitions of becoming minister of finance, he was passed over.

Dr. Pirnia became my mentor. Although I was hired at the lowest possible grade, my position as his assistant gave me a broad perspective on the operations of the entire department. All of Iran's concessions—oil, mines, and fisheries—came under his purview. The British petroleum concession in the south was by far the largest—and most politically treacherous—brief in the portfolio. But the Russian fisheries concession, with its valuable haul of caviar, was also significant.

Dr. Pirnia was a superb administrator, the essence of the capable technocrat. Under his tutelage I received my first lessons in the art of epistolary administration: how to compose a report, justify a point, change one word to transform the spirit of a memo from negative to positive, address a minister directly, or devise correspondence that would get past the adjutant to the desk of the boss. Dr. Pirnia and I pored over the ministry's old files, which gave me a lifeline into my government's past. I discovered that I had arrived on the cusp of a great upheaval in Iran's bureaucracies.

Historically Persia's public sector was an outgrowth of the agriculture sector. Members of Parliament, ministers, and their staffs all obtained their money from land revenues—and hence had hands-on knowledge of how the land was managed, what the problems were among the people, and what the real value was of goods, services, water, and transport. They then came to Tehran to serve.

The twentieth century changed all that. The new class of technocrats got their education in Europe or the United States and came back with theories based on social and political organizations that bore no relation to the situation at home. Though they lacked any general knowledge of Iran, they thought they knew it all better than their elders; they had books to prove it and the names of social theorists to bring any argument to a halt. Rather than solving problems they created them and became skilled at sidestepping responsibility by shuffling files from one desk to another. Eventually none of us could live in an Iran managed that way.

I came back from England knowing no more than succeeding generations about Iran. But I learned its historic ways nonetheless, having the benefit of the last of the old generation as my teachers. Besides Dr. Pirnia there was my uncle Ahmad Khan, my mother's brother, who appeared at my door within the first few days of my arrival at the ministry. He brought a stack of law and regulation books that he deposited on my desk as a welcome gift. He was undersecretary of the budget—had been for thirty years—and would stun his visitors by quoting the codes by heart: "According to the addendum of such and such a law passed on such a date fifteen years ago," he would say, puffing a cloud of smoke into the air from his hand-rolled cigarette, "what you claim is actually not right." Not surprisingly, over the years he received fewer and fewer visitors.

Ahmad Khan, his old face drawn like a dried lemon, offered me a piece of advice as well. "You have just joined a caravan which is going slowly through the desert. You are young and you are on a stallion, and you ride back and forth, pushing and impatient all day long. But you cannot go faster than the caravan, for every night you must return to it for food. Occasionally those who stray too far become separated and die of thirst and hunger."

I thanked him for the advice and then, using the *taarof,* or verbal etiquette, requisite to any Persian conversation, begged him to tell me how the miserable scale I had brought him from England was serving his illustrious household. In the last letter I'd received from my mother before leaving Birmingham, she had specifically requested that I bring Ahmad Khan a two-pan handheld scale with weights that could measure to the hundredth of a gram. Ahmad Khan, inclining his head like a bird, said that the scale was excellent and that I should stop by some evening to see it at work.

AN OPIUM TALE

I was the youngest man by forty years the night I went to Ahmad Khan's house. He and his cronies sat in a circle around an elegant copper brazier, or *mangal.* That morning the servants had lit a fire of charcoal in the pan, and now the embers were dusted with ashes. Ahmad Khan tapped the mangal, causing the veil to drop from the iridescent coals. He singled out one of the embers and, using a long, graceful pair of tongs, lifted it from its bed and placed it on the porcelain mouth of a water pipe that stood on the floor surrounded by dishes of sweets and fruit. Beside him lay two boxes—one of gold, one of inlaid woods. In addition I could see the tooled leather case of the scale.

Ahmad Khan took up the wooden box first and, springing the lid, selected a mouthpiece for the pipe. From the gold box he lifted a bar of opium, yellow as the gold itself. He then opened the scales, and I sighed with relief that I had found a set lovely enough to match the ritual. They bobbed in his hand like a marionette as he slid a weight onto one of the pans and a nut of opium onto the other. Satisfied, he lifted the opium with another pair of tongs, this one filigreed, and placed it gently on the coal. It sizzled and bubbles formed at the edges. The room filled with its aroma.

As the pipe was passed around, a servant brought a tray of tea and set it next to the brazier to keep it warm. The tea was as important to the ritual as the opium. The glasses were set in silver holders with handles, and when the tea was poured you could judge its quality by looking at its color through the glass. I refrained from taking the opium pipe, but I did take some tea and settled back to listen to the conversation. It started with politics and wound gradually into a discussion of Persian literature. By the time dinner was served I had identified two of the guests as lawyers from the Ministry of Justice, and it was toward them that I bent my ear.

They counseled caution. The old and the new bureaucracies were fighting to stamp their own identities on Iran, they said. At issue was self-preservation. It was not a question of decay, of an old system with rotten foundations having to be replaced by something new. To believe that was a mistake made by foreigners—and the young: *"Kafar hameh-ra bekish khod mipendarad*—The infidel always thinks others believe what he does," said Ahmad Khan, quoting an old saying. The foundations were still strong, they said; the challenge was to build the future on the base of tradition.

They were tough old men. By looking at me they tried to see what their country might become. I left not knowing whether they trusted what they saw.

In addition to Ahmad Khan I got in touch with my old tutor from the harem, Agha-ye Jafar Khan, who was now a clerk at the ministry. This man, who had beaten my hands every day as a child, would now, out of deference, not even sit down in front of me. I ordered tea and at last prevailed upon him to take a seat. I wanted to brush up my Farsi, I told him, improve my writing, and become better acquainted with Persian literature. I asked him if he would come to my house and give me lessons. My mother did not like him, remembering too clearly how he'd beaten us as children. But from the moment he opened the book of Hafez, I was smitten. What Western expressionists did on canvas in the twentieth century, Hafez had done with words in the fourteenth. Agha-ye Jafar Khan became the lens through which I learned to understand the lyric, abstract symbolism of his poetry.

My induction into the Ministry of Finance was very different from

Nosrat-Doleh's, who had become minister at the age of thirty-four. Very soon, however, Dr. Pirnia decided that I had inherited some of my brother's diplomatic traits and put me to use as his liaison. Dr. Pirnia himself was not a smooth negotiator. He was too independent, too frank, and, when it came to dealing with foreigners, often too brusquely patriotic.

One person Dr. Pirnia did not get along with at all was Melville Munk, the adviser Arthur Millspaugh had placed in charge of taxation and concessions. Munk had wounded his right hand while on assignment in South America, but he loved tennis so much that he had taken it up with his left and become a surprisingly good player. So we played tennis together, and good relations between our departments were maintained.

THE TALE OF A NEW OIL STAMPEDE

My first real challenge in the department came only a few months after I joined. In late November 1943 the Big Three, Roosevelt, Stalin, and Churchill, converged on Tehran for a summit to decide how the world would be structured in the war's aftermath. The summit was an insular affair confined to the adjacent compounds of the British and Soviet embassies, and only a quick visit to the Shah by Stalin and Churchill acknowledged that it had taken place in Iran.* The meeting became even cozier when, after the first day, the Russians claimed they'd heard rumors of an assassination plot against Roosevelt, and the president hurriedly moved from his own embassy a few blocks away to stay at the Soviet mission. A tent was constructed over the alley dividing the Soviet and British embassies, and we didn't so much as catch a glimpse of the visiting dignitaries during the four days they were there.

The main issue of the summit was the role the three powers would assume in Europe, Asia, and the Middle East after the war. At the last minute—so unexpectedly, in fact, that a version was never translated into Russian for Stalin—they signed a declaration pledging to shore up the Shah's government after the war and respect "the independence, sovereignty and territorial integrity of Iran."[1]

The saccharine words sent out over the world's wires after the summit

---

*President Roosevelt, breaking the strict international protocol of visiting heads of state, never went to the palace to call on the Shah. Instead he met the Shah at the Soviet Embassy when the latter returned Stalin's courtesy call. This angered the Shah, and he thereafter harbored ill feelings toward Roosevelt for his lack of etiquette. By contrast the Shah much appreciated Stalin's gesture and subsequently made an effort to maintain cordial relations with Moscow.

belied the undercurrent of competition among the powers that had already started to play itself out on Iranian soil. This competition eventually developed into the cold war.

One of the cold war's first conflicts had in fact already begun as a result of Iran's perennial efforts at self-preservation. As a parry to the continual British and Russian attempts to carve up the country, Iran had courted the Americans since the 1920s to develop an oil concession in the north. Four companies had tried and failed to develop a foothold, thanks in large measure to British threats and Russian interference. Now, in the early forties it was common to see eager-eyed, flint-nosed negotiators from all three powers trying to score an oil deal about town. Occasionally undercover prospectors would also slip in. My cousin Hossein Dowlatshahi became an expert desert scout after guiding a Dutch group around for almost four years as they sank sounders, ostensibly for mining leads but in fact for oil. During the occupation, in 1943, a new area in the south, close to the Indian frontier, became the subject of wild speculation. The British, in the form of Royal Dutch Shell, and two American companies, Standard-Vacuum and Sinclair, immediately dispatched representatives to Tehran to bid for concessions.

The Iranian prime minister, discomfited by this bitter rivalry suddenly being evinced by two of the powers still occupying Iran, decided to engage a pair of American oil consultants to review the situation and provide recommendations. Herbert Hoover, Jr., and A. A. Curtice duly arrived in early summer 1944 and settled into offices in the Ministry of Foreign Affairs.

Dr. Pirnia, immediately sent me over to the Ministry of Foreign Affairs to establish contact. I invited the two Americans to tea.

Hoover, the son of the former president of the United States, was big and broad-shouldered and by profession a mining engineer. Curtice was small, though like Hoover he laughed a lot and had a disarming, unbuttoned style. They were private businessmen whose company, Amareda, had been founded by a famous Texas oilman named Everette De Golyer.* It seemed a dubious position from which to offer objective advice, but though Dr. Pirnia and I badgered them with questions from every angle, we were unable to glean much about the nature of their assignment.

Hoover maintained that oil consumption after the war would drop, tak-

*De Golyer had returned to the United States six months before from an investigative mission to Saudi Arabia for the U.S. State Department. His estimate that 30 billion barrels of oil (and likely a lot more) lay under its inhospitable sands blew the top off all previous estimates and sealed the U.S. commitment to Saudi Arabia as an all-American, big-budget investment.

ing prices down with it. How wrong he was! In the United States a post-war boom in motor vehicles would push gasoline sales up by 42 percent in five years, and the price of crude oil worldwide would double between 1945 and 1948. Congressional suspicions of oil company skulduggery prompted more than twenty investigations in Washington. Oil's short, tumultuous history had never yet shown a drop in usage. Hoover's view, later distributed in a report, only increased my suspicion that he was angling to get a cheaper rate on a concession for private ends.

But Hoover was not wrong about everything.

"The British dominate the Gulf," I told him carelessly. "If they want to throw you out of Saudi Arabia, they will."

He laughed. "You overestimate British power," he answered. "The day will come when they will have to share oil in the Gulf."

"In Iran?"

"Yes," he said.

"Never! They will throw you out and drown you if it pleases them," I said.

Hoover knew the might of the American oil companies and the power of America's imperialistic temperament. I didn't and thought he was mad. The influence of the British in the Middle East was so great that we couldn't imagine a world without them.

The meeting with Hoover and Curtice made me uneasy, and I decided, with Dr. Pirnia's blessing, to speak about them to my cousin Dr. Mossadeq. He was a deputy in the Majles and, if he thought it was in the Parliament's interest, could use his post to demand an explanation.

Dr. Mossadeq was preparing to attend a Majles session the morning I walked through his door. He waved me to a seat in his bedroom and called for tea.

He was a comfortable character, modest and easy to talk to, and though he must have been in his sixties at the time, he didn't make me feel in the least embarrassed at the difference in our ages. I'd known him all my life and was especially close to his older son Ahmad, with whom I had lunch every Wednesday.

With his droopy, basset-hound eyes and high patrician forehead, Mossadeq did not look like a man to shake a nation. But even as a boy he'd had a strong and eccentric character and been a particular favorite of my father's. Before I was born he served as Farman Farma's personal secretary, a position he capitalized on masterfully to get to know the political establishment.

Like Nosrat-Doleh, who was only one year his senior, Mossadeq was passionate about government and politics. Before he turned thirty, on his return from Switzerland, where he'd obtained a doctorate of jurisprudence, he passed through Shiraz. Though he'd been on Persian soil for less than a week, he set the wheels turning in his favor so effectively that he was appointed governor. Thereafter, until the rise of Reza Shah, he was rarely out of office. Farman Farma appointed him minister of finance during his brief premiership in 1915, and in 1921 Mossadeq served in the same cabinet as Reza Khan when the latter was minister of war. He was also governor of Azerbaijan during the Russian-inspired separatist movement following World War I.

But Mossadeq preferred the role of people's deputy in the newly minted Majles to any government-appointed administrative position. To his mind the Parliament was the only mouthpiece of the people of Iran. No matter how rigged the elections or how corrupt its members, it was the only body that did not depend for its power either on outside influence or on the court, but on the authority of the Constitution. The Majles became his soapbox. Elected to it time and again by the people of Tehran, he used it to denounce the misconduct of the British and Russians, and later the Americans. When he said, "The Iranian himself is the best person to manage his house," he was stating not only a conviction but a policy that he was to pursue with unwavering purpose until his picture appeared on the cover of *Time* magazine and he had thoroughly shaken the foundations of the world's oil establishment.

Although Mossadeq championed Iranian self-determination, he had little faith in his fellow deputies, and few escaped the lash of his tongue. He accused them of cowardice, of lacking initiative, and worst of all of being unpatriotic. His fulminations at the podium were both frightening and theatrical. Gesturing wildly, his hand unconsciously wiping away the famous tears that sprang unbidden from his eyes at times of nervousness or rage, he pilloried his listeners with the righteousness of a priest who suffers with his victims even as he unmasks them.

Mossadeq eschewed political parties and partisanship and instead walked his own line down the center, championing a creed that would later be called nationalism. Most of all he despised the absolutism of the Shah. The Constitution had been designed to limit the Shah's authority.* But the Constitution had been ignored. Mossadeq had been on hand in 1925 when Reza Khan approached the Parliament for its kingly blessing. With eleven others, he'd voted no. It was not a parliamentary right to elect shahs, let

---

*Article 44 of the Constitution states unequivocally, "The King bears no responsibility; only cabinet ministers are responsible and accountable in all affairs of state to the two houses of Parliament."

alone their "male descendants in succession."[2] To Mossadeq doing so meant that the Pahlavi reign was inaugurated by an act of treason.

The Parliament became a cipher after that. For fifteen years outspoken men like Mossadeq were either killed or gagged. Yet even when Reza Shah's men took him to prison, Mossadeq's courage did not fail him. While he was surrounded by guards in the police station, standing in front of a picture of the monarch, the words of Saadi sprang to his lips, and he recited loudly, *"Dar panje shirre khunkharre-yi, joz sarre taslim-o reza kuchare-yi—* When thrown into the paws of the bloodthirsty lion, what remedy is there but agreement and approbation."*

In Persia when a man of note was arrested, the grandees closest to him interceded on his behalf by petitioning the Shah for clemency. The tradition had continued through the rule of Reza Shah, and such men as Teymourtash, Nosrat-Doleh, Sheikh Khazal, and Seyyed Hassan Modaress had all had their cases brought before the Shah by the grandees—though in none of those instances to any avail. When the crown prince returned to Iran from Switzerland, the grandees turned to him to approach the Shah in their stead. And so it was that Mohammad Reza spoke to his father about releasing Mossadeq from jail. This time the Shah was moved, and he ordered that Mossadeq be transferred to house arrest on his properties outside Tehran.

After Reza Shah's abdication Mossadeq reinstalled himself in his residence across from Heshmat-Doleh's—and reinstated his famous afternoon political salons, which he conducted up in his bedroom while he lounged in bed in pajamas. Two weeks later he went to thank Mohammad Reza Shah for his intercession. The years of quietude under the shroud of political exigency had not softened his temperament. Standing a good head taller than the sovereign, frail and stooping a bit, his paper-white skin ghostly under the lights of the audience hall, he spoke with feeling to the young monarch. "Do not pursue the policies of your father," he admonished. "Choose the people around you carefully, and don't back the same people he backed. Disassociate yourself from the unacceptable past and make your own history. Act like Ahmad Shah, who, though young like you, followed the letter of the Constitution."

Mohammad Reza Shah looked quizzically at the older man standing before him. "Following the Constitution did not serve Ahmad Shah very well," he said. "He was thrown out, don't you remember?"

"Indeed," said Mossadeq, his eyes blazing. "But Ahmad Shah was

*A play on words, since *reza,* which means "approbation," was also the name of the Shah.

thrown out by the English, and left with his name intact. He was the first and only constitutional monarch this country ever had. Even his enemies have nothing to say against him. It does not matter if you are thrown out as long as you are respected for having done right."*

It was vain of Mossadeq to give such advice. The Shah was not going to betray the memory of his father, who in fifteen years had transformed medieval feudalism into a modern state, sent a hundred students to Europe every year to study, and restored his people's belief in themselves. Had Mossadeq instead tried to capture the confidence of the young monarch, perhaps he could have helped mold Mohammad Reza Shah's character—and he might have fulfilled his own dreams more easily as a trusted statesman.

But Mossadeq and the Shah would never see eye to eye, and suspicion rather than trust marked their relationship. For thirty years the name Mossadeq, or "Old Mossy" as the British came to call him, would be like poison in the Shah's ears and was never mentioned in his presence. Ironically, in the end both men would abuse the Constitution, and both would fall in ignominy.

For the moment, however, Mossadeq's star was ascending, and the newly elected Fourteenth Majles would mark the beginning of his ten-year rise to explosive prominence. The deputies who took their seats in March 1944 were a contentious lot. The confirmation process that preceded its formal opening was searing—a preamble to the bitter infighting that would characterize its tenure. Members of the Communist Tudeh Party who arrived from the northern provinces were fiercely attacked, and their leader, Jafar Pishevari, was finally rejected for having cooperated too closely with the Russians.

Seyyed Zia Tabatabai's credentials also sparked heated debate, and Mossadeq took the lead as his most persistent opponent. Mossadeq considered the Constitution as the one rock on which Iran could build a future, and he lambasted Seyyed Zia for ignoring its principles. Not only had the people of Yazd had no say in choosing him as their deputy, he pointed out, but it was Seyyed Zia's coup that had led to Reza Shah's dictatorship and the subsequent suspension of the Constitution.

At one point Seyyed Zia, beside himself, jabbed a long finger at the tears that had begun to course down Mossadeq's face. "You are nothing but a woman," he stuttered furiously.

---

*Dr. Mossadeq almost always traveled with his second son, Gholam Mossadeq, who was a surgeon. Gholam went with his father on this visit as well and told me about it afterward.

"Who's the woman?" retorted Mossadeq, his eyes glancing for a shattering moment over Seyyed Zia's shoulder-length hair.

There was an aura about Mossadeq, a consuming heat that none of his opponents took lightly. His hair, tightly cropped and receding over his temples, was fine as corn silk, his mouth a cupid's arabesque. The morning I sat in his bedroom with him, his expression was almost beatific, his demeanor open, accessible, and interested. But cross him and he could turn into a dismissive, caustic, dictatorial monster. His spirit, barely bound in the tenuous housing of his lanky frame, was overwhelming. Mossadeq was a man who literally burned with vision. The shackles on Iran weighed him down as though manacled to his own feet, and he fought harder than any man until Ayatollah Khomeini to get them removed. Distinguished, highly emotional, and every inch the aristocrat, he believed so totally in his own country that his words reached out and touched the common man. Mossadeq was Iran's first genuinely popular leader, and he knew it. To the continuous astonishment and discomfort of his colleagues, he would take his cause to the streets when he couldn't manipulate the Parliament from within and there precipitate a showdown from his perch atop the shoulders of the people.

It was not that he was invincible; Seyyed Zia squeaked through the confirmation process despite Mossadeq, though he was never elected to Parliament again. But Mossadeq was a veteran and as I spoke to him about Hoover and Curtice he shook his head. "I am beholden to you for bringing this important affair to my attention. But victory and patience are old friends," he said, quoting Hafez. "It is not for the deputies to challenge the government. We must wait until the matter is brought to us."

He did not have to wait long.

In September 1944 the Russians, not to be outdone by having two Americans in residence at the Ministry of Foreign Affairs, sent Sergei Kavteradze onto the scene. Kavteradze was the Soviet Union's assistant commissar for foreign affairs, and his arrival instantly moved the negotiations from the back room to the public stage. His mission was to obtain an oil concession in the north, and he lost no time in producing a formal note from the Soviet government suggesting terms. (From Iran's perspective, this was the big difference between the Anglo-American approach and the Soviet: The Soviets were always straightforward in their demands; the British and Americans were more Machiavellian.)

Caught between the Americans and the Russians, Prime Minister Sa'ed did what any good oriental politician would do: He procrastinated. But Kavteradze was not to be put off. Claiming that the government's stance was an outright rejection of the Soviet overture, he turned to the Tudeh

Party for support—and got it. Demonstrations were organized in the north, where the Tudeh Party was the only legal party allowed by the occupying Soviet forces, and transported to the capital. Goaded by a barrage of anti-imperialist and anti-Sa'ed propaganda, a huge rally gathered before the Majles—my sister waving a banner in its midst—demanding the prime minister's dismissal.

To the deputies inside, the hard-line tactics of the Soviet Union indicated that there was more than just the oil concession at stake. It smelled of political consolidation—the preamble to another division of Iran into north and south territories. As long as the British had their oil wells, they would not lift a finger against Russian expansion. The specter of Balkanization that had haunted Iran since the beginning of the war was now at the very gates of the Majles.*

Then, on December 2, Mossadeq walked into the Majles with a bombshell. The weather that day was raw, and whenever Dr. Pirnia or I approached the windows of my office we saw waves of Tudeh demonstrators tramping stoically down Shah Avenue. Over the past few days marches had carpeted the city, and the situation had become desperate. At the Majles, however, the scene abruptly changed. To the amazement—and then delight—of his colleagues, Mossadeq proposed a bill that made it a crime for any minister to discuss a new oil concession until six months after all foreign troops had evacuated Iran. In addition, no new elections would be held during that period, making it physically impossible to pass or ratify any laws or concessions once the Fourteenth Majles had expired. By this trick Mossadeq's bill gave the people of Iran added impetus to rid their land of foreign troops as soon as possible.

The deputies passed Mossadeq's bill overwhelmingly. Overnight he became a hero.

Kavteradze, spluttering but outmaneuvered, packed up and went home. So did Hoover and Curtice, and the smoldering question of a northern oil concession was put on the shelf.

The British government, for its part, was not content to let it go at that. Perturbed by the Soviet army's consolidation in the north, it decided to cozy up to the tribes in the south in case a fallback position was needed. Tacitly supported by the Americans, the British encouraged the tribes to band together, hinting broadly that should Iran be divided, a tribal con-

*Prior to becoming prime minister Sa'ed had served as ambassador to Moscow. During his posting Soviet officials had approached him to become president of the Republic of Iran—once such an entity was realized with the help of Russian forces. Sa'ed, seeing another Hungary in the making, had turned them down.

federation could take over the south. Alan Trott, Ambassador Reader Bullard's right-hand man, was transferred to Ahwaz, the capital of the oil province of Khuzistan, to conduct the operation as consul general. British army officers, many of them from the intelligence unit MI6, were posted throughout the area and also engaged by AIOC. Colonel Fletcher's tactic of siphoning rationed goods, particularly sugar, directly to the tribes for resale was put into general practice so that the chiefs would have ample funds to purchase arms. The Qashgahis alone made $3 million a month on the arrangement.

In Germany British agents contacted Mansur and Hossein Qashgahi and persuaded them, despite stepped-up Nazi promises of money and arms, to abandon their government-in-exile and return to Iran via Istanbul. In Istanbul the two brothers were met by Seyyed Hassan Taqizadeh, the Iranian ambassador to London, who informed them that their eldest brother, Nasser, the Il-Khan of the tribe, was in on the plan and that they could travel under British protection via Cairo back to Iran. Taqizadeh was the man who had signed the 1933 oil agreement. Avowedly pro-British, he had been appointed ambassador to the Court of St. James's the very day Reza Shah had abdicated.

The Qashgahis disappeared without mentioning a word to their friend Hassan Goreshi, who was immediately nabbed as a spy and imprisoned by the Germans. After Berlin fell, Goreshi was picked up by the British, who in turn threw him into jail for conspiracy.

By contrast the Qashgahis benefited hugely from their abrupt flight from the Nazis. They lived like kings, without a shred of contrition, for they felt nothing for either the Germans or the British. According to their enemies they even double-crossed the Nazi agents they had harbored during the war, offering them a sumptuous luncheon and then stepping away from their chairs as British soldiers stormed into the dining hall. The Qashgahis were like that, and everyone in Iran knew it. Even if you were fond of them—which was easy, since they were jovial and friendly, a bit madcap, and always entertaining—you never trusted them an inch.

The Qashgahis were extremists, and they ended up spending every cent of the millions they had. They bought fleets of American cars for their subordinates and friends, purchased splashy new residences, acquired the most beautiful gardens in Shiraz, and swashbuckled through society with rough-edged bravado. I once walked into Hossein Qashgahi's living room to see him squatting on his haunches shaving with a huge straight razor. He was squinting into a minute hand mirror held up by a servant, forcing him to bend and stretch to see his reflection. It was a scene from the desert, transposed to the lush carpets and damasks of town—an oxymoron even then.

The Qashgahis are gone now, the stuff of legend, much like the American cowboys, whose restless independence enabled them to outwit the elements and the land—but not the changes of the twentieth century. Ayatollah Khomeini levied the last blow. Nasser had died and was fortunate not to witness the sordid end. Khosrow, the youngest brother, was the last Il-Khan and had been elected to Parliament after the revolution, in 1981—a shoo-in since the Qashgahis had always been anti-Shah. Khomeini, suspicious of anyone not dedicated to the Islamic Republic, had him captured in Shiraz and sent to his tribe in chains. There, in front of his own people, he was hanged.

THE INFIDEL PEACE

In 1945, however, Nasser Qashgahi was still very much alive and, despite being a member of the Majles, doing his utmost to undermine the power of the central government. In this he was joined by the Kurds to the northwest, the Bakhtiaris to the west, and all the other nomadic players who, afraid that the government was destroying them, rallied to Nasser's cause as a tribal crusade. Their goal was to return to what in Qajar times had been called "the United States of Iran [Mamalek-e Mahrous-e Iran]," where the provinces, held in balance by the Crown, had each enjoyed a modicum of independence and self-sufficiency. When outside interference had amplified territorial unrest, Reza Shah's wholesale divestiture of the states' power had held the country together. But the tribes had never found his system palatable, and with the war coming to an end it seemed a propitious time to revert to the ways of the past.

When in 1941 Iran became the only country in the world to be invaded by all three Allies—and to have its throne forcibly handed off to a young monarch—the still embryonic centralized system collapsed, confirming to the tribes that the Pahlavi system was unsound. By 1945 the country had become virtually ungovernable. The north and south were polarized between the ostensibly friendly but in fact intensely antagonistic Russian and British forces. The countryside had returned to a chaotic state of banditry and brigandage. Gasping under the pressure of the occupation, Iran's fledgling industries had shriveled through lack of raw materials, its roads had worn thin under the weight of the trucks transporting goods to Russia, its currency had collapsed, its poor were starving by the hundred thousands, and its villages wallowed under the yoke of widespread extortion. The Majles, having nothing to govern, had rows and threw out the prime minister every few months.

The young Shah lived removed from it all. Shy, powerless, and married to an Egyptian princess who pined for the cosmopolitan life of Cairo, he stayed tightly closeted in his new palace. At the peak of the country's desperation he threw a costume party at the court, where his sisters came dressed as cats and the tables groaned under their burden of food. Even members of the royal family were outraged.

A few weeks later a friend approached me with an offer from the Shah to become a court adjutant. I turned it down, afraid of incurring family reprimand. The Shah wanted to gather around him a shadow cabinet of young bloods from the country's most powerful families. It was a good idea, and he should have insisted I comply.

Unlike other dynasties, which had gained supremacy on the shoulders of a tribe and drew their strength from tribal loyalty, the Pahlavis had no independent power base. They had risen through the national army, itself an entity without historic precedence and one that always failed in the face of crisis. As Mohammadvali Mirza once said, the Pahlavis came out from under the coattails of the British ambassador. To the British their very lack of family and territorial roots recommended them. In the case of Reza Shah, his upbringing on the land and his single-minded drive gave him the strength to rule. But for his son, who had been brought up like a noble but without the hereditary buttressing of land and family—and without his father's brazen self-confidence—the lack of an independent power base made for perpetual insecurity. Putting together a cadre of young grandees was one way to develop a personal base. But the Shah, we would discover, never knew when to use and when not to use his royal prerogative to best effect, and over and over he would shoot himself in the foot by misjudging.

The war's end passed almost unremarked in Iran. May 8, 1945, dawned like any other day: It was mild, and the fragrance of new growth hung heavy about the trees. I had an appointment at AIOC that morning and headed out early in my big blue Oldsmobile. The grates on the stores were just going up for business on Kakh Street. I hung a right at Shah Avenue and passed an emporium of little shops that Mozzafar Firouz had invested in—and that, to everyone's amazement, had become a runaway success. A few blocks farther on was the construction site of the new Park Hotel being built by Mossadeq's half brother. Across the street my aunt Najmeh-Saltaneh's house had been turned into a hospital, the Mariz Khuneh Najmieh, where Mossadeq's son Gholam was chief surgeon.

Just before turning onto Avenue Sepah, I nosed past the Sheikh Hadi Saga Khuneh, a shrine and fountain where U.S. vice consul Robert Imbry had been assassinated twenty-five years before. It was said he was killed because he was taking photographs of the faithful as they prayed. However,

Mostafa Fateh, the head of distribution at AIOC, had mysteriously appeared on the scene astride a motorcycle. It was just at the time of the first Standard Oil concession talks. In the wake of the assassination, the Americans abruptly terminated discussions, wanting nothing more to do with such a cruel people. The Persian government, on the brink of bankruptcy, was forced to pay compensation to the family. It was a strange incident, hushed up, and the cause of a brief break in relations with the United States. The fountain was Imbry's only memorial. What money could justify a murder? I wondered as I pulled up to the gates of AIOC. Would death always be a by-product of oil?

I had hardly been handed a glass of tea in the reception room when a call came through from Fateh himself. The man I had come to see put down the receiver with a stunned expression. The Germans had surrendered, he said. Fateh had invited us to join him for some wine in the grand salon.

We all trooped downstairs and, though it was just 11 A.M., drank to the end of the war. Fateh got up, the brilliantine in his hair shining, and gave a little speech. He seemed to be the only one genuinely pleased. Out in the streets there was little celebration. It had never been our war. The Allies, our "friends," had brought far greater devastation to our country than the Nazis ever had.

As I headed home for lunch I thought of Seyyed Zia's brother, Seyyed Allah, who had accompanied us once on a trip from Tehran to Qom. Throughout the drive he'd mumbled to himself in a corner, occasionally interrupting his flow of words to blow softly into the air in a sort of arc, a habit of those reciting the Koran to spread around God's beneficence. At last I asked him to speak up so that we too could enjoy the sound of the Word.

"Oh, I'm not reciting the Koran, Shahzdeh," he said. "I'm thanking God that he is making the British infidels give arms to the Russian infidels so that together they can all be destroyed fighting the German infidels."

People were sad not because Germany had lost but because Britain and Russia had won. What none of us—not the Shah, the tribes, or even the Majles—could know was that although the war in Europe and Asia had ended, a new war had already begun in Iran. The conflict was now between the victors. Spheres of influence and precious resources, particularly oil, were the spoils at stake.

By war's end the U.S. controlled more than half the world's known oil reserves, the Soviet Union just over 10 percent. One third of the world's oil lay in the Middle East, with England controlling the lion's share of these reserves. All three powers had troops in Iran, the country where the greatest and oldest Middle East oil industry was operating. The clash between divergent political and economic aspirations was inevitable. Although

Iranian actions would have a material effect on the outcome, we were in many ways just stand-up players in what would become the first serious drama of the cold war. The introduction had been the oil controversy between the Russians and the Americans the year before. The next act, ready to begin once hostilities with Germany were officially terminated, broadened the theater.

AZERBAIJAN: A TALE OF SECESSION

The first indication that the Russians would not honor their pledge to evacuate Iran came just two weeks after V-E Day. Tudeh demonstrations suddenly erupted again in Tehran, and forty members of Parliament walked out of the Majles in a boycott that lasted four months. The cause this time: the independence of Azerbaijan.

Azerbaijan is a vast green province—a crossroads of mountains and wide plains. During the Qajar dynasty its capital, Tabriz, was the home of the crown prince and his testing ground. For although it is prosperous, Azerbaijan is politically complicated, wedged between the Turks and the Russians, between the Armenians and the Kurds, an inland country with the Caspian Sea on one side and the Black Sea on the other. Its language is Azeri, the root of Turkish, and its tough, hardy people for centuries composed the backbone of the Shah's personal army. In the nineteenth century Russia conquered half of Azerbaijan. Ever since, the northern bear has coveted the other half.

At the head of the independence movement was Jafar Pishevari, the Tudeh delegate who had been rejected by the Fourteenth Majles. He had contributed to the breaking away of Gilan, a province neighboring Azerbaijan that had pronounced its independence (with Russian backing) until the movement was crushed after World War I. Now, backed by the resident Red Army and a well-organized, Soviet-funded Tudeh Party, Pishevari began for the second time in thirty years to campaign for independence.

For Mohammadvali Mirza, our family patriarch, Pishevari's strident politics made for a quandary. He'd already witnessed once the Russian takeover of Azerbaijan—when he'd had to slip up to Moscow incognito to save his properties—and now he saw the whole process coming around again like a repeating nightmare. As one of the biggest landowners in the province, he knew he would be a primary target of Pishevari's new Democratic Party of Azerbaijan (which had incorporated the local branch of the Tudeh) and its program of land redistribution. At first he tergiversated, but when the party demanded allegiance he finally professed cooperation, playing the game as Persians had for centuries—hoping that in so doing he would not be the first to lose his properties or his cotton gin. The party called him *Shahzdeh Communist,* or the Red Prince, and with gusto pointed to him as the aristocratic confirmation of their ideals.

On December 12, 1945, a newly elected Azerbaijan parliament, composed exclusively of Democratic Party members, proclaimed their province an autonomous republic. Azeri became the official language, a new flag was designed, and the Iranian national anthem was scuttled. As the Red Army stood by, Pishevari was elected prime minister, and Red Army uniforms were adopted for the People's Army of Azerbaijan.[3] Three days later a Kurdish People's Republic was also proclaimed.

THE TALE OF THE FIRST
SECURITY COUNCIL CASE

It was at the Tehran Summit that Roosevelt, Stalin, and Churchill first agreed to establish a United Nations after the war. In mid-1945, just after Roosevelt's death, the UN Charter was signed in San Francisco. The Security Council met for the first time in London six months later, and its first case was brought by Iran.

After the war Dr. Pirnia started sending me with some frequency to Abadan as liaison between AIOC and the Finance Ministry. In early autumn 1945, after one of these trips, I hopped over to Baghdad to visit my sister Mehri and Mohsen Khan, who was there serving as ambassador. By chance my visit coincided with a stopover by Iran's UN delegation on its way to Tehran from San Francisco. Mohsen Khan's friend Fazlollah Nabil, whom I had not seen since our train ride together from Abadan, was among the group. He spread his arms and shrugged in dejection when the topic of the United Nations came up.

"What United Nations?" he asked rhetorically. The five permanent members of the newly formed Security Council—the only countries allowed a veto to protect their own interests—did not represent the world's peoples, he explained; they represented only arsenals. The Russians, peeved that the French were seated on the Security Council, had insisted on bringing in Chiang Kai-shek's China. But two continents, South America and Africa, had been ignored completely. Islam, one of the world's great religions with more than half a billion believers, was represented only by the Soviet Union, whose very ideology condemned religion as the opiate of the masses.

The delegation was going on a pilgrimage to the Moslem shrines of Najaf and Karbala, and he asked if I wanted to come along. I agreed, and we headed into the stony desert of southern Iraq.

Karbala and Najaf are the cities of Ali and his son Hossein and form the foundation of Shii Islam. Their splendid golden domes and turquoise spires belie the blood that was spilled there in the seventh century in the civil strife that henceforth divided Sunni from Shii Islam.

When the Prophet Mohammad died in Medina in 632, he left no will, opening his succession to conflict. On the banks of the Euphrates River, midway between Karbala and Najaf, Mohammad's son-in-law, the fourth caliph Ali ibn Abu Talib—to Shiis the Prophet's legitimate heir—was felled by the knife of an assassin reputedly sent by a competing caliph, who enjoyed the following of the Sunnis. Anticipating death, Ali asked to be put astride a camel and to be buried wherever the camel stopped. The camel halted at Najaf, where Ali's tomb, caged in gold, memorializes Shiism's first martyr. He was a pious, desperately poor man, who represented the dispossessed among the Prophet's fold and whose death inspired the first strains of revolutionary Islam.

Ali's son Hossein, zealous and outraged by his father's murder, took up the standard. In the scorched desert outside the city of Karbala he and his small band of followers were first tortured by thirst and then cruelly massacred. The schism between Sunni and Shii Islam was complete. The slaughter of Hossein, like the Crucifixion of Christ, became a symbol of willing sacrifice, the subject of passion plays, and the beginning of the cult of Shii martyrdom so fundamental to the Persian spiritual heart.

As we approached the cities all we saw for miles around were tombs, for the Shiis' ultimate wish is to be buried at Karbala or Najaf. Many Iranians say sarcastically that the Iraqis have one prosperous industry: importing the dead from Iran. Many Iranians have property and homes there and come yearly on pilgrimages. My mother once made the pilgrimage when I was very young. She traveled with three or four other women and stayed at the house my father bought there when he was exiled to Iraq.

Spirals of dust whirled up suddenly among the sepulchres as we approached. Pictures of Ali hung along the walls of the great mosques, inside under the candles, and in every street-side stand. The images were all the same: a young man in flowing Arab headdress with a round, warm face, a dark beard, and liquid eyes.

Najaf has a preeminent mosque school—the other great one being in Qom—and as we wandered its alleyways and bowered squares, we could feel the aura of religious learning that distinguishes all such cities the world over from their secular urban sisters.

The words *Allah-o-Akbar*—Allah is great—floated from the minarets and the tongues of the pilgrims as we sat on a bench and discussed the UN. "The Security Council will open its inaugural session in London," said Nabil. "You will see, it will be a farce." Turning a little stick he'd picked up from the sand over and over in his fingers, he added, "After all, how can you clarify a situation when the aggressor is also one of the judges?"

Six months later, the four great winners of the war and France sat in a semicircle behind their placards at the first Security Council meeting. Ambassador Seyyed Hassan Taqizadeh, laying aside for a moment his robes as envoy to the queen of England and donning instead the garb of ambassador to the UN, presented Iran's complaint on January 19, 1946. So began the *Official Records of the Security Council, First Year, First Series, Number 1.* Taqizadeh, speaking in English, the imperial tongue, accused the Soviet Union of "interference . . . through the medium of its officials and armed forces, in the internal affairs of Iran."

As Nabil had predicted, the Soviets denied it all, and even made the preposterous claim that agreement had already been reached between the two parties to the full satisfaction of Iran.

On January 30 the Security Council delivered its recommendation: continue bilateral negotiations and report any results to the council. To Iranians it was an echo from an earlier time: Edvard Beneš of the League of Nations had used almost the same words in his judgment of Iran's 1933 oil dispute with Britain. In effect, by washing its hands of the issue, the Council condemned the weak to the maw of the powerful.

A TALE OF WIZARDRY

By then, however, events had already taken a turn in Tehran. The premier had resigned, and in his place the Majles had elected Ahmad Qavam-Saltaneh. The election had been a squeaker—victory going to him by a margin of only one vote. The narrowness of his support did not bother Qavam-Saltaneh at all. He was a wolf who had seen much rain, as the Persian saying goes, and knew he would outlive the Majles, whose plenary session was scheduled to end on March 12. Thanks to Mossadeq's bill, the election of the Fifteenth Majles was delayed due to the continued presence of Russian troops. This opened a window of opportunity in which Qavam-Saltaneh could act with his hands free.

It is said that times of crisis bring forth great men. The vote that had opened the door just wide enough for Qavam Saltaneh to slip through was historic, for he would prove himself a decisive and effective prime minister. Like Winston Churchill he was a leader distrusted during times of peace and turned to for relief in times of danger. The Shah found him unmanageable and threatening and was most uncomfortable when he was elected premier. The British too were miffed, having pinned their hopes once again on Seyyed Zia.

But the Russians were delighted. Viewing Qavam-Saltaneh as an able, straightforward negotiator, they instructed the Tudeh Party to give him its support.

Qavam-Saltaneh was the oriental epitome of the Renaissance man: His calligraphy was renowned as being among the most beautiful in Iran, he was a scholar of the Persian language, he collected art—particularly precious Korans—and his notion of a strong Iran was one maintained by an enlightened elite. As a young man he had served as court secretary to Mozzafar-edin Shah and was the one who had formulated and written the Constitution of 1906. He saw politics as a game like chess, not a crusade as it was for Mossadeq. He played the game artfully, motivated by the challenge of each maneuver rather than any overriding personal ideology. This confounded his adversaries and supporters alike and made him considerably more controversial than his basic political beliefs might have warranted. Over six feet tall, like his brother the former premier Vosugh-Doleh, he was bespectacled, haughty, and shrewd. When he was not in power, he was usually out of favor and living quietly as a country gentleman on his rice hills in the north.

Qavam-Saltaneh was sixty-eight when the Majles handed him his new post, and he took it up with the confidence of a man who had already acted three times as prime minister during periods of crisis. In 1921 when Seyyed Zia fell, he was the one who accepted the premiership when my father turned it down, going directly from his prison cell to his seat at the head of the government. Faced with an empty treasury after the demise of the 1919 agreement, he suggested bringing in a third power and thus undertook the first negotiations with Standard Oil for a northern concession. Under British pressure (compounded by Imbry's assassination) the negotiations were halted and his cabinet fell, only to be reinstated six months later in August 1922. This time he hit on a new plan and hired Dr. Arthur Millspaugh to revamp Iran's finances, hoping the American would not be expelled by the British and the Soviets, as his predecessor, W. Morgan Shuster, had been eleven years before. The gamble paid off, and Dr. Millspaugh's first two-year mission was a success, opening the door to many years of U.S. involvement in Iran.

In 1942 Qavam-Saltaneh again engaged Dr. Millspaugh, along with Norman Schwarzkopf, when he was elected to bring the country through its darkest hour in the midst of war. The cities were being torn by bread riots, and spiraling inflation was devastating the country. This time, however, though Qavam-Saltaneh's medicine was efficacious, it was deemed too harsh, and he was labeled despotic. Enraged crowds, incited by the Shah, who felt ignored and intimidated by his overpowering premier, descended on Qavam-Saltaneh's house and set it on fire.[4]

I remember that day as though it were yesterday—smoke billowing into the street, shouting demonstrators rushing past our house down into Kakh Street. As soon as the scene calmed, my mother insisted we go and see to the safety of his wife. I was in the army still and, carrying my revolver, accompanied her to their door. The carpets were smoking and disfigured by burn spots. Porcelain, which Qavam-Saltaneh had collected for years, was everywhere, all smashed and piled in heaps on the ground. The furniture had been broken into pieces and set on fire. The kitchen was in a shambles.

At last we found his wife, sitting alone in an upstairs room, tears running down her face. She was holding a Koran to her head—the ultimate gesture of one who believes they are about to die. We helped her to her feet, and for the next few days she stayed at our house.

The lessons of 1942 were not lost on Qavam-Saltaneh as he took up the reins of power for the last time four years later. He chose a cabinet that was strongly anti-Shah, wanting there to be no mistake that he, not the pro-British court, was the government and that he was acting on his own accord. His task was to seduce the Soviets into evacuating Iran, and to do so he had to earn their trust. But it was a decided risk, for it would mean alienating the British and possibly the Americans. As his deputy prime minister he chose my nephew Mozzafar Firouz, whose fallout with Seyyed Zia had taken place in a flurry of public recriminations a few months before. He also handed Mozzafar the critical job of director of propaganda. My brother General Mohammad Hossein Mirza, who had headed up the gendarmerie and worked with Schwarzkopf during the war, became minister of communications. He spoke perfect Russian and as a boy had studied at the Imperial Military Academy in Moscow.

On February 18, 1946, the day after receiving a vote of confidence for his cabinet, Qavam-Saltaneh flew to Moscow. Stalin received him with enthusiasm, promising that he would withdraw a small number of Soviet troops by March 2, the official evacuation deadline agreed on by the three powers in Yalta (and which both England and the United States honored). But until he was convinced that he did not have a hostile neighbor to his south, he said, he was going to leave the majority of his garrison in place. It was not that he was discriminating against Iran, Stalin assured Qavam-Saltaneh; he was doing the same thing throughout Eastern Europe.

In his talks with Molotov, the Russian premier brought up the subject of the northern oil concession. At the very mention of it Qavam-Saltaneh backpedaled, explaining that he could be jailed for even discussing it. Molotov was nonplussed.

"Then change the law!" he demanded.

Qavam-Saltaneh explained that only the Majles could do that.

"Then change the Majles!" cried Molotov.

When Qavam-Saltaneh explained that new elections could not take place until all foreign troops were off Iranian soil, Molotov turned beet red.

"I *can* help you with that," he snapped.[5]

But Molotov did not immediately help. On March 2, instead of moving out troops, fresh Soviet forces poured into Azerbaijan. At the same time heavily armed columns of Soviet soldiers started marching from Tabriz toward Iraq, Turkey, and Tehran.

Qavam-Saltaneh remained unflustered, even though he returned to Tehran ostensibly empty-handed. In fact he now had a plan: He would offer to barter Iranian oil for the removal of Soviet troops.

Back in the capital Qavam-Saltaneh began to play a double game. To the American ambassador, Wallace Murray, he gave assurances that Iran would renew its complaint in the Security Council, for it was now an open-and-shut case of breach of treaty.

To the Soviet ambassador, Ivan Sadchikov, Qavam-Saltaneh proffered a carrot. Though he could not discuss an oil concession directly, he saw no reason why a Soviet-Iranian company could not be proposed to carry out joint-venture prospecting in the north. Once the new Majles was in place, it could ratify the formation of such a company, creating a de facto concession.

Meanwhile, government forces began to close in on anti-Soviet activity in the capital and shut down newspapers hostile to the Communist cause. At the same time, Qavam-Saltaneh had Seyyed Zia, who was then at the vanguard of the anti-Communist movement, arrested as he walked out of a meeting at the palace. It must have been a moment of sublime irony for the prime minister, who had been arrested by Seyyed Zia during Reza Shah's coup twenty-five years earlier.

Although the Americans were perturbed by Iran's mating dance with Russia, it was a happy if inscrutable Qavam-Saltaneh who announced two days before new Security Council deliberations were to begin that direct negotiations with the Soviets were bearing fruit. The negotiations were still at an extremely delicate stage, however, and in subsequent consultations with Ambassador Sadchikov, Mozzafar threatened that unless Iran received immediate satisfaction, "we would arm the people and then resign . . . the country would fall into a state of anarchy . . . and the world would well understand that a new imperialism was being practiced by Lenin's successors."[6]

The ambassador was suitably impressed, and on April 4, 1946, he joined Qavam-Saltaneh and Mozzafar in signing a communiqué pledging that Soviet troops would evacuate Iran by May 9. In addition the Azerbaijan dispute would be peacefully resolved, and a joint Irano-Soviet oil company would be formed pending ratification within seven months by the Fifteenth Majles.

I went over to Mozzafar's house to wait out the evening with his wife, Maheen. Mozzafar came in about 1:30 A.M., jubilant and ravenous, and informed us over dinner that all had been resolved.

The communiqué, signed with smiles and handshakes across a Kashmir tablecloth, seemed to confirm that the crisis had never been more than a blown-up border conflict. What more could anyone hope to milk from the situation?

Much more, as it turned out, for the British, who had not been consulted, were not pleased.

A HOUSE DIVIDED

Stop telling tales of repentance at the feast;
For the arrows of magnificent archers will pierce
you with the bows of their eyebrows.

—HAFEZ

Tehran 1946

The Tudeh Party was by definition a labor movement, and the largest concentration of labor in the country was employed by AIOC on the swampy island of Abadan. As the Azerbaijan crisis unfolded in the north, the Tudeh had seeped south into the oil province of Khuzistan and there found fertile ground. On my first trip down for the Ministry of Finance in 1945, I could see right away that the situation had become explosive.

During the war conditions had deteriorated markedly. Oil companies were not known for their generous treatment of local workers—Mexico's nationalization in 1938 was a direct result of labor discontent over unlivable conditions—and AIOC was acting no better. Wages were 50 cents a day. There was no vacation pay, no sick leave, no disability compensation. The workers lived in a shantytown called Kaghazabad, or Paper City, without running water or electricity, let alone such luxuries as iceboxes or fans. In winter the earth flooded and became a flat, perspiring lake. The mud in town was knee-deep, and canoes ran alongside the roadways for transport. When the rains subsided, clouds of nipping, small-winged flies rose from the stagnant waters to fill the nostrils, collecting in black mounds along

the rims of cooking pots and jamming the fans at the refinery with an unctuous glue.

Summer was worse. It descended suddenly without a gasp of spring. The
heat was torrid, the worst I've ever known—sticky and unrelenting—
while the wind and sandstorms whipped off the desert hot as a blower. The
dwellings of Kaghazabad, cobbled from rusted oil drums hammered flat,
turned into sweltering ovens. The temperature climbed to 130°F in the
shade. At the refinery the boilers and open flares stoked the already sizzling
air another 20 or 30 degrees; at the wells the grease ran down the pumps
like sweat; the ground cracked; the water in the exposed piping literally
boiled. In every crevice hung the foul, sulfurous stench of burning oil—a
pungent reminder that every day 20,000 barrels, or 1 million tons a year,
were being consumed indiscriminately for the functioning of the refinery,
and AIOC never paid the Iranian government a cent for it.

To the management of AIOC in their pressed ecru shirts and air-
conditioned offices, the workers were faceless drones—just as they were in
the meatpacking plants outside Chicago, the coal mines of Wales, and the
sweatshops of Hong Kong. The habits of the "natives"—eating food with
their hands, for example—disgusted the British officials. Not only were
the British blissfully unaware that their own customs—eating with a fork
that had at one point been in someone else's mouth—were in turn considered unclean and uncouth by the Persians, but they failed to see that fresh
water for the workers to wash their hands before and after their meals was
therefore critical. Piping water to Kaghazabad so that it could be wasted
on foolish ablutions was not in the company plans. And so the workers
were reduced to getting their water from pumps that ran only a few hours
a day, and their lives became a constant fight against the very filth that
their superiors so witheringly condemned.

In the British section of Abadan there were lawns, rose beds, tennis
courts, swimming pools, and clubs; in Kaghazabad there was nothing—
not a tea shop, not a bath, not a single tree. The tiled reflecting pool and
shaded central square that were part of every Iranian town, no matter how
poor or dry, were missing here. The unpaved alleyways were emporiums for
rats. The man at the grocery shop sold his wares while sitting in a barrel of
water to avoid the heat. Only the shriveled, mud-brick mosque in the old
quarter offered hope in the form of divine redemption. Even British foreign secretary Ernest Bevin felt compelled to remark in 1946 that "although we have a Socialist Government in this country, there is no
reflection of that fact in the social conditions [of] this great oil production
in Persia."[1]

Nonetheless the British government, feeling maligned by Qavam-

Saltaneh's anti-British stance, his arrest of Seyyed Zia, and his subsequent incarceration of the British ally and chief of staff General Hassan Arfa, chose not to meddle in AIOC's affairs.

Labor unions, suppressed under Reza Shah, bloomed during the war and, watered with Tudeh encouragement, began to clamor for higher wages and better living conditions. But since the unions were still illegal, AIOC chose to ignore the galling discrepancies between the luxuries enjoyed by the British nationals and the misery of the Persian workers. Eager to hide this from the government, it sent company planes to fly me to Abadan and entertained me in the private all-British clubs that had been closed to me as a recruit. Yet the 1933 Concession specifically stipulated that the company provide workers with schools, hospitals, telephones, roads, decent salaries, and the opportunity for advancement. Its failure to meet these obligations were points I raised every time I flew in from Tehran. Whenever I brought up the subject, however, the officials became evasive. So much was in dispute, they said. There were financial disagreements to settle, such as the Iranian government's preposterous claim that the company was shirking its tax responsibilities. Not until all the issues were resolved could they possibly consider changing conditions on-site.

The workers were not willing to wait. Within days after the evacuation of Britain's forces from Iran in March of 1946, they began a series of wild-cat strikes. The company, scrambling to protect itself, encouraged Arab minorities to organize into a separate union, possibly with a view to splitting the province of Khuzistan off from the rest of Iran and folding it into Iraq. This only encouraged violence in the streets, and one night several Arab businessmen and their families were massacred.

By July the unrest culminated in a widespread riot. Forty-seven people were killed and more than 170 injured. The British fortified their troops in Basra and sent two warships into Abadan. E.G.D. Northcroft, the local AIOC director, sent a famous letter to the Iranian government complaining, "The company has ceased to be an organization."[2]

Tehran's reaction was swift. Mozzafar flew down with two Tudeh officials in tow. Ordering the release of all prisoners, he succeeded in bringing the strike to an end and oversaw the withdrawal of the British destroyers. Then began some hard bargaining with AIOC officials. "I gave them formal notification of the new labor code," he later recalled, "and informed them officially that they would be obliged to pay the workers on a seven day basis for a six day week. When the head of the company replied that he would refer to London for instructions, I replied that respect for Iranian laws by the company was imperative and no concern of London."[3]

What Mozzafar achieved was the first imposition of a minimum wage in

Iran and, by force majeure, the payment of salaries rather than exploitive day rates. For the moment tension was diffused. But the incident left the officials at AIOC feeling both irate and vulnerable. Stalin had, after all, gotten his political start in the oil town of Baku, and at the time of the Russian Revolution his men had torched the fields, turning oil for the first time into a political weapon. Communist penetration, company officials contended, was growing in Iran—not just in Abadan but in Qavam-Saltaneh's government and through Russia's ongoing influence in the north.

At the same time the chairman of AIOC, Sir William Fraser, did not believe that labor loyalty was important and hence saw no reason to compromise company profits to finance reform. A hard-boiled Scotsman whose control over the vast funds that AIOC poured into the British treasury gave him considerable clout in London, he persuaded the Foreign Office that cooperation with Iran's government would lead nowhere and that England's primary purpose was to protect its own interests. As a result the British government further tightened its grip on the south. Using the same technique that had proved so effective with the tribes, British officials now lured landowners to their side by offering them sugar at 1.5 rials a pound, which they could then resell at 28 rials to purchase arms. And the consuls general in Khuzistan and Isfahan were given the go-ahead to incite sedition.

THE SPECIAL AMIR

Turmoil in the south spread like forest fire. Taking a quick vacation, I headed down to Kermanshah in August 1946 to see the lay of the land. The three-million-strong Kurdish Kalhor tribe was jittery and forging allegiances with Kurds in the north and possibly with some of the southern tribes. Amir Maksus, the tribe's chief, had spent fourteen years in prison under Reza Shah, who had also confiscated all his property. He was a bitter man, and though he had no money, he had persuaded many of the leading men of Kermanshah to sign a manifesto for Kurdish independence. He asked that I sign it too.

"The north has already separated," he said. "We must get our share before it's too late. We are on the cusp of a civil war. Part of your properties are composed of tribal lands and peoples. And your brother is the Il-Khan of the Zuleh tribe."

I thought of my father, faced with a similar situation thirty years before. And just as Salar-Doleh had done to my father, Amir Maksus offered me a bribe. "Should we separate totally," he said, eyeing me, "your family will benefit from a big slice. Imagine, three hundred square miles at least."

It was then that I turned on him.

"You are making a big mistake," I said. "A government is a permanent institution, at times weak, at times strong, but it remains a mountain upon which we are just incidental trees and stones. Storms may blow us down; there may even be an earthquake that tears some of the cliff away. But the mountain stays on. Whether the state is a shah or a parliament, people recognize it and know it to be the government.

"In this very state of Kermanshah thirty years ago, my father was asked by his cousin Salar-Doleh to divide Iran. And he refused. He subsequently smashed Salar-Doleh.

"Your father and all the Kalhors were with Salar-Doleh. They too were vanquished, just as you will be. That is why I refuse to sign this. I am following my father's legacy and will never act as a tool to dismantle Persia!"

Amir Maksus (whose name I loved, for it meant "Special Amir") was very disappointed and became afraid that, having shown me the document with the signatures, I might inform the government. I told him to have no fear, for many of the names on the manifesto were those of friends. "But don't be surprised," I warned him, "if some desert you at the last moment."

At last he turned to leave, but I held up my hand. "Before you go I have something to show you too," I said. I pulled from my pocket a letter from Qavam-Saltaneh, written in his own beautiful hand. It stated that a decree be passed awarding Amir Maksus a portion of his properties so that his life would be easier until a solution was found for the balance.

"Qavam-Saltaneh entrusted me with this letter and the power to carry out its purpose," I told Amir Maksus. "The quandary now is how to restore property to a man in revolt."

It was a peace offering, an effort by the premier to soften Amir Maksus's attitude toward the government. But Amir Maksus was untempted. He had lost all faith in Tehran. He was so sure that the country was disintegrating that he chose to hang on to the manifesto rather than claim his land. Poor man. Despite everything I liked him a great deal. A few months later he died in a car crash.

Amir Maksus was not the only one to solicit my support for cutting up the country. A prominent landowner and right-hand man to my father for many years had appointed himself big man about town and during my stay threw a lavish lunch for the tribal chiefs to coordinate strategy. I refused to attend. So did the fierce Sanjabis, a tribe whose chiefs had always been well educated and highly suspicious of the British. They had been close allies of my father's, who twice gave them refuge in our Tehran compound during disturbances.*

After the lunch the tribal chiefs sent a series of demands to Tehran, asking in essence for autonomy. In response Qavam-Saltaneh dispatched General Mohammad Ali Saffari, the chief of police, to Kermanshah to make inquiries. He first stopped by our house for a quick reconnaissance. We discussed the incredible spell the British missions were casting over the area and their ability to play on the greed of the grandees. Declarations of autonomy were pouring into Tehran from tribes all over the country. Arms were everywhere and easily available from British sources. By mid-1946 the country was armed to the teeth and more divided than it had ever been.

A BROTHER'S TALE

The demarcation between the north and south of Iran ran just north of Hamadan along the border of Azerbaijan. There in the mountains clashes between the Communist-backed insurgents and the British-supported tribes had become frequent and bloody. Before I left Tehran for Kermanshah, Abol Bashar, still at Janatabad and concerned for the safety of our villagers, had asked me to send some ammunition. Through a British contact I obtained five thousand rounds of shot for some old French-made *canne à pêche* rifles that had been stored at the fort since World War I. I also ordered a few tommy guns and a crate of light arms, mostly revolvers. Now Abol urged me to pass by Hamadan myself, for he needed some advice.

I arrived to discover that the situation there was much worse than it had been in Kermanshah. Tudeh rebels based in the city of Qazvin, an hour's drive north, were traveling the countryside on horseback inciting the peasants to revolt. Whole villages, filled with the fervor of Communist visions, were rising up in battle. The landlords, backed by the British and the Iranian government, were fighting hand-to-hand battles against their own people. In our area the situation had become particularly tense around Assadabad, where my own properties lay.

Abol and I sat before the fire in the great hall talking late into the night. News had arrived that the Zolfagharis, huge landowners to the west in the province of Zanjan, had mounted a countercoup against the Tudeh Party. They were four brothers, big shots, proud, and in the past fiercely inde-

---

*It was a point of honor in Iran that anyone offering refuge protect their guests to the point of death. This was why the Qashgahis were so condemned when they released their Nazi charges to the British.

pendent of the Shah. But this time, when the area fell under Soviet occupation, they had accepted support from both the government and the British. Forming a private army, they fought a pitched battle in the fields and took over the capital of the province.

Abol said he wanted to do the same in Hamadan, which had become a hotbed of sedition. Like most landowners in the area, he already had armed and organized a private force of two hundred men from our properties. His plan was to march in and seize Hamadan.

Abol sat with his chin balanced on his fingers as huge, soft shadows from the fire danced behind him on the walls. I marveled at this firebrand of a brother who had chosen to take on the life of a tribal lord. Even now he was wearing a bow tie—his unique trademark, for absolutely no one else in Iran wore one. Abol had always been unorthodox and incorrigibly mischievous, as if the six-year-old boy he'd once been was still alive inside him. Some years later, when my two-year-old daughter complained about her porridge, he turned the bowl upside down on her head. He was always getting into scrapes, not in small part because he enjoyed spending time at the bazaar. Yet there was another side to him: the scholarly Merlin with a unique knowledge of poetry and, after his return from Columbia University a few years later, a commanding grasp of international law. He had the capacity to listen too—rare in our family—and to take things in stride. Our father must have known all this, for the name Farman Farma gave him, Abol Bashar, means "Father of Mankind."

Abol had taken on the life of Janatabad as if Iran were still a country of khans, and under his tutelage much had changed. Stones had been cleared, roads laid where only horse tracks had been, and village houses had new roofs. Under Reza Shah a visa had been required to move from one town to another, and for twenty years that visa had been denied to anyone in our family. Janatabad had fallen into neglect. Now a renaissance of sorts was taking place. With the help of our mother, who became involved in the health care of the villagers and tribes, a doctor was engaged, as well as a young medical student from the university. Until then the peasants had suffered from malaria, and their only cure had been to peel the bark from the willow tree and drink its bitter juice. Now the undersecretary of health, a staunch Communist as well as a close childhood friend, provided us with quinine to fight the malaria, as well as vaccines and first aid equipment such as aspirin, cotton balls, and alcohol. He was the only minister ever to offer such aid.

The most important thing we did was to repair all the baths in the villages. These were domed buildings housing a pool of water about a yard deep, heated from underneath. Even at my father's house there had been such a bath, a *khazineh,* and everyone got in it together—the men of course at a different time from the women. Because there was a lack of timber in the Hamadan area, the villagers heated their houses—and later the baths—by burning a mixture of cow dung and straw, which they formed into cakes and baked in the sun. The baths became like clubs, where everybody gathered once a week to soak, gossip, and drink tea.

Yet the fact of the matter was that Iran's feudal system had died with the nineteenth century. Although we still managed the land, our holdings were not independent fiefdoms anymore. And in times such as these, it was no longer our place to mobilize our people to take over neighboring towns. The government might be weak and helpless, but taking up arms against it was still treason.

Abol wanted to imitate the Zolfagharis, but I reminded him that our situation was very different from theirs. They were on Russian-occupied territory and had mounted their revolt in the name of the government—even though we all knew that they would be the greatest beneficiaries. Nonetheless it was legal. Taking over Hamadan would not be. It was still in government hands—even if only barely. If we were to march in, the government would muster whatever troops it had and make it a showcase. We would be considered rebels like the Qashgahis.

That night I was wracked by nightmares. The next morning, when a great commotion in the courtyard shook my windows, I thought I was still being haunted by dreams. When I looked out I saw twenty or thirty people near the well making an incredible noise. *What new calamity is this?* I wondered in dismay. Abol was just emerging from the house, and hurriedly throwing on my shirt, I ran down to see what was going on.

Fortunately there was no cause for worry. At the center of the crowd a local medicine man was engaged in healing a backache. The patient was astride a donkey with his legs tied tightly around the animal's belly. The donkey, we were informed, had not had anything to drink for twenty-four hours and now, at last having been led to the well, was drinking ravenously. The more it drank, the rounder its stomach became, and the rounder its stomach became, the more the man's legs were stretched, causing him to emit bloodcurdling yowls of pain to the loud amusement of the crowd. The medicine man, smiling savagely, assured me that the next day his patient would be as good as new.

That evening Abol and I talked again. We climbed to the roof of the castle and strolled around the inside perimeter, surveying the dark scene stretched out around us. Guards manned the watchtowers in each of the corners, their guns ready, their eyes searching the restless countryside.

My heart was heavy, for I did not want to draw on that argument of last

resort—that Abol must give up his plan because as his older brother I said
so. What's more I could see his point. Had the line of conflict run through
Kermanshah rather than Hamadan, I would have been tempted to send our
men into battle and join the tribes. Kermanshah was a fractious tribal center, with lawlessness common even in the best of times. Hamadan and the
areas north into Azerbaijan on the other hand were more sedentary, and one
could, if careful, stay aloof and uninvolved.

And yet, as Abol and I circled the ramparts of Janatabad's old brick
walls, I knew in my heart that even here, there was no central government
left. If the conflict finally came down to the British or the Russians, it was
obvious that we would side with the tribes who supported the British.
However, if we played our hand too soon . . .

Abol was eating seeds: One crack, an almost imperceptible swallow, and
the empty, perfectly split shells would drop onto the ground. He looked
up, shrugged his shoulders, and, with a sad, comical look on his face, tilted
his head in a gesture of acquiescence. "They have closed all the doors of the
wineshops," he said, using the words of Hafez. "So why have they left open
the houses of the liars and double-crossers?"

I grasped his shoulders. Yes, the double-crossers were still at large and
free to act, but he understood that we had to exhibit the loyalty that our
family heritage demanded. Suddenly I felt as one does the first day after a
sickness, free and glad and marvelously virile. That night I went to bed
convinced that for the moment our munitions would stay home.

A TALE OF FALSE HOPE

Negotiations between the government and the Azerbaijani separatists, designed to bring the discord to a close, were touch-and-go throughout the
summer. As they'd promised, the Soviets pulled their troops out with com-
mendable docility by May 9, leaving the province in the hands of the insurgents. Once they were out, pressure from Moscow to begin the election
process intensified, the hope now being to achieve politically what the
Russian army had failed to do militarily. The strategy was straightforward:
influence the selection of candidates so that the Majles would favor the Soviet Union. That way Moscow would not only get the vote for the oil deal,
but it could manipulate domestic and foreign policy from the inside, little
by little bringing Iran—or at least the north—back into the Soviet orbit.

In the evacuation agreement, however, Qavam-Saltaneh had specifically
stipulated that no elections could take place until all of Iran was under central government control. By this scheme everything was linked together:

Elections could not take place until Azerbaijan was tethered, and the oil deal could not be approved until the Majles was in session.

In June, one month before heading to Abadan to quell the strikes, Mozzafar went to Tabriz and signed a fifteen-point agreement with the separatist leader Pishevari that seemed to solve all the major issues within the framework of the Iranian Constitution. A picture shows Mozzafar being carried on the shoulders of a cheering crowd as it sweeps him jubilantly toward his plane after the meeting. His right hand is up and waving; his left clutches a bouquet of flowers as another is thrust his way and confetti flies in the air. A placard of Qavam-Saltaneh bounces behind him. Natty in tie and hat, he wears an expression of sheer joy, diverted only by the need to keep his balance.

Another picture shows the welcoming committee called together by Qavam-Saltaneh, waiting for Mozzafar's return at the Tehran airport. Maheen, Mozzafar's wife, in her wide straw hat and platform pumps, stands out like a spring flower in the midst of our gray suits. Mohammadvali Mirza sits next to her on the left, the focus of the camera blurring across his unreadable eyes; I'm standing on the right, cocky in my stylishly short tie and pencil mustache. We all wear a look of pleasure, relief, and anticipation that at last the country will settle down, the guns will be laid aside, and the election campaign will begin. If time had stopped there, one might have imagined a dénouement in which everyone got what they bargained for. But Britain's hard-line position in the south allowed the solution suddenly to slip away like a cockroach scuttling under a loose doorjamb.

A TALE OF ARRESTS

"Long and carefully laid British plans to detach the oil fields from Persia and incorporate them into Iraq appear to be maturing," wrote a diplomatic correspondent of the London *Daily Worker* in September. By then open rebellion was sweeping the south.

On the morning of September 8, 1946, I stopped by Mozzafar's house, as I often did, for a quick cup of coffee, only to find his anteroom full of people. Hilda Arfa, the British wife of the general whom Qavam-Saltaneh had arrested on charges of treason, was entering with her daughter as I arrived.

"Shahzdeh, my father is in solitary confinement," whispered the girl, running up. "We have not been allowed to see him, and now they are preventing us from seeing the minister."

Hilda clutched my arm. "I knew your father, and his house was open to everyone," she snapped in her clipped English accent. "Now your family is in power, and yet your treatment of others is disgraceful."

I patted her hand, trying to console her as I settled her into a chair and escaped upstairs. In the bedroom I found Mozzafar shaving and breakfast being served. As I threw myself into a chair, I told him I'd brought Hilda Arfa along and that she was waiting to see him in the hall downstairs.

Mozzafar became extremely cross and began shouting orders to the servants that no one was to be allowed inside the house. "They are British spies," he said, rushing about with a towel to his chin, "and I absolutely refuse to see them. Arfa is to be court-martialed—the sooner the better—and you will see, he will be properly condemned." Mozzafar and Arfa had long held each other in healthy contempt, and I realized it was useless to have brought Hilda to his attention.

"In any case," Mozzafar said, calming down and perching on a chair to eat some toast with plum jam, "I can't possibly see any of these people. I have to go to Isfahan." He smiled his foxy grin, his humor restored. "Why don't you come with me? It's going to be quite a trip." Mozzafar's expression was always bemused, as if he'd just turned away from a wonderful intimate joke. Just to see him was to smile without any idea why. As so often happened, I found myself beaming at him like a Cheshire cat, but I shook my head.

"I wouldn't go anywhere with you, even to paradise," I joked. "I have work to do—my own small part in keeping the British under surveillance."

He asked me to wish him luck, which I did, and we went our separate ways.

As I lunched that day with my mother, the radio announced that Mozzafar had arrived in Isfahan to military honors and a large welcome by the town dignitaries and Bakhtiari leaders. Then, to our astonishment, the report said that the visit had taken an unusual turn. Instead of giving the regulation airport speech, Mozzafar had suddenly had the tribal chiefs arrested, handcuffed, and thrown onto his plane. He'd then turned on his heel and returned to Tehran.

What had Mozzafar wanted me to do? I wondered as I headed back to the office. Entertain these guys in their manacles in the back of the plane? After all, a number of them were my friends.

Well, that day, apparently, they weren't friends. The southern tribes had, with British backing, been about to stage a full-scale uprising against the government, which would surely have split Iran in half. "Division" had been on every tongue as the chiefs had ridden into Isfahan.

Instead the tables were turned. The Qashgahis, alerted by the British to possible government reprisals, at the last moment sent their excuses. The Bakhtiaris, armed to the teeth, walked into a trap.

The invitation for the gathering had come from General Motazedi, head of the Isfahan garrison, whose loyalties no one had bothered to question. He was a confidant of the Shah's and had even gone to Egypt for the royal wedding.* On the surface it had seemed just another excuse for pomp. In fact, the general, who was married to my sister Masamah, had received special orders in advance from Mozzafar. When the latter arrived in Isfahan, General Motazedi met him at his plane and shadowed him as he stepped into the hall to face his victims.

Mozzafar, tailored and genial, had plunged into the rough company before him and without a moment's hesitation grasped the hand of the first Bakhtiari in line. Behind him General Motazedi slipped on a pair of handcuffs and, before anyone knew what was happening, had one, then another, and finally all the tribal chiefs manacled, escorted from the room, and thrown onto the plane. With incredible courage Mozzafar, his ebullient smile in place, continued to move around the horseshoe of notables, seemingly oblivious to the winnowing taking place in his wake. In fact one raised eyebrow, one slight hesitation on Mozzafar's part, could have caused those still free to turn on him like wolves to the kill.

There were moments like that during those tense days, moments of showmanship and bravery. But the aborted showdown in Isfahan was just an epitasis. Less than two weeks later the Qashgahis openly revolted. The Hayat Davoudi tribe seized the Gulf ports of Bandar Abbas and Bushir and the island of Kharg. Government troops throughout the south were routed. On September 22 Nasser Qashgahi, magnificent at the head of the clamoring tribal confederation, issued Qavam-Saltaneh an ultimatum: Grant autonomy to the province of Fars, or more bloodshed would follow.

---

*The return from Cairo—which to those in Tehran seemed a gloriously royal affair—was, according to General Motazedi, rather a fiasco. The bride, Princess Fawzieh, was accompanied by her mother, Nazli, an extremely beautiful woman who brought along a man thought to be her lover—a very strange state of affairs to our eyes in Iran. In Abadan a special train had been arranged to bring the wedding party to Tehran, but at the last minute it was found to be without water or food, and they had to appeal to AIOC for provisions. The weather was extremely hot, and before the emergency delivery arrived, a lady-in-waiting fainted from the heat, prompting someone to pour a bottle of lemonade over her face to revive her, which left her sticky and uncomfortable for the rest of the trip.

A PALACE TALE

Every Saturday the American ambassador, George Allen, and the Shah played tennis. On Monday evenings the Shah often invited Allen over for dinner. Frequently the Shah's twin sister, Ashraf, joined them for tea or a glass of whiskey on the terrace to watch the sun drop over the Elborz Mountains. Now, in September 1946, the air was already crisp and the leaves were turning. The summer dust had settled, and the lights in the palace illuminated the garden.

To Allen the Shah was an easy man to get along with. Urbane, Europeanized, and clearly wanting the best for his country, he was less difficult to fathom than many of Iran's other leaders, elder statesmen like Qavam-Saltaneh or the puzzling Mossadeq, whom Allen found intractable and overly suspicious of American aims. The Shah was less artful, more direct. His mounting angst over Qavam-Saltaneh's dangerous pas de deux with the Soviets, now the cause of serious repercussions in the south, matched Allen's own sentiments—and those of his government. Within the year the Truman Doctrine would be issued in response to communist threats in Turkey and Greece,* codifying Washington's policy of communist containment and establishing the frontiers between the Soviet and American worlds as surely as would the Berlin Wall. The Shah's exasperation at his premier's pro-Soviet stance convinced Allen that the United States had found an ally in the young monarch.

The two talked at length about Qavam-Saltaneh's reshuffling of the cabinet in August, when three members of the Tudeh Party had been handed portfolios. Neither Allen nor the Shah approved of this move despite the prime minister's claim that he could manage the Party better from inside the government than as an opposition force. Nor did they buy his argument that by placing the Communist politicians in the same government as aristocrats such as the two Firouzes, Mozzafar and Mohammad Hossein Mirza, they would be compromised in the eyes of the masses.

For that matter neither man trusted the Firouzes. Allen's predecessor, Wallace Murray, had called Mozzafar "Qavam's evil genius," an opinion not far from Allen's. It was common knowledge that it had been Mozzafar's idea to bring the Tudeh Party into the government. The Shah was as

---

*Coincidentally—or was it?—President Harry Truman issued his declaration before Congress the same day, March 12, 1947, that Standard Oil of New Jersey, Socal (Standard Oil of California), Socony (Standard Oil of New York), and Texaco signed a historic joint venture creating the Arabian American Oil Company (Aramco), an agreement that had almost been derailed by concerns that Soviet influence was causing political instability in the surrounding area.

eager to rid the cabinet of the Firouzes as he was to throw out the Communists.

Princess Ashraf also denounced the prime minister, calling him a martinet with dubious motives. She was sure it would not be beyond him to plot the overthrow of the throne and declare himself dictator.[4] The party he'd set up a few months before reflected his intentions to pack the Majles with his own supporters. Called the Democratic Party of Iran, it had outwitted the Azerbaijanis by stealing their party name and nationalistic rhetoric. He was a power to be reckoned with, she said, crossing her fine legs at the ankles and sipping her cocktail; a serious threat to the monarchy—surely the ambassador agreed.

Princess Ashraf often expressed her opinions with greater fire than her brother. Petite, square-jawed, with a hard glint to her widespread eyes that reminded people of Reza Shah and a smile that rarely reached beyond her cheekbones, she was the one who had inherited her father's toughness and ambition even though her twin had inherited the throne. Condemned to grow up in his shadow, she fought all her life for recognition, outriding him whenever they raced their horses or fast cars and adopting his friends as her own. When he'd left for school in Switzerland, she'd been devastated. "I felt I had been separated from a part of myself," she later wrote in her memoirs.[5]

Ashraf did not begrudge her brother the Crown. She was too devoted to him, too highly possessive, and too aware of her own unique position as his conscience to be jealous. Instead she considered the task of his life hers as well and believed that Allah had split the soul of sovereignty between them. To Ashraf that meant carte blanche to bolster the Shah in any way she could, and often she acted as his alter ego, provoking him into being decisive, sometimes even taunting him to act against his own wishes. Over the years she also appointed herself personal public relations representative, special international envoy, political liaison, cultural director, and behind-the-scenes negotiator. In April, after Qavam-Saltaneh returned from Moscow, Ashraf made a state visit of her own to Stalin to remind the Soviet leader that the Shah was as much a player as the prime minister in relations between the two countries. Stalin was apparently captivated by the steely princess and, after taking her to a sports review, sent her home with a magnificent sable coat.

Newspapers in Europe were already dubbing Ashraf "The Black Panther of Iran" and "The Power Behind the Throne." By then the Shah's first wife, Fawzieh, "The Tame Kitten," as Ashraf liked to call her, had escaped back to Cairo, and a divorce was being quietly arranged. Ashraf herself was about to embark on a second marriage, but her focus remained her brother.

By September 1946, as the country twisted itself into an armed standoff between north and south—between Britain and Russia—Ashraf was furiously politicking, meeting with members of the Majles and lobbying hard against the coalition cabinet of Qavam-Saltaneh.

The week the ultimatum arrived from Nasser Qashgahi, the mood at the palace was somber. Yet when the Shah and the ambassador came in from their tennis, they each wore a hint of a smile. Nasser Qashgahi had for once chosen a path that coincided with that of the Crown. In addition to his demand that Fars be granted the same autonomy as Azerbaijan, his note to Qavam-Saltaneh called for the immediate resignation of the Tudeh ministers and a general clampdown on the Communists.

That evening the Shah reiterated a theme he had brought up often to Allen: his desire for money and arms to bolster his army.[6] Schwarzkopf's gendarmerie, he felt, was the one anchor holding Iran steady in the storm. If only the United States would help him provision a more effective force under the command of his generals, he could move the army into Azerbaijan and bring the nightmare to an end. As it turned out, Allen was unable to arrange an American loan for military aid until a year later, in 1947. But when it finally came, a mere $10 million droplet, it marked the beginning of a love affair between the American administration and the Shah's war machine that over the next thirty years would transform the Iranian army into the world's fifth-largest fighting force.

Allen's tenure also introduced another element into U.S.-Iran relations. Thanks to his close personal rapport with the Shah, U.S. policy began to exhibit a subtle though significant contradiction: While professing support for democratic principles, it increasingly favored the monarchy and its authoritarian position over leaders elected to undertake parliamentary change.

REVERSALS

Unlike the Shah, Qavam-Saltaneh did not feel that a larger army was necessary to bring Azerbaijan to heel. Whether he had anticipated events in advance or simply knew how to play for time, the wily premier now closed in for the kill. Nasser Qashgahi's ultimatum, instead of alarming him, gave him an excuse to change strategy. For six months he'd flattered the Russians in order to ease their stranglehold on Azerbaijan. Now he instituted a wholesale purge of the Tudeh Party.

The premier's first move was to reshuffle his cabinet and oust the Tudeh ministers from his government. The Shah, however, was not going to let it go at that. The Firouzes, he insisted, must go too. Allen, who was present at the meeting between Qavam-Saltaneh and the Shah, wrote afterward that Qavam-Saltaneh pleaded to keep Mozzafar "at least for a short while." But the Shah "became furious, banged [the] table and told Qavam that mention of Firouz again would end any cooperation between himself and Qavam forever. Shah said he wanted Firouz either in prison or out of [the] country immediately."[7]

A week later Mozzafar and Maheen left for Moscow. In his suitcase, packed in tissue, was the ornate black and gold uniform and the ostrich-feather hat worn by the Shah's ambassadors plenipotentiary. Qavam-Saltaneh had saved Mozzafar's face, but his political career at home was finished.

Although Mozzafar's departure was a setback for Qavam-Saltaneh, he did not let it slow his momentum. With a new cabinet in place, supported by both Allen and the Shah, he closed down Tudeh offices all over the country. He then suddenly announced that the presence of Iranian troops was a requisite for elections in the provinces. As commander in chief, the Shah then ordered General Zahedi into the south and Schwarzkopf's gendarmes, under the command of General Ali Razmara, into Tabriz. The maneuver, a masterstroke, caught the Russians in a vise. Retaliation would mean losing the oil concession, while the international outcry provoked by any type of military response would be severe. Schwarzkopf, who unlike Allen held Qavam-Saltaneh in high regard, marched into Tabriz to cheering crowds. Within twenty-four hours the autonomous republics collapsed.

At last Azerbaijan was back in the Iranian fold. To celebrate, the Shah, surrounded by his generals, left for Tabriz to personally welcome his people back. It was a sweet victory. The army's prestige, badly battered by the Allied invasion, had been restored. And the Shah's power, compromised while the army faltered, was back on track. The sovereign who waved so triumphantly to the crowds in the great square in Tabriz knew that thanks to the uniforms massed behind him, he, not Qavam-Saltaneh, was now supreme.

The nation of Iran had been saved. The British, relieved, relaxed their support of the tribes, and the south soon settled down. On January 17, 1947, almost a year to the day after the case had first gone to the UN Security Council, the Shah pronounced the opening of the campaign for the Fifteenth Majles.

The election proved, however, that by the Shah's order, not just Mozzafar Firouz but the entire family was politically finished—at least for the time being. Mohammadvali Mirza and Mohammad Mossadeq both lost their parliamentary seats. In Kermanshah, where I ran as the provincial

president of Qavam-Saltaneh's own Democratic Party, I experienced the
same fate that Mozzafar had encountered two years earlier: not a single ballot for me in any of the urns—not even my own.

A TALE OF PLUCKED CHICKENS

I was outraged. Democracy! It was a farce in my country, and it was the
Shah's doing. "Is he blind?" I asked my friends. Couldn't he see that his
best allies were the aristocracy—that self-interest made us staunch supporters of the Crown? Didn't he read the message our family had sent by
holding firm at Hamadan—that we were trustworthy supporters of the
state and were on his side?

"No!" said Sadeq Hedayat as we sat at lunch one day. "No!"

Sadeq was a storyteller, and though he died young—by suicide in
1948—he became, by some counts, the most famous writer of modern
Iran. He was Maheen Firouz's uncle. His eyes were veiled, focused beyond
me somewhere. His bony mouth twitched. "You saw the chicken man as
we walked down Ferdowsi Avenue?" he asked.

"Yes."

"He stands there with his basket shaped like a half cylinder, five or six
chickens inside. Whenever a customer arrives, he opens the wicker door,
reaches in for a chicken, and cuts its throat. The people of Iran are just like
those chickens. They live together quite nicely, not thinking of danger.
They may be hungry, they may be thirsty, but they go along living. Then
suddenly one of them is grabbed, and they are shocked. They make a big
noise, *khot-khot-khot-khot-khot.* To the chicken man it makes no difference
which one he takes, and the other chickens don't realize that the chicken
that's disappeared is getting its throat cut, and that in time their own turn
will come. The chickens calm down after a bit and return to normal, until
the next time the man puts his hand in and plucks one of them away. That's
what it's like in Iran. A dictator shows up, kills a few people, and the other
people, like the chickens, just walk the street, feeling calm, oblivious of
the fact that they too are condemned."

Sadeq's story made me even angrier. I would not be a philosopher-
chicken. I'd had enough of the ruses, the lies, the maddening deceptions.
I wanted to talk to someone who could do something; I wanted to change
things. That someone was suggested to me by Ghaffar Vaziri Tabar, a
Birmingham friend who was Ambassador Allen's secretary. "I'll arrange a
rendezvous for you to see him," he suggested one day in response to my anguish.

The United States occupied the old German Embassy at the time (the huge compound where Khomeini's hostages would be taken had not yet been built). Ghaffar accompanied me to Allen's office. The ambassador was tall and relatively young; his manner was relaxed. I started off right away, dispensing with the *taarof,* or verbal niceties—the "What a lovely office you have here, Mr. Ambassador" and "Strange weather, don't you think?"—knowing that Americans were used to getting right down to business. I told him I'd come to find out whether he was in fact a defender of the people and of democracy as we imagined Americans to be.

"Of course," he said. "But what is your point?"

"My point," I told him, "is that liberty is a myth in this country. In my own experience, in Kermanshah, I have seen first Colonel Fletcher and now the Shah rig the elections. After Azerbaijan we had hoped there would be a modicum of freedom in the campaign. We believed that you would influence the Shah and the government—and that things would change."

He eyed me thoughtfully. "What, in your opinion, should have been done?" he asked.

"The government should have allowed every candidate to compete equally," I answered forcefully, "as it does in your country, instead of rigging elections to install its own people. No one in this election can claim to have been elected by the populace. Look at Dr. Mossadeq, the most popular man in Tehran. Even he has had his seat stolen from under him."

Ambassador Allen leaned forward in his chair. "Elections have always been interfered with in countries like yours," he said. "But if you think about it, there has never been a Majles that has acted against the interests of the country."

His directness brought me up short. Rather than protesting that the election had been free and that I, Mossadeq, and all the others had lost fairly, rather than talking about democracy and retreating into subterfuge, Allen was being a realist. His honesty stunned me, and I looked at him with admiration. What was he insinuating? That the oil law would not pass? That this Majles too would wriggle free of the Russians? When the half-hour interview came to a close, I shook his hand in gratitude.

The next day I went to visit my father's grave. "When you are happy," my mother would say, quoting a phrase of the Prophet Mohammad, "you should go to the cemetery, for you will be reminded that one day you will die as well. And when you are sad, you should also visit the graves, for you will see all those around you are dead, and you are still alive."

My father's grave lay about ten miles from town near the Shrine of Hazrat Abdol Azeem, where Nasser-edin Shah was buried. Although the government had denied him a resting place in the shrine, the family had obtained a burial spot nearby.* It was the first time I had gone to visit his grave, and I went as much to pay my respects as to salve my anger. My father too had faced treachery from the Crown, and yet he'd always gone on. I looked at his headstone and made a pact with myself. I would no longer rely on my family legacy or inheritance to create my future, for too often they let me down. Neither would I marry a woman for her wealth or connections, for that also could undermine me. My life was mine to make. I would do it on my own. All around me the dead lay quiet, while I stood on my feet, alive.

THE TALE OF AN ORIENTAL HAT TRICK

Ambassador Allen turned out to be right. The Fifteenth Majles was intensely patriotic and an embarrassment to both the Russians and the British. When the Soviet oil concession came up for a vote in October 1947, the Majles rejected it overwhelmingly. It also commanded the government to review AIOC's 1933 Concession and reestablish Iran's rights to its own natural resources.

The Russian play for oil in the north was dead.

The British, thinking the reference to their concession a ruse to throw off the Russians, ignored the Majles decree and continued business as usual. Rather than addressing any of the Iranian government's complaints, AIOC decided it needed a public relations officer and gave the job to Mostafa Fateh. It was a fundamental misreading of the situation, and one that they would deeply regret.

---

*Today the whole area has been wiped out to make room for a mosque—the largest in the world—commemorating the Islamic Republic's martyrs. Ironically the Koran specifically condemns destroying the resting place of the dead. Nonetheless my father's grave, Nasser-edin Shah's shrine, Nosrat-Doleh's grave, and the resting ground of hundreds of others were demolished.

REHEARSAL FOR A
BREAKUP

Give me geisha, the wine which the Great Shah Jam
Claimed that by drinking, he could divine the unknown.
—HAFEZ

Tehran 1948

Qavam-Saltaneh lasted only two months after the oil vote. The Shah had
had it with strong prime ministers and, with Ashraf working the back corridors, engineered his fall. The old premier left on a note of warning. In a
broadcast the day before his resignation he lambasted AIOC's failure to
abide by the concession and called on the public to demand redress.

Awareness of AIOC's infractions had grown since the Majles oil vote in
October 1947. Figures on royalty discrepancies and reports of the company's exorbitant tax payments to the British government had begun to
appear in the press. The public's natural distrust of British colonial practices was rekindled, and for the first time since Reza Shah had come to
power more than twenty years before, a mollah, Seyyed Abol Qassem
Kashani, surfaced as a strong leader demanding reform. His father had
fallen under the British sword in Iraq before World War I, and Kashani
himself had been a victim of the Arak concentration camp during the occupation. Now he fanned a rising flame of nationalism.

The first prime minister the Shah chose to succeed Qavam-Saltaneh was
a yes-man known for his pro-British sentiments. He proved no match for
the public's demands and fell in June 1948 after six months. The next,

Abdol Hossein Hajir, the minister of finance in Qavam-Saltaneh's last cabinet, was by contrast a force to be reckoned with. He had gone to England in the early 1940s, it was said, to rescue Reza Shah's fortune—some £20 million to £30 million or more—which the British government had locked up until after the war. He had a dead eye, over which he wore a dark spectacle, and was cunning and universally unpopular. One of his deputies, Jalal Shadman, had also lost an eye, and it was whispered that together they peered at the world with just one pair.

Although Hajir's own views mirrored those of his predecessor, the Majles impressed upon him the need to start talks with AIOC, which he did. They got nowhere. The company, discounting the Majles, refused to improve conditions in the south or review its own accounting practices. It listened instead to the Shah, who, anxious to maintain his throne, tried to appease the British.

The breakdown of the talks ended Hajir's premiership, and he was made minister of court, where he remained extremely powerful until he was assassinated a year later. The new prime minister was the weak-kneed Sa'ed, who'd served as premier earlier in the forties.

In the Majles the voice of a new opposition orator emerged. Abbas Mirza Eskandari was from Hamadan, a prince of the Qajar family. My brother Abol Bashar and I had strongly supported his candidacy, and he often invited me to the Parliament's sessions. From my seat in the visitors gallery I watched him command his audience into silence by the sheer virtuosity of his speech, ridiculing the ministers for dragging their feet and demanding the immediate restoration of Iran's oil rights. In a parliament usually as tumultuous as the British House of Commons, I could hear my own heart beat in the tense pauses between his sentences. Fear of British retaliation haunted the government's corridors, he declared, turning its officials into cowards. It was time the ministers realized that it was their own people, not the British, who were their true masters.

In January 1949, when a second round of oil talks foundered, ten deputies presented a bill to cancel the AIOC concession outright. The Majles temporized, but angered by the company's inflexibility, the members established a commission to formalize Iran's complaints for the next round. Dr. Pirnia, promoted to undersecretary of finance, was assigned to head up the commission. At the same time, foreign legal experts were hired to present their views.

As the hearings progressed, it became clear that one of the main points of irritation for the Majles was the concession's sixty-year extension to 1993. Originally Reza Shah had adamantly opposed extension, and the early drafts in 1933 had not contained such a clause. Then, at the last minute, it had been included.

On January 25, 1949, the hearings erupted in turmoil. Seyyed Hassan Taqizadeh, retired from his ambassadorial post in London and now a member of Parliament, was on the witness stand. Confronting him was Eskandari, snarling as he paced back and forth on his short legs before the dais. Quoting liberally from the Koran and Persian literature and constructing his arguments with the power of a Demosthenes, he brought the hearings to a climax, battering Taqizadeh for his role in signing the 1933 Concession. "Why," he bellowed, "as minister of finance under Reza Shah, did you sign knowing it contained a sixty-year extension?"

I was lunching at Victoria's that afternoon, and I headed through snow flurries to the Qajar palace she'd inherited from her father, Sarameh Doleh. As usual, there were many people chatting around the fire in the salon, for Victoria was the wittiest, most intelligent hostess in town. She had a talent for engineering introductions, which made her one of Tehran's best power brokers. She was telling a story as I came in, opening her arm in a wide arc, and as she did so, she caught my eye. I found her enchanting. She was not a classic beauty, but she had an allure, the seductive appeal of a woman who dresses exquisitely, listens well, and speaks with consummate sense. People trusted her, for she was neither a gossip nor a fool. What made her so special was her grasp of the importance of honor. "What is honor?" asks Falstaff in Shakespeare's *Henry IV*. Victoria, the daughter of Sarameh-Doleh, knew.

Victoria and I had been friends since childhood. Her husband, Hassan Akbar, was a clever, gregarious man, beloved in his own right, and one of the young hawks in the Majles. That day he burst through the door, almost incoherent with excitement.

Taqizadeh's testimony had shaken the Parliament up to the rafters, he announced. Badgered by Eskandari, he publicly admitted that he'd signed the concession under duress. "Feared for his life," snickered Akbar, gulping down the drink a servant handed him as he stripped off his snow-covered overcoat. " 'No one could stand against the will of the Almighty Ruler,' Taqizadeh whined," Akbar said, laughing. "What a condemnation! He was like a person going to the *kishish* [confessional] and admitting all his sins."

"It's the end of the concession," shouted Ali Dashti, another member of Parliament, as he came into the room.

"And a good thing too," said the bucktoothed Abdollah Daftari, a minister and ex-director of the Central Bank, swinging his pinched head around like a camel.

"The Majles was a madhouse," continued Akbar, signaling his wife to move us into lunch. "An absolute madhouse. Taqizadeh revealed that the British 'on the last day' appeared with the proposed extension and then threatened to walk out unless it was accepted. No doubt they told Reza Shah 'Sign, or else. . . .' The next time they did that, of course, he refused, and they kicked him out. The Majles is calling for blood. The AIOC is going to be scrambling. If the guy who signed it admitted he was forced into it, well! Old Northcroft . . ."

"Northcroft?" asked Daftari's extraordinarily beautiful wife.

"Yes, my dear lady, Northcroft," answered Akbar, absentmindedly raising her hand to his lips. "He's the local director of Anglo-Iranian. He will be shaking in his bed. And he'll get Taqizadeh to retract the testimony. Taqizadeh is part of the British clique after all, the lily-livered bastard!"

"This is war," growled the ex–prime minister Ali Soheili, his jowls shaking as he sat down heavily in the chair opposite me at the table. "No telling what will come of this. *Aval cha-ra hekan, had menarre-ra bedozd*—first dig the well to hide it in, then steal the minaret. We're acting too soon. We're going to get stuck holding the minaret. The British will retaliate. They always do. We will end up paying—and we will pay dearly."

PROMOTION

As Akbar had expected, Taqizadeh backpedaled the next day, claiming his words had been misconstrued. No matter, the concession had been thrown into question.

Dr. Pirnia and I worked feverishly putting together a roster of points to discuss with the foreign experts when they arrived—Gilbert Gidel, president of the Academy of International Law in The Hague, and Jean Rousseau, an accountant recommended by the French government.

Meanwhile, Dr. Pirnia's promotion had left a gap at the Finance Ministry. Every day as I rushed past the open doorway of his old office I eyed the empty room. Often I went in and used the files. For one month, and then another, the position remained open. Even so I knew I didn't have a chance. The family was under a cloud, my own defeat in Kermanshah still fresh in people's minds. Mossadeq, meanwhile, though out of Parliament, was rallying together what was looking more and more like a nationalist party and, at every flex of the Shah's new muscle, becoming more critical of the court.

It came as a surprise, therefore, when I was asked by a friend of the family's, a lawyer and member of Parliament, why I had not been appointed to the post. "You know how it is, people are afraid of our name," I told him. "Mozzafar and Maryam have made us even more of a liability. It's rumored the Shah is against me. My minister, I'm sure, doesn't want to risk it."

He laughed. "Nonsense," he said. "What is today? Monday? I'll be seeing His Majesty tomorrow and will arrange an audience. Be ready to see him later on in the week."

That Wednesday I received a call summoning me to the court the following day. I was told to wear a morning suit.

The Shah received me in his office in the small summer palace of Sa'adabad. I kissed his hand and remained standing, according to protocol, feeling extremely nervous. Not owning a morning suit, I'd had to borrow one from a friend's father, who turned out to be a good deal shorter than I. The only way I could keep the trouser legs over my shoes was to bend my knees. This made me very unsteady, and I worried throughout the audience that I'd suddenly forget and stand up straight, shamelessly exposing my ankles to my sovereign. The Shah too remained standing, with all the poise and arrogance of a monarch accustomed to receiving jittery subjects in borrowed morning suits.

He began by asking me questions, first about our estates, then about my younger brother Jamshid, a classmate of his from elementary school. At last he turned to the purpose of my visit.

Carefully I told him that the position of director general for petroleum and concessions had been vacant for some months and mentioned his reported hostility toward my appointment. He looked surprised. He said he did not even know that I worked in the Ministry of Finance. "Why should I be against your nomination?" he asked. "Consider it arranged."

I walked out of the audience with half-bent knees, unconvinced that the Shah would lift a finger.

I was wrong to doubt him. Two days later an order from the minister was delivered to my office. The Shah had kept his word. As of April 1949 I was the new director general of petroleum, concessions, and mines.

A SHOOTING

My new position conferred more status, but the job I had just taken on was a bitter one. My files contained the truth about AIOC's accounting practices—the very statistics the public was clamoring for—and it could not have been more sordid. But as Dr. Pirnia had too often discovered, the government was not willing to force the issue. Many ministers were afraid of British reprisals and considered it their job to keep the Majles in check. At the time I was hot-blooded and thought them unpatriotic. Later I came to understand that they were probably right. If we protested too loudly, AIOC could have stopped paying us the £7 million a year we depended on so much. They were the masters—just as the United States is in the Gulf today.

The Shah too was right to be afraid and, with the army behind him, went to some lengths to restrain the anti-British groundswell. But he was young and inexperienced, and his tactics were heavy-handed. Soon there were attacks in the press and protests in the street accusing him of being nothing more than a servant of the British Empire.

Then suddenly, on February 4, 1949, all criticism ended. As the Shah alighted from his car at the entrance of Tehran University, he was shot and wounded.* The country went into a state of shock. The would-be assassin, himself immediately gunned down by the Shah's bodyguards, was accused of being a Communist. The Tudeh Party was banned. My sister Maryam's new husband, Noureddin Kianouri, was imputed to have been one of the masterminds of the operation. Overnight they and their friends were forced into hiding. The mollah Seyyed Kashani was exiled, his effect on the populace considered too incendiary.

The Shah considered his escape a sign of divine intercession and became more confident after the incident. In April, encouraged by Minister of Court Hajir, he ordered the Majles to amend the Constitution to give him more power. Now he could dissolve Parliament—giving him control over the cabinet and prime minister. At the same time he decided to convene the senate, a body that was described in the Constitution but had not been seated since the first Parliament in 1906. Half the senators were to be elected, while the other half were appointed by the Shah. This gave the Shah enormous power over national policies—including the politics of oil—for the Senate had to approve all acts passed by the Majles.

Qavam-Saltaneh, who was traveling through Europe with his niece, re-acted strongly when he heard the news. From Deauville, a French seaside resort, he wrote two moving, historical letters, which in his exquisite hand admonished his sovereign for going against the law of the Constitution. "The trend throughout the world is toward democracy," he wrote. "You are moving our country into a dictatorship."[1]

For the Shah it wasn't a question of dignity or honesty—or democracy. It was a question of power. The Shah's ruthlessness—more polished and

---

*Ironically it was a Qajar prince, Nader Arasteh, who threw himself in front of the as-sassin to protect the Shah. The Shah never acknowledged his act of bravery, resentful of his lineage despite the fact that the man had saved his life.

less consistent than his father's—kept him on the throne for almost forty years. His dismissal of great statesmen such as Qavam-Saltaneh and later General Zahedi, after both were publicly lauded for their service to the country, cast grave doubts on the Shah's integrity. But was he wrong? Every time he loosened his hold, he was nearly overthrown. When he allowed even an iota of liberty, his authority was challenged. There was no middle ground. Constitutional monarchy doesn't exist in the third world. He chose oppression for his own survival. Would I have done the same? Wouldn't anyone in Iran? I've often wondered.

A TALE OF ROBBERY

On the day of the assassination attempt Neville Gass, one of AIOC's London-based directors, arrived in Tehran to resume negotiations. This time the Iranian government was prepared to confront him. The list Dr. Pirnia and I had drawn up contained twenty-five points. Many of the issues had been discussed, but a full roster had never been compiled before. Nor had the legality of each point been examined by foreign experts.

When Dr. Pirnia and I presented the document to Gidel and Rousseau, they found that in practice AIOC was ignoring many of the stipulations of the 1933 Concession and that it was being exploitive and at times blatantly dishonest—a judgment distressingly reminiscent of Armitage-Smith's almost thirty years earlier.

From beginning to end there were discrepancies, some caused by the war, others by England's abiding conviction that its overseas holdings existed purely for its own pleasure. The Boston Tea Party of 1773 had taught it nothing. England's demands remained exorbitant and its accounting abusive.

Iran's complaints were straightforward. First, there was the gold clause, which in 1933 pegged our earnings per ton to the price of gold—in essence an antidevaluation measure. But in the eight years since the beginning of the war the Bank of England had fixed the price of gold at the artificial rate of £8.40 per ounce, almost £3 ($8) less than the world market rate. The result was that the Iranian government was being paid only 7 shillings a ton when it should have been receiving 12.

The company's treatment of taxes was equally manipulative. First, AIOC refused to distribute our share of profits before paying its taxes to the British Exchequer. This meant in essence that the British government was taxing the Iranian government, a breach of international law. Second, since the war had begun, Whitehall had levied a surtax on all corporate profits, which AIOC was paying without first dividing out Iran's share. Iran was thus being made to pay for Britain's war effort. The amounts in question were staggering. In 1933 the company had paid roughly equal taxes to the Iranian and British governments. By 1949 the figures were £1 million to Iran, £28 million to Britain!²

And there was more. AIOC was supposed to pay 20 percent of its profits to Iran, which in 1939 came to £1,074,000. Each year profits had risen, and by 1949 the Iranian government was due £10.6 million. But since the beginning of the war the British government had frozen profit distributions by all U.K. companies to 1939 levels, requiring whatever came in above that to be placed in a kitty called "general reserves"—to be used either for war expenditures or reconstruction. Since 1940 Iran's profit increases had disappeared into "general reserves," and we were still receiving just £1,074,000 a year.

Because the British government owned 51 percent of the company, these were sticky issues. The division of profits and taxes paid to the British Exchequer was hazy, and a large portion of the funds in "general reserves" had already been spent.

Then there were the old conflicts that had plagued the D'Arcy Concession. One was the deep secrecy in which the company kept its books. They were open to Britain's government because it had two members on the AIOC board; since Iran had no representatives on the board, the books were closed to us. This made it impossible for us to check profit and revenue figures and hence to really know what our share should be. It also gave the British negotiators ample opportunity to accuse our officials of being ill-informed.

Of a different nature but just as egregious was the generous discount AIOC continued to grant to the British Admiralty. In 1949 the price of oil on the open market was £3 per ton (about $8, or $1.50 a barrel). But the Admiralty paid only 10 shillings a ton (or just 20 cents a barrel). This cut deeply into the company's overall profits and meant that for more than thirty years Iran had subsidized British defense.

Another deal, struck in 1947, was equally unfair to Iran. To pay off a war debt London owed Washington, AIOC's chairman, Sir William Fraser, had agreed to sell oil at a discount to a number of American companies operating in the Middle East. The debt had nothing to do with us, and yet once again our income was being used for British national purposes.

Unfortunately the financial discrepancies were not the only area of disagreement. In matters of practical management the company was failing miserably to live up to the terms of the concession—at great financial and political cost to the Iranian government. AIOC refused to pay royalties on any of the oil products consumed in its operations. And, it was flaring (or otherwise wasting) the natural gas released as a by-product of drilling, disregarding our repeated requests to reinject it into the fields or to pipe it to nearby towns for use as fuel for heating and cooking.

The company also continued to disregard the Iranization clause, which specified that Persian workers be trained and placed in positions of rank and responsibility. Meanwhile AIOC imported workers, and at one point the Ministry of Finance had applications for three thousand visas for unskilled workers from Palestine—a British colony with a high rate of unemployment.

The final two points of the twenty-five were perhaps the most crucial: the computation of royalties and the length of the concession. Since 1933 the price of oil on the world market had risen substantially, but our income had stayed fixed at 4 shillings a ton. Iran was asking for £1 a ton, one third the current market price, to be adjusted every fifteen years to reflect the market. Better yet would have been to halve the profits, much as Venezuela was doing with a number of American oil companies. We would take a percentage of royalties in kind (i.e., oil) and share the risks of marketing. The company would not then need to guarantee a yearly minimum payment and could dispense with the convoluted computation of royalty tax and profit distribution. With such an arrangement we favored continuing the sixty-year extension. Otherwise we wanted it reduced.

This option—the equal sharing of profits and risk—was entirely ignored by our British counterparts; later they claimed that their offers were better. Finally, when it was far too late, the BBC claimed that the British had offered such a plan and that we'd rejected it. I never witnessed such a proposal. The irony is that if they had considered it at this stage, all the other points would have resolved themselves and AIOC would probably still exist.

As it was we had two other extremely difficult problems to resolve. One was the "subsidiary companies" issue—the clause Nosrat-Doleh had gone to bat for in the 1920s. Despite Armitage-Smith's report in 1919, AIOC was not paying us income on the subsidiary companies, claiming that our rights were confined to properties actually on Iranian territory. Yet since 1923 AIOC had not raised a cent of outside capital, even though it had undergone enormous expansion. Although we had no access to the books, it was no secret that AIOC made a practice of churning profits back into the company to underwrite what had reached close to one hundred other ventures. By 1949 the company's worldwide assets were valued at £254 million (despite the low rates offered to the Admiralty and the U.S. oil companies). Only £30 million of that was actually in Iran. The rest, funded by Persian oil, lay beyond our borders. Though we were not privy to the details of these holdings, particularly those in Iraq, Qatar, and Kuwait, the concession guaranteed us profits from these ventures. Sadly this was poorly understood by our own politicians, including Mossadeq, and in the future turmoil over nationalization they failed to fight for these companies—to the enormous detriment of Iran (and Britain's great gain).

The last point had to do with royalties. AIOC was robbing us, we contended, and to prove it we computed our royalties using the method AIOC had adopted for its own subsidiary, Iraqi Petroleum Company, as well as that used by Creole Oil, a subsidiary of Standard Oil in Venezuela. Instead of the £7 million we actually received in 1947, we should have earned, according to the Iraqi method of calculation, almost £12 million;[3] the Creole method of calculation would have given us £22 million!

In 1947 AIOC made a profit of £40 million. Our share was £7 million. The British government and the company pocketed £33 million between the two of them!

Little did we know, as we prepared our brief, that Foreign Secretary Ernest Bevin was himself unhappy about the standoff between AIOC and the Iranian government. After meeting with my brother-in-law Mohsen Khan, who had been appointed ambassador to London as Taqizadeh's successor, Bevin sent a long note to the secretary of the Exchequer, in which he stated in no uncertain terms that the situation was intolerable. "The division of profits is inequitable," he observed. "We are not on good ground taking the Persian Government's profits and withholding their share . . . by limiting the amounts the Company can distribute. In general, our attitude looks . . . imperialistic."[4]

Nonetheless, the gulf between the two sides could not have been greater. Within three weeks the talks had broken down.

THE TALE OF 50/50

Iran's fight with AIOC was not unique. Governments and companies all over the world were fighting over rights and revenues. The maturing oil industry was proving wildly profitable, offering a better return to its delighted shareholders than gold, diamonds, or any other natural resource ever had. By the late forties a barrel of oil was selling for $2.50; royalties, production costs, shipping and handling, and taxes rarely exceeded 75 cents. The result: $1.75 pure profit on every barrel sold.[5] And millions of barrels were being sold every day, oil being, despite its enormous profit margin, the cheapest of all fuels.

Most of that profit went straight into company coffers, thanks to old arrangements that reflected on the one hand the heavy investment and risk the companies had initially taken, and on the other the low value of the property in what had been isolated, often useless regions of backward countries.

By the forties risk was no longer a factor. The huge costs of prospecting, setting up refineries, and establishing marketing networks had been repaid, and new investments were rapidly being underwritten by the enormous revenues. At the same time the land—those stark, empty ranges—had become extremely valuable. What had been equitable contracts had become anachronisms.

Knowing they had a good deal, the companies were loath to change the terms, claiming that what was legal was just. International law was on their side. The concessions, signed by all parties, stretched well beyond the forties without provisions for change. Representing not only the superior technological prowess of the West but also the clout of their governments—England, the United States, Holland, and France—the companies felt secure and smug. After all, they argued, thanks to their industry they had brought unexpected riches to the poor countries they straddled, not to mention employment, infrastructure, and global recognition. And so they complimented themselves for "happily combining a sense of public service with the fruits of huge profits."[6]

The first signal that realpolitik would haunt these huge multinational companies and shake their very foundations came in Mexico in 1938. Nationalistic fervor was running high. Disagreements over royalties, taxes, and production levels had intensified after a buildup of almost twenty years. To Shell and Standard Oil of New Jersey, along with a handful of other American companies, Mexico was still a colonial backwater. More concerned about setting a global precedent than about conditions in the oil slums, they ignored the strikes that wracked the industry and refused to compromise. When the government ordered them to meet worker demands for better housing and higher wages, they said no. To their astonishment the next morning they found themselves catapulted out of the country.

Yet President Lázaro Cárdenas's extraordinary decision quickly turned into a fiasco when the companies closed ranks and refused to buy a single drop of Mexican oil (an experience Iran would too soon share). It took PEMEX (Petroleum of Mexico) thirty years to get back on track. A preferable solution was clearly for the companies and the producer nations to work together so that both could receive roughly equitable returns. Such was the conclusion the U.S. government drew from the Mexican debacle, and although the Mexicans themselves never reaped the rewards of their bold stand, other nations hosting U.S. oil companies did.

This thinking came into play first in Venezuela—and with great success. Venezuelan oil had become increasingly critical in the wake of Mexico's dwindling production. In 1946 almost 80 percent of Europe's oil came from the Western Hemisphere, much of that from Venezuela. By 1948 the insatiable thirst for cars in the United States turned it for the first time into a net importer, and its closest and best source was just across the Caribbean in Venezuela. A country of coffee and cocoa before the discovery of oil, Venezuela had in the 1930s turned into a single-industry economy wholly dependent on petroleum. When the government decided to exercise greater control over its most critical source of income during World War II, the U.S. government offered support and encouragement. The two experts sent to help keep negotiations on track were Herbert Hoover, Jr., and A. A. Curtice. The year was 1943, exactly twelve months before the same two men would come to Iran.

Representing the Venezuelan government was Juan Pérez Alfonzo, a geologist and economist with extraordinary vision. Pérez Alfonzo's solid grasp of the realities of the oil market led to an agreement that would be a landmark in concessionary arrangements and a standard used by all future American oil companies. In effect, Pérez Alfonzo worked out a deal in which the government's taxes, royalties, and currency conversion earned about the same amount per barrel for Venezuela as it did for the companies. Standard Oil of New Jersey's subsidiary, Creole, anxious to avoid a repeat of Mexico, willingly went along. Shell, less enthusiastic, came around after U.S. undersecretary of state Sumner Wells leaned on the British government to bring pressure on the company.

The result, called 50/50, changed the oil business. There was a harmony to it, a sense of equal partnership that made for stability. For the first time the conflicting demands of economics and politics, of private enterprise and national pride were balanced. Within two years 90 percent of Creole's workforce was Venezuelan. Labor unrest and its accompanying complaints about living conditions, bad wages, wasted human resources, and all the other trappings of exploitation disappeared as if by magic. The Venezuelans now felt that they were working for themselves. The deal also gave their government enough money—six times what it had earned in 1942— to invest in what it now considered its own industry.

The enlightened Pérez Alfonzo added one more codicil that would have serious ramifications beyond the working relationship between country and company. Rather than taking all the royalties in dollars, he arranged for 25 percent, 36 million barrels at the time, to be paid in kind—which

Venezuela then sold directly on the open market. It was a revolutionary move, since the sale of oil had never before been handled by anyone other than the companies. Venezuela earned between 11 and 15 cents more per barrel than the average market price that first year.[7] When the next year it hinted that it might like all its royalties in kind, the companies blanched and were forced to up their rate. No longer could the price of oil be set through clandestine agreement. At last it had gone public, and its value was set by market forces.

Over the next few years 50/50 moved to the Middle East. Deals were struck in Saudi Arabia, Kuwait, and what was known as the Neutral Zone—a shared territory of vast oil reserves located between the two. Except for a minority position in Kuwait held by AIOC, all the companies were American. AIOC, like Shell in Venezuela, came around after pressure was brought by the U.S. government—but only after a sharp outburst by its chairman, Sir William Fraser.

The U.S. government's decision not to get involved was the secret to the success of these negotiations. By refraining from putting pressure on the market, the banks, or the politics of the countries involved, it allowed the two sides to strike a lasting arrangement that served U.S. national interests better in the end than any forceful government wangling could have—a fact that Britain's interference in Iran proved all too strikingly.

Unlike the United States, postwar Britain was still mired in the old colonial order, and countries working with British enterprises fared less well than those working with Americans. Britain was the only Allied power to fight from the beginning of the war to the end, and the conflict left it devastated. It was a poor and ruined country as it looked up from victory in May 1945.

The Marshall Plan brought new hope to England. But it was soon followed by the loss of India in August. Within months, despite Churchill's ranting that he was not going to auction off the British Empire, Palestine too was spun off. These were bitter dismemberments, jolting to the country's self-image as the nerve center of a vast empire.

But the sacrifices were necessary, according to Whitehall, to ensure the survival of the empire's other prizes: Suez and above all the Iranian oil fields. To the sheared and disheveled Britain of 1948, they were its due not just for their emotional value but because of the cold, hard cash they brought in.

Coal, Britain's old bulwark, was no longer a substitute for oil. Not only was it unable to power the cars and trucks that flooded the highways, but its higher cost made it less appealing to industry. Pit strikes and union battles further reduced its allure—industry upheavals sparked by the same maltreatment and low wages that were causing uprisings in the oil fields in Iran. While struggling with the labor unrest in England, the British government jealously collected the riches pouring in from Abadan, convinced that what it could not solve at home was not worth noticing abroad.

Dogged by a lack of convertible currency and fuel, Britain became completely dependent on AIOC. Not only did the company contribute half its revenues to the Exchequer, but it paid millions of pounds in taxes—not to mention the fuel it supplied the Admiralty. Very simply it became England's lifeline to the future. "Without the Middle East and its oil," Foreign Secretary Bevin observed, "[there is] no hope of our being able to achieve the standard of living at which we are aiming in Great Britain."[8] But though the revenues were prodigious, they were never enough.

Adding to London's discomfort was the debt it owed the United States for providing 80 percent of its oil during the war. It was to balance this debt that Sir William Fraser acquiesced on the 50/50 deal in Kuwait and signed a long-term contract with Socony and Standard Oil of New Jersey to sell them Iranian crude at below market prices.* The deal gave AIOC access to new European markets and the chance to join the sorority of six other megacompanies—Socony, Standard Oil of New Jersey, Socal, Gulf,

---

*The Kuwaiti situation was complicated by an astute discovery by King Saud next door in Saudi Arabia. American companies could deduct any income tax they had to pay to foreign governments from their U.S. tax bills (a law originally designed to give American companies a competitive edge in foreign markets). Capitalizing on this, Saudi Arabia began taxing Aramco the exact amount the company had hitherto been paying to the U.S. Internal Revenue Service. In 1949 the U.S. Treasury received $43 million in taxes from Aramco, and Saudi Arabia received $39 million in royalties. In 1951 King Saud collected $110 million in royalties *and* taxes, while the U.S. Treasury received only $6 million (Yergin, *The Prize*, page 446). When the same tactic was adopted by Kuwait a year later, AIOC, not having the benefit of such a law, was left holding the bag. After a similar deal was struck in Iraq in 1952, however, British Inland Revenue softened its position and allowed for compensatory tax credits.

Interestingly, allowing U.S. oil companies to write off their Saudi (and later Kuwaiti, Bahraini, and Iraqi) taxes in effect meant that the American taxpayer subsidized those countries to the tune of more than $50 million a year. In subsequent congressional hearings company lawyers pointed out that if such monies were not paid as "taxes," the U.S. foreign aid bill to those countries would have been much higher. To the U.S. executive branch, the "Golden Gimmick," as it came to be called, neatly sidestepped the need for congressional allocation of such funds and therefore any discussion of Arab versus Israeli aid. It seemed to be a case of having one's cake and eating it too, although it did mean the oil companies, as private enterprises, began, from the 1950s on, to serve as a direct arm of U.S. foreign policy—a position that accorded them power well beyond any other U.S. industry.

Texaco, and Shell—the famous "Seven Sisters,"* in forcing down the price of Middle Eastern oil.

Still Britain had neither enough dollars nor enough oil. Fully 20 percent of the Marshall Plan's aid was going to pay for fuel. By 1948 Prime Minister Clement Attlee realized that the only way to stay afloat was to devalue the pound.

THE CHAIRMAN'S VISIT

Sir William Fraser arrived in Tehran in May 1949 to revive the talks that had foundered in March. He brought with him a new contract, an addition to the 1933 Concession that was later called the Supplemental Agreement. It addressed three points: First, profits would be distributed before the deduction of British income tax—though there was no mention of rescinding the onerous surtax or compensating for the payout in previous years. Second, funds would no longer be funneled into the "general reserves," and 20 percent of what was left in the kitty would be paid to Iran as compensation. Third, the fixed royalty base would be raised to 6 shillings a ton (half what we were asking for), and the Iranian government could tax the company an extra half shilling per ton if it so wished. The problem of the gold clause remained unaddressed. The rest of the twenty-five points Iran had brought to the table were ignored.

Sir William Fraser was not an easy man to work with—a fact observed not only by the Iranians but by his own British counterparts in Whitehall. Glasgow-born, with a forbidding brogue and an austere manner, he was an obdurate negotiator who hated compromise. The Foreign Office files and Majles records are filled with his ultimatums, backed up by his unbending conviction that he alone knew how to handle affairs in Iran. To quote U.S. secretary of state Dean Acheson's remarks after it was all over, never had anyone "lost so much, so stupidly, and so fast."[9]

Fraser had been an oilman all his life and would hold the chairmanship of AIOC longer than anyone in the company's history. His father had owned the largest shale oil company in Scotland in the twenties, and when it, along with all the other Scottish shale oil companies, was acquired by AIOC, the young Fraser joined the company with a substantial block of shares and a reputation for knowing more about oil than anyone in the British Isles. By 1933 he was a member of the AIOC board and right-hand

*The first three would change names over the next few years to become Mobil, Exxon, and Chevron. AIOC would turn into British Petroleum, or BP, after Iran's nationalization.

man to Chairman John Cadman. One of his tasks was to formulate the 1933 Concession. When Cadman died suddenly in 1941, Fraser stepped in to fill his shoes.

The dour Scotsman, with his baleful glare and white wispy eyebrows, approached the job with the fastidiousness of a boarding school accountant, disavowing any knowledge or appreciation of politics. He seemed strangely blind to the fact that the war had in part been fought for energy control and that in its aftermath Britain's oil monopoly in the Middle East had been broken. In his view if England had lost its imperialist edge, AIOC had not, and he devoted his best efforts to reconstructing the past rather than preparing for the future. He considered the gentlemen of Whitehall meddlesome and kept them informed of events only insofar as it might persuade them to bolster the company's objectives. These aims did not include developing a better relationship with Iran. AIOC never worried about domestic stability in the way its American counterparts did, confident that if circumstances should dictate, the government would intervene militarily to protect British interests, either adding the oil fields to Iraq or dividing Iran in half. In his reports to Whitehall Fraser never failed to contend that his brainchild, the 1933 agreement, was more than generous and that the Iranians were ingrates.

It was with this attitude that he came to Tehran. He presented us with the Supplemental Agreement as a fait accompli. When Prime Minister Sa'ed suggested that the royalty proposed was inadequate, Fraser stated that the company would not add a penny more, then turned on his heel and flew home.

It was yet another ultimatum. The chairman even failed to present options that the British government itself had suggested. A memorandum circulated in the Foreign Office after his return noted, for example, that "Sir William Fraser has not as yet used the discretion we have given him to agree that . . . the sum placed to General Reserves should be . . . *before taxation,* which would give the Persian Government another £2 million annually."[10]

This was a discretion Fraser never would use. Instead he scoffed at the Iranians, informing the Foreign Office that "they're really only interested in more money" (as though the British government was not). Fraser then claimed he'd arranged it "so the Persians would suffer nothing from United Kingdom tax" and that he'd offered "the highest royalty payments in the Middle East."[11] Both were outright lies. The observation in the Foreign Office memo itself indicated a loss of £2 million a year to U.K. taxes; as for the royalty the deals in Kuwait and the Neutral Zone guaranteed more than £1 a ton.

Arbitration, it now seemed, was the only answer.

With the encouragement of the minister of finance, I contacted Mohsen Khan in London and asked him to suggest an appropriate legal expert who could give an opinion on Iran's rights, particularly concerning the income tax AIOC was paying to the British government. He recommended the highly respected barrister Sir Cyril Radcliffe, who swiftly handed down the opinion that Iran was being wronged and that the matter could be successfully brought before a British court.

The Shah, however, was concerned that even if the chance of losing was minuscule, a negative judgment would permanently undermine the government in the eyes of its people, leaving it helpless in any further negotiations. He therefore ordered the cabinet to accept the Supplemental Agreement and let the Majles decide whether to sign it into law.

Dr. Pirnia and I were the only members of the government to declare ourselves unequivocally against the agreement. Iran had no hand in writing it, we told the reporters who flooded into the ministry for interviews. It was submitted to us as a unilateral contract. At issue was not just how much or how little the Iranian government was going to be paid. The agreement also did not address—let alone resolve—outstanding disagreements over labor, gas flaring, and the Admiralty discount.

Yet, on July 17, 1949, all remnants of the triumph that had followed Taqizadeh's confession six months before were eclipsed as we witnessed the minister of finance, Abbasgoli Golshayan, a wise and honest man, unwillingly sign the Supplemental Agreement for the same reasons that Taqizadeh had put his grudging signature to the 1933 concession.

The agreement came to the floor of the Majles four days before its term was to expire. But the Majles, skeptical of its value, mounted a filibuster. After a series of windy speeches it closed without a vote, delaying the decision until the next Majles was seated.

The British were livid. As Neville Gass later admitted, it had been a "voluntary revision by the company primarily to take account of devaluation."[12] Now devaluation would take place before the Majles vote, revealing the Supplemental Agreement to be little better than a hoax.

On September 8, 1949, the pound sterling lost a third of its value against the dollar. Any gains offered by the Supplemental Agreement were wiped out—a point made by Prime Minister Sa'ed to Fraser at a meeting in London. Sa'ed also took the liberty of observing that the deal, even before devaluation, was less generous than Venezuela's 50/50. It was a series of half measures, which Sa'ed illustrated with statistics: Using 50/50, Iran would have earned £40 million in 1950; under the Supplemental Agreement's best scenario (37.5 percent of net profits) we would have earned £10 million less.

A DIRECTOR GENERAL'S TALE

By then the campaign was in full swing for the Sixteenth Majles. I didn't even bother running. Over the past few months I had gotten into scrapes with both my minister and the press—and had had a close shave with the court. I felt lucky to have my job.

The first incident occurred in September 1949. Every year AIOC sent a contingent of Iranian students to England to study with the understanding that upon their return they would work for the company. As director general of petroleum I thought it important to give them some contact with the government, so I invited them to Tehran for tea at the ministry. It was the first time such an invitation had been extended, and I prepared my speech carefully, knowing I was setting a precedent for what I hoped would be a good relationship between the government and future alumni of the oil company. The boys had each passed a battery of tests in the selection process, and they were a bright bunch. Among the group was Parviz Mina, who later became a powerful director of Iran's nationalized oil company.

"You are not just being sent to the United Kingdom for book learning," I told the group of scrubbed, eager faces that afternoon, "but to see British society and civilization as well." I gave them what I hoped was an encouraging look. "And don't forget to amuse yourselves, for that will teach you how to live, which will be useful to you—and to us—when you return to Iran. As Hafez says: 'Take advantage of this measured night / For after our own day closes / The promenading world will spin on / And many nights and noons will follow.' "

The next day the newspapers tore me apart. "Look at the brother of Nosrat-Doleh," they screeched, "telling our students to amuse themselves in England!"

Minister of finance Golshayan refrained from making any comment in the wake of the outcry. He had in fact ignored my existence completely since my promotion, peeved perhaps that I had gone over his head to get the appointment. Not long afterward, however, he sent me a summons late on a Thursday afternoon, just as I was heading out to Hamadan for the rest of the weekend.*

I knew why he'd called me and, canceling my trip, presented myself with great excitement the next morning at the ministry. A few weeks earlier I had discovered that Venezuela had a double standard of currency ex-

---

*Friday is the Moslem holy day, so the weekend in Iran is on Thursday and Friday; the new week begins on Saturday.

change: the regular bank rate and an "oil rate." Creole, Gulf, and Shell used the oil rate to buy bolivars, the Venezuelan currency, for their working capital inside the country, and that rate *cost more dollars per bolivar than the regular rate.* During the first year of my tenure as director general, AIOC was exchanging £1.5 million a month into local currency for operating expenses. If we could institute a similar system—i.e., charge more pounds sterling per rial than we were currently charging—we could earn millions more a year just in exchange. Excited by this prospect, I had sent a note to the minister explaining the concept and suggesting that we call the difference "oil currency."

As I waited for his call that Friday morning I felt charged. I paced back and forth across my office picturing the course of the upcoming interview as I rehearsed my arguments, already relishing the look on his face as I showed him the documents and figures.

But the morning wore on, and he did not contact me. Nor did he contact me the next day . . . or the next. Finally, on Monday, I was called into his office. He remained seated when I entered, leaving me standing like a schoolboy in front of his desk.

He was furious. "Who suggested this note?" he barked. "Don't tell me it was your idea!"

I looked at him dumbfounded. I was annoyed and stared straight into his black-rimmed glasses, refusing to drop my gaze.

"Take it back immediately and tear it up," he growled. "And delete it from the registry of ministry memoranda. I want no record of this left hanging about." Golshayan was a dark-complexioned man, and his face looked like thunder. "I am being helpful to you," he went on, returning my unwavering stare. "Your brother Prince Firouz was once in my position, and he lost his life refusing to conform. You, young man, had better watch yourself. Now, get out."

As warnings go that was a blunt one, and I stalked from the room with my pride very much wounded. With thinking like that, no wonder we never got anywhere. I was mortified by my government. What were we, a bunch of moth-eaten donkeys?

My mother doused my anger by pointing out that I was lucky not to have been fired. "Don't underestimate Golshayan," she said. "He's been around a long time—he was there when Nosrat-Doleh was minister. He's capable and honest. If he dismissed your idea out of hand, it was probably because it didn't have a chance. Just because you're right doesn't mean he's wrong."

Ah, my wise mother. I was to have many run-ins with Golshayan, and each time he surprised me. He was a master of the oriental sleight of hand.

His avuncular, toe-the-line mentality exasperated me, as my cocky enthusiasm clearly exasperated him. Yet the very differences that made us clash contributed to a grudging mutual respect. My uncle Ahmad Khan was right; I was constantly galloping out ahead of the caravan on my stallion, and Golshayan was always reining me back. Once he sent around a classified report by an anonymous English oil expert labeled SECRET, PERSONAL, CONFIDENTIAL, FOR HIS MAJESTY'S MINISTERS ONLY. It was the famous brief that described AIOC as "a sovereign state masquerading as a tradesman." I jokingly scribbled "Burn Before Reading" at the top before returning it to his office. Golshayan fired me on the spot. He couldn't believe my lack of respect and cavalier attitude toward the confidence he'd displayed in sharing such a secret document.

Ten days later he called me back. I agreed on one condition, young scoundrel that I was: that I get an official car.

"The son of Farman Farma now wants a car," he said sarcastically, pursing his lips and calling his secretary.

Mumbling and shuffling, the secretary at last whispered, "Sir, but there is no car available."

"Then he shall have mine!"

Suddenly I felt ashamed. "I can't take your car," I said. *"Arz mikonam—* forgive me—but it's not the car that's important, it's the prestige."

"Ahh," nodded Golshayan sagely. "A chauffeur with a cap from the ministry is what you desire. And that is what you will get. And he shall drive you about with all the prestige imaginable in your own car."

A few weeks later, toward the end of May, a hitherto secret document appeared in the press. It was signed by the manipulative Hajir when he was minister of finance in 1947 and addressed to the Anglo-Iranian Oil Company. To my horror the letter expressed full satisfaction with a set of annual accounts presented during Qavam-Saltaneh's premiership. Written in Hajir's exquisite hand, it was a unilateral declaration that settled all the claims that the government and his minister had been making against AIOC.

As I read the letter my heart dropped. It was a betrayal—another self-inflicted setback—and one that explained why company officials had so stiffly refused to discuss any accounts prior to 1948. In one sweep of the pen it wiped out all Iran's contentions that the company had cooked the books since the signing of the 1933 Concession and hence owed us vast sums of money. Thanks to Hajir we couldn't collect a cent of the millions owed for the years between 1933 and 1947.

My blood racing, I realized that I would be the one blamed for leaking the letter. I had all the files. No one would believe that I had never seen this odious document before. With growing anger I remembered the time Hajir had offered me a job. It had been Qavam-Saltaneh's idea to promote me, and with ill grace, Hajir, as minister of finance, had dangled the position of undersecretary before my nose. I'd turned him down. I didn't trust him. He was a cynic, the epitome of the plump, smiling, wizardly vizier cut straight from the pages of the *Arabian Nights*. Never have I met anyone so Machiavellian. Under his tutelage the Shah not only repossessed all the Crown lands that had reverted to the state after his father was deposed, but he also acquired more constitutional power than any shah since Mozzafar-edin before the constitutional revolution of 1906. Hajir could be witty when he chose to be, a strong speaker when it suited him, but mostly he preferred the role of old-style courtier, manipulating the strings from the shadows. Had he lived, he would have dominated Iranian politics for years. His one private passion was Hafez, so I'd quoted him a passage from Hafez when I'd rejected the job: " 'Come, the prosperity of this workshop will not decline, either through your devotions or my sins' "

How could I know his devotions would condemn us all?

I drove home wondering how I was going to rescue the situation this time. Nothing came to mind. Cursing, I turned the car past the police station.

Almost as I passed it, I saw the chief of police, General Saffari, open the door and start down the steps. I slammed on the brakes and backed up. General Saffari had visited Kermanshah and spoken with me and my uncle during the tribal disturbances. I rolled down the window and called out a greeting. We hadn't seen each other since, and he immediately walked over, slight and proper in his uniform, his face breaking into a big smile.

After a few pleasantries I asked him if we might have a private chat. "Of course," he said, climbing in. Briefly I outlined what had happened. "What I suspect," I said, summing up, "is that my boss, Minister of Finance Golshayan, leaked the letter to spite Hajir, not realizing that I would take the heat."

General Saffari shook his head in disbelief but promised to look into it. We agreed to meet the next day.

"You are very lucky," he told me in his amusing Rashti accent when I walked through his door the following afternoon. "Yesterday at the Council of Ministers, everybody was accusing you of the leak. 'Not so fast,' I told them. 'What possible motive could he have as head of the Oil Department in getting such a document published?' Then I explained what a setback this was for the current negotiations. But the coup de grâce was when I told them to look at the reference numbers. 'Those,' I said, 'are the reference numbers of the minister himself!' "

He gave me a triumphant pat on the back. "Not only are you lucky," he chortled, "but you did me a good turn as well. The ministers thought I had been most diligent and praised me for checking up on the source of the leak so fast."

DR. MOAVEN'S SECOND WIFE

At the adrenaline-filled age of thirty-two, I saw such sparring with fortune as simply an occupational hazard. The Kermanshah elections had reduced my innocence but not my ambition. I was healthy and rich and had a budding career. And I had made a pact with myself at my father's grave that I intended to keep. Yet just days after my visit to the cemetery, I was thrown into a conflict that by the summer of 1949 was squeezing me between two of the most powerful forces of Iranian society. Again I faced jail—only this time with my eyes wide-open and with a sentence stretching into uncounted years.

It was my first lesson in the laws of God.

The problem started in Kermanshah. Another candidate in that ill-fated election, a surgeon named Dr. Moaven, invited me to tea a week before election day. I'd never liked Moaven much; he was a cad who had destroyed a school once, saying the peasants should be kept ignorant. Unfortunately many of the elite thought that way. He was married to Mansureh Vosugh, one of the eight daughters of Vosugh-Doleh and a sister of Maheen Taba's.

When I arrived at the house, Moaven pointed to a woman sitting on the floor wearing a prayer veil. "My wife," he said.

"Your wife?" I asked in surprise, seeing a woman who was tall and dark and *not* Mansureh Vosugh.

"Yes," he said, without further comment.

The election took place a few days later. The Shah sent down a general named Kia to stop my bid, but Moaven was luckier and was elected with British backing. The next morning, however, as he headed to Tehran, he was hit by a truck and killed.

Some months later I had just come home from work when a woman was announced at the door. It turned out to be the "wife" Moaven had pointed to in Kermanshah. She had a baby on her arm, a son, but because there were no official marriage documents, she told me, she could not register the boy as Moaven's heir.

The Moslem religion, however, provided her with a weapon: *shahed-e aadel,* the word of a reliable witness. She had drawn up a list of ten such people and brought it to a judge. The only one on the list the judge considered a just and honorable man was me. "Will you act as my witness?" she asked.

I didn't ponder long. "No," I said, then showed her the door.

I was not going to go against the daughter of Vosugh-Doleh. And it wouldn't just be her. It would be all eight of them—that powerful, beautiful, sexy sorority married to half the great families of Iran. Many of their husbands were my cousins. Going against them would be suicide.

A few days later I came down to breakfast and saw the woman sitting across from my mother. It was cold outside, a fire burned in the grate, and I could smell the hot bread on the plates. "This woman has come to us for help," said my mother. "You are the only one who can offer her her reprieve. I know you have refused her already, but I'd like you to think again about your duty to a woman who has no one else to back her up. If she is in the right, you cannot abandon her. As a mother I ask you to reconsider."

I shot the woman a cold look and turned on my heel, leaving the hot bread on the table. That afternoon I decided to go see the judge.

The woman was clever and had chosen a judge well known to my family. He was a *haakemeh sharee,* a judge of Koranic law, which operated as a separate stream of jurisprudence alongside the state's code of civil law. In a long-winded speech he laid out my options, saying I was under no legal obligation to make a statement. "But should you decide to make a statement," he said, "it is final and you cannot ever retract it. Should you retract it, the sentence is jail." Then he quoted Saadi: " 'The judge, receiving your affirmation, will not receive your negation.' "

"Think about it," he counseled. His turban was the size of a modern-day satellite dish. "I have been in this post since your brother Nosrat-Doleh put me here twenty years ago. I must warn you that should you decide to speak, it will be a great liability to you in the future."

"No, I'm not going to think about it," I said, already sick of the whole affair. "I'll make a statement now and sign it and finish with it."

He nodded. "The question you must answer is this: Did you hear this man, Dr. Moaven, say this woman was his wife?"

"Yes," I answered, with a twinge of horror. "I was so surprised, I even repeated, 'Your wife?' and he said, 'Yes.' "

I read the statement. The woman could now lay claim to half of Moaven's estates, for according to the Koran daughters receive half of the maintenance of sons—and Moaven had two daughters by his first wife. The son would also now receive the legitimate name of his father. "I would like to make signature conditional on one point," I said. "I never want the woman to call me again for anything whatsoever." The judge nodded, assuring me he would make that clear.

I took up the pen and signed the paper. Never has a signature brought me so much trouble.

Mansureh Vosugh was a close friend of Princess Shams's, the Shah's older sister. Both had converted to Catholicism. It was from Princess Shams that I received my first call. She invited me for tea. Shams was more demure than her sister, Ashraf, shyer and very lovely. I had met her some time before in Abadan when she'd come down as the head of a charity visit. "The woman is a nurse at the Najmieh Hospital," she told me. "She is a common woman [Wasn't Shams's father once a common man? I thought] with no right to Moaven's inheritance. At the same time your statement has deprived his first wife of what is rightfully hers." She proffered me a salver of cracknel candy. "I want you to revoke your statement," she said sweetly. "My friend is suffering. Besides, as a Catholic she feels doubly wronged, for she does not believe in the laws under which you have done this."

I had difficulty saying yes or no and left the palace in confusion.

A few months passed. I began to hope that the whole affair had blown over. Then I got a call from Ernest Perron.

Perron was Swiss and one of the luminaries of the Tehran social scene. He had met the Shah when they were both students at Le Rosey in Switzerland and had accompanied him back to Tehran as a protégé. He lived in a room at the palace and was probably the Shah's closest friend. I'd met him at a dinner and found him marvelous company—amusing, well-read, and highly diplomatic. He was a man without personal ambition, and although his position of intimacy with the court was unparalleled, he never used it to acquire money or power. After we'd met, I'd started receiving frequent invitations to tea and dinner at the palace. By the time he called I considered him a good friend.

Perron told me he was coming over to talk about the wives of Moaven. "You must think seriously about this," he said when he arrived. I explained the difficulties I faced. "Then you should see a lawyer. Go see Dr. Hedayati, the court's counsel. I'll back you up. I'm sure there's a way out of this."

I saw Perron to the door with a sense of impending doom. It had been almost six months since I'd made the statement. Yet the court had obviously decided not to let the matter drop. What was this building into—a full-scale war with the family of the Shah? What a prospect! Prison couldn't be worse.

Thoroughly distraught, I went to see Hedayati, who was about to be named minister of justice. He lived just down the road. His assurances were uncannily like Perron's. "We'll find a way out," he said, implying that the civil law could overrule the Moslem one. I wasn't so sure. I needed the advice of an objective observer.

It was summertime. My friend Fuad Rohani, a young lawyer working for AIOC, and I sat in his little garden drinking beer. The strains of Mozart floated from his Victrola as I told him my story. "There is no way out," said Rohani after some consideration. "Revoke your statement and your sentence is jail."

Meanwhile, the second wife took on a big-shot lawyer who was also a member of Parliament. Everyone in Tehran was taking sides. I was in over my head.

But I wasn't going to be bought out. I wasn't going to disappear to Europe until the first wife had trampled the second and the whole thing was forgotten. My career was at stake, my name, my reputation as a "just and honorable man."

The next to call was Princess Ashraf, who invited me to dinner. I couldn't refuse, but with what reluctance did I put on my bow tie and cummerbund that night. Intelligent, powerful, and breathtakingly beautiful, Ashraf began the barrage as soon as I had a drink in my hand. "I'm disappointed in you," she began. "This is rancor against your election loss to Moaven. It's not right for you to take such steps against his wife."

Then, in a more soothing tone, she repeated the words that had become like acid in my ears: "But, Manucher darling, maybe there's a way to adjust this affair. I'm sure there's a way out."

By March 1949 I couldn't walk into a party without people turning their heads . . . or running up to encourage me effusively to hold strong. On No Rooz, the Persian New Year, my cousin Ali Amini, who was now director of Iran's first seven-year economic plan, visited my mother. His wife was also a Vosugh daughter, and he had power of attorney for what he considered his "jilted" sister-in-law. My mother refused to interfere. At a dinner right after I'd signed the statement, I'd suggested to Amini that he make a deal with the second wife and pay her a good sum. He'd flatly refused. Now he wanted to buy her off with 100,000 toman (about $30,000) and asked me to handle the job. I said I wouldn't touch it.

Over a year and a half had elapsed, and the pressure was intensifying. I had to do something. The next time I spoke to Ashraf, I made a suggestion. "The only one who can protect me is the Shah," I told her. "If he orders me to revoke my statement, I will listen. If I'm thrown into jail, he's the only one who can get me out."

"Yes," she agreed. "I'll get him to talk to you right away."

That was what was so good about Ashraf. She always had her wits about her. And you could count on her. Within a couple of weeks she invited me for dinner and told me that the Shah would be present. This time I dressed with enthusiasm.

The Shah preferred buffets so that he could take his plate around the room and mingle with the guests. I positioned myself directly across the table as he served himself, making it as easy as I could for him to catch my eye. First he talked with someone to his right, then to someone to his left. I got the distinct feeling he purposely avoided looking straight ahead to where I stood. When he moved away, still having made no sign, I circled to his side of the table. He immediately turned his back and walked in the other direction. And so it went the whole night.

I left the dinner incredibly relieved. I was off the hook. The Shah himself had refused to succumb to the pressure of his family. His choice not to interfere gave me the strongest possible argument against them. I felt very grateful to him. An enormous weight had been lifted. I was once again a free man.

THE TALE OF THE
VENEZUELAN OIL DELEGATION

Against this background, Golshayan called me into his office one day in early November 1950 and handed me a telegram. It was from Ambassador Ala, my old mentor in London, who as our envoy in Washington had just granted visas to four Venezuelans wishing to visit Iran on an oil mission. I raised an eyebrow. The telegram implied that Ala had ignored instructions *not* to give them visas—even though three of them bore the rank of ambassador.

There was a long moment of silence. Then, very curtly, Golshayan said, "I don't have time to receive them. These ambassadors enjoy long holidays abroad and think I do the same."

"But sir," I ventured, "these are oil experts granted the rank of ambassador for the sake of this mission. Aren't you going to receive them at all?"

"Only for a few minutes. You take care of them," he replied impatiently, already waving me away.

I couldn't believe it. Venezuela had become a land of Oz for the rest of the oil-producing nations. Pérez Alfonzo had become a hero, and the deals he struck, though we were often hazy on the details, defined our own aspirations.

We did not know that getting those details into our hands had become a priority for Venezuela. Its stupendous negotiations had had one negative effect: Venezuelan oil was now more expensive than the depressed prices of crude oil coming out of the Middle East. The visit offered an opportunity for both sides, and I was dismayed that Golshayan felt so concerned about British retaliation that he was once again playing it safe.

I went to the airport to greet them. Contrary to protocol the Ministry of Foreign Affairs had sent no one and provided none of the customary services usually awarded visiting dignitaries. I thought it outrageous and resolved to do everything possible to make their visit pleasant.

From the minute they stepped off the plane it was friendship at first sight. Leading the delegation was Dr. Edmundo Luongo Cabello, vice minister of hydrocarbons and mines, an impish man with an impetuous laugh whose propensity for quoting poetry turned out to be as prodigious as mine. With him were Dr. I. Monsanto, the Venezuelan ambassador to Rome, a dashing, cultured man clearly assigned to the delegation to give it diplomatic flourish; and Dr. Monsalve Casado, a professor of petroleum and mining law who later became president of the Venezuelan Supreme Court. The fourth man was a secretary who lugged a big valise. The Venezuelans said it was filled with documents translated into both English and Arabic, since they were hoping also to stop in Saudi Arabia, Kuwait, and Iraq.

On the way to the hotel Dr. Luongo Cabello explained that this was purely a courtesy visit. Venezuela considered the time ripe to begin an informal exchange of ideas among oil-producing nations. "The companies speak to each other all the time. We should be doing the same," he said. "At the moment none of us compare notes, as though we were just so much real estate. This must change. The more we can learn from each other, the better our position will be."

"This is very moving," said Monsanto, tearing his eyes for a moment from the window. "No Venezuelan has ever officially been sent to the Middle East before; it is our first contact with what is becoming the petroleum center of the world. We are alone in the Western Hemisphere, unlike you who have oil brothers all around." He laughed delightedly. "We have come to join the family."

We wound along the steep drive to the Darband Hotel, perched on the mountainous slopes of Shemiran north of the city. On the way up each of them in turn made the point that they in no way wished to inconvenience our government or AIOC. Whatever we felt we could discuss was a first step. The Venezuelan government was anxious to provide us with information on any aspect of its oil business that we might consider useful.

As I helped them unload at the Darband, I glanced about with concern. It was really a summer place and looked damp and forlorn under the winter skies. But we had no other choice—it was the only first-class hotel in

Tehran at the time. I checked them in and promised to be back for dinner. On the way to the office I pondered what they'd said. The Gulf Arabs were our neighbors, but we'd always thought of them as enemies rather than family. I almost laughed out loud. Surely these "oil brothers" would use whatever information we exchanged against us. Iraq in particular was ruthless, squeezing us into a few meters of shoreline along the Shatt-al-Arab, and AIOC had encouraged distrust between us. I couldn't picture them as partners. But the Venezuelans had a point. We were all on the same side; we shared a common industry. Our suspicions of each other were heightened by our lack of contact. I silently thanked Ambassador Ala for having gone against his orders. How cowed we all were, how afraid and alone inside our borders. What the Venezuelans were suggesting was revolutionary and would drive the British government crazy!

"So what do they want?" Golshayan sniffed once I'd told him they'd arrived. "Why do they say they are here?"

Ask your British contacts! I wanted to yell at him. Instead I blandly said, "Friendship. They're willing to show us everything they've got. As they rightly point out, we share mutual interests." Golshayan could not have looked more dubious. With difficulty I wrung a promise from him to see the delegation for a half hour the following day.

The Darband restaurant looked out through plate glass windows onto a large open-air dance floor. In summer lanterns winked in the trees, and a band played under an awning. Now the tables were lashed together with chains, and the dance floor was covered with puddles. The restaurant was cold and, apart from our party of five, as empty as a coffin.

We had hardly sat down to dinner, however, when a ravishing blonde appeared and took a seat facing us a few tables away.

"Good God!" exclaimed Dr. Luongo Cabello in a loud voice, smiling broadly. "They've even sent a Mata Hari to keep an eye on us."

"Well," I answered in a stage whisper, "there are five of us, so she can't kill us all at once. Let's ask her to join us."

"Capital idea," said Ambassador Monsanto, gracefully getting up to issue the invitation. But though he and I both tried, the lady categorically refused our advances. It made me wonder whether one of the many waiters around might not be reporting on us as well—and that his presence was keeping her in her seat.

That evening we began what became a four-day marathon of conversation, the first open exchange of information ever held between two oil-producing nations. It was invigorating and inspiring—the first step in the emancipation of the oil industry and the seed of what ten years later would flower into OPEC, the Organization of Petroleum Exporting Countries.

Fath-Ali Shah.

Nasser-edin Shah.

Farman Farma as a teenager and student at
the Austrian Military Academy in Tehran.

Farman Farma and his sharp-tongued
eldest sister, Najmeh-Saltaneh, the
mother of Dr. Mohammad Mossadeq.

Hazrat-Oliah, Farman Farma's second-
eldest sister, who married Mozzafar-edin
Shah and was the grandmother of
Dr. Ali Amini, wearing a "miniskirt."

Farman Farma (right) with Sir Percy Sykes of the South Persia Rifles and his sister,
Ella Sykes, who afterward wrote *Through Persia on a Side-Saddle*.

Farman Farma (center) just before being named premier, with Dr. Mossadeq (second from left).

Farman Farma (seated) surrounded by the Sanjabi tribe, to whom he gave asylum during World War I. The Il-Khan (standing, left of center) was the father of Dr. Karim Sanjabi, minister of foreign affairs in the first cabinet after the Khomeini revolution.

Mohammadvali Mirza (third from right) in Kermanshah aiding Farman Farma against the rebellion by Salar-Doleh. Reza Khan (center), a rifleman in Farman Farma's army, later became Reza Shah, the founder of the Pahlavi dynasty.

Farman Farma (left of center) as governor of Shiraz, having resolved the conflict between the Qashgahi tribe and the British. Sir Percy Sykes stands at center, in a pith helmet; to the far left stands the young Mansur Qashgahi, who became a "guest" in Farman Farma's house to secure peace.

Nosrat-Doleh (far right) in Nice, France, in 1912, during the Flower Festival. Seated in the back of the car is Entezam-Saltaneh, father of Abdollah Entezam, future chairman of the National Iranian Oil Company.

THE SHAH OF PERSIA ON A VISIT TO LONDON

The Bulletin announced Ahmad Shah's visit to England before the signing of the 1919 Agreement. Included in the photo are Nosrat-Doleh (far left), Ahmad Shah (center), Prince Albert (fourth from right), and Lord Nathaniel Curzon (far right).

Farman Farma and Manucher, at age six, both wearing the *farmanfarma'i* hat.

Maryam (left) age ten, Mehri (center) age eight, and Manucher, age six.

Farman Farma with his eldest son, Nosrat-Doleh, and his youngest son, Abdol Ali.

Manucher as a student in Birmingham, holding Trudi, the daughter of his landlords and friends, Derek and Winnie Philips.

Mohsen Khan Raiis, ambassador to Germany (left); Mohtesham Saltaneh Esfandiari, speaker of the Parliament and later head of the Farmanfarmaian family board (center), stopping off in Berlin on his way to the coronation of King George VI of England; and Adolf Hitler (right) in 1937. Mohsen Khan was married to Manucher's sister Mehri; Esfandiari was father-in-law of Manucher's sister Maryam.

Manucher's mother, Batoul Khanoum, poses with Farman Farma in 1936 for a picture commemorating the abolition of the veil. She made him buy a tie for the occasion.

The welcoming committee in Tehran anticipating Mozzafar's return from Tabriz. Manucher is in the back row (far right). In the front row are the family patriarch, Mohammadvali Mirza (second from left); Maheen Firouz, Mozzafar's wife; and the mayor of Tehran, Mehdi Mashayekhi (right).

Three wives from Farman Farma's harem. Left to right: Masumeh Khanoum (from Tehran, in north-central Iran); Batoul Khanoum, Manucher's mother (from Kermanshah, in the west); Fatmeh Khanoum (from Shiraz, in the south).

Dr. Mohammad Mossadeq.

Verla Gean Miller, who married Manucher in 1952, in a Kurdish tribal headdress in Kermanshah, 1954.

U.S. vice president Richard Nixon (left) inscribed this picture personally for Manucher (right) in 1954. The man in the middle is F. Amir Alaii, adjutant to the Shah.

Herbert Hoover, Jr. (left), and Manucher in 1954 when both served on an oil commission laying the groundwork for the Consortium agreement.

Manucher with Dr. Ali Amini (right), minister of finance, who signed the Consortium agreement in 1954.

The inauguration in 1960 of Pars Oil, which was founded by Manucher's youngest brother, Abdol Ali. Left to right: Baroul Khanoum, Dr. Yahya Adl, the Shah, Abdol Ali.

Six Farmanfarmaian brothers at one Salaam, 1962. Left to right: Abdol Ali, vice president of the Chamber of Industries; Alidad, president of the New Pars Engineering Company; Alinaghi, president of the Bank of Industries; Manucher, director of the National Iranian Oil Company (NIOC) and president of the Chamber of Oil; Dr. Khodadad, governor of the Central Bank; and Dr. Kaveh, vice president of the Chamber of Commerce.

Mohammad Reza Shah (left), Agha Khan Bakhtiar (center), and Manucher at the opening of a pump station on the new Tehran pipeline at Bidrouyeh.

In Holland during one of the Consortium trips, Jack Berlin, the first American chairman of the Consortium (second from left), and Manucher pose with Dutch villagers.

Amir Abbas Hoveyda, prime
minister 1965–1977.

Wedding of Manucher and Petronella
Kahmann, winter 1965. Standing, left to
right: Mehri, Safieh Khanoum (wife of
Mohammad Hossein Mirza),
Afsaneh (daughter of Maryam), Haideh.

Mecca, April 1966. Manucher (left, with cigar)
and his uncle Etezad-Soltan.

Inspection of an oil installation,
left to right: Queen Farah; Abdollah
Entezam, chairman of the NIOC
board; Mrs. Entezam; Manucher,
a director of the board.

Manucher and his last and favorite house, in Farmanieh.

To my loving Daughter Roxane first picture goes!
R. [signature] 2/26/1972

Manucher in ambassadorial
regalia before setting out for
Venezuela in 1972.

Venezuelan president Carlos Andrés Pérez
(left) and Manucher, 1973.

Mehdi and his children at his house near the Kurdish border with Turkey.

Manucher with Luben Belof in
Sofia, Bulgaria, in 1980, right after
hearing the news of his release.

A lineup of brothers in Majorca, Spain, after the revolution. Left to right: Dr.
Qaffar, Dr. Cyrus, Dr. Khodadad, Farough, Alidad, Dr. Abol Bashar,
Dr. Kaveh, Manucher.

The very concept was anathema to the British, and their diplomatic reports on that visit are still closed in the Foreign Office files—and will remain so until the year 2010!

Dr. Luongo Cabello had brought copies of Venezuela's hydrocarbon law, tax law on royalties, labor code, and concessions—all meticulously translated into English. "Whatever else you wish to see will be at your disposal whenever you feel you can come to Caracas," he said. He willingly revealed to me how their system worked, the specifics of the 50/50 deal, what their arguments had been in the negotiations, and what the ramifications were. Dr. Monsalve Casado, the lawyer, filled in the legal aspects: how they got their money, how the tax worked, and what the rights and responsibilities were of both the companies and the government.

Over and over again I cringed at the terms we had compared with what the Venezuelans had obtained. When I showed them our concession, they practically spat on it and became all the more anxious to show us what we could achieve instead.

Their workers were paid four times what ours were, worked a half day less per week, had medical and retirement benefits, and could even purchase a house on credit against their salaries. Food, housing, and clothing were subsidized—unlike the situation in Abadan, where workers often went about in rags. Venezuela's oil income was based on the internationally posted price of $2.22 per barrel. Our 1933 Concession did not even mention a posted price. The only posted price we encountered was when we bought back refined gasoline from AIOC for our own internal use.

The Venezuelans were fascinated by what I could tell them about our oil business, for until then AIOC had kept the details tightly secret. "It gives you an idea of the terror the British feel," said Luongo Cabello, his mouth working as though he were twirling the idea under his tongue before letting it go. "What different souls the British and Americans have. There is no comparison between their companies: The company in our country is civilized and an open book, in yours it is mean. We can talk to ours without killing each other. Americans understand the psychology and interests of Venezuela. The British do not bother. They are so unchangeable, so . . . enigmatic!"

I observed his discomfort with interest, having become so callous to AIOC's attitude myself. "Their mistake is to create a tempest in a teapot." His eyes flashed. "They think we're revolutionaries—and so have tried to keep us out of your countries. They fear we will try to improve our group position. They're right! We must get our ideas together." He flashed his sudden, droll smile. "Thank God for Ambassador Ala's initiative in issuing us the visas for Iran. Thank God for you, *caramba*! You have been the savior of this mission in the most important country in the area. What we will do in the Arab countries I don't know. So far we haven't even received visas."*

The meeting the next day with Golshayan did not go well. He received them with an even darker, more unsmiling demeanor than usual. We spoke in French, since he did not speak English, and though he was about to resume negotiations with AIOC, his whole approach was one of unabashed resentment. I had alerted the Venezuelans that the meeting was to last exactly half an hour, and in thirty minutes on the dot Dr. Luongo Cabello stood up. At the door Golshayan seemed to pull himself together. "What's your hurry?" he asked abruptly, as though the delegation might slip through his fingers.

Dr. Luongo Cabello brushed him off. "Your Excellency," he said, "your director general has informed us you are a busy man." He'd had enough of Golshayan's sourness. "We will give him a full report—and all the details on how our government's royalty adds up to three times what you receive!"

Luckily the Golshayan meeting was the nadir. The next meeting was with Dr. Pirnia, and he received them with open arms. He was intrigued by their idea of maintaining an ongoing exchange of ideas among the oil-producing nations. Although he too was doubtful about the Arabs, he was game to try. Dr. Pirnia questioned the two oil experts closely about the 50/50 deal, and they revealed a number of points we had hitherto been unaware of. "How advanced Venezuela is," he remarked at one point, "that your university offers a course in petroleum law." He turned to me, shaking his head. "Really, we have a long way to go to catch up."

As always, I was overwhelmed by Dr. Pirnia's performance. Had we had the Americans as our interlocutors, he would have been the Pérez Alfonzo of Iran. Unfortunately every time we came to the table with AIOC, we not only gained nothing, but we usually lost ground. The British were old hands at colonialism. They were used to twisting a few arms at the top, knocking off a few people in the street if they needed to, and then taking home the spoils. The Americans were different. That is why they were so loved at the time. They approached business in foreign countries exactly as

*From Iran they flew to Saudi Arabia, where they were not even allowed off the plane. "The Saudis were suspicious—they thought we were extraterrestrial," Luongo Cabello told me later. In Kuwait, still a British colony, "the consul accompanied us to see the sheikh, so we couldn't discuss petroleum." In Baghdad they were well received by the prime minister, Nouri Sa'id Pasha—a good friend of my father's from the old days—as they were in Syria and Egypt. But in Baghdad, Luongo Cabello fell ill with appendicitis, and oil was not discussed. The other two countries were not oil producers. The result: The ideas discussed by Iran and Venezuela for a mutual exchange of information remained unique, and the dynamic between them would significantly affect OPEC's founding ten years later.

they approached it at home. To them Venezuela was in effect an extension of the United States, with rights to the same laws and legal redress. They played fair. That's why Pérez Alfonzo had been able to achieve what he did. Only later did America learn the British trick of relying on force rather than the fair deal. We all have suffered for it. As I look back I remember the admiration we felt for the Americans and their diplomacy based on commercial common sense. I remember hoping that soon we too would be able to work with U.S. companies because then someone like Dr. Pirnia would finally have a chance to shine.

The next day the Ministry of Foreign Affairs belatedly decided to recognize the delegation and assigned a friend of mine, Manucher Marzaban, as their aide. The minister of foreign affairs even arranged for a visit to the palace. In their audience with the Shah they spoke of exchanging diplomatic missions. Little did we know that it would take nearly twenty-five years for that to happen and that I would be sent as Iran's first ambassador to Venezuela.

On the last afternoon before they left I took them to the Tehran Museum. It was an impressive place, housing bronzes and terra-cottas from Persepolis and Susa, monoliths of stone, tiny figurines of ancient glass, exquisite miniatures and calligraphy, mosaics, and, of course, stunning carpets. Although Monsanto lived in Italy and knew the beauties of Roman art, all three were awed. Suddenly I could not imagine what it must be like to spring from a world without aeons of ancestors and their relics stretching into the hoary past. It was a moving moment for each of us as the representatives of a new civilization confronted the riches of an old one.

The next morning I filled their arms with gifts from the bazaar, and we promised to stay in contact. Even as they climbed into the plane I knew their trip had been one of the most important events in my life—and in that of my country.

CHAPTER
X

NATIONALIZATION

Destiny bestows to the ignorant the reins of government;
You are learned and erudite—and that is your sin.
—HAFEZ

Tehran 1951

A lot happened between those last months of 1949 and the beginning of
1951. The Shah announced he was divorcing Fawzieh and then left on his
first trip to the United States to see President Harry Truman. Elections
were held for the Sixteenth Majles, but police beat up candidates not favored by the Shah and riots broke out. The minister of court, the calculat-
ing Hajir, was assassinated. After the elections, Dr. Mossadeq claimed that
the vote had been rigged and in protest started a sit-in on the palace
grounds. His supporters put aside their party differences and formed the
National Front, a coalition that would not only vote Mossadeq into the
Majles in a by-election but eventually lift him to victory against AIOC.

The mollah Kashani, though still in exile, also was handed a seat. It took
him six months to return to Iran. When he finally did so, he came in great
pomp; a million people poured into the streets to greet him. Although he
was a very short man, he stood up with fire burning in his belly and de-
claimed that Hajir had gotten his due. I admired him for speaking his
mind. So did Mossadeq, who read his messages out to the Majles, since
Kashani chose not to appear in Parliament for that whole session—or for
the next one either, even though he had been elected speaker of the house.

It was also in the winter of 1949 that my stepmother, Princess Ezzat-Doleh died. The funeral was a very special event in my life. The spirit of the family that day is imprinted on my mind: all of us lined up, the young sons of Farman Farma standing solidly together at the Fakhre Doleh Mosque, a simple but old family mosque named after Ezzat-Doleh's sister and located near the Majles. People streamed in to pay their respects to the older members of the family, walking past us as we stood outside the door. An old man approached and surveyed us, then mumbled under his breath the ancient Zoroastrian saying: A flame burns in this house. It was the first time we had stood together like that—or perhaps the others had stood like that when Farman Farma had died, but I had not been among them and so had not witnessed the strength that comes when a family assembles in sorrow and is lifted up, seeing its new generations gathered like fresh green wheat, their eyes sparkling with hope for the future.

A TALE OF IRISHMEN

That winter I started dating Mary Hollis, the private secretary of American ambassador John Wiley. Mary was a young divorcée from the Midwest, long-legged, gutsy, and thoroughly entertained by life in Tehran. She ran the embassy from top to bottom and knew everyone in the American community. It was a wonderful time to be American. The United States was at its postwar apex, and all the best cars, shoes, film stars, and airplanes came from there. The United States was basking in a haze of unexpected worldwide popularity, and its unblemished innocence gave countries such as mine great hope. Unlike the British, who had commanded respect at the end of a gun, the Americans were cherished. Texas in particular was legendary—the state of extravagance, with its ten-gallon hats and rugged oilmen who looked like John Wayne. Mary had a number of Texan friends who lived in a house on Takhte Jamshid that everyone called the "Texas Embassy"; it even had a plaque on the wall to that effect. They gave me my first experience of the Texas drawl. Their confidence was reassuring, as was their sense of country.

Mary and I became very close and went frequently to Bagh-e Chal, my cousin's country estate. It was dotted with huge tents erected in the old Persian fashion near running water, with figures of horsemen and dancers drawn in fanciful penstrokes, called *qalam kar,* on the inside walls. My cousin used the place rarely, but it was always well stocked and staffed by hordes of servants. As the weather grew warmer with the beginning of spring and later in the flat heat of summer, we escaped there to the water jets and pools, spending the nights with the tent flaps thrown open to the garden. Stretched out on a couch covered with Persian embroidered cushions, we watched the faerie moon, and I know Mary felt transported into the love songs of Omar Khayyám.

I am not a romantic, and finding the setting comfortable, I would become drowsy. But Mary, who wanted to capture another husband, would begin to gossip in the moonlight.

Unfortunately, by the time dessert was being cleared away, my eyelids were drooping and my ears going deaf. Once or twice I tried valiantly to stay awake, hoping to discover some useful gossip. But in those days it was still too much for me to be with a woman for more than eight hours on end—no matter how attractive and entertaining she was or how perfect the ambiance—and I would become somehow ill-tempered because I wasn't in my own bed. In any case real secrets must be learned obliquely, since direct questions elicit suspicion.

One afternoon Mary invited along an embassy colleague, First Secretary Jerry Dooher. He talked big and was big, with a shock of ginger hair and teal eyes set broadly on a rather fleshy face. He was a "go out and get 'em" sort of man, and already had a reputation about town for his strong ideas about British meddling, AIOC's unfair policies, and America's role as likely savior. Under Ambassador Allen his views had been constrained to talk; under Wiley, who described working with Iranians as being "like eating soup with a fork,"[1] Dooher's ideas began to turn into action.

"Throw the AIOC out," Dooher said that day, as he would say every time I saw him. He did not even wait till we had reached the property and had stretched out in the sun after a swim. In the car, half an hour after we'd met, he began to bombard me. "Negotiate new terms. What does it matter?" he said scornfully, scoffing at the spiderweb of threads that tied us so tortuously to Britain. "We'll take up the slack. American ships will pull into dock tomorrow and buy your oil. Don't you guys worry."

Seeming to add clout to Dooher's chest-beating was the new undersecretary of state, George McGhee, who passed through town for a brief visit while the Shah was in the United States. He was an oilman, married to the daughter of the Texas oil magnate Everette De Golyer, and he made it a crusade of sorts to badger AIOC and the British Embassy to offer Iran more generous terms.

Dooher openly advocated bringing in a strong prime minister to whip the country into shape. He was later credited as the driving force behind the appointment of General Ali Razmara, the army's chief of staff, to the premiership in May of 1950. Razmara's was certainly the first government in which three ministers were so openly sympathetic to U.S. aims that everyone called it the "American cabinet." But Dooher's brazen claims that the United States would fill any gap left by the imperialistic British eventually engendered retaliation. His nemesis was Geoffrey Keating, and the tool was Keating's camera.

Keating was the head of public relations for AIOC, and it was in that capacity I had met him on a visit to the oil fields some time back. He was a crack bridge player and had an easy wit. Like Dooher he had the sandy skin and fiery coloring of many Irishmen. Keating had been one of our era's first real war reporters, traveling on the front lines with the British army and ending up as General Bernard Montgomery's official photographer in North Africa. I found him an extremely friendly character, cool in his shoes like so many self-made men, with an address book the size of a dictionary and a sanguine view of the British postcolonial empire. He tried hard to bring Dooher around to a softer view of British intentions but failed. Dooher's hatred of the British stemmed from his own Irish roots, and he simply found his fellow Irishman a traitor.

One day in early summer, Keating and I met for lunch at the British Club. I was one of only four Persian members, and I appreciated the privilege enormously. The building had an air of seclusion about it, even though it was right on Ferdowsi Avenue above one of the busiest circles in the city. Gentlemen read in the corners sunk in overstuffed chairs while waiters in white coats glided quietly along the sisal-covered floors bearing drinks on trays. There was no prowling and preening, no dangling of reputations, just peace, and I often took my Persian girlfriends there, grateful for a hideout with good food and deferent company. On this particular day Keating and I met in the bar. He smiled a bit strangely and tossed a copy of a local newspaper in front of me. Dooher stood proudly at the center of the picture on the front page, garbed in a colorful cummerbund, surrounded by gun-toting Bakhtiari tribesmen.

"So it was a good trip," I said to Keating.

"Capital," he answered. "First class. Americans have a thing for the tribes, you know." He paused significantly. "It must be their sense of independence, a kinship for the wide-open stretches. Pity you couldn't make it." He eyed me as though expecting some reaction on my part.

I didn't know what to say and so pointed to the photograph in the paper. "And how did this happen?" I asked.

He shrugged. "Vanity, dear chap. You know, that typical American hankering to spread the fairy dust of manifest destiny. Neodiplomacy, I'd call it; a bit rash maybe." His expression was oddly bleak.

"Noblesse oblige," I said, turning the paper over and sniffing at Keating's somber mood. "Bring this man another drink," I said to the bar-

tender. "And make it strong. He's wearing the guilty expression of the
damned—though God only knows why."

I completely underestimated the impact of that innocuous photo. It was
Dooher's undoing. Ever since the uprising when the tribes had formed
their confederation and declared autonomy, ever since the attempted coup
against Qavam-Saltaneh and Mozzafar, the Shah had been hypersensitive
about the tribes. They were the underbelly of his power, his weak spot, the
only ones who could make deals behind his back—as they had with the
Germans and then the British—and he was not going to countenance any
flirting with the tribes by the Americans. It had been an innocent trip—
and an innocent picture—but the implication, if one wanted to read anything into it, was clear. Dooher was transferred to New York to head up
the Middle East desk of Voice of America. Keating had deftly fired the cannon without any noise, as the Persian saying goes. The man who'd spoken
most adamantly against British oil was gone.

TALES FROM THE OIL COMMITTEE

Dooher may have contributed to Razmara's rise, but his departure in no
way deterred the crusty old general from climbing on many other shoulders to reach the premiership. Razmara was a master at making promises
he couldn't keep. Tiny in stature, extremely polite, and staccato in his actions, he had a face-splitting smile from which his teeth seemed practically
to fall out. He'd served as commander in Kermanshah some time back,
where he'd distinguished himself for having looted a great deal. Oddly
enough both the Americans and the British thought him an honest man.
How misguided we can be in judging values in other cultures.

Mozzafar, who was married in Razmara's house, supported his appointment as chief of staff to Qavam-Saltaneh. Yet Razmara, ever the operator,
immediately declared himself loyal only to the Shah. After leading the
troops into Azerbaijan to oust the Russians, he survived even as Mozzafar
and Qavam-Saltaneh fell. Negative politics were his forte, and he fought
wars of attrition in the halls of government with no higher goal than his
own aggrandizement. The Shah regarded him with suspicion and only reluctantly acquiesced to his premiership in May of 1950. Having a general
as premier was not a Persian tradition, but the pressure exerted on the sovereign by the outside powers—especially the United States—was intense,
Razmara having promised to each the plums they most desired. To the
Americans he vowed to stand firm against communism and to involve
them in government. To the Russians he promised to free the Tudeh pris-

oners who still languished in jail after the assassination attempt on the Shah. To the British he pledged the most impossible of all: passage of the Supplemental Agreement and resolution of the oil problem.

Razmara's tenure began badly and ended worse. Because the public held his American support in dubious regard, the arrival twenty-four hours after his swearing in of the new U.S. ambassador, Henry Grady, led to street fighting, and a number of people were killed. Thereafter Razmara tried to downplay his military image; he wore civilian clothes and opted for conciliation rather than decisive action. The strategy backfired. In a country rent by political quarreling, in which the players had steeled themselves for the ruthless saber strokes of an army commander appointed to bring order, Razmara was soon judged a softy.

Even I lost my patience at his dithering. We were discussing the Supplemental Agreement. As happened occasionally he'd called me and the minister of finance to his office to discuss tactics. The turncoat radio announcer Bahram Sharogh was there too. During the war, Sharogh had spoken first for the Germans and then for the British. Now he was head of the department of propaganda.

Razmara strutted back and forth and declared that the oil debate had gotten out of hand, the opposition's arguments were incendiary, and it was time we brought the government's position to the media. After half an hour of this I became exasperated. "Your Excellency," I said, "you have attained power as a general with the backing of those who hoped you would act with authority. So why don't you exercise the rights given to you? Propaganda is useless. People will not listen even though we talk sense. The opposition accuses the government of acting treacherously, and the very daring of the charge inspires the crowds." Razmara's eyes narrowed, but I plunged on. "Why don't you stop the opposition from its constant interference? Why don't you stop them from obstructing whatever decision the government takes? People do not want words, they want leadership. Where is the stick we all thought we saw in your hand? *Shotor savari, dolah dolah nadare*—once you're up on the camel, you can't try to hide."

"We don't live in times when such power can be exercised," he said. He'd stopped pacing and begun to snicker out of habit. "You are young and think I can act like your ancestors did." His smile widened to the ends of his ears. "Those, young man, are outdated ideas."

Razmara had no stick. It came as a shock. It is a common delusion that a uniform bestows special power to a government leader—even more that it hides violence and potency. For the most part, however, uniforms hide straw men. Faced with the rebellions that are a natural part of civilian governance, many generals fall apart, their regimental experience providing them no practical skills to combat the disobedience of the mob. No doubt that is why America eventually snubbed such men and backed "democratically elected leaders" instead. What we all discovered was that uniforms are disguises and that the weak don the most impressive ones—men like the Shah, who bedecked himself with all the medals he could find, or the ill-fated Nicholas II of Russia. In fact the uniform only made them weaker, for it was one more flashy thing to live up to. The really formidable bosses never bothered. Hitler, the ultimate tyrant, remained all his life a sergeant in an unassuming uniform. In Razmara we had a sheep in wolf's clothing.

Razmara appointed my brother-in-law Mohsen Khan as minister of foreign affairs. In seeking a man to keep the peace with the British, Razmara had chosen well, for Mohsen Khan was the ultimate diplomat who believed in compromise to the bitter end.

The new minister of finance was Taghi Nasr, the most "American" of what came to be called the "American cabinet." He lasted only a few months. Announcing suddenly that he was going to the United States for a conference, he left and never returned, thoroughly shaking public confidence in Razmara's fledgling government. Nasr was replaced by my intimate friend Gholam Hossein Forouhar, for me a propitious appointment, for he was from an old family and a close member of Victoria's inner clique.

With Razmara's promise to the British hanging over his head, Forouhar's mandate was to find accommodation at any cost. Fighting against him was Dr. Mossadeq, who had taken up the standard where Eskandari had left off, his rhetoric against AIOC developing little by little into a full-fledged crusade for nationalization.

After the Sixteenth Majles took its seat, an eighteen-member parliamentary oil committee was set up. It was a strange group. Although Mossadeq's party had only eight deputies in Parliament, he and four others were represented on the committee. On the other side of the political spectrum was the tribal representative Khosrow Qashghai and our neighbor in Hamadan Nasser Zolfaghari, both supportive of the agreement.

The Ministry of Finance represented the government. Dr. Pirnia, who normally would have attended, did not see eye to eye with Forouhar and little by little was shunted aside. We attended a wedding together that summer in which Dr. Pirnia's behavior was typical. It was an oil wedding if there ever was one—joining Northcroft's niece and Eric Drake, Northcroft's second in command at AIOC (he later became chairman of British Petroleum—the company that resulted after Iran's nationalization of oil). Mary and I laughed when we got the invitation, for Drake had been a most anxious suitor of hers, though she would have none of him. She loved to mimic the way he called her "Mary" with the stiff chin and long, deep-throated *y* of upper-class English. I told her the funny story of his announcement to me of his marriage a couple of months earlier.

"To whom?" I'd asked, surprised, having never seen him with a woman.

"I don't know yet," he'd answered.

Now two months later he was marrying his boss's niece.

During the wedding a picture was taken of us standing in the garden It was later published in the papers. Dr. Pirnia holds a turtle he'd fished from the pool and is addressing Drake. "The British are advancing like this turtle while the world rushes by," the caption quoted him as saying. "If I were the government, I'd make a new contract and scrap the Supplemental Agreement!"

You had to have the heart of a lion to speak that way in those days, but it did not win him points in the ministry. And so in place of Dr. Pirnia, I was sent to the oil committee.

We met twice a week in a boardroom of the Parliament building. We convened around a long table; I sat at the head, and to my right was Dr. Mossadeq, who, though he represented a minority party, had been named chairman. Each time I walked into the Majles I felt a surge of pride. At last I was crossing the threshold that I had been prevented from entering as an elected deputy.

The committee was ostensibly set up to investigate the Supplemental Agreement and find grounds for settlement, but the technical and economic aspects of the agreement were rarely raised. The deputies were not well versed in oil and were interested in it only insofar as it related to politics. Instead, they fixated on the human costs, publicly spotlighting one of the weakest links of the concessionary arrangement. Soon the committee became an emotional jousting field that often degenerated into attacks on me as the spokesman for a government they considered plodding and fainthearted.

Dr. Mossadeq dominated the proceedings. He criticized everything with great sarcasm, a technique he'd mastered in the twenty-five years in which he'd done nothing but carp and bestow blame. At first the discussion focused on the plight of a group of employees who had been dismissed by AIOC. These "unfortunates" had posted themselves at the gate of the Parliament building and heckled everyone who entered. No matter what we tried at the ministry, we were unable to get them removed either by having the company reinstate them or by having the police disperse them. The Mossadeq opposition repeatedly—and rightly—pointed to them as a prime example of company abuse—and I eventually started to wonder whether the company's intractability in the matter indicated a deeper political agenda. It was not the last time I would notice discrepancies in its actions that made me question its motives.

The emphasis on quotidian mismanagement, which monopolized the committee's exchanges, imbued the discussions with a political intensity way beyond the actual merit of the evidence. Medical doctors in the oil fields were recruited mainly among Iranians, but because there were too few of them available, a number of Indians and Pakistanis also had been engaged. To discredit the system and create political mayhem, the Communists and anti-British nationalists encouraged groups of up to a hundred workers to queue in front of the clinics run by the Pakistani and Indian doctors. As a rule the doctors could see one patient every fifteen minutes— or a total of thirty patients a day. When by day's end the exhausted doctors faced a belligerent crowd massed at their doors, they resigned on the spot, offering the ostensibly ailing workers ample cause to accuse the company of not providing adequate medical care.

Mossadeq and the other four National Front deputies on the committee spoke heatedly against the company's ineptitude in such matters and declared that negotiation with such a heartless firm was pointless. As a body whose purpose was to find grounds for a settlement, the committee had turned into a farce. Mossadeq did not care about dollars and cents or numbers of barrels per day. He saw the basic issue as one of national sovereignty. Iran's sovereignty was being undercut by a company that sacrificed Iranian lives for British interests. This is what infuriated him about the government's willingness to compromise—and it was what made him decide unequivocally that AIOC had to go.

I was torn. I believed in Mossadeq, not just because he was a member of my family but for what I perceived as his genuine sincerity. By being negative he had achieved much good for Iran. But his bitterness—and that of his followers—against the British was turning everything into an issue of black and white, and as the months passed I listened to them talk themselves into a dream world. The American approach in Saudi Arabia came to represent a fairy tale of goodness. The hints that continued to emanate from the American Embassy—despite Dooher's departure—implying that once the British were out the United States would fill the gap only exacerbated the situation.

One day the committee asked me how much oil Aramco produced in the deserts of Saudi Arabia. I hesitated to tell them outright, for I knew how much they prized their steadfast belief that the world would collapse without Iranian oil. So I showed them a copy of *The Lamp*, a magazine published by Aramco. Rather than read from it myself, I asked Allahyar Saleh, one of the National Front deputies, to do so. Saleh read out the production figure of 17 million tons a year. The committee exploded in outrage. One of the members, a particularly rabid nationalist named Hossein Makki, shouted that it was a lie concocted by the British. No such production level was possible. And then, galvanized by his rage, the whole committee turned on me like baying dogs for passing out British propaganda.

THE JUDGE

One summer evening in the midst of all this I went by Mary's flat. A man was already there. He turned out to be U.S. Supreme Court justice William O. Douglas, who was traveling through Iran and writing a book. He was tall and craggy, and though he lacked the top hat made of an American flag, he looked like Uncle Sam. He was stiff too, like the poster, and showy, and he had developed the habit of trying to act and look younger than he was. I found this odd in a judge, for sages in my country usually tried to look their age.

Mary shooed me into a chair with a "watch your tongue" look and told me they were talking politics. Very soon it became apparent that Douglas was strongly biased in favor of Razmara, while his comments about Mossadeq were most disparaging.

"Have you met either of them?" I asked at last.

"I'm scheduled to meet Razmara tomorrow," he said. "I have no intention of meeting Mossadeq, for he is a Communist."

Right then I should have shut my mouth and not said another word. At the very least I should have remembered I was a representative of the government and had no business interfering. But I couldn't stand the attitude—at the time so prevalent in those days of early McCarthyism—that everyone opposed to the government was automatically a Communist.

And so I began my tirade. "Mossadeq is not a Communist, and you should not judge him by his clothes or his tears," I admonished. "To you his emotionalism may seem weak; to us this very humanity makes him endearing. Iranians are prepared to die for Mossadeq. He is one of the very few freely elected leaders in our history. How is it possible that you don't want to meet the legitimate leader of the opposition, a man whose strength is drawn entirely from the support of the people? Isn't this the foundation of democracy—to give conflicting voices a fair hearing? How can you be true to your democratic principles and ignore him? You will leave understanding nothing of this country."

After a fervent hour, I felt I had convinced the justice to keep an open

mind, to see Mossadeq as a national standard-bearer and not prejudge him
as a Communist. Too eagerly, no doubt, I told him that should he wish to
meet Dr. Mossadeq, I could arrange it.

Somewhat reluctantly he agreed, and early the next morning I went to
see Dr. Mossadeq, who obligingly promised to meet Douglas about noon.
But when I rang Mossadeq at lunchtime, he told me Douglas had not
come. When at last I got hold of Douglas, he claimed he'd been in the car
and on the way to see Mossadeq when he'd realized they did not speak a
common language—and so had turned back.

"Are you serious about wanting to see him?" I demanded.

"Absolutely," he insisted.

So I fixed a second meeting for later that day. In the evening I stopped
by Mossadeq's house to see how it had gone, but Douglas had not kept that
appointment either.

Mossadeq was not amused. Though he was gentlemanly about it, I could
see he thought I'd become overly friendly with the Americans and was trying to push them on him. He did not understand my sincere belief in him
as an opposition figure and my determination to set the record straight. I
did not realize at the time that it would be something he would hold
against me.

As for Douglas, he spent several weeks in Iran, much of the time traveling through tribal areas. In his book *Strange Lands and Friendly People* he
describes with a swagger "a toast to the rearming of the Bakhtiari" and re-
counts a story of Soviet troops massing on the Russian border—their invasion halted apparently in the nick of time thanks to a Russian setback in
the budding Korean War.[2]

After the nationalization of oil, when Mossadeq traveled to the United
States, Justice Douglas appeared on television asserting that he was a good
friend of Mossadeq's, whom he'd met in Tehran. (No one asked why the
meeting was never mentioned in his book.) Later, I read in *The New York
Times* that Douglas had resigned from the court under a cloud, having mis-
appropriated public funds for his own use.

A TALE OF CAT AND MOUSE

As fall approached, Razmara's hold on the country became increasingly unsure. His ministers lost confidence, and Mohsen Khan even tried to resign.
Pressure from Britain, the United States, and the Soviet Union was mounting. All pretense of postwar friendship among them had expired. The
United States, clothed in the silks of the UN, was in an all-out war in

Korea. Moscow, meanwhile, decided to make noises toward us about trade and political conciliation. Razmara, seeing little warmth or money coming from either Britain or America, decided to make good on his promise to the Russians.

One evening I was dining at the home of my brother General Mohammad Hossein Mirza. He lived downtown on a small slice of ground left over from the old compound. A stupendous Qajar frieze of warriors on horseback going into battle ran the length of the dining room wall. Carpets covered every inch of the floor, many of them overlapping as was customary in old Persian houses. In the middle of the meal the telephone rang and my brother excused himself from the table. He returned with the news that a general had been seen pulling up to the main prison in an army truck with the authority to release all the important Communist prisoners. From there the prisoners had disappeared. Clearly the Soviet Embassy had been primed; its massively padlocked doors had been opened a crack for them to slip through, then shut again with a bang. Although Razmara was already calling for an investigation and threatening to punish those who'd allowed the escape, it was obvious who had ordered the operation.

Keeping the promise paid off. Two months later, in November 1950, the Russians signed a trade agreement with Iran.

Washington considered the British more than a little to blame. Their stinginess vis-à-vis AIOC, argued McGhee on a trip to London just two months earlier, was putting unnecessary strain on Iran and encouraging it to look favorably toward its Communist neighbor. The United States wanted stability—as the best defense against communism—and AIOC's behavior was not helping. To pressure Tehran into approving the Supplemental Agreement, the British government was even withholding a loan of $25 million pegged for Iran by the multilateral Eximbank. The United States wanted the loan to go through so that Iran could start reaping the rewards of investment—and by association feel good about the West. In addition, said McGhee, it was obvious that the oil company could improve its terms while still enjoying enormous profits.

Sir William Fraser was hardly more cordial to McGhee than he had been to us Iranians. Unmoved by McGhee's oil background or position, he even went so far as to suggest that Whitehall encourage Washington to get rid of him. Like a lighthouse programmed to send out only one message, he told the undersecretary, "One penny more and the company goes broke."

"It can only be concluded," wrote Ambassador Grady to Dean Acheson, U.S. secretary of state, "that the UK is bent on sabotaging our efforts to strengthen Iran [in order] to preserve its [own] dubious supremacy and control there."[3]

Yet from England's perspective it was the Americans, not the Russians, who were causing the problem in the area. Thanks to the Americans, England's greatest nightmare was at that very moment turning into a reality. Just across the Gulf, Aramco was about to offer a 50/50 deal to King Saud—in addition to the extraordinary tax windfall from the "Golden Gimmick."

In Tehran the matter of oil was coming to a head. With Kashani drawing crowds in the streets and Mossadeq hurling thunderbolts in the Majles, we had reached an emotional climax. Legal arguments were being brought up almost as afterthoughts, while the technical arguments were tabled as superfluous. On November 25, 1950, a crystal day of sunspangled snow, Mossadeq brought the Supplemental Agreement to a vote in the oil committee. The 1933 Concession was, he argued, a fraud, signed under a dictatorship that had been imposed on the country for that very purpose. The Supplemental Agreement was a further ploy to keep Iran in bondage for the next forty-three years. His voice was low. He was in failing health; his disease of the nerves was getting the upper hand, making him dizzy and sometimes faint. But the power of his spirit was plain despite his weak voice. Even those not in his camp considered the British offer a halfway measure and were against it. The agreement was unanimously rejected.

A few weeks later, on Christmas Day, Forouhar called me into his office. Dr. Pirnia was already there. The minister was to present the government's final position before the Majles the following morning, and he wanted us to help him prepare the speech. Despite the oil committee's vote, Forouhar's position—strongly encouraged by the Shah—was pro-agreement. He intended to explain the terms to the Majles and highlight the advantages: We needed the extra money; there had been no further options forthcoming from AIOC; from a pragmatic viewpoint we had no alternative.

It was well after midnight when the address was finally completed; the lights in the ministry were out, and the secretaries had all gone home. After saying good night to Forouhar I drove downtown with one of the minister's aides to roust a typist from her bed and get the document typed by morning. We wound through the kinked streets near the bazaar, our tires squealing in the deadly silence. At last, after a number of wrong turns, we found the house. A good deal of banging on the door finally brought the typist's husband to the window. He leaned out in his underwear, shouting and cursing, and threw a bucket of water on our heads. Only then did he listen to our story. Still looking very fierce, he accompanied his wife into the back of the car and to the ministry. There we left them in front of a typewriter as we headed for home.

The next morning, as I pulled out of my mother's driveway, I noticed Forouhar's car a few yards ahead of me. We drove in tandem for a while, until Forouhar's driver turned into the prime minister's office, located some blocks before the Ministry of Finance. Checking the speech with Razmara, I thought as I continued on to the office.

Later that morning Forouhar presented the speech to Parliament. I slipped up to the visitors gallery to watch. He was heckled badly. Every figure he quoted—even the production figures he used to illustrate how Mexico's nationalization had set back its economy—was booed as a British fabrication. But he went on stolidly, supporting past government efforts to obtain the best deal for the people and pointing out the positive sides of the current agreement. It came as an enormous shock, therefore, when he read the last line: The government was unhappy with the AIOC proposal and was withdrawing its support.

I was not the only one stunned. After a moment of complete silence, the house exploded in an uproar. Mossadeq's National Front, primed to condemn the government, had been preempted. Although it was clearly what many of the ministers wanted, they ganged up on Forouhar and said they thought it a mistake. Razmara, the greatest coward of all, denied having seen the speech—though I knew he had looked at it that very morning and had obviously written in the change. Forouhar didn't stand a chance; by the end of the day he was fired.

I felt deeply for the man who had been made a scapegoat. The government, I realized, did not stand for anything. The politicians had sacrificed him, and they would sacrifice me too. That same week I went to Razmara and tendered my resignation. He did not accept it. It was the first of many times over the next few months that I would try to withdraw. I wanted nothing to do with the spirit of revenge that was taking over. The clash of leadership between Mossadeq on the one hand and the forces of the Shah and Razmara on the other had deteriorated into theater, with no hope of getting back to the issues. We had become lost in demagoguery.

The next time I tried to resign was a week later. The news finally broke that the Aramco deal had been signed. We were devastated. Not only had the British categorically denied that any such deal could be given in the Gulf, but as the oldest producer with the biggest refinery and highest output, we felt ill-used and shamed. The next oil committee meeting was tragic. With blind vindictiveness the members first dismissed the Aramco deal as a British plot and then, turning on me as the handiest victim around, levied a barrage of abuse at me as the representative of the government. Makki, once again in the lead, turned personal, insinuating that my family had been the architects of British domination in Iran since the beginning.

I shouted and fumed right back, said a number of things I later regretted, and thought of many more that I later regretted not having said. When I couldn't stand the abuse any longer, I stalked out of the room and presented my resignation to Forouhar's successor. He gave it back to me, saying mildly, " 'When the moon shines, dogs howl.' Get used to it. You won't get anywhere by being so sensitive."

THE UMBRELLA MAN

In truth, I was pleased that the Supplemental Agreement had been scrapped, though nationalization—the only alternative, it seemed—did not make me any happier. I was not against nationalization per se but rather against any irrational move that would compromise our long-term interests. Nationalization would calm the country's raw political nerves. But acting rashly would rob us of everything beyond our borders, since one can only nationalize what is actually on one's own territory. By nationalizing we would lose all the subsidiary companies that our oil revenues had enabled AIOC to acquire. That would be a mighty write-off by any account—and an enormous gain for AIOC. It's what made our situation so different from that of Saudi Arabia, Venezuela, or any of the other oil-producing countries. Nationalization would finally give the company what it had been angling for since the negotiations in 1918 with Nosrat-Doleh: full claim to all the affiliates.

But we were past the point where anyone would listen to such arguments. Each day the chanting crowds became more aggressive, the newspapers more obstinate, the placards more strident. And as the impasse continued, I wondered whether the British themselves were secretly encouraging the move toward nationalization.

I wasn't the only one who was uncomfortable with the turn of events. My cousin Hossein Dowlatshahi was likewise distressed, though for different reasons. Like many others, he was a staunch supporter of the Shah, and he believed that the oil affair and Mossadeq's growing strength boded ill for the throne. Hossein was an arms dealer, the official representative of Winchester and Remington, and had a large gun shop on Avenue Saadi. Often I'd stop by there after work, and we'd go upstairs to his office for a coffee, surrounded by rifles and revolvers in their felt-lined cases. Hossein would always show me the latest arrival, often a collector's item in an inlaid box. Once he showed me the gun that George V of England had given to Ahmad Shah in 1919, and which in turn the young monarch had bequeathed to Nosrat-Doleh. It had a crystal bottle with an ivory plug to hold the gun oil and had birds and flowers chiseled into the metal. I held it solemnly, admiring the craftsmanship, and felt chagrined that I could not afford to buy it.

Hossein had always been crazy about guns. It was a legacy from his father, a grisly colonel in Reza Shah's army. Despite being Farman Farma's brother-in-law, Hossein's father had been so close to the sovereign that at one point Hossein's brothers had been engaged to Princesses Shams and Ashraf. Hossein was the one who had taken the Dutch geologists around the desert in 1939 and then found out later they'd been illegally sounding for oil. We used to go hunting together, and he would get out of his jeep after hours of driving through featureless flatlands and, from the look of a knoll or far-off ridge, identify exactly where a water hole was to be found. It was uncanny. So was his skill with a gun. I took pride in not being too bad a shot myself; I could pick off an ibex from a ridge seven hundred feet away. But that was nothing for Hossein. Once I invited him to Hamadan, where a type of buzzard inhabits the plains. The bird can see a predator from miles away and has plenty of time to lift up and, with wings clattering, escape to safety. Yet Hossein got one; he had the eye.

Hossein's reputation as a gunslinger was well known in Tehran. While in his twenties he caught the attention of U.S. counterintelligence forces and did a turn or two for them in Baghdad. Later in Tehran, during the occupation, he hooked up with an American major named Alex Gagarin, and the two dressed like Soviets and drove through the gates of the Russian encampment to make a report. Hossein was the "chauffeur," while Gagarin barked out orders to him in Russian. They drove all over the camp and afterward drew a map for the Allies describing the communications layout and weapons. Had they been caught, they would have been shot on the spot.

Hossein was a genuine patriot. His values were clearer and simpler than those of most men: adventure, duty, and above all devotion to the sovereign, for whom he would have sacrificed his life. Yet even Hossein was not immune from the political deceptions of the day, and it was his reputation as a gunslinger that got him embroiled.

It was late when I walked into his store one afternoon. An icy wind sifted a coating of dry snowflakes along the carpet before I could shut the door. A coal stove warmed the place, and though it was a large shop, with Hossein's second-floor office hanging above it like Juliet's balcony, it had the snug, woody feel of a ship's hold. Hossein called from above, and I climbed the steps, my heart heavy with the day.

He was holding his round, heavyset face in his hands; a cigarette burned as always in a dish nearby. "I have something to show you," he said. "But first have yourself some coffee."

A servant had come up behind me with a metal tray rattling cups and a dish of cookies. After he'd placed these on the table between us and withdrawn, I told Hossein that Ernest Perron had stopped by to see me. "Reconnaissance for the Shah, though he doesn't say it and I don't ask."

"Does he stop by often?" Hossein asked, interested.

"Yes. Once a week, maybe more. A quick visit an hour or so after the oil committee adjourns."

"I'm glad you oblige," he said.

"I don't know how much it helps," I returned darkly. "I've told him how ineffective the government is in the face of all this infighting and how desperately we need a clear policy. Poor man. You know he's come down with some paralyzing muscle disease. It's becoming quite an effort for him to move around."

Neither of us said anything for a moment. Then we heard the door downstairs open and someone walk in. Hossein jerked up his hand in a gesture of silence. No greetings were exchanged between the new arrival and the shop attendant.

"Come on," he said softly. "We're going down."

An elderly man without a hat sat in one of the chairs leaning on an umbrella. He wore large brown shoes, too big for him, and was poorly shaven. He was German or maybe Swiss. Hossein introduced us without using his name and explained that I was a cousin and that I would be accompanying them. The man eyed me suspiciously. Hossein ignored him. "Let's go to my house," he said. "There we can talk in private."

On the sidewalk Hossein stopped me and whispered in Farsi, "When we get to my house, walk in behind me. Indicate for him to go first so that I can walk in second and you last."

I nodded and climbed into the car.

Hossein's house overlooked the city, and as a spin-off from his desert hunting expeditions he had turned the grounds into a zoo, with lions, alligators, and many other strange animals in cages. The hobby had turned into a venture, and he'd recently caught the biggest panther ever measured in Iran and sold it to the Hamburg Zoo in Germany. As we pulled up I saw the cheetah that Hossein occasionally brought with him into town when he had difficult business with the government. The zoo was the first in the city, and during the day it was open to the public. Now the visitors had gone home, and we drove silently through the gate.

When we alighted from the car, I did as Hossein had instructed and ushered the man in first. Hossein gestured him toward the stairs, indicating that he leave his umbrella in an urn near the banister. I had barely reached the door of the upstairs lounge behind them when I saw Hossein draw his revolver.

"Stop right there," he said, his voice icy and even. "Put your hands up and get over there by the wall."

The man didn't even turn as he put his hands up.

"Stand with your feet apart," Hossein ordered, "and lean forward."

Hossein quickly frisked the man and felt out an automatic hanging from a shoulder holster. It looked to me like a Belgian Browning. Snapping open the clip, he dropped out seven bullets, which he put in his pocket.

"You can turn," Hossein said, "and take this." He handed the man the pistol. "Now we can talk business."

Looking surprisingly unruffled, the man took his seat.

"Why did you want to see me?" Hossein asked.

"I come to you for one thing," the man said cautiously. He glanced at me with unveiled discomfort but nonetheless went on. "We want the mollah, Seyyed Kashani, eliminated. My contacts in Europe inform me that you are the one to do the job." He looked down at his shoes, rubbing one toe over the other. "Money is not an issue," he added. "We can put the money in your account anywhere you wish. We need the job done fast."

"Let me tell you something," said Hossein, calm as cold yogurt. "I like adventures. I really do." He looked straight into the man's eyes. "The problem is, I've never killed anybody. And I don't *plan* to kill anybody now." He paused, as if turning the matter over in his mind, though I knew he was just wriggling the bait. "It's true I don't like Kashani. He's a fanatic and a supporter of Mossadeq. If there was anybody I should like to eliminate, it would be him. But I'm not going to indulge in a crime just to see the world rid of him. What's more, I would not do it for money. You, sir, have come to the wrong man."

"I'm sorry about that," said the man. "We'd hoped to come to some arrangement."

"I'll tell you one more thing," said Hossein. "There is no arrangement to be made around here. Either with me or anybody else. I advise you to go back where you came from, right away."

The man pursed his lips. He seemed suddenly shrunken in his chair. "Actually," he said, "I had planned to stay a few more days."

"No," said Hossein. "There is a plane leaving tonight at eight P.M. for Switzerland. A seat has been reserved on it in your name. I will accompany you to the airport."

"I see," said the man. "But there is the problem of my effects, still at the hotel."

"No problem at all," answered Hossein. "Your two valises are in the trunk of the car we drove here in."

The man took a second to digest this, then nodded gravely. "I am at your disposal," he said. "And looking at the barrel of your gun."

We trooped out of the room and down the stairs. At the bottom I noticed that the urn with the umbrella in it was now empty. The man became very agitated. "My umbrella!" he demanded.

"Your umbrella," Hossein scoffed. "From that first day when you came into my store and sat without speaking, and the next day when you came, I could see from my office on the second floor that your umbrella wasn't an umbrella! I knew your game right away. I don't do business with people who carry hidden guns onto their host's premises. Now, shall we go?"

Hossein and I spoke of the incident only once, and that was some years later. In the meantime Kashani claimed a number of assassination plots against him, which I never doubted. He eventually died in his bed.

"You remember that man with the umbrella?" Hossein asked me out of the blue one day. "Well he's dead."

"Dead?" I asked in surprise. "How do you know?"

"Because he left a draft in my name for twenty thousand pounds, according to his bank executors in Geneva."

I laughed out loud. "You going to go get it?"

"Hell no!" His eyes twinkled, and I waited for him to say more. "But the bankers have been adamant. They badger me, call me up at all hours, insist they are legally bound to give the money to me." He pulled on his cigarette and blew out a spiral of smoke. "So I have come up with a solution."

I was sure he was going to tell me he was sending it to some floozy. Hossein was a typical Middle Eastern businessman—fond of cheap women and cabarets and always getting into fistfights late at night in shabby bars.

"I have told the bankers to pay it directly to a foundation that I set up some little while ago," he said slowly. He averted his face. His voice sounded almost shy. "The money will go to feed the children of southern Tehran."

I looked at him amazed, marveling that even when you think you know someone intimately, he can have facets you never even imagined existed. The foundation he mentioned was well known in Iran, but I had no idea it was Hossein's creation. I was one of the very few ever to find out. We said no more, and he never mentioned the matter to me again.

A TALE OF MISSED OPPORTUNITIES

The month of March, leading up to No Rooz, 1951, was a landmark in Iranian history. On the fourth Razmara attended an oil committee session. He looked tired, like a bull goaded by picadors, and had obviously lost much political blood. He insisted the British were now more amenable to profit sharing, though he stopped short of saying they'd consider a 50/50 deal. Then he presented the opinions of "experts" to show how catastrophic nationalization would be. Afterward we all got up to speak with him informally. At one point I saw him pass a piece of yellow lined paper containing, he said, the list of experts to a man named Faramarzi, the editor of the big morning newspaper *Kayhan*.

The following morning I dropped by to see an old friend who had just returned from Europe. Seyyed Jalal Tehrani was an astronomer and the type of person who was friends with everyone, including the most vicious enemies, such as Mossadeq and Razmara. He had served in a number of cabinets, and though he'd been asked to join the present one, he'd turned the position down. Years later, as head of the Regency Council, he went to Paris as the last envoy from the Shah's government in a futile attempt to negotiate with Ayatollah Khomeini.

The morning I went to see him he came to the door with the prime minister. The night before, the radio had broadcast Razmara's speech to the oil committee, and already there were angry demonstrators in the streets calling for nationalization. But the prime minister looked relaxed and, after we exchanged greetings, said his good-byes.

Tehrani confided to me that morning that he thought Razmara was failing. The people are against him, and he will never succeed in living up to his promises to the British, he said. "You know what I told him just now? That tomorrow I have an audience with His Majesty the Shah and that I will tell him that the prime minister wants to resign. It is better for us all if he goes now."

Tehrani was, among other things, a collector of antiques. That morning we sat in a room filled with clocks and a number of old stargazing instruments on rollers and swivels. Through the window I could see orange trees that he'd imported from Europe and planted under a glass gazebo.

"Will he resign?" I asked.

"Yes," said Tehrani. "He said he would."

Later that day Razmara telephoned me in great agitation. He spoke rapidly and peremptorily told me the note he'd given to Faramarzi was the wrong one and that he needed it back. Since I would see Faramarzi at the oil committee meeting the next day, I was to ask him privately for it and arrange its return.

There were rumors that before coming to the oil committee Razmara had held discussions with the new British ambassador, Sir Francis Shepherd, and that at last a 50/50 proposal had been handed over. I put down the phone, wondering whether this "wrong note" had perhaps contained information on that deal.

Faramarzi shed no light on the matter. He denied that the note was the wrong one and refused to hand it over. But my suspicions of an imminent 50/50 deal were confirmed that night at a dinner at the home of the first secretary of the British Embassy. The former director of AIOC's students Charles Myles was in town from London, and he greeted me warmly, listening with amazement to my escapades on *The Merchant of Venice*. Over dinner the conversation was all about oil, and after a while I realized my hosts were testing my opinions.

"If 50/50 were to be offered, do you think it would be a viable solution?" asked Myles.

"Perhaps," I answered carefully. "But it addresses only one aspect of the problem. There is still the money owed to our government from past years, the Admiralty discount—and all those other issues."

"Yes, those would have to be settled," George Middleton, whose home it was, said vaguely.

"If it were only so easy," I said smiling. "And what about the profit sharing from the subsidiary companies?"

"That too would have to be worked out," Myles said. "It is of course unthinkable that the Iranian government claim a fifth of the consolidated profits of our oil operations in Iraq, Kuwait, or Qatar. What would your suggestion be?"

"I think we will eventually have to bring it to court," I said. "I think that's why the company has refrained so far from offering us the 50/50."

In the library over cigars I observed that back in the 1920s Armitage-Smith had adjudged the company's offspring fully within Iran's claims. Since his time AIOC had not had to raise a single cent; its phenomenal growth over the past thirty years had all been capitalized by reinvested profits—money that had been siphoned off before Iran was given its share of the proceeds. The company, I reminded them, now owned refineries in France, Israel, and Australia; a worldwide tanker company; and partnerships in oil companies throughout the Gulf and as far away as Burma. Wouldn't it be considered very bad business—from Iran's perspective of course—if the country were now to step away from assets that it had funded almost unilaterally?

They nodded politely but returned to the question of Iran's own oil, the real crux of the problem, they said. By the time I left, they'd more than intimated that a 50/50 proposal was already in play.

As fate would have it the whole discussion was moot by the next day—as was Razmara's anticipated resignation. It was a cold, clear day that Thursday, March 7, 1951, and spring seemed far away. Outside my office demonstrators massed along the sidewalk, denouncing the prime minister and chanting "Death to the British."

A report on my desk revealed that at last the British government was willing to release the Eximbank's $25 million, which it had heretofore frozen until the Supplemental Agreement was voted through. It seemed further confirmation that the terms had changed. But the papers mentioned nothing, and I wondered whether the prime minister was keeping it a secret. I decided to alert Mossadeq, hoping to use this new development as proof that patience and pressure were bringing results and that nationalization was not the only answer. But Mossadeq would hear none of it. His mind—and that of the people in the streets, he said—was made up.

Just minutes after I returned to my office, my secretary handed me the phone. As I listened to the voice on the other end, my mouth went dry. Prime Minister Razmara had been shot and killed as he was entering a mosque with one of the Shah's closest friends. No one else had been hurt. His assassin was a religious fanatic. Already it was being rumored that the Shah's friend had brought Razmara to the slaughterhouse.

I laid the phone down carefully. Once again a life had been lost as the price of oil.

I didn't believe the rumors about the Shah's involvement, but I did know that the man who was supposed to have brought order to Iran had instead brought the country to the brink of chaos. Although Razmara was incompetent, he was the last bulwark against nationalization. Now the gates were open. Providence seemed to favor Mossadeq, for his enemies had all been wiped out.

THE TALE OF NATIONALIZATION

The next day the oil committee voted unanimously for nationalization. "With 50/50 we'll only be able to pay half our debts," quipped one of the members. "With nationalization we'll be able to pay them all." Previously he'd been a staunch supporter of the Supplemental Agreement, and I was intrigued by the change. Had he come to realize that it was political suicide to be against nationalization? Did he fear he would be lynched if he voted otherwise? I looked at him with a quavering heart, wondering whether he realized what an enormous sacrifice we were about to make.

A week later, on March 15, Mossadeq triumphantly brought the bill for nationalization before the Majles. My old mentor, Ambassador Hossein Ala, had been appointed prime minister upon Razmara's death. Although he was one of the few who understood the catastrophic loss Iran would suffer by severing the mother company from the subsidiaries, he was sanguine enough to know that any possibility of compromise had already been lost. Fifty-fifty, brought to the table too late by AIOC, had now become too little. Although Mossadeq and Kashani were not above exerting pressure on the deputies, the anti-British furor prevailing in the Parliament was enough to send every last representative into a headlong stampede for nationalization. There was sweet vengeance in it too, for many thought that without Iranian oil Britannia would fall.

I heard the news of the vote just as I was leaving the office for a lunch at Northcroft's home. It was snowing when I got there. A big fire burned in the grate, and many of the town's luminaries, both in and out of power, stood about the room. I saw Forouhar in one corner and nodded. My brother Mohammad Hossein Mirza, splendid in his general's uniform, entertained a group by the door. I asked Northcroft whether he had heard the news.

"Of course," he replied, with the ease of one who knows everything. "What about it? Have a whiskey!"

His calm demeanor did not sit well with me, and nervously I moved from one group to another, hardly listening to their conversations. Nationalization was not going to be the cataclysm we had made it out to be for the British. The hardship would be ours, for we would have to pay compensation to AIOC with money we did not have. Seeing Northcroft across the room, I could tell he felt that AIOC had actually won the first hand. As the bubble of chatter flowed around me I suddenly realized we'd walked into a trap. AIOC was going to avoid paying us any of the money it owed while holding on to the subsidiary companies we legally shared claim to. And, from an international standpoint, it would come out smelling like a rose.

Nationalization inspired euphoria in the streets, and everywhere Mossadeq went he was surrounded by a frenzy of adulation, stirring speeches about the future, and strong words about the present. The Communists jumped on his bandwagon—an ironic twist since he'd always claimed he'd created the National Front to provide the disaffected masses with an alternative to the Tudeh Party. The tribes, always anti-Shah, supported Mossadeq in the hope that he would weaken the government and thereby offer them greater autonomy. Seyyed Kashani, whose clout with the clerics gave Mossadeq religious legitimacy, exhorted his followers to show themselves in the street for the man who had done the impossible by ousting the British and saving Iran. Mossadeq's National Front coalition, balanced loosely on the shoulders of such diverse interests, so dominated the Parliament that every bill it considered was his and every vote cast was according to his plans. *The New York Times* called him a dictator (a term that in the next twenty years it ironically never used to describe the Shah). And, for a short while, with full popular support, he was.

By mid-April 1951, Prime Minister Ala had had enough. "A prime minister has no business being in the job if he can't control the Parliament's agenda," he told me privately, and tendered his resignation.

The move caused consternation in the Majles. Word had gotten out that the Shah's next candidate for prime minister was the old eccentric Seyyed Zia. He was the British government's choice as well. To indicate how serious it considered the situation, AIOC abruptly cut wages in Abadan, igniting riots; two British frigates then moved into the Gulf, ostensibly to restore peace. Without mentioning nationalization Ambassador Shepherd let it be known that any further talks with AIOC would be conditional on Seyyed Zia's appointment.

Seyyed Zia went to the palace—as was usual for the candidate about to be named premier—to wait with the Shah for Parliament's ratification of his appointment. In the Majles Jamal Emami, a prominent member of the right wing, faced a quandary. On the one hand was the powerful Mossadeq, whose enmity toward Seyyed Zia had already been played out once in Parliament with tears and finger-pointing. On the other was the Shah, whose candidate few trusted. How could he prevent an ongoing confrontation between these two that would permanently hobble the Majles at this critical time? Public shame, Emami decided, was the best tactic. And so, with a saturnine scowl, he took the podium and accused Mossadeq of hindering all parliamentary action he did not like. Mossadeq had brought the Majles to a standstill, Emami complained. He only criticized, never constructed. If he was going to set the course of the Majles and its oil policy, *he* should serve as prime minister.

Emami's taunt was not a recommendation for Mossadeq's candidacy. Mossadeq had always disdained holding office, maintaining categorically that the only way to serve the people was as a deputy. He had never accepted previous offers of the premiership, and Emami was sure he wouldn't accept this one.

Emami was wrong. In a surprise move Mossadeq accepted and on May 1, 1951, it handed the Shah a fait accompli. It was a historic moment. For the first time a prime minister had been elected without the Shah's approval. The Shah had no option but to accept. It was a humiliation he would never forget.

The Shah, so concerned about juggling the foreign powers to protect his throne, had at last been undermined by his own people. His power struggle with the Parliament was humiliating, for we had never witnessed such conflict between the two arms of government. And this just at the time when the country needed strength, for it was suddenly on its own, having finally sent its old colonial adversary packing. Nationalization was in essence independence, a heart-throbbing, honorable, and glorious step, but one that stirred deep-seated qualms and doubts. It was a bad time for the nation's faith in the Shah to waver.

A TALE OF REACTION

What followed was the calm before the storm. From the Iranian perspective all the pieces were in place for a seamless transition. Mossadeq, impatient but realistic, had a clear idea of the legal ramifications he faced both at home and abroad. It was not, he told Ambassador Shepherd, a bilateral confrontation. Iran had nationalized its main industry just as postwar Britain had done under Clement Attlee. The British government needn't get involved. He wanted direct discussions with company officials, and he wished to address only two issues: compensation and evacuation. British nationals, he said, would be encouraged to renew their contracts with the newly formed National Iranian Oil Company (NIOC), which would honor them unchanged. The books should be handed over, and incoming funds would immediately be placed in a British account to start paying compensation.

To this end a joint committee was formed in mid-May. It immediately set up a provisional board to manage the newly minted NIOC and invited AIOC's representative in Tehran to sit in on its sessions. At its helm was Mehdi Bazargan, dean of the University of Tehran's Technical College and the founder of what was considered the core intellectual group within the National Front. A soft-spoken, sober man of strong liberal conviction, he twice in his life took on the task of attempting a miracle at the head of a fledgling enterprise. Heading up the brand-new NIOC was the first effort.

The second was as Ayatollah Khomeini's first prime minister after the departure of the Shah in 1979. In both cases he fulfilled his role with dignity, but both jobs were impossible and in both cases he failed.

The British government was flummoxed by Iran's extraordinary behavior. Nationalization as a legal step appeared to mean nothing to it. The action was interpreted as a threat, a ruse, an act of larceny, or an act of extreme stupidity. Sir Oliver Franks, the British ambassador to the United States, described it as "the insolent defiance of decency, legality, and reason by a group of wild men in Iran who proposed to despoil Britain."[4] Never once was it recognized as a straightforward "breach of contract [that] involved payment of damages or compensation," as U.S. secretary of state Dean Acheson put it.[5] Ambassador Shepherd, who previous to his appointment to Iran had served in a number of British colonies and countries with strong dictatorships, refused to recognize Mossadeq's distinction between government and company, and he recommended that Whitehall adopt a "stiff attitude." In London, military intervention was seriously considered and provisionally dropped only after strong resistance from Washington.

For the moment events on the international front were suspended. Down in the oil fields, however, the workers wanted drastic action. Confused over the ambiguity of their management, the men poured into the city demanding that the government take over operations. On June 11, 1951, Mossadeq responded. The provisional board occupied the central office in Khorramshahr and hoisted the Iranian flag. Fifty thousand workers cheered in the streets, facing down a raging sandstorm. The nameplate of AIOC was changed to NIOC, and a statement was issued that all employees, Iranian and foreign, were henceforth on the payroll of the National Iranian Oil Company. It was a heady day, and when the sun rose the next morning it seemed a new dawn was breaking over Iran.

But the harsh light of morning was to reveal only quicksand ahead. Eric Drake, AIOC's general manager, refused to hand over the books. On Fraser's orders he instructed all the tankers at dock not to sign any NIOC receipts. Then, in an odd move, he slipped off to Basra under cover of night, leaving behind hundreds of British nationals to fend for themselves. Cowardliness was not a trait associated with the British, and Drake's ill-timed departure, which many Iranians viewed as poltroonery, was a severe setback to their position.

In Abadan, despite all the American talk of supporting Iran's nationalization, U.S. tankers held fast with their British counterparts and refused to sign any NIOC receipts. Ships filled with oil began to pump it back into holding tanks at the refinery. One after another they weighed anchor and filed out of the port of Abadan empty. By the end of June all export of Iranian oil had ground to a halt.

A TALE OF DISMISSAL

A nation's triumph is an awesome thing. For one precious moment the whole population is buoyed up, carried by a common bond of pride in country. Like the fans at a soccer game who watch their team make the winning goal, a shot of delirium sends everyone to their feet, and everyone cheers, somehow feeling that they contributed to the victory. Sudden energy surges through the crowd; strangers hug each other, laughing and dancing. So it is for a country. After a victory a sun burns in one's chest, one speaks lightly and sleeps well, and there is a sense of release. The nation has come together; no one remembers who was for or against the move that led to the triumph, and no one knows or cares what the next step will be. For the moment people are united and joyous, celebrating with their families, jumping over bonfires, thanking God for his care and benevolence. And so it was for us. The British Empire had been slapped in the face, and Iran felt a triumph it had been awaiting for fifty years.

It is only later that it becomes clear that not everyone is part of the victory. The nation begins to divide like an amoeba. Memory returns, condemning those that were against the course that was taken. Division over what step to take next occurs. The people, leaving behind the littered stadium, the bunting now torn in the wind, go home to make dinner, wash dirty dishes, face the humdrum of the evening. After the ecstatic afternoon, the mood drops, revealing fear, anger, the sentimentality of despair. The comradery dissolves. The witch-hunt begins.

Though I was ambivalent about nationalization, once the bill passed and Mossadeq stepped into the premiership, I was carried along by the wave of euphoria. At last a member of my family had reached the spotlight of power; we were back in the saddle, and we were going to start moving the country forward.

It came as a total shock, therefore, when a friend of mine, a deputy of the Majles, called the same day Mossadeq became premier and told me that I had been dismissed. I said that it must be a mistake. I had already weathered seven premiers and eight ministers of finance; no one in the ministry had survived for so long. In addition I was an admirer of Dr. Mossadeq's.

Nonetheless, when I was summoned by the minister of finance an hour later, he confirmed the report.

"Your job is political," he said. "Now that oil has been nationalized, he feels it must be managed in a different way. Your cousin is replacing you with someone else.

"I have argued your case to the prime minister," he continued. "I spoke highly of your ability. I suggested you be transferred to Washington as commercial attaché at the embassy."

I was too incredulous to respond. I rose quietly and thanked him for his time. Like a shadow I left the room.

That afternoon I called Mossadeq's son Gholam Hossein. He already knew of the decision. "I wasn't even allowed to resign," I said with indignation. "I have been shown the door like a traitor. Why, Gholam, why?"

"It is people like Makki, fanatic nationalists," he said with a sigh. "You represented the government; they are branding you a British sympathizer. There is nothing you can do now but wait."

I hung up the phone devastated. The accusation of being pro-British did not particularly bother me. Everyone in Iran had been dubbed pro-British at one point or another. The Shah had accused Mossadeq of being pro-British; Mossadeq had returned the insult. Qavam Saltaneh had been accused of it. My own brother Nosrat-Doleh. . . . What bothered me more was that I had been kicked out for arguing patience, for showing the downside of nationalization, for being frank. I had been kicked out for refusing to conform.

As the process of nationalization gathered steam, I stayed home in semi-retirement. Nothing came of the suggestion that I go to the embassy in Washington. Makki, it seemed, had stifled that idea too.

Some weeks later my brother Abol Bashar, who was studying law at Columbia University, sent me three articles on the legal aspects of nationalization. They involved countries that had nationalized against American companies. The United States' acceptance of compensation offered an important precedent. I translated the articles, annotated them with observations about the Iranian situation, and submitted them to the newspaper *Kayhan,* which promptly published them on the front page. It kept me involved and in the public eye, a good position for my next step—whatever that would be.

The articles immediately elicited a reaction from AIOC. It came in the form of my lawyer friend Fuad Rohani, who stopped by for tea. Rohani had a face that looked as if it had never been young. He had grayed completely, though he was not more than thirty-five, an asset that, in conjunction with his carefully chosen spectacles, he used to convey the image that he was wise beyond his years. He had developed a number of mannerisms to bolster that impression, among them the habit of reading while he walked—until he was hit by a car and almost killed. Another was his propensity to discuss any subject in a priestly manner, which he now proceeded to do concerning my articles on nationalization.

I did not begrudge him his role as messenger from AIOC, but I was not going to let him walk all over me either. Despite our friendship, I knew he could not give up his inner feelings of support for the British—who had paid for his education and given him his job at AIOC. So when he told me that AIOC had expected better of me, I gave him a hard look. "Why should they expect anything from me?" I asked. "Are they planning on hiring me in London? No. Are they planning to do something for me here? No. Have I ever been on their side? No! I have just argued the merits of the case and acted like a gentleman, and if in the past that has given them the impression I'm a supporter and friend, well, they're wrong."

Rohani blushed in anger but said nothing. He was a master at maintaining his equilibrium. Where I would speak out, he would keep his own counsel and avoided contradicting others. It was a difference in approach that would later have an enormous impact on our careers—and our friendship.

As the summer wore on, the British government decided the situation in Iran had gotten out of hand and took over the negotiations from the officials at AIOC. As a first step it brought the matter to the World Court in The Hague. Mossadeq protested. The World Court, he said, had no jurisdiction in a case between a country and a company (an opinion later confirmed by the court itself). U.S. secretary of state Dean Acheson, seeing the hardening on both sides, suggested sending Franklin Roosevelt's old shuttle diplomat, Averell Harriman, to try his hand at finding common ground.

Harriman arrived in the heat of mid-July, accompanied by a famous international oil expert and government adviser, Walter Levy. It was Levy who had discovered during the war that Hitler was secretly making airplane fuel out of potatoes (something he miraculously deduced by comparing train schedules). We met one evening at the American Embassy. Behind his wide face and well-pondered words was a razor-sharp mind. He was one of the cleverest men I've ever met. His grasp of the conflict was unclouded by extraneous political interests, and right away he understood that the oil issue in Iran was one of sovereignty and wounded national pride. He and Harriman both thought Fraser a fool. I filled him in on Mossadeq's idiosyncrasies and warned him not to judge by the surface but to look at the purpose of the man underneath. Levy did not suffer from the same prejudices I had noted in Justice Douglas, and I left that evening with high hopes in their ability to mediate a settlement.

Harriman's mission, however, was not a success. Although it stretched over many weeks and helped to forge a tight friendship between the Americans and Mossadeq, finding common ground between the Persians and British proved elusive. Harriman's most quoted comment after his final return: "I feel we spent more time in Iran than all the officials of AIOC put together."

Harriman's failure had a negative impact on the politics in Iran. It left Mossadeq more exposed to fanatic demands and lessened his room for maneuver. With the oil spigot turned off, the country's financial reserves began to shrink. Goods became scarce and inflation soared. Blame and condemnation began to fly. One day my friend and former minister Gholam Hossein Forouhar called, asking me to come and see him. It was a dangerous request, for his house was being watched and accusations that he had cooperated with AIOC were rife. Nonetheless I went. Sorrowfully he admitted that he had mentioned my name in Parliament to shield himself. He had been questioned by the police, he said. He knew he would soon be arrested and warned me I might be too.

"Get out of the country," he whispered, his face white with fear, "or you will end up in jail with me."

"Mossadeq is not an assassin," I said. "If we go to jail, we will come out as heroes. To be a political prisoner is not a bad thing in our country. Don't worry. I'm not going anywhere. And no matter what, you'll be fine."

I was to eat my words. A few days later I received a call from Dr. Pirnia. Having been sidelined, he now enjoyed the trust of the current regime and was back in the game. He told me a telegram had arrived from the Venezuelan government. It was from Dr. Luongo Cabello, who had become minister of mines, personally inviting me to an oil conference in Caracas.

"Then I shall go," I said to him, "though God only knows how I shall arrange to get a passport."

By sheer coincidence I was invited to dinner the next evening by the Shah's brother, Prince Abdol Reza. His mother, a relative of ours, had invited me often to the palace after Reza Shah's abdication, and Abdol Reza and I had been close for a long time. To my mind he had the soundest judgment of all his siblings. He wore his title with dignity, and I always felt he could be trusted. The Shah was there too, and when the men withdrew to the library for cigars, I drew alongside him. Was it possible, I asked, in these difficult days, for His Majesty to give the order granting me a passport? He nodded. It was to attend a conference in Venezuela, I explained. I had been invited personally by Dr. Luongo Cabello, the Venezuelan minister of mines, who had visited Tehran the year before. I then explained a few of the difficulties I had encountered with Mossadeq and the government's negative attitude toward me.

The next day, just as I was sitting down to lunch, Ernest Perron burst in, his face radiant. Though normally he did not drink, he asked for a beer. "Let's celebrate!" he declared. "Here's your passport!" He produced it from his vest pocket and waved it in front of my nose. "It's a semidiplomatic one for government dignitaries. You can leave anytime."

I left Tehran two days later. My sisters Leila and Haideh accompanied me, the latter to get married in Paris, the former ostensibly as my secretary. Leila was on her way to Barnard College. Caracas would be an adventure. I was to act as her chaperon and deliver her afterward to New York.

His Majesty the Shah sent a colonel from his personal guard as an escort to the plane. We left at night, having mentioned our departure to no one. As the plane lifted off over the plain, banking west away from the Elborz Mountains, I looked out of the window with a feeling of anguish. I had been tossed off and was running from the turmoil with no idea how long I would be gone. I don't know whether the word *exile* formed in my mind, but the feelings were all there. As so often happened when emotion caught me, a stanza of Hafez came to mind:

Pretty words and recitations are not cherished in Shiraz
Come, Hafez, let's hurl ourselves into a more appreciative land.

CHAPTER XI

A LOSING BATTLE

Hafez gave his life for wine and was consumed by love
Where is Christ to rehabilitate us with his breath?
—HAFEZ

Tehran 1953
The image of Nero playing his violin as Rome went up in flames has always struck me as a powerful metaphor. The frenzied abandon before disaster: It was in the films of Berlin's elite in the 1940s, with the platinum blondes dancing the nights away before the fall of Hitler. And it was in Tehran during the last days of Mossadeq, after I returned in 1953.

For two years Iran had not sold a drop of oil—and it showed. Its sterling balances had been frozen by the Bank of England, and the government had no money to pay the armed forces, let alone its civil servants. Paper money rolled off the presses, and every day prices rose. The rial had lost almost half its value, dropping from 75 to 130 rials to the dollar by July 1953. Only the rich could afford the exorbitant prices of medicine and food. The poor, always the first to feel shortages, suffered that much more.

After my two years in the United States the city looked ill and tattered to me. The streets were all torn up for the water pipes that were at last being laid in Tehran. It was a project of the Shah's that stumbled on despite the country's financial disarray. Heaps of earth and deep trenches interrupted the flow of traffic, and where the work had been finished, the cars drove up and down along deep ruts in unpaved roads. Beggars filled the

streets in greater numbers than I remembered. They gathered at the corners—mothers with babies in their arms, the children's eyes rimmed with
flies. There was not a single new car to be seen. The vehicles in the streets
wheezed and clanked, ramshackle victims of a market in which spare parts
were scarce and extremely dear. Ironically, this created a fuel shortage in
the capital. No pipeline yet connected Abadan to Tehran, so fuel still had
to be trucked in or sent by rail. As the transport fleet grew dilapidated, less
oil reached the city and long lines, particularly for kerosene, became a common sight.

People were angry—but not at Mossadeq. They blamed England and
the international oil cartel for refusing to honor the country's right to nationalize its oil. They felt vaguely disillusioned with the United States, the
great protector of the underdog, whose motives were now a bit suspect.
Mossadeq, in an appeal that would be echoed many years later by Ayatollah Khomeini, called this time of hardship a "holy war" and promised victory through perseverance. Posters of Mossadeq, looking sage and stern,
dotted the walls of bakeries and pharmacies and hung above the black-
boards in schools. A smiling portrait would have been considered undig-
nified—even weak—and there were none of those. Posters of the prime
minister were particularly evident around the university, but they were becoming worn, and the old man himself was acting more like a mad dog
beset by wolves than the triumphant leader of a nation newly free.

When I returned to Iran no one knew that Mossadeq's remaining days
would be so few. It was an odd confluence of events and people that
brought about his downfall. Had Churchill not won the election in England or had Truman run again in the United States; had Stalin not died
or the Korean War not wound down just when it did; had Senator Joseph
McCarthy been silenced just a bit sooner or Congress not been rocked by
an oil cartel scare—history would have been different. Most bizarre of all,
had the CIA not had an operative named Kermit Roosevelt, a grandson of
President Theodore Roosevelt, who would turn out to be the living em-
bodiment of "the Quiet American," as the British double agent Kim
Philby liked to call him, Mossadeq might at last have won. There are still
many mysteries. The greatest is the resonant silence of the Soviet Union,
which was fighting the United States and the rest of the UN on its eastern
flank in Korea yet remained mute about Washington's flagrant activity on
its southern border in Iran. History books ignore this detail, and the
British archives on the subject are closed until 2050. No doubt there is
much to hide.

VENEZUELA

When I reached Venezuela after my long, grim flight out of Iran in 1951, I was welcomed as a hero. It was a nice change. Dr. Luongo Cabello had filled everyone in on our concessionary choices and our frustrations with Sir William Fraser. The Venezuelans thought that AIOC was monstrous and congratulated me heartily on the nationalization. I didn't know how much their mood was inspired by their own windfall profits as a result of our disappearance from the market, but it seemed sour grapes to belabor that now. I laughed with pure pleasure when I saw Dr. Luongo Cabello's puckish face at the airport. We hugged each other warmly, and he and the rest of the Venezuelans treated me as a guest of honor.

My sister Leila and I were installed at the Hotel Avila, a gracious modern building overlooking the lush green valley of Caracas. Parrots and sloths hung about the trees. Everything in the city was new, and it was clear that much of it had been cut out of raw jungle just a few years before.

This was the first conference I had attended in an oil-producing country, and the experience was invigorating. U.S. undersecretary of commerce Oscar Chapman opened the proceedings, and afterward we met for a private talk. Trying to suggest something useful, I proposed that the United States set up a new system of oil sales that would help Iran save face—and perhaps induce Mossadeq to sign an agreement with the American oil companies. What an illusion! How little I understood then what the big oil companies were really after. But Chapman was a gentleman, and we both agreed that under the current status quo Mossadeq would fail. Afterward I wrote to Mossadeq and the Shah, reporting on Chapman's opinion that for the moment the U.S. companies had no choice but to support AIOC, dashing any hope that Iran could sell and export oil independently. I sent the letters care of Dr. Pirnia, who later informed me that Mossadeq had laughed outright when he got his, shouting, "Look at what he's writing to me—that I will never succeed. Ha!" and then stashed it under his pillow. Dr. Pirnia suggested that in the future it might be wise to keep such opinions to myself.

The conference closed with a visit to Maracaibo, the coastal drilling and refinery site of Venezuela's oil industry. It lay about as far from Caracas as Abadan does from Tehran and reminded me very much of our own petroleum installations. But here rigs rode the rainbow-slicked surface of Lake Maracaibo, pumping crude oil through hundreds of feet of water in a miracle of modern engineering.

At the dinner dance that evening, Dr. Luongo Cabello opened the first waltz with Leila. To my surprise, the Saudi delegate, Abdullah Tariki, strode to my side and hissed in a barely concealed whisper that Moslem women were not supposed to dance. Before I could gather myself to reply, a Venezuelan, overhearing the comment, answered acidly, "Then perhaps you should put down that whiskey in your hand, Mr. Tariki."

Tariki and I would meet at a number of conferences in the future. He was Saudi Arabia's top oil expert, an intelligent, outspoken man but too leftist for his time—an attitude that eventually brought his downfall. One of his eyes was bad and protruded oddly from his face, a defect that in no way affected his self-image as a highly eligible bachelor, not the least because he was rich, which all Saudis of that rank were. Being used to the limelight, he was clearly miffed at the attention that my sister and I received throughout the conference.

Too soon the idyllic days in Caracas drew to a close, and we flew first to Mexico and then on to New York. There we arrived to hear that a military coup in Caracas had immediately followed our departure. Under the dictatorship of General Marcos Pérez Jiménez, Dr. Luongo Cabello was appointed minister of oil. Four years of extraordinary progress for Venezuela followed, though at great cost. Pérez Jiménez was finally overthrown by a revolution, and never again would my friend Luongo Cabello hold office. For years he lived under house arrest. His fate was a tragic comment on the capricious politics of developing nations, which out of fear and inexperience destroy their own best and brightest.

New York, when I got there, was in a frenzy over Mossadeq's imminent arrival. The British government, failing to get a quick judgment out of the World Court, had decided to bring the case to the UN Security Council. To its horror Mossadeq announced that he would himself head up the Iranian delegation.

The impasse between Mossadeq and the British government had become more pronounced over the previous weeks. By September 22, 1951, Herbert Morrison, Prime Minister Attlee's minister of foreign affairs, had made it patently clear that London had no intention of negotiating with the current Tehran regime and in fact actively sought its replacement. Feelers were sent out probing the strength of the aged Qavam-Saltaneh and the ever-hopeful Seyyed Zia as alternative prime ministers who might reverse the nationalization law. British ambassador Sir Francis Shepherd let the Shah know that should he not be cooperative, the British government could and would replace him too.

Such backdoor politicking did not escape Mossadeq's notice. When the Foreign Office requested and then dismissed a new set of his proposals— terms the U.S. State Department called "not far from a basis for settlement"—Mossadeq's patience snapped. The British personnel still at

Abadan would have to go, he decided. They refused to work for the re-vamped NIOC, and besides, he had no money to pay them. The eviction was set for October 4, 1951, with the injunction that the Iranian officials responsible should "see them off with the most friendly of feelings."

Removing the last expatriate staff from the oil fields was a trump card that the Attlee government had itself planned to play. But Mossadeq stole the show. Requesting a ten-day delay until his delegation could arrive in New York, he succeeded in postponing the Security Council's debate until after the expulsion. By the time Mossadeq touched down at La Guardia Airport, there was not a single British oil employee left in all of southern Iran.

NEW YORK

Having just arrived in New York myself, I wondered how Mossadeq felt as he stepped for the first time onto American soil—the symbol of the brave and the free. He did not enjoy the benefit I did of speaking the language. He relied on an interpreter or, whenever presented with the opportunity, spoke in bad French. Neither did he have the benefit of good health. From the airport he was whisked to New York Hospital, where he passed much of his time in bed, negotiating incessantly with Assistant Secretary of State George McGhee.

I, on the other hand, moved about easily on bus and subway, relishing the broad American accent of the streets. I liked the United States. I'd al-ways felt that anyone who could should live there at least for a while. I im-mediately found an apartment through the newspaper—a large, bright room in a brownstone on leafy East Ninety-fourth Street, right around the corner from Central Park. It was an easy hop to see my sister Leila at Barnard and Abol Bashar, who was still at Columbia Law School. By now a number of my other brothers and sisters had moved to the United States to study: Cyrus and Khodadad were in Boulder, Colorado; Alaverdi was at Stanford; Hafez was in Washington, D.C.

In those days an apartment off Fifth Avenue could be rented by the month, and the arrangement suited me perfectly. Although I expected lit-tle change in my status vis-à-vis the Mossadeq regime, I didn't believe I would stay out of favor for long. At first I set out to find an engineering job with an oil company. This proved impossible since I had no work permit, only a tourist visa valid for six months. The people interviewing me were kind, however, and held none of the animosity toward Iran that they would develop after Khomeini came to power.

My chance to test the waters with Mossadeq came sooner than I'd anticipated—and for a brief moment I thought my term of exile might end almost as soon as it had begun. As usual the prime minister was traveling with his son (and resident physician) Gholam Hossein. Since he and I were close, we soon got in contact by phone. Mossadeq, Gholam Hossein told me, was slated to go to Washington, D.C., after the Security Council debate to meet with President Truman and Secretary of State Dean Acheson. I asked if it might be a good moment for me to meet with Mossadeq and talk about the future. Gholam Hossein said yes.

Mossadeq appeared before the Security Council on October 16, 1951. The presentation he delivered was masterful. Furthermore the audience he addressed was inclined in his favor. The Soviet delegate had already publicly stated that nationalization was a domestic affair that did not fall under the Security Council's jurisdiction. The Chinese—representing Nationalist China, not the vast Maoist mainland—said that it seemed nothing more than a flap about "property" and hardly a question of "peace and security" as claimed by the British delegation. Many of the others seated on the council were representatives of nations that themselves had suffered under European imperial rule and were dubious when England described AIOC as benevolent, magnanimous, and evenhanded with Persian and British employees. When Mossadeq called AIOC a "latter-day parallel of the former East India Company," one of those who sat nodding in complete understanding was the delegate from India.

Mossadeq took the floor as both political leader and international lawyer. Drawing on the dramatic skills of his long parliamentary experience, he presented tough legal arguments with consummate ease. This was the ideal international forum in which to describe the oppression still being practiced by Great Britain in a country that had never been a colony, and he made ample use of the opportunity. He laughed at England for construing the nationalization of oil as a threat to world peace. It was the United Kingdom that had sent warships to Abadan, he pointed out. "Iran has stationed no gunboats in the Thames."[1] Nationalization was an internal matter, no different from Britain's own repeated nationalization of its industries. If Whitehall accepted the *principle* of nationalization, which its Security Council representative claimed it did, then there was simply nothing more to dispute. The only question outstanding was its *application*—specifically, wangling over proper compensation.

When the British representative, Sir Gladwyn Jebb, took the floor, he had already lost. Mossadeq had by then become a TV sensation, and whenever Jebb accused the Iranians of being "insensate," "intemperate," "suicidal," and "intolerable," he only offered more grist for that night's news mill. Jebb's statement that AIOC had not only been generous to Iran but was acting as a "trustee" for the Iranian people until the 1933 Concession terminated in 1993 was perhaps the last straw. "The profits of the Company in the year 1950 alone," said Allahyar Saleh, another member of the Iranian delegation, "after deducting the share paid to Iran, amounted to more than the entire sum of £144 million paid in royalties to Iran in the course of the past half century."[2]

Jebb had no reply. When the French delegate suggested that the whole debate be delayed until the World Court determined whether it was a domestic or an international matter, Jebb grudgingly acquiesced.

In London the *Financial Times* was withering, describing the English representative as "utterly incapable of dealing with the Persian Prime Minister, who has won a succession of resounding diplomatic victories."[3] In the United States the press, though infatuated with the wizardly "Old Mossy" as it liked to call him, was not quite sure just what kind of success he represented. When *Time* magazine chose him as "Man of the Year," the worried cover line identified him as "The man who oiled the wheels of chaos."

To Mossadeq the Security Council debate was a triumph. Steadfastness of purpose had paid off, and it was with a real sense of hope that he headed to Washington.

THE TALE OF AN INTERVIEW

The Shoreham Hotel is a sprawling, modern building near Rock Creek Park, not far from Washington, D.C.'s elegant Embassy Row. It was here that Mossadeq climbed once again into bed, propped up against puffy white pillows, and was surrounded by a covey of supporters and hangers-on. Aside from having lunch with President Truman at the White House, he went out little, preferring to see Dean Acheson, George McGhee, and a new addition to the team, Paul Nitze, the State Department's policy planning director, at his bedside. Truman told Mossadeq he was worried that the impasse with Britain was weakening Iran. If a solution was not quickly found, he warned, the Russian "vulture" would move in, grab the oil, and be well placed to launch a world war.

In fact the vulture of communism was nothing but a scarecrow, which inflamed U.S. foreign policy for years until it fell dilapidated from its pole. Mossadeq, himself unworried about the Communists, nonetheless listened carefully and decided to play the vulture card to his own advantage. The British embargo was sorely taxing Iran's economy, he said. Much more of this and the government might collapse. Then the Communists would walk right in. It had almost happened under Qavam-Saltaneh just a couple of years before.

Mossadeq's gamble paid off. To Truman and his aides the real problem was never oil but the spread of communism, and they hastened to inform the British government that a settlement had to be reached forthwith. Soon McGhee was at Mossadeq's side informing him that the only obstacles left were the price Iran wanted for its oil and his intractability in not allowing British nationals to be reemployed at the refinery. All the rest—including nationalization and compensation—had been accepted.

It was a victory. And yet at this crucial moment—all the more crucial since across the Atlantic Winston Churchill, who had helped create AIOC in the first place and was among that dying breed of English statesmen who still felt viscerally that Britain should remain an empire, had once again become prime minister—right then, Mossadeq lost his footing. Always the opposition politician rather than an oilman, he did not know how to compromise. He did not know the price of oil, the cost of production, the amount of margin he had to play with. In fact he did not care. It was prestige, not economics, that mattered to him, and having decided on a price that was completely unrealistic, he refused to back down. Ironically the price he was offered was 25 cents per barrel more than Iran would get after his fall. Twenty-five cents was a lot when each barrel was only fetching a dollar.

I went to see Mossadeq at the Shoreham in the midst of these negotiations. I still felt that there was hope for a breakthrough between us. Mossadeq was in a magnanimous mood. He gestured me over to his bedside and gave me a frail but genuine embrace. Then he began to praise my father, remembering the days when Farman Farma had named him minister of finance. Everyone in the room began to look at me with admiration, thinking perhaps that I might be appointed minister in recognition of the past. But as Mossadeq talked, I could feel the worm begin to turn. Suddenly, looking over to the rest of the group gathered in the room, he declared, "Well, gentlemen, for no reason my uncle called me one day and I was dismissed."

The goodwill that had permeated the air abruptly evaporated. Everyone glared at me. Still Mossadeq talked. "You must go back to Iran," he said to me. "We need people like you."

For what? I felt like shouting at him. To be arrested?

I returned to New York convinced that there could be no understanding between us. Mossadeq had accurately divined that I did not agree with his policy on oil or with his new bargaining stance. In fact, I realized, though Mossadeq was a redoubtable warrior, I did not like the battles he fought. His crusade was misguided. The power of his personality obscured the fallacy of his objectives. He was just ambitious—a politician, not a statesman. His tactic was to constantly take action so as to remain in the public eye. His handling of the British was like the installments of a soap opera: first nationalizing oil, then closing the consulates, now kicking the employees out of the oil fields. He maintained ongoing conflicts with everyone—Seyyed Kashani, the Shah, the Majles—relying on turmoil to feed his political career. When later in the year he finally broke diplomatic relations with Britain and closed the embassy, every Iranian thought the sky would fall in. Yet such brash fearlessness was what made Mossadeq great in the eyes of his people.

It was also what destroyed him. He wanted to be a hero. He spoke constantly of democracy and instead became a tyrant. He was the most dictatorial prime minister Iran ever had. When he couldn't get something through Parliament, he dissolved it. Unwittingly he more than anyone played into Britain's hands. Ever since the days of Nosrat-Doleh the AIOC board had pursued a policy of forcing Iran to abandon its claims to the subsidiary companies. It was Mossadeq who finally threw in the towel. He justified the act as being good for Iran. In fact he lost more for Iran than anyone in history.

A few days after returning to New York, I was invited to a dinner with Undersecretary of State McGhee, set up by friends of Leila's. It was a small affair and an unexpected opportunity to speak with McGhee directly about Mossadeq. I could see that he expected there would be a crack in Mossadeq's position. I told him there would be none. Ironically, he believed in Mossadeq much more than I. But I did not want to discredit Mossadeq in front of the American negotiator and so held my tongue.

McGhee did not understand that the movement in Iran was a popular outcry against the British. He also failed to see that Britain would never make a deal with Mossadeq no matter how good the terms. McGhee had attended Oxford, and his old dean and tutor, Sir Oliver Franks, was at that moment ambassador to the United States. McGhee had a soft spot for the English—much as I did—though his favorable opinion extended to the good he felt the British Empire had brought to the world's "underprivileged." When I tried to suggest otherwise, using Iran's present state as an example, he would not listen. He accepted facts about Venezuela he would not about Iran. By the end of the dinner I'd decided that he was a stubborn, closed-minded man and I did not like him.

I was not unhappy to hear that he was about to leave Washington to become ambassador to Turkey. A man of such unrealistic perceptions would never be able to broker an agreement. When Churchill's government rejected McGhee's proposals, I was not surprised. McGhee was not even able to convince Truman to offer Iran a tide-over loan until it could start selling its oil. His empty optimism at last served no one.

A TALE OF MAKING ENDS MEET

The fallout with Mossadeq made me realize that my stay in New York would be an extended one. But I had no income, since the embargo on Iran made it impossible to export currency for living expenses. For a while I worked with an Iranian from Shiraz who had a shoe shop near my apartment. He was a good salesman but a bad accountant and soon went under. He offered me a shady deal exporting goods to South America. I told him I was not the man, and we parted ways.

At this time I began attending seminars and talks at the Association of the Friends of the Middle East, and I would often speak out strongly during the question-and-answer sessions. As fate would have it my outspokenness attracted the attention of the association's director, who asked me one evening if I would give a lecture on oil.

The hall was full when I arrived. Sitting in the front row was the consul general, Mahmoud Foroughi, whose younger brother had sat next to me during our *baccalauréat* exams in France. I started out by saying that although a representative from my government was in the audience, I was not going to change my speech; I was still going to talk about why I thought Mossadeq was making a mistake. But I did welcome Foroughi politely before proceeding.

After the speech a man named Clark Getz, the head of a public relations company, came up to me and said, "I want to hire you for a three-month series all over the United States. And I'll pay you three hundred fifty dollars for each speech because I liked your frank approach."

I was stunned. The top rate for famous people in those days was $400. The best hotels in New York at the time—the Plaza and the Essex House on Central Park South—cost just $10 a night. He was offering me an absolute fortune, and I thanked him effusively. In the end I earned almost $6,000 and traveled all over the United States, speaking at Rotary and Lions Club meetings about Iran's politics, oil, and history. I have seldom enjoyed my work so much. My audiences came from all walks of life. Iran was a new country to them, and they were eager to learn about it. Many of them kept up a correspondence with me long afterward.

In Chicago the American Petroleum Institute was hosting a conference at the same time I was speaking to the Rotary Club. Walter Levy was there, and I invited him for lunch. I also invited an old Birmingham pal, Ghezel Ayagh, one of the most academically brilliant of our group. Afterward I went over to Ghezel's place. I found him living in a cellar, a bare twenty-by-twenty-foot box. The walls were plastered with diplomas, all framed. First he'd gotten every engineering degree possible. Then he'd moved on to industry and commerce. Nonetheless he was starving. He was from a poor family in Iran, plucked by the government and sent to Birmingham because of his intelligence. But when he'd returned to Iran, he hadn't been able to adjust to the conflict between his roots and his education and had left for America. I remember going to his mother's home for dinner with all the other Birmingham graduates to say farewell. We sat on the floor. There was a kerosene heater in the corner, its sooty fumes filling the room. A pan of water steamed on top to keep the air from drying out. That evening I was pointedly reminded how fortunate I was and what hardship it was to live in poverty.

Now, in Chicago, he was again a failure. I found it a tragedy. What could I do for him? I took him to a good restaurant for dinner and then hid a $100 bill in his apartment.

A TALE OF THE WORLD COURT

Mossadeq returned to Tehran at the end of 1951. He traveled via Cairo, where he spoke against British control of the Suez Canal and had a picture taken with Prime Minister Nahas Pasha at his bedside. The tide of nationalism in Egypt was running high, and Whitehall was livid when the news reached London. To the ailing Churchill it confirmed that Mossadeq had to be eliminated. Otherwise his crazy chattering would not only permanently rob England of Iranian oil but could lead to the loss of the Suez Canal as well.

In Iran, contrary to London's dire predictions, the Abadan Refinery was operating well. Dr. Reza Fallah, a gifted oilman, was in charge, and though capacity had been reduced, efficiency was maintained. This gave the lie to Whitehall's insistence that no agreement could be reached without the provision of British personnel on-site to sustain output.

On July 22, 1952, the World Court finally issued its judgment in the case. The 1933 Concession was a contract "between a government and a foreign corporation," it ruled, and the government of the United Kingdom had nothing to do with it.[4] Iran had every right to nationalize as long as it offered adequate compensation. Five judges dissented, including the one from the United States. Nine judges assented, among them the justice from Great Britain.

To the jubilant Iranians it was the triumph of David over Goliath, a hard-won victory by a weak nation against the seemingly invincible British Empire. From a psychological perspective it was an enormous coup for the people of Iran. Particularly it proved to them that their leader, Dr. Mossadeq, had not just been heroic, he had been legally right. The British would now have to come to a settlement.

Or would they?

THE TALE OF THE
FOUR-STEP PINCER

The World Court ruling came as the Korean War was moving into its second year. The British embargo on Iran's oil the year before had reduced Western energy stocks and caused a scare. To make up for the shortfall a joint pool of English and American oil companies went into high gear to shuttle around supplies. Washington momentarily suspended antitrust laws to allow the companies to cooperate legally in the effort. Production was boosted in Saudi Arabia, Iraq, and Kuwait, as well as in Southeast Asia. This was one of the reasons Undersecretary of Commerce Chapman intimated to me in Caracas that the U.S. companies were supporting their U.K. counterparts in the embargo on Iran. Not only did they wish to discourage national movements that might complicate their own contracts with source countries, but at that very moment they were actually benefiting from the collaboration with AIOC in securing a worldwide network of oil supplies.

The oil company partnership turned out to be wildly successful. Worldwide oil production rose by 2 million barrels—more than three times Iran's total output in 1950. When Mossadeq claimed his victory from the World Court, he wanted to exact vengeance against the British by selling his oil to independent shippers outside the "Seven Sisters" oil cartel. What he did not recognize was that the world didn't need Iranian oil.

The consequences were dire. Production in Iran was at 20,000 barrels a day, down from 666,000 at the start of the embargo. Revenues from oil had dropped to almost nothing in 1952. The government, strapped for cash after paying the salaries of the oil workers, had little left over for law and order. Brigandage in the countryside was on the rise, and the tribes, feeling a weakening of the government, were once again acting up.

Upon his return from Europe Mossadeq faced new elections. Anticipating unrest and disillusionment, he appealed to the people on June 29, 1952, to stand strong and "not shrink from deprivation [and] self sacrifice."[5] An austerity program was instituted, imports were cut, and exports of nonoil products were increased.

Despite losing a number of seats in the countryside, the National Front swept a majority of delegates into the Majles, and Mossadeq was again voted prime minister. It came as a shock, therefore, when a week later he tendered his resignation. The prime minister, though constitutionally entitled to choose all cabinet ministers, had always deferred to the Shah, as honorary commander in chief, to serve as minister of war. Mossadeq was wary of the army's loyalty to the sovereign, however, and so chose to keep the post for himself. The Shah, outraged, rejected the entire cabinet. In protest, Mossadeq resigned.

The British Foreign Office was delighted. Its hope of getting rid of Mossadeq had unexpectedly been granted. And being sure that a more amenable prime minister could arrange a settlement that included putting British nationals back in Abadan, it had already identified Qavam-Saltaneh, now eighty-four, as the man to swing the deal. If not, "and there is a breakdown of the Persian administration and Russian intervention in the North," one assistant undersecretary observed, "we can, if need be, set up a British sphere of influence in the South on the lines of past history."[6]

On July 17 Qavam-Saltaneh was voted in by a Majles lacking a quorum. I received a call the next day from a good friend in Paris informing me that I was a candidate for vice premier responsible for matters of oil. My friend Abbas Mirza Eskandari, the fiery Majles delegate from Hamadan, had suggested my name. He was himself a candidate for vice premier in charge of Majles relations. I was flattered but doubted that Qavam's premiership would last. Too obviously supported by the British government, illegally elected, and plagued by a deep-seated distrust of the Shah (a sentiment that was returned with interest), Qavam's government, I decided, was not worth rushing home for. When three days later strikes crippled the country, Qavam was forced to resign.

Mossadeq strode back into his second term on the winged feet of victory. Yet the political atmosphere in Tehran had become tense and dangerous. Mossadeq sensed that despite his massive popular support and the judgment awarded him by the World Court, the situation would become more turbulent before it eased. He therefore approached the Parliament for special legislative powers, which it granted him for six months. These made him in all but name a dictator. Eventually he would use these powers to dissolve the Senate and institute a curfew. Adamant that his tack with the

British was the only one to take, he muzzled the country into silence. The only voice raised against him was the daily diatribe of the BBC.

With money short and the black market once again flourishing, it was a time of mirrors, when people's loyalties were not what they seemed and everyone worried about what was happening behind their backs. Even in Mossadeq's choice of cabinet there were flaws that would eventually destabilize his regime. My friend Saifollah Moazemi, who had come to my room that fateful morning in England when I'd heard of Nosrat-Doleh's death, was appointed minister of posts and telegraphs. He and his brother Abdollah were both staunch members of the National Front, and Abdollah was named head of the Majles. Abdollah was a clever man, the type who could fit into any keyhole, as we Persians say. He urged Mossadeq to appoint another Birmingham friend, a vile man named Khalil Taleghani, as secretary to the Council of Ministers. Despite their National Front affiliation, the Moazemis were privately very pro-British, as was Taleghani, and it intrigued me that Mossadeq entrusted them with ministerial duties at such a critical time. Taleghani was a confidant of the Rashidian brothers, that wealthy pair of contract spies I had met when Seyyed Zia had arrived in Kermanshah in 1943. Soon it was rumored that Taleghani had himself become an agent, passing the notes he took at each meeting of the Council of Ministers directly to the American Embassy.

Mossadeq's turncoat cabinet was not just a result of bad judgment. It also reflected how effective the British Embassy was becoming in its anti-Mossadeq campaign. The postwar United Kingdom was still a formidable power. The United States, though continuing to hold out hope for a settlement, was gradually being bullied into adopting the British stance. Unless Washington helped to create a united front, London hinted, it would not be able to strike a deal with the Iranians. There was also the issue of Korea. What went unsaid but was certainly implied was that if the United States did not take Britain's side in Iran, Whitehall might not support the United States in Korea. The possibility of making a deal with the Soviet Union to divide Iran was never out of the question. Moscow was not much happier with Mossadeq's nationalist movement than London was, and an agreement over Iran might work out well for both.

The British government, though on the losing end of the World Court ruling, had no intention of sitting down with "Old Mossy." Very simply it considered his terms preposterous, which in some ways they were. Another man, such as Qavam-Saltaneh perhaps, could have pushed through a deal, but he would not have had the Persian people behind him. To bring the country around and discredit Mossadeq, a four-step pincer program was put into action.

First, the embargo was widened to include a worldwide interception of all tankers carrying Iranian oil obtained in any fashion, including barter. An advertisement in thirty-three newspapers in twenty countries announced that Iranian oil was stolen property and any tanker carrying it was doing so unlawfully. Deals Mossadeq had struck with India, Turkey, and Italy were abruptly terminated by those governments. To illustrate the danger of challenging the British position, an Italian tanker carrying Iranian oil was seized in January 1953 by British inspectors in the port of Aden. Its load was impounded, and a court judgment was issued against the Italian firm.

Second, foreign technicians, lawyers, and accountants hired by the fledgling NIOC were constrained from leaving their countries to go to Iran. Pressure was brought on the governments of Germany, Sweden, Austria, and Switzerland to deny their nationals visas. In the United States British Embassy lobbying helped kill a bill before the House Foreign Relations Committee encouraging U.S. oil companies to provide technicians to Iran. The State Department even constrained American technicians working in other parts of the world from obtaining visas.

Third, the Bank of England froze all Iran's sterling balances and withheld overdue payments of outstanding royalties due prior to nationalization. This came to a total of £49 million, without which Mossadeq was unable to pay any military or government salaries, let alone service Iran's foreign debt.

Finally, as the months passed with little change in Mossadeq's position, Operation Boot, a military plan to oust the premier from power, began to take shape. It was not presented to the U.S. government until November 1952, at which time General Omar Bradley, chairman of the Joint Chiefs of Staff, and other key players condemned it as unrealistic and too military in tone. It did not stand a chance of being accepted in Washington, in fact, until the Democrats were voted out and Eisenhower was voted in.

Meanwhile, though Iran's economy was deteriorating, Mossadeq refused to budge. After receiving a joint message from Churchill and Truman at the end of August that seemed to question once again the legality of nationalization, he decided he'd had enough. On October 22, 1952, despite anxious urging by the Shah to reconsider, Mossadeq severed diplomatic relations with the United Kingdom.

Mossadeq was equally unyielding in his approach to oil pricing. A number of countries, including China and some of the other Communist bloc nations, were anxious to buy Iranian oil if the price was right. Serviced by independent tanker companies, they were less concerned about the embargo than obtaining energy at a bargain. Had Mossadeq sold the oil at 35

cents a barrel—a 65 percent discount—he could have broken the block-
ade, set up his markets, and then raised his prices.

When I was in Venezuela I'd met a famous oil expert, Professor Wilbur
Nelson from Oklahoma University, who subsequently contacted me in
New York about just such an opportunity. He informed me that PetroBraz,
Brazil's national oil company, was very interested in buying Iranian oil.
Two refineries had been built in Brazil, for which he'd been called in as a
consultant, and since they were government owned they could purchase
Iranian oil without danger of prosecution. It was an ideal opportunity to
make a deal, and he encouraged me to follow it up.

This was in the summer of 1952, and Allahyar Saleh, Mossadeq's right-
hand man at the Security Council hearings (and one of the delegates I had
worked with on the Majles oil committee), had been named ambassador to
Washington. He was a first-class diplomat. When I mentioned the proposition to him on the phone, he invited me to Washington for lunch.

Once there, I realized that Allahyar had grown disillusioned with
Mossadeq. Mossadeq was trying to sell at a 40 or 50 percent discount to
the Italians, Argentines, and Japanese with only minimal luck, and Allahyar suggested strongly that I stay away from any new negotiations. The
prime minister was suspicious of outside propositions, he said. It was unlikely I'd get very far, no matter how good the deal—and I'd probably
damage my own reputation in the process.

Allahyar then went on to tell me that Makki, the sharp-tongued parlia-
mentarian who had engineered my ouster, had just arrived in Washington.
"He wanted to hold a press conference here in the embassy!" Allahyar said.
"I had to tell him no. 'Why?' he asked. 'You're a parliamentary representative,' I told him. 'Your opinion is your own. This building represents the
nation and can express only the official opinion of the government. Besides
I have my orders.'

"You should have seen his face. 'Orders from whom?' he demanded.
'From Mossadeq himself!' I told him. 'You'll have to hold your press conference in your hotel.'

"Mossadeq is alienating even his staunchest friends," Allahyar concluded. "He is picking fights with the mollah Kashani, and the two are not
seeing eye to eye at all anymore. He has of course never had real support
from the Communists. So where does that leave him? With a few intellectuals and the changeable mob in the street. Soon Mossadeq will have nobody behind him."

Back in Tehran Makki fell out with Mossadeq over the press conference,
and the two became enemies. After Mossadeq fell, General Zahedi, the first
prime minister of the postnationalization era, invited Makki to become

vice president of NIOC to represent the old nationalization group. Makki turned it down. I was sorry he did. He was acquainted with the terrain and had learned that politics can't run the oil business. But he was vindictive, resented the offer, and refused to get involved. In his own way he was like Mozzafar—a flash in the political pan, then out forever because of his inflexible convictions.

A TALE OF MARRIAGE

It had been almost a year since I had taken up residence in New York and I was thirty-five. Without planning it, I suddenly realized that I was in love with a woman I wanted to marry. I had met her at a production of T. S. Eliot's *Murder in the Cathedral* staged at the Columbia University chapel. Verla Gean Miller had dark hair and bright blue eyes and was an accomplished pianist. She had been born in Salt Lake City, Utah, a part of the world similar in both geography and religion to Iran. She was born a Mormon but had decided to leave the fold, and for the past eight years she had been working for a Hungarian family that owned a vast shipping network and represented the Coca-Cola franchise in Egypt. She had spent the last few summers on their farm in Alexandria, and though she was every inch the vivacious American, she had learned a little about what life was like for women in the Middle East.

Gean's employer, Alexander Pathy, was an exceptional man. He'd been a lawyer at the Nuremberg Trials before moving to the United States as a result of the Communist takeover of his native Hungary. We became instant friends, though apparently, as I became increasingly attentive to Gean, he grew concerned and had an Interpol investigation done to make sure I was not an undercover agent or a fly-by-night hooligan. Reassured by Interpol that I was not dangerous, he gave us his blessing and we were married in May of 1952—first in a mosque, then in the Iranian Embassy, and finally at New York's city hall. Gean was at the time studying for her master's degree at Columbia, and though I was becoming increasingly eager to return to Iran, we decided to stay another year so that she could finish her studies.

We took an extended honeymoon throughout the United States, and I began to write occasionally for the Voice of America and *The Oil Forum,* a magazine touted as being "the best minds of the petroleum industry between two covers." I also tried to offer my services to a number of smaller oil companies that were eyeing Iran as a new market left wide open by the Seven Sisters' embargo. Among those I approached was City Services Oil

Company, whose president, Alton Jones, was a confidant of both Truman and Eisenhower. Jones refused to see me, even though my sister Satareh was working in his office. He was the only American oilman to visit Iran during this time, arriving in August of 1952 with an offer to bring technicians to Abadan. As it turned out his meeting with Mossadeq had a disastrous effect on the premier's thinking since it led him to believe that Jones spoke for a number of independent American companies and that his eagerness to do business represented a break in Anglo-American solidarity. If anything Jones's visit made Mossadeq more obstinate—the very opposite of what Truman had intended.

Since getting full-time, worthwhile employment was proving impossible for me, Gean and I decided in July 1953 that I should go on ahead to Iran by boat. She would join me a couple of months later. The opposition movement had grown in Tehran to such a degree that I no longer feared for my safety. The split between Mossadeq and Kashani had become much more marked, and Kashani had begun to declaim that it was the will of Allah that Iran become a fundamentalist state organized along religious lines. Many of his tenets would be echoed twenty-five years later by the much more successful Ayatollah Khomeini.* As it was, he was leading demonstrations in the street and publicly refusing to cooperate with Mossadeq.

Meanwhile, General Zahedi, an ally of the Shah's, had begun leading the right-wing opposition to Mossadeq. The old general, who had arrested Sheikh Khazal in Abadan for Reza Shah back in the 1920s and then been jailed by the British during the war, was a tall, strong, imposing man with a very oriental personality. A longtime senator, he now operated undercover, with real muscle in both the Majles and the army.

In 1953 the country I was leaving was no less extremist than the country I was heading to. Joseph McCarthy's rhetoric boomed incessantly from the radio; Congress was hauling in actors, scholars, playwrights, and a slew of others in a show of public abuse and name-calling; people were afraid to speak their minds, and all political discussion revolved around communism. The greatest witch-hunt in U.S. history was in full swing. I was undoubtedly better off in my own land.

---

*Ayatollah Khomeini lionized Kashani, and today Iran's official history books credit him, rather than Mossadeq, with many of the achievements and political experiments of the nationalization years. Mossadeq is not a hero in the annals of the Islamic Republic; Kashani very definitely is.

As for Ayatollah Khomeini's views on oil, he appeared on television right after the 1979 revolution and flatly asked, "Why are you talking about oil so much? What does it count for? So someone nationalized it once in a perfectly ordinary act. So what? The question to ask is, What is it worth to Islam?"

The ship dropped me off in France. From there I sailed to Beirut, where I jumped on a bus to Baghdad. The city was plastered with pictures of Mossadeq in a show of brotherly support. To my amazement—and delight—the bus pulled into a garage in Baghdad called Farman Farma, which turned out to belong to my family. Within minutes I'd extracted some overdue money from the astonished caretaker before continuing on my way to Kermanshah.

At the Iran-Iraq frontier, however, I was told I could not cross the border without an exit visa from Baghdad. I was flabbergasted and, having no intention of backtracking, began ruminating about ways to slip over the border. Just then a large limousine drew up, and to my great surprise one of my nieces, who was married to a high-ranking Iraqi official, stepped from the car. It was an extraordinary coincidence. My niece's husband arranged my visa, apologized profusely for not being able to take me in their car since it was packed to the gills, and gave me a large jug of water to quench my thirst on the rest of the trip.

A TALE OF RETURN

In Kermanshah I made straight for the home of my uncle Etezad-Soltan, hoping to hide out there for a while. He dissuaded me, however, saying that a small town had more tongues than a large one and it would be better to go to Tehran. It was early on a dark morning at the beginning of August when we set out on the four-hundred-mile trip with me behind the wheel of my uncle's new car.

For twenty-five miles the road ran through semi-desert and was slightly elevated above a ditch. We had not gone far when I saw a man—really just his silhouette—in the middle of the road waving for us to stop. Instinctively, I slowed down. Then I saw another man with a shotgun scrambling out of the ditch, and a little farther on a third. As I slowed, my uncle began shouting to drive on quickly since he was sure they were robbers. Not wanting to argue with him, I stepped on the gas.

The first man appeared to be standing his ground in the middle of the road, and I knew that if I kept on without braking I would hit him and very likely kill him. Then, just as we were almost on him, the second man, the one with the shotgun, lost his footing on the sill of the ditch and fell. In that split second, the man in front of us jumped aside. I swerved wildly, grazing him on the right. "Shoot! Shoot!" he shouted, and a splutter of gunshot immediately followed. But by then we were already past the third man and heading into open road.

I was dumbfounded by the narrowness of our escape. The roads had not been this dangerous in years. What state had my country fallen to?

In Tehran I moved in once again with my mother, who had prepared my rooms upstairs just as if I'd never left. She was delighted that I had at last gotten married and immediately offered to help me find an apartment and prepare it so that Gean and I could live in some privacy once she arrived.

The first day after my arrival I went to see my brother Sabbar, who had been named acting minister of health. Sabbar had always been a staunch supporter of Mossadeq's. He had become a doctor, a specialist in malaria, and had traveled all over the world studying mosquitoes. As the oldest son of his mother's nine children he had inherited a sizable part of the family fortune, which he spent primarily on mosquitoes and donations to the government. We had drifted apart since our shared summer in Geneva, primarily because of political differences.

I spoke to him of my apprehensions about the growing influence of communism in the country and then cautioned him about Khalil Taleghani, who was rumored to be reporting everything that transpired in the government to the American Embassy. He remained unworried and insinuated that my concerns over communism stemmed directly from my recent stay in the United States under the shadow of McCarthyism.

I then reminded him of his oath of allegiance to the Shah and offered a piece of unsolicited advice. "Once you are settled," I counseled, "let the Shah know of your continued loyalty. Tell him you are at his service. He won't ask for anything. What does he need from the Ministry of Health? But we know one thing about the Shah—he's here to stay, and he'll remember."

Sabbar shook his head and told me he could not do such a thing. Then he added kindly that perhaps I should not have returned to Iran under the prevailing circumstances.

I next visited my friend Saifollah Moazemi, now minister of posts and telegraphs. His personal secretary was waiting for me at the entrance to the ministry when I arrived, and when I walked into his office Saifollah jumped to his feet, showering me with warm words and praise. Clearing his desk of business, he motioned to the sofa, where we drank tea in silver cups. It was not the first time I had been in the room, and I told Saifollah of my last visit there, when my friend Seyyed Jalal Tehrani had been minister. It was a December morning, and a big coal furnace burned in the office. Tehrani was shouting at a man with a thick, disorderly file under his arm. Apparently every winter the ministry provided wool coats to all employees who worked at night; however, that year the ministry had yet to buy the fabric, let alone sew the coats. Each time Tehrani asked him a question in this regard, the man opened his file, trying to find an argument to confirm his innocence. At last Tehrani, pointing menacingly, instructed, "Go open the stove." Reluctantly the man did so. "Now," Tehrani shouted, "throw in your file!"

Saifollah and I both laughed at the story. When a half hour later I took my leave, I said, "Saifollah, you know my problem! And when friends are in power, one can only hope . . ."

"Yes," he answered immediately, his eyes twinkling. "As a matter of fact there was a little telegram about you, reporting that you had crossed the frontier a few days ago. It is still here on my desk."

Somewhat taken aback, I could only ask how it was that the secret service operated so well.

"My dear friend," he said, "it is the only service that works well in Iran these days. But don't worry. The telegram will be left on my desk for a very long time. You can count on me for that."

THE PRINCE AND THE PRIME MINISTER

Once assured that the government was not going to make my life difficult, I made an appointment, through Mossadeq's son Gholam Hossein, to see the prime minister. On the appointed morning, as I called at his house, a chauffeur-driven car stopped in front of me and Nosrat-Doleh's old friend Prince Sarameh-Doleh got out. He was white-haired now but still towering at six foot three and handsome in his dark tailored suit and custom-made shoes.

"I did not know you were in Tehran," he said, his voice ponderous and slow. Like so many Qajars he wore thick glasses and exuded an overarching air of gentility. "How lucky that we should meet, though it is not under the best of circumstances here in front of the house of Dr. Mossadeq. But no matter. We will consider it a sign of good fortune for us both."

He took my arm, and with dignity we entered the house, where we waited for a few minutes in the secretary's vestibule. Then, strangely, we were called in at the same time. Dr. Mossadeq lay in bed. As usual he gave me a kiss and once again remarked, after we were both seated, "My cousin reminds me of his father, who was a great man. Surely Your Highness remembers him?" In consternation I recalled the last time the conversation had started off in this vein and immediately opened my mouth to say something to reroute it.

To my chagrin, however, Sarameh-Doleh had already jumped into the exchange. "Yes," he said. "How could I forget him? If you recall, we both served in his cabinet when he was prime minister, and neither of us was up to his standard."

I looked at them both aghast, knowing that things were going from bad to worse, and started to blather an apology, to no avail. Apparently deciding to overlook Sarameh-Doleh's indiscretion, Mossadeq fixed a beady eye on him. He ignored me completely.

"I hear you are going to Europe, to London in fact. Perhaps you are going to sound out your British friends on our situation here?" Mossadeq's voice was very quiet. "Why don't you tell them to come off their high horses and walk with us?"

Sarameh-Doleh's face became very tense, and I could see the anger surging through him by the way he turned his body. The insinuation that he had retained British government contacts through the many years since he'd been minister of finance—years that he had spent in silent exile in Isfahan, completely removed from politics—and that he would now use those contacts against the government, was a vile insult to his patriotism and his honor.

"There is no need for the British to talk to me," he said, enunciating each word quietly and slowly. "When the time comes, they will settle, one way or another."

"The people are on my side," Mossadeq hissed emphatically.

"You make a mistake," the prince answered. "Nobody is on your side. The British and the Americans are not friends of yours because of the oil situation. The Russians know you are at heart an aristocrat and so against them. As for the Persian people, they have never lifted a finger against a despot, but now finding the Shah weak they pretend to back your democracy. When once again they feel the strength of the Shah, they will be ready to make peace. Remember Seyyed Modaress, the great and humble friend of the people and delegate to the Majles. When he stepped down from Parliament, the people kissed his feet. When Reza Shah took him and killed him, no one uttered a word. They are the same people. They move like sand, and they will move from under your feet too."

He got up and bowed with great solemnity, then left the room without another word. There being nothing more to say, I too got up and took my leave. I never spoke with Dr. Mossadeq again.

On my way home I stopped off to see my elder brother and family patriarch Mohammadvali Mirza. He was as frail as always, and I was careful not to crush him when I greeted him with a hug. I told him I had been to see Dr. Mossadeq and that Sarameh-Doleh had been there as well. The exchange had been shocking and had left me most disturbed.

"If I had known you were planning to see him, I would have dissuaded
you from going," said Mohammadvali Mirza. "He has always been a difficult man and has really never liked our family. It would have been better
if he had forgotten you altogether. Do not go to see him again." He looked
out the window, the flat planes of his narrow face catching the light like a
black-and-white photo. "He cannot last," he said almost to himself. "His
government will fall, for he is not a constructive leader and his negativism
will destroy him."

I left Mohammadvali Mirza's house feeling like a whipped schoolboy.
Yet it was his final words that kept churning through my head. Mohammadvali Mirza was a cautious man who would not easily attempt to pre-
dict the future. Did he know something we didn't? Or was it simply
intuition?

A SPY'S TALE

The year 1953 dawned with the inauguration of a new crew to the leadership of the United States. President Dwight D. Eisenhower was a Republican, and the men he brought to his cabinet were business tycoons with a
clear sense of the world value of oil. Among them were Charles "Engine
Charlie" Wilson, the president of General Motors, who became secretary of
defense; George Humphrey, a banker from Cleveland, who was appointed
secretary of the treasury; and John Foster Dulles, a senior partner at the
powerful law firm of Sullivan and Cromwell, who was named secretary of
state. Dulles in particular, along with his brother Allen, then deputy secretary of the CIA, had a healthy fear of world communism and was much
more dubious than his predecessor, Dean Acheson, of Mossadeq's ability to
keep Iran from falling to the Reds. At the very least, he said, Mossadeq's
dictatorship would be followed by a Communist takeover unless the
United States acted to prevent it.

At first Eisenhower's government was no more amenable to British
plans for a coup than Truman's had been. But after a quick trip by Winston Churchill to New York in January, the tune changed. Churchill wisely
focused the discussions on the Communist threat rather than the problem
of oil, and to his surprise he found a ready supporter in John Foster Dulles.
Until then Churchill had considered Dulles a "stupid man." Now he
thought otherwise and furthermore observed that whatever Dulles suggested on foreign policy, Eisenhower tended to follow.

Though old and decrepit, Churchill had lost none of his craftiness as a statesman. He now determined that one of the most effective ways to get the United States to help overthrow Mossadeq was to let it lead the operation. In November 1952 Kermit Roosevelt, head of the CIA's Middle East operations, had met with AIOC representatives in London on his return from a trip to Tehran. He had been the first American to be told of Operation Boot. It was now proposed that he spearhead the operation. In March 1953 British foreign minister Anthony Eden traveled to Washington with a number of agents from the British intelligence unit MI6. Allen Dulles, now head of the CIA, thought Roosevelt's appointment as the coup's mastermind a capital idea and immediately dispatched him to Tehran.

Roosevelt had already visited Iran three times as a member of the Office of Strategic Services before taking on the coup assignment. He'd met Herbert Hoover, Jr., in 1944, and the two had traveled to Ethiopia together before Hoover came to Iran for his first oil negotiations. He also knew Alex Gagarin, the U.S. military attaché who had made the crazy dash through the Russian camp with my cousin Hossein Dowlatshahi that same year. Roosevelt—happily married, slightly balding, with thick-rimmed glasses—was, in British double agent Kim Philby's words, "the last person you'd expect to be up to his neck in dirty tricks."[7] He spoke neither Farsi nor German, the only languages spoken by General Zahedi, whose premiership he was out to obtain. He knew the Shah and U.S. ambassador Loy Henderson, and he was close to Zahedi's son Ardeshir. He was also not a man to give up—a crucial characteristic in the face of ensuing events.

Although the details of the planned coup were secret, the Eisenhower administration's involvement was not without strong opposition in Congress. On June 29 Senator William Langer of North Dakota made a sweeping indictment of John Foster Dulles's foreign policy, accusing the administration of pandering to dictators, "spoon-feeding a group of European allies who are willing to do little more to help themselves than to blackmail us periodically with the threat of communism." As Langer went on he asked, "Would we tolerate such a punitive action against our neighbor Brazil, which is also nationalizing its oil resources? . . . If imperialism as utilized by the Russians is vicious and hateful, it is just as vicious and hateful in the hands of European colonial usurpers wherever they may operate, for in each case what is depended on is the unlimited use of force, corruption and intrigue. . . . To this scheme, our State Department obviously has been a party."[8]

It took guts to speak like that during the McCarthy era. But Langer's audience was small; the Senate did not want to hear such things.

Since Roosevelt's last visit to Tehran in November 1952, the situation had changed radically. The Rashidian brothers, in the pay of the British government to the tune of £10,000 a month, had been fanning opposition to Mossadeq and were at last affecting the Majles. Mossadeq's own haughty demeanor had further fractured his support. Besieged and irritated by his inability to control the deputies—70 percent of whom he had hand-picked—the prime minister demanded a year's extension of his emergency powers. The Majles balked. To get his way Mossadeq organized massive street demonstrations that descended on the Majles and mobbed the gates. The emergency powers were extended, but at great loss to Mossadeq's prestige. The man who had talked for thirty years about democracy was now ruling by "mobocracy."

Things only got worse. In February the Bakhtiaris, armed with rifles provided by British intelligence, occupied gendarmerie posts in Khuzistan near the oil fields. Their revolt was short-lived, and they were soon crushed by government forces, who jailed their leaders along with a number of pro-Shah officers, including General Zahedi. But their uprising and their anti-Mossadeq statements came as a sharp reminder to the prime minister that he could not control the countryside as effectively as he did the city. A few days later a crowd organized by Kashani, who was now in open opposition to Mossadeq, marched to the Shah's palace in a show of support for the sovereign, then descended on Mossadeq's house. There the people hurled stones at his windows and tried to break through his gates. Mossadeq escaped through a back window and made straight for the Majles, where, still in his striped pajamas, he claimed that men sent by the Shah had tried to assassinate him.

The Shah, feeling helpless, had already told Ambassador Henderson that he wanted to leave the country. The number of Communists supporting Mossadeq in the streets alarmed him, he said. But Kashani's demonstration at the palace gates and a personal note from Churchill dissuaded him from leaving for the moment.

Roosevelt's assessment was that the British plan to oust Mossadeq was too military for a covert operation. Reinterpreting the plan as a "counter-coup" by the Shah, since it was Mossadeq, he felt, who had initiated the "coup," Roosevelt devised Operation Ajax. The candidate chosen to replace Mossadeq as prime minister was General Zahedi, whom the Shah trusted completely. The British government and AIOC agreed.

What carrot the CIA and MI6 extended to Russia to keep quiet while the Western powers engineered a coup on its southern border is unknown. Stalin had died in March, temporarily leaving a power vacuum in Moscow that was quickly filled by the melon-faced, mercurial Nikita Khrushchev.

On Russia's eastern flank the bloody, drawn-out Korean War was finally winding down. A treaty bringing the war to a close was signed and made public on July 27, 1953. On that day Mossadeq broadcast a speech to the nation claiming that foreign powers were covertly planning his overthrow with the intent of putting their own supporters in his place. It seems unlikely that when the coup attempt was made less than a month later, the Soviet Union would have turned a blind eye if some payoff had not already been made. It was after all the threat of Iran turning Communist, the danger of Iran's oil falling into Soviet hands, and Moscow's use of the Tudeh Party in the streets that had convinced the Americans to intervene in the first place.

A SPORTING TALE

Thanks to an initial invitation from my friend Ernest Perron, I began at the time to regularly attend functions at the court. Since I had no nine-to-five job, social events were as much my "business" as staying abreast of daily political developments. The Shah usually received a group of friends on Sundays and Thursdays for sport and dinner at his summer palace in the hills, and so it was that I found myself often heading up to Tajrish, the northern village now encompassed by Tehran's urban sprawl, where I'd once passed my summers at Rezvanieh.

There were about twenty of us, all friends since childhood, and always a couple of Bakhtiaris, since the Shah had remarried the year before and his new queen, a stunning beauty named Soraya, was half German and half Bakhtiari. We'd enter the beautiful gardens about midafternoon. Although much of the glitter of the palace had been removed, there were still armed guards posted at the entrance.

Once we had all gathered, the royal pair would appear and we would greet them by bending down low while clasping our hands behind our backs. The Shah was shy but tried to project an image that was both friendly and dignified. The result was that he always came off a bit stiff, despite his obvious warmth. Queen Soraya, though she dressed flamboyantly, was very quiet. Lacking education and a strong personality, she was more a pretty statue than a real presence. Yet the Shah clearly adored her.*

---

*Queen Soraya could often be seen playing with a baby lamb, which she kept in her lap. She held on to the lamb until she was divorced two years later. After she was gone, the lamb lost its special status and eventually was slaughtered and served for dinner at the palace. What a symbolic change of fortune—going from the lap of a queen to mutton on a plate!

Soon after arriving we would change into shorts and move into the gardens to play His Majesty's favorite game, volleyball. The Shah had always been athletic. Broad-shouldered and slight of build, with strong muscles in his arms, he had played soccer avidly as a young boy and now enjoyed tennis, bowling, skiing, and weight lifting, performing every sport with the indefatigable vigor of a born athlete.*

Once when he invited me to his palace on the Caspian Sea, he put us through such a marathon that afterward I referred to the weekend as Dien Bien Phu. At nine o'clock in the morning he had us run for an hour along the beach. Then we water-skiied, played volleyball, and had a short lunch. After lunch we played bridge, water-skiied again, and went horseback riding. At night, after dinner, we played parlor games and cards until eleven, followed by dancing until three in the morning. By this time we were so worn-out we could barely move. But His Majesty was still going strong, and when his eyes caught us flagging, he decided to stay up until four, making us suffer for our weakness. "What a lovely moon," he said. "Let's go for a sail." And out we went.

Like the Shah a number of the other guests at his weekly luncheons were expert volleyball players—which I wasn't—and all played with great seriousness. Among them was my brother-in-law Manucher Garagozlu, a tall, dashing adjutant to the Shah. He was married to my sister Haideh, who for a while was a lady-in-waiting to Soraya.

I generally left the others to play, for I did not want to blunder when the stakes were so high. Another frequent guest who shared my feelings was Mohsen Foroughi, the son of a former prime minister and a passionate collector of Persian art—including pottery, bronzes, miniatures, and decorative pen boxes. We became fast friends, and he greatly influenced my own growing love of collecting. Foroughi later exhibited his collection at the Louvre in Paris. He was unfortunately promoted to minister of higher education at the tail end of the Shah's regime and arrested by Khomeini. He spent two years in jail, where he painted to keep himself sane. He emerged a broken man and died soon after his release.

After the initial thrill of being invited to court I began to find the routine tiring. We had been advised not to talk politics, though we all insulted Mossadeq in the Shah's presence. There were always the same

---

*Sport was one of the things the Shah most successfully encouraged among the people of Iran. Under his direction the Zurkhaneh, the ancient schools of weight lifting and wrestling, were reintroduced into vogue, and weight lifting became one of the areas in which Persians excelled at the Olympics. In the 1960s he built a $500-million stadium outside the city, designed by my brother Aziz, for the Asian Games. One of his most cherished hopes was to host the Winter Olympics in Tehran—a dream he never saw fulfilled.

people and the same games, and since we could not really talk, smoke, or sit as we chose despite the Shah's friendliness, I found the afternoons a strain. Neither the Shah nor Queen Soraya had any interest in art or literature, and so the day's entertainment was limited to game playing or listening to someone trying to be funny. To be fair, the Shah was under great political pressure and looked to us to lift his spirits. But the hours dragged, and after dinner, until we could honorably take our leave, I could barely stay awake.

One Sunday afternoon in the second week of August, our game of volleyball finished, the Shah, newly changed into a fresh pair of tight jeans, settled into a chair to read *Etela'at,* the afternoon paper. Every few minutes he would look up and join in the conversation. As usual at that time of year the weather was mild, and we all stretched out under the trees in lawn chairs, relaxing and drinking tea. At one point the butler approached and began to whisper something into the Shah's ear. Very loudly the Shah said, "Tell him to come in."

A minute or so later, a man whom I did not recognize appeared from behind the plane trees. He was dressed neatly in a dark suit and after saying a few words to the Shah presented him with a document. The Shah rose and asked tersely if anyone had a fountain pen. I offered mine. When he returned the pen he remarked that it was a good pen, and now that he'd signed the document with it, it would be worth much more.

"A fortune?" I asked, joking.

"Perhaps. Perhaps it will bring us all luck as well."

Nothing more was said. I found out later that the messenger had been sent by Kermit Roosevelt and the document the Shah had signed appointed General Zahedi prime minister. Mossadeq's fall was imminent. Operation Ajax was about to begin.

That night at dinner the Shah seemed calm, and the conversation turned to how lovely the Caspian weather must be.

"Are you going north, Your Majesty?" one of the group asked.

"Yes," he answered. "I have given orders to have the horses readied to ride. You must join us in a few days."

He said good-bye that night with every indication that we would be seeing him again soon. The next morning the papers reported that he and Queen Soraya had gone north, just as he had told us.

THE TALE OF THE COUP

In those final days before Mossadeq's downfall the relationship between the premier and the Majles became increasingly turbulent. But as we say in Farsi, in muddy waters one catches fish, and Mossadeq had always in the past proven that he could walk away with a good catch whenever the waters were troubled.

In June his dispute with Kashani reached the breaking point, and deputies loyal to the prime minister relieved Kashani of his post as house speaker. In his place they elected the brother of my Birmingham friend, Abdollah Moazemi. Still the Majles remained hopelessly divided and unable to conduct any business.

Taking advantage of the turmoil the Tudeh Party adopted an increasingly public role. Ostensibly the party supported the prime minister, but by the very act of taking his side it knowingly contributed to his downfall. Communist papers appeared openly in the streets, slogans dotted the city walls, and Tudeh Party members drove around in jeeps calling to the people through loudspeakers. Mossadeq, hoping to shame the United States into coming to his aid, encouraged Moscow to send an ambassador to discuss the sale of oil, allowed the Tudeh papers to be sold, and left the Tudeh slogans unwhitewashed on the walls.

On July 22 a large demonstration, composed primarily of Tudeh supporters, clamored for the closing of Parliament. This followed closely Moscow's posting of Anatol Lavrentiev as ambassador to Tehran, a significant move since he had been the point man in Prague when Communist tanks had thundered into Czechoslovakia in 1948. The heavy Communist showing convinced the American administration that Mossadeq had lost control and that the Soviets were about to take over. Its premonitions were only strengthened when Abdollah Moazemi dissolved Parliament.

A few days afterward, as we had sat around on lawn chairs, the document appointing General Zahedi prime minister was handed to the Shah for his signature. Twenty-four hours later he had flown from the scene.

But over the next few days the coup did not work out as planned. On Saturday, August 15, the night Mossadeq was supposed to be arrested, I was invited to dinner by his sons Gholam Hossein and Ahmad at their house in the mountains. We all enjoyed ourselves so much that we decided to meet a few days later to see some old rock carvings and bas-reliefs near Tehran. Even as we were having dinner, however, Colonel Nassiri, commander of the Imperial Guard (and later, head of SAVAK), arrived at their father's house with a contingent of officers to arrest the premier. Mossadeq, always suspicious, found the midnight visit strange and had his own guards arrest Nassiri's men instead. The next morning he accused the Shah over the radio of fomenting a coup with the help of foreign elements. The Shah, hearing the news from the Caspian, took fright and fled to Baghdad. From there he flew to Rome, where he arrived bedraggled, without servants or baggage, much to the amusement of the Italian press.

Kermit Roosevelt was not deterred. What seemed like a disaster to the British Foreign Office, and even to Allen Dulles at the CIA, was to him just the first step. In conjunction with General Schwarzkopf, who was once again in Iran, he devised a follow-up plan. Copies of the Shah's document appointing Zahedi prime minister were distributed throughout the government and the army. Leaflets describing Mossadeq as a Communist collaborator flooded Tehran. A huge demonstration was organized, ostensibly of pro-Shah sympathizers but in fact primarily of hired thugs (by Roosevelt's own account in his controversial memoir, *Countercoup*).

On August 17 I went to have lunch in Poonak, the orchard village where my sister Haideh and her husband, Manucher Garagozlu, had a house. It lies across a broad gulch from the city proper and commands a spectacular view. We could see fires burning in town and listened to reports of rioting on the radio. By midafternoon, too curious to stay out of the city, Manucher and I decided to drive in.

Street fighting was almost unheard of then, but several thousand Tudeh Party members, capitalizing on the news of the aborted coup, had poured into the streets, many carrying flags on thick poles like clubs. We saw truckloads of soldiers along the streets, and as the crowd surged the soldiers jumped from their vehicles, taking up positions against the people. It was then that the rioters threw away their flags and began to attack the soldiers, striking them with their short weapons. Mossadeq, however, had forbidden the soldiers to shoot, and they could only fend off the crowd by using their cumbersome rifles as shields.

Suddenly we heard gunfire and, jumping out of the car, we escaped into a nearby house for shelter. But the people inside turned out to be members of the Tudeh Party, and they immediately started to threaten us. Fearing for our lives, we hurriedly left. Outside, bands of rioters were tearing down statues of the Shah and showering the mosques with rocks. I wondered who was instigating all this action in the streets—and why—since my sister Maryam and her husband, Kia, along with many of the other Tudeh heavies, were still in East Germany.

The timing of this Tudeh riot played right into Roosevelt's hands. Mossadeq's popularity among the masses, until then untarnished by either economic hardship or political mayhem, suddenly waned. The deep-seated fear of communism so endemic to the Iranian character had been kindled. Was it possible, people began to wonder, that Mossadeq had really succumbed to the Reds?

Wednesday morning, August 19, I went as planned to rendezvous with Mossadeq's sons for our outing. To my surprise no one was there. Confused, I started walking toward the center of town. At the main post office I saw several truckloads of soldiers shouting pro-Shah slogans. Crowds of people (many of them Roosevelt's hired thugs, I later learned) were massing in the streets, and many carried pictures of the Shah. Every time a car drove by, the crowd surged to stop it, insisting that the driver put a 10-rial note on the windshield with the picture of the Shah facing out. Soon there was a traffic jam, with all the cars honking and flashing their lights.

Back at my mother's house we could hear the roar of the crowd as it converged spontaneously around Mossadeq's place just down the street. We could also hear tanks rolling down the street and the sound of gunfire. Anxious for our own safety we barricaded the house with wooden planks. About four P M the radio announced that General Zahedi had been appointed prime minister and that Mossadeq had fled.

When the dust at last settled, more than twenty people had been killed. Mossadeq had escaped across the back wall of his house into a neighbor's garden. We watched the crowds coming back up the street loaded with loot: tiles from the walls of his house, a washbasin, pots and pans from the kitchen, even trees from the garden. What they couldn't take they smashed.

Later my cousin Hossein Dowlatshahi told me that the CIA had contacted him to help with the operation. Along with a number of friends he had gone to take over the radio station. Commanding the radio was key, since until then every time Mossadeq had made a broadcast, he'd crushed the opposition. To ensure that the pro-Mossadeq front could not get through, Hossein's group had parked a number of cars in the middle of the main road leading to the station, instantly creating a traffic jam.

That evening General Zahedi formally proclaimed himself prime minister. The next day Mossadeq gave himself up.

The fall of Mossadeq marked the end of a dream. It was both a tragedy and a godsend. Mossadeq had given Iran confidence. With his ouster, tainted as it was by outside engineering, that newfound sense of self dissolved. Yet ironically, like so many politicians, Mossadeq had become successful not so much because of his own strengths but because his opponents were so mediocre. Though powerful in opposition, he was out of his depth once he became leader of the country. Although the ship, whose captain he was, could have been saved, he preferred to sail it gloriously onto the rocks rather than relinquish command. And we, his people, had believed in him, certain that he would guide us out of the British quagmire. How we were deceived! In the words of Hafez,

> When falling into the whirlpool of sorrows,
> With his vision there was always the hope of finding a shore.
> But they don't say anymore that Hafez is farsighted
> For we all saw that Hafez was totally ignorant.

Tales of the

Later Years

CHAPTER XII

THE EAGLE LANDS

Hafez, did you see the laughing partridge roaming in the hills
Who was so unaware of the claws of the eagle of destiny?
—HAFEZ

Tehran 1953

The British era was over. From the moment the coup succeeded, the United States became the prominent foreign power in Iran. For the next quarter century it would send shiploads of arms, millions of dollars in aid, and thousands of experts, assuming a presence that eventually proved too suffocating to bear. For many Persians the coup was a crucial turning point. By intervening to overthrow Mossadeq, the United States sacrificed the real love it had enjoyed among the people. Overnight our trust in it evaporated. Now many looked upon the United States with suspicion and dismay, unnerved by its covert role in overthrowing the only democratically elected government the country had ever had. Democracy apparently was just a political label and, when not expedient, dispensable.

Having seen its oil pour into British and American tankers while it collected only a fraction of the proceeds, Iran had long felt cheated. Having been occupied by British and American soldiers to protect the world first from the Nazis and then from communism, Iran felt used. Now, having forcibly evicted AIOC after fifty years of occupation, Iranians were once again seeing a foreign power move in. All that Mossadeq had stood for and achieved was lost. Twenty-five years later, when the United States was humiliatingly expelled by Ayatollah Khomeini, it was left to those in Washington think tanks to observe that the seeds of the rejection had been planted in 1953.

In August 1953, however, the coup was heralded the world over as a big success—the victory of Western democracy over the great Soviet threat. The Shah flew back from Rome on the 22nd, protected by a military phalanx. Martial law was declared, and Dr. Mossadeq was brought to trial for defying the Shah's order to step down. In consideration for his age and international reputation—and the deep popularity he still enjoyed—the military tribunal waffled and worried and at last gave him a relatively light sentence of three years in jail. Afterward he moved to his properties in Ahmadabad, where he remained under house arrest for the rest of his life.*

I attended the trial. The courtroom was very small, and entry was tightly controlled. A friend of mine arranged to get me a ticket, and after being screened (they wanted no fuss or demonstrations by Mossadeq supporters) I was allowed in. The proceedings were carefully staged, but it was a noisy court, and the tribunal was only halfhearted. People came in and simply cried. Mossadeq, cocky and fearless, frequently broke in on the testimony. When his chief of staff, a general named Riahi, took the stand, he was asked why the soldiers had stopped including the Shah in their nightly prayers. "Because," answered the general, "the prime minister ordered it so."

Mossadeq sprang to his feet. "Yes, General, I accept that," he said sarcastically. "But not everything you did that was wrong was on my orders."

The coup itself was said to have cost several million dollars.† Immediately after the Shah's return to Tehran, the United States granted Iran a

---

*Ahmadabad was near a property owned by my brother Farough and his American-born wife, Jean. Jean remembers that after his exile Dr. Mossadeq wanted to set up a clinic in the village. But he needed access to water, and the nearest water in the area ran through Farough's property. "Of course we gave him the water rights," Jean recalls. "By way of thanks he gave us a carpet. He also gave me a turkey every year after that for Thanksgiving. But these weren't like American turkeys. They were Persian turkeys, which ran around freely and were scrawny and skinny. When the revolution came, I packed the carpet into my suitcase. It was the only one I saved. Other people look at it and think, What a beautiful carpet. I look at it and think of turkeys."

†Various figures have been given, starting with Kermit Roosevelt's understated $75,000. Yet, according to Ambassador Henderson in an interview in 1984, General Zahedi alone was paid $2 million. The Rashidian brothers were thought to have received a similar amount for their crucial role in arranging secret meetings between Roosevelt and the Shah. The relationship between Roosevelt and the Shah remained active throughout the following two decades, with Roosevelt visiting Iran up to twice a year. Every time he came, he stayed with the Rashidians. They continued to serve the Shah throughout his reign.

loan of $45 million. This was separate from the river of aid being funneled in under the auspices of Point Four (and later, USAID), a program that had begun in 1950 during Mossadeq's premiership but increased rapidly in size after the coup.

The British government was irritated by what it called Washington's generosity. Mossadeq's fall did not immediately carry with it a solution to the oil problem, and so Britain continued its embargo on Iran and kept the doors of its embassy tightly shut.

THE TALE OF THREE OIL COMMISSIONS

For Iran the first order of business after the coup was to negotiate an agreement to get its oil flowing again. Given the saturation of world markets, this was no easy task and required the cooperation of the world's major oil companies. The man John Foster Dulles chose to facilitate the job was Herbert Hoover, Jr. To add clout to Hoover's negotiating position Dulles elevated him to the status of undersecretary of state, indicating how much the United States valued Iranian oil in its long-term energy plans.

Hoover arrived in Tehran in late October, bent on devising a deal that would create a consortium of companies to handle all aspects of Iran's oil industry. The idea had initially been floated by Walter Levy back in 1951 when he and Averell Harriman had come to Tehran the summer after nationalization. Now Hoover adopted it as the only feasible solution.

Earlier that fall Prime Minister Zahedi had formed a four-member commission to examine the oil situation and advise the government of its options. Dr. Pirnia and I were asked to serve as members, and after meeting briefly we wrote a report. Immediately thereafter a second commission was assembled, this one to meet with Hoover and discuss alternatives, though not to act as a decision-making body. It was headed up by Abdollah Entezam, the minister of foreign affairs, and, besides Dr. Pirnia and me, included a couple of cabinet members, two ex-senators, and representatives from the oil industry.

Although it was good to see Hoover again after so many years and we felt confident in his long-term knowledge of the Iranian oil situation, I sus-

One of them went as his special envoy to see Indira Gandhi, causing outrage among the Shah's more seasoned diplomats. The Rashidian name also appears in U.S. government records dating as late as 1976 concerning a sale of F-14s by Grumman Aerospace. Some $2.5 million in untallied commissions were paid to a company that turned out to be owned wholly by the Rashidians.

pected that he had already worked out the main points of the deal with Zahedi and was not particularly interested in our perspective on British compensation or a 50/50 division of profits (two of twenty-four discussion
points we brought to the table). He briefed us fully on the state of the international oil market and provided statistics of refinery capacity and
world output. His main purpose, however, was to promote his proposal for
a consortium of companies to take over where AIOC had left off, while still
granting AIOC (now rechristened British Petroleum, or BP) the majority
share.

At this we balked. Under the current political situation no agreement
that gave BP such a large percentage would ever pass the Majles. We discussed the point for two meetings, and since Hoover always came with a
secretary who took full and copious notes, I got into the habit of taking
notes as well.

At the third meeting Hoover clearly felt that the proposal had been discussed long enough and suddenly shifted tone. He had just described the
financial difficulties posed by a consortium to show us why it would be
preferable for BP to dominate the arrangement. All at once his voice took
on an edge and he said, "I want the assurance of the acceptance of these
principles."

There was a moment of confused silence. Then Dr. Pirnia spoke. "Mr.
Hoover," he said, "we are here to clarify Iran's position. We never talked
about principles, and we are not mandated to give any assurances."

Hoover glanced around the room, then flatly denied he'd made such a
statement. I looked at him in amazement. He and I were friends—as
friends go in the oil-negotiating business. This was neither the forum nor
the moment to be making deals or issuing ultimatums. Yet here he was
bullying us, with the obvious intention of making us agree to something
we couldn't support.

Dr. Pirnia was not one to back down. "You never said such a thing?" he
countered, sitting bolt upright. He swung his gaze to the rest of us at the
table and started to ask each person in turn what he had heard. What cowards! Not one owned up to having heard Hoover demand our acceptance of
the principles he'd been describing. One man said he really didn't understand English very well. Another said he hadn't been listening.

Dr. Pirnia's face turned ashen as he realized he was being let down by his
compatriots. Finally he sat back defeated.

It was my turn to speak. "I have been taking notes," I said, drawing my
sword. "With your permission I will read back what was just said."

I started a bit higher up on the page. As I read the proceedings, the others commented on how clear and accurate the notes were. Then I got to "I

want the assurance of the acceptance of these principles." It was an awkward sentence, but Hoover had said it.

"Oh, all right," Hoover admitted. "But that's not what I really meant."

What a tragic moment. Suddenly I knew for certain that he was betraying us. Dr. Pirnia and I had shamed him in front of the others by showing that the commission was only so much window dressing and that we were there only to add legitimacy to a plan Hoover had already decided to adopt.

Entezam suggested that we break for tea and cake in the lounge, then stood up immediately to prevent any further discussion. On the way out I stepped into the washroom with Dr. Pirnia. When we came out, I saw a servant standing with our hats and coats in the vestibule. I took Dr. Pirnia's arm and pointed. "We better get out before they throw us out," I said. We could see the others already drinking their tea in the room across the hall. Dr. Pirnia hesitated.

"You can stay," I said, "but that's my hat, and I'm leaving."

In the car Dr. Pirnia sat in silence, his face contorted with despair. "What kind of country are we living in?" he mumbled miserably. "Our compatriots are traitors. You and I defend this country. We want it to move forward. And yet we never find a partner to help us."

When we reached his house Dr. Pirnia got out quickly. But before he shut the door he leaned back in and said pathetically, "I'm not concerned about what has happened for my sake. I'm concerned about you. They have taken enough reprisals as it is against your brother. This is the type of incident that could lead them to take reprisals against you too."

That was truly friendship. I reached over and took his arm. "Don't blame yourself," I said. "It was the only thing to do."

Many years later I received a letter from Dr. Pirnia recalling that meeting. "You were like a cloud in the desert that falls on someone who is thirsty," he wrote. "I will always remember Hoover's words, which you wrote down and threw back at him in front of everybody. By backing me up, you miraculously destroyed the meeting that would have established a consortium hopelessly skewed in favor of the British.

"Everything is a setup by the big powers," he went on sadly. "Democracy is a pill they force us to swallow by kicking us in the pants. These pills not only do not bring us good health; they bring us disturbance and grief, which at last, cannot be cured."

The commission disbanded soon after, the point obviously having been reached where decision making was necessary. The finance minister, Dr. Ali Amini, subsequently assembled a ministerial commission composed of cabinet members such as Ali Soheili, an ex–prime minister, and Dr.

Fakhre-din Shadman, who had been our government's oil commissioner in London when I was at Birmingham.

THE TALE OF THE DEEP THROAT

A friend from New York, an interesting man named Emad Kia, came to visit me one day soon after the third commission had been assembled. Over tea and cakes he told me he was a close friend of Ali Soheili's and asked whether Soheili could visit me. I had just published a book (in Farsi) called *Considerations on the Problems of Oil,* which established me as an authority on the subject, and Soheili, Kia said, wanted to pick my brain.

It was just the type of matchmaking that was typical of Kia. I had met him years ago, but it was in New York, where he was consul general, that we got to know each other well. He'd been on Nosrat-Doleh's political staff and knew a lot of big shots in Iran. He never wanted money or position for himself; he just liked politicking—making introductions, gathering people together, and quenching their quarrels. He was an intriguing thinker and intermediary—a man who could be counted on to make the business fat, as we Persians say. What's more he had a very attractive wife named Gotzi.*

Kia was not asking me a big favor, and yet I hesitated. Soheili was large and sloppy, with a pockmarked face and a tough, mulish look. He had been quite young when he'd served as prime minister during the war, and as a result I'd always assumed he was a British stooge and faulted him for engineering the sugar shortages and financial difficulties that plagued us during his tenure. But I was peeved that I had not been asked to serve on this newest commission. Ali Soheili, I realized, could become my front man. If I briefed him well, he could become the contrarian on the commission, the voice to trumpet Iran's future when all the others abandoned it.

The next day was the first of Soheili's many visits to my apartment. I did not know him well and found him to be a very clever man. He was a real

*Gotzi divorced him soon after he left New York for Tehran. Only later did I find out that she had been a close friend of Soheili's. She went on to marry an American in Tokyo, and after divorcing him she married the Colombian ambassador in Beirut. Through her the Colombian began to do undercover work for the Shah, which in the 1960s included keeping an eye on Teymour Bakhtiar, the ousted head of SAVAK, Iran's secret service, when he tried to stage a coup against the throne from Beirut. The Shah rewarded Gotzi and her husband by making him consul in Bogotá, the only foreign consul we had in the world. When I became ambassador to Venezuela, the Colombian government asked if I could be accredited as ambassador to Bogotá as well. It was then that my minister of foreign affairs told me this story, saying, "We can't touch the consul. He's there by order of the Shah."

sponge, able to absorb information quickly, then repeat the concepts in his own words. He had a knack for distilling the complicated into the simple, and once he learned something, he would speak with the confidence and assurance of an expert. On the commission he became so voluble that he was shifted to the role of spokesman.

One day I heard him laughing on the stairs as he approached my apartment.

"I'm laughing," he told me, "at the memory of one of the commission's oil 'experts' sitting with his fork in the air with a piece of meat on it, stunned that I knew so much about oil and could spout so many statistics. Truly, in the land of the blind the man with one eye is king."

Soheili's colleagues, particularly Dr. Amini, knew there was a deep throat somewhere. But *who* it was they didn't know.

Sometime toward the middle of November Soheili called and said he needed to see me urgently. I was lunching that day at my mother's and asked him to join us. He arrived with Kia, making us five at the table, for my youngest brother, Ali, now twenty-two, had just returned to Tehran from Oxford. My mother was pleased to see me with such a circle of friends, and her eyes widened when Soheili announced he'd been nominated to open diplomatic relations with England and asked if I would accompany him to Zurich to meet in secret with key British officials.

I was startled by the suggestion. "Mr. Soheili," I said, "in all honesty I'm taken aback by your proposal, especially coming from such an experienced man as you. If you go there with me—the brother of Nosrat-Doleh—you will be accused of being a British pawn and of secretly trading for a future nomination as prime minister. We will both be accused of all sorts of double-dealing. I'll lose my chance of riding on your coattails, and you will never again become premier." At this I grinned, knowing I'd tapped a secret hope of his.

Soheili saw my point and decided to go right away and tell Zahedi he'd changed his mind about meeting the British in Zurich. At the door he embraced me. "I'm amazed at your insight," he said. "How is it possible you have not gone further in the government? For the first time I understand how handicapped you are by your heritage—hobbled by the Shah and by everyone else."

My mother, however, was not so taken by my words, and as she helped me with my coat as the others waited outside on the stoop, she spoke to me as if I were still a little boy. "Why do you contradict *Agha* Soheili?" she asked. "He is such an important man. You never approve of anything."

I gave her a hug but brushed her off. The system dictated that when the big man talked, the younger ones listened. But I was not like that.

I dropped Soheili off at the Officers Club, where Zahedi was residing at the time. The next day he told me of their conversation. "It would be better," he'd told Zahedi, "to approach the British through their Swiss representatives here. We cannot afford for the British Parliament to claim all the credit once relations are reestablished."

A few days later British foreign secretary Anthony Eden announced in London that relations between England and Iran would be reestablished. By the middle of December a chargé d'affaires, Denis Wright, was dispatched to Tehran.

THE TALE OF A DEAL

Most of the real negotiating on the oil deal took place in London, where the major oil companies haggled over how much each would get in Hoover's consortium and whether what they'd agreed on would be acceptable within the current political climate in Iran. Eventually British Petroleum's share was set at 40 percent of what was christened simply the Consortium—a multinational conglomerate that would handle Iran's oil industry. Another 40 percent was divided among five U.S. majors (the four Aramco partners—Standard Oil of New Jersey, Socony, Socal, and Texaco—plus BP's partner in Kuwait, Gulf Oil). Shell got 14 percent, and a French company, CFP, got 6 percent.*

Sir William Fraser, arrogant and rapacious as always, insisted not only that BP's new partners should pay it more than $1 billion for its losses in Iran but that Iran itself should provide BP with 110 million tons of free oil over the next twenty years as a tithe "for rupture of agreement."

The U.S. State Department found Fraser's demands so unreasonable that it threatened to pull out of the Anglo-American alliance—the informal front the two maintained in Middle Eastern policy. The resulting uproar forced Foreign Secretary Eden (who had become so exasperated by Fraser's Scotch narrow-mindedness that he described him as being in "cloud cuckoo land"[1]) to prevail upon BP to reduce its claims. Nonetheless, after the last signature was affixed to the agreement, Fraser's haul for BP was

---

*Very soon after the agreement was reached, the major American companies released 5 percent of their holdings to a miniconsortium of fifteen independent U.S. companies, including Alton Jones's City Services. This was partly to allay U.S. government fears of monopoly, particularly in the face of an ongoing investigation of the oil companies by the Justice Department. It was also partly to pay off the independents, which maintained they had supported the majors in their embargo of Iran's oil in order to receive some of the spoils now.

significant: The five U.S. companies, Shell, and CFP together eventually paid it $600 million cash for their 60 percent share—a fortune considering that by the company's own financial statements, all existing assets (valued at $93 million) had already been paid for by the export of Iranian oil. Furthermore Iran ended up paying BP more than $40 million in compensation over the next ten years.

Though not very pleased with the size of BP's holding and angry at having to pay for interests it felt BP was reselling to other Consortium members, Iran had little choice but to agree to the deal.

On the other side of the table were oil company representatives from France, Britain, Holland, and the United States, who arrived in Tehran accompanied by a swarm of journalists. Among them was Wanda Jablonski, petroleum editor of the *New York Journal of Commerce* and later correspondent for the influential magazine *Petroleum Week*. I had met her in New York through Walter Levy and had seen her several times since. A brunette from Czechoslovakia, she had a mind like a steel trap, a nose like a toucan, and a smile that could crack open an oyster. We got along famously.

NIXON

In the first blush of the new government, with all the foreign dignitaries pouring in, the city took on a carnival air, with the hotels fully booked and parties every night to entertain the visitors. Persian society celebrated and paraded in style. My cousin Dr. Ali Amini, the minister of finance, who eventually signed the Consortium agreement when it was finalized in September 1954, was in great demand. His glamorous wife, Batoul, one of the eight Vosugh sisters and a frequent companion of Qavam-Saltaneh's, was a great friend of mine (even though Amini and I were not), and she regularly invited me to their glittering dinner parties, where she entertained in gowns by Lanvin and Dior.

In December 1953 Vice President Richard Nixon and his wife, Pat, arrived in Tehran. He came to solidify U.S. relations with Iran and show how strongly Washington supported the Shah. Prime Minister Zahedi fêted him with a gala dinner at the Ministry of Foreign Affairs, to which I was invited. When Zahedi introduced me, he asked me to act as Nixon's interpreter and companion during the dinner. The picture taken of us that evening shows us all with pasted-on smiles. I found Nixon insipid—uninterested in meeting people, uninterested in talking about petroleum. I switched the conversation to Persian art, Persepolis, even world politics. He would bite on none of it. He had come to see the Shah, and the friendship established between the two would affect U.S.-Iranian relations for the next two decades. The country itself, however, held no interest for him.

My wife, Gean, arrived in Iran in January of 1954, on the day that running water finally reached my mother's house and the rest of Tehran. Though it had been thought an impossible task, particularly in this financially difficult period, the Shah had insisted on laying mains and building a dam to pump fresh water into the houses of Tehran. For my mother it was an extraordinary luxury; for me it was a godsend to be able to offer my new wife the convenience of regular plumbing when everything around her was strange and new. At first we could only wash with the new water; drinking water was still brought to us in copper urns by a little man on a donkey, drawn from streams way up in the mountains above Darband.

Gean and I moved into our new apartment on Reza Shah Avenue as soon as she arrived. It was close enough to my mother's house so that she often sent over hot meals or one of the servants to do the cleaning. We had a coffee table consisting of a board placed on top of two huge bottles normally used to collect kerosene. To jazz the place up Gean put goldfish in the bottles. Their bright scales caught the light as they swam about, brightening the flat like mirrored mosaics.

A SOCIAL LESSON

We did a lot of socializing in those days, since I had no regular job and I made it my business to keep abreast of events through personal contacts. We also frequently went on hunting parties with my cousin Hossein Dowlatshahi, shooting duck along the rivers, or mouflons, with their twisted horns, or the goat-like ibex in the mountains. In the winter desert we would see gazelles and onagers (Asian wild asses). The variety of the game and the vastness of the landscape were breathtaking. There is nothing as pure as the desert, with no sign of human life anywhere—just clear sun and blessed silence. Many times we went into the desert at four o'clock in the morning, and once I shot an ibex, its horns arching high over its head, far up in the hills against the dawn. Everyone congratulated me on the shot except Gean, who burst into tears. "It was the only thing alive for miles, and you killed it," she sobbed. Neither of us was finding marriage easy.

One evening we were invited to court for a black-tie dinner with about one hundred guests. At one point, as I was chatting with my friend Agha Khan Bakhtiar, Dr. Amini came up and asked me abruptly whether I was interested in a job. When I told him yes, he offered me my old position as director general of oil and concessions at the Ministry of Finance. I flushed with anger. I did not want a job I had done two years ago, I told him. I wanted to be challenged by greater responsibility.

Amini, sarcastically I thought, turned to Agha Khan Bakhtiar and said, "Imagine. What's going on in this country? I offer this young man a good job, and he doesn't accept it."

The offhandedness of his remark set me off. I didn't care that he was minister of finance or my cousin, and I began to insult him. Had we not been in the Shah's house, I probably would have punched him in the nose.

Later that evening the Shah beckoned me over and asked about the incident. Someone had reported the altercation to him, and he found it amusing, as he himself had little love for his finance minister. Eventually I began to find fault with everything Amini did, and our relationship became frigid.

In the summer of 1954 Soheili was nominated ambassador to London. He asked me to go along as his commercial attaché, but I turned him down, once again hoping to become a member of Parliament from Kermanshah. Soheili warned me that I had no chance. "The Shah will never allow you or any other Farmanfarmaian to become a member of Parliament," he said. "A minister, yes, because then he can throw you out whenever he likes. But a member of Parliament, elected by the people, planted and unmovable for two years inside the government? Never." Nonetheless I insisted on trying.

We both felt sad at the thought of parting, for we had become extremely close. Wanting to spend his last moments in Iran in my company, he asked me to drive him to the airport.*

When I went to pick him up, I saw that Emad Kia had come as well to accompany Soheili's wife, a very eccentric Russian woman. Poor Emad. Soheili had just one bag, but his wife had mountains.

When we got to the airport a slew of dignitaries were there to see Soheili off, including Dr. Amini. They were surprised to see me arrive with him, and I watched as they suddenly realized that I must have been his oil source. I walked right past Dr. Amini, refusing even to say hello.

After Soheili departed, Amini came up to me. "Manucher, I never expected such behavior from you," he said. "Insulting people never pays. How is it possible that you are acting this way, you the son of Farman Farma, who never insulted anyone and got along with everybody? He

*Soheili's political star was then very bright, and he stood a good chance of becoming prime minister in the following years. Many times he told me that when he was elected, I could be sure of a ministerial post. Unfortunately he was diagnosed with cancer while in London and died soon after, taking my political dreams with him.

didn't have this impetuosity that you are allowing to get the better of you. You are truly a Kurd. He must be shaking in his grave to see you so quarrelsome."

Amini spoke so warmly and was so kind and brotherly that I felt suddenly ashamed. He was right, and I was mortified. He was being genuinely conciliatory—the sign of a mature man—and I realized he was giving me a much-needed social lesson. It was more than I had a right to expect even from my own kin.

Amini was from an old family who for a hundred years had been serving the Persian government as high-ranking officials. He was related to us through his mother, Fakhre-Doleh, an extremely intelligent woman who kept the family fortune clutched tightly in her hands, demanded respect without reciprocation, and was overly proud of her aristocratic descendance. She was a sister of Princess Ezzat-Doleh (my father's first wife) and like her one of my father's cousins. Yet the two families shared little love, and the relationship between us was marked by a good deal of jealousy. Therefore all the more extraordinary was Amini's generosity of spirit toward me. I had never been anything but trouble to him, causing anguish to his wife as I'd stood my ground against her sister in the affair of Dr. Moaven's second wife and aggravating his already strained relationship with the Shah by arguing with him in the palace. When he extended an invitation to come for dinner that very night I accepted humbly, filled with remorse, and vowed never again to exercise malice so senselessly and in public.

A TALE OF THE SHAH

As Soheili had predicted, I lost my bid for Parliament. The new Majles took its seat in September 1954. Its first order of business was ratification of the beleaguered Consortium agreement. After all the haggling Dr. Amini signed it grudgingly, explaining to the Majles, "It was the best I could get—and the best to be obtained." Although Iran was to receive 50 percent of the profits, its oil industry was still to be managed by foreigners. And because of the structure of the deal Iran still had little say as to how much oil would be sold and at what price. Thanks to Mossadeq's ignorance Iran had lost forever its claim to 20 percent of BP's worldwide profits and its stake in the subsidiary companies. The United States also gained less than it could have had it responded when the country first nationalized oil. It certainly hadn't needed a coup to achieve what it got through the Consortium.

Immediately after the agreement was ratified the Shah went to Washington to thank President Eisenhower for saving his throne. He was feeling very secure, having gotten rid of General Zahedi in March and replaced him with Hossein Ala, his minister of court. Though Zahedi had shown every loyalty to the Pahlavi dynasty, he was a powerful character and his very presence made the Shah nervous. His son Ardeshir, who later became famous as ambassador to the United States, had recently married the Shah's daughter Shahnaz, but rather than improving relations between the two fathers-in-law, the marriage only served to make the Shah more suspicious. The Shah did not dismiss the prime minister himself. In a tactic increasingly typical of his dealings with subordinates he ordered his close friend Assadollah Alam to do the dirty work.

General Zahedi was appointed ambassador to the UN and shipped off to Geneva, where the UN still had its headquarters. A couple of months later, on a trip to Switzerland, I ran into him in the street. He asked me to come for lunch or dinner, but I already had plans. Instead we took a short walk together through the Old Town. It was an overcast afternoon, the threat of snow hanging in the air. He put his gloved hand into the crook of my arm and admitted without rancor that he could easily have kept the Shah in Rome for weeks after the coup if he'd wanted to solidify his own position. I told him it was a secret everybody knew. "From the minute His Majesty returned, he acted against me, fearing he would be eclipsed by a strong premier. But the good of the country depended on the Shah's regaining power," he said, and he would never have stood in the Shah's way.

"Very few times in my life have I misjudged a person because I was under the spell of someone else," he said a little later in the conversation. "In your case I made such a mistake. I took you off the commission when I should have kept you on it to negotiate our stake. I made an error, and I'm sorry about it."

Zahedi's apology was so unexpected and heartfelt that I found myself at a loss for words. He was a very special man: a symbol of bold courage and devotion to the Shah. Now, once again, he was doing the Crown's bidding—his last assignment as it turned out, for disease and old age would overtake him in Geneva.

It was the fall of 1954, and as I still had no regular job, I arranged to do another set of lectures with Clark Getz's outfit in New York. When I got there, Manucher Garagozlu, my sister Haideh's husband, called to say that the Shah's party was staying at the Waldorf-Astoria. Manucher was the Shah's public relations officer and told me that Howard Page, the president of Standard Oil, was scheduled to see him that evening. Knowing nothing about oil, Manucher asked if I'd come along. I told him I'd be delighted.

I'd met Page earlier that year at the Aminis'. He'd been one of the main negotiators of the Consortium deal, and of all the people I'd met throughout the process he was the nicest and the most willing to help Iran. It turned out that Page wanted to throw the Shah a big dinner party in San Francisco, but the Shah refused.

A few days later the Shah decided to go to the West Coast anyway, though without fanfare. Coincidentally I was in San Francisco finishing up the lecture tour when the royal entourage turned up at my hotel. The hotel bar was full when His Majesty and Queen Soraya appeared there one night. When I saw the Shah, I got up and offered them my table, telling them I was leaving. Thereafter we ran into each other at every turn, as though we were destined to dine at the same restaurants and visit the same sites.

Since I was in San Francisco, I decided to go back to Iran via Southeast Asia. As a result I entered Iran from the east at Zahedan, a horrid little town on the cuff of the desert along the Pakistani border. I arrived with several cameras and a lot of American goods in my bags, and right away I could tell that the border guard, a rough fellow, was going to give me a hard time. He had me open all my bags and, with heavy hands, began rummaging through my things. Suddenly he gave a start as he saw a little volume of poetry by Hafez that I always traveled with. "You have a Hafez?" he asked. I nodded dumbly. I had become addicted to Hafez and could not sleep at night without reading a passage or two. I was not alone in this appreciation. The guard took the book reverently in his hands and, opening it, read a page silently to himself.

His eyes shone as he looked back at me. "You may close your bags now, sir," he said with respect, handing the book to me on the flat of his rough, cracked palms. For a moment we stood looking at each other, such vastly different men who nonetheless were brothers through the love of poetry. Invigorated, he helped me to shut one of my more obstinate trunks and went out of his way to make everything as easy for me as possible. He even took my address and some months later sent me a bag of saffron.

A TALE OF THE CONSORTIUM

Less than a month later Dr. Amini invited me to become a member of the Consortium board. I was extremely flattered and agreed immediately. Amini was not a vindictive man—a rare quality indeed and fundamental to the makeup of a good statesman. He was astute and of strong character, and one week after the signatures were affixed to the contract he pressured the Consortium into exporting its first cargo of oil—a fortnight earlier than scheduled. Unfortunately Amini's strengths were never appreciated by the Shah, who refused to change his opinion of him, and like so many good men in our government, his talents were never fully tapped.

Amini also appointed me to the Board of Accountants at the National Iranian Oil Company (NIOC). This turned out to be a major job, with a car and a good salary. Finally I was back in the saddle again.

According to the terms of the agreement, the Consortium managed all technical and international operations—exploitation, refining, and export. Routine, nonbasic business such as health, housing, and internal distribution were left to NIOC—giving NIOC the impression it was somehow involved, even though it really wasn't. The Consortium Refinery Board was composed of six directors and one chairman. Two of the directors were Persian. Our chairman was Jan Brouwer, who had represented Royal Dutch Shell during the negotiations. John Loudon, the chairman of Shell, had chosen Brouwer as his fair-haired boy, and it was assumed that he would follow in Loudon's footsteps to become Shell's chairman—which he did. He was tall and sleek, with long fingers and a chilly gaze. Nonetheless, during his two years as board chairman, I became quite close to him and went often to his house in Shemiran.

I appreciated that a Dutchman had been nominated to the chairmanship, representing a neutral party among the Consortium partners. It dignified the operation and gave welcome recognition to the fact that anti-British feeling still ran high in Iran. Later an American took the position, and still later an Englishman. Once the English took over they never left, and their leadership was dismal. The Dutch, however, proved outstanding.

The other Iranian on the board was Dr. Reza Fallah, a member of the NIOC board and director of the Abadan Refinery under Mossadeq. He was an inspiring colleague, brilliant and somewhat contrarian—which I identified with, though unlike me he was not impetuous. His arguments were so compelling that everyone ended up voting his way. Fallah was ten years older than I and also had studied at Birmingham, where he had obtained a doctorate in oil engineering. He was so renowned there that I had heard of him well before I actually met him while working for the Ministry of Finance. At the time he was chancellor of the Technical School of Abadan, where Mossadeq plucked him to head up the refinery as NIOC was born.

Fallah was always very proper and, though he was my superior, always called me Shahzdeh, or Prince. His own name literally meant "peasant." He was reputed to have come from a family of brigands from the city of Kashan to the southwest of the central desert. In the nineteenth century

two of his ancestors were hanged by the government for turning the area
into an armed state and stopping anyone they wished from traversing their
land to get to Isfahan. This was ironic since the Kashis (as those from
Kashan are called) were known in Iran for their timidity. There was even a
story of one hapless Kashi who decided to parade outside the gates of the
town festooned with knives, guns, and bullets. On the road he ran into a
Bakhtiari, who whipped him so thoroughly that he took all the Kashi's
arms and knives. When the Kashi returned to town people asked, "What
happened to you? You had all the arms!"

"But," he said, "I did not have a whip."

Nonetheless Kashan produced the two most notorious outlaws Iran has
ever had, and both were related to Fallah. His own rise to the pinnacle of
the oil industry was testimony to the lack of social discrimination in
Iran—the son of a thief could, on his own merits, become an invaluable
civil servant.

As director of production Fallah accomplished a number of enormous
projects and eventually became the main inspiration behind the construction of the Tehran Refinery. His desk was a sheet of glass, and it was always
clean—not one paper was ever on it. He had a pencil that he would pick
up occasionally while he pondered some question, though I never saw him
take a single note. He had no staff either. He would listen to a report and
then make a decision without further study. He could speak on legal matters as lucidly as any lawyer and was completely cognizant of his power to
convince anyone of anything. We became pals, though even as his friend I
rarely knew what he was up to, he was such a private man. Often he carried out special assignments for His Majesty. He wrote confidential reports
to the Shah on scraps of paper, frequently dashing them off on a fold-out
tray on an airplane. Rarely have I enjoyed traveling with anyone so much.
There was a rationality to him, a mathematical harmony to his thinking.
He made me feel calm. I called him "The Genius."

Fallah and I frequently traveled to Abadan together. The refinery had
grown into a vast city of thirty thousand employees and encompassed four
hundred acres, not including the storage tanks, the electric power installations, and the housing facilities. We often laughed at the memory of the
single derrick that we'd learned to operate at Birmingham and the electric
power station that everyone who took mechanical or oil engineering had
had to run.

He was amazed that a decade after he'd left Birmingham we'd still had
the same power station, with its old submarine engine captured from Germany during World War I. One person had to shovel in the coal while another adjusted the meters, a third controlled the pipes, and a fourth acted

as boss. Shoveling coal for two or three hours was backbreaking, but I'd enjoyed it. Every summer we also had to work in a mine or manufacturing plant. The pit of the mine was a thousand feet underground, and there were ponies in it that had been there all their lives. We went down on elevators that simply dropped like a stone to within a foot of the ground. The first couple of times I felt as if I was going to die: My stomach fell, everything was dark, and the car jolted to a stop with a bang.

Fallah smiled wryly in recognition. We discussed the old days in Abadan, when there were English employees who'd lived there for twenty years and never visited Tehran. They would work, go to the club, drink, sleep, work, drink, and so on every day, until they finally returned to England. There was even one fellow who left his boat in his air-conditioned house all summer while he was on home leave—while the Iranians outside didn't even have a fan.

One of the new plans Fallah and I instituted was a month on, fifteen days off, for all foreign and university-educated employees. A special plane shuttled employees from Abadan to Tehran in under an hour. Fifteen days in the capital, away from the intensity and isolation of work, made for better employees. It was an American idea.

A number of new schemes had been incorporated into the system, and to its credit the Consortium (with Amini's prodding) quickly brought us back to pre-Mossadeq levels of output. It was not as though there had ever been a total shutdown under Mossadeq—Fallah had kept all on-site operations moving. But export sales and marketing were critical to increasing our capacity and income and reclaiming our position as a preeminent Middle East producer. For that we had needed the Consortium. Within five years our revenues jumped from $10 million to $285 million—despite the fact that the price of oil, which was fixed by the companies, never rose above—and sometimes dropped below—$2.22 per barrel (and we only got 50 percent of it).

POINT FOUR

Helping Iran help itself by paying more for its oil was not on the American agenda. Sending over experts and aid was, and by 1954 we were inundated by the philanthropy of Point Four. It was an unmitigated disaster.

Point Four, a U.S. government program to bring American scientific and industrial progress to underdeveloped areas, was originally President Truman's idea (the fourth point in his 1949 inaugural address). Congress allotted $25 million for the program, which was administered through a number of agencies as well as the UN. Plagued by corruption, riddled with waste, and rent by internal rivalry, Point Four became the subject of a congressional investigation in 1956. By then more than 200 advisers had been sent to Iran and 102 locals had been hired to work on its projects. Managed by William E. Warne, Point Four (later, USAID) occupied offices in a series of large buildings that looked like a good-size ministry.

Warne lived more luxuriously than the American ambassador. His house was on Pahlavi Avenue, a main residential street lined with towering plane trees. Outside stood a big generator that supplied extra electricity for the films Warne liked to project. It was a damning symbol of the luxury enjoyed by a man who had come to help the poor.

Besides the big office in Tehran branches were opened in every major town, and at least one or two Americans were sent out to head each local office. Few of the Point Four advisers had any experience, let alone any idea of what would work in Iran. They knew nothing of farming and agriculture and were unfamiliar with Iran's language and culture. Alone in these small, faraway towns, they felt isolated and miserable. There was no movie theater, library, soda fountain, or corner hotel. Nothing could have been further from their homes in Iowa or Ohio than Kermanshah or Yazd.

The Point Four agent posted to Kermanshah came to my properties in Assadabad one day to discuss tractors. "Tractors?" I said. "Where will they come from? Who will import them? Who will teach the peasants how to use them, care for them, repair them when they fail?"

He talked of storing grain in silos.

"We don't have any silos," I told him, "or cement to build them either." For thousands of years the Persians had dug deep holes in the dry earth and stored their grain there. They were in effect reverse silos. No animal or insect could burrow into the grain beyond a depth of six inches. These storage holes were still in use because they worked.

The best thing about Iran was that no one had tampered with such simple solutions since the days of Cyrus the Great or the Mongols. Now people who did not have a clue were giving us useless advice, often through translators who were themselves American and also couldn't relate to the terrain or culture. The mission was more than fruitless. The changes the advisers did bring about were devastating. Had they had the wherewithal to do more, they would have destroyed Iran.

The Russians, also recipients of Point Four aid, complained bitterly that it was a front for espionage.* We understood their frustration. The Point

---

*In fact one man who was transferred from Kermanshah to Azerbaijan turned out to be from the CIA. "He's a journalist now," Mohammadvali Mirza told me sometime later.

Four Program sent "experts" into the countryside who weren't experts, didn't have diplomas in agriculture or infrastructure, and didn't even have good judgment.

One of their recommendations in Iran was that we improve transportation by bringing in a better breed of donkey. The donkeys in Iran, particularly in the south, were hardy and strong. Nevertheless the Point Four representative decided to import donkeys from Cyprus—at great cost. After much fanfare they arrived—and turned out to be indistinguishable from the ones we already had. Not only were they a complete waste of money, but they in no way "modernized" our transportation system.

Point Four's greatest source of pride was its health corps, of which my niece Nahid, a medical expert, was a member. Birth control, aspirin, and personal hygiene were its three main contributions. The Communists, however, counteracted the health corps's efforts by spreading rumors that the Americans were trying to kill people. Nahid noticed that every time a Point Four ambulance reached a village the people scattered and refused help. Speaking in Farsi she asked a few of the people what was happening and was told that the pills and injections were poisonous. And not only were they deadly, but they rendered a person infertile as well. The men, they said, would be impotent if their wives took birth control pills. Aspirin also would rob the men of their virility. When Nahid pointed out that a woman who had taken an aspirin a year earlier was still alive, they said it was just a matter of time; eventually she would die.

The fallacy underlying Point Four and the U.S. technical aid programs that followed was the assumption that because a country was not industrially developed, anybody recruited in the United States had something to teach the local people. In fact the mediocrity of the staff patently illustrated that the United States did not have enough experts to send around the globe. The greatest abusers of the program were people like Warne, who wrote a book called *Mission for Peace.* In a nation that had to beg the American ambassador for a few million dollars because hospitals were at the point of closing and the railway was grinding to a stop, Warne literally threw away his yearly budget. He succeeded only in besmirching America's name, while enjoying a life of luxury at others' expense.

THE SECOND CHAIRMAN

In the middle of 1956 Jan Brouwer left the Consortium to succeed John Loudon as chairman of Shell. I was concerned that the prestige of the Consortium would suffer, but his replacement, another Dutchman named K. Scholtens, turned out to be a man of great ability and an excellent chairman in his own right. Scholtens had spent thirty-five years in the Dutch East Indies, where he'd been president and managing director of Shell's operations in Indonesia. When I met him he was not married and was always flanked by beautiful secretaries. His was an image and lifestyle I appreciated. Though I was still married, things were not going well, and Gean and I were spending much time apart. We'd had a daughter in 1955, a wondrous experience that positively affected my attitude toward children but did not save the marriage. Since I was now effectively a bachelor myself, Scholtens and I spent much time together and became friends.

On the surface we could not have been more different. He must have been in his late fifties or early sixties, with sandy hair and white, finely lined skin. He wore heavy, square, black-rimmed glasses over his twinkly blue eyes, which could turn frosty in a minute. He emanated at once a sense of efficiency and kindness. He was comfortable with himself and full of ideas, which he had the strength to carry out.

It was really Scholtens, not Brouwer, who modernized the oil business in Iran—expanding the drilling, exploration, exporting, and development. One day he told me he was building ten thousand housing units. In all of Mossadeq's time not six hundred had been put up. "I've built a part of the world," he told me with pride once. "Thirty thousand housing units and a refinery in Indonesia—and now this." He expanded the airports in all the oil fields so that a four-engine plane could land and take off from every drilling site. He left a great legacy behind; no one else would achieve anything comparable. "I don't have time to justify my actions to every Tom, Dick, and Harry," he'd say. "I have to get on with the work." It was typical of Scholtens that within a few months of his arrival he arranged for me to take the office next to his at the Consortium—and, without ever saying a word, assigned a beautiful secretary to the desk outside the door.

A TALE OF EXPLORATION

Oil was once again filling our national coffers, but with the promise of progress and development stirring the collective imagination, the country's treasury seemed painfully inadequate. It would be awhile yet before our oil would generate anywhere near the income we had had prior to nationalization. As for foreign loans or aid, Europe was still rebuilding itself, and the United States preferred to send help in the form of political reward rather than as a response to need. (Money arrived, for example, the month after Mossadeq was thrown out, a week after the Consortium agreement was signed, and in 1955 right after we joined the Baghdad Pact, a military defense organization composed of Pakistan, Turkey, Iraq, Iran, and Great Britain.) Left to our own devices we decided to increase our oil revenues in a different way.

Any oil found outside the area of the Consortium (the old AIOC concession lands) was Iran's to keep and sell at any price it could get. It did not take long for exploration to start in various spots around the country, including the north and in the Zagros Mountains. After quite a bit of exploration we found oil in 1956 in the vicinity of Qom, the religious center an hour to the south of Tehran. One hundred thousand barrels shot out in a magnificent stream on the first day. I drove over by car with Scholtens and saw this enormous jet rising 120 feet on the horizon— oil splashing the area for many yards around. It was sensational.

The "hit" was a huge victory, and everyone was terribly excited. The dis covery not only confirmed that Iran could command the requisite technical competence for such an undertaking locally, but it also gave the fledgling NIOC a welcome boost in credibility and prestige. Immediately there was talk of establishing a refinery, stopping the pipeline that was projected to bring oil to Tehran from Abadan, and experimenting with all sorts of other projects. We called the one firm in Tulsa, Oklahoma, that had the know-how to cap the well until we could control its use. We then entertained bidders from abroad to undertake all the various projects that were being discussed.

Only Fallah and Scholtens were doubtful. "If I were you, I'd sell the rights to it now," Scholtens said. I told him that he was completely out of gear and we were going to do it ourselves.

"I wonder about the reserves," Fallah said. "If we're not careful, we could go down in history as fools. This could become a textbook case. We build the refinery, and then the well runs dry. We should wait and see what it does." I remember him sitting with his head in his hands, his fingers on his forehead, and then looking up. He was a man who looked at the horizon, finding his way through problems no one else could solve.

As Fallah predicted, the gusher dropped—then stopped altogether. After drilling all over the immediate area, not another drop of oil was found. If we'd sold the rights as Scholtens had suggested, we'd have made a clear $100 million for the company.

That same year, 1956, Enrico Mattei appeared on the scene, a famous

Italian who single-handedly ran his government's medusan energy con glomerate, Ente Nazionale Idrocarburi (ENI). He had cooperated with the Seven Sisters in embargoing Iran during nationalization, hoping that when a settlement was reached ENI would be part of the deal. When he was excluded from the Consortium, he vowed to get even. It was not just a question of pride. Italy, he felt, needed a guaranteed source of oil.

The Shah was taken with Mattei, a little man who wore tight-cut suits, and soon the Italian and NIOC were talking terms. Mattei offered Iran significant risk and investment capital, as well as an infrastructure of tankers and markets. Iran could offer Mattei an exclusive deal. The ensuing contract was a landmark in oil history. It gave Italy a foothold in the Middle East and Iran 75 percent of the profits. Known thereafter as 75/25, the deal sent shivers of concern through the boardrooms of the seven major oil companies and catcalls of derision that Mattei was paying dearly for nothing but a few bones.

"There is much marrow in those bones," he replied, and he zealously set out to prove it.

By the end of 1957 the Italians had discovered a drilling site on their concession almost a mile up in the Zagros Mountains. I took a helicopter in to inspect it, landing on eighteen feet of snowpack, and saw that the site was literally on a pinnacle. Everything had been airlifted in. The drill needed a pump to get the oil up the mountain. They told me they'd developed a machine that could bring up twenty thousand barrels a day. I couldn't believe my ears; such a pump was unheard-of. Three hundred barrels, yes. Twenty thousand, no. But when I inspected the place, I saw they'd done just that. It was a perfect design and supereffective in such extreme conditions. When we took off in the helicopter, the precipice dropped three thousand feet below us in five seconds.

Mattei's people also developed a site in the Persian Gulf at Bahregan Sar. It was on the continental shelf and produced thirty thousand to forty thousand barrels a day. Though neither of the sites was a huge producer, they did provide the Iranians with added income and the Italians with a direct link to Iran's oil reserves.*

As Scholtens and I worked together I gradually learned the dynamics of managing a board. He never avoided controversy and always made the final decision. This was a departure from the oriental system, where no one ever

---

*Mattei would not live long enough to enjoy the fruits of his efforts. In 1962, while flying his private plane from Sicily to Rome in a storm, he crashed under mysterious circumstances. Earlier a bomb had been found on the aircraft. The Shah always felt that the 75/25 agreement had earned him the hatred of the big oil companies and privately blamed them for Mattei's death.

wanted to contradict or humiliate another person. Scholtens was straightforward and practical, and moved ahead with purpose. He immediately started a big project to redo the housing and urban development of Abadan. He also single-handedly started the Kharg Island port and refinery.

Under Scholtens Consortium rules became clearly defined and were strictly adhered to by everyone. Like many Dutchmen he had an ironclad belief in moral rectitude and believed that one could be more constructively imaginative within stringent rules than without them. He could not stand drunkenness, laziness, or imbecility, and he ran the Consortium exactly as he had run Shell—without making allowances because we were a third-world country. As a result he was a fairer, more effective administrator than other chairmen who did.

Once a year the Consortium partners sent their directors to Iran to tour the facilities. We called it "the circus," and privately I referred to the directors as "the absentee landlords." During Scholtens's first year he mentioned Kharg, a coral island about forty miles offshore, as an ideal place for a supertanker port. The visiting directors wanted to place a port on the coast. Scholtens said, "No! You come here without knowing the position of the land, and you want to decide these things in five minutes. I know the situation, and I should be the one to decide." So Kharg it was.

I saw Kharg for the first time with Scholtens in 1956. We arrived by helicopter. It was a stunning slip of an island—one mile wide, two miles long, rising vertically out of the sea. It had originally belonged to the Hayat Davoudi tribe but was subsequently nationalized and the inhabitants brought under government control. There were no houses, and Scholtens and I were put up in caravans for the night. We scouted out the area for the best spot to place the port, listening to the arguments of the various surveyors and looking at maps. At last Scholtens chose the northeast point because of its deep waters. Thanks to the slow, steady downhill grade of the continental shelf from the coast to the island, the oil could flow along a pipeline pulled only by gravity. At the port site the oil, propelled by its own momentum, would rise to the surface and right into tanks that could hold a million barrels each. It was cheap and effective, and Kharg's deep northern waters would provide ample room for the 500,000-ton tankers that had now become a fixture of the industry.

A TANKER TALE

One of the perks of being on the Consortium board was attending meetings two or three times a year in The Hague, where the Consortium had been officially incorporated. These were always gala affairs, with luxury tours to local sites and sumptuous dinners at castles and estates in the countryside.

At the meeting on July 13, 1958, Iran made history. Sparked no doubt by our handicap in having no way to transport our oil during the embargo that followed nationalization, the government had been contemplating for some time the idea of going into the maritime business. Now a private Iranian company was bringing that dream to fruition. It was the first time a Middle Eastern oil producer obtained its own transport vessels—two 40,000-ton tankers built by the Dutch but paid for and christened by Iran. One was called the *Reza Shah,* the other the *Mohammad Reza Shah.* Queen Juliana and Prince Bernhard of Holland were on hand. As was the Shah, who pressed the button for the bottles of champagne to fly against the hulls to christen the ships before they slipped gracefully into the water.

The next day, I was planning to leave for Sweden for a few days' vacation where I hoped to relax with a lovely woman I knew there. Meanwhile the Shah and his entourage were flying on to Istanbul for a meeting of the Baghdad Pact. When I came downstairs for breakfast with Fallah that morning at the Hotel des Indes, however, I could see before I crossed the room that his face looked like death. When I was still some distance away he held up the morning paper. A banner headline announced that a bloody coup had taken place in Baghdad. The king had been beheaded; the crown prince, Prime Minister Nouri Sa'id Pasha, and his son (a good friend of mine) Sabbah Sa'id, who was head of the air force, and many others had been shot. A military junta had taken over.

The news came as a shock and sent a cold shiver throughout the Middle East and even as far as India. As an oil producer Iran worried that something similar might happen there. And Abadan was within the sights of Iraqi guns should the new junta wish to destroy the refinery. In any case, our relationship with Iraq, religiously osmotic and industrially intertwined along the Shatt-al-Arab, would necessarily be affected. The news also raised a number of other questions. Would it change the price of oil? Would there be less oil on the market for a while? How would it affect the other Middle Eastern producers? And would it alter the Baghdad Pact?

Instead of going to Sweden I returned to Iran with Fallah. The Shah went on to Turkey as planned but for only one night. It was, he felt, more prudent to proceed with the schedule than to exhibit fear by canceling the trip.

Just before our plane landed Fallah took my arm and said half-jokingly, "How do we know that when we arrive, it won't be another Baghdad affair? The revolutionaries will meet us and say they've reserved our spot in the trees next to all the ministers and NIOC officials hanging there." Indeed even in the airport I could feel anxiety in the air. There were street demonstrations signaling opposition to the government, but the military remained loyal to the Shah and was out in force. On the evening of July 15 Prime Minister Manucher Eqbal (who had replaced Ala in 1956) appeared at the Darband Hotel restaurant, where he danced with his wife to show that events in Baghdad had had no effect on him. The next day the Shah arrived from Istanbul to a huge show of military support on the airport tarmac and along the streets.

In Iraq the coup led to a number of major changes. The junta summarily threw out the British, who had created the Iraqi throne and the royal family out of thin air when they'd carved up the Turkish Empire after World War I. The junta also unilaterally revised the terms of the Iraqi Petroleum Company concession—much as we had done in Iran, though without eliciting similar international retribution. Finally it cozied up to the Soviet Union, eventually withdrawing from the Baghdad Pact, which henceforth was called CENTO (Central Treaty Organization).

Meanwhile Iran took advantage of the coup to tell Iraq that it wanted the Shatt-al-Arab divided in half. It was the age-old question of rights. Although Iraq had no port on the Persian Gulf (Basra was twenty miles up the Shatt-al-Arab), it had inherited all the coastal and water rights when the British had divided up the Turkish Empire. This division left Iran with rights to only a few yards of water off its coast. As a result, all tankers coming in and out of Abadan had to be towed by Iraqi tugs because the waterway came under the Basra Port Authority. (While accepting the Gulf waters inheritance, Iraq on the other hand never recognized the British separation of its old southern province of Kuwait, as Saddam Hussein rudely reminded the world in 1990.)

The new Baghdad junta was not to be pressured and informed Iran that it was maintaining the same water rights as the previous British-controlled government. This angered Iran, which announced that it was not going to use Iraq's tugs anymore—putting NIOC, and all the port businesses in Khorramshahr in a jam. I was sent down to have a look, and to no one's surprise I reported that we couldn't build tugboats overnight and that the government's ire, though understandable, would harm business. We had to back down.

A British contractor, Ian Bowler, suggested that we build a short pipeline between Abadan and the sea so that we could become independent of Iraq once and for all. Eventually that is what happened.*

I felt awful about the Iraqi coup. Sabbah Sa'id had been a friend for many years, and though I saw him rarely, I felt his loss. He was a very good pilot, and every time his wife, an Egyptian beauty, threatened to leave him, he would fly his plane under the Baghdad Bridge and have the papers take pictures; when he sent her copies, she would always come back. The Sabbahs had been good and respectable men, and Iraq would see many dark days ahead without their wise leadership.

Some years later my brother-in-law Mohsen Khan introduced me to a young Iraqi general named Daghestani, who was head of the general staff when the coup took place. We met in London, and over lunch he told us that the coup had actually been a cover-up. Originally the military had planned to mount a campaign to invade and take over Kuwait. But as the troops began moving south, conflicting orders had reached the generals to turn around and march on Baghdad. They were orders, he said, that had been generated by the British to save Kuwait. The ensuing chaos had enabled a junta to take over Baghdad, and he had had to flee.

I found it an extraordinary story, but I liked Daghestani, and the next time I was in London I rang him up and invited him for lunch. During our meal I guessed that he was planning on returning to Iraq to lead a countercoup against the junta. About two weeks later, on a trip to Baghdad, I learned that he had died. Had the British killed him? The Kuwaitis? The

---

*Bowler, who built the pipeline from Abadan to Tehran, got the contract for the coastal line. But before construction began, the Consortium, which had initially turned down the job, decided it didn't want anyone else involved. It made for a sticky situation, which could have turned out badly had Bowler not acted with impeccable integrity. But Ian wasn't your everyday pipeline contractor with a preference for hard hats over Homburgs. At that very moment he was courting a flamboyant Persian girl named Hamoush, who had recently divorced my own brother Kaveh. They married, and he soon became a fixture of the Tehran social scene.

We offered to compensate him $100,000 for services rendered, and he agreed without demanding that we pay him a break fee. In gratitude the Iranian government later awarded him a highly lucrative contract for a natural gas line between the southern fields of Iran and the Russian frontier. Called IGAT, it was a landmark project, with the line running a thousand miles across snowcapped peaks more than fifteen thousand feet high. Upon its completion Iran sold natural gas to the Soviet Union, making money for the first time off a natural resource that until then had been flared at the well site and wasted. Ironically what started out for both Iran and Bowler as a tugboat problem with our western neighbor ended up as a moneymaking deal for us both with our neighbor to the north.

Iraqis? I had no clue and forgot all about it until Iraq invaded Kuwait twenty-five years later.

A NEW JOB

My position on the Consortium board had turned out to be infinitely more challenging than I had expected, and I was happy with the variety of my responsibilities. In 1958 my luck improved still more. That year two directors on the NIOC board were removed, creating an opportunity I hoped to capitalize on. I couldn't, however, approach the Shah directly regarding the matter; I would have to find another avenue.

One night during dinner at my sister Haidch's, I mentioned the subject to my good friend Professor Yahya Adl. His sister was married to my brother Mohammadvali Mirza, and we had known each other for years. He was a medical doctor and the first real surgeon Iran had ever had. The Shah had taken a great liking to Adl, as had Princess Ashraf, probably because he was one of the very few who spoke his mind without flattery or dissemblance. The Shah had invited Adl to accompany him on his first trip to the United States in 1949. Since then the sovereign had wanted to make him a minister and even premier, but Adl had demurred. It was not his way to seek personal gain, and he wanted to remain a doctor. As a result he was admired as a man of integrity.

Tall and lean, with deep-set sad eyes, Adl had volunteered some years before, at the Shah's request, to run the huge downtown hospital of Sina, a facility that catered to the poor. Once I visited him there, and as we walked the wards the other doctors followed him like a prophet, hanging on his every word.

"We have no room," he said sadly. "Look there, two people in one bed, one head up and one head down. Now look underneath. Another sick person lies there." I was appalled. Such was the extent of our country's poverty.

Though he never agreed to act as the Shah's own physician, Adl did like to play bridge with His Majesty, and he could regularly be found at the court two nights a week. He agreed to speak on my behalf for the NIOC board appointment, and I knew I could not have found a better advocate.

A few weeks later, in the fall of 1958, I was named to the board. My job was to head up sales and distribution in Iran and abroad. Ten years after walking into Fateh's corner office in the impressive AIOC building hoping he would have a job for me, I sat behind that very desk myself, responsible for the same task but on a much larger scale.

THE NEW DESERT MASTERS

His vista is as great as the sea
You who have lost time, the season of learning is imminent
Profit from the moment, for your triumph is nigh.

—HAFEZ

Tehran 1958

The fifties in Iran, as in much of the rest of the world, were years of rebirth. Despite the flicker of worry sparked by the Iraqi coup, the Shah's position had become increasingly secure. After the Mossadeq fiasco he felt a spiritual reprieve and seemed to grow stronger by the day. The fifties were in fact a watershed decade for the Shah, and the marked improvement in his self-esteem had significant repercussions for the entire country. Backed by the military and warmly embraced by the United States, he felt, for the first time since he'd taken the throne, free to act as he wished.

The Shah was unique among the monarchs and dictators of the Middle East, for his country had been independent for twenty-five hundred years and had never once been colonized. His outlook, therefore, was more self-assured than that of other third-world leaders. He saw himself, like Cyrus the Great, at the dawn of a new Persian civilization. His destiny, he believed, was to make Iran more competitive so that it could become a prosperous industrial nation before its oil reserves ran out. Paralleling this was his desire to become the most powerful military presence in the Gulf—and perhaps in the whole Middle East. Casting himself as a visionary hero, he zealously set out to lead his country out of the darkness of the third world and into the light of the first.

Like Mossadeq, the Shah wished to deliver the country from the shackles of the past. But Mossadeq was a man of the nineteenth century, an idealist who never fully accepted the harsh new ways of the modern era. Though equally idealistic, the Shah believed wholeheartedly in the achievements of the twentieth century and dedicated himself to bringing widespread reform to his country. He had the illusion, typical of the young, that if he only hurried, he could change the world.

At the age of thirty-eight, energetic and confident, the Shah began to initiate his first real political program. He still enjoyed widespread popularity as a symbol and an idol—an untested leader whose defects had not yet been revealed. His people adored him simply because he was their sovereign. What he wanted, they wanted. And what he wanted was westernization, industrialization, and modernization—which he hoped would turn him into the dominant leader of the Middle East and earn him the respect he so coveted from his Western peers.

The pace he set himself was relentless. In his autobiography, *Mission for My Country*, he describes his accomplishments in a typical month:

> On the outskirts of Tehran I dedicated a newly-completed orphanage for 2,000 children. One of my sisters opened a clinic and a canteen. On the occasion of my birthday, 28 new schools were opened in various parts of the country. New power stations went into operation in 15 provincial towns. Street-paving was completed in seven towns. Installation of electric signals was finished at twelve railway stations in south-central Iran. A mechanized agriculture center was opened in the province of Kurdistan. Work started on a gas pipeline from one of the southern oil fields to Shiraz to serve both the city and the new fertilizer factory under construction there. A clinic was finished in one town and a sanitorium in another.[1]

In the mid-fifties the Shah began to give the peasants deeds to their own land in a set of reforms that would culminate in 1963 in what came to be called the White Revolution. By 1958 ten thousand taxis were shuttling around Tehran, double-decker buses had begun to travel the streets, and the number of telephones had tripled (with demand at ten times the level of supply). Oil revenues were mounting rapidly, and the country was operating under an economic blueprint called the Seven-Year Plan.

Yet these social and economic advances were not mirrored by corresponding political strides. Although the Shah wanted to appear democratic and painted himself as a constitutional monarch backed by an elected parliament, he acted more and more like a dictator, convinced that his reforms could be accomplished only through the force of his authority. Repression was the inevitable result. The Shah's innate shyness and rigidity led him first to cut all but a few close advisers from his inner circle. Next he rendered the Majles a sham. Its members were handpicked based on their readiness to rubber-stamp any order issued from above. Few ever visited their constituencies, for they owed their voters nothing, and not once in the twenty years between 1958 and 1978 did the Parliament vote down the Shah's dictates.

The Shah also changed the structure of the bureaucracy, breaking once and for all the tradition of having to work one's way up from the bottom. Instead jobs were awarded to people who had studied abroad regardless of whether they had experience. This broke the hold of the old landed gentry over the institutions of civil government and created a whole new cadre under the direct management of the Shah. But the Shah proved to be only a mediocre manager—lacking the genius of a reformer such as Peter the Great, for example—and Iran soon fell into the same trap as so many other developing countries: an overdependence on Western influence and an underappreciation of its own seasoned civil servants. Dissatisfaction and corruption grew, even as the United States became the new Mecca toward which everyone prayed.

In 1957 the Shah authorized the formation of SAVAK, the National Organization of Information and Security. Devised with the assistance of the United States and Israel and headed by the ambitious and extremely loyal Teymour Bakhtiar, SAVAK rapidly developed into a highly efficient secret service that fed the Shah's increasing paranoia of internal dissidence. What started out small quickly grew, as agents spread throughout the government and began interfering in all areas of life. Soon it became a vast blanket organization, like Britain's MI6, with agents serving as ambassadors, envoys, and all manner of public and private servants.

The same year he founded SAVAK the Shah announced the formation of a two-party system as the first step toward a working democracy. Prime Minister Manucher Eqbal led the Nationalist Party; in opposition was the People's Party, led by Assadollah Alam, an old school chum of the Shah's. Soon, however, it became clear that the parties were a farce and that true opposition had no place in Iran.

No one in Iran was fooled by the railroading of this new party system. Any belief in free elections had long ago withered into a profound cynicism about democracy in general and its appropriateness for a developing country in particular. People were simply not created equal in a place like Iran; the powerful remained powerful, and their political parties, heavily tainted by foreign interests, had consistently betrayed and cheated the public. It was no surprise, therefore, that the Shah's democracy became a vehicle only for the greedy.

At the time those of us in the upper class saw the Shah's dictatorship as the only safe alternative to the Communists, and we supported it whole-heartedly. As it is written in the Koran, "Any injustice shared by all is jus-tice." We were tired of turmoil and hoped that a controlling government would end the disturbances that had wracked our streets for the past sev-eral years. We also were wary of what was happening in next-door Turkey, where the two-party system had brought the country to the brink of civil war, with people from both parties being killed, at last provoking a mili-tary takeover. We therefore became anti-party and raised no objection when the Tudeh Party was brought to heel and its leadership banned from the country. Nor did we react when the clergy were divested of political power and restricted to their mosques.

A ROYAL DIVORCE

At first we did not notice that the stronger the Shah got, the more he lost touch with the country. We did not realize that what was slowly develop-ing was a personality cult, separating the Shah from his people as he re-treated to his ivory tower. Most people saw him only in the pictures religiously passed out by his officials with the exhortation that they be hung on every ironmonger's wall and in every school hallway and office throughout the country. During the Qajar reign monarchs had maintained a close connection with the people. Qajar shahs ruled according to old tribal habits and sat with the people at lunch or in the mosque—since they were all worshiping the same God, after all. In those days the shahs trav-eled constantly from province to province, much like American presiden-tial candidates today, and it was not uncommon to see them on horseback in the streets or at their seasonal levees. They often married their enemies' daughters, and contact—rather than charisma—reminded the people of their loyalty. There were fewer people then, and more time, and of course, more wives allowed.

The Pahlavis changed all that. Mohammad Reza Shah, like his father, was handed the crown and therefore lacked the tribal support that would have brought him closer to the people. Unlike his father he grew up entirely sheltered and kept a great distance between himself and everyone else. The Shah's introversion, which eventually deteriorated into paranoia and egomania, was the fatal flaw in a man otherwise so conscious of his royal duties.

It was Ashraf, his twin sister, who typically put into words the attitude that characterized the monarchy in those days. "What do these people want from us?" she asked us peevishly at dinner one night, referring to the populace that her brother ruled. "They never gave us the crown! They acted against us and did not even invite us back after the coup in 1953. We came and took our crown and by returning saved them from communism. You think we owe anything to anybody here? No! We're entitled to do everything and anything that pleases us."

Like Czar Nicholas II, who could communicate only with his wife, Alexandra, the Shah could never talk to anyone but Ashraf. He never had close friends and felt no real love for anyone. He kept Ernest Perron and even his wives at a distance. As for his other siblings, such as his highly capable brother Abdol Reza, he never turned to them for advice or trusted them with positions of responsibility.

At first the Shah's image was so inspiring, his motives so patriotic, and his schedule so full that we dismissed his increasing estrangement as due to overwork, an irritating fact of modern royal life. If at times his behavior was insulting, we hid our reactions even from ourselves. I remember once when he came for a visit to the Kermanshah Refinery. The governor and my uncle, as well as all the rest of the grandees, lined up by the plane to see him off, dressed to the hilt in their old finery. My uncle's black suit had turned dark orange with age, but he wore it proudly since he had the chance to attend such special functions only once in a decade or so.

I thought the Shah would walk among the grandees and talk to them— find out what they had to tell him about his people and life in the countryside. Instead he sprang from his limousine and spoke only briefly to the first two in line as the rest, their hands clasped respectfully in front of them, bent forward, craning their necks to see. Then rather than moving down the line to greet the others, he hopped on the plane and flew away.

It was outrageous. No speech, not even an acknowledgment that they were there to honor him, those men of importance in a good-size provincial town. They remembered his father, rough and tough, but at least he knew how to mingle. Stunned by the Shah's lack of respect, which would have cost him so little and meant so much to them, they felt ashamed, and closed their mouths tightly against the indignity.

Not long after, the newspapers reported that the Shah and Soraya were driving through Tehran when their car broke down. Immediately the people massed around him, and for a few minutes, the paper wrote, the Shah was among the people.

In those days the Shah still rode without a cavalcade through the streets of Tehran and we would see him occasionally at parties. One night Ambassador and Mrs. Ala threw a masked ball at their jewel of a villa near the bazaar, way down in the bowels of the city. Late in the evening four people entered, all heavily masked, and sat down at a corner table. I recognized none of them as they called for drinks. Shortly afterward Madame Ala came over and asked if I would dance with the lady in the group. I walked over immediately and presented myself with a short bow, then led the lady to the floor. She was gorgeously attired in a typical Spanish trouser suit, pearl-gray and slinky with matching brimmed hat. A large black mask covered most of her face apart from her flashing green eyes. We danced and I spoke to her, trying to find out who she was. But she kept her distance and refused to say a word, pursing her tantalizing lips tightly over her teeth. Finally, taunting her, I said, "If you don't tell me who you are, I'll kiss you right here in front of all these people."

"Don't be presumptuous!" she whispered hastily, turning her face away. Her voice hard, she added, "I am Soraya."

I stopped dead. A kiss would have been the end of me. The Shah was most jealous of her and watched her every movement. Thank God she spoke.

Those were the days when the Shah was somehow still one of us. Within the decade this would end. The Shah's close entourage soon became a shield protecting him against the rest of the world. He went everywhere with them, traveled with them, and talked only to them.

But like all men the sovereign was a paradox. His ambitions for Iran were real and boundless. He felt the constant pressure of time and was willing to make sacrifices for his country that even Edward VIII of England had not been ready to make. Soraya had been his queen for six years, and it was clear to all of us how deeply he loved her. Nevertheless she had failed to bear him an heir.

One evening in March of 1957 I was invited by the court to dinner at Ab-e Ali, a ski resort just thirty miles outside Tehran. It was a beautiful place with a small hotel tucked against the side of the snow-covered mountain. There had been talk about Soraya not producing a child, but it was so casual that I went innocently to Ab-e Ali for dinner.

The evening was much like many I'd passed at the palace, only the venue had changed. The Shah played cards; Soraya chatted with friends on a couch in the corner; the guests were the usual crew. A small band played for an hour or two of dancing before we headed back into town. The next morning the papers reported that the queen had departed for Europe. Immediately thereafter their divorce was announced.*

THE TALE OF A WATCH

Within the week the Shah appeared on television and made a speech. "I have been advised," he said, "as reigning monarch, that I should name a successor to the throne. However, I have decided instead to have a son who will follow in my footsteps and reign over Iran."

This was a fantastic statement. Few men would venture to make such a declaration, especially after two marriages had failed to produce an heir. He was at that very moment in the process of a divorce and in public appeared morose and lonely, obviously shaken by the whole affair. Yet he clearly had no intention of considering a regency and as a result was eliminating his brothers from the scene. Instead he obviously planned to find a new wife who would conceive a son.

The Italian oil magnate Enrico Mattei thought he had just the answer. There was at the time a daughter of the former Italian king Umberto who was still unmarried and of just the right age. Although the Italians had thrown her father out and the family was living in Spain, Mattei clearly thought that there could be no better opportunity for matchmaking than between the Iranian and the Italian thrones. Of course there were a few difficulties to overcome—religion, money, divorce—but nothing, he felt, that could not be taken care of discreetly. The Shah was encouraging, since marrying a member of European royalty would gain him acceptance into their clique.

In any event, the princess and her entourage came to Tehran to pass a few days on the Shah's royal yacht, a lovely vessel that had come from Germany through Russia, down the Volga River to the Caspian Sea. One evening I was invited aboard for dinner, along with my sister Haideh and her husband. There were only a few guests. The princess was tall and insipid and behaved amorously toward the Shah all evening. She threw herself around him whenever she could and encouraged him to take her outside for a romantic moment at the railing to watch the moon. But it did not seem to me that the Shah was much taken with her or the rest of her

---

*The Shah had made the decision earlier but could not face telling Soraya himself. She found out in St. Moritz, where he sent an emissary to tell her only hours before the official announcement was made. Thereafter he worried that she would write a book about all the petty intrigues at court. But when the book came out, it was not malicious, only sad.

retinue—flint-nosed pretenders who had nothing and knew nothing and yet treated us like beggars and dogs. After dinner a strange incident took place that extinguished the Shah's ardor once and for all.

It was about eleven o'clock when the Shah got up from his flirtations to go to the bathroom. The quarters of those staying on board were separate from the public rooms to which we had access as visitors. The Shah had barely rejoined us when he realized that he'd forgotten his watch in the bathroom. With a quick sign he sent one of his aides to retrieve it. But the man returned empty-handed and worriedly murmured into the Shah's ear that the watch had not been found. Immediately everyone began to whisper, and for a moment I thought we would all be searched. But the Shah was too gentlemanly for that, and he knew it could not be one of us since we did not have access to his private rooms. Clearly one of the Italians staying on board had stolen the watch—even as he was enjoying the Shah's hospitality.

Not three months later it was announced that the Shah would marry Farah Diba, a beautiful architecture student and daughter of one of Iran's aristocratic families. A year later the Shah's hopes for an heir were realized.

I was having lunch with the workforce in Rey near the Tehran Refinery when news came over the radio that a son had been born to the Shah. It was cause for great celebration, and I ordered lunch to be served all around. In the city people poured into the streets, and in Maydan-e Kakh, in front of my mother's house, there was music and dancing. Over the next few years three more children followed—two daughters and another son.

A HISTORICAL BETRAYAL

It was about this time, in 1958, that a brilliant young man named Gholam Reza Nickpay, whom I had hired to work with me at NIOC, stopped by my office one morning. The Carnegie Endowment for International Peace, he said, was funding a study to analyze Iran's nationalization of oil. Nickpay's name had come up as a possible participant, but knowing that I was a more senior official and better informed, he'd suggested that I attend instead. NIOC's lawyer, Fuad Rohani, was also chosen.

In due course I was making my way to Geneva to meet with Professor Sven Henningson, a Danish historian who was writing up the project as a neutral observer. We met at a roundtable, Rohani and I as well as a couple of British representatives, including Sir Reader Bullard—who was little changed from his days as ambassador to Tehran—and Archibald Chisolm, an ex-official of AIOC and the prime negotiator of Kuwait's oil deal with

Shell and Gulf. The Carnegie Endowment's goal was to study third-world movements that had changed the balance of power in the world. Iran's oil nationalization was one such movement; another was Tunisia's rebellion, led by Habib Bourguiba, against France. In both cases the question was, how could a people without money or arms and with no outside help manage to throw out a large, internationally powerful country? Our assignment was to develop a report that covered the history as well as the outcome.

I brought a number of important documents and notes with me for the first few meetings so that the nationalization of oil could be understood within the context of the larger British colonial strategy, as well as Britain's desire to cut Iran out of the profits of AIOC's subsidiary companies. It was perhaps the first major divestiture in history—with AIOC, an international company, trying to become a purely national company because it did not want Iran to be a fellow shareholder. Though I was not pro-Mossadeq, I did not want history to follow the British interpretation that he was a traitor and a madman. Here was a landmark opportunity to prove that we were not as bad as the British made us out to be. I looked forward to the job.

But the Carnegie study turned out to be a crushing disappointment due to double-crossing from an unexpected quarter.

Prior to each discussion Henningson wrote a précis of the topic at hand and gave it to each of us to read. I always studied it thoroughly and made copious notes. At the time of the second set of meetings Rohani flew in late and, saying he'd not had time to read his précis, asked to borrow mine. The next morning, to my amazement, he offered opinions based on my notes as though they were his. For the first time I began to question Rohani's motives, but I kept my own counsel and said nothing.

At the third meeting Bullard was replaced by Ann Lambton, who had worked at the British Embassy in Tehran and who spoke fluent Farsi as well as a number of tribal dialects. Ann and I knew each other well. She was a big, solid woman who always wore sensible shoes and said sensible things. She had often come to my mother's house for lunch, and once I'd taken her to Kermanshah to meet the tribes. She'd even put in a good word for us to that louse Colonel Fletcher. When she left Tehran she threw a party and introduced me to many of the powerful men I was subsequently to count as friends, including Seyyed Jalal Tehrani.

The third meeting with Ann in attendance went very well, and I felt that our perspective was beginning to gain favor. I left energized, and looked forward to the next installment of Henningson's notes.

A few weeks after I'd returned to Tehran I ran into Rohani, who offhandedly said that he had something to show me. He pulled a letter from

Archibald Chisolm from his pocket. Chisolm complained that Henningson was incompetent and too slow in conducting the study. "He's chewing much more than he can swallow," Chisolm wrote, despite the fact that Henningson had already gone to the United States to interview Truman and despite his gift for succinctly recording our separate views. Chisolm concluded, "The British side is withdrawing and not contributing any more."

"What was your answer?" I asked, shocked by this turn of events.

"I said we didn't want the study either and that we would happily give up the project."

I was so taken aback I couldn't say a word. I felt defeated, and to this day I don't know why Henningson and the Carnegie Endowment let go. But to me, for an Iranian to withdraw was the ultimate betrayal.

Rohani came from a family of Baha'is, a religious sect born in the mid-nineteenth century whose base was in Shiraz. Most Moslems considered them heretics, and many in Iran believed that the Baha'is were specially protected by the British. This made them very unpopular, and they were badly persecuted. Under the Pahlavis, however, the Baha'is were gradually integrated into society, and resentment against them waned. The Shah relied heavily on Baha'i advisers, and at the time he fell in 1979 half the cabinet and many prominent generals were Baha'is.

Rohani's Baha'i beliefs had never been an issue in our friendship. Once when he'd approached me in the mid-1940s to ask for a favor for his brother-in-law, a fanatic preacher of Baha'i principles who had gone to Azerbaijan—an extremely devout Islamic province—on a missionary tour. There he'd incited a mob that attacked him, and he barely escaped before the police intervened and threw him in jail. Rohani asked if I could approach Mohammadvali Mirza, at the time a Majles deputy from Azerbaijan, to intervene on his behalf. Mohammadvali Mirza immediately wrote a letter to the authorities, and soon after, Rohani's brother-in-law was released, though we never received a word of thanks for rendering such a dangerous service.

Unfortunately the story did not end there. A short while later, when the Shah's army reclaimed Azerbaijan from the Russians, Mohammadvali Mirza's letter was discovered, and it was seen as a black mark against the family. Mohammadvali Mirza never again served as a member of the Majles. The tragedy was that it was all for naught. Having learned nothing from the experience in Azerbaijan, Rohani's brother-in-law went on to preach in the villages south of Tehran, where he was killed.

Fuad and I had been friends for many years, but the Carnegie affair permanently altered my view of him, and thereafter we never saw eye to eye.

A TALE OF KHARG

In the middle of 1958 Scholtens's tenure as chairman of the Consortium ended. He had served with such integrity and accomplished so much that I lobbied the Shah to try to get his term extended. The Shah sent a letter to Howard Page, the chairman of Exxon and a major decision maker for the Consortium. We arranged to have it delivered in New York at the very hour that Page and Scholtens were scheduled to have lunch together. The letter was delivered, and afterward I spoke with Page myself, but Scholtens's term was not extended. I was extremely sorry to see him go, though his replacement, a hearty Texan named Jack Berlin, was a good man.

Scholtens came back to Iran once more in 1958 for the opening cere-monies of his special project—the great port terminal at Kharg. This was Iran's opportunity to honor the man who had done more for its oil business than anyone before or since. The ceremony was small but impressive. Flags flew, a big lunch was served, and the mood was jubilant. The Shah and Prime Minister Eqbal attended, and both looked very pleased. The Shah decorated Scholtens with a Homayoon medal, a great tribute and one of the highest forms of recognition Iran could pay a foreigner.*

Scholtens and I stayed in close touch, and I saw him every time I visited Holland, which was frequently, since Gean had chosen to settle there with our daughter, Roxane, after she and I decided to part ways and eventually to divorce. When he died suddenly of a heart attack in 1961, I felt I'd lost the best friend I ever had.

A TALE OF SUEZ

Early in 1959 Abdollah Entezam, the chairman of NIOC, asked me to go to Cairo to attend an Arab oil conference. The government hesitated to send an accredited delegate, he said, because of the Arabs' cupidity in the aftermath of Mossadeq's oil nationalization. I was therefore to go as an ob-server. I had been chosen for my experience in international relations as well as my position on the Consortium board. Under no circumstances, however, was I to speak for the government or imagine that I was there

---

*The Shah bestowed two different types of decorations: the Taj and Homayoon. The Taj, or Crown, had four levels: the first two were bestowed on a limited number of recipi-ents; the third and fourth had no restrictions. The Homayoon, or Royal, also had four lev-els, with no restrictions on the nationality or number of recipients.

with any official rank. I could take along an adjutant, and I chose Dr. Gho-lam Reza Nickpay. SAVAK also wanted to send someone with me, but I said no; either you trust me or I won't go.

Egypt itself had little oil, but under its new leader, Gamal Abdel Nasser, it had become a beacon of change for the entire Arab Middle East. Rising from the ashes of British colonialism, Nasser's war cry was nationalism. He addressed his own countrymen as well as his neighbors with such fiery passion that a sense of common identity, later called Pan-Arabism, began to be felt throughout the Arab nations. What's more he incited the Middle East to recognize that oil was a weapon it could use to manipulate the imperialist West.

Nasser took the helm in Egypt when he toppled a military junta in 1954. A staunch admirer of Dr. Mossadeq's and a dedicated student of his radio rhetoric, Nasser was the original army officer turned nationalist crusader (he would be followed by numerous others, including Libya's Moammar Qaddafi, Cuba's Fidel Castro, and Tunisia's Habib Bourguiba). Nasser urged his people to take to the streets and reject Israel, the West, and in particular Britain's colonial hold on the Suez Canal. By 1955 he had arranged an arms deal with the Soviet Union and was supplying aid to a rebel uprising in Algeria. Later that year plans went forward to build the biggest dam in the world at Aswan with World Bank funding. Early in 1956 Nasser told British foreign secretary Selwyn Lloyd that if Britain wanted to retain control of the Canal, it would have to arrange a 50/50 deal with Egypt along the same lines as its deals with the oil-producing countries.

By this time British troops had withdrawn from the Canal following a previous agreement, leaving the waterway (to Western eyes) extremely vulnerable. Some two thirds of Europe's oil passed through the Canal; sabotage or, worse, a takeover could instantly cut its energy lifeline. With Nasser behaving like a bombastic nationalist while cozying up to the Soviet Union, neither Washington, Paris, nor London felt at ease.

The straw that broke the camel's back came when U.S. secretary of state John Foster Dulles decided on July 19, 1956, to nix the World Bank's funding of the Aswan Dam. Livid and vowing revenge, Nasser struck back. Seeing no other way to fund his dam than to use the tolls from the Canal, the Egyptian army took over Suez the following week.

But nationalization did not interrupt traffic. Although the ships' pilots were now Egyptian rather than British, the heavy tankers continued to float grandly through the Sinai Desert. To the British and French this made the situation in Suez seem even more threatening. It meant that Nasser was more in control than they'd thought. His success, unblemished by a slowdown in operations, swelled his popularity in his own country and consolidated his appeal among his neighbors. If today it was the Suez Canal, then tomorrow it might be the oil wells.

Their fears seemed confirmed when in October Syria and Egypt formed a military pact, which Jordan joined the next day. Then Syria cut the flow of oil for twenty-four hours through the Tapline—the huge pipeline traversing its land that carries Iraqi and Saudi oil to the Mediterranean.

It was too much. The Israelis attacked the Canal Zone in late October 1956, and the French and British soon backed them up. Nasser immediately blocked the Canal, and oil supplies were finally interrupted. But Eisenhower, who was then in the midst of a presidential election, had no stomach for embrangling himself in another war. His decision to remain neutral marked the first time the United States failed to back up its allies despite Moscow's support for the other side.

Without Washington's backing and with oil supplies precipitously dropping throughout Europe, the operation fizzled. A month later the British and French withdrew their troops.* As for Israel, its ill-advised military action succeeded only in further antagonizing its neighbors and reinforcing its status as archenemy.

Suez was an enormous victory for Nasser—and a shot of adrenaline for the rest of the Middle East. Unlike Mossadeq, Nasser had truly succeeded. He adeptly showed the leaders of the Arab oil world that their precious natural resource held the West in a hammerlock and that this in and of itself was power.

The Iraqi coup of 1958 added another associate to Nasser's circle. And when Egypt and Syria officially merged to form the United Arab Republic early in 1958, the partnership gave Nasser control over all the main oil transport lines from the Middle East into Europe. The next step was to develop a union with the countries that actually produced the oil.

The greatest divisions among the Arabs lay in their choice of superpower support. Saudi Arabia and Kuwait favored the United States, Iraq and Egypt the Soviet Union. But even as the Congress of 1959 drew near, this division faded in the face of an unprecedented act by British Petroleum. Without regard for the upcoming meeting of oil-producing nations

*The war, though only a month long, created an energy crisis in Europe. The United States refused to start a bailout until British and French troops withdrew, which is why the war came to such an abrupt end. A highly efficient "Oil Lift" was instituted, but even though Europe was blessed with a mild winter, it took four months before the crisis was averted—and this at a time when oil accounted for only 20 percent of Europe's energy requirements.

in Cairo, BP unilaterally cut the price of oil as a reaction to a flooded market. Overnight the still-meager income of these nations dropped. The insult was palpable, not only because they had not been consulted but also because the cut constituted a very costly economic setback. It was in this charged atmosphere that I arrived in Cairo in April to attend the Arab oil congress.

A GENTLEMEN'S AGREEMENT

The Congress and Exhibition of Oil Products lasted five days and was attended by a vast array of delegates. The largest delegation was from Venezuela, headed by their minister of oil, Juan Pérez Alfonzo, who like me was there only as an observer. There were also many journalists and representatives from all the major oil companies as well as a handful of Arab businessmen.

Nasser opened the congress as we stood in a stiff line in the exhibition bleachers. He drove up in an old, chipped Cadillac, so worn that it had turned from black to violet-gray, and stepped out of the car without the help of a chauffeur or bodyguard. Before coming over to greet us he surveyed the scene, all the while fishing around in his breast pocket. At last he pulled out a cigarette, and then began tapping his pockets for a lighter. Finally he found a match and slowly lit his cigarette.

This carefully choreographed performance was designed to show us that he was not a dictator but a man of the people. He greeted each of us warmly, with a friendly handshake and a crooked, toothy smile that never left his face. He welcomed me specially, having not expected Iran to send a representative. Next he turned to the Arabs like a master surveying his lieutenants. Nasser was tall and towered over everyone else. In my report to the Iranian government I observed that the other Arabs had looked like his vassals. Yet he was relaxed and friendly, and I liked him immediately. He struck me as a great man.

There were many old friends at the congress, including the journalist Wanda Jablonski and the Saudi sheikh Abdullah Tariki. Tariki acted splashily and bragged endlessly about his swank new apartment in the only skyscraper in downtown Cairo. Wanda stuck to him like a burr throughout the congress, making me feel neglected as one of her oldest friends. Tariki, who was now Saudi Arabia's minister of oil, acted diplomatically toward me, however, despite the incident in Venezuela, and I came to appreciate him as a solid representative of his government.

The days were spent reading prepared papers, with little spontaneous discussion about how to respond to BP's price slashing. The only delegate who said much was a businessman from Beirut associated with the British company Motherwell Bridge & Engineering. Emile Bustani had pulled off some good jobs drilling in the Persian Gulf and now fancied himself a budding banker. He proposed that an Arab bank be established (which he offered to chair) in which 10 percent of our revenues would be invested in a pool that would be distributed to poorer Arab countries. To prove that he knew a great deal about petroleum finances he began a diatribe against the Iranian government for underselling its oil at a discount (something all the producing countries were doing).

Bustani was not aware that I was in the audience and took a swing at Iran simply to ingratiate himself with the Arabs. I immediately rose and refuted his argument point by point, then formally objected to a private individual's being allowed to offend a government in such a forum. The chairman of the congress backed me up and pointedly told the rest of the delegates that Bustani was talking nonsense.

Bustani had invited us all to a big dinner that night, but after his absurd performance I refused to go. Dr. Pérez Alfonzo, whom I did not know well but whom I'd admired for years as the father of the 50/50 deal, decided that he too would refuse the invitation and instead have dinner privately with me.

We met at his hotel. He was an extraordinary thinker, and our dinner together was one of the most important in my life. "We oil producers," he said at one point, "have no means of exchanging views to discover the advantages and disadvantages of our respective contracts. This is why I have brought a copy of our contract with me—translated into Arabic."

Dr. Luongo Cabello had done the same thing when he'd visited Iran nearly a decade before. The Venezuelans were so open with their information, I told him, that it made me wish the Iranians and the Arabs could be more trusting and do the same.

"You can," he said with a twinkle. "We all can—and we must. We owe it to ourselves to get together regularly and discuss these matters. We must even start informing the others when we get better terms so that they can do the same and we can all be stronger as a result. At the moment we all operate in secret—partially, I know, because the companies have pressured us and threatened us. Nonetheless the time has come to go beyond that. The monuments of Paris and London are lit by the energy we supply at insignificant prices. We must stop this waste. We must get together and formalize an agreement to our mutual advantage. Like you I am just an observer here. But the government of Venezuela is ready to sign such a protocol!"

It was an amazing idea, and I sat back, wondering how much authority I had in such a matter.

"Are the Arabs ready to do such a thing?" I asked.

"I will approach them," he said. "But Iran is the key. You are of the Gulf without being Arab. You are the oldest producer of us all. I need to know first that you are with me."

I drew in a breath, my thoughts racing. Then, throwing caution to the winds, I said, "Yes, you can count on me."

"We must proceed with the utmost care," Pérez Alfonzo warned. "This must be done in complete secrecy. No journalists. Not a word outside our little group. I'll set up a meeting tomorrow and let you know the time."

The next day, arriving from separate venues and in separate cars, we gathered at the Mahdi Yacht Club. It was a dry, dusty conclave of buildings next to the Nile with only one tree shading the property. It was under this tree, far from prying eyes and ears, that we sat down before lunch to discuss the terms of the agreement. We gathered around a rickety metal table: Pérez Alfonzo and myself; Dr. Bernardo Flores, Pérez Alfonzo's assistant and Venezuelan minister to Beirut; Tariki of Saudi Arabia; and the representatives of Kuwait, Iraq, and Qatar. Ironically three of our group were just observers at the conference, the third being the Iraqi, whose government had had a sudden falling-out with Nasser and had sent him at the last moment as only a delegate from the Arab League.

Dr. Flores wrote up a short draft on the spot, just one page long, with every line beginning with "Whereas."

"Whereas the representatives of Iran, Venezuela, Iraq, Saudi Arabia, Kuwait and Qatar. . . ."

"Whereas they, as oil producing nations. . . ."

The draft established our agreement to confer among ourselves regularly on matters of oil and on the logistics of running the industry. It specified that we would discuss aspects of administration, including labor issues such as wages, pensions, and amenities. Finally it mentioned that we would exchange ideas about our financial arrangements and any advantages our governments obtained from the companies. It made no mention of pricing structures or price pressure. Neither did it imply in any way that we were creating a front against the companies.

We each read through the document, then Pérez Alfonzo handed me a pen. Suddenly I got cold feet. "I do not have the necessary authority from Tehran," I said. "I am after all just an observer here."

"I am an observer too," said Pérez Alfonzo. "We are doing this to help our countries. We do not need to be empowered. This does not imply responsibility. All the conditions are optional. If you do not sign, no one will."

"Why don't we write that we are under no obligation—that adherence to these principles is voluntary?" I said. "If we do that, then I will sign."

Everyone agreed, and this final "Whereas" was added at the bottom of the page.

"Now I can sign it," I said, snatching up the pen without another thought. All the others signed their names after me.

This was the Gentlemen's Agreement that developed into the Organization of Petroleum Exporting Countries, henceforth known as OPEC. Copies of the agreement were handed out, and we all pledged secrecy, knowing that oil company representatives and journalists would be suspicious of our disappearance. Then saying nothing more, we went in to lunch.

When I ran into Wanda Jablonski later that evening, she said pointedly, "You all came back from Mahdi looking very secretive. Dear Manucher, do tell me what's going on."

"Well, Wanda," I said, "why don't you go ask your good friend Tariki? Why ask me?" Strangely, many years later I discovered to my great surprise that some oil experts wrongly credited Wanda for having started the whole idea of OPEC.

Although a trip up the Nile had been organized for the delegations, I rushed back to Tehran, anxious to report to the government what had transpired in Cairo. I was apprehensive—as it turned out, rightly so. The NIOC directors attacked me bitterly, pointing out that I had been sent as an observer, that no authority had been vested in me, and that I had overstepped my bounds. They contended that Iran should "ride its own horse" and never cooperate with the Arabs, who had deserted us in our hour of need. No one wanted to talk about collaboration, and so when I turned up with the Gentlemen's Agreement, they condemned me as a quisling.

A couple of days later Entezam, the chairman of NIOC, called me to his office and, saying that my situation had become difficult, told me he was referring the matter to His Majesty. Two or three hours elapsed before he called me back to his office. I could tell by his smile that all had gone smoothly. He sat behind his desk smoking a cigarette while coffee was brought to me on a tray.

"Go ahead, drink it," Entezam said, laughing. "It is not a Qajari."*

---

*In the eighteenth century the Qajar shahs sometimes served their enemies poisoned coffee. If they refused the cup, the Shah would accuse them of not trusting him and have them killed. If they drank it, they died. Such coffee came to be called "Qaffe Qajari."

He then told me about the meeting. "Is it detrimental to Iran to be part of this protocol?" the Shah had asked.

"No," Entezam had answered.

"Has Farmanfarmaian done anything injurious to the state?" the Shah had then asked.

"No," Entezam had said again. "He signed something that he may not have been empowered to sign, but it is not against the interests of Iran."

"Then let's leave the matter be," said the Shah.

It saved my job.

Nonetheless NIOC made it known that the Shah wanted Iran to have no part in cooperating with the Arabs. As a result we did not send a delegate to the next meeting in Beirut. It was a grave oversight, for at that meeting Pérez Alfonzo revealed details of Venezuela's oil deal with Exxon that had earned the country millions of dollars—information we remained oblivious to for many years. As I only found out later, when Pérez Alfonzo swung the 50/50 breakthrough in 1946, he'd managed to squeeze 100 million more bolivars (about $20 million) from Exxon as back dues before signing the contract—something Mossadeq should have known before he began threatening AIOC with nationalization. In addition a secret clause specified that if the companies paid more for a barrel of oil to another country than they were paying Venezuela, they had to deposit the difference into a special fund. That fund later paid for the building of major roads and government offices.

Oblivious that such sharing of information had begun, Iran maintained its hard line. This was Entezam's position, therefore, during an interview with Wanda Jablonski a few weeks later in New York. Wanda had decided to dedicate an entire issue of *Petroleum Week* to the new agreement and was focusing on Entezam as the chairman of Iran's oil company. But Entezam stated flatly that we would not be actively involved despite having signed what he derisively called the "Farmanfarmaian Agreement" in Cairo.

A couple of days before the magazine hit the newsstands, the Shah abruptly changed his mind and decided that this was not the image Iran wanted to present. The Shah was no fool, realizing that Iran would not be able to get very far by itself. If he cooperated with the Arabs, he might dominate the group, and the oil world would fall into the palm of his hand.

Entezam, still in New York, faced the daunting task of having to rectify the situation. The only solution he could think of was to buy up the entire printing. It was rumored to have cost close to $100,000, but no one ever saw a copy of that issue.

A TALE OF OPEC

In September 1960 an invitation arrived from Baghdad to attend the next oil meeting. To my surprise all those in Tehran who had been such vociferous opponents of the agreement now lined up in favor. I was nominated to go as the Shah's special representative. NIOC sent Fatollah Nafici and Fuad Rohani, both fellow board members. Since Rohani had recently been elevated to vice president of the oil company, he headed up the delegation.

We were welcomed by General Qassem, the president of Iraq, who had bright blue eyes and a Persian wife. Pérez Alfonzo had come from Venezuela, and Tariki was there from Saudi Arabia, accompanied by an American adviser. With the Kuwaitis and Iraqis there were five of us; Qatar had not been invited. It was here that we formalized our objectives and obligations—with Tariki's American doing much of the talking as he explained how we should organize ourselves.

The main topic on our minds was the recent seesaw in prices and how badly it had affected our national budgets. Once again it had illustrated that as long as we had no control over prices, the companies owned our countries. Stopping their unilateral control over this important part of our economy would be our next aim, we decided, so that our budgets wouldn't be rendered meaningless each time prices fluctuated.

Our final act was to coin a name. We chose the Organization of Petroleum Exporting Countries.

It was clear from the beginning that OPEC would not immediately be an effective forum. The governments of the founding nations were divided over what steps to take—beyond preventing further price cuts—and worried about the political consequences of their actions. Many of the officials had difficulty deciding how to balance national priorities with international ones. All of us had a past with British or American companies, and some still tried to play a double game: paying lip service to OPEC while being conciliatory toward their old masters.

Saudi Arabia was particularly responsive to U.S. pressure, especially once Tariki was replaced by Yamani. And to my chagrin Iran was more obsequious toward the Consortium than I had hoped. The Shah, in fact, forewarned of this, said in an interview with Wanda Jablonski that he did not expect OPEC to have much clout for some time. The result was that OPEC became little more than a circus, offering its members the chance to travel around the world while accomplishing nothing. It took thirteen years for this to change.

After Baghdad our next big gathering was slated for January 1961 in Caracas. Naturally I was scheduled to be on the mission. When no preparatory meeting was arranged to discuss priorities, I went to the minister of finance and asked him for a policy briefing and written explanation of our objectives. He vaguely said that Rohani would take care of everything, just as he had in Baghdad. In Baghdad—as in Geneva during the Carnegie Endowment study—Rohani had kept everything very close to his chest and refused to share any substantive information. It would be useless, I realized, for me to go to Caracas if I was to be kept once again in the dark.

Sadly I told the minister that these were not terms I could comply with and tendered my resignation. In Caracas Rohani was elected the first secretary general of OPEC, a position he held for three years. The headquarters of OPEC were temporarily established in Geneva,* and to my surprise—as well as that of many others—he more or less decamped there, returning to Tehran only briefly each month to attend meetings of the NIOC board.

One of the difficulties was that Iran did not have an oil ministry, and therefore no obvious governmental body responsible for OPEC's affairs. When Rohani suggested to the minister of finance, Abdol Hossein Behnia, that it should reside there since that would bring the ministry great prestige and power, Behnia backed the idea and separated NIOC from OPEC. Behnia knew no English and had never been in the oil business, and he was completely unaware that severing the ties between the two oil entities would pit them inexorably against each other.

As a supporter of a strong national oil policy, I had repeatedly gotten myself into hot water for my outspoken opinions. Now once again I was falling out with the government over its position on oil, this time on its handling of OPEC. I wanted to deal directly and seriously with the issues and did not believe in going on the merry-go-round of state trips at my government's expense simply to be there, wear the name tag, and become an habitué of the world's five-star restaurants. But others did, and my government backed them up. Though disappointed I felt no remorse in going my separate way. OPEC was here to stay, and I knew that as long as I was in oil, I'd be involved.

---

*Switzerland, however, refused to give OPEC diplomatic status, and after a few years, the headquarters were moved to the equally neutral Vienna.

A PALACE REVOLUTION

No one has opened—or will open—
with logic, this mystery.
—HAFEZ

Tehran 1960
Despite my divorce from OPEC life was good. I was forty-three years old
and it was time, I decided, to build a house. I chose a piece of property just
north of Tehran and called my new home Villa Roxane. I loved that house,
not least because of the large library and the beautiful old faïence tiles de-
picting my father and ancestors that I painstakingly collected and placed
in the walls and oriental pools. But the neighborhood soon became con-
gested and was plagued by bad sewerage and potholed roads, so I sold the
house to my youngest brother, Ali, and built another, and then a third, in
Farmanieh, a suburb that still bore our name and had once belonged entirely to my family.

This last house, which I lived in for fifteen years, had a magnificent garden backdropped by the Elborz Mountains. I brought in beautiful granite
columns from a broken-down house I discovered (and bought for this purpose) in the southern part of Tehran. I also came across a pair of stone lions
while driving around in a remote area outside of Shiraz, where I'd gone to
inspect a new pipeline. They were in a cemetery lost in the desert, sitting
for what must have been centuries on two tombs overgrown with weeds

and washed in sand. I sent them by truck to Tehran and placed them on either side of my entrance door.

Dr. Roman Ghirshman, my archaeologist friend, encouraged my appreciation of such treasures. I saw him regularly at his fortress castle in Susa, where I often spent weekends and many memorable New Year's holidays. He called us his "wealthy cousins," since we all worked in the same area, we drilling for oil while he excavated for stones. Susa was near the vast oil fields of Masjed Soleyman, where a huge Achaemenid arena had been built some twenty-five hundred years before around a fire that sprang spontaneously from the ground. Ghirshman and his wife had come to our castle in Assadabad some years back, and she wrote a book about the archaeological ruins on the property. After finishing up at Susa he went on to discover Chagh-e Zambil, a three-thousand-year-old lump that housed many civilizations. Like many cities of the time, it boasted a large tower (like the one in Babel) of bricks decorated with cuneiform writing. Ghirshman's dig in Susa was supported by the Louvre and involved cutting through fourteen layers of earth, each representing a different town. Once he showed me a school dating from 1500 B.C., complete with adding blocks and mud erasers. You could see the children's sums marked on clay tablets and the teacher's finger marks crossing out the ones that were wrong.

A TALE OF FAMILY FORTUNES

By the end of the 1950s my father's youngest children had finally grown up and most had returned from university in the United States, plugging right into the Shah's program of Western progress. Thanks to Farman Farma's insistence on education, we were one of the best-trained families in the country and immediately brought to our jobs the modern practices and ways of thinking His Majesty valued so highly. This was a big advantage not only because we spread across the professional map in a range of fields but also because in some areas, such as politics and banking, two or three of us actually held related positions.

My brother Khodadad, who had studied in Colorado and at Stanford, was now governor of the Central Bank. Two other brothers, Abdol Ali and Cyrus, had started Pars Oil, an independent company that produced lube oil in conjunction with Shell. Ali also cofounded the Chamber of Industries and was currently serving as its vice president, while another brother, Kaveh, was a director of the Chamber of Commerce. Aziz had risen to become an internationally prominent architect and was designing many of the city's largest buildings, including the airport and the new headquarters for NIOC. Later he would design the Shah's Niavaran Palace and Iran's pavilion at the World's Fair in Montreal. Alinaghi had been named the first president of the Bank of Industries of Iran, while Alidad had started what would become the highly prosperous New Pars Engineering Company.

There is an unusual picture of six of us brothers taken at one of the Shah's Salaams, at which the heads of all the major companies and government institutions paid their respects to the sovereign. The Salaams were an ancient tradition dating back to Cyrus the Great and Darius, who had the ceremony illustrated in bas-relief on the walls of the great stair of Persepolis. Succeeding dynasties had retained the custom, and throughout his reign the Shah had made a point of keeping the tradition going, receiving people on No Rooz as well as on three religious occasions (Mabass, the anniversary of Mohammad's institution as a prophet; Fetr, the last day of Ramadan; and Ghadir, the anniversary of Ali's succession to the caliphate). The receptions were held in the large state room of the Golestan Palace, and a hundred people were received at a time at hourly intervals. Traditionally the intent was to establish meaningful contact between the monarch and his people. Now the explosion in population and the emphasis on privilege had made it more superficial.

Nevertheless it was an honor to go and unique for six members of the same family to appear together before the Shah. In the picture we are all dressed in morning suits and standing outside in the courtyard sun. Our expressions suggest that the world lies before us. We are young and confident, and our numbers add strength to the enchantment of our lives. How could we know that in twenty years it would all be over, that Alinaghi, who stands in the middle next to me, the ultimate banker who never spoke much, took a long time in thinking over his ideas, and was scrupulously honest, would be imprisoned during the revolution for having lent money to the royal family, and would survive only because someone standing near the prison wall shouted, "No, not that one," as he was being herded toward the firing range? We could not know. We pulsed with the adrenaline of being at the forefront of a country that needed everything done and had the means to do it. Even the turmoils that would erupt over the next few years did not faze us. We considered them the growing pains of a new country and marched on.

Professional prominence and proximity to the court were as much a part of our lives as they had been of my father's. Nonetheless we were not shielded from the vicissitudes inherent in being Farmanfarmaians—powerful members of the old order. My nephew Bahram, who had risen through the Ministry of Interior to become a top official in Tabriz, had some years before married the sister of Assadollah Alam, the Shah's closest friend and right-hand man. It was considered an ideal match until the woman was found to be unstable. Several times she tried to commit suicide. Then one evening Bahram came home to find her dead. He went into shock and didn't call anyone until the next morning. Immediately rumors began to fly, and Bahram was suspected of foul play. My brother Abol Bashar, who had returned from his studies at Columbia Law School, acted as Bahram's lawyer. Bail was set at the equivalent of $3 million, an astronomical sum beyond any ever posted—and a direct slap at the family.

At Bahram's wife's funeral the Alam family and friends were ranged along one side of the mosque, we on the other. They glared at us as though we were murderers, and anyone glancing in might have imagined that at any moment we would come to blows. The burial itself took place in the holy city of Mashhad, a stronghold of the Alam's, whose family seat lay to the south in Birjand. Some twenty of us rented a DC-3 and flew in to support Bahram, making such an impression and giving so much to the poor, who typically come to burials knowing that alms and food will be distributed, that the Alams felt uncomfortable in their own land.

To their credit the Alams eventually settled amicably. Bahram was exonerated of blame, and good relations between the two families were restored.

A TALE OF BUILDING NIOC

My job as director of sales and distribution was turning out to be the biggest job at NIOC. The foreign sales were more or less routine; the challenge lay in internal distribution. The British had left virtually no infrastructure for internal use—no pipelines, few rail lines, and the roads were hardly dependable. Because of the large desert in the middle of the country, the roads were not constructed north to south or east to west but always around the desert and through mountainous terrain. This made the travel time between the already scattered towns even longer. The main port of Iran is Khorramshahr, next door to Abadan on the Persian Gulf. To send oil from there to Shiraz, for example, which is just four hundred miles as the crow flies, meant sending it all the way around via Tehran—a distance of more than fifteen hundred miles.

As most of the larger towns lie in the north, transport by truck from the south was costly and dangerous. In winter the roads were snowbound, and it was often impossible to reach any part of Azerbaijan in the west or Khorassan and Kerman in the east. The border villages near Afghanistan and Pakistan were virtually isolated and so poor that people still used camels to travel and transport goods. Most of the roads were unpaved and regularly washed out by sand. There were no facilities for repairing trucks, and any vehicle that broke down either had to be abandoned or repaired on the spot. As a result many of the NIOC's drivers developed into some of the best mechanics I've ever known.

We were constantly frustrated by the difficulties of expanding without adequate materials or competent personnel. NIOC employees were often illiterate and took months to train for routine work. Many of them had lived in isolated villages and had never seen a telephone or a refrigerator. Without a trace of malice they managed to destroy everything around them, particularly anything involving electricity, cars, or appliances. It was not their fault—how could we expect a man who had never lived with electricity to respond properly to a ringing telephone: know to pick up one part of it, speak into the correct end, and then put it back on the cradle? In my own house I would often find that a new servant had left the receiver sitting next to the telephone box. And usually the servant had been chosen from among the most intelligent and responsible people on our properties!

Living with such ignorance was the price of getting up to speed. But we had no choice—there were no other pools of labor to turn to. Whereas private industry could keep a closer watch on their staffs, it was impossible for a huge government complex to exercise the same vigilance over the complicated scheme of pipelines, depots, installations, service stations, pumping houses, and other facilities being installed and serviced throughout the land.

In the meantime I was responsible, although there was little I could do in response to the deluge of telegrams and complaints in the newspapers whenever shortages affected one area or another of the country. As one solution we tried anticipating the increased winter demand for supplies by holding extra goods in store from the summer onward. But this meant not only building storage facilities but maintaining them as well. Then there was the unpredictable winter weather, which could block mountain passes for weeks at a time. Once we even sent kerosene by military air transport as a sign of goodwill to people who had been cut off from fuel supplies for weeks. But it was a mere drop in the bucket.

Over time we laid a number of pipelines connecting Abadan to Tehran and Tehran to Mashhad and Rasht. The British entrepreneur Ian Bowler built the first trans-Iranian pipeline, and I remember flying over it with him. We invited the Shah to make a tour, which he did, and I very proudly showed him our achievement. We were in the middle of nowhere, surrounded by scrubland, the pump houses and the shacks where the workers lived huddled together against the wind. The engineer in charge stood stiffly while I explained to the Shah how the flow of oil was maintained and the pressure was checked. He listened and asked questions, as always very interested in the technicalities of oil.

Then I told him, "The people who live in these oil outposts need more than the employees in the towns. The man who finishes eight hours of work comes right back into the pump house after dinner because there is nothing else to do. Many of the villagers smoke opium to relieve the boredom. We need to remedy that. We should provide facilities for sports and entertainment—television, for example."

The Shah supported the idea but failed to follow up. He lacked perseverance and the spirit to follow through to the end of an operation. It was a handicap that affected all our jobs.

The Shah also came to the opening of a pumping station in Bidrouyeh, in the south-central part of Iran. I told him there was a large, beautiful lake right behind the mountain called Oshteranku. He was immediately intrigued and asked if it could be used for electricity to help develop the area. He told his adjutant to follow up. I offered to do a report and made a special trip to the lake to scout out the possibilities. But again nothing came of it.

I honestly do not know what to make of these dead-end projects of the Shah's. Did he express interest in reforms solely to please us? Out of a desire to be seen as modern? Or did he honestly think that everything he decreed would be carried out without question or any need for followup?

The Shah's management of these small-scale ventures reflected in microcosm his overall approach to governance. He had no sense of organization, no real system or method. Because he was unchallenged by close advisers and overconfident of his power, his good intentions remained for the most part mere dreams. His hope was to transform the country just as Japan and Singapore had been transformed, but he was ignorant of what had accounted for those countries' success. His greatest handicap was that he lacked a real education and had never spent enough time in the societies he was trying to emulate (as Peter the Great did) to learn how they really worked. In fact he did not even know his own people. He had delusions about their capacity to adapt to ways that were not their own and overestimated their allegiance and willingness to cooperate. The Persian character had not changed just because Western practices were being introduced.

The people needed time and training, and the guidance of good example. Yet the Shah's own style of governing was haphazard and inconsistent, and as often as not he failed to deliver what he set out to achieve.

AFGHANISTAN

Once pipelines were constructed in the east to Mashhad and Rasht, we began to consider the possibility of exporting gasoline and kerosene to Afghanistan. In 1960 the Soviets were supplying oil to the north, including Kabul, while Shell was sending it to the south at great cost from Pakistan. Still the country suffered extreme shortages. We therefore began to send in more than fifty thousand barrels a month, though I knew the need far exceeded that. Afghanistan is a very cold country—much colder than Iran—and most of the trees near inhabited areas had been felled. With no means to transport wood from the mountains, people throughout the countryside suffered from inadequate heating.

For centuries Afghanistan had been one of our provinces, until the British, wanting to create a buffer between Iran, Russia, and India, tried to take it over in the nineteenth century. In two successive battles, twenty thousand Englishmen and forty thousand Indians were slaughtered at the Khyber Pass. Thereafter Britain gave up its takeover plan and instead helped Afghanistan gain independence.

Even so Iran and Afghanistan remained close. The Afghans speak the same language as we do and we share a common religion and culture. The border between us is a vast arid desert more than 500 miles long that has never been tightly guarded. It seemed obvious to me that we could cement the friendship by supplying them with as much cheap oil as they needed. Their consumption was ludicrously low—just 100,000 barrels a month. And unlike the Russians or Shell, we could supply it easily. We had a pipeline that ran within 150 miles of the border. From there the oil could be trucked across the frontier.

In 1960 and again in 1961, I traveled to Kabul, where I was introduced to Sardar Soltan Mohammad Ghazi, brother-in-law of the king and head of the airline. We hit it off and soon agreed that Iran should supply Afghanistan with a good part of its fuel requirements.

The next step was to see my old colleague Jan Brouwer, now president of Shell. We met in Paris, where I was scheduled to go for a back operation. Over lunch at Restaurant Fouquet I asked him how it would affect his business if we were to supply Afghanistan with oil. He admitted that Shell was taking a loss on its Afghan operations, but as with so many oil arrangements it had done so for strategic reasons. He was delighted to learn that we were interested in taking over the business there, and immediately sent two people from London to talk to me.

That left the Soviets, who could never supply oil at the price we could. I came back to Tehran full of hope that we would soon make Afghanistan commercially and industrially dependent on us. Not only would it be good policy for Iran, but it would save the Afghans from the Soviets.

But the geopolitical position of Afghanistan was considerably more charged than I realized. First the Americans and then the Soviets had fixed their eyes on the area, and any plans for Iran to increase its influence there were immediately scotched. When I brought my suggestions to the chairman of NIOC, he dismissed them on the bogus grounds that they were neither financially feasible nor suitable. Clearly he had been told that Afghanistan was too hot to touch. As a result, the Soviets and Shell continued to do business there. To add insult to injury I was branded a meddler for making the suggestion that we get involved.

As I was now seasoned in the ways of bureaucratic thinking, I did not take this too personally, knowing it would soon blow over. I was not surprised when a few months later NIOC assigned me to do a survey for the Afghan government on an airport by Kandahar, a town a few hundred miles across the border. Iran Air and Afghan Air were establishing a line between Kabul and Tehran and hoped to use the airport as a fueling stop.

Kandahar was once a great Mongol city. Now it was barely a smudge in the desert—a few hundred miserable houses with neither water nor forests nearby, sandswept and subjected to extreme summer heat and horrible winter cold. I wondered why anyone would want to live in such a place.

The airport was equally astonishing. The minute I saw it I knew that it could do the job. Built by the United States, it was a vast monolith that spread across the frozen desert. By 1950 Washington had sunk more than $100 million into it (the equivalent of $1 billion today), even though its existence was kept a secret. Nobody knew why it had been built, but it had obviously been intended as a base for major military operations. Bigger than many international airports at the time (certainly bigger than the one in Tehran), it was dotted with several landing fields, houses for the staff (all fitted with liquid gas stoves, even though there was not an ounce of gas within two thousand miles), and storage facilities large enough for a fleet of aircraft. Right after it was built it was abandoned.

As I looked at the huge neglected complex, I wondered whether it might have played a part in the deal between the United States and the Soviet Union when they'd negotiated the end of the Korean War and the role each would play in the coup against Mossadeq that followed just days later. Clearly Washington had had serious plans for this place. Had the United States decided to withdraw from Afghanistan and hand the country over to the Soviets to keep Moscow out of Tehran?

The Soviets had lost no time in moving in. Immediately they began to construct a massive north-south superhighway that traversed the crests of the Hindu Kush, some twelve thousand feet high. The highway was the most daring feat of engineering I had ever seen; its staggering cost could have been justified only by military strategic interests. The road crossed right over the flank of the mountains, where sharp winds could bury it in a field of snow within minutes. As a result it had been constructed in such a way that in winter it was fitted for miles with window panels, which were removed in spring and summer. The Russians called it a gift to the Afghans. Yet like the airport at Kandahar, it was twenty times bigger than anything the Afghans would ever need. The U.S. government never said a word about the highway, just as it never mentioned the arms the Russians were sending along it to the Afghan tribes, and, publicly anyway, it seemed genuinely surprised when Soviet tanks began to rumble south along the road some years later.

Such were the enigmas in countries like ours. As pawns within a larger global game we often did not know what plans were being spun or what money was being wasted on our lands. I gave the go-ahead on the airport as a fueling stop and hoped that over time our export of oil to Afghanistan would increase. How could I know that instead, just a few years later, the country would become the site of another superpower war?

A TALE OF DERVISHES

Although my effort to expand our role in Afghanistan proved fruitless, it did not deter me from devising other schemes that I thought could help Iran. I was a rambunctious talker and the youngest member of the NIOC board, and often my exuberance pitted me against the other directors.

This did not ruffle Abdollah Entezam, the chairman, who appreciated different opinions. He would have a lasting impact on the industry at a critical time in its development. He also influenced me significantly, just as Scholtens had before him. Entezam had ecclectic gifts: He was a math-ematician and an expert in optics, a wise administrator (of which there were too few in Iran), and a dervish—a mystic dedicated to honesty, poverty, and courage. His father had been my father's best friend. I'd met him after the war when he was ambassador to West Germany. By the time he became minister of foreign affairs under Prime Minister Zahedi in 1953 I knew him quite well.

Abdollah Entezam had a keen sense of humor and spoke plainly, refreshingly unfettered by political paranoia. Once, when a number of us were in audience with the Shah, His Majesty complained that his statues in the street were being vandalized and destroyed. Puffing out a steady stream of blue smoke from his ever-present cigarette, Entezam asked innocently, "What do you want statues for, Your Majesty? Pigeons sit on their heads and leave their droppings running down their noses and into their eyes." (Was he making a veiled reference to the unacceptability of statues in the Moslem religion? Was he also implying that pigeons could do to statues what real people would have liked to do to the Shah?) I choked back a laugh, anxious to show respect in front of His Majesty.

The Shah smiled. Entezam would be Entezam.

More than once I went to open houses hosted by Entezam. As a dervish he disdained materialism and owned no property. While he worked at NIOC he was given a luxurious company house and a Cadillac, but afterward he lived in a shabby little place with a small flight of stairs leading to the door. Usually it was jammed with visitors and other dervishes, many of whom came from out of town to see him, some crawling the whole way on their knees.

Once while on an official visit to the Kermanshah Refinery, I invited Entezam to visit a community of dervishes in Uraman, about thirty miles from the Iraqi border. They belonged to a special sect that prized the ability to transcend pain. It was early morning when we arrived. The dervishes had already begun their rituals and were dancing around a fire gesticulating wildly. The fire and their frantic movements reminded me of old Zoroastrian ceremonies. Entezam whispered to me that after three or four hours of this dizzy dancing near the heat, the glands in the ear expand, making the body lose its feeling. This enabled the dervishes to accomplish the incredible feats that I witnessed that day.

Some hurled themselves headfirst at a wall; others walked barefoot on glass. One man took a red-hot piece of wood in his bare hands, stuck it in his mouth, and swallowed it. Another broke a glass and ate it as I stood there. A third took up a piece of white-hot metal, the smoke rising from his hands, and began to lick it. A fourth man grasped a sword and passed it back and forth through his stomach; only a drop or two of blood fell from his wounds. It was extraordinary to me, though to them it was commonplace—an act of stoic worship.

I respected Entezam as well as his beliefs. Invariably the discussions at his house were about religion, politics, and literature, and even as the years went by and the monarchy became more rigid, we always felt that we could express our opinions freely at these gatherings. Sometimes unidentified guests would appear, most likely agents of SAVAK, but even then we spoke without fear. I found myself questioning the idea that Iran was turning into a dictatorship. Did democracy mean that the newspapers could print whatever they liked? Was freedom of expression among friends not sufficient? Perhaps, I decided, we had liberties unappreciated by those who accused the Shah of dictatorship.

Everyone on the NIOC board was inspired by Entezam. His judiciousness gave us strength, and while he was chairman no one, not even the Shah, interfered in our decisions or our work. Entezam gave us a rare sense of confidence and independence and encouraged us to exercise initiative. This meant that we could carry out our responsibilities without worry of reprisals and focus on our objective of raising oil revenues.

A TALE OF ISRAEL

One of the burning issues that came before the board soon after I joined it was the United States' insistence that we provide oil to Israel. After the Suez conflict the Arabs refused to sell oil to Israel. Its only alternative sources were Venezuela and Iran. Venezuela had no objection, but the distance between the two countries was great, and the price reflected the cost of transport.

To avoid paying this surcharge Israel turned to Iran, which had been neutral during the war. The deal had to be government to government, since the member companies of the Consortium handled Arab as well as Iranian oil and therefore could not be party to the agreement.

Yet recognizing Israel as a sovereign country was a problem for Iran. When Instanbul had done so, claiming that Turkey was a lay society, it had immediately earned the wrath of the Arab states. Iran, as a Moslem country, was in an even more compromising position.* Nonetheless, with heavy U.S. prodding, Iran at last grudgingly agreed. As director of sales I was put in charge of the operation.

It was a multifaceted problem, and as I was known to be tough and impetuous, I was flanked by two other directors, Fallah and Nafici. We knew

*In response to Arab sensitivities Iran never formally recognized Israel. The two countries exchanged missions strictly on a consular level, though in fact the consulates acted as embassies. During the revolution in 1979 one of the first targets of the demonstrators was the Israeli mission, just down Kakh Street from my mother's house. It was immediately transformed into a Palestinian mission, which it has remained ever since.

SAVAK would be watching us like a hawk, since the Israelis had been and were still heavily involved in its training. Then there were the regular invitations to visit Israel with all expenses paid. I never went because the Israelis were known for extending bribes and I did not want to run the risk of being falsely accused of accepting one. But it was a no-win situation, since I then ran the risk of being labeled anti-Jewish.

We knew the Arabs would react bitterly when they heard of the setup, and they did. It gave me heartache. We owed Israel nothing, but the Arabs were our neighbors and colleagues in OPEC and we had every reason to support them. Furthermore, though we were Israel's only source and last resort, it didn't want to pay us full price for our oil. Instead it wanted a 10 percent discount, as though it were still getting the oil from the Consortium on the open market.

Things got nasty until Fallah's temper finally snapped. At a meeting with an Israeli delegation in Tehran he said, "Look here, you can't obtain oil from Venezuela or the Arabs. We are your only source—and we have to weather the retribution of others for providing you with the energy you need. You are like the man dying of thirst in the desert. Someone shows up and offers you a bottle of water and saves your life. Then you refuse to pay for the water. How can you imagine you will get a discounted price when the Consortium itself pays us the full rate? In fact we want you to pay us a few percentage points more than the market rate to cover our discomfort in supplying you against the will of our friends."

Miraculously Fallah's tough stance smoothed everything out, and the deal was struck. Because the oil could not be piped through Syria it had to be shipped around Saudi Arabia and up the Red Sea. Later, when a pipeline was built from the Gulf of Akaba to Tel Aviv, Israel included us in the contract and paid us an extra 10 cents on the barrel.*

ANOTHER SHOWDOWN

As a full-fledged member of the NIOC board I felt it my duty to regularly point out the inconvenience of having OPEC managed by the Ministry of Finance. NIOC had to approve OPEC's budget, so I insisted that the di-

*The relationship between Iran and Israel remained cordial until the revolution, despite the pressure it put on Arab-Iranian relations and the deep discomfort it triggered in much of the Iranian public. Goods and services, including arms, moved freely between the two countries. Ironically it was the huge stockpile of Uzi submachine guns the Shah acquired from Israel that Iran later used to supply the Moslem forces in Croatia and Bosnia in their war against the Serbs.

rectors needed access to all information and reports. Rohani retorted that the material we asked for was secret and could not be disseminated.

At the time OPEC was focusing on how to get out from under the yoke of the big companies. Three reports were written. The first, by an Italian named Fua, was published in toto by Wanda Jablonski's *Petroleum Week*. The second, written by Stanford Research Institute in two volumes, I obtained from a secretary at the Ministry of Finance who'd been assigned to translate it for the files. The third, written by the consulting firm of Frankel in London, had little substance.

Since I knew of the existence of these reports, I asked to see them one day at a board meeting. I was told that they were secret and confidential.

"They are so confidential," I answered acidly, "that one has already appeared in *Petroleum Week*. The second, by Stanford Research, I have already obtained and read. I will of course make both available to the rest of you on the board."

Entezam and the other directors looked at me hard but said nothing.

The conflict between the management of OPEC and NIOC went on for some years. Each time I refused to back down, but as long as Entezam remained chairman nothing was resolved. It was not until Manucher Eqbal took over the chairmanship in 1963 that the situation suddenly changed. Finally the time had come to take revenge. All of us on the board attacked Rohani openly, asking what he was doing with OPEC, why he was in Geneva all the time, and what he was doing for NIOC. When no straight answers were forthcoming, Eqbal brought the meeting to a close. Rohani was let go, and OPEC management was taken over by NIOC.

A TALE OF RENEWED CHAOS

From my position inside the NIOC directorate it was becoming increasingly obvious that our oil revenues were insufficient to take our country from its state of poverty to something approaching prosperity. Though we had raised our output to three million barrels a day, the price had not changed. For this we faulted the big oil companies and the governments that stood behind them. They were keeping the oil prices down so that they could reconstruct Europe. Not until ten years later did our oil royalties rise above $1 a barrel—or a little over $1 billion a year. Such revenues could hardly support the expenditures of a government that administered a million square miles—three and a half times the area of Britain—with a population of thirty million, most living in underdeveloped conditions.

I made this point in 1975 at an OPEC conference in Quito, Ecuador.

The Algerian delegate made an impassioned plea to keep the price of oil down because the French could not afford an increase. I sprang to my feet. "In two hundred years of French domination, have you in Algeria ever had the money to buy a Rembrandt or a Renoir? If the French are so poor, let them sell you one—just one—in exchange for a shipment of oil. France is not a poor country. It has serious assets. Stalin once sold a Rembrandt to buy wheat. Let the French sell a Renoir or a Gauguin. It is not after all such an outrageous exchange."

Needless to say no such exchange took place, and the government was unable to bring about sufficient social change with the oil revenues it had. Only slowly, with the help of foreign corporate investment, was light industry, such as tire, cement, glass, and automobile assembly plants, able to develop by the end of the 1950s.

Meanwhile Iran was increasingly suffering from a plague that was affecting almost every other developing country after the war: an influx of the rural poor into its cities. It was the beginning of a terrible urban problem. At the end of World War II the capital had 1 million people; fourteen years later, in 1959, it had 2.5 million; today it has over 10 million!

How to accommodate such numbers? How to supply electricity and water, pave the new streets, build schools and hospitals, and supply kerosene to the slums when there was three feet of snow? Villagers arrived empty-handed, hoping to find work. But because they lacked skills, they were a liability from the minute they set foot in the city. The expanding slums reeked from the detritus of poverty. A vicious circle was being set in motion: Once in the city, though underemployed, hungry, and dependent on others, these people would not return to the village. In fact they encouraged those back home to join them, as though their urban misery was to be coveted over anything achievable on the land.

The uprooting of people in the villages turned into a stampede in the mid-sixties as a result of the Shah's White Revolution. This was the first step toward the regime's ultimate breakdown less than twenty years later. Ironically it was viewed by the West as a mark of great progress, a sign of industrial development. In fact it signaled great discomfort, as villagers fled from a countryside they no longer recognized.

By the early sixties the United States had dropped a billion dollars into Iran, most of which went to building up the army. Thousands of Americans arrived to take up residence as military advisers, bringing along Western values as well as a demand for Western culture. To the middle class the military buildup constituted a shocking waste of money that could have been better spent on education, health, and housing. Yet the danger of saying so had grown, and there was little outlet for complaint.

The villagers arriving in the cities were overwhelmed by the onslaught of Westerners. They felt threatened by what they saw as the moral laxity of Western values. In Tehran they saw vulgar movie marquees of half-naked actresses, bars, and hotel swimming pools where men and women bathed together. Men who, like my kadkhodah at Janatabad, kept their money under their mattresses and showed their wealth in their smile were now exposed to bank advertisements on television. The sole continuity for the peasants was the unbending rituals of their clerical mentors—and the overarching strength of Allah.

The clergy, led by Ayatollah Mohammad Hossein Burujirdi, counseled tolerance of both the Pahlavis and the Shah's introduction of Western culture. And so the distress of the villagers and their city brethren was kept under wraps until a confluence of events allowed the pot to boil over.

Right after No Rooz in 1961 Ayatollah Burujirdi died. Suddenly the lid that he had kept on the younger clergy was removed. This new generation was deeply disaffected by recent changes in Iran and quickly began to expound a political message of defiance from their minarets.

The same month that Burujirdi died, John F. Kennedy took the presidential oath in Washington, D.C. Kennedy's views differed substantially from Eisenhower's when it came to countries such as Iran. Military might, he felt, was not the greatest weapon against communism; instead he favored economic and social reform, a message he lost no time in communicating to the Shah. For his part the Shah was not enamored of Kennedy. He much preferred Richard Nixon and the Republican Party and did not take kindly to a man two years his junior telling him how to run his country from five thousand miles away. Kennedy's administration was adamant, however, and sent a string of officials to Tehran to hammer the point home. Their words, picked up in the press, gave hope of impending change to Iran's intellectual middle class. A similar convergence of events took place in the late seventies during the Carter years, culminating at that time in a revolution.

For the first time since 1953 the National Front started organizing rallies and issuing proclamations, and Mossadeq's picture even appeared in the newspapers. Riots erupted at the University of Tehran, and the car of Manucher Eqbal, one of the Shah's confidants and chancellor of the university, was burned.

Concerned that things were getting out of hand and feeling pressured by the United States, the Shah recalled my cousin Ali Amini, then ambassador to Washington, and appointed him prime minister, giving him a free hand to fight corruption and appease the masses. At the same time the Shah dismissed the hated head of SAVAK, Teymour Bakhtiar, and a bevy of military leaders, including Abdollah Khan Hedayat, Iran's first four-star general and a court favorite (as well as a good friend of my family's).

The reason for the military dismissals was not immediately clear. Later it came out that both Bakhtiar and Hedayat had secretly traveled to the United States to meet with John Foster Dulles to discuss U.S. support for the Iranian military. During the meetings it became apparent that a good chunk of the money being sent to Iran was ending up in the private accounts of many of Iran's top brass. When Bakhtiar informed the Shah of this, the sovereign became furious that his generals had met with the Americans behind his back and dismissed them all forthwith.

Amini, pro-American and radical, moved quickly once he took office. He appointed reform-minded politicians to his cabinet, instituted a policy of economic austerity, and began the process of redistributing land. He gave speeches every night and made sure he was accessible, even to those who were against him.

But the Shah still felt a deep-seated dislike for Amini and did not appreciate either the nature of his choices or the speed with which he acted. He also felt unnerved by the rallies that rocked the streets once censorship was eased and political liberties increased. He worried that the cabinet was too liberal. The minister of agriculture, Hassan Arsanjani, a rough, crude, clever chap imbued with a sense of mission, was cruising around the provinces, particularly in the northeast, turning land over to the peasants. The minister of justice, a staunch Communist, was sending his officials out with arrest warrants to apprehend civil servants for engaging in corruption and failing to do their jobs.

Such strong-arm tactics brought about quick change but at great cost to Amini's popularity. By January 21, 1962, sick of the chaos in the streets and the criticism in the press, the Shah sanctioned a takeover of the university. Military commandos stormed its gates during a demonstration, and several students were killed. Four months later, his reputation tarnished and his power undermined, Amini resigned.

THE TALE OF AN ILLICIT PROPOSAL

Just before Amini's fall in May I went to a Consortium meeting in London. I'd gotten into the habit of spending the weekend before these meetings in Geneva, where I'd met an English girl named Fiona who lived in the Old Town, on the top of a hill. She set my slippers out, didn't talk much, and laid the London *Times* next to my coffee in the morning.

Before my departure I stopped by to see a friend who was also my banker. I told him I was leaving the next day for Geneva. When I left, he got up to accompany me to the door some ten yards away. But when we reached the middle of the room he stopped and made a gesture with his hand not to talk, indicating he thought the place was bugged. Then he bent over and with his face close to my ear whispered, "Can you take a check for Teymour [Bakhtiar] to Geneva when you go?"

I nodded in assent.

He pulled a check made out for 100,000 Swiss francs (about $50,000) from his pocket along with an accompanying phone number. "Tell him," he whispered, "that I'll be sending a check every month."

I nodded again and slipped the check into my pocket. My friend then loudly wished me good-bye and Godspeed.

I went to Geneva planning to avoid Bakhtiar until my last day, at which time I thought I'd drop by his house on the way to the airport. He was after all an exile and a menace to the regime. How did I know he wasn't being watched by members of his own SAVAK—or worse the Swiss government? It was better not to have any more contact with him than was necessary.

Bakhtiar had been commander of the Shah's forces in Kermanshah and had made a name for himself during Mossadeq's last days for declaring that he would march his troops against the prime minister to protect the Shah. After the coup he was named a general. I first met him when I passed through Kermanshah on my way to Tehran from New York. I did not know whether he was pro-Mossadeq and so was very careful with him. He had little time for me. Later, when I became a director of the Consortium, he found me more interesting.

Soon after he was appointed head of SAVAK there was a purge against the Communists, and his men came to my mother's house looking for my sister Maryam. It was summertime, and we were eating lunch in the hall, where it was airy and cool. Uniformed men poured through the gates and up the stairs, their Colt revolvers cocked as we rushed to the door. I was in a lighthearted mood that day and knowing that Maryam was nowhere about, I ribbed the major in charge quite mercilessly in front of his men. I made him go upstairs and check the rooms, even though they'd all been closed up as each of the children had moved out and the furniture had been put under dustcovers.* Unnerved, the major insisted that I accompany him to Bakhtiar's office, where I complimented him heartily, saying he'd

---

*In one of the rooms where the major did not look, I still had a stash of arms from the old days of conflict at Janatabad. Ironically this included five thousand rounds of Savage bullets, the same ammunition required by the Colts the major and his men were using that day. After this incident I got rid of the stash immediately.

done a good job and should be promoted. It was then that Bakhtiar realized I held an important job in the oil industry, and thereafter he invited me to the parties he threw whenever one of the sheikhs from the little oil countries in the Gulf visited Tehran.

I was never very impressed with Bakhtiar, though I admired the conviction he'd shown in support of the Shah. He was a typical Iranian army man who lacked a basic education and held little regard for anyone who was not in a position of power. It was clear he thought the best way to run the country was by shouting and waving a whip. After he was thrown out he wrote letters on No Rooz reminding everyone that he was in Geneva. While in exile, however, he got involved in a number of underground arms deals, and there was even talk that he was plotting a coup.

Despite this I was not worried about the check I was to deliver. My banker friend was an honest man and clearly just trying to transfer funds to Bakhtiar from his private account.

As usual I spent my first day in Geneva with Fiona, enjoying the comfort of her little apartment and the quiet grace with which she prepared our afternoon tea. She was in many ways a typical Englishwoman, very beautiful and very chic, and I was grateful that she never expected anything of me and seemed happy just to spend time together.

The next day I walked to my bank on the Rue du Rhône, and then took a stroll by the lake, window-shopping and stopping for a coffee at a café. As I came out of the café I saw that Bakhtiar was in the street and coming straight toward me. Behind him in the shadows I could see a couple of Persians, confirming my worst fears that SAVAK was on his tail. Bakhtiar saw me immediately and embraced me in a bear hug. I had no choice but to return the greeting, right there in the middle of the Rue du Rhône. Luckily I had my wits about me sufficiently to whisper in his ear that I would ring him up later on.

That evening I thought I'd better go to Bakhtiar's and get the whole sordid business over with. After dark I hailed a cab and, taking along a suitcase as though I were on my way to the airport, went to his apartment. I told the driver to wait for me while I went upstairs.

A Bakhtiari maid met me at the door, dressed in baggy black tribal pants as if she'd just come in from the desert. She served me tea as I glanced about the apartment. It exuded the bleak neglect of a single man with neither taste nor interest in his surroundings. There wasn't a book or a tablecloth, nothing but a few sticks of cheap furniture and some Bakhtiari art that was no more appealing in Geneva than it was in Iran. A platter on the table was filled with apples cautiously piled into a pyramid more than a foot high, as though we were still in a Bakhtiari tent.

When Bakhtiar came in I gave him the check and the message. Then sitting on one of his uncomfortable chairs I asked, "Why, Teymour, have you become a rebel? The Shah has never taken a step against his servants. He may even call you back one of these days if you let him. It's a mistake what you're doing."

"Manucher," he answered, "you are a civilian. You don't know what it's like to live and work in uniform. I am heart and soul a military man. I cannot exist without my stripes and braid. Look at how I wear this suit. It is crying on me. I feel ashamed to leave my apartment. The Shah has reduced me to nothing. I can't bear it any longer."

"That's happened to many people," I returned, "not just to you. You are making yourself into a nuisance and a danger, and the Shah will be forced to take steps against you. You should patch things up. Live quietly and your turn will come."

"Your voice is so sincere," he said, almost sighing. "But I cannot continue this way."*

I told him I had to catch a plane and needed to go. He offered to drive me to the airport. I told him my car was waiting downstairs. He said, "I'll come with you."

"Teymour," I said as calmly as possible, "I'm accompanied by a woman."

He came downstairs anyway to wave me off. I ordered the driver to go to the airport. Once we got to the middle of town, however, I told him to go to the Old Town instead.

Suddenly I felt worried that the driver might be an informer, and I asked him to drop me at a restaurant called Chandelier. The street was one-way, and I knew that once I got out he'd have difficulty seeing where I went. Standing in the vestibule of Chandelier, suitcase in hand, I felt like a fool. The place was deserted. The maître d'hôtel, whom I knew, came out, and we laughed a bit as he reminded me that he never opened before eight.

"Then I'll come back," I promised. "I'll just go drop off my bag." Fiona's apartment was just fifty yards away.

The next morning she prepared a perfect English breakfast and placed *The Times* as always next to my cup. Though I was not being very demonstrative, she acted most loving. Little did I know she had more in store to jangle my nerves than Bakhtiar ever had.

"Do you know what I do here in Geneva?" she began.

*Bakhtiar eventually moved to Iraq and in 1970 was assassinated by two Iranian agents. Though they were sent by SAVAK, the men posed as opponents of the Shah, hijacking an Iranian plane and then asking for asylum in Iraq. There they approached Bakhtiar and a few days later shot him on a hunting expedition between Baghdad and the Iranian border.

"Yes," I said casually from behind my paper. "You're a secretary at a bank."

"It is not as simple as that," she said, running her hand up and down my arm. "I work for the bank president. I was brought here from London especially for this job. I speak German and French and even some Italian."

I was listening with only half an ear, more interested in the day's news than in her morning prattle. But what she said next jolted me into rapt attention.

"Because of my job I have access to all the top secrets of both the president and the bank. The president has a private account. He is a clever manipulator of the stock market, and according to the information he gets he buys and sells certain stocks and makes a lot of money. Why don't you come to Geneva and live with me, and I'll supply you with all the relevant information whenever he buys or sells his stocks. You won't have much to do—a couple of transactions every month—and we will live well and have a very good time."

By this time the newspaper had dropped to my lap. Staggered, I stared at her blankly. She knew nothing about me. We'd met in a restaurant a couple of years back. She did not know that I was an oil company director, that I had a large family and a full life in Iran.

My mind racing, I fumbled for the right words. "I am very touched," I said as gently as I could. "But I have a job—I work for a living. I come from a different country. I cannot just throw everything overboard and disappear. I regret it deeply, for I have a lot of feeling for you."

She said nothing and never pronounced another word on the subject.

My plane was scheduled to leave at eleven o'clock that morning. Usually she would drive me to the airport, where we would part lovingly and she would ask me when I was due to return. This time, when I told her I had to leave, she picked up the telephone and called a taxi. At the door she gave me a cold kiss. I knew we would never see each other again.

Still every time I am in Geneva I never fail to go to the Old Town and look up at the windows where she lived. The street and the building have not changed, and I always wonder with nostalgia whether she is still there.

THE TALE OF THE
WHITE REVOLUTION

By the time I returned to Tehran Amini had resigned and the Shah had appointed Assadollah Alam in his place. Alam was a trusted friend whose loyalty the Shah could count on and whose conservative outlook closely matched his own. The tide had turned; now the Shah could undertake reform on his own terms.

On January 9, 1963, the Shah outlined a six-point reform program he grandly called the White Revolution, or the Revolution of the Shah and the People. Its goals were to create a literacy corps, nationalize forest and water resources, institute land reform, establish suffrage for women and minorities, and introduce employee profit sharing in industry. Land reform, however, was the cornerstone of the program. The Shah hoped that if he nationalized land, he would become as popular as Mossadeq had been when he'd nationalized oil.

But the people did not want the land nationalized. Neither did the clergy, who denounced it as contrary to Islam, which protects private property. They also belittled the enfranchisement of women, saying it violated their special role in Islam. Particularly vocal was a cleric named Ruhollah Khomeini.

The Shah, incensed by the clergy's attack, went to the holy city of Qom and called the mollahs a pack of reactionaries. Half the people—that is women—had been denied the vote and now should get it. So should Armenians and Jews, who until then had been allowed to vote only for one representative each.

A week later the program was supported by a nationwide referendum. But everyone whispered that it was rigged.

The White Revolution succeeded only in alienating everyone from the throne. Shoddily planned and haphazardly carried out, it caused waste and disappointment in equal measure. The elite felt undercut because it took away their land and privileges. The middle class resented it because it offered them little and made no provision for extending political or social liberties. It hurt the peasantry because overnight they became responsible for their own land (and well-being) even though they lacked the requisite tools and know-how, which until then had been provided by the landlords. Finally the clerical class condemned it because every aspect—the confiscation of land, the inclusion of other religions into the suffrage, and the rigging of the referendum—went against the precepts of the Koran.

Nine of the most powerful mollahs in the country wrote a joint letter to the Shah sharply criticizing the plan. "If in the past women and minorities were not allowed to vote, then all the laws passed until this point in history were wrong," they observed. Referring to land reform, they wrote, "Why is such a thing not done in England or the United States? We are not communists here. Only the communists have ever done such a thing."

Finally they quoted a line from the Koran: "*Al-nas mosalatouna ala kol am-valehem va anfosehem*—the people are supreme over all their possessions and their conscience."[1]

At No Rooz in March a big uprising against the Shah took place in Qom. His anger mounting, the Shah sent troops to break it up. The soldiers attacked a religious school and, using sticks and batons, threw the students out.

Now it was Khomeini's turn and he wrote an open letter to Alam accusing him of being a heretic. Getting no response, he began delivering a series of speeches in which he boldly attacked the government.

Khomeini didn't care that his open opposition was the first of its kind in Iran. Fanatic and brave, he wanted to be heard. "Why do you take such reprisals against the Moslem religion?" he asked rhetorically of Alam. "You do not even have a school certificate [indeed, Alam had never gone to university], and yet you are trying to rule the country. I warned the Shah. "Sir, don't do such a thing." [To address the Shah as "sir" was unheard of.] We want the Shah to be believed, so that when he says something the people can agree with him. The Shah said 6 million people voted for the referendum. In Qom, in the Bazaar, not a vote was cast. Attacking people and beating them—was that his order? If it was, he is against Islam and the Koran. If it was not, then why doesn't he stop such activities? It is not possible to be king of Iran and against Islam."[2]

In June 1963, on the religious day of mourning called Ashura, the populace poured into the streets for the annual demonstrations of grief and ritual self-flagellation that marked the massacre of the Prophet's grandson Hossein.

That morning I went to NIOC headquarters. I had chosen my office to look south toward the bazaar and refinery. From the windows I saw smoke rising near the bazaar in the vicinity of a pump station where a great deal of gas and kerosene was stored. If the pump caught fire, there would be a disastrous conflagration. Very worried, I went to Entezam's office and rang the head of police. He wasn't there, which made me even more concerned, since it was a golden rule that in a crisis the chief must stay in his office to issue orders. Entezam called Prime Minister Alam, who breezily told him not to worry.

"The military," Entezam said to me after he'd hung up, "has been sent out to stop things."

"Then why aren't they stopping it?" I practically shouted, not thinking of the political consequences.

"How can they stop them?" Entezam shouted back.

"By shooting if necessary! If the pump blows up, we'll lose thousands of people."

The pump station did not blow up, but it was a black day anyway. The streets were clogged with the devout, who wept and chanted—and died, for the military attacked them with guns and clubs, and the gutters ran with blood. In Qom, Khomeini spoke harshly against the Shah and referred to him as "that man." On the third day of bloodshed, as Ashura came to an end, he was arrested and taken to Tehran, where he was reportedly beaten and then expelled from the country.

Khomeini's speeches were published only after the Shah's fall in 1979. At the time we knew nothing of the substance of his attacks. We had no idea what was percolating in Qom; the speeches were never reported and the nature of the uprisings never explained.

It was the last time for fifteen years that an uprising of any magnitude would occur in Iran. From then on the papers were tightly censored and the Majles was even more rigidly controlled. The landlords, without their land, lost their hold on the countryside and their understanding of its people. The clergy were banished to their mosques; those who could not be counted on to keep their tongues quiet were sent to prison or thrown out.

THE TALE OF OUR LAND

For some time we had watched our land being distributed to the peasants—though the White Revolution was the last and greatest severing. Under the method of compensation that was devised we came out comparatively well. Land was appraised according to the taxes one paid, then multiplied by ten, and that amount disbursed over ten years. Ironically, because my family had been persecuted since the time of Reza Shah, we had been forced to pay more taxes than we should have, and as a result we received more than our land was worth. But many people had failed to pay sufficient taxes and so received only a pittance. Several thousand families who had no other income were completely destroyed.

The capital expenditure for the government was huge—$950 million for 25,000 villages—which it hoped eventually to recoup in taxes from the peasants. But that's not what happened. The villagers, who had been given fifteen to twenty acres each (for the most part plots too small for them to make a living), immediately encountered difficulties. Maintenance of the water supply, farm equipment, oxen, the roads, and even homes, which had been overseen by the landlords, was now the responsibility of the community. But the village co-op, as it was called, lacked the coherence, experience, and organization to manage such matters and was quickly overwhelmed. The ancient balance of the five basic elements—land, water, seed, tools, and beasts of burden—and the old ways of dividing water in times of drought practiced since the days of the Mongols, all were dismantled in a number of months. Qanats (the ancient underground canal systems) silted up, fields were left fallow and turned to dust, and farm equipment rusted away.

Unused to the responsibility and hardships of managing their land, many farmers sold their newly acquired property to richer ones and left. The richer ones now became the new landowners. But the depopulation of the countryside left them with insufficient manpower to till the fields. Much of the land reverted to desert. Output dwindled and taxes were not paid. Those who sold their property moved to the cities to sell melons in summer and nuts in winter. The luckier ones found regular jobs and received weekly salaries. They were happy not to have to worry about crop management, rainfall levels, and property maintenance.

And so were we. When our lands were nationalized in Kermanshah, Hamadan, and Azerbaijan, we no longer had any reason to go there. To visit now meant dealing with all the peasants' problems while enjoying none of the advantages. The social fabric changed. Without the overlay of supervision that we had provided, disobedience and disorder took hold. The Voice of America talked incessantly about the benefits of land reform—perhaps to counterbalance Soviet pronouncements about the achievements of communism. But in the end democracy was not served by these much-trumpeted measures. The people were interested not in land but in services, and the services disappeared.

After the first summer when we realized everything had changed, we gave up going to our properties. For thousands of years the main business of Iran had been land, but now that the modern world had moved to the city, we were happy to be relieved of the constant burden of dealing with peasants, land laws, and taxes. The decline of Kermanshah and many other provincial capitals was one of the unexpected side effects of the White Revolution. Reduced both politically and commercially as the focus shifted to Tehran, they gradually shrank into the desert, forgotten in the mad rush toward modernization.

The Shah thought he would gain popular support by handing over our land to the peasants. But without an infrastructure for training the peasants to manage their own land or a co-op from which they could get credit or rent machinery, they were even worse off than they'd been before. Just as building a schoolhouse will not educate anyone in the absence of teachers, so the great land giveaway did little for the peasants since it provided insufficient support. They were left vulnerable and resentful. The upper class and the clergy (who also had been substantial landowners) never forgave the Shah for illegally giving away their property. Like the tribes we were broken, but to no benefit to the government.

And so Iran, which had always supported itself agriculturally, began importing increasingly large quantities of food from abroad. Furthermore, in the absence of the landlords, the government—that faceless bureaucracy with the Shah at its head—now became the butt of every complaint and grievance. When the final reckoning came, the anger of all those the Shah had disenfranchised would leave him friendless when he most needed his country's love.

A LITTLE TALE OF INTRIGUE

A few days after the Ashura debacle the Shah called a meeting of dignitaries to discuss what had happened. Among those invited were Prime Minister Alam, Minister of Court Hossein Ala, General Yazdan Panah (an old mentor to the Shah), and Entezam. A few thought that strong action should be taken and all opposition crushed. Ala and Entezam, on the other hand, expressed the view that the people's will ought to be respected. They rejected the use of police brutality and advised the government to change its hard-line policy in favor of a more conciliatory approach. That was the end of Ala and Entezam.

The next night Ala invited me to dinner.

At the dinner Ala drew me aside. After the meeting with the Shah, he said, he had been relieved of his post as minister of court and named senator. He then told me something else. It concerned an award of medals that was to be given to all the directors of NIOC on the occasion of the Shah's birthday. The head of personnel, Amir Abbas Hoveyda, had for some reason excluded me from the list. I had mentioned this to Ala and told him how badly I felt about being left out. Ala now told me that the Taj, third level, had been authorized for me especially by His Majesty. Hiding a smile, he added, "What's more he has refused the medals assigned to all the other directors!"

Such were the backstairs intrigues of the court. All of us constantly struggled to maintain and improve our positions. As often as not our maneuvering worked against us. Luckily this time I came out ahead.

A TALE OF BACKSTABBING

Two days later my brother Khodadad and I had lunch. He had recently left the governorship of the Central Bank to become director of the Plan Organization, an ill-advised move, I bluntly told him, because central banks the world over were powerful organizations whose chairmen were on a par with presidents and prime ministers, while plan organizations existed only in primitive countries to carry out economic reforms. But he was excited by the challenge and took the job anyway.*

In his position at the top of the financial community Khodadad was privy to many secrets. Entezam, he told me, was going to be fired. Like Ala he was being sacrificed because of the views he'd expressed at the council of dignitaries. It was very hush-hush, Khodi said, because of the impending visit of French president Charles de Gaulle to inaugurate a costly French-funded fertilizer plant that was to be operated by NIOC near Shiraz. Only after de Gaulle left would Entezam be dismissed. Khodadad warned me to keep it a secret, though he probably knew I would tell Entezam.

De Gaulle arrived before I could speak with Entezam. It was not until we were all headed down to Shiraz that I found an appropriate moment to warn him. He immediately laughed. "I'm used to hearing such talk," he said. "Rumors like that have circulated before, and yet I'm still in my job."

"No, Agha-ye Entezam," I said gravely. "This time it's serious."

For all his bravura I could see that Entezam was severely shaken. Nonetheless he delivered an excellent welcoming address in flawless French to de Gaulle and the French contractors gathered at the opening ceremonies. During Entezam's speech I saw de Gaulle bend forward and ask the Shah some questions. When he got up de Gaulle named Entezam and all the other important dignitaries without a single glance at his notes. Next, little girls from a nearby school sang the French "Marseillaise" in broad Persian accents, which made everyone laugh, including His Majesty. Only de Gaulle never cracked a smile.

Afterward each of us from NIOC shook hands with de Gaulle. Until then I'd never admired him, but I did that day. He was a gentleman, and had developed the habit of concentrating completely on the person in front of him, as though nothing else in the world mattered. De Gaulle was a very

*Khodadad, who had taught economics at Princeton, went on to have one of the most illustrious careers in the family. He became chairman of the board of the Bank of Industries and was named a Ford Foundation fellow. After the revolution he became a professor at Tufts University's Fletcher School of Law and Diplomacy.

tall man, so big in fact that whenever he traveled special arrangements had to be made to accommodate him, including the procurement of an extra-long bed.

The morning after we returned from Shiraz, Entezam called and asked if I could confirm the rumor of his dismissal. I rang Dr. Yahya Adl, who said he was playing cards with the Shah that night and would ask. At eight o'clock the next morning Adl phoned and verified that Entezam was out. In his place the Shah had assigned Manucher Eqbal.

A few days later, after the secret of Entezam's dismissal became public, I went to his house. He had left the sumptuous mansion NIOC had provided him and moved into a small, miserable apartment. A line of people waiting to see him stretched fifty feet from his door. When I finally got inside he thanked me warmly for my warning. "Sir," I said, "life is full of vicissitudes. You have more experience than I. In the past some of my brothers and sisters—and I—used to be invited to court two or three times a week. Now we never get an invitation. A new group is there, and those of us who stood by during the difficult times have been forgotten. This is human nature."

He smiled and said, *"Khoshk, va tar, ba ham misouzand*—Where there is a fire, both wet and dry will burn. In crisis the good and the bad often go down together. The Shah had to take a stand. I hold no grudge. As for you, your family is so large that there's always one of you around no matter where one goes. Your brother Tari is a favorite at court even as we speak."

That was what was great about Entezam. He could appreciate a man's qualities even if the man opposed him. Eqbal was different. His appointment spelled the beginning of the end for me.

A TALE OF BETRAYAL

The White Revolution's legacy of misbegotten aims and disillusioned people would take many shocking turns. The first came the following year. In March 1964 Prime Minister Alam was replaced by a young, ambitious politician named Hassan Ali Mansur. He was a tall, cocky character who had formed the Party of the White Revolution, the party singled out by the Shah as the only one now acceptable in Iran. He said he'd always wanted to be prime minister, and it was clear he was determined to change the country in a few months.

Two weeks after he took the post he doubled the domestic price of oil. A general transport strike immediately ensued, and the public refused to use their cars. Within a few days the strike had the desired effect, and the measure was overturned.

In October 1964 the Majles passed a bill giving American military personnel and their dependents full diplomatic immunity. Called the Status of Forces Agreement (SOFA) in the United States and the Capitulations Agreement in Iran, it came before Parliament after an intense two-year campaign by the American Embassy and only barely passed (despite the fact that the Majles was filled with handpicked Pahlavi yes-men).

The reaction in Iran was bitter. The Capitulations Agreement meant that any crime committed by an employee of the U.S. Department of Defense working in Iran—or any of his dependents—could not be prosecuted under Iranian law. Even if the United States chose not to prosecute, the Iranian government could not take the case. When two weeks later, on the Shah's birthday, the United States extended a $200 million loan to Iran specifically for the purchase of military equipment, the Iranian public felt doubly betrayed. Once again their national sovereignty had been sold in the interest of an outside power. The United States had no such agreement with any other country, which the Iranians quickly realized, increasing their shame.

Ruhollah Khomeini, whom Premier Mansur had invited back to Qom on the premise that he could be better controlled inside the country than from Najaf in Iraq, responded with vituperation. Already he had lambasted Mansur's one-party government; now he waged a frontal attack on the Capitulations Agreement. His speech was a cry from the heart. Not many of us heard it, and Khomeini was immediately thrown out again once it was delivered. But reading it now I realize how much he voiced the pain we all felt. He spoke of how the law had been passed without our ever having heard of it. Never once was it reported in the press or debated in the Majles. And it gave rights to Americans—strangers, as he called them—that no other country in the world had ever granted to any foreigner.

"My heart has been shocked," he said to his audience in the mosque. "I can't sleep. The Americans, including secretaries and technical workers, are exonerated of every crime in my country. The people of Iran are now lower than the dogs in America. If an American cook killed the Shah here, he would not be arrested. We did this because we asked for a loan from America and it said you must sign on this line before we give the loan. Our ministers and deputies belong to America. If you say they do not, then why don't they stand and shout to obtain our rights? According to the Constitution's laws, we in the clergy must see every law before it's ratified. If there was one mollah in the parliament, he would have thrown this law out. We don't recognize this government—it is traitorous to Iran."[3] Khomeini would spend the next fifteen years in exile abroad, but when he returned triumphant, the Capitulations Agreement still smarted. In his speeches in the new Islamic Republic he referred often to the moral decrepitude the country had fallen into when its local laws were no longer respected by foreign countries and its own people were reduced to the status of serfs. It was an insult for which he never forgave the United States and which deeply colored his actions once he obtained power.

Prime Minister Mansur exiled Khomeini and thought no more of it. In January 1965 he instituted price increases for basic commodities such as bread, rice, and kerosene. For the people of Iran it was unbearable. On January 21 an assassin's bullet found its mark, and Mansur died five days later.

When I visited the hospital to sign the book of condolences, I ran into Dr. Yahya Adl, whom the Shah had immediately called to perform the abdominal operation required to save Mansur's life. But Adl had not been found in time, and the operation was performed by the resident doctor. Nonetheless, American, French, and Austrian specialists had been summoned to examine the prime minister. The operation was botched, and the French surgeon, asking to be booked on the first flight back to Paris, said, "There's nothing more to be done. They have assassinated him twice over."

The general malaise affecting Iran did not lessen with Mansur's death. Though the most politically outspoken elements of society had gone underground, a sense of resentment continued to permeate the populace. The violence was far from over.

A TRIBAL EXILE

Contributing to the unrest was the wholesale destruction of the tribes, whose ancient lifestyle had at last been permanently dismantled by the White Revolution. Several million people had been dispersed around the country, destitute and homeless. Many of their chiefs had been arrested and some executed. And their flocks were run off the hillsides by the Ministry of the Environment, which instituted a plan of reforestation—on land that had been bare for thousands of years!

My friend Hossein Khan Qashgahi, like many tribal leaders, was suffering severe political reversals at the time. His three brothers were in self-imposed exile, having departed in early 1958 to avoid charges of embezzlement and conspiracy. Opposed to the Shah and agitating, as all the tribes did, for independence, they had supported Mossadeq and had even offered him military support and revenue—information that was divulged in a letter made public after his fall. What little the Qashgahis had left after the fallout from that revelation was all but obliterated by the White Revolution.

Tribes did not have a place in Iran anymore. People who wandered about the countryside were considered politically dangerous and possibly subversive. As a result few people in government would see Hossein Khan now, apprehensive that the secret service would report on them. But when he called and asked to see me, I told him straightaway to come to my office, having weathered many such brush-offs myself.

Hossein Khan arrived accompanied by a young man dressed completely in black, whom he introduced as Hayat Davoudi. He was the young khan of a southern tribe that used to live on the island of Kharg. His name was familiar to me because the arrest and execution of the tribe's leaders on allegations that they were traitors had been front-page news. Working with the Qashgahis, the Hayat Davoudis had backed the wrong horse and committed treason. Unlike the Qashgahis, however, no one abroad had ever heard of them, so retribution against them had been unusually severe.

We exchanged hugs and compliments and then sat down. An awkward silence ensued. I looked at my desk, they looked at their shoes. Tea was served. Finally Hayat Davoudi spoke. "I have come for your assistance," he said quietly. "My father and uncles have been executed and my properties confiscated." I understood now why he was dressed in black. "My wife and children are hungry and living in the streets. We've become like lepers in this town. What am I to tell them? That no one wants to see me or help me because of my name? Why don't they just get rid of us," he said bitterly, "rather than leaving me to beg—and at last to die?"

His face was piteous, and I could see he'd exhausted all means of appeal before coming to me. But helping him would not be easy. I explained the difficulties. I too was vulnerable; I could not act on my own. "Yours is an acute government case," I said. "I can't offer you a job, but I can and will explain your situation to higher authorities. I promise I'll do what I can."

I had hardly finished speaking when I was interrupted by the phone. Excusing myself, I picked up the receiver. The voice of a friend of mine in Parliament excitedly and almost incoherently informed me that one of the Shah's guards had, but a few minutes before, opened fire and tried to kill His Majesty as he entered the palace. The Shah had managed to escape by ducking behind a palace door. The guard had been arrested. So far nothing more was known.*

I put down the receiver as calmly as possible and, knowing that the news had not yet spread, decided to say nothing about the call. Nonetheless my position was extremely delicate. Officers of SAVAK surrounded me in the building. Two tribal leaders, known to be dissidents, were sitting in my office at the very moment the Shah had been attacked. We could be accused of conspiracy. People had been condemned for lesser crimes. The memory of Prime Minister Razmara's assassination flashed through my mind. His alleged killer had claimed to have been sitting in a friend's office, and he had an alibi to prove it. Now the same thing could be said about us.

"I can't do anything more for you today," I said, quickly getting to my feet. "You should leave immediately and separately. We are all so vulnerable that in the future you should come see me individually. I suggest you leave from different exits. Hossein Khan, my secretary will take you to the front door of the building. Agha-ye Hayat Davoudi, an office boy will accompany you to the north entrance, where you can leave unobserved." Both men thought my caution natural and politely took their leave.

A few days later I saw Hossein, but neither of us dared speak a word to each other. I did, however, bring the subject of Hayat Davoudi up with Eqbal, the new chairman of NIOC, and presented him with all aspects of the case. "People cannot be left to starve in the street after all," I told him. "Otherwise they have every right to plot against you and become subversive. You want to keep surveillance on him? Send him home where you can watch him—and give him a job." Eqbal agreed, and with his blessing I wrote Hayat Davoudi a strong recommendation that would serve him in the southern oil fields, close to his ancestral home. He left Tehran soon after and carried out a number of independent jobs for NIOC.

In a manner of speaking he survived. But his tribe didn't. Absorbed into the oil company, they lost all that had ever characterized them as Hayat Davoudis—their culture, their clothes and habits, their lives as a migrant people, and most important their properties on the island of Kharg. The tribe had existed for two thousand years—only to be destroyed by the enlightened twentieth century.

---

*What happened at the Marble Palace that day was never fully uncovered, though fourteen men were tried on charges of masterminding a plot. A few years later the Shah was about to go out one night when a chandelier fell from the ceiling where he had walked just seconds before. The matter was never even investigated, and we were all told to hush it up. Assassination attempts made bad press for the Shah, and he didn't want his supporters—particularly the United States—to think he wasn't universally loved.

THE EMPEROR AND
THE AMERICAN DREAM

Kiss only the lips of a lover and the cup of wine
To kiss the hand of those who sell faith is misguided
—HAFEZ

Tehran 1965

It took me seven years to get married again. I met Petronella Kahmann on
a trip to the south organized by my nephew Eskandar Firouz and his stunning wife, Iran. Petronella was the daughter of a respected Dutch businessman. She had a cosmopolitan education and worked at the Dutch
embassy in Tehran. Tall and blond, she had a knack for languages and an
insatiable love of travel.

We had set out to visit some of the more inaccessible monuments in the
country, including the massive statue of Shapur, the second shah of the Sas-
sanian dynasty, fashioned from a single stalactite and stalagmite that had
joined together in the middle of a large cave. We traveled by mule and then
walked up a hill. Deep inside the cavern the five-foot-wide stalagmite/sta-
lactite had been carved into a statue almost thirty feet tall. Years previously
it had been broken in half, some said by an earthquake, though it could have
been during the Arab Conquests. Reza Shah had had it reconstructed by
local soldiers, though Roman Ghirshman told me they had originally put
the feet on backward. Now, however, the statue was perfect. Thanks to the
orientation of the cave the light falls all the way to the back and illuminates
the face of the king. It is one of the most stunning monuments I've ever seen.

Visiting such a site seemed an auspicious way to begin a friendship. Petronella had style and presence, and she brought to all she touched the flair of old Europe. But marriage was not an easy thing for me. I wanted children but did not really want the ties of wedlock. Nonetheless it was time, we both decided, to take the plunge.

We were married in a typical Persian wedding in my own living room, with a mollah chanting the Koran and my sisters holding a cloth over our heads as they rubbed cones of sugar together to bring sweetness to our union. As the poet Iraj Mirza writes, "If there were no women, there would be no love among us." Before I knew it we had two sons, Alexander and Teymour. The house was suddenly filled with children's laughter—and the happiness that comes with it. I was a family man at last.

THE TALE OF A *HAJ*

There are some things you talk and dream of doing all your life, thinking you have all the time in the world to do them. The years pass, and then one day you realize you must do them now or they might never happen. So it was for me with my pilgrimage to Mecca.

I had talked for years with my uncle Etezad-Soltan of going with him. Visiting Mecca is one of the five pillars, or requirements, of Islam. I had often heard of my father's pilgrimage. He took along Princess Ezzat-Doleh, and on the way back they passed through Cairo, where they bought slaves and were entertained by the Turkish pasha, then the governor of Egypt for the Ottoman Empire.

Was it that I was now the father of two sons? That I was almost fifty years old? That my uncle was nearing the end of his life? I do not know. But in 1966 we decided to go.

It was the best trip I've ever taken. We went in a group, or caravan, of fifty people, two drops in the cascade of forty-five thousand pilgrims whom Iran Air shuttled every year to Jedda. Everything was expertly organized by a man named Sharbat Orly, who ran a caravan business just as his father had done before him, as an act of charity. I was not acquainted with many of the other people in the caravan, though afterward a number of us became friends and got together regularly for lunch at my house in Tehran.

From Jedda we drove by car to Medina and then on to Mecca, a distance of some three hundred miles. In Medina we spent the night in tents out on the great desert. Each tent contained five hundred to a thousand people. There were thousands of caravans as well as thousands of Saudis, who go on the pilgrimage every year. It was like a vast, annual Woodstock, with all the same problems of sanitation and the same need for clean water, food, and emergency medical care. Yet the Saudi government was used to this annual inundation and cleaned and fumigated each area as we moved, like a horde, from one spot to the next throughout the week of rituals. The performance was all the more impressive considering that for the other fifty-one weeks a year, the area was completely empty.

Immediately upon leaving Medina we donned the outfit of the *haji* (the pilgrim), a white sheet, or longhi, which we wrapped around ourselves like a Roman toga. I found it very difficult to keep on, not being used to wearing such a thing.

Between Medina and Mecca lies the village of Mena, where we stopped to pass the night outside on the hills. It is customary to collect seven stones from these hills and throw them at a stone marker called the "Great Satan"* in the village. There must have been a million or more of us on the hills. In the morning when everyone got up, it was as though the whole hill went into motion, fluttering like a huge flock of birds.

To be honest, I am not a staunch believer, but it was a fabulous experience to see so many people roaming around, reciting their prayers to themselves and yet moving all together. Often during the ritual I would see the same people in different spots, their eyes focused on an inner vision, enraptured by the place and the feeling that Mohammad was there.

I thought a lot about Mohammad, a man who had come from the desert, couldn't read or write, and had at age forty—about my age—conceived of the Koran, with all its poetry of language and thought. Historically we know a great deal about him: how tall he was, the details of his face, what he did in daily life, what his wife was like. He had visions, but he never claimed to be divine. There are many interpretations of what he said, many theories and descriptions, because he always denied any special relationship with God. Instead he claimed just to be a messenger, bringing news from the angel, another messenger.

Mohammad was a great man, and his wife was great as well. She, in fact, knew the Koran by heart and could recite every line. After Mohammad died, it was reputedly from her mouth that the words were written down and became a transmittable book.

From Mena we drove to Mecca, passing a million people walking along the road. There my uncle and I moved into a small guest house. That night, at 2 A.M., we went to the Kaaba (Cube), the symbol toward which

---

*This was named well before America was discovered—and Khomeini's fondness for the term during the revolution.

every Moslem the world over turns to pray. It houses the famous black me-
teorite that Abraham is supposed to have set in the center of the city. The
plaza was thronged with people, walking the ritual seven times around the
Kaaba in a huge wheel. Those who couldn't walk were carried by others in
baskets high on their shoulders. The Kaaba was once a pagan temple containing a hundred graven images, which were destroyed by Mohammad
when he brought Islam to the thriving merchant city of Mecca in 630. It
is a big square building, hung with a new damask cloth sent each year by
Egypt. And each year the king of Saudi Arabia, as the servant of God, goes
to the Kaaba and sweeps it with a broom to show his humility.

It took us four hours to walk the seven turns. Suddenly at 5 A.M. the
Azan, who calls the morning prayer from the minaret, began to shout, and
abruptly the whole wheel stopped. The day broke, and the sun peeked over
the horizon, bathing us in light. Everyone in the crowded plaza turned to
the Kaaba, the house of God, and began to pray, bowing and scraping the
dirt with their heads. The morning prayer is the shortest, so that people
can go to work, and as in a dream it was over, the day had dawned, and the
wheel began to turn again.

Near to the Kaaba is the famous spring ZamZam, a small trickle of
water where Mohammad drank. Each Moslem must drink from ZamZam,
for it is the reason Mecca sprang up on this otherwise barren site. Taking
the tin cup that hangs there, I held it under the soft gurgling water and,
catching a few drops, drank. It may not sound like much—but it was. I
was filled with enthusiasm and the energy of all the people reaching and
turning around me and the sense that every minute we were putting our
feet on the stones that Mohammad had trod and drinking the very water
he had drunk.

The next day we went to the grotto where Mohammad often escaped to
seek answers to the problems he faced. He had many of his visions there.
It was a dry, hot place of burnt volcanic rock without any greenery, but it
was a wonderful feeling to go and stand in the spot where he had received
the messages from God's angel that make up much of the exquisite poetry
of the Koran.

Our trip was half over. We visited the plain of Arafat, and then performed the last ritual that awaited us: walking seven times between the
markets of Safa and Marveh. A plaza about fifteen hundred feet long lies
between the two markets, which have stone pillars marking each end. We
walked around these markers according to the ritual, following an elon-
gated circle from one end of the giant plaza to the other.

After the rituals were over I visited the bazaar and spent some precious
time alone in the house, reading my books. There is a picture of my uncle

in his pajamas and me in an Arab outfit with a hat, taken in the street. I
have a big cigar in my mouth and look very happy.

"THE HUNCHBACK"

In Iran the allure of progress was blinding. The Shah, having taken the first
steps toward the precarious goal of self-aggrandizement, was gradually iso-
lating himself in the rarefied air shared only by other heads of state and the
immortals of Persian history. He imagined himself well loved—a sovereign of the people who had, by imperial order, distributed land to the poor,
nationalized the forests and waterways, brought literacy to the countryside, and built a raft of universities, including ones in Shiraz, Ahwaz, and
Qazvin. U.S. president Lyndon Johnson certainly thought that what the
Shah was doing was terrific. "What's going on in Iran," he announced in
June 1964, "is about the best thing going on anywhere in the world." Better than any other ally, the Shah was fulfilling the American dream. In
1966 Johnson's cabinet declared Iran a "developed" country economically,
ignoring for the moment that the average income was still $250 a year and
that only 28 percent of the entire population (and only 16 percent of
women) was literate.

Johnson, who had visited Iran a couple of times, clearly chose to ignore
what he'd seen, for it was impossible to compare Iran to a developed country. The poor were still in rags; beggars, wracked by disease, still swarmed
around the cars at traffic lights, asking for alms; and the streets were
chaotic. Once, coming out of a Salaam, I was unable to find my car and driver in the mayhem of haphazard parking and jammed streets and instead
drove back to the office with a friend. As we sat stuck in rush-hour grid-
lock, he remarked that Tehran's traffic reflected the state of the Iranian bureaucracy. Everyone disregarded the rules of the road. Driving on the left
and right sides of the street was exactly the same. To turn right at a light
the most expedient place to position oneself was on the left in order to arc
around everyone bunched up at the intersection. Taarof, the exaggerated
Persian etiquette that was so much a part of our social habits, had disappeared on the roads. Nobody thought of others. The streets, narrow and
labyrinthine, only added to the mess. It was, after all, easier to sell cars than
to build roads.

The word *democracy* began to drop less frequently from the royal lips,
until at last it was heard only in combination with the word *economic* and
never with the word *political.* The Shah believed that he had not only the
divine right to govern but the intellectual right to decide national destiny.

He did not know that on television his shyness and reserve made him appear arrogant and pompous. He did not realize that his lackluster religious commitment had alienated the very poor he purported to represent. The minister of court, Assadollah Alam, claims in his memoirs that he warned the Shah of the danger of this tack: "So much of our self-advertisement is patently untrue, and as for the rest, it's so mixed up with adulation of Your Majesty's own person that the public grows tired of it."[1]

The Shah, like any man whose mind and nature raise him above others, stood alone and lonely. Anyone who opposed his views was labeled an opponent and dispatched, until he had whittled down the cadre of people around him to include only sycophants: advisers without education, politicians without the ambition to think and act for themselves, masters foremost in the art of intrigue.

Amir Abbas Hoveyda, who was appointed prime minister when Mansur was assassinated in 1965, epitomized the kind of man the Shah chose as confidant. Hoveyda's primary qualification for the job was that he had been a friend of Mansur's. The only cabinet post he ever held before being named prime minister was minister of finance during Mansur's brief premiership. While he was there it had become abundantly clear that he was incapable of reading an account or judging an expenditure.

When Hoveyda was appointed premier we were all stunned. Mansur had committed such blunders and discredited himself so quickly that we had all expected the Shah to learn from the experience and appoint a true statesman. Instead, despite the opinion of Parliament and in flagrant disregard of the bevy of competent people willing to take the job, the Shah chose Hoveyda. It seemed an act of pure spite, as though he was bent on getting back at the people who had assassinated Mansur.

Years later Hoveyda admitted to me that he had overshot his own goals. He didn't know who was in Parliament, what legislation was on the table, what the people wanted. What he did know was how to serve his master, and this he did with absolute dedication and cunning. He viewed the position of prime minister as having no duties beyond anticipating and executing the Shah's wishes. No humiliation was ever too much to bear, no wait in the sovereign's anteroom ever too long, and no task ever beneath him. He told the Shah whatever the sovereign wanted to hear and shielded him from all else, an approach that fit perfectly with the monarch's increasingly capricious and autocratic rule.

Once Hoveyda became premier the Shah lost his hold over the government. From then on he knew only his minister of defense (since he personally ordered all the military hardware), his minister of finance (since he monitored how the oil money was spent), and his minister of the interior (to control the elections). The rest of the ministers belonged to Hoveyda, who regularly reshuffled them so that none could develop a personal power base or an inside line to the Shah. He was an expert at setting people against each other and dealing out influence like face cards in a stacked deck.

Entezam had first discovered Hoveyda and Mansur when the two younger men had worked for him at the embassy in Germany. Impressed by Hoveyda's industriousness, Entezam had brought him along as a secretary when he became chairman of NIOC. When Eqbal took over, Hoveyda was immediately let go, though by then Mansur had already assured him of a ministerial post. His subsequent rise stunned Entezam, who thereafter blamed himself bitterly for bringing such a man to the fore. "*Sadta chaghu misazeh, yekish dasté nadareh*—He makes a hundred knives, but not one has a handle," he'd mutter at Hoveyda's exasperating propensity to make promises and never deliver.

Hoveyda spoke bad Farsi, having spent most of his life abroad. He lived for a while in Palestine near Haifa, where his father, a staunch Baha'i, had emigrated some time before. He studied in Belgium, where he was in the same school as my brother Jamshid, but he never went on to obtain a higher degree. He was short, balding, and stooped. And as he was lame in one leg, he walked with a stick, which earned him the epithet "The Hunchback." That was perhaps the kindest of the names people called him behind his back. Some referred to him as "The Court Jester." Alam, the minister of court, called him *Khajeh Haramsara,* "The Eunuch"—a play on words since *khajeh* means a respected statesman, while *khajeh haramsara* means man of the harem, or eunuch. He was married only briefly, and ever after wore a fresh orchid in his lapel, a testament to his ex-wife's love of orchids.

Most people thought Hoveyda would fall rapidly, but he lasted for twelve years—the longest reign of any prime minister—his tenure spanning the most prosperous and most wasteful period of modern Persian history. More than anyone else he helped weave the web of self-deception and disdain for public opinion that led to the Shah's downfall—as well as that of the whole country.

At one of the Shah's Salaams on No Rooz Hoveyda was presented with the highest level of the Taj, which he wore proudly across his chest on a gold shoulder strap. Afterward he came out to show off his decoration to the rest of us who were waiting to be called in. Always simpering and self-deprecating, he came over to where I stood talking with Eqbal. We congratulated him on the medal, and then almost as an aside, I recited a line of poetry (attributed to Hafez, though in fact written by an unknown poet): "The greyhounds and the stallions are becoming injured under the donkey's saddle."

Hoveyda laughed out loud and then completed the verse: "But the chains of gold hang from the necks of the asses." I was surprised to hear him recite it, for he hardly knew any Persian poetry and so must have heard the verse already more than once that morning. (Eqbal, on the other hand, was peeved, and complained to me afterward that I was always saying things I shouldn't, and in front of him to boot.)

Hoveyda always tried to be witty, without much success. But as his power grew, more and more people laughed at his jokes. That he should be the butt of the joke only amused him more.

The most distressing part of the situation was that the Shah, an experienced statesman who had been on the throne now for twenty-four years, could see through Hoveyda as well as we could. And yet he thrived on Hoveyda's buffoonery. He found it amusing. Once, while watching a production of Shakespeare's *Henry IV* at Stratford-upon-Avon in England, I was struck by a statement made by the king's son as he defined the meaning of sovereignty. "What is the crown but a piece of metal?" asks the prince of his dying father. "It is *you* who are England." I walked the streets after the play as though haunted, thinking of the Shah and how he had gained his throne, and how he defined Iran. He had no notion that he should represent the pride and honor that we as his people felt to be Iranian.

And so the manipulative Hoveyda flourished untethered. During his seemingly endless premiership the rule of law became arbitrary and the cult of the Shah supreme. Together Hoveyda and the sovereign made for a lethal combination, and we all suffered for it.

Did I recognize all this then? Yes . . . and no. Like the rest I paid lip service to it all. I was a director on the NIOC board, doing something of value, living well, and like any man selfishly wrapped up in my own life— my children, my house. We were all part of the same caravan, traveling together so as not to die of thirst alone in the desert. We supported the Shah not out of love or conviction, for he had forbidden us as grandees to join Parliament or as landed gentry to serve on the land; we supported him because it seemed our only option, and not a bad one at that.

One of my brothers, Hafez, a professor at the University of Tehran and director of the Middle East Center, found the situation too stifling and left. He felt that his ability to teach the truth was being compromised. Propaganda rather than learning had become the goal of the university. Hafez had set up a research library in the family's name, was publisher of the University of Tehran Press, and had done seminal work on the Qajar period.

Yet as his independence as a professor was circumscribed and the integrity of the university tarnished, he felt he had no option but to go. He left with great foreboding.

Hafez was the first to leave. My brother Alaverdi, a professor of science specializing in marine life, soon came to the same conclusion. The rest of us, who were in business, thought that the opportunities still far outweighed the growing pressures.

Right or wrong I forgave the Shah many of his drawbacks. As the poet Saadi said, "The enemy who is learned is better than the friend who is a fool." I considered it my destiny that he should be my sovereign and knew that any disapproval I expressed would change nothing.

Or so I justified my silence then.

A TUNISIAN TALE

The tensions on the NIOC board under Eqbal were in any case using up all my energy. Eqbal was a medical doctor and one of the Shah's most devoted minions. He'd held every imaginable ministerial position, every one of which he'd obtained by pulling strings. His approach was diametrically opposed to everything that had gone before him at the company. Previously it had been run according to rigid rules. Now it became Eqbal's private domain. Secret budgets were set aside for gifts to such people as the Shah's chauffeur and to finance trips for court friends—all for the sake of Eqbal's own comfort and popularity. He was a meddlesome manager and undercut people's power until, at last, NIOC deteriorated into a shambles.

Yet the Shah had decided he liked having a figurehead running NIOC, since he wanted to shape oil policy himself. NIOC was a unique animal. Though ostensibly a company and not a ministry, it was the most productive element in the economy and it financed the majority of the national budget. It provided the main contact Iran had with the outside world. And it was managed by the elite of the educated class. As such the Shah wanted to keep it under tight scrutiny. He was well versed in the international problems and policies of oil and knew himself to be very effective as a negotiator both for Iran's own position and as a leader of OPEC.

When Eqbal took the helm I felt right off that we would have differences. He was a good-looking man who wanted to dominate the situation without being challenged. The board he inherited was composed of Entezam's men, and he quickly moved to bring in his own team. Initially he relied on Dr. Fallah to manage most of the international side, but soon the two clashed and Eqbal looked elsewhere for support. The best choice he made throughout his tenure was to promote a young engineer named Parviz Mina. Mina had been educated through the auspices of the old AIOC and had been among the group of students I'd spoken to over tea in 1949 while I was at the Ministry of Finance. He was sharp and good with people, and clever enough to work well with Eqbal while preserving the interests of NIOC.

At first Eqbal and I got along well, and he would often send me on missions abroad. The Shah was frequently behind these assignments, since he wanted contact with all the leading oilmen of the world, not just the representatives of the major companies. One of the endeavors I undertook was to go see Jean Paul Getty and extend an invitation to him to visit Iran. The Shah hoped that NIOC could buy out Getty's oil interests, but Getty was at the end of his oil ventures and declined.

Perhaps the most curious of all the trips I took during those years was in 1968 to Tunis to meet President Habib Bourguiba. It was an important and somewhat touchy visit, as it was the first official encounter between our two countries since Iran had begun providing Israel with oil.

The situation between the Arabs and Israel had deteriorated greatly, and in June of 1967 the Six-Day War had once again brought the conflict to a head. Iran had maintained a neutral stance, though its position was the cause of great tension among its own people. Once again most Iranians, including my family, felt that we should be helping our neighbors and fellow OPEC members rather than a country thousands of miles away.

The Shah, however, stated on television that he would never use oil as a political weapon. His refusal to join the embargo against Israel foreshadowed his rejection of the much wider oil embargo of 1973. What galled us in Iran, however, was that the Shah's support of Israel indicated that he was more concerned about his standing with the American government than with his own people. The United States, worried about Communist containment and watchful of Soviet-Arab rapprochement, encouraged as much distance as possible between Iran and the Arab world. This is why we had no embassy in Tunis—to my mind a serious oversight. At the very least we should have had formal representation in every Moslem country.

Bourguiba received us with open arms. He was very short and badly dressed in a lousy suit. Immediately he turned to me and said jovially, "Mr. President, why do you think we North African Arabs didn't lose our fight for independence against the French?"

I looked at him blankly. First of all why was he calling me Mr. President? Perhaps because I was president of the mission? I worried that my staff would think I was putting on airs and might report back unfavorably about my leadership. I immediately, therefore, scribbled a note to the Tunisian minister of foreign affairs requesting that Bourguiba just call me "sir," since "Mr. President" might be misinterpreted.

And how should I respond to that awful question about independence? Bourguiba was a hero of the Tunisian revolution, a guerrilla fighter who had led his men in their revolt against the French. He was a man of the people, a scrappy, blustery character, wildly popular and deeply loved. Only later would I find out that he gleefully asked this same question of every visiting dignitary, reveling in the chance to relive France's humiliation and his own country's success.

Hoping for the best, I said, "Mr. President, you had no backing and no money. The French had resources and technology and the support of their European allies. We never imagined you could win such a fight."

"Mr. President," he said, his smile triumphant. "We never fought a battle! The French lost the war all by themselves. We knew exactly where they were the whole time, thanks to their turncoat spies. All we did was carry out guerrilla operations." He rubbed his hands together and went on cheerfully. "The French have not won a war since the time of Napoleon. That's one hundred and fifty years! There was no reason they should have defeated us!"

I stood with my head bowed. What could I add to such a discussion, having come to talk about oil?

The next day Bourguiba refrained from calling me Mr. President. But to my horror he launched into a soliloquy praising Mossadeq as a great hero for having nationalized oil. Once again I had to send him a note, this time informing him that the government of Iran no longer took such a positive view of Mossadeq and that such eulogizing might cause His Majesty the Shah a twinge of discomfort. Although Bourguiba could not have been more hospitable, I left Tunisia with relief after visiting the oil fields and offering some advice, wondering how many more notes I'd have had to send if we'd stayed any longer.*

---

*Another funny incident occurred in Tunis, though completely unrelated to Bourguiba. I was returning to my hotel room after dinner when I saw a beautiful girl waiting at the elevator. When it arrived she hesitated at the threshold and finally decided against stepping in. I took the elevator up alone with regret. When I arrived at my floor I saw a door down the hall open a crack and to my surprise, saw Edward Kennedy quickly stick his head out, clearly thinking the girl had come up in the elevator. Never did two men look at each other in such dismay! He closed the door with a snap, as though someone had approached him with a gun, and I went to my room, where I spent the night alone.

THE CORONATION

The year 1967 ended with a bang: the formal crowning of the Shah and the Shahbanou Farah as emperor and empress of Iran. The coronation was the harbinger of a series of flamboyant and glamorous ceremonies that the Shah hoped would symbolize the greatness of his reign—and the rebirth of Iran. From the coronation he moved, four years later, to the glittering party at Persepolis to commemorate the Persian Empire's twenty-five-hundred-year anniversary. After that he hosted, with Empress Farah, a modern art festival in Shiraz, and commemorated the fiftieth anniversary of the Pahlavi reign. He then hoped to host the Olympics.

By this time the country had gained the image of being, as Jimmy Carter would later put it, "an island of stability" in a chaotic region. It also enjoyed the reputation of having successfully engineered an economic miracle similar to that in Japan. It was, the Shah felt, a good moment to celebrate. A mere dress rehearsal to the party in Persepolis four years later, it was an act of pure theater, and though overlaid by a patina of Persian aesthetic, it had no precedent in Persian history.

The ceremony took place in October on the day of the Shah's forty-eighth birthday. I was invited as an official of NIOC. The morning broke fine, and most of the fifty-five hundred Iranian dignitaries were seated outside on the lawn, from where we could see the ceremony unfold through the large open windows of the Grand Salon. Foreign visitors, the press, and the entire diplomatic corps had front-row seats inside.

The venue he chose, the old Golestan Palace downtown, was a quintessential Qajar palace. I imagined he might have constructed a new Pahlavi palace to commemorate the occasion, but the Shah was not a builder of palaces, any more than he was a man to appreciate Persian art and literature. To the old Golestan Palace, therefore, where the Shah's father also had crowned himself, I went in a morning suit, at what seemed the crack of dawn for the ceremonies at eleven.

In Europe coronations are religious rituals that take place in the greatest churches of the land—Westminster Abbey in London or, in the past, Notre Dame in Paris or St. Basil's in Moscow—and it is the highest religious leader who carries out the crowning. In the Middle East there is no such tradition; there is simply the placing of the crown on the head. But the Shah wanted more of a ceremony. The Imam Jomeh Tehran (literally, Friday Prayer Leader, the highest mollah of Tehran) directed the proceedings (ironically, he was closely related to Dr. Mossadeq). There was an Iranian chorus as well as a bugle fanfare and military music. A long, dreary poem praising the Shah and his family was delivered by a mediocre poet.

Somehow the ceremony stretched to an hour. As the clock struck noon the Shah placed the Pahlavi crown on his head to a gun salvo announcing that the deed was done.

Afterward the newly anointed emperor and empress, whom he had named regent, crossed the Hall of Mirrors and appeared on the steps in front of the invitees sitting outside. The crown prince, ten-year-old Reza, followed close behind, clad in a military uniform hung with medals—a ridiculous and anachronistic sight. Empress Farah's dress, designed by Christian Dior, had a sleeveless cloak in midnight-green velvet embroidered with gold and gems. It stretched into a vast train carried by six pages. Her tiara, crafted by Van Cleef & Arpels from loose stones in the vaults of the crown jewels, was a mass of pink and white diamonds and truly exquisite. The Shah donned his father's crown, topped with an egret's feather like Fath-Ali Shah's. He wore a military uniform in the court's colors of light blue and white emblazoned with ribbons and medals. From his shoulders hung a sumptuous cloak embroidered with rows and rows of pearls that his father had worn during his crowning forty-two years before. At the door and along the pathways palace guards stood at strict attention, dressed in Austrian uniform with plumed hats and shining hip boots, holding lances.

The royal family descended the steps to a round of unsteady applause. We would have been glad to clap longer and louder, but we hesitated since there was neither a program nor a master of ceremonies to tell us what to do. Then the Shah and Empress Farah climbed into a golden coach, crafted in Vienna, and drove through the city streets. Carpets had been laid along their route, and flags hung from the trees. In reminiscence of Europe foot soldiers in blue uniforms ran alongside the coach as an escort.

People lined the avenues and climbed the telephone poles for a better view, thrilled by the opportunity to see the Shah and to celebrate—though they were a little unsure of what it was they were celebrating. To them the title "Emperor" meant nothing. The only title that meant anything to Iranians was the exclusive title "Shah," and that their monarch already had. No doubt they hoped he would step down from his coach, talk to someone, kiss a child. Had he done so he would have been the most popular man in the world.

THE TALE OF A BRITISH DIPLOMAT

The emulation of European tradition by the court provided a strange contrast to the outright rejection of such traditions by the sixties generation in Europe and America. Since Iran was a critical stopover on the famous Silk Route, we were being inundated at the time by the West's hippies. And for us what a strange sight they were.

The British hippies were particularly shocking. To our amazement they parked their trucks and cars on the sidewalk outside the embassy, set up tents and picnicked, and acted for all the world like the beggars at the gates of our own bazaar. Then they demanded to camp on the embassy lawn. The ambassador closed the gates and refused to allow them in. Left outside, they made placards and began to demonstrate.

"Down with the embassy," they chanted, marching up and down Ferdowsi Avenue in the center of town. "Death to Queen Elizabeth. We demand our rights."

Soon the demonstrators gathered a huge crowd. Passersby couldn't believe their eyes. These scraggly hippies, with their torn jeans and limp hair, were doing what we had never dared to do: question the force and power of the British government. The embassy, sequestered behind high walls and towering trees, seemed to cower. Awed but emboldened by the marching hippies, and sympathetic to anyone defying British might, the Iranian bystanders gradually joined in.

The ambassador, Sir Denis Wright, was a learned, witty man and a friend of mine. I had met him when he was first assigned to Iran as chargé d'affaires. In an effort to make the embassy more open and accessible, he had the two lions removed from the front gates. The move had subtly changed the public's impression of England. In style Wright seemed very different from his predecessors. Brushing aside the stuffiness and pomposity that characterized most British diplomacy, he tried to popularize Britain's image.

When his post as chargé d'affaires was over we were sorry to see him go—and delighted when, a few years later, he returned as ambassador. There was little he could do, however, to maintain the embassy's diplomatic mien in the face of the uproar caused daily by the hippies. Over dinner one night he told me he'd just been dealing with the son of a prominent jeweler who had come to Tehran on his way to Afghanistan. The boy had gotten himself into a scrape and been thrown into jail. By pulling strings and using a great deal of influence, Wright had finally arranged his release. But when the jailers went to let him out, he refused to leave his cell, saying he enjoyed the Persian rogues he'd found in prison.

"Imagine," said Wright, laughing, "to be an ambassador and face such problems as these!"

The antics of the hippies were only one of the many headaches Wright faced during his tenure. In 1968 the British government announced that it would be pulling its forces out of the Persian Gulf by 1971. The Shah dearly hoped to fill the power vacuum this would leave behind. But before he could take any steps to do so, disagreements over Iran's long-standing claim to Bahrain and various small islands, such as the strategically located Abu Musa and the Greater and Lesser Tunbs, had to be resolved. It was, after all, our control over these islands and far-off shores that had earned the waterway its name.*

Finding an acceptable settlement with the Gulf sheikhs was one of Wright's jobs. The British government, which had seized the islands from Persia less than a century before, had handed them over to a clutch of Arab sheikhs, some as recently as 1937, and they were now claiming these bits of land as their heritage.

The negotiations might have been quite easy if Iran had not been engaged in a disagreement with the Consortium. Embarked on a massive program of industrial development, which included the building of large dams, petrochemical plants, iron and steel complexes, and gas lines—as well as the Shah's extremely expensive program of military acquisition Iran needed greater revenues. Being wholly dependent on oil to finance these projects, it was pressuring the Consortium to increase output to $1 billion a year. But the Consortium was digging in its heels. Each of its members was more heavily vested in a Gulf Arab country than in Iran (Standard Oil in Saudi Arabia, for example, and British Petroleum in Kuwait) and had little incentive to increase Iran's output at their expense (particularly since labor, and hence production, was cheaper in the Arab countries). The Shah found their offer of $900 million ($50 million more than Iran's current income) unacceptable and threatened to bring legislation to the Majles that would rewrite the Consortium's brief. As so many of his predecessors had done before him, Wright became an intermediary—a thankless job at best.

Dealing with the Gulf Arabs was never predictable. One day I was driving downtown from my house when I saw Wright's tall, angular form striding along the crowded sidewalk instead of being driven grandly through the streets in his Rolls-Royce. "What's going on, Denis?" I called out. "Did you lose your car?"

---

*The division of the waters of the Shatt-al-Arab also remained a thorn. In April 1969 the Shah decided to abrogate the old treaty with Iraq that gave it dominance over the inlet and sent a ship into Iraqi waters carrying a Persian flag. The two countries almost went to war over this maneuver. Then in January 1970 a coup attempt in Iraq, backed by Iran, failed, and relations between the two countries deteriorated again. They did not work out any kind of agreement until 1974.

"Yes," he answered. "It just never turned up—so I decided I'd better walk."

"Get in," I said, throwing open the door. (Wright's driver eventually showed up at the embassy, admitting he'd been caught in traffic.)

Wright folded himself into the front seat and started shaking his head. "I must tell you what happened this morning," he said. "There was a reception given for the Gulf Arab sheikhs in the Shah's palace. I honestly must say I have never seen carpets such as His Majesty had on the floor." He touched his eyes over and over, squinting as he said this, obviously still overcome by the sight in his mind's eye. "The sheikhs were drinking Turkish coffee—terrible stuff, can't stand it myself. Then I saw them get up, as though they were going outside their tents, and throw the muddy leftovers into the corner of the room—right on those beautiful carpets!"

The Shah was so fond of Wright that when his posting drew to an end he personally approached the British government requesting that his term be extended (the request was denied). Wright always professed a deep love for Iran and the Persians, and when he finally left in 1972 we all felt we'd lost a good friend. To our surprise and horror, after the Shah's fall Wright wrote a series of articles in which he denounced the Shah and dealt extremely harshly with his regime. We also learned that Queen Elizabeth did not attend the festivities in Persepolis after he told her the Shah was getting too big for his britches. Like Cyrano de Bergerac, who could scoff at his own huge nose but allowed no one else to say a word about it, we felt Wright's negativism was a betrayal. It was one thing for us to find fault with our government; it was something very different for a diplomat and friend of the Shah's who professed such admiration for our country during his tenure to be so disparaging after he left.*

A TALE OF SUCCESS

The dispute over the Gulf territories was finally resolved through the creation of the United Arab Emirates, which allowed Iran to recover Abu Musa and the Tunbs while diplomatically relinquishing Bahrain. It was a significant achievement, especially since the islands were thought to carry substantial deposits of minerals and oil.

*After Wright left Tehran he wrote two books, *The English Amongst the Persians* and *The Persians Amongst the English.* In these he took an extremely supercilious attitude toward the Qajars, which after an exchange of correspondence led to a complete breakdown in our friendship. Finally, it was Wright, dressed in a disguise, who went to the Bahamas after the Shah fled Iran in 1979 to inform him that he could not seek asylum in England.

The question of oil output, however, took much longer to resolve. In 1969, after much haggling, the Consortium agreed to raise output to the $1 billion mark. The long, drawn-out negotiations made it crystal clear, however, that the time was fast approaching for us to take control over our production and decide on our output level ourselves. As long as the Consortium had control we were condemned to a fight whenever we wanted an increase in revenues. Only by determining the level of production ourselves could we control our budget and oil income.

This change in roles took place four years later in March of 1973, just in time for us to cash in on the bonanza created by the Arab oil embargo.

Meanwhile, in 1969 the price of oil was marginally increased. The following year an OPEC meeting in Caracas turned out to be a watershed—the first time the member countries felt sufficiently strong to threaten an across-the-board shutdown in production if the companies did not raise revenues. New men had joined the organization and felt more strongly that OPEC could play a proactive role. Finally OPEC, it seemed, was coming into its own.

Even so it was not lost on any of us that in its ten years of existence, OPEC had succeeded in raising the price of oil by only 45 cents a barrel, to $2.25. Inflation and cost of living the world over had grown by ten times that. Each year it cost us more to import the goods and services we needed for development, while the actual value we received for our oil lessened. Twenty-five years later, when the price of oil finally reached $15 to $17 a barrel, it was easy to calculate that had the price kept up with the decrease in the value of the dollar, oil should have been selling at $140 per barrel!

The Caracas meeting was followed by another in Tehran in January 1971. The Shah made a speech in Parliament, attended by all the OPEC representatives, demanding an increase in the posted price as well as inflation indexing so that the value of our expenditures would stay in line with the value of our revenues. It was a bold stance, but the Shah felt well supported by the other OPEC members who considered they had sacrificed enough.

Over the previous decade the West's consumption of oil had skyrocketed to more than 20 million barrels a day. This had created a seller's market, and left the oil companies much less leeway to negotiate with us. What's more, political upheavals in Libya and Iraq had reduced the amount of oil on the market, while a rupture of the Tapline in Syria had temporarily shut off the delivery of 500,000 barrels a day of Saudi oil to Europe. Meanwhile Europe and the United States had grown increasingly dependent on Middle Eastern oil as U.S. reserves dried up. It was all in all a very different situation from that in the fifties.

The main negotiators at the Tehran meeting were Iran's new oil czar, Dr. Jamshid Amouzegar, the minister of finance and our delegate to OPEC; George Piercy of Exxon; and Sir William Fraser's son, Lord Strathalmond—a sloppy character who stepped off the plane waving a bottle of whiskey—who was representing British Petroleum.

THE SAUDI SHEIKH

Although I was not currently involved with OPEC, I was privy to many of the behind-the-scenes deliberations due to my close friendship with Dr. Amouzegar. When, as minister of finance, he was appointed our delegate to OPEC, I was delighted, not only because I respected him as an economist and a shrewd man in the affairs of oil but because, in contrast to his predecessor, we had a close personal rapport. The government had also at last appointed someone with a rank equal to the ministers of oil who were the OPEC delegates from the other member countries.

The meeting in Tehran was the first at which Sheikh Yamani, the flamboyant representative from Saudi Arabia, appeared on the scene. He was an extravagant individual who was responsible for the image of profligate wealth that dogged OPEC throughout the early seventies. He was always showing off with big cars and big planes, and though he was clever, his style could not have been more diametrically opposed to Amouzegar's. Whereas Amouzegar was renowned for his modesty, Yamani made a point of magnifying his status. He maintained a bevy of special guards and flew to meetings in a private four-engine plane—frequently emblazoned with the Exxon logo. If he stayed the night, he usually spent it on board rather than joining the other delegates at a local hotel. He held the OPEC meetings in such disregard that as often as not he would walk out in the middle of a session.

Every time he came to Iran he spent some $100,000 on carpets. In Vienna he made a lasting impression on the citizenry by coming down the stairs of the Imperial Hotel with his arms filled with Pekingese dogs. He was so ostentatious that he made international headlines when he arranged for Harrods, the great London department store, to stay open one night so that his family could shop there alone. That evening the Yamanis reportedly spent $500,000.

Yamani was the most flagrant of all the Saudi ministers, though none were easy to deal with. They were different from the rest of us. They acted like potentates within OPEC, refusing to cooperate or compromise. Yamani was particularly peremptory with his colleagues, and only Amouzegar succeeded in never quarreling with him. The Saudis had vast amounts of money, and their needs were fewer than those of us with higher populations and more developed societies. They were unique in that they had both the power and the capacity to flood the market—and didn't really care if prices plummeted as a result. We did, and tried our utmost not to get into the dangerous race of investing in surplus capacity. We could never quite count on the Saudis in this regard, however, just as we could never quite count on them to hold the line against the American companies. Their relationship with Aramco remained strong, and they were avowed allies of Washington, which, heavily dependent on Saudi oil, made every effort to nurture the link (in stark contrast to the British, who never made any effort with our government during the days of AIOC). Knowing that they could afford to lose a few million dollars here and there for political expediency, the Saudis often argued for lower price increases or higher production quotas, seemingly unmoved by what everyone else needed or wanted. And because their market share was so much greater than anyone else's, they usually won. It was frustrating and made us all feel that in the Saudis, we had the equivalent of an American company delegate sitting in OPEC. At the Tehran meeting Yamani threw his weight behind the OPEC position however, impressed no doubt by the Shah's tough stand and the unanimity of support among all the other members.

Amouzegar always invited me to dinner at his house on Friday nights, where his charming German wife presided as the best hostess I have ever known. I was there on the night of February 12, 1971, when the OPEC negotiations ended in triumph. As he told me the details of the deal—a 33-cent-per-barrel price hike and subsequent annual increases—I couldn't believe my ears. In addition, the famous 50/50 profit sharing was changed to 55/45. (Libya and Algeria were the only exceptions, holding out for a 60/40 split since they were on the Mediterranean and their oil could be shipped more cheaply to Europe than ours from the Gulf—and more safely too, since it didn't need to go through Nasser's Suez Canal.) It was the beginning of a new era, which would guarantee us a secure economic future. Amouzegar had masterminded the plan and brought it into being. When a couple of days later I heard that he'd been awarded the highest level of the Taj—a decoration usually reserved only for prime ministers—I felt that it had never before been so wisely given.

A TALE OF PERSEPOLIS

The Shah was at his zenith. An effective and persuasive force within OPEC, a valued ally of the United States, and a perfect example of why the Nixon

Doctrine encouraged local leaders to assume greater geographic initiative, he was now also rich. It was the perfect moment to celebrate his prowess as the sovereign of the oldest monarchy in the world. With the glow of the OPEC deal still lingering, preparations began in earnest in 1971 for the most glittering party in history.

My own feeling was that the whole idea was bunk. The concept of continuous monarchy lasting more than twenty-five hundred years was a perversion of history. Persia had always lived by destroying what previous rulers had constructed. There had been a plethora of dynasties, many of them overthrown by internal revolution, and there had also been huge gaps in between. In the past two hundred years alone, only three out of nine shahs had died on the throne (something neither of the Pahlavis would do). The Shah's emphasis on continuity was designed, therefore, purely to enhance his own standing. Just as he had assumed the title "Aryamehr"— "Light of the Sun"—to strengthen his image among his subjects, so his insistence on tying himself to the long and shadowy lines of empire was pure bravado. His hope was that the West would view his reign as a constitutional monarchy rooted in tradition. In fact his rule was neither constitutional nor rooted, and the pageantry of Persepolis only stiffened internal dissension against him. Iran's real continuity was religion, a force so strong that it would eventually unseat him—though at the time he and we of the elite were blissfully unaware of its smoldering power.

For three years the minister of court, Assadollah Alam, worked to organize the party. Invitations were sent to every ruler and president in the world—accompanied by feverish arm-twisting on the part of the Shah, who wanted only the crème de la crème to attend. Seventy-one dignitaries agreed to come, including Marshal Tito of Yugoslavia, Vice President Spiro Agnew of the United States, Prince Philip and Princess Anne of England, President Ferdinand and Imelda Marcos of the Philippines, and President Nikolay Podgorny of the Soviet Union. Singular in their absence, however, were Queen Elizabeth, President Richard Nixon, President Georges Pompidou of France, and Chancellor Willy Brandt of West Germany.

To the amazement, and then growing outrage, of the Persian people, everything from food to services was imported from abroad. Tents and marquees were constructed by the French artisan Jansen. The banquet hall marquee alone cost $1 million. All the food was catered by Maxim's of Paris, and more than 165 chefs and waiters were flown in for the occasion. Some twenty thousand bottles of French wine and champagne also were airlifted in. The crockery came from England and the curtains and drapes for the tents from Italy. Total estimated cost: between $50 million and $100 million. The only thing there that was "made" in Persia was Persepolis—and its destruction had begun with the attack by Alexander the Great two thousand years before.

The monarchs, presidents, and other nabobs were housed in fifty-seven tents spread like a chivalric painting across the plain fronting the great ruins of Persepolis. The rest of the guests stayed in Shiraz, just twenty minutes away. As a member of the NIOC board I was included on the guest list, but instead of staying with my colleagues at the new Hotel Dariush I stayed with a friend. In the mornings he and I rode horseback for a couple of hours; in the afternoons and evenings I attended the ceremonies at Persepolis and joined my colleagues for dinner in the hotel.

On the first day we were given a tour of the tents before dinner. In the tents every head of state had his or her own set of china and linens especially designed to match the furnishings, including the carpets. At the end of the celebration each head of state was given the china as a lagniappe.

That first evening after dinner a sound and light show was held among the ruins of Persepolis. It was one of the most spectacular monuments in which to see such a display. The program was designed by the French, and as a result the voices booming from behind the pillars and equine cornices claiming to be Cyrus, Darius, and Xerxes all spoke in French. We Iranian dignitaries, dressed in black tie, took our seats first before the royal entourage arrived with their guests. When they appeared the sight was truly staggering; never had I imagined that I would see so many heads of state in one place. Medals glittered, jewels shone, long dresses swirled, and in the reflected light I could see many of the ladies wore deep décolleté despite the sharp desert breeze.

They alighted from buses, which had shuttled them from the tents to the steps of the ruins. Empress Farah, with the Ethiopian emperor Haile Selassie on her arm, led the procession up the grand staircase to the seats on a special platform below us. Haile Selassie was the senior head of state, having held on to his throne longer than any of the other monarchs. As such he enjoyed the place of honor on Farah's arm, despite the fact that his rule had been one of the bloodiest and most corrupt in the annals of history. (He was deposed just a few years later.) They made a sorry couple, for he was short and slow, and weighed down by his military overcoat and blazon of decorations, had great difficulty climbing the succession of high stone steps. The empress, embarrassed, almost had to drag him up the last few. Behind them kings, queens, and presidents bunched up in a crowd, unable to see what was happening up ahead.

The show, projected against the evening twilight over the great stone ruins, animated the history of the Medes and Achaemenids, whose great kings had built the ancient Persian Empire and the palace of Persepolis.

Everything humanly possible had been done to make it a stunning program—save one. A cold wind had begun to blow off the desert, and everyone began to feel the chill. I could see the ladies below me on the platform,
their shoulders bared to the breeze, begin to shiver. Yet no one had thought
to provide blankets. There, at the foot of the ruins of Persepolis, surrounded by flat desert plains, the city of Shiraz thirty miles away, blankets
could not be gotten, even if it had been at the request of Darius himself.
Although the audience was composed of presidents and kings, there was
nothing anyone could do but let them shiver.

The next day was the highlight of the celebration: a spectacle of military pageantry stretching across twenty-five hundred years. A regiment
from every dynasty in Persia's past was represented, as well as tribal warriors and royal guards. Five hundred to a thousand men marched by at a
time, brightly dressed in traditional garb, beards flowing and swords
glancing in the sun. Meticulous care had been taken to re-create all the cos-
tumes and armaments directly from the paintings and miniatures left by
our ancestors. The men had grown their beards for more than a year, and
the beards were now as thick and long as if they'd always worn them. Their
coats and shirts, meanwhile, had been designed and sewn in Paris.

The procession took place along a fairway parallel to the great wall of
Persepolis. As a Persian dignitary I sat in the viewing stands facing the
wall, while the royal entourage sat opposite looking out over the plains. By
four o'clock the sun had become so hot that umbrellas brought especially
for the purpose were passed out to shade us. The arc of the sun continued
to turn, however, and by six o'clock its rays were full in the face of the royal
guests. Court adjutants were sent to reclaim the umbrellas, but they were
relinquished only grudgingly, and usually only after threats and loud exhortations, since many of the spectators had hoped to hold on to them as
souvenirs. The sun had dropped behind us, however, and we were able to
see the parade far better than those for whom it had been staged. Even with
umbrellas the illustrious guests were blinded by the slanting rays of the
Mede's great god Ahuramazda until it finally set behind the horizon a good
hour later.

The festivities in Persepolis were complemented by celebrations in all
the major cities throughout the land. Pictures of past shahs were attached
to streetlamps along the main avenues and parks. For a while the Qajar
shahs were singular in their absence. Then, in the last couple of days Alam
gave the order to hang pictures of the dynasty's founder, Agha Mohammad
Khan, inadvertently bringing him much more attention than if he'd been
included in the first place.

To commemorate the occasion the Shah built a huge arched monument called the Shayad Memorial, just outside Tehran's city limits. It was glazed in blue tile, modern in design yet reminiscent of ancient forms. The Shah also decided to change the calendar, backdating it twenty-five hundred years.

Changing the calendar was disastrous. Already it was confusing enough to be using the Islamic calendar and do business with the West. Now, beginning with 1971, all our documents, newspapers, calendars, and books would be dated beginning 2530.* This meant that three years hence the dating on our papers would be 1974, 1352 (the Islamic date), or 2533, depending on which calendar we used. In a country already dogged by disorganization and inefficiency, this made for complete mayhem. The move also incensed the clergy, who considered it not only a heinous insult to Islam but also one more indication that the Shah was neglecting his constitutional obligations to uphold the Shii faith. How much better would it have been if he had done what Atatürk did in Turkey: adopt the Western calendar and Western alphabet for the sake of true reform. The clergy would have bitten their lips—but at least they would have understood and respected the motivation.

Did the festivities at Persepolis live up to the Shah's expectations? Gathering together such a group of luminaries would have been a logistical nightmare anywhere in the world, and the fact that Iran was able to pull it off without hitch was in itself a great success. If the Shah's purpose had been to create a sense of comradery among the world's immortals, however, he failed. Almost before it was over the gathering became the source of ridicule and peevish complaint, an excuse for the world press to blame everyone who had attended for living lives of ostentation and extravagance. The European monarchs, having spent centuries as wealthy, autocratic despots, had since World War II been trying to convey an image of modesty and of doing a job much like those of their subjects. They had also been downplaying the extent of their inherited fortunes. The feasts of Persepolis jeopardized this effort. Once again their luxurious lifestyles were brought under scrutiny, and the public was reminded of the millions they had stashed away.

If the Shah had hoped that by hosting such a party he could induct himself into the inner circle of old-time sovereigns, the event was again a failure. Rather than breaking the bonds of conceit, it only accentuated them. The contrast among leaders was too great. Rubbing shoulders in a social context with Communist presidents and rude-mannered dictators such as

---

*The actual twenty-five-hundred-year anniversary had occurred thirty years before the celebration.

President Marcos only denigrated the status the European royals accorded themselves. Having to pander to Haile Selassie, a black African and a murderer, was unbearable.

And so the European royals found fault with everything, and the press had a heyday. To be fair had the food not come from Maxim's, it would have been called inedible. Instead it was denounced as too expensive. There was one thing, however, that was roundly said to have been unimpeachable, and that was the caviar.

A TALE OF LOSS

The cracks that would eventually destroy the Iran we knew had already begun to appear. But they were hairline thin and seemed more like the craze in the enameled surfaces of our blue porcelain pots than fissures that would rend the structure asunder. The country still had one major success ahead of it, the windfall from the Arab oil embargo in 1973 and the subsequent catapult in prices to $12 a barrel. This was almost $10 more than we were receiving in 1971 and would literally inundate Iran with billions of dollars in cold, hard cash.

These were good times, when everyone made money and lived well. As a family we had our moments of pride. We were extremely pleased when my brother Hafez donated the library in our family name to the University of Tehran. A few years earlier my brother Ghaffar, a doctor of economics, won the Alfred Noble Prize (named after the American civil engineer who built the Panama Canal). Khodadad, as managing director of the Plan Organization, was developing Iran's important five-year plan—the blueprint of development for the whole country.

But our family also suffered a series of tragedies at this time. Death, that cruel snuffing out of young, jubilant life, suddenly became a common visitor. The tragedies were so frequent and unexpected that they came to seem like a curse. Yet never did the appearance of death prepare us for the shock and pain of each subsequent encounter.

The first loss was Mehri's son Fereydoun, a fresh, gregarious boy who had just finished his studies in London. He was to leave two days later for university in the United States. I happened to be passing through London just then and invited him to lunch at the Dorchester Hotel. "Can I bring some of my friends?" he asked. I readily agreed, bemused that from one generation to the next we all took advantage of our uncles whenever we could. He invited twelve of his friends, and I rented a special room for the occasion. The next day he was killed in a car accident.

A few years later, in the summer of 1969, another disaster hit. My sister Maryam's daughter Afsaneh and her husband, Mansur Gidfar, were vacationing on the Caspian Sea, where we had a large family enclave of cabins on the beach. Ali was a strong swimmer, and though a warning had been issued about the vicious undercurrent, he decided to go out anyway. He could not have been in more than four feet of water when a riptide wrapped itself around his legs and swept him out to sea.

My brother Tariverdi was next. A sociable, easygoing regular at court, he had become a close friend of Princess Ashraf's. He was hunting in the desert town of Shahrud. Seeing a couple of poachers on the property, he walked quietly up to them and asked them to give themselves up. One of them lifted his gun threateningly, but Tari did not stop walking forward. The man fired, shooting Tari dead at point-blank range.

The last, and thank God it was the last, was my youngest brother, Ali. How is it possible to suffer loss so much? Already Ali's first wife, a Greek beauty named Julie, had been shot in Athens by a jilted lover. Now, remarried and with two boys the same age as mine, Ali was killed in an avalanche while skiing in Shemshak, a ski resort just an hour from Tehran.

Each time we received words of condolence from the Shah, which was a great consolation. Yet, each time we were devastated. We went through the motions of our daily routines, numbed, waiting in horror for the next tragedy to come. Pain is like a disease, it wracks the body with fevers and shivers, it robs one's appetite and reduces one's concentration, and it leaves one frail in both body and spirit. For my mother losing her youngest son was a cataclysm from which she never fully recovered, and it surely contributed to her passing the following year. Mehri at last wrote a book about the loss of her Fereydoun, a sad, moving testament that only partially helped diffuse her pain.

As a family only gradually did we emerge from the cloud and realize that the fickle hand of disaster had at last moved on. It left us scarred and torn, but miraculously life continued.

THE TALE OF AN APPOINTMENT

It was 1972, and I had been at NIOC for more than fifteen years. Looking back, I was proud of the work I had done. The company had changed significantly while I'd been there: The Tehran Refinery had been built and a network of pipelines had been laid across the country. Looking into the future, however, I was less sure of my path. Under Eqbal the company had mutated into a different animal. I was tired of all the interference that had become a constant part of the job. I had reached a point where I needed a change—a position removed from the constant tensions of dealing with NIOC's five-hundred-strong staff and thousands of laborers. I wanted a job with autonomy, something in which I'd be able to operate outside Eqbal's involute system.

Some years before, in the late sixties, the Venezuelan government had sent an oil lawyer, Dr. José Navarete, to serve as its ambassador in Iran. Iran never sent a matching mission to Venezuela, even though we had posts in Brazil and Argentina. This policy contrasted with that of the Turks and Egyptians, who, though ill able to afford the cost of formal representation, had embassies in every country of South America. It reflected Iran's lack of awareness of the benefits of international contact when common interests such as oil linked two countries together.

Underlying Iran's hesitation was the commonly held view that the diplomatic corps was a pack of upstarts—friends of the court or the cabinet who would gallivant abroad for four years. Even I suffered from this opinion—despite the good example set by my brother-in-law Mohsen Khan. The government set a low priority in funding embassies and felt little incentive to start new ones.

Not surprisingly, therefore, when Ambassador Navarete pointed out during one of the Salaams that he had been in Tehran for some time and that his country still hoped Iran would send an ambassador to Caracas, the Shah demurred, saying he did not know whom to send. Navarete, who had already spoken with me, answered with a certain degree of presumption. "If I may, Your Majesty, let me suggest you send Farmanfarmaian."

At the time of the Salaam I was in London with Eqbal for a meeting of the Consortium. The Shah, taken with Navarete's suggestion, fired off a telegram informing us both of my nomination to the post. The news exhilarated me, but I was hesitant. Ardeshir Zahedi, our ambassador in London, was about to be named minister of foreign affairs. We were not friends, and I knew he would avoid signing my appointment as long as he held the post.

Throughout the years my career had been touched by Venezuela, and I felt deeply that by starting an embassy there I could serve my own country as well as the oil community at large. For the moment, however, I had to bide my time. Ardeshir Zahedi was very different from his father, whose friendship I had cherished and who had held a special love for my family. Ardeshir was cocky and regarded everyone else as beneath him. As a young man he had enjoyed a number of significant successes, among them marriage to the Shah's daughter and appointment as ambassador to London. Although the marriage had not lasted, he had become a close friend of the

Shah's. To his credit he had many of his father's best qualities. He was tall and good-looking, spoke easily, and was extremely generous. (Sometimes he was overly extravagant. According to Alam, in 1970 alone Zahedi bought nine hundred Vacheron watches to give away as gifts.)

Zahedi and I were not meant to be friends, however. Both of us were made of the same hard, uncompromising metal. The real falling-out took place in London. As ambassador he traditionally hosted a dinner for the Consortium board during our biannual financial meeting. One night he placed me at a table below my rank. After dinner I left the embassy in a huff. Had I liked Zahedi better I would not have been so bothered, but his negligence concerning other people's position made me very angry—so angry in fact that six months later, when another such dinner was scheduled, I refused to attend.

I knew this was a slap in the face, but I could not help it. I am one to hold grudges, and though Dr. Amini shamed me into learning not to be hotheaded about them, I still to this day do not forgive a slight easily. For the next two years Zahedi invited me to his dinners, and for the next two years I refused to attend, creating a huge rift between us.

And one has to pay for one's sins. I had been rash and had not heeded the advice of the poet Saadi, who wrote, "Before drawing your weapons for battle take care that the pathway to peace has been discreetly cleared." When, two days after my nomination as ambassador to Venezuela, Zahedi was appointed minister of foreign affairs, I knew I would have to wait until the end of his post to see the realization of my dream.

Meanwhile a job had opened up within the larger umbrella of NIOC that was just what I'd been looking for. Eqbal, quite happy to let me go, accepted my resignation from the board. My new job was chairman of SIRIP, an Italian-Iranian joint venture that was the legacy of Enrico Mattei. Years earlier the Italians had discovered oil in the south and now worked two platforms in the Persian Gulf, as well as a number of fields along the coast. Although SIRIP was a multinational venture, 95 percent of the employees were Iranian.

When I took the job, I could not believe how different the Italians were from the British. I would arrive in the fields and be unable to distinguish between the Italians and the Iranians—they looked the same and moved so similarly. The Romans never conquered the East, and as a result the Italians still held us in high esteem. They admired us for having taken their emperor Valerian prisoner in the third century and for holding the line on our empire. Unlike the English, who thought of us as servants, the Italians admired our culture and sophistication and thought of us as equals.

I waited three years for Zahedi to be reassigned. Ironically, when he was relieved of his job, I admired him for the final battle he fought—and lost. Throughout his tenure he never attended a single meeting of the Council of Ministers due to his low regard for Prime Minister Hoveyda. He was not alone in this. Hoveyda was badly handicapped during his premiership by people such as Zahedi who established their own fiefdoms and openly refused to cooperate with him. It was during a trip to India that the final break occurred. Zahedi and Hoveyda managed to get into a horrendous quarrel and Zahedi insulted the prime minister, using a slew of unprintable words. The Shah, forced to take action, relieved him of his ministerial post and appointed him ambassador to the United States.

I had been assigned at the time as acting chairman of an NIOC investment corporation in the south that was operating under the auspices of the Ministry of Finance. Often I would find myself on the same plane going back and forth from Abadan as my friend the minister of finance, Jamshid Amouzegar. It was on one such flight that I mentioned to him the proposed opening of an embassy in Venezuela. It was really thanks to him that my appointment became a reality. He advised me to refrain from saying anything more until he could set aside the requisite funds in the budget. Further, he said, he would speak with the new minister of foreign affairs, Dr. Abbas Ali Khalatbari, and persuade him that Iran's leading role in OPEC made it imperative to have an ambassador qualified in oil affairs in Venezuela.

I was in Italy when the cable arrived informing me of my official nomination as ambassador to Venezuela.* At last, my dream had come true.

Back in Iran, Khalatbari, whom I'd known for a number of years, accompanied me to see the Shah for his blessing. The royal offices were on the second floor of one of the old Qajar palaces downtown that I had known since childhood. I contemplated the arch windows as we waited in the vestibule. My new uniform was already at home, the official plumed hat and gold-embroidered jacket exactly like the one my beloved nephew Mozaffar Firouz had worn when he'd been banished from the country and sent to Moscow as ambassador. This was only the second time that a member of the family had become an ambassador, and thankfully I was going under much more auspicious circumstances.

After a very long wait, which the minister assured me was not unusual when coming to see the Shah, we were finally ushered in. It was eleven o'clock. Khalatbari bowed and said, "Your Majesty, allow me to introduce our new ambassador to Venezuela." The Shah smiled and came over and shook my hand. I brushed his fingers with my lips in homage.

---

*Ambassadors had a higher rank than ministers, since an ambassador was appointed by the Shah as his representative, while a minister was appointed by the prime minister.

The Shah's desk was at the far end of the room near the window. Old Persian arms, helmets, swords, and shields from the time of Nader Shah in the late seventeenth and early eighteenth centuries, hung on the walls. As was his wont when receiving Persian dignitaries, the Shah stayed on his feet throughout our audience, precluding any sense of ease in the discussion. His voice remained low, almost monotonous. He made no personal gesture and gave no indication that I had been in the inner circle of his social acquaintances at various times in our lives.

His Majesty briefly expressed satisfaction with my family's services to the country. He then said, "Look here, you'd better take this job seriously. There are ambassadors who don't promote Iran with the money we pay them and instead put it in their pockets. Others only look at their posting as a holiday and don't do any work."

I stole a glance at Khalatbari. It was very discourteous, I thought, for the Shah to levy such accusations in his presence without following them up with any real course for change. Khalatbari, however, was an extremely mild and dutiful man and showed no expression on his face. The Shah continued. "You are not of the ministry and so will do a good job I am sure. We rely on the cooperation of Venezuela—as a friend, not a rival—of Persia." He again shook my hand and wished me success. He then went back to his desk, signaling that the meeting was over.

The whole interview lasted just ten minutes. There was no discussion of goals or policy, no request to watch for certain developments, no indication of what my priorities should be. I walked out happy it was over and vowed to myself to serve the Shah and my country as best I could.

The next week I spent at the Ministry of Foreign Affairs learning how to send encrypted telegrams, while trying to absorb as much about the place as I could. I was amazed at how chaotic it was. Used to the rigid organization of NIOC, I imagined the ministry would be the same, with the embassies classed into tiers: first the big ones (London, Washington, Paris, Moscow, and Istanbul); then at mid-level Brussels, Rome, Baghdad, and, as an OPEC partner, Caracas. But there was no such organization.

A GOOD OMEN

It was October, and the weather in Tehran was magnificent—sunny and cool. I decided to depart right after the Shah's birthday on the 26th so that I would not arrive in Caracas—without a residence, driver, or staff—and have to throw a party right off.

Just before the packers came, a carpet dealer visited the house. It was a serendipitous visit. As he unfolded his wares I saw him pull out an unusual prayer rug. Instead of flowers and medallions, it bore a picture of a king from one of the bas-reliefs of Persepolis. Indicating no special curiosity, I glanced at the rug until I found what I was looking for: the name of Farman Farma written in the top left-hand corner.

I felt a sense of vindication. I remembered these rugs as a child, stacked on the terrace of Farman Farma's palace. He had had a dozen of them made in Kerman, all with different bas-relief pictures. He used to give them away as gifts. In 1905 they had been featured in an exhibition in Paris. Since then most had disappeared. Mohammadvali Mirza had one; there was another in the Tehran Museum and one in the British Museum. Now, here was a fourth.

I smiled as I looked at it. My father had had them made to give to his European friends, not realizing that they'd much rather have had a traditional carpet than one with a postcard picture on it. Now, ironically, his children were anxious to buy them. The carpet in front of me was a particularly nice one. A couple of the others I'd seen had Farman Farma's name woven into them in mirror writing, the poor illiterate weaver, unable to read the writing on the slip of paper he'd been given to copy, having woven it in backward.

I asked the dealer the price. Not knowing how valuable the carpet was to me, he asked for 80,000 toman (about $12,000) in cash. It was a price I was willing to pay, but I didn't have the money on hand. Then I thought of my neighbor and friend Ali Moalizadeh, who always kept cash at home and had offered to make it available if I ever needed it. I'd always poked fun at him about it, but now I called him up and asked him to bring some over. He arrived within minutes with a suitcase filled with bills—at least $50,000 worth—and was genuinely disappointed that I needed so little.

As I looked at the carpet later that evening, I thought it was a good omen. It was as though my father knew I was setting off on a new adventure and was sending me on my way with his blessing.

CHAPTER
XVI

IN THE KING'S SERVICE

No one in this world has a servant such as Hafez
Because no one in this world has a king such as you.
—HAFEZ

Caracas 1973

I arrived in Caracas in November 1972, a month before Petronella and the children. Four weeks later a first secretary from the ministry, Abbas Rostamizadeh, was sent over. He spoke no English, and neither of us spoke Spanish. I insisted he go every day to the American Venezuelan Institute, and that if in six months he hadn't learned English I would throw him out—the oil business needed English. I too attended daily classes in an effort to learn Spanish, for in a country like Venezuela it was imperative for an ambassador to speak the language. I hoped my dedication would serve as an example to Rostamizadeh. In fact he learned good English and later Spanish, which he came to speak better than I did.

A SAVAK man also was sent over. He spoke only Farsi and didn't even know how to hold a spoon. His education was poor, and he lacked any knowledge of the workings of the ministry. Why did they send such a man? I wondered. To spy on me—or on Venezuela? I hardly saw him, but he apparently learned something, for today he has a relatively high post in the government (or perhaps they just have a greater tolerance for fools).

Two weeks after my arrival I presented President Rafael Caldera with my credentials at Miraflores Palace. Because Venezuela is a republic, the dress code called simply for a dark suit, which meant I never did wear my wonderful uniform.

I liked Caldera immediately, and invited him to visit Tehran. Unfortunately he could not accept, since he was close to the end of his term.

When the ceremony was over the band played the Iranian national anthem. I slipped the bandleader a big tip, knowing he'd had to practice the anthem many times to play it this once—however badly—for the ceremony.

A few months later the Caldera government finished its term and was replaced by Carlos Andrés Pérez's Acción Democrática party, which won the election by a landslide. Pérez was a staunch supporter of OPEC, and with the help of his minister of oil, Dr. Valentin Hernandez Acosta, he had a strong influence on the organization, helping to hold it together even when Venezuela's production was reduced in favor of a higher quota for the Persian Gulf.

THE TALE OF THE ARAB EMBARGO

The world oil situation took a drastic turn just as I arrived in Caracas. A shortage of oil resulting from increased demand doubled the price by the summer of 1973. Both Iran and Saudi Arabia took advantage of the situation by at last taking control of their output, which significantly reduced the power of the Consortium and Aramco, respectively. Meanwhile Libya's Qaddafi appropriated the contracts and concessionary rights of all the companies operating in his country. This meant that the price of oil would now be influenced as much by supply (now wholly in the hands of the producing countries) as by the market.

This realignment was the culmination of years of conflict. In the beginning the oil companies operated as quasi-governmental offshoots of their own countries, while disassociating themselves from the governments with whom they had contracts. As a result, the host governments were forced to approach the European and American governments directly whenever they wished to establish a more equitable division of income and resource control. But the consumer countries were less interested in our requirements than in guaranteeing a supply of cheap oil to fuel their own economies. Already, by early 1973 the supply of oil in the United States had become so tight that the term *energy crisis* was beginning to slip into the national lexicon. It was ironic, therefore, that after years of jockeying the producing countries asserted sovereignty over their oil just as the West began to feel the first stifling pinch of an energy shortage.

With the economic balance of power shifted, the political balance shifted too. Since the companies could no longer act as intermediaries or provide a buffer between the producing countries and the consumer countries, conflict between the two increased. The companies now had to carry out the policies of the producing countries, even if that meant hurting their own home governments (as in the case of an embargo). This meant that the governments of consuming countries now had no choice but to become actively involved in the process of ensuring sufficient supplies at affordable prices—a process that involved political alliances with the producing governments. The importance of oil to the world economy thus resulted in an about-face: Having begun as a completely commercial enterprise, oil became, first in the producing countries and then in the consuming countries a government enterprise through political necessity.

In the first test of this new balance of power Saudi Arabia's King Faisal summoned the directors of Aramco in May of 1973 and told them that the company's assets and U.S. interests would be severely imperiled if Washington did not tone down its support for Israel.

On October 6 Egypt and Syria launched military operations against Israel. It was the beginning of the October War. By chance, on the same day, an OPEC meeting convened in Vienna. Scuttling the two-year-old Tehran and Tripoli agreements, now outdated by price jumps on the open market, Saudi Arabia's Yamani, Iran's Amouzegar, and the rest of the delegates demanded that the companies significantly revise the posted price so that the windfall in profits could be shared by both sides. The companies refused. Their intransigence led to the use of a new weapon in the October War: the oil embargo.

The embargo was carefully conceived by the Arab producers. It was to begin with a 5 percent decrease in production, followed by a rolling cutback of 5 percent each month until the Israeli army evacuated the Sinai Peninsula and the Golan Heights, and Palestine was given its independence. In fact, after hearing that the United States was resupplying Israel with arms and contributing to an escalation in the war, Saudi Arabia decided to act immediately and reduced its oil production by 10 percent right away. Export was completely cut to the United States and the Netherlands, both openly involved in aiding Israel. Later South Africa and Portugal were added to the list.

The Iranians were not party to the embargo. When the cutbacks began, more than 5 million barrels of oil a day dropped out of the market. Iran immediately raised its output to help make up for the shortfall. By breaking ranks with its Arab neighbors, the Shah went out on a limb for the sake of his alliance with the United States. It was a gesture for which Washington never gave him credit.

The embargo caused panic in the United States, Japan, and Europe, where long lines snaked out of every gas station and signs saying SORRY, NO GAS hung ominously from the pumps. The surplus that the United States had always used to offset shortages in the past (not only domestically but in Europe as well) had dried up, causing not only a run on whatever gasoline was available but also a jump in prices. The Watergate scandal, which was just beginning to heat up, exacerbated the situation by contributing to the public's general distrust of government and big business.

The October War wound down three weeks after it started, but the embargo continued on, its goal—to recover the Israeli-occupied territories—having still not been achieved. In December 1973, a little over a month after I arrived in Caracas, price was again discussed at an OPEC meeting in Tehran. The question this time: whether to milk the market for all it was worth during the crisis or establish a price that would hold steady. The per-barrel price since October had been $5.12 (though when Tehran auctioned some of its oil on the open market, bids went as high as $17). The Shah suggested almost doubling the official price to $11.65. To the ministers gathered at the meeting (including all the Arabs, who were there despite the difference of opinion on the embargo) it seemed a fair compromise. The suggestion carried. Washington never forgot that the Shah spearheaded the move, and it never forgave him for it.

By March 1974 the embargo had petered out. Europe and Japan made policy statements supporting the Arab position on the occupied territories and Palestine so that their oil deliveries would resume. The United States eventually followed suit, pledging to bring the Palestinian issue before the UN Security Council. The crisis was over, though the effects were everywhere apparent. One result was that OPEC had gained the reputation of being a cartel so powerful that it could control the industrial world's economies and so rich that it could influence its banking system. Reviled for causing the ensuing 1974 recession (which in fact resulted primarily from the United States' scuttling of the Bretton Woods agreement in 1971 and allowing the dollar to float rather than stay pegged to gold), OPEC became the scapegoat for all the West's financial complaints.

In June I was notified that I should attend the fortieth OPEC meeting in Quito, Ecuador. I had recently been accredited to Ecuador and Trinidad, since neither had Iranian embassies and both had oil. My first secretary, Abbas Rostamizadeh, accompanied me, bringing along the embassy's encoding machine, which we zippered into a bag and then handcuffed to his wrist.

The discussion at the conference was bitter. The topic was the high rate of inflation in the West and how it was eroding our income. But when all the other ministers voted to raise the royalty, Yamani threatened to withdraw from OPEC, and then flew off in his four-engine Aramco jet, snubbing the Ecuadorian oil minister, who was hosting a dinner that night.

Upon my return from Quito the Venezuelan president, Carlos Andrés Pérez, summoned me to his office. He was concerned about OPEC's future. The Shah too was worried and had sent instructions not to push for the price increase if Saudi Arabia really meant to walk out. "The survival of OPEC is worth much more than a few cents—or even dollars—on the price of a barrel," said Pérez. "Please inform the Shah that I am going to search for a compromise. OPEC is our only forum for dialogue. We must reinforce its strength at any price."

Pérez's arguments saved the day, but his stand was a difficult one, since none of us wanted to back down from the new price hikes. Oil was like the goose that lays the golden egg, delivering more money into our coffers than we'd ever imagined. In fact our governments' incomes in royalties and taxes on each barrel of oil had risen from 90 cents in 1970 to $7 by 1974. For the Middle East exporters as a group this translated into a jump in net profits from $4 billion to $60 billion over four years.

THE GREAT CIVILIZATION

Our sudden financial power was cause for great concern in the West. Now that we were feeling wealthy, would we turn off the oil spigot to conserve our resources? Would we use our new power for political ends? Would we build up munitions and armaments that might threaten global security?

To counteract OPEC's power the West created the International Energy Agency in 1974. Huge storage tanks were built on the Caribbean island of Bonaire, and various industrial nations began to stockpile oil to avoid future shortages or sudden price increases. With Japan leading the way the consumer nations also began a program of energy conservation.

The influx of vast sums of oil money into our treasuries presented an equally knotty problem for us. How should we spend our riches? How could we invest in real development that would ensure prosperity and self-sufficiency by the time our oil reserves ran out? Our needs were enormous, and yet the speed with which our fortunes had turned left us little time to consider mature ways to apply our sudden wealth.

Not surprisingly the whole thing went to our heads. In Iran we began to think that we deserved this windfall, that we were a chosen people who could re-create society from scratch and explode upon the twentieth century full-blown and perfect. The Shah began to speak of the "Great Civi-

lization," a state Iran would reach within ten years. A pamphlet published
by the Ministry of Information in 1974 explained exactly what the Great
Civilization was:

> The first thing will be the complete absence of illiterate people in the
> whole territory. Every Iranian will be able to write his or her letter, or
> read the papers or write his own report.
>
> In addition, every citizen will own his own house or apartment. Irani-
> ans love to own their own house, which symbolizes for them the positive
> idea of a shelter, a refuge, and also the idea of a family and of a haven, so
> necessary for the keepsake of dear memories.
>
> Following the Shahanshah's recommendations, all the *kevirs* or deserts
> will be transformed into woods and put to exploitation by the inhabi-
> tants.
>
> Social justice will be renamed "Pahlavi Justice" and this title will des-
> ignate whatever is just, righteous, inspired, human and beautiful, either
> in Iran or throughout the world. Theft, corruption, lies, deception and
> ugliness will vanish.
>
> Workers syndicates will grow to the extent of replacing ancient cor-
> porations and perfect concord will be established between employers and
> employees.
>
> The production of artificial rain for dry farming will make the wait-
> ing for seasonal rains superfluous.
>
> Longevity will be the treasured possession of every Iranian, disease
> will have completely disappeared and men and women will live more
> than a hundred years.[1]

This of course was utopia. To achieve even a fraction of this imaginary
state, however, necessitated a lot more than money. It required time, expertise, infrastructure, and management—none of which were available.
As a result the problems and challenges encountered by Iran and most of
the other OPEC nations attempting to overhaul their societies were unprecedented and overwhelming. Explosive development and unharnessed
spending created a miasmic soup of bottlenecks and delays, corruption,
waste, false starts, and unproductive ostentation. Internal inflation skyrocketed. Increased pollution, congestion, and violence were justified as
necessary side effects of progress and growth. A shortage of manpower—
reaching almost 600,000 jobs by mid-1975—severely hampered the ful-
fillment of the country's vast economic plans.

For the next three years the oil-exporting countries went on a buying
spree the likes of which the world had never seen. This translated into long

lines of ships at sea unable to unload the goods on their decks. Money spent on demurrage—and storage and all that had rotted after it had sat around for several months—was senselessly thrown away. While other countries thrived on our commerce, our people had nothing more to show for it than useless trinkets that did little to improve their standard of living.

Ports, warehouses, roads, and railways became overcrowded, overloaded, and overworked. What was unloaded was often just piled on the quay and left to the elements or the swift hands of vandals. Over time it became impossible to find anything in those piles, and with each passing day the disorganization became more acute. The infrastructure was simply not there to distribute the massive amounts of materials that entrepreneurs and bureaucrats in Tehran, with their open checkbooks and open mandates, were ordering into the country. They thought that materials could be purchased, manpower made available, and administration bought without appreciating the importance of organization. They did not realize that bricks, cement, and steel piled up on a building site do not correspond to a house or a factory.

Everyone talked about Japan, but no one had studied how the successes there had been achieved. Besides, our society was at heart still tribal, fragmented, and disjointed, like an orchestra in which everyone sounded a different tune. What we lacked was leadership—and training—to turn the cacophony into music.

The money that poured into Iran from 1973 to 1977 totally changed the country, distorting the institutions, the social structure, the economy, and the outlook of the people to such a degree that it brought about a complete rupture with the past. In 1970 rural life was still largely untouched, and life in the provincial cities of Isfahan, Mashhad, and Shiraz was much as it had been a century before. In ten years all that changed. With the deluge of money, the birthrate soared, villages drifted family by family into the cities—or were subsumed by them—and the rapidly growing cities soon outstripped their ability to provide water, electricity, or sewerage, let alone schools, parks, or training facilities. The growth was neither planned nor centrally coordinated and took place in an atmosphere increasingly marked by insecurity and distrust.

In the midst of plenty Iran, much like Venezuela on the other side of the world, began to suffer from shortages caused by faulty government planning. Food was perhaps the most salient shortage. A series of dams were built in various parts of the country to improve irrigation and promote large-scale mechanized farming. Deeming the peasants unfit to handle the huge machinery or manage the large farms that could be irrigated with the newly available water, the government appropriated the land—the very land that had been given to the peasants ten years before in the White Revolution. Seeing no place for themselves in the new agribusiness, the peasants drifted toward the cities in search of work.

The Shah, who was no longer in touch with his people, had no clear idea of the ramifications of these decisions. "Produce one hundred thousand tons of sugar," he said, and imagined that it would be done. But the government was little better than the peasants at farming and fell far short of its projections. With consumption growing—the average per capita consumption of red meat jumped from sixteen pounds a year in 1960 to forty-eight pounds in 1975 (and this in a country where meat used to be regarded as a luxury!)—the government was forced to import increasingly large amounts of wheat, barley, soybeans, meat, and rice, to the tune of $3 billion a year. The situation was not unique to Iran. This was also happening in Saudi Arabia, Venezuela, Nigeria, Kuwait, and the other Persian Gulf states.

And yet as Simón Bolívar said in the 1800s in reference to South America's development in relation to Europe, "Don't try to have us do well in twenty years what you did badly in two thousand." The Shah cannot be blamed entirely for what he did or failed to do. Even developed countries, with all the facilities at their disposal, have many times thrown themselves over white elephants, constructing monstrosities such as Chernobyl and Three Mile Island. In Iran the regime did its best to solve the bottlenecks. Truck drivers, doctors, and construction crews were brought in from India, South Korea, and the Philippines. Track lines were laid to increase transport facilities from the ports to the cities. More dams were built to bring water to the cities. And as for agribusiness, it was not a homegrown idea. It was funded and researched by the World Bank, which after seeing it fail in a number of underdeveloped countries realized that depopulating the countryside was not a tolerable side effect. By then of course, in Iran and Venezuela, it was too late.

TALES FROM PERU

About the same time I was accredited as ambassador to Trinidad and Ecuador, my government took a very friendly step toward Peru. Peru had sent a mission to Iran requesting a loan and asking that diplomatic relations be established between the two countries. It also formally requested admission to OPEC, having recently discovered a small amount of oil on its land.

The Iranian government responded by lending Peru $100 million at low interest and accrediting me as ambassador. This fit well within the Shah's larger international aims. In tandem with his aspirations for the Great Civilization, he set his sights on turning Iran into the fifth power in the world. His goal: to develop an empire of lost countries. As such Iran would become the primary protective force in its region (the Persian Gulf and Indian Ocean) as well as a benefactor to needy developing countries. He sent troops to Yemen (at the request of its leader) and financed $10 million in development in Africa—hoping to launch a federation that would counterbalance the Arabs and South Americans. Iranians didn't even know where the Horn of Africa was, but he didn't care. His ambitions were fueled not by the needs of his countrymen but by his own vision of grandeur and the flattery of men such as Hoveyda and Alam, who would say to him, "Ah, how brilliant. We could never have thought of that."*

To carry out my appointment to Peru I arranged several times to go to Lima to present my diplomatic credentials. But each time some sort of political disturbance broke out, and I was never able to deliver them. Peru had a military government, and all the ministers were generals. On one occasion when I went to present my credentials I met with the minister of education, of course another general. Over lunch the minister asked whether in Tehran we'd had a lot of upheaval at the university.

"Yes," I answered, "and it is endless."

"We do too," he said. "Our students don't study. They pass their time demonstrating and striking, and they end up costing the government heavily since they have to return year after year to complete their studies. Unlike in the United States our students don't stop demonstrating."

I knew exactly what he meant. In countries such as ours the universities became bastions of upheaval. There was no tradition of campus-based learning as there was in the United States or Europe, no historical respect for the degrees being offered or the reputation of the universities. The concept of higher education was imported from abroad, and as a result our universities were still young and considered second-rate. The students who went did not have a long family tradition of education or even the conviction that a university degree could better their lot. Most were there because the government funded graduates from the teeming urban schools.

The government had allocated vast sums to establish the system of higher education—something the Shah rightly took very seriously—but

---

*Iran had in fact stepped beyond these bounds to grant a loan of $500 million to France—eliciting much grumbling in Iran. Budgets were cut across the board to finance the loan, while people complained that France, a rich country, would never have done us a similar favor if we'd cried poverty.

like all sectors in Iran the universities suffered from poor staffing and arbitrary state interference. There were not enough teachers or administrators, and all had to be educated or imported from abroad. There was also no competition between schools to keep up the standards. In the United States private colleges played a significant role in maintaining the quality of education. In third-world countries private colleges were even more embryonic and less well regarded than state schools. Taking advantage of the fact that the universities were one of the few places in which frustration could be organized and mobilized, the students turned them into hotbeds of political dissension. Boycotting class was a perfect way to confront the system and make the government pay.

In Iran we considered much of the unrest at the universities to be sponsored by the Communists, and I mentioned this to the minister. He shook his head, saying, "We have made inquiries and have found that certain embassies are financing these uprisings. But we have discovered that it is not the Soviet bloc but European embassies, which suggests the grave implication that the West is hampering the development of South America—and perhaps your country too."

The minister explained that he hoped to call a conference to discuss the difficulties the third world was having with its students and wondered whether we would be interested in attending. I told him I thought it was a good idea. "I have to report our discussion to my government," I added. But I cannot imagine that we would not welcome such a plan."

To my chagrin the response to my report was not what I'd anticipated. "We have no disturbances at the universities in Iran," it said, and therefore no reason to attend such a conference. I smiled sadly at the government's blindness. Prevented from taking the subject any further, I dropped a note to the Peruvian minister wishing him well.

I returned to Peru again in August 1975, this time with Dr Amouzegar, who was now minister of interior, though he was still our delegate to OPEC. He came first to Venezuela to receive the Order of the Liberator from President Carlos Andrés Pérez; then we went together to Lima, where he was decorated with the Order of the Sun.

Amouzegar arrived in Caracas on August 27. The next day Pérez invited us to lunch at La Casona, the presidential residence. It was a very private affair. Over soup the president looked quizzically at Amouzegar and said, "Did you see the speech the Peruvian president gave at the Conference of Nonaligned Countries yesterday in Lima?" And he pulled a newspaper cutting from his pocket.

"Since you are going to Peru, maybe you can talk to the president about it. He attacks OPEC and the investments the member countries are making with their surplus money—such as Iran's recent purchase of twenty-five percent of Krupp, and calls for a reorientation of this policy. He accuses us of behaving like the nations that until recently kept us subjugated and demands we invest in the underdeveloped world instead."

Pérez looked up from the clipping. "OPEC is contributing a great deal to helping the third world," he said. "Look at Iran, which has lent Peru $100 million at low interest. Peru really has no grounds to be raising such a dust.

"I have instructed my minister, Pérez Guerréro, an observer at the conference, to cut short his stay. Perhaps when you go you will consider telling the president that OPEC cannot countenance such attacks."

In the car afterward Amouzegar wondered out loud whether he should go to Peru at all. "Jamshid," I counseled, "don't assign too much importance to that speech. Such statements don't mean much in these countries. Better to go and discuss it with them directly and encourage them to tone down their rhetoric."

He agreed, and that afternoon we caught the plane to Lima. Amouzegar instructed me to draw the Peruvian oil minister aside at the airport and tell him the great concern the Iranian and Venezuelan governments felt about the president's speech. He even suggested I mention that he had hesitated to come to Lima under such circumstances.

The Peruvian oil minister, General Fernando Maldonado, had become a good friend of mine. He was energetic and highly patriotic, and he had excellent ideas. When he heard what I had to say he became concerned and said he would do his best to rectify the situation. It was, he said, a point of personal importance to satisfy the members of OPEC, since he dearly wanted Peru to join the organization.

Lima, unlike Caracas, does not enjoy a beautiful climate. For six months the sky is covered in a dense, gray fog. The rest of the year it is clear and very warm. But the city is grand, with wide avenues and large, stately buildings. The ancient monuments of Peru were all built on a massive scale (like Persepolis), but although we Persians had lost the art of producing such huge structures, the Peruvians had continued the tradition, and nowhere else in South America were such impressive new constructions to be seen. What's more Lima had none of the traffic jams and ramshackle housing that made Caracas so similar to Tehran.

At 10 A.M. the next day, Amouzegar and I departed for our first meeting at the Ministry of Oil. We were halfway there when the car radio announced that a coup had just been staged and the president had been overthrown.

"This is typical," I said to Amouzegar, as the driver made a U-turn and sped back to the hotel—and I told him of so far being unable to present my credentials for just this type of reason.

We stayed at the hotel for the next few hours. At last General Maldonado called and apologized for the morning's delay. He had just been named prime minister and sounded very pleased. The ceremony at the Ministry of Foreign Affairs had been rescheduled, he said, for five o'clock, and afterward we would meet the new president. All was very calm, and not a single shot had been fired.

Amouzegar received his decoration in a small ceremony in which I did the translating. The room was filled with generals. I was happy to see my friends in power, especially General Maldonado and Admiral Parodi, whom I'd met in Caracas and who was now minister of the navy. Every one of them smoked, however, and I coughed throughout the ceremony.

Afterward we went to the president's office, where he welcomed us warmly. General Maldonado got up and said the new president would close the Conference of Nonaligned Countries with a speech that would rectify the ex-president's statements.

That evening over dinner with General Maldonado I said teasingly, "Fernando, don't tell me I gave you the idea of a coup last night."

"By God, no," he answered. "We had made the decision to do it after the Conference of Nonaligned Countries so none of the delegates would be around to face possible danger. But you did precipitate things." He smiled. "We all know, Manucher, that you are always in a hurry and you push everyone around. This time it was for the good of everyone—and the timing was right." The next day, however, the absurd rumor got around that the interior minister of Iran had come to Peru to demand an explanation and had been the reason for the coup!

Back in Caracas Carlos Andrés Pérez couldn't have been more pleased by the outcome of our visit.*

As for my credentials they had to wait. The next time I went to Lima another disturbance—this time by striking government employees—prevented their presentation. At last I gave them to the wife of Admiral Parodi, an influential woman who reminded me of my friend Victoria in

---

*As it turned out the following year OPEC established a loan facility for third-world development programs—partially to offset those countries' burdens in the face of oil's higher price. In September 1975 Iran proposed that the oil producers and the industrial nations jointly establish a special multimillion-dollar fund to help poorer countries. Nothing came of that proposal, and a few months later OPEC went it alone. According to an Organization for Economic Cooperation and Development (OECD) report for that year, OPEC gave 2 percent of its income to aid poor nations, compared to 0.3 percent by countries in the West.

Tehran. She promised to transmit them to the minister of foreign affairs, finally solving, after two years—and at least five different sets of disturbances—my problem.

THE TALE OF THE
SHAH'S VISIT

President Carlos Andrés Pérez and I became good friends, and we often talked about the possibility of his visiting Iran—and of the Shah's coming to Venezuela. Invitations were exchanged, and in the spring of 1975 the Shah decided to visit Caracas as part of a tour that included a stop in Mexico and a few days in Washington, D.C., to see President Gerald Ford.

Never in my life has the planning of three days been so painstaking or the hours to be filled seemed so long. His Majesty's retinue, and that of Queen Farah, was to number more than seventy. Thank goodness the security problems were nothing like what they would be today.

General Amini-Afshar of SAVAK arrived from Tehran to coordinate safety measures. I found him thorough and hardworking, and truly dedicated to protecting the Shah. Sadly, during the revolution he was one of the first people to be executed at the Ayatollah Khomeini's command.

General Amini-Afshar adeptly put my embassy staff at ease by telling them he would take care of all protocol matters and security and that we had only to arrange the schedule and do our best to help the Shah enjoy himself. For security reasons the sovereign was to stay at the State House at the Military Club. Rooms were arranged so that everybody attending His Majesty and Queen Farah, including Petronella and myself, would be close at hand. The rest of the entourage would stay at the Caracas Hilton.

The general arranged a direct phone line to Tehran in the sovereign's personal chambers and set aside a special room nearby for his personal physician, Dr. Ayadi. It was well known that the Shah was a bit of a hypochondriac and would spend the day in bed for even the slightest cold, insisting that his doctor be close by. Dr. Ayadi had a difficult part to play, for he spent most of his time with the Shah and was present at all formal occasions and private parties. During the Shah's visit, although the Iranian minister of foreign affairs accompanied His Majesty and I was there as his ambassador, all Prime Minister Hoveyda's communications were addressed to Dr. Ayadi. I always wondered whether Dr. Ayadi, a staunch Baha'i and for twenty-five years one of the closest confidants of the Shah, knew of the sovereign's cancer before it became public knowledge.

In the weeks leading up to the Shah's arrival, a very Middle Eastern thing began to happen. Iranians began to pour into Caracas from around South America trying to wangle an invitation to the festivities. They rang me or Rostamizadeh, saying they just happened to be in town and could they be put on the guest list.

"No!" I told Rostamizadeh when he came in and said so-and-so had called and could he be invited. "If I see any of these characters at the receptions, I'll have the guards throw them out as gate-crashers. I'll have to blame you for passing them an invitation—and then I'll have to dismiss you, too!"

Rostamizadeh knew I would never do such a thing—he was my right-hand man and fast becoming my friend—but he got the message and made sure to post someone from my staff at the door of every reception to vet all the guests coming through.

As the date approached everything seemed to be moving according to plan. But then, just before the Shah's arrival, an incident occurred that could have blighted the whole occasion. A new American ambassador had been named to Caracas. Harry W. Schloudeman was to arrive the same day as the Shah. He had been in Santiago, Chile, in 1973 during the overthrow of Salvador Allende, and when his appointment was made public in Caracas posters and graffiti appeared on the walls, condemning the ambassador and the United States for engineering the coup. Worse still there were rumors that he would be met by demonstrators at the airport.

I called the Ministry of Foreign Affairs, concerned that we might have to cancel the Shah's visit, since crowds shouting protests against America might be mistakenly assumed to be shouting insults at the Shah. Nelson Hernandez, the chief of protocol, agreed to look into it. He rang me up an hour later. Schloudeman would arrive three days earlier, he said, and all demonstrations would be forbidden.

On the big day, May 5, an advance party of forty or fifty special guards, secret service agents, secretaries, cipher experts, and royal household staff flew in on a separate plane from Tehran. One of the embassy secretaries greeted them, and then all but the guards and secret service agents were transported by bus to the Caracas Hilton.

The Shah's plane arrived about midmorning. The main road to the airport was decked with green, white, and red banners (the colors of Iran's flag) carrying the Shah's portrait and welcoming him in Spanish to Venezuela. It looked very festive and made me exceedingly proud as I drove the forty minutes to meet him.

Protocol required that I go on board to meet the Shah and welcome him to Venezuela on behalf of the embassy and the Iranian community. We then descended from the plane to where President Carlos Andrés Pérez stood on the tarmac. The Shah presented Queen Farah to the president, and then reviewed the honor guard.

A formal lunch followed, after which we went to place flowers at the Bolívar Mausoleum. From there we went to a private meeting between the Shah and Pérez at the president's office at Miraflores.

The Shah had brought a gift of a Persian carpet, and the president gave him a beautiful duplicate set of Bolívar's swords. After the formalities the two leaders began their talk. The problems they faced as leaders of rich, developing nations were very similar. High on the agenda was how to tackle the growing pains both countries were experiencing. Then they spoke of oil and OPEC. The Shah had recently enjoyed a geopolitical victory in an accord signed in Algiers with Saddam Hussein, vice president of Iraq. In exchange for withdrawing all support for the Iraqi Kurds, who were fighting a war against the Iraqi government, Iran was at last granted full rights to half the Shatt-al-Arab. This was one of the most significant achievements of the Shah's reign, removing a thorn that had plagued the country for years. For the first time since the discovery of oil Iraq and Iran were at peace, an important factor in the stability of OPEC.

At the end of their exchange President Pérez observed that the industrialized countries were waging an intense propaganda campaign against OPEC. To counteract it, he said, he had engaged a public relations firm in New York, and he suggested that Iran do the same.

The Shah was intrigued. Just a month previously the much-touted Conference on International Economic Cooperation, hosted by the French, had turned into a confrontation between the industrialized countries and the third world. The third world had hoped to initiate a north-south dialogue to establish minimum prices for their primary raw materials. The industrialized countries, with France at their helm, had paid lip service to such a dialogue going in, but during the conference made it patently clear that what they really wanted was a guarantee of lower oil prices and that they were uninterested in discussing anything else. The OPEC countries had sided with the third world, and the conference had ended in a shambles.

I was glad that the Shah could see the need for the services of a public relations firm. Not only had I had a tiff myself with the French ambassador over the conference in France, but it struck me that Iran's image could do with some shoring up. The benign picture of the Shah held by U.S. presidents Johnson and Nixon had become somewhat tarnished since he had developed his role as OPEC strongman, arguing for higher oil prices while sounding self-righteous (to American ears anyway) about all the pain the producing countries had suffered in the past. The American and European publics now blamed the Shah for the high prices at the gasoline pumps, and all their other mounting energy bills. Secretary of the Treasury William Simon was even huffing that the United States was being "strangled" and had threatened to invade the Middle East if energy grew scarce again.

That evening the president hosted a seated dinner for two hundred. Both leaders gave speeches, Carlos Andrés Pérez in Spanish and the Shah in English. From my seat I watched the Shah while the president spoke and was struck by his exceptional attentiveness, his eyes focused unwaveringly on Pérez throughout, indicating sincere respect and support even though he did not understand a word that was being said.

After dinner the Ministry of Foreign Affairs threw a reception for more than a thousand guests, who packed into the building so tightly that it became a subject of much press criticism the next day. Before descending into the reception area Pérez led His Majesty and Queen Farah to a window overlooking the Place Bolívar, where a few hundred people had gathered to observe the festivities. As she looked out the window Queen Farah asked, "Where are the crowds? We have yet to see a large gathering here. And when we do see people in the street, like the few out there, they're quiet rather than shouting or cheering."

"Your Majesty," I said, knowing she was used to thunderous welcomes whenever she appeared in public, "Venezuelans do not come out in response to official orders. The government has no say or interest in such matters and does not call the public to rallies through the television or radio. Even if it did, the people would probably not listen."

She turned and gazed at me, and I could see she thought it strange that there was no crowd to whom she could wave.

The next day was rainy, and I knew we would have to cancel the outing I'd planned to the Volmer hacienda, a huge sugar plantation and rum distillery owned by one of Venezuela's oldest families. I had decided to invite the Shah to the properties of a couple of friends of mine so that he would see that like the United States, Venezuela had many large landowners and thriving private companies. Unfortunately the deluge rendered it too dangerous for the helicopters to land among the hacienda's wooded hills. By eleven, however, the sun had come out, and we decided to go straight to Mostrencos, a King Ranch two hundred miles outside Caracas owned by Gustavo de los Reyes, a Cuban exile. A lunch was hurriedly organized there so that the royal party could spend the day relaxing in the country.

Gustavo, tall and distinguished and an impeccable gentleman of the old school, greeted us as we stepped from the helicopters. He led Their Majesties to chairs set up outside to view a typically Venezuelan entertainment called a *coleo*. Twenty bulls were released into the open fields, followed by six riders, who tore around at great speed, catching them with ropes and throwing them to the ground. Everyone was very impressed. Queen Farah took a movie of the event. And the Shah's chamberlain, Mr. Atabay, an old-timer of Turkoman stock who was in charge of the royal stables, told me he thought it the most incredible riding he'd ever seen.

After the show we had a barbecue—a provincial lunch where everyone served themselves and protocol was mercifully at a minimum.

The following day we all flew to the Venezuelan province of Guyana, the center of that country's heavy industry. Unlike Iran—or, in fact, most other countries—Venezuela is blessed with a multitude of natural resources, including vast rivers, gold mines, an iron mountain, and huge bauxite fields. With the president acting as proud tour guide, the Shah visited the mammoth steel and aluminum plants that had been hewn out of the jungle, and the industrial city, Ciudad Bolívar, about three hundred miles from Caracas.

Over lunch that day with Dr. Ayadi, the Shah, and our minister of foreign affairs, I made the apparent mistake of addressing the last as *Agha-ye Doctor* Khalatbari, since he was a doctor of letters. Almost angrily he turned on me and said, "I'm not a doctor. These titles have been abolished in Iran."

"How strange," I answered—right in front of His Majesty. "These titles are not given by the Persian government but bestowed by universities." Dr. Ayadi looked at me aghast, since I was speaking in direct rejection of the Shah's orders: He had abolished all titles of doctor save for dentists and physicians.

Having already gotten myself into hot water, I decided to further risk mentioning a couple of points to the Shah that synthesized some of the observations I'd made over the past two years.

"Your Majesty," I ventured, "in the typical four-year posting an ambassador is never given a single plane ticket to return to Iran. How are my sons to learn Farsi? How are they to find out about the extraordinary changes taking place in Iran? Other countries, like England, send their ambassadors home with their whole families at least once a year. We should do the same."

"They won't take advantage of it," said Khalatbari flatly. "They'll just go to Europe on vacation."

"Not if you have them report to you and give you a mid-tour update. Arrange for them to visit new dams, schools, ports, whatever—so they know what our great country is doing."

The Shah nodded and said, "I agree. Mr. Khalatbari, make a report on it and I will sign it."

"Second," I went on, "I am the only Persian ambassador in all the northern part of South America, and there are only two others in the whole continent—in Argentina and Brazil. We are heavily outweighed by the Arabs. Iran should produce public relations materials to send to the prominent people of each country so they can learn about our country and what we are doing. Other countries do this to great effect. It helps trade and international business. What's more when someone comes here from Iran, the South Americans won't look at him and say 'Arab?' "

Again the Shah nodded, but this time I could tell he was not committed. He thought these countries below Iran and not worth the effort. As I might have expected, Khalatbari never wrote a report about either idea, and the Shah never followed up.

That evening the Shah hosted a dinner for the president at the Military Club. It was a sit-down dinner for a hundred people, with a reception for about eight hundred to follow. The dinner, staged by Petronella and myself, was a great success, primarily because we invited only people we knew well. I stood at the door to make sure there were no gate-crashers (and in fact turned quite a few people away). Everyone filed into a line to meet the Shah and Queen Farah. Many of them even had a bit of a chat. The dinner was a luxurious affair, the stiff protocol was relaxed, and a sense of real enjoyment permeated the evening.

Three days pass quickly, and before I knew it the Shah's visit was over. When the plane took off I felt terribly relieved. All had gone smoothly, and no terrible incident with a sharpshooter or crazy attacker had marred the event.

A couple of days after the Shah's departure I went to see the chief of protocol, Nelson Hernandez. I thanked him and then related some suggestions from our head of protocol, which apparently were routine and took place after each royal visit.

Nelson and I had become friends. He had a sharp wit and was at heart an academic, a trait we both shared.

"My ministry has asked whether a street or plaza should not be named after His Majesty to commemorate the visit," I told Nelson. He said no, Venezuela never named a street or plaza after a living person.

"My ministry further suggests that your government print a stamp of His Majesty in memory of the visit." But he again said no, such an act had no precedent in Venezuela.

"All right, Nelson," I said, "then I'd like to invite you out for dinner." To this he agreed at once.

On my own initiative I went to see an orchid specialist named Abraham

Jesurum and asked him to name an orchid after Queen Farah. He told me that it was an involved process. He would have to develop a hybrid and then send it with a request for the name to the world headquarters in London. It would probably take three years.

Toward the end of my stay in Caracas, Jesurum came to me with the documents and a picture of the orchid, which was bright yellow. I gave him lunch at the embassy and then, as I was overwhelmed by other events, forgot all about it.

By coincidence a year later I was visiting friends at the Ministry of Foreign Affairs in Tehran when one of them showed me a letter from my successor, describing all the effort that he was going through to obtain an orchid named for Queen Farah. He made no mention of the fact that I had initiated the project and instead took all the credit himself. By then we were in the midst of a revolution, and my friend and I agreed it was probably better to have someone else's name on anything involving the court.

THE TALE OF KISH ISLAND

In December of 1975 I returned to Tehran for a few days. It was the first time I'd been back since my appointment to Caracas two years earlier. I found my country booming, growing so fast, in fact, that it seemed to be splitting at the seams. On the one hand there was great excitement: With each passing day a new company was established; a new museum was opening its doors; a new dam, hospital, or school was being inaugurated. Yet a tension, a discontent, lurked beneath the hectic surface. It seemed to me as though my countrymen were compensating for the inanity of the legal system by ignoring it and the severity of their modernization effort by defying it. The city bulged in all sorts of new directions, and the difficulty of traversing it had become so acute that to drive the two miles between my house in Farmanieh and my mother's in Takhte Jamshid now took two hours.

My mother's house, empty since her passing the previous year, was now in the middle of town and stood like a shrunken widow surrounded by apartment blocks. Rezvanieh, the garden where I'd passed my summers as a child, also was enclosed by the city, and cranes brought in to construct a brand-new subdivision hung in the air across the street. Everywhere one looked there were cranes and piles of sand and bricks; villages were being subsumed by urban sprawl, and corridors of buildings had replaced the old streambeds and open fields. The new subdivision, called Sharestan Pahlavi, was slated to become the new city center, for the bazaar area in the south was too far from the banks and villas in the north and no longer served as the commercial hub of a city that had shed its past.

It was wonderful to see my family and friends—prosperous, at the forefront of the crusade—but the cancerous growth all around made me vaguely uncomfortable. There was much talk of the Shiraz art festival that had taken place the previous summer, an effort by the queen to bring foreign culture to Iran. But something had gone awry when a French theater company had staged a play in a storefront using nude actors—a sight that had sent the pious Shirazis reeling and the Tehran intelligentsia muttering that such a display wouldn't have been acceptable even in France. To me it was just one more example of a dream turned into a nightmare, more the rule than the exception in Iran. When Dr. Amouzegar invited me to visit the island of Kish in the Gulf, I gladly accepted.

At the time I did not know the island, though it soon became famous as the winter resort at which the Shah spent No Rooz and getaway weekends. Financed entirely by government funds, it was conceived in the same vein as the Persepolis festivities: Everything was imported from Europe. The food was from Maxim's, bricks and cement had to be sent in from Tehran, and everything from shoeshines to cocktail nuts was imported and terribly expensive. An active publicity campaign touted Kish as the perfect paradise for rich Arab vacationers who would no longer have to travel as far as the south of France or Beirut for some fun. So far the resort still had a long way to go. Besides the residences of the royal court, a couple of hotels and a casino had gone up, but little more. Nonetheless I passed a delightful weekend there, though even if I had had all the money in the world I would never have bought a house in Kish with the Caspian coast just a hundred miles from Tehran and Beirut or Paris just a flight away. Besides, the sea was infested with sharks, and the weather got so hot and muggy that the place was uninhabitable for four months of the year.

While I was in Kish I was approached by a car dealer, who offered me a Cadillac for $15,000 (in Tehran they cost $45,000). But the island was hardly three miles long and one mile wide. "My friend," I told him, "where would I go in a Cadillac on an island like this? If I was trying to steal a few moments with a girlfriend, everyone would know exactly where we were."

The problem was that there were no women in Kish, a key element for any vacationing Arab. Madame Claude, the famous regent of the Paris demimonde, supplied a constant stream of women, though it was hardly sufficient to put Kish on the Arab map.

Kish, however, held a special appeal for the Shah, who used it as a base from which to view the air force and navy exercises every spring—and spend a few weekends on his own away from family and work. Of course instead of escaping to Kish, he should have stayed for dinner on board the navy's destroyers after the exercises and passed some downtime with the military brass. But unlike his father, who often spent evenings talking and drinking tea with his generals and would visit the Tehran garrisons every morning at 5 A.M., the Shah had no stomach for such comradery. Although he always prided himself on being a military man, he never spent much time with any of his men in uniform. Often, particularly in the early seventies, when the equipment and technology were new, the maneuvers would be shoddy, the bombs and cannons entirely missing their targets, and he would become furious and replace all the top officers with younger men—something he did over and over.

The Shah was passionate about military hardware, and he spent much of Iran's great oil wealth acquiring more and more. He genuinely felt that by offering his men Chieftain tanks and F-4 Phantom jets (not to mention F-5s, DC-10s, and a whole range of helicopters, torpedo ships, and cutting-edge missiles), he deserved their loyalty and admiration—and even their love.

But the fierce loyalty that comes with personal contact cannot be bought. When the great challenge to his reign came just four years later, his soldiers abandoned him.

To be fair the Shah was just an ordinary man, with ordinary strengths and faults, burdened by sovereignty and the human desire to make a difference during his lifetime. He was constantly exhausted by the public demands of his rank. His marriage to Farah was good, but she was the empress, and he could never expect the lighthearted banter and sexual caresses that for him constituted a relaxing evening from the woman whose son was to be the next shah. For that he had to escape to Kish, and if it meant leaving the military brass at full salute at the airport, so be it.

My father faced much the same dilemma. Married to eight wives who diligently bore his children and kept company with all the upper-class ladies of society, he could never let down his guard with them—let alone expect them to deliver any fun. For this he had to go to Zahra Khanoum. He'd call all his best friends, including his oldest sons, Nosrat-Doleh and Salar-Lashkar, and tell them there would be a dinner that night at Zahra's. He would send over his cook and his valet while food was transported from his own kitchen by truck.

At Zahra Khanoum's the girls danced, played the tar (a melon-shaped guitarlike instrument with a double chamber), joked with the men, searched their pockets for money, sat in their laps, and smothered them with kisses. To them these great statesmen, to whom everyone groveled and bowed, were just men to be teased and tickled. No one in all of Iran could laugh at my father and Nosrat-Doleh and play with them like these women. And neither my father nor any of his friends could have enjoyed such a good time among themselves at home with their wives.

Zahra Khanoum, like Madame Claude, must have been a very intelligent woman, and she was highly respected. Sarameh-Doleh bought a house for her. Nosrat-Doleh gave her a droshky. She was a friend of theirs, and she always kept a keen eye out for what would make them happy.

Madame Claude must have been much the same. She sent her girls all over the world. She had quite a network—and knew how to follow up. One day I was traveling from Tehran to Geneva via Istanbul when I noticed a beautiful girl sitting next to me. After I'd gotten over the loveliness of her face, we got to talking. She asked me whether there was any place in Istanbul she could change dollars into francs and, opening her purse, showed me a stack of bills, as though she'd just robbed a bank. Deciding to ask no questions, I told her surely she could find someplace, but it would be better to wait until she got to Switzerland.

Two days later I received a call at my hotel from Madame Claude, whom I had never met or dealt with. "One of my girls met you on the plane," she said through the crackling line from Paris, "and I was wondering if you might not enjoy some of our services. I see in my records that there are many of you brothers but that you have never come to us."

I thanked her heartily, respecting her very much for her efficiency. But, I told her, so far I'd had plenty of luck on my own.

THE TALE OF CARLOS THE JACKAL

After our few pleasant days in Kish, Amouzegar invited me to the OPEC meeting that was opening the following week in Vienna. I told him no; it was December, and I had to get back to my family. My daughter would be coming to Venezuela from university, and we would be spending the Christmas holidays all together for the first time in many years. Plans had already been made for us to stay at a friend's house on the Caribbean island of Tobago, just off the coast of Trinidad.

How lucky it was that I did not go. The very morning I was planning to leave for Tobago I received a call from my right-hand man, Rostamizadeh, who excitedly told me that terrorists had entered the OPEC offices in Vienna and taken all the ministers hostage. I rushed to my office, delayed my departure, and called the editor of *El Universal,* the biggest and most influential newspaper in South America. But he was out of town. The whole of Caracas was empty. Everyone had left for the Christmas holidays.

The next day newspapers all over the world were buzzing with the news and speculating on what had happened. Carlos the Jackal, the notorious Venezuelan terrorist, was the ringleader. After bundling the ministers into a plane, he had flown from Vienna to Tripoli, where he'd released the hostages and escaped unharmed.

A few days later I spoke with the minister of oil, Valentin Hernandez Acosta, who had been in Vienna. It was, he said, a harrowing experience. Yet the Venezuelans had had the least distressing experience of all the delegates, since Carlos, warming to his fellow countrymen, had released them before flying with the rest of the hostages to Tripoli. At the door of the plane he'd handed a letter to Hernandez Acosta for his mother, who now lived in Caracas. "And you'd better deliver it to her in person," he warned. "Otherwise I will come down and find you. . . . "

Later I spoke with Amouzegar, who with Yamani had been the last hostage to be released after Carlos took them on to Yemen and Tunis. Whether Carlos had been waiting to receive a ransom and whether he finally got it has never been revealed. Amouzegar asked the Shah point-blank whether he'd had to pay any money, and the Shah said no. "But if they'd asked," he told Amouzegar, "I would have gladly paid." Nevertheless there were rumors that Carlos made $20 million from the escapade.*

Terrorism and insecurity were rampant at the time. The first year that I was in Caracas a government jeep with three uniformed men tailed me for almost six weeks, following me to my office, to restaurants at night, and to every appointment or out-of-town amusement. A few other ambassadors also were being watched, and none of us could understand why. Then suddenly, to my enormous relief, the tail was removed.

Sometime later I was informed that a Venezuelan gangster had been arrested and that a list of people targeted to be kidnapped had been found in his pocket. I was on that list. Oddly this made the ambassadors of some of the Arab countries very jealous. Meanwhile I could only thank God that these armed shadows had at last been removed from my life and that of my family.

A TALE OF CLOSE TIES

I liked being an ambassador, and Caracas was a wonderful place to be one. Petronella and I entertained constantly and soon gained the reputation of

*Carlos was finally arrested in Sudan in 1994 and was still awaiting trial in Paris in 1996.

having one of the most glamorous embassies in town. We both made a real effort to learn Spanish, and I insisted on speaking it whenever I was asked to give an address or a talk. The Venezuelans appreciated this, and we made many friends well beyond the normal scope of the diplomatic corps.

I was delighted, therefore, when toward the end of my posting President Carlos Andrés Pérez told me he had decided to accept our invitation to visit Iran. It was January of 1977, and the situation within OPEC had again become critical. Although OPEC was exporting close to 30 million barrels a day, inflation and the drop in the value of the dollar had virtually wiped out the gains made in 1973, while further price increases had not kept pace with the price of other goods on the world market. Not surprisingly many producing countries were getting restless. During the previous two OPEC meetings it had been suggested that the price be pegged to inflation. But Saudi Arabia had dug in its heels, insisting on a six-month freeze. When the other members chose to raise their prices by 5 percent anyway, with another 5 percent to follow six months later, a rift had developed that was threatening the organization. Saudi Arabia was continuing to supply the United States with cheap oil while the rest of the OPEC members charged Europe and Japan more.

Once again Pérez wanted to mediate. "Many times you have asked me to return the Shah's visit," he said. "But I didn't want to go on just a pleasure trip. Better to go at a time when I could accomplish something useful. That time has come. I want OPEC to remain strong and powerful, and that is why I must travel to the Middle East now to speak with its members and try to find a solution."

He handed me an envelope. "Please send this to your government," he said. "It contains information about a note we received today from Iraq, proposing an extraordinary meeting that would exclude Saudi Arabia and the United Arab Emirates. I have declined to go. I believe we must all act together, or OPEC will be doomed and all the efforts of the last ten years wasted."

Pérez planned to depart for Europe in mid-April and then to continue on to the Middle East, where he hoped to visit every member of OPEC. He expected to arrive in Iran toward the end of the month.

Tehran immediately accepted his plan and sent our new minister of finance, Houshang Ansari, to Caracas at the beginning of March 1977. Ansari was a flamboyant self-made man who had previously served as minister of industry. He was close to the Shah and so prominent that he'd been named to a three-person arms-purchasing commission (along with Henry Kissinger) that was entrusted with spending $15 billion over the next four years. I did not know him well, though I quickly discovered we had very different ideas and ways of doing things, and our personalities soon clashed.

Ansari's first meeting with the president did not go well. Pérez said he was considering a proposal to funnel all future increases in the price of oil into a new OPEC fund to aid the third world. Ansari said little until we were out of the president's earshot. But once in the car he blew up. "How does Pérez expect the other oil-producing countries to react if future increases go to other countries? He is being completely unrealistic. Why should the producing countries be blamed for price increases when others would be the beneficiaries?" he demanded. "And why, worst of all, should we put ourselves in a position to be pressured by the needy nations hoping to get more out of the fund?"

His points were all valid. But much as I had done with Amouzegar I cautioned Ansari that such statements in Venezuela were often just a testing of the waters.

Ansari, however, was impatient. He wanted to contact the Shah immediately and tell him that Venezuela's policy was opposed to ours and the rest of the OPEC members'. He even suggested advising the Shah to cancel Pérez's trip to Iran. By this time we had reached his apartments in the Hilton. On the way up the elevator I noticed that he must have had only $100 bills in his pocket because he used one to tip the bellhop. Our discussion was becoming heated. Exasperated, I told him he had no right to interfere in matters that were in my purview.

Tense and angry, we both paced his room. Suddenly he turned on me and began a harangue about his shoddy accommodations—that he expected the royal suite and that I was the one responsible. This was too much, and turning on my heel, I strode from the room, slamming the door.

I had barely reached my car when a sorry-looking undersecretary scurried up wringing his hands. "The minister is very cross," he said, shaking to his very toes.

In no mood to argue I answered, "Go to hell," and I drove away.

The next day we were scheduled to visit a number of industries outside the city. But when I got to the minister's hotel, he said that he preferred to stay in Caracas.

"Let us leave aside our differences and forget yesterday's exchange of words," I said.

Ansari laughed. "You are the first ambassador ever to have crossed me," he said. "I was very impressed."

Almost in the same breath we then both suggested that our top priority that day was to clarify the Venezuelan position. "We should visit the president a second time," he said.

That was easier said than done. The president was giving his annual message that morning to the Congress. I drove to the Congress building, but instead of going upstairs to my official place, I stood with the reporters downstairs. As the president walked through the entrance he saw me and realized immediately that I had something to say. He stopped in front of me. "Mr. President," I said after greeting him, "my minister of finance has something urgent to discuss with you. Would it be possible to have a few minutes of your time?"

He nodded and told me to be at his office in two hours.

Outside a huge mayhem of cars—hundreds of vehicles parked helter-skelter—met my eye, and with a sinking feeling I knew I would never be able to find mine in the mess. At that very moment the Brazilian ambassador drew up, and rushing over to him I asked if I could borrow his car. The traffic was horrendous, but the Brazilian's driver was very wily, dodging and weaving and using his horn, and at last we emerged onto the open highway. I picked up Ansari, along with a translator to make sure there would be no more misunderstanding, and we were ready and waiting for the president at his office at the appointed time.

Ansari opened the conversation by asking for a clarification of the president's intent. "What I am concerned about," Ansari said, "is that the lesser-developed nations will pressure us to raise prices even further and we will become even more unpopular. Yet it is my understanding that you plan to give away all further increases to a fund for the benefit of other nations."

"That *was* my initial intention," Pérez agreed. "But after your visit yesterday I changed my mind. In fact I deleted that section from the speech I delivered this morning."

We all relaxed, and the talk turned to his visit to Iran and his mission to maintain unity within OPEC. I was very impressed by Ansari, and clearly the president was too. Better appreciating each other's roles in the affair, Ansari and I forgot our quarrels and became good friends.

President Pérez arrived in Tehran on April 27, 1977. I flew in a few days before. The first evening of his visit, during cocktails, I went around the salon at Niavaran Palace with Queen Farah to look at the modern paintings she had collected over the years. We came to a portrait of her by an Italian artist, which she said she disliked. I had to agree with her. In Venezuela I had met a number of very good painters, and I mentioned that if she wished I could arrange for one of them to come to Tehran to do another portrait. She agreed, and the next day I invited Carlos Fernandez Escribano to carry out the commission. He arrived a couple of days later and, setting up his easel and paints in the palace, had the queen pose for several sessions. She was delighted with the results.

The queen also was very taken with the gift presented to her by the Venezuelan president. Knowing of her love for modern art, he had arranged a surprise: a piece by the famous Venezuelan abstract artist Jesús Raphael Soto—a geometry of lines and colors that played tricks on the eye.

The next day Pérez gave an account of his visit to the countries on the other side of the Gulf. Saudi Arabia, he said, had agreed to increase its price by another 3 percent beginning in July of 1977, bringing its rate almost to the level of that of the other OPEC countries. But it had agreed to do this only if Pérez guaranteed that there would be no further price hikes in 1978. "I told them I would talk with you and see if we could jointly issue a statement that would accommodate the Saudi view," he told the Shah. "It is not parity, I know—but almost—and it's worth it to keep OPEC together."

"The main danger to the whole world and particularly OPEC is Saudi Arabia's future financial policies," the Shah said. "With its vast monetary reserves it could easily destabilize the world's money markets. I appreciate your idea of reestablishing price uniformity, but closing out any option for increasing the price in 1978 is not a good idea. Even if we raise it just 5 percent we are not keeping pace with inflation."

And so the discussions went. The president hoped that if Venezuela, Iran, and Saudi Arabia could issue a joint declaration, the other members of OPEC would follow suit. He had intentionally left Iraq and Algeria to the end of his tour in the hopes of persuading them to drop their hard-line policies once the others had reached agreement. Iran was the linchpin—a fact the Shah fully appreciated—and though the two did not reach full agreement that day, a meeting later with Amouzegar did result in a mutual declaration.*

The four-day visit came rapidly to a close, and before I knew it we were all at the airport wishing Pérez a safe trip to Baghdad. The Shah and his retinue were there, as well as the entire diplomatic corps.

As the presidential plane drew away, the Shah asked why there were seven stars on the Venezuelan flag. As usual, he had not made sure that I, as his ambassador, stood anywhere near. (In fact, he had been so surrounded by his retinue during the president's trip that I never even got a picture of the two leaders and myself to commemorate the occasion.)

Immediately a whispering began, and the question passed from one ear

*Between 1975 and 1995 the amount of oil produced by OPEC declined by almost one half (from 30 million barrels a day to 16 million), despite a steady increase in world consumption. Today the industrial nations produce close to 20 million barrels a day and gain more income from the sale of oil than the members of OPEC.

to the next until at last it reached me. Having no real answer I said, entirely off the cuff, that it was because Venezuela had started its republic with seven states. When the message finally reached the Shah, he turned and glanced back at me and, catching my eye, indicated he knew I'd improvised. Thank God I later proved to be right.

On the way back from the airport to central Tehran the streets were so blocked with traffic that it took two hours to complete the journey. Three years previously it would have taken fifteen minutes. I drove back with the assistant minister of court, Homayoun Bahadori, an erudite man and my main contact in Tehran while I was in Caracas. He was also a fellow collector of books on Iran, and what a collection he had—there were few books in my library that he could envy. As we drove he told me the public transport services had become hopelessly inadequate and pointed at the people trudging in the streets or waiting listlessly at the bus stops. I observed them with apprehension, knowing that revolutions begin at bus stops and other such places where people gather, complain, and eventually ferment trouble.

I also noticed that the air was so polluted that I had developed a constant cough. The beautiful snowcapped mountains were obscured by a smog so thick that it hung like a black curtain in front of us, making it seem unimaginable that a town, a capital city, lay beyond the gloom. The towering peak of Mount Damavand had disappeared entirely. I could not imagine that Mexico City could be any worse.

The urgent demand for bread, sugar, tea, meat, and housing, Homayoun said, had eclipsed the need for social reforms. Inflation had hurt the salaried classes of government officials, who previously had been among the most privileged. Although there was an air of continued work and progress, the bureaucracy had exploded, and petty bribery had grown with it. Influence, which had worked well when the bureaucracy was a tightly knit group of landed nobles with independent incomes, had become a cancer, riddling the government with corruption and greed. Many civil servants, now in possession of easy money, were sending their plunders abroad. The internal situation was becoming so bad that even honest citizens, alarmed by the irregularities, were transferring out capital, not only as a hedge against inflation (which was rampant) but as a security measure.

The Shah was neglecting the less glamorous needs of his country, and since no one else had been authorized to do the job, the general malaise could be seen everywhere. On this trip I realized that no social system or people could have been less prepared for the deluge of wealth that had been thrust so suddenly upon them. It poured down like a huge river and drowned Iran. His Majesty saw weakness and confusion but could not decide which way to turn to channel it or stop it.

A TALE OF DEPARTURE

By 1977 I had been in Caracas for five years. It was time to go home.

I anticipated the return with some trepidation. I decided to continue leasing my house in Farmanieh and bought an apartment in a new downtown complex called Saman, built by my brother Aziz, where many of the family had taken up residence. Petronella and I had decided to go our separate ways, and she had already returned to Europe, putting the boys into boarding school in England.

While I was in Caracas I had begun a number of new collections, including pre-Columbian pottery and early Peruvian Christian paintings. These treasures, along with the carpets and Persian calligraphic pottery that I had brought from Tehran, were packed into three large containers and shipped to Iran.

Before leaving I made a farewell trip to Ecuador, Peru, and Trinidad and Tobago to bid adieu to their respective presidents. In Caracas a whirlwind of parties and heartwarming send-offs tied the knot on some of the best years of my life. I felt particularly honored when I heard that I was to receive the Order of the Liberator, the highest medal awarded by Venezuela. In a small, moving ceremony the minister of foreign affairs tied the decoration on its blue ribbon about my neck.

It was with a heavy heart that I packed my suitcases, said good-bye to my staff, and took a last, lingering look at the beautiful embassy residence. I boarded the plane slowly, drinking in the dry salty air for what I thought would be the last time. Then feeling as though I was leaving part of myself forever in Venezuela, I flew out across the azure waters of the Caribbean.

REVOLUTION

Don't be struck by the revolution of time
For the wheel of the world remembers a thousand thousand of
   these turns.

—HAFEZ

Tehran 1977

I returned to Iran in November 1977, at the tail end of fall, when the trees are bare but the sun still shines and the dry air is cool. Snow had collected on the peaks of the mountains and cleared away some of the smog. In the mornings frost sugared the grass.

I came via the United States, where I stopped in Washington, D.C., to see my daughter, Roxane. She had just graduated from Princeton and was working at the Kennedy Center. My trip happened to coincide with that of His Majesty the Shah and Queen Farah, who were visiting President Jimmy Carter.

Every hotel in the District of Columbia was booked, and I ended up spending the nights on Roxane's sofa bed in her living room. At first I thought it was the Shah's entourage and secret service that had packed all the hotels, but I soon learned it was Iranian students who had flown into the city to stage demonstrations against the Shah's rule. By then there were more than sixty thousand Iranians studying in the United States, most of them financed by the Iranian government. By supporting their freedom to express anti-Shah slogans and sentiments, the U.S. press and government unwittingly helped create a monster. Most of the students maintained close ties with Tehran (by 1978 Iran was the fourth-largest consumer of AT&T long-distance lines) and played a significant role in the opposition's growth back home. The Shah and his ministers brushed them off as insignificant. I tended to agree, as did President Carter, whose administration soft-pedaled the Shah's alleged human rights abuses during the visit.

On the morning of the ceremonial speeches at the Rose Garden, where Carter and the Shah posed for photographs, a large crowd of students gathered at the White House gates. Many wore white cylindrical masks and waved placards that read SHAH IS A FASCIST BUTCHER and STOP ARMING THE SHAH. Their pushing and chanting reached such a frenzy that police dispersed tear gas over the crowd to break it up. It was a breezy day, and soon the gas wafted into the Rose Garden, leaving an enduring picture of the two leaders and their wives wiping tears from their reddened eyes.

Back in Iran the discontent and anger were palpable, even among the privileged classes. Sir Edward Grey, head of AIOC in the twenties, once described Russia as despotism without discipline. The same could be said of Iran. The Shah imagined he was helping the poor when instead he only upset the affluent without satisfying the impoverished. As a result a feeling of great injustice pervaded all levels of society. Inflation was still out of hand, and oil revenues had leveled off. The money had been spent; the dreams, however, remained unrealized.

Now that I was back I began experiencing the daily discomforts and frustrations that in the past I'd only observed from afar. Every day there were power outages that lasted two to three hours. Cars choked every winding side street, nerves were frayed, and the resentment was reaching the breaking point.

One day I took a cab from downtown to the northern suburb of Shemiran. Normally taxi drivers picked up more than one passenger going the same way, but this time there were only the two of us. The driver complained bitterly about how high prices were, how there was not enough housing for his family and friends, and how low the quality of life had become. He banged his fist on the dashboard a couple of times, yelled at the motorcyclists squeezing their way between the cars, and then told me he was generally a mild-mannered person. I believed him.

It was winter and cold. "But you're lucky," I told him. "You're sitting in a nice warm taxi, out of the weather. Now tell me, does the taxi belong to you?"

"Yes, yes," he said. "I've paid part of it already, and I'm paying off the rest."

Hoping to show him a different angle, I made up a story. "My father was a droshky driver," I told him. "He drove horses. The poor man had to sit outside under the snow just to earn a piece of bread. Now here you are, sitting in a nice car that's warm and that's yours, and I'm paying you for the service of driving me uptown. And still you are disgruntled. What do you want the government to do for you? Your lot has improved so much from that of my father."

But he would not be swayed. He said he deserved to have more and that his money should stretch farther. He did not realize that his own needs had risen substantially and his own demands were contributing to the overall shortages. Then he told me, conspiratorially, the prevailing rumor in the city. "Hundreds of millions of dollars have been sent out of the country," he said, glancing over his shoulder with a knowing look. "What I could do with just a slice of that. . . . "

As I got out of the car I felt I'd known this man for a long time. He was just like the villagers on our properties in Hamadan—now displaced. He was prosperous by all accounts, since he had his own car and a job, and yet he was lost, his whole life turned upside down in the short time since he'd come to this chaotic city, his nerves afire with the noise, his good humor shorn by the daily plying of his cab through the crowded streets, his sense of hope unable to be restored by the respect of his fellow villagers or the silence of the fields. Everything in Iran was so unnatural—like a tree blooming in the wrong season.

A TALE OF BUILDING

I had returned to Iran with big plans to build a couple of hotels and cash in on the economic boom that everyone else had been enjoying while I was in Caracas. Very soon, however, I began encountering difficulties.

In Tehran the municipal authorities had issued new zoning regulations dividing the city into five concentric circles. Every five years, moving from the inside out, a new zone was released for construction. If your property fell outside the current construction zone, you could not obtain permits to repair or expand it, let alone build something new. The authorities claimed that a master plan was being designed for the city, and until the plan was finalized it was unlawful even to sell a property. The poor suffered from this as much as the rich, for there was an acute shortage of housing and the authorities turned a blind eye to the right of the needy to obtain shelter.

Just repairing the wall fronting my house in Farmanieh turned out to be a nightmare. Since my departure five years before, the civil bureaucracy had doubled to more than 800,000 (the military had ballooned to almost

700,000) and was now incapable of coordinating or dealing coherently with any situation. In many respects the government was at a standstill. As I had feared I was told there was no chance of receiving a repair license. The road was going to be widened sometime in the future, and the entire wall would then be demolished and taken back thirty feet. Until the plans were drawn up I would have to wait.

My situation was typical. Huge bribes were being paid to negotiate a route around the bureaucracy. Many homeowners resorted to repairing their buildings at night, even though a demolition squad would often arrive later and destroy their work. There were stories of people who even lay down in front of the oncoming bulldozers.

I called up my friend and previous employee Gholam Reza Nickpay, who had left NIOC five years earlier to become lord mayor of Tehran. He asked me out for lunch, and on the way I arranged for us to drive by my wall so that he could see it—and so I could talk him into giving me a repair license. I complained to him that just ten years before, I had gotten a license to build the wall, which the government was now revoking for the sake of a road. I would lose more than three thousand feet of property and would have to replace the entry gate, the garages, and the servants' quarters. I would have to redig my well, and I would lose a great number of trees. Who would pay for the work? What would be the compensation? And when would the work be done?

Nickpay, who had a degree from the London School of Economics, was one of the most honest, dedicated men I have ever known. Out of principle he refused to grant me an interim permit to repair my wall. I implored him to be more humane.

"It is not enough to be just," I told him. "We are in a crisis. You cannot continuously alienate everyone. You are hurting the government, yourself, and me. There is no court of appeals for me to establish my rights. Therefore it is you who must be more flexible and listen to people's needs." I even suggested that the municipality do the work and that I'd pay. But he refused that too.

At last, at wit's end, I called the family mason, who repaired the wall in four nights and made it look old. I had pursued every avenue in trying to comply with the municipality's requirements and had failed. I felt no remorse.

Influence, mostly at court, and bribery did produce permits for big-ticket projects like apartment buildings and shopping malls. At first when apartment buildings appeared in Tehran, the aristocracy never thought they would live in them. But then the idea caught on, and there was a great rush to have an apartment. The middle class—bureaucrats, small business owners, and the new cadre of middle management—followed suit. Now apartment complexes were going up all over the city, many of them sprouting right out of the desert.

The middle class also had popularized the Caspian coast as a new resort area. For centuries the mountains dividing Tehran and the sea had been inaccessible. Now they could be traversed in four hours by car or half an hour by plane. Malaria, which had thrived in the coastal jungles and kept people away, had been eradicated. American troops brought the first DDT to Iran in the forties, and my brother Sabbar, working with the World Health Organization during Mossadeq's time, had finished the job. Now everyone was trying to grab a piece of land near the sea.

My own family had bought a huge tract of ocean frontage back in 1959, with each of us brothers purchasing fifteen thousand feet. Over the years we had developed a summer camp called Farmansara, where everyone in the family gathered for two weeks in July. Now I barely recognized the place. The village of Chalus had become a town. People didn't know one another anymore. Hyatt had built a first-class hotel there. Discotheques thrummed loudly on Friday nights. There was even a casino on the beach.

Yet when I saw Chalus and the type of development prevailing in Tehran, I knew I had made the right decision before coming home. In Caracas I had formed a partnership with some bankers involved in the ownership of Holiday Inn. I'd signed a contract to build two hotels in Iran, one in the city proper and one on property I had in Vardavard between the city and the airport. A number of my brothers were bankers, so financing would be easy. Besides the problem of licenses nothing in those first weeks after my arrival indicated that it would be anything but a good business venture.

Within four months, however, I realized there was no chance. Half the banks had been stormed and closed. The mob was attacking anything that smacked of foreign investment. I'd been preempted. Had I returned just a year earlier, it would all have been so different.

A TALE OF TROUBLE

Iran was quiet—almost deathly quiet—through the New Year. Jimmy and Rosalynn Carter spent December 31 with the Shah and Queen Farah at Niavaran Palace, ushering in the ill-fated year of 1978 together.

Slowly, first in Qom and then in Tabriz, Tehran, and Isfahan, demonstrations began to ripple across the country. A couple of students were killed in one location, a strike took place in another, a major cleric lodged a public protest in a third. There was genuine indignation at the excesses of capitalism, and neither the Shah, the law, nor the elite was capable of plumbing the culture for the necessary moral guidance. To the Iranian people the Great Civilization was turning out to be an affront to their dignity as the influx of foreign expertise clashed humiliatingly with the old ways of doing things. The common man was lost, and the country began to veer like a drunken sailor between the Shah's increasingly unsteady authoritarianism and the promise of a more spiritual life proposed by the clergy.

The Shah sent in troops to quell the disturbances but held off from imposing a large-scale clampdown, chary of incurring criticism from the human-rights-conscious Carter. At the same time, under pressure from his Western allies, he promised reforms and allowed the press a little more leeway. But the long-awaited freedoms anticipated by the opposition failed to materialize. Both sides were at fault. The population expected instant change without understanding the problems; the government made promises it could not deliver.

Then in August the Rex Cinema in Abadan burned down, trapping four hundred people inside. It was a catastrophe—and a turning point for the gathering forces of revolution. Grief and horror gripped the general public, who demanded an explanation. Riots broke out, and an angry movement collected around the stricken mourners in Abadan. I thought surely the Shah would fly to the south and quell the distress by personally visiting the victims' homes and promising amends. He had never done such a thing before, but I remained hopeful. It was the only way to solve the problem. But he never went.

In the midst of the turmoil a friend of mine, Dara Zargar, came to Tehran from New York. We talked of the Shah's apparent inability to take action and his loss of face. "Why doesn't he do something?" I asked in frustration. "How can he not react?"

"I was just glancing at a book on your shelves about Churchill," he answered. "He gave a speech to the House of Commons after World War II that seems to answer your question. As Churchill says, 'The British Lion, so valiant, so fierce in bygone days, so dauntless and unconquerable through all the agony of Armageddon, can now be chased by rabbits from the fields and forests of its former glory. It is not that our strength is seriously impaired. We are suffering from a disease of will. We are the victims of a nervous collapse, of a morbid state of mind.' "

This indeed described the Shah.

Four months earlier Alam, his closest friend and minister of court for fourteen years, had died of cancer. Some months earlier he'd resigned his post, and the Shah had put Hoveyda in his place (despite the fact he'd been such a failure as prime minister) and assigned Jamshid Amouzegar to the premiership. Hoveyda was no substitute for Alam, whose advice and sincere loyalty had been an irreplaceable mainstay for the Shah. Without his stalwart support the Shah was bereft—and unmoored.

His own health also was not good. What was wrong with him was unclear—at the time he showed no outward signs of the cancer that would eventually kill him. My friend Dr. Yahya Adl and I talked after the monarch had left Tehran and the matter of his disease was aired publicly in New York. Adl, who became even closer to the Shah after Alam's death and saw him almost every night for cards, said lymphatic cancer has obvious symptoms that he could not have failed to observe. It causes swelling in the face, weight loss, itching, and weakness. The Shah, he said, exhibited none of these. Even so a French specialist, Dr. Jean Bernard, who came to Tehran to care for both Alam (who suffered from the same form of cancer) and the queen mother, began to treat the Shah for various ailments during this time. Whatever conclusions he drew he kept to himself. Adl, who was assigned to take care of Bernard when he was in Tehran, never heard him mention a diagnosis of cancer. If there was such a thing, it was kept secret from the Shah and Queen Farah as well, though there is some question as to whether the French president was informed. In any event the secrecy could well have killed him, for had he been informed and treated early in the disease, his life could perhaps have been saved.

A TALE OF HOLY WAR

The Shah's response to the Rex Cinema fiasco was to replace Amouzegar with Jafar Sharif-Emami, another of his old standbys. Sharif-Emami immediately announced a return to the Islamic calendar, the closing of all casinos and gambling houses, and, for the first time, freedom for all legal political parties. Ex–prime minister Hoveyda and General Nassiri, the previous head of SAVAK, were incarcerated, though no reason was given for their arrests. Finally a government investigation was begun into the Abadan disaster.

Sharif-Emami's moves were too little too late. The religious leadership, the only group in Iran with an effective network of communication, deplored the government's handling of the situation. From Najaf in Iraq Ayatollah Khomeini sent over tape after tape of his sermons, criticizing the moral degradation of the Shah's rule, its sellout to the West, its debauchery and corruption, and its hidden agenda in Abadan. Sharif-Emami, the son of a leading religious family but known to be very corrupt, became a target of Khomeini's ire.

At the same time, discourses against the Shah's repression poured with greater frequency and fire from the State Department in Washington, D.C. President Carter and Anwar Sadat, the Shah's friend and president of Egypt, were in the midst of negotiating the Camp David accords and hence too busy to give the Shah the personal support and assurances he so needed. The CIA had meanwhile informed Carter that there were no grounds for worry, since Iran "is not in a revolutionary situation, nor even in a prerevolutionary situation."

That summer Ramadan ended on September 4. People poured into the streets in massive demonstrations to mark the last day, calling for the expulsion of the United States from Iran and a return to more religious principles. Disconcerted by the size and anger of the crowds, the Shah approved the imposition of martial law on the evening of September 7 and banned all unauthorized gatherings. The next day working-class poor from Tehran's southern slums, guerrilla fighters who had long been targets of SAVAK, and students from the university, unaware of the new regulations or perhaps emboldened to confront them, massed in Tehran's Jaleh Square. This time the security forces opened fire. More than a hundred people were killed, and three or four hundred were injured. The incident became known as "Black Friday."

Black Friday was the beginning of the end. The military, posted in tanks and jeeps along the roads and in front of targets such as the British and American embassies, gradually lost their resolve to confront their own citizenry. Designed for warfare against the Russians, the cannons were so huge that they would in any case have demolished a whole block with a single shot. As the weeks passed the soldiers became bored. Passersby showered them with flowers, making them feel foolish behind their guns under the hot sun. Schoolgirls flirted with them on the street. Restaurateurs and café owners sent out food for them to eat.

It was a holy war, although we did not recognize it then. It seemed at the time more like a general uprising, directed as much by the intellectual opposition as by religious groups. Khomeini, whose name was still largely unfamiliar to us, was only one of many voices. What seemed more insidious at the time was the BBC Farsi Service, which appeared to take genuine glee in Iran's turmoil and which, with a conscientiousness that belied objectivity, reported every demonstration, interviewed every opposition leader, and criticized the Shah's every move. The BBC carried enormous weight with Iranians. The legitimacy it gave to the forces massing against the Shah was a benediction—and implied Western support if not outright involvement. "The people are expected to gather tomorrow at the Shayad Memorial and walk to the university," the BBC would report, and after hearing this, crowds would show up to march.

The BBC had been a factor in our political dramas since the time of Reza Shah. It had played a role during Mossadeq's time and had often been a thorn in the Shah's side during the 1960s and 1970s. The BBC medium-wave station, beamed into Iran from the Persian Gulf, lies on the band right next to Tehran Radio. In 1972, for example, I happened to hear a report about the generals in Chile being broadcast in Farsi. Anyone not paying close attention or who had tuned in a little late could easily have mistaken it for a report on the generals in Iran. I went to see Hamid Rahnamah, the minister of propaganda, and alerted him that this was a veiled attack on the Shah and the military. Three days later, when nothing had been done, I went to Alam. The next morning the BBC correspondent was thrown out of Iran. When I saw Alam again a week later I thanked him.

"It is I who should thank you," he said. "The British have been wanting to sell us Chieftain tanks. There were a few generals against the purchase. This may have been an attempt to discredit them."

"I don't usually listen to the BBC," I told him. "You should have someone monitor it all the time. Countries like ours receive broadcasts from the United States, Britain, and the USSR all the time, but we cannot send our views back to London or Washington or Moscow. We cannot communicate with their masses. We can barely communicate with our own."

Alam nodded sadly. "The people of the United States don't realize how Britain—and the BBC—have shaped the Middle East," he said. "They don't understand Britain's very real ability, even today, to lynch governments. The BBC, funded by the Foreign Office, interprets the news as it sees fit. And when the BBC speaks, the people of Iran and the rest of the Middle East listen."

Now Alam was gone, and the Shah was too weak to expel the BBC correspondent, a young Englishman named Andrew Whitley, who was little older—or wiser—than many of the Iranian youths demonstrating in the streets.* The Iranian media were under strict control, and therefore the BBC became Khomeini's mouthpiece. Without it he would have enjoyed much less access to the country's widely scattered population. The cassettes of his sermons that came in regularly from Iraq would not have had the

*Some years later I had dinner with Whitley in New York, and he told me he was writing a biography of the Shah. I warned him that many Iranians would not read it, since he was neither a scholar nor an expert on modern Iranian history and his role with the BBC would discredit his views. Whitley discovered that few Iranians would cooperate with him for interviews, and he dropped the idea soon after.

same impact. And although there were mosques in every village and the mollahs enjoyed tremendous influence, Khomeini's own voice would not have been heard with such immediacy. He would not have been able to speak to the people every night in their homes, direct the uprisings with such precision, or react to every move made by the Shah. Thanks to the BBC Khomeini was able to transform the people's resentments and prejudices into action and inflame them with an idea that was then still unthinkable: getting rid of the Shah.

Demonstrations were now taking place every day in cities all across Iran, but the government responded halfheartedly: Shoot the gun but make no noise. Very soon the people realized that martial law was not holding and that they could easily disobey it without great risk to their lives. And so we watched the rebellion gather with increasing strength. We were the spectators—and what an incredible spectacle it was: thousands of people marching down the avenues chanting slogans, first a group of men, then a group of women in black chadors, and then more men, and then more women, praising Khomeini, armed only with flowers, lauding the smiling soldiers in their tanks, the whole river of humanity flowing across town, angry and yet contained, for Khomeini had urged them not to be violent. "Every life is precious," he told them through the radio, "and if provoked the police will kill."

At night the people climbed onto their roofs and called out, *"Allah-o-Akbar, Allah-o-Akbar,"* and the whole city seemed to echo the refrain.

Then in early October, at the instigation of the Shah, who thought Khomeini was more dangerous in Iraq than somewhere else, the Ayatollah was forced out of Iraq and moved to Neauphle-le-Château outside Paris. The effect was exactly the opposite of what the Shah had envisioned. Suddenly Khomeini had reached the world stage. The news media swarmed around him. Opposition supporters based in France organized a political cadre around him and began to direct the revolution as though from a shadow cabinet abroad. People we had never heard of became household names: Yazdi, Gotbzadeh, Bani-Sadr. Opposition emissaries began to go back and forth between Tehran and Paris, and every word Khomeini said became a matter of record.

It was about this time that my cousin Hossein Dowlatshahi and I added our names to a letter written by a number of the old nobility expressing our allegiance to the Shah and offering to support him in any way we could. A few days later someone from the Shah's office called and invited us to visit His Majesty at Sadabad Palace.

The audience was one of the most tragic scenes I have ever witnessed. Over the previous few days the Shah had been receiving members of the

old landed gentry whose vast properties had at one time blanketed most of
Iran. The news was obviously not good. The Shah looked shrunken and
tired, and he spoke very quietly. At first I thought he would suggest that
we form a committee to cooperate with the government.

Instead he said, "I need your help. I need you to go back to your old villages and rally the people there for the good of our country. They trust you.
They will listen to you. I need you to act as my representatives."

We looked at him with stricken faces. At first I could say nothing. Then
finally I spoke. "We have not been back to our villages for over fifteen
years," I said. "At the time of Your Majesty's Revolution of the Shah and
the People I left, having no role there anymore."

"We no longer know the people in those villages," said Hossein, whose
lands had been in the north. "The villages have changed. Many of the farmers have left and come to the city. We have no connections there anymore."

"If anything we are despised in those places," I added. "It is only the
preachers of religion who have influence there today."

"But we are willing to do whatever we can, Your Majesty," said Hossein,
who had already been in touch with the military and was better versed than
I was in such matters.

The Shah shook his head and looked away. The other landowners had
told him the same thing. At last, with wrenching finality, he understood
what it meant to have weakened us by his own hand.

Silently, heads down, we took our leave. It was the last time I saw him.

The Shah's land reforms and the massive industrialization programs
pushed on him by the United States and organizations such as the World
Bank had brought his regime to the edge of the precipice. It was his own
governors, mayors, and representatives whom he should have been able to
call on to act as his lieutenants. But they had never been effective. Now,
too late, he was having to face the horrible fact that his government had no
one left in the villages.

After land reform the mollahs, unnoticed by the government, had
stepped into the vacuum we had left behind. Their land confiscated, just
as ours had been, they were outraged by the Shah's decrees and had assumed the moral high ground. The Shah had made a great mistake in
thinking that religion was unimportant and that patriotism and material
reward could replace devotion. When the state took over some of the
clergy's traditional functions, such as the administration of charitable be-
quests, it just added a nail to its own coffin. Throughout the turbulent period of reform and the rapid economic expansion that followed, the
mollahs had provided the community services so badly needed by the disenfranchised and the urban poor. Their mosques had come to resemble so-

cial clubs, where their devotees could gather, obtain assistance, and listen to the encouragement of Khomeini, the saint of the "barefooted," as he called them. No matter how often SAVAK expelled the mollahs, others invariably replaced them, committed to the same cause. There had always been money for them, for the Koran requires that one fifth of all profits be paid to the mosque in taxes. The people who were able had paid this through the years, and the money had been used to organize relief throughout the country, all independent of the government.

Much had happened in fifteen years. Having failed to stand up to the Shah, we had lost our country. The Shah was even more alienated than we. He traveled everywhere by helicopter and so did not know the pandemonium of the streets—the potholes, the twisting traffic. His children were schooled on the royal premises and knew almost nothing of the world beyond their walls. Only occasionally did they even play with children of the elite—and always on their own premises. Queen Farah, perhaps the most involved of all the royals in her efforts to visit schools, hospitals, and orphanages, was nonetheless always surrounded by the pomp and display put on for a queen on her rounds. The rest of the Shah's family disdained the life of everyday Iran and instead focused on the vast profits that came with facilitating international investment in the country.

THE SHAH'S LAST DAYS

By November the Shah had given up on Sharif-Emami and appointed a military government headed by General Azhari, the army chief of staff.

By then it would have made no difference whom he appointed. The revolution had taken over. Spontaneous demonstrations were erupting on every corner and street. The crowds attacked banks, cinemas, and hotels, and parts of the city were often on fire. Shoot-outs were common. Many shopkeepers closed down in case they too would be targets. Whole streets looked abandoned, the commerce of their customers gone, their stores bolted and shielded by thick metal gates, the broken windows and boarded doors on a building gutted by fire indicating the onetime presence of a bank or hotel.

In October the Abadan Refinery went on strike, and by the end of the month production had dropped to 150,000 barrels a day—a quarter of the usual output. Over the next few weeks the oil situation worsened, sparking long lines at fuel pumps for both gasoline and kerosene. At the crisis's nadir the wait was two days; the traffic in Tehran never looked better.

Power outages had now become regular, lasting four hours every day between six and ten in the evening, just as people got home from work and turned on the TV for the news. With only candles and a battery-operated radio to welcome them home, everyone now listened exclusively to the BBC.

Although General Azhari was not an acquaintance of mine, I called on him one day to discuss the beleaguered political state of the country. The conversation turned to the bands of young people roaming the streets while the police and army did nothing to intervene.

"I was standing in the street just yesterday," I told him, "and a gang of youths stepped off a bus yelling 'Death to the Shah.' The police standing there didn't raise a finger to disperse them. And they still didn't move even when the demonstrators started to loot the shops nearby!"

"It is useless to fight," said Azhari. "Though a few well-trained men could have stemmed the disturbances in the past, the Shah has forbidden the police and army to interfere. It is now too late, and hour by hour the rioters are taking over."

Azhari was an old general who had come up through the ranks and had no pretensions of knowing how to run a government. He was not the spitfire the Shah needed at the time if drastic action were to prevail. I mentioned the disastrous effect of the BBC broadcasts on the population and how they were turning the people against the government. "You should start broadcasting critical commentary on British policy and the royal family—which wouldn't in any case be hard. That would shut the BBC up," I advised.

Azhari said he'd mention it to the Shah and that he'd already talked to the British ambassador. "Radio France and the French newspaper *Le Monde* are also attacking the Shah," he said. "I asked His Majesty if I could throw out their correspondents, but he said no, that he was a close friend of President Giscard d'Estaing. The Shah wants to keep power in his own hands, even though he does not act."

Azhari and I warmed to each other, and our mutual frustration created a greater bond. Feeling that he could trust me, he confided something I had never heard before, though it came as no surprise. Years later he provided more details.

While he was chief of staff in the mid-seventies, he was invited to meetings at the Pentagon chaired by General Alexander Haig, then head of the North Atlantic Treaty Organization (NATO). The discussions centered on the purchase of arms and the activities of the Ministry of Defense. One day, said Azhari, Haig pulled out a file containing a letter from King Fahd of Saudi Arabia, in which the king stated that he hoped the Shah would step down since he was the main instigator in OPEC for higher oil prices.

"In fact," said Azhari, "the Saudis do not care about the price of oil. They are scared of the Shah and worried about their own security. The Saudi generals, who met with Haig just like I did, had been petitioning for the Shah's removal for some time. They were convinced that the arms being funneled to Iran from the United States were not going north to protect against the USSR but were instead being concentrated in the south, so the Shah could carry out some grand plan of taking over the Gulf. When the Shah sent military help to Sultan Gabous of Yemen to throw out the Communists, the Saudis took it as an omen. With a foothold in Yemen, just south of the Saudi border, the Shah, they claimed, was now threatening all the Arab states.

"This view was only strengthened when a few months later the Shah granted an interview to an Israeli journalist, who asked him, 'In case of conflict which side would you back, the Arabs or Israel?' and the Shah answered, 'Israel.' Just today," Azhari continued, "I see the representative of Israel, who comes twice a week to give me all the latest information from their security networks—almost all of which, I must say, turns out to be right. In any case the Arabs took a very dim view of this statement—even though the Shah has always supported Israel for the sake of the U.S.—and resolved to combat Iran in Washington. Haig and the rest of Washington took King Fahd's letter very seriously."

Saudi Arabia and the United States were longtime friends, he pointed out. They scratched each other's backs. The Shah had become very independent, had gotten up on his high horse; he had his own program—talking one day of becoming the gendarme of the Gulf, the next about the Indian Ocean, the next about the Horn of Africa, and boasting that his army was the fifth-largest in the world (after those of the United States, the Soviet Union, the United Kingdom, and China). He was a thorn to Europe and America when it came to oil negotiations, and though he was unfailingly supportive of Israel, the United States didn't trust him anymore. "There are many examples," Azhari said, "including the appointment of Richard Helms, who was previously the director of the CIA, to Tehran as ambassador.* Little by little the CIA's maneuvering has bolstered the opposition to such a degree that it is leading to the Shah's fall."

I walked out of the meeting marveling at the duplicity of our neighbors. Was OPEC then for nothing? I remember telling the Venezuelan Luongo Cabello, when he had come to Iran nearly thirty years before, that we did

*Helms left Iran in 1977 and was succeeded by Ambassador William Sullivan, whose embassy openly held talks (with Secretary of State Cyrus Vance's approbation) after June 1978 with opposition leaders, including militant Khomeini supporters.

not trust the Arabs, and he had said, "Nonsense, we *must* trust each other; our only hope is to work together to prevail against the Great Powers." Well, we had worked together, but we still did not trust each other.

And what were we to make of America's policy of forcing democracy down our throats even as it humored the monarchy of Saudi Arabia? Its condemnation of the Shah's track record in human rights and its silence on the Saudi front? Besides, how had the United States suddenly become the world's arbiter of human rights?

I thought of some poetry I'd once read: "What is the monument erected by the architect of time which he himself does not overturn through the whirlwind of events?"

Later Azhari told me he had often had to implore the Shah, in those last weeks of November, not to leave Iran. The Shah was losing hope. The signals coming from Washington were so confused he did not know whether President Carter and the rest of the West supported him or not. France certainly seemed to have abandoned him, counting no doubt on its ability to settle amicably with whoever succeeded him.* England and the others also had gone mum. The Israeli representative who had come regularly to report to Azhari had abruptly stopped his visits. It was as though a vacuum had suddenly been created around the Shah.

Meanwhile members of the opposition were flooding into Paris to speak with Khomeini. Those who went included Karim Sanjabi, a leader of the reconstituted National Front, Mossadeq's old party. Sanjabi was the son of the tribal leader who, with his brothers, had taken refuge in my father's house to escape British persecution after World War I. He was a man of substance, educated, and well thought of by the secular opposition forces.

Sanjabi's arrival in Paris coincided with a speech by Carter, in which the U.S. president said he hoped an agreement would be reached between the two opposition leaders in the name of democracy. Never was a statement more ill-timed. Khomeini's reaction was immediate. He would not be a pawn of U.S. policy, he announced.

It was the first time that we and the rest of the world became aware of Khomeini's uncompromising character and his goal of becoming the only leader of the revolution. The anti-Shah forces had until then seemed a sin-

*There were a number of huge deals about to be struck (three or four atomic energy plants, the Tehran subway), which both the French and the Americans had bid on before the turmoil in Iran put everything on hold. The French, convinced that they would get the contracts if the Americans were out, abandoned the Shah in the hope that they could come out ahead with his successor, particularly if it was Khomeini, to whom they were providing asylum. Their position was more anti-American than anti-Shah. Their gamble paid off. The Americans were eliminated, and today most of these projects have been handled by France, which worked closely with the ayatollahs right from the beginning.

gle, amorphous mass. Khomeini was now drawing a thick line between himself and the other opposition groups. His was not a revolution for democracy or for any other ideal promulgated by intellectuals, Communists, or students of Mossadeq. His was a revolution for Islam, and he was going to make no concessions.

The talks came to nothing, though later Sanjabi served in Khomeini's first government.

Sometime later my old friend Seyyed Jalal Tehrani went to Paris to see Khomeini as head of the Regency Council, an advisory body set up after the Shah's departure. He fared little better. A cleric from an old family of religious leaders, he represented a substantial group of powerful clergy who still supported the Shah. In Paris Khomeini sent Tehrani a message saying, "I will see you only if you resign from the Council of Regents." Tehrani resigned. Khomeini met with him but again the talks went nowhere.

On December 6, 1978, and repeatedly in the following days, President Carter stated publicly for the first time that he was uncertain whether the Shah could hold on to his throne. For the Shah this was the ultimate betrayal. The nightmare that had haunted him throughout his reign was now coming to pass. What he had seen happen to his father was now happening to him. The West had turned its back on him. In his hour of need his allies had decided he could be dispensed with like an old shoe.

The Shah's high command, however, was still behind him. In an effort to find a solution the military's top generals—Kamal Habibollahi, Gholam Ali Oveysi, Nader Jehanbani, and others—went to the Shah and proposed that he retire to Kish Island and let them handle the situation. They suggested strong military action: a clampdown on all the uprisings—to hell with the blatter from Washington—and a complete cleanup of the streets. They even suggested bombing Qom—a plan that may, in fact, have worked.

The Shah shuddered and turned them down. In his heart of hearts he was not a fighter.

The generals' offer was the last hope. A few weeks later President Carter sent a military mission to Iran in the form of General Robert Huyser. He came with no clear agenda beyond informing the generals that the United States would countenance no major clampdown. Huyser, ill-informed and politically inept (Haig was adamantly against his appointment to the job), misinterpreted the situation so severely that less than a week before Khomeini's triumphant return he still talked of victory for the Shah's forces.[1] The generals, caught between the Shah and the Carter administration, had no room for maneuver. Within days many of them were forced to

flee. Those who stayed were arrested and executed by Khomeini's victorious forces just weeks later. Nader Jehanbani, a Qajar prince, even shouted,
"Long live Mohammad Reza Shah!" as he faced the firing squad.

As the last days of 1978 ebbed away the Shah, despondent and vague,
stayed holed up inside his palace, the radio blaring beside him, unable to
make a move, unable even to decide whether to go or to stay. King Hussein
of Jordan, an ally to the last, came to Tehran in those last days to help bolster the Shah's confidence. "Go into the streets and face your people," he
counseled. "Tour your cities. Use your voice to lower the flames of discontent. Whenever I have done this, even in the worst of times, the situation has
calmed. Your presence alone will settle the people. They need only to see you
and know you are with them. They will not attack you. They will recognize
you as their sovereign. I know. I have been in such situations myself."²

But the Shah could not bring himself to go into the streets and show his
face to the people. Instead, when Azhari suffered a stroke at the end of December, the Shah appointed his last government, this time headed by an
opposition leader named Shahpur Bakhtiar. He then made it known he was
going to leave the country for an unspecified amount of time.

Bakhtiar's government, generally referred to as the "Kerensky government,"* was utterly powerless. Bakhtiar had neither experience nor stature
and got the job only because no one else would take it. Sanjabi, Amini,
even Entezam turned it down—though Entezam suggested Bakhtiar.

To the Shah's credit Bakhtiar's appointment represented a real departure
from the establishment. His ministers were members of the bourgeoisie,
Mossadeq admirers who believed in constitutional government and liberal
reform. If anything they were too far to the left for the prevailing mood in
the country. But Bakhtiar was doomed by the very fact that the Shah had
selected him. And Khomeini had told the people not to compromise. The
Shah, Mossadeq, and all of their followers were the same, he said: pro-
Western, imperialist, and anti-Islam. "Why do you talk of the Shah,
Mossadeq, money?" he asked in a radio broadcast. "These have already
passed. Islam is all that remains."

Khomeini, who by now had become the leading voice of the revolution,
then fired another salvo: He would not leave France for Iran until the Shah,
"the root of all evil," had left. His homecoming would signal the beginning of a new era, he said, one in which he would act as the nation's spiritual leader.

In anticipation he had already put together a shadow government,

---

*The Kerensky government was the last government under Nicholas II of Russia be-
fore the Communists took over, and as hobbled as Bakhtiar's by political counterforces.

which was waiting in the wings to take over. Everyone knew exactly who was in this new government. They were being quoted in the newspapers as often as—if not more often than—those who actually held office.

His new premier would be Mehdi Bazargan, the man who had taken over the management of the Abadan Refinery when Mossadeq had kicked out the British in 1951. Wizened now, intensely religious, and well respected by a wide range of groups in Iran, Bazargan was an ideal political choice as the first head of a new post-Shah government. Also in the cabinet was Dr. Karim Sanjabi, who was slated to become minister of foreign affairs. At the same time, with Bazargan's help, a religious council of prominent clerics was assembled, but although we knew of its existence, its role was shrouded in mystery.

As Christmas approached many of my family left Iran to spend the holidays with their children abroad. Few ever returned. Iran had become dangerous—and melancholy. The schools were closed, and the streets were filled with guns.

As the grim days of December followed menacingly one after another, I too left to join my family for a skiing vacation in Italy. First, however, I had another task to attend to. Since my return to Iran I had waited with great anticipation for my belongings to arrive from Caracas. But months had passed, and they had never come. So I headed to New York to see whether I could track them down. The trail was cold, and I found nothing. I felt defeated and began to wonder, as I passed the holidays with my children in Europe, whether I should return to Iran. What awaited me there? The Shah was finished. Would there be anything left for us after his departure?

On January 16, 1979, accompanied only by his family and a few close servants, the Shah quietly left Iran for Egypt. He would never see his country again. The Pahlavi era had come to an end.

THE TALE OF THE AYATOLLAH

The day the Shah left, I was in Rome, where I walked aimlessly through the streets, debating whether I should abandon Iran once and for all. There, a good friend of mine, Parviz Azemoun, persuaded me that our time in Iran was not necessarily over. "We do not know what will happen now," he pointed out. "Iran is our country. We betray ourselves if we do not at least wait to see whether there is some opportunity left." And so together we booked tickets on the last KLM flight to Tehran. The airport closed just a few hours after our arrival. It would not open again until Khomeini touched down in victory a couple of days later.

Khomeini came like a dragon, evaporating everything that lay before him. He had achieved the miraculous—he had ousted the monarchy—and his triumph was boundless. At the airport he was greeted by millions of people who jammed the highway for miles, shouting their jubilation in all the roads and in the plaza around the Shayad Memorial.

Khomeini alighted from the plane with the help of several Air France assistants, signaling that for France it was already a case of "The King Is Dead; Long Live the King!"

The crowds reached out to touch him, hoping to catch a glimpse of this man of God who had done the impossible and brought them freedom. Boarding a helicopter, he immediately headed toward his first stop, the cemetery of Behesht Zahra in the desert on the road to Qom. There another crowd of thousands had gathered to watch him pay homage to the martyrs who had lost their lives to topple the Pahlavi devil. It was a clever move. The Shiis love death and mourning, and this first tribute conformed perfectly to the people's desires, showing them he valued their sacrifice and was one with them.

I watched the Ayatollah's arrival on television, as stunned by the images that flashed across the screen as anyone living in Paris or New York. And yet what I saw did not immediately presage disaster. I expected the revolution to follow the French rather than the Soviet model and imagined that only the top layer of society would change.

At first Khomeini said and did little, biding his time, holding his cards close to his chest. The press was suddenly free and acted as it wished. The curfew that had been imposed during the last months of the Shah's rule was lifted.

The people, meanwhile, went on a rampage, taking the law into their own hands and occupying government offices. By then NIOC had stopped functioning and the state administration had ground to a halt. Foreigners were fleeing, as were upper-class technocrats and government officials. The army was crumbling, and every day news came that a different regiment or corps had gone over to the opposition. Army jeeps, used as passenger cars, raced along the streets carrying heavy machine guns stolen from the barracks. Even my mason obtained two or three rifles and came to me one afternoon to offer me one. There was shooting in the streets every night. The number of guns available was overwhelming, making it easy to settle personal feuds without anybody knowing. Revenge became just one more act of liberty.

Then, on February 11, 1980, ten days after Khomeini's triumphant return, the final curtain was lowered on the old regime. The Imperial Guard, until then loyal to their sovereign, were attacked and won over. The last barracks in the cities of Tehran, Isfahan, and Tabriz fell to the crowds, who swarmed over the walls, reappearing in exaltation with guns clutched in their arms like bouquets, and then set off, horns blaring, to celebrate in the streets. Boys of all ages waved AK-47s and G-3 machine guns as though they were toys. Fires burned late into the night.

The next day it was all over. The Islamic Revolution had been won.

THE NEW REVOLUTIONARIES

One of Khomeini's first acts was to set up revolutionary committees in the style of those of the Russian Bolsheviks. Where had he learned of this? we wondered. The heads of the committees were mollahs, and as each competed against the others to prove his religious fervor, they became increasingly aggressive and brutal. Suddenly the government didn't exist anymore. The committees had their own firing squads and guards and held complete power over the life or death of anyone who came within their districts. Immediately they began to commit acts of savagery of a kind unparalleled for centuries. Never had such cruelty been perpetrated by Mohammad Reza Shah or his father, nor had the Qajars ever commissioned such indiscriminate crimes. At the very moment when they should have been addressing the needs of the poor and the needy, the mollahs were executing the innocent right alongside the criminal.

Within the first few days four generals were executed by firing squad. Once four were killed, why not forty more or four hundred? The next to die were Hoveyda and Nassiri, whose show trials were broadcast on television. The Ayatollah's condemnation was a phrase from the Koran: *"Mofsed fel arz"* meaning "Those who corrupt the earth." Hoveyda and Nassiri were dragged from the court and shot half an hour later.

These six deaths gave the green light to the committees to kill anyone they wished. With another of Khomeini's telling phrases ringing in their ears, "Government is the law of religion," the Ayatollah's lieutenants began executing people right in the streets: ministers and members of Parliament, cinema owners, bankers, government employees, and landowners. Committee heads throughout Iran did the same, and in many insignificant towns as many as fifty or a hundred people were executed. The Ministry of Justice and the courts were dissolved in all but name. Most notorious of all was a mollah named Khalkhali, called "The Butcher of Tehran," who traveled about the country and, with the Koran in his hand, condemned anyone who caught his eye to instant death in the street. Each day the pictures of those who had been killed were published in the newspaper.

It was horrible and frightening. As with the Bolshevik revolution, all precedence, rules, and laws were wiped out. With one clean sweep Khomeini turned everything upside down.

Very soon a plethora of new revolutionary entities were established, all with Khomeini's blessing. Most powerful was the Revolutionary Council, the advisory group of ayatollahs formed before Khomeini's return, which now emerged from behind its veil of secrecy and was supposed to be the religious conscience of the government. But it soon began to act as an independent political force, countermanding government actions and undercutting its authority. The Revolutionary Council put real teeth into its dictates by establishing a new extragovernmental security force: the Pasdaran. This was the equivalent of the gendarmerie, although it operated with no formal structure and answered to no one except its religious mentor and manager, Ayatollah Khamenei—a big player on the Revolutionary Council.* Initially the Pasdaran was set up to collect all the arms that had been seized by the population from the fallen barracks. Very soon, however, it began to infringe on the committees, and at times the two openly clashed, contributing to the sense of general chaos and insecurity.

Meanwhile, under cover of the Bazargan government, Khomeini was developing his plan for an Islamic Republic. It would have no place for Communists, moderates, the bourgeois successors of Mossadeq, or even mollahs not committed to his vision. These would in time all be ousted, run underground, executed, or expelled with a ruthlessness that would make the Shah's rule seem positively benign.

Khomeini worked with only one instrument, and that was religion. Alas religion—how many crimes are perpetrated in your name! His conviction was fanatic and sincere. He crushed all argument and imposed his views by refusing to compromise. Religion, as Khomeini interpreted it, was transferred into a political doctrine the likes of which neither Iran nor any other Islamic country had ever known. For Khomeini Islam *was* democracy. Unlike the Bible the Koran prescribes many of the rituals of daily life, and to Khomeini the immediacy of its tenets had not changed despite the passage of fourteen hundred years. Khomeini suffered no doubts that the people of Iran wanted Islam to guide them not just spiritually but in every aspect of their lives. They had marched in the streets and demanded it. Now they deserved the redemption that he had promised them.

For Khomeini bringing an Islamic Republic to Iran was the ultimate revolution—the first completely new chapter in twenty-five hundred years

---

*When Khomeini died in 1989, Ayatollah Khamenei succeeded him as president of the Islamic Republic and highest religious authority in the country.

of Persian history. But it would succeed only if the iniquity that had driven the country into its present state of moral degradation was destroyed. Khomeini coined a phrase to describe the situation in Iran: *garb zadeh,* meaning "struck by the West." The old idols and oil boom era standards had to be demolished. It would take vigilance and force. It would take an inquisition.

Like Lenin and Hitler, Khomeini came to power uncontested, supported by a delirious public. There was no one and nothing to counterbalance him. The Shah was gone; Bakhtiar had evaporated into the night;* the government had dissolved; even the army had collapsed. And of course the Parliament no longer existed. Into this vacuum Khomeini came with his own men and his own doctrine. With each passing day he drew on that doctrine much as Lenin drew on Marxism, interpreting the Koranic laws as he saw fit and gradually building up a body of precedence. Khomeini legitimized mock trials and street-side executions by saying that Islam had no need to refer to corrupt secular laws to pass judgment. He condemned those who did not follow in his path by labeling them deserters, not just of a regime but of a religion. And so people were hunted down and shot, property was seized, civic laws were overturned, new codes of dress were imposed, and alcohol was banned—all in the name of Islam.

Yet ironically Islam was not the thread that tied the diverse opposition groups to Khomeini. It was instead his choice of "imperialism" as the enemy, that all-embracing word that embodied Western values and materialism as well as Western historical might. Hatred of imperialism inflamed not only the poor and the religious but also the intellectuals and the bourgeoisie, the fanatic guerrilla groups, and the religious left. Anti-imperialism also effectively neutralized Khomeini's enemies—the Tudeh Party, the secular moderates, and any who opposed his executions and reprisals. Further it neatly set the tone for Iran's new foreign policy—aligning it with the less developed, more radical third-world nations both inside and outside OPEC.

Khomeini's coup d'état changed society from top to bottom. The people became hotheaded and intolerant of everything that had gone before—

*After Khomeini's triumphant return to Tehran Bakhtiar escaped to Paris, probably because his wife was French. There he set himself up as the symbol of opposition. A couple of years later assassins hunted him down at his home and slit his throat. The murder was shrouded in mystery, however, since his son had for a long time worked with the French secret police and had been specifically assigned to protect his father. Yet on the day of the assassination his son was out of the house. What's more, the French police, who found and arrested his murderers, later released them—under pressure, they said, of threats from Khomeini's government.

even of those things that had been good. One of the most ridiculous examples of this was the overnight reversal of all laws passed under the Shah's regime (on the premise that anything he'd signed was bad). More telling was the extreme difficulty—and ultimate failure—of Mehdi Bazargan's government (and its successor, the freely elected Bani-Sadr government) to exercise any control over the various power centers that sprang up after the revolution.

Once the revolution had rooted out its enemies, it turned on many of its friends—supporters who were less fanatic or less religious than the rest. There were many victims, though perhaps most surprising was another ayatollah, the highly respected cleric of Tabriz, Shariat-Madari. His prestige was so great that he was the only person Khomeini visited when he first went to Qom a few weeks after his return to Iran. But Shariat-Madari preached tolerance, and as the poet Saadi said, two kings cannot rule the same realm. As disappointment in the new regime inevitably began to be heard, a plot was uncovered that was supposedly traced to Shariat-Madari's followers. On his next pilgrimage to Qom from Tabriz, Shariat-Madari was put under house arrest, stripped of his title, and forbidden to communicate with his city. Gradually he disappeared into oblivion. When he died his funeral was attended by only his closest relatives.

THE TALE OF A BROTHER IMPRISONED

At first, after the initial elation and inevitable return to daily life—when the stores began to reopen, people began going back to work, the electricity came on again in the evening, and the gasoline lines subsided as the Abadan Refinery resumed operation—we thought the body of Iran had simply molted, throwing off its old coat but remaining essentially the same. We did not realize that in fact a whole new animal had been born.

We did not know then that the old elite would always remain under suspicion. We could not imagine that factories would be confiscated; that companies, land, and commercial buildings would be seized; and that even private homes would be taken over. We had not read Khomeini's writings and therefore did not know that he had for years envisioned the Revolutionary Council becoming the real wielder of power and that clerics would henceforth govern Iran. Instead we sought a way to find a niche for ourselves within the new structure.

Then suddenly one of my brothers was arrested. It was Alinaghi, the president of the Bank of Industries, and his crime was usury—lending money at a rate of interest. His wife was in Geneva with their children. The local committee came to his office unannounced and marched him off to Evin Prison. We were informed that as siblings we could go and visit him, but the outlook for his release was bleak, and the threat of execution hung ominously over his head. As new atrocities swept the city, many people panicked and rushed madly to escape. For some it was too late. A list at the airport immigration booth became infamous for containing the names of those who were to be arrested at the departure gate and sent directly to Evin Prison. Lists of people who were *mofsed fel arz*, "corrupters of the earth," also were published in the newspaper. Henceforth their assets, bank accounts, and property were frozen, and they were barred from engaging in any form of business, including the selling of a car or even a wristwatch. Some of the lists were so hastily composed that they contained the names of people who had been dead for fifty years. But this did not make it any easier for those still alive.

Terribly anxious about Alinaghi, I made an appointment to see Dr. Karim Sanjabi, the minister of foreign affairs and the only person in government with whom I had a deep connection. Visiting the ministry was eerie, for there was barely anyone left from my days as ambassador two years before. Where had all these new people come from? I wondered. How could they do the work, particularly in the area of foreign affairs?

Sanjabi's office was the same one that had been Khalatbari's for a good ten years before he was executed. I knew every detail of that office; only the rotating chair had been changed, and the picture of the Shah was gone. The waiting room was full, but the secretary, who also was the same, told me I'd be ushered right in. Even though I had not seen Sanjabi for almost a decade, he came to the door the minute he heard my name and greeted me warmly, giving me hope that, revolution or no revolution, the aristocracy still had a hand in the game.

Nonetheless he looked at me with apprehension, probably thinking that I had come to ask him for an ambassadorial appointment or government post. When we sat down, we looked at each other in silence for a moment, he thinking as I was, perhaps, how different our paths had been over the years.

I broke the silence. "Rest easy," I said. "I am not here to ask for a job. But I am here to ask you an awkward question. Have you forgotten your debt to my family?" He looked at me pathetically, and I could tell he knew exactly what I was referring to.

"How can you possibly say such a thing?" he asked reproachfully. "Though we have different political opinions, I'm ever reminded that my family owes yours everything. Your father saved my father and uncles, and at great risk to his own family. It served as a black mark against Nosrat-

Doleh and contributed to his fall. How can I forget such a sacrifice? All my life I have tried to keep my name above reproach. Now you accuse me of being ungrateful, which I cannot bear."

"There is no question of your honesty or good intentions," I said. "But recognizing the sacrifice of my father and brother, how can you now witness the imprisonment of a member of my family without raising a finger?"

"How do you know I haven't already taken action on that matter?" he returned. "Even as we speak my men are trying to obtain the release of prisoners who have been arrested without any proof of guilt. I am making a special investigation into your brother's case and will let you know whatever I find. But so far I have had little impact." His face fell. "The government's hands are tied because everything is run by the committees. I must admit to you I am on the verge of resigning."

"Don't resign at any price," I said quickly. "We don't know anyone else in power today. You are the only one. And yours is one of the few moderate voices we hear anymore."

Our friendship restored, he accompanied me to the elevator. Three days later he resigned, finding himself powerless to free anyone or carry out the rest of the duties of his job. For him and many others of a more liberal bent, the Khomeini revolution brought nothing but disappointment. He had fought all his life for social reform, only to realize that at the very moment that the country could turn toward democracy, Khomeini had hijacked the revolution. Soon, like those of us who were damned from the beginning, he too fell under suspicion and had to flee.

My sister Maryam and her husband, Kia, were victims of the same disillusionment. As the Shah fell they returned to Iran from East Germany, filled with the hope that the Tudeh Party would finally have its day. During the uprisings the party enjoyed a resurgence, particularly in the oil fields and in the north along the Caspian coast. Yet the Soviet Union was careful not to assume too public an image, not only because Khomeini damned communism as no better than capitalism but also because it had its own agenda of taking over Afghanistan once the Shah's formidable military collapsed, a move it duly made at the end of 1979. After the revolution the Soviets heavily supported the Tudeh Party's activities, as well as other communist groups such as the Fedayeen Khalq, a militant guerrilla force, convinced no doubt that it was just a matter of time before its followers prevailed.

Upon Khomeini's return, when all political activity was allowed, Kia found himself at last the head of a legitimate party. Under his guidance the Tudeh Party immediately made itself felt, publishing a newspaper called

Mardom (People), establishing a headquarters downtown, and demonstrating in the streets. But soon it too was repressed. Khomeini made it clear that communism was a threat, a foreign ideology that denied God and could only destroy Iran. The paper was banned, the offices closed, and once again the Tudeh Party was run underground. Within the year Kia and Maryam were imprisoned as traitors to the state, and they served many years behind bars.

It was late February 1980 when I had my own brush with the committee. I was at lunch with Mohsen Foroughi, the art collector whom I'd gotten to know during the Mossadeq days when we'd both sidestepped the Shah's volleyball games at court. Suddenly a group of gun-toting youths showed up at the door and dragged us off to committee headquarters. Revolutionary guards and committee henchmen were breaking up parties all over town and arresting the guests for crimes that ranged from hoarding alcohol to ill treatment of their gardeners. Extortion was becoming commonplace, the false charges sometimes being dropped upon an exchange of money. Meanwhile supervisors, many of them boys as young as fifteen who barely knew which way to hold their guns, were appointed to all the residential buildings and assigned to watch and report back on all movements of the occupants.

This time we were immediately released once we got to the committee headquarters. The next time the committee came to Foroughi's house my brother Khodadad was there, and they were both held overnight. The third time they put Foroughi in jail for several months.

With Sanjabi out of the government I tried to obtain Alinaghi's release by contacting the brother of Prime Minister Bazargan. I had met him years before through my brother Mohammadvali Mirza. Their father had been a merchant in Azerbaijan and at one point had bought land from my father. But my efforts were to no avail. Once again the Farmanfarmaian name had become a signal light of danger. A new list of traitors published by the central committee had our name at the top, condemning us all, since the compilers of the list had made no effort to specify us individually, as they had with all the other "corrupters of the earth." We were falling deeper and deeper into disfavor while knowing nothing of the mentality of the religious leadership and lacking any connection to anyone in power.

Incapable of obtaining Alinaghi's release, we did the only thing that was allowed—we took turns going to see him each week at Evin. Face-to-face behind a wall of thick glass in a small cell, we talked on a monitored telephone. The saddest part was that we had nothing to say. We were so shocked by the situation that we could only look at each other in bewilderment. We tried to give him hope and comfort, but in truth we seemed to need it more than the lonely man we saw on the other side of the glass.

The visits were over quickly. Afterward we suffered for hours in despair. Alinaghi looked pale and on the verge of collapsing whenever we delivered news of his wife and children in Europe. When news was scarce we fabricated it. But he seemed to sense when we were making things up, though he pretended to believe us, knowing that would make us feel better.

Outside the prison gates a crowd waited all day to enter. We would stand there for hours, shivering before the massive doors in winter, sweating under the harsh sun in spring. A bazaar had sprung up along the road, where kabobs, cheap trinkets, and cassettes of Khomeini's sermons were sold from tented kiosks. Sharpies claiming to be intermediaries tried to fool people into paying huge sums to have their relatives released.

Occasionally a mollah sitting in state in the back of a chauffeur-driven Mercedes would pull up, flanked by a group of zealous guards. While the guards covered the crowd with their machine guns, the mollah stepped majestically from the car. Attendants pushed the people back with the butts of their rifles and trampled on their feet. It reminded me of the grande dame of the Tata family in India throwing her coins into the crowds, though now I was one of the beggars.

The mollah, with obvious disdain, would sneer at the onlookers, who were too terrified to know whether to acknowledge his presence with reverence or to turn their heads in mock respect. Perhaps the Shah himself had acted like this, but his entourage could never have gotten away with it. Once a notorious prostitute was executed and her yellow Mercedes-Benz confiscated. The very next day the assistant governor of Evin Prison was seen riding in it. The mollahs had become no better than petty tyrants, putting on airs and despising their followers.

A CLOSE CALL

As the net tightened around us, we adopted an increasingly low profile. We did not go out much, and the only people we saw were relatives and close friends. In one of his radio talks Khomeini impelled the populace to embark on another wave of calumny. "Everyone has a duty," he said in bellicose reverence, "to denounce counterrevolutionaries so that we may punish them." Now even longtime servants were turning on their masters, and a campaign of anonymous letters, accusing people of every imaginable crime, had brought a new spate of arrests. Thank God my own loyal servant and driver, Shirkhan, had remained trustworthy, for he was privy to many secrets and I had grown heavily dependent on him. Nonetheless we knew that phone calls had been made denouncing our family and that letters had been written about us to the local committees. Central authority and the law as such no longer existed; our fate was in the hands of young revolutionaries whose honor and prestige—and perhaps even their income—hinged on the number of arrests they made and the importance of their game.

It was just a matter of time before news came that another member of the family had been seized. This time it was my nephew Eskandar Firouz, who had been vice minister of the environment under the Shah. He had succeeded in limiting the indiscriminate hunting of gazelles and other wild game in Iran and had set up a program of reforestation in the north that had contributed to the revival of wildlife in the Caspian Sea area. He had turned the Department of the Environment into one of the most efficient government departments in Iran. Yet now Khomeini's thugs confiscated his property and threw him into jail for turning Iran "green." As with Alinaghi the only thing we could do was go see him and hope to God that he would soon be released.

A number of my family—brothers, sisters, and several nieces and nephews—had bought apartments in the same block where I lived. As a result we saw one another often, and our lives became increasingly bunkered. It seemed safer to take an elevator from one floor to the next rather than venture into the streets. One evening one of my nieces who lived a few floors below invited me for dinner. Before going down I left her telephone number with the concierge in accordance with the new rules requiring us to inform the committee where we were at all times.

We were eating the first course when the telephone rang. The committee wanted to see me. Everyone's face went white. I could see in their eyes the fear that something drastic was going to happen and they might never see me again.

I took the elevator up to my apartment on the fifteenth floor. As the automatic doors opened I saw four submachine guns pointed at my face.

"You are under arrest," said one of the guards. "You must come with us to committee headquarters." The guards were clad in ragged uniforms. Their shoes were mismatched and torn. They were peasants, poor people from the slums who'd been handed a gun and were anxiously doing their duty, even if it meant killing.

I asked if I might pack some underwear and my shaving kit, and they agreed. As I opened the door to my apartment one of the guards muttered, "Poor devil. He thinks he'll need to change and shave. He doesn't even know how many days he has to live."

While they sat and waited for me in the lounge I hurriedly got some things together. Just as we were leaving the telephone rang. Seeing a flicker of a nod from the head guard, I picked it up. It was my friend Ali Moalizadeh, who had brought me the suitcase of cash for the carpet before my departure for Caracas. Many years before I'd given him a license for a gas station, which had prospered, and ever since he'd called me his lucky star.

He was calling to say good-bye before leaving for New York the following morning. My greeting, though warm, was brief. He could hear the tension in my voice. After a couple of sentences he broke in and asked what the matter was.

"The revolutionary guards are here to take me to committee headquarters," I said. "I must go, for they are in the living room right now."

He was very distressed and offered to postpone his departure to see if there was anything he could do for me.

"No, Ali," I said. "Get out of here now. Who knows, you may face this same predicament tomorrow."

He mumbled agreement and seemed about to hang up when suddenly, almost as an afterthought, he said, "Ask what the name is of the mollah heading the committee."

I turned and asked the guards.

"Mollah Shahabadi," I told Ali. "Why do you ask?"

"Mollah Shahabadi?" he said, his voice incredulous. "It is a miracle! The mollah is related to my family. Keep the guards occupied for a few minutes. I will call you back."

Diverting the guards' attention was not difficult. They were already working their way through my silver and other knickknacks on my tables.

Within minutes the telephone rang again. This time it was Mollah Shahabadi himself. He addressed me with great respect. "*Agha-ye* Moalizadeh has often spoken of you and even before the revolution told me of your kindness toward him. Please do not bother to come down to our headquarters this evening. Tomorrow will be fine. I shall receive you myself."

It was almost an invitation rather than an order. I appreciated his dignity and thanked him.

"Pass me please to the leader of the guards," he said. "I look forward to seeing you tomorrow."

The guards left immediately, robbing me of some of my small silver boxes, which they surreptitiously slipped into their pockets. It seemed a small price to pay under the circumstances. Minutes later my friend Ali rang again, and with great emotion we said our good-byes.*

The following morning Shirkhan drove me to Shahabadi's office. It was a little two-story mud-brick house on a very narrow street in the old part of town. There were two guards with submachine guns at the door. A cellar below served as a prison. There I saw desperate, worried faces peering through the bars.

That could have been my prison too, I thought as I climbed the stairs to meet the mollah. He sat ceremoniously in his turban and gown, surrounded by a crowd of people. He got up and greeted me, then asked me to wait, saying he had to settle everyone else's case before he could attend to mine.

Someone was complaining that a tire he had bought was too expensive. Another accused his neighbor of advancing his wall a yard into his property. I recognized these small problems as the same ones I'd dealt with as a landowner in Hamadan. None were really the mollah's responsibility but rather the government's. Nonetheless in each instance he said he'd send a guard "to make a report," one more pretext to divert the dispensation of any real justice while he kept power in his own hands.

The room was cleared of people when the mollah finally turned to me. "Your friend *Agha-ye* Moalizadeh, who is married to my cousin, thinks highly of you, and so I wanted to see you. Write your name and telephone number on this paper so I can find you if I need to."

I wrote my name as Haji Farmanfarmaian, indicating with the "Haji" that I had made a pilgrimage to Mecca. The mollah looked at me with surprise, apparently unaware that people such as myself ever made the pilgrimage. He then admitted he lived in Farmanieh, and so was my neighbor, and had often encountered the charity work I had done for the villagers.

He walked me to the door to say good-bye. But upon seeing my driver he called to Shirkhan to come in for what he said would be a few words. I waited an hour before Shirkhan returned. As we drove home he told me he had been extensively debriefed on how I treated my staff. He said he'd told the mollah that he had no complaints and that he felt very satisfied to be in my employ. He assured me he'd added that he felt someone had maliciously and falsely accused me of crimes against the revolution and that I

*After the revolution I searched in vain for Ali Moalizadeh, but he knew none of my friends, and no one had any idea where he was. Then, quite by accident, ten years later in Washington I ran into him. It was an emotional reunion, for I considered him someone who had truly saved my life. Unfortunately it was our last reunion; shortly thereafter he died of cancer.

was not guilty. I realized then that I should have passed the mollah a gift, for it was all a sinister game of blackmail.

We drove home past the American Embassy. I remembered as a child going north with my father and seeing the house when it still belonged to the Garagozlus, an old family whose property was filled with pines. The place had seemed far away and very beautiful. When the city had grown to meet the property, the Garagozlus had sold it to the U.S. government. It was just down the road from my mother's house. The same street, Takhte Jamshid, ran past the university farther on. There were still a few pines left, though the wall that encased the embassy was now covered in graffiti. I would be long gone by the time it became notorious as the center of the American hostage crisis in 1979–1981.

A TALE OF UNBEARABLE MADNESS

Strangely, the fervor that had led up to the ouster of the Shah did not subside with the triumph of the revolution. Iran was gripped by a fever—a madness—that grew more acute with every passing day. The opposition forces now turned on one another and were fighting to the death for dominance. Daily demonstrations filled the streets in support of one group or another; often they ended in skirmishes and deadly gun battles. An outright war had erupted in Kurdistan, where the revolution had been fought for autonomy. The minister of defense, Ali Chamran, personally led what had been reconstituted of the army in helicopter gun battles strafing the Kurds. Horrifying pictures appeared in the newspapers of men hanging from rafters or shot in sequence against a wall.

Meanwhile the executions in all the major cities seemed to increase in number and absurdity. An old army general, long retired, was executed for having been involved in the coup d'état of 1921, when he was only a junior lieutenant. Homosexuals and thieves were gunned down. Prostitutes and adulteresses were publicly stoned to death.

The clear winner in this new round of bloodletting was Khomeini. Pictures and posters filled the streets proclaiming him a virtual deity. People no longer called him Ayatollah but Imam, meaning prophet. Daily demonstrations exalted his wisdom, his judgment, and his mercy. Radio and television broadcasts exhorted the people to believe that the past was only darkness and the future only light. The history of Iran, it was maintained, had begun with the history of Islam.

When my brother Rashid was arrested, it brought the number of family members in prison to three. I knew I would be next. I decided to go see Mollah Shahabadi again in case there was something he could do.

After waiting a long time in his vestibule I handed him an envelope containing more than $1,000 in Iranian currency.

"Sir, this is for your charity expenses," I said. "You know better than I who are the needy."

I then spoke of my brothers and nephew and asked if he could help. He opened the Koran and read for a little in silence. The omens were apparently not favorable. "Let's think about it," he said when he looked up, "and we will be in touch."

My hopes were shattered. Did he read signs of my own arrest just a few days down the line? So far I had been lucky, but luck has a way of running out.

THE LAST ROAD
TO FREEDOM

On the day of tragedy, sorrows should be discussed with wine
Trust no one on this earth;
Sit and observe with optimism through the turmoils of the time,
the face with sweetness on its tongue.

—HAFEZ

Istanbul 1980
And so I left, my escape turning into a harrowing journey across the Iranian border and the snow-choked wastes of Turkey. The cold, inhospitable city of Istanbul seemed like another hell. How strange life is. Thrown together with Sa'id, a coarse, vulgar ruffian with a heart of gold, we were trapped like rats in dangerous territory. Never in my wildest dreams could I have imagined such a thing. More than anything in the world I wanted to leave Istanbul for Paris. I was tired; I had had enough.

Already Sa'id and I had whiled away an extra day in Istanbul waiting for the train. Now, with our luggage once more in hand, we were told by the platform master that the train was two hours late. Sa'id and I consoled ourselves with the thought that once it arrived and we waved our first-class tickets at the conductor, we would enjoy its little luxuries: its brass fittings, its polished wooden banquettes, its pink lampshades. How shattering it was to discover that the train had no first class and that the ticket master, now nowhere to be seen, had simply relieved us of our money.

I shouted angrily at the conductor, frustrated not just by the ineptitude of the Turkish train system but by all the setbacks and trials that had dogged my flight from Iran. The lavatories were indescribably filthy and would not flush. The windows were hazy with grime. The ashtrays overflowed with foul-smelling cigarette butts. Still the train was almost empty, and Sa'id and I were able to find a compartment all to ourselves.

In the early dark of the next morning the door burst noisily open and a short, stout frontier guard asked for our passports. We had crossed the Turkish frontier into Bulgaria. Right away I could tell there was something wrong.

"You don't have transit visas to cross Bulgaria," he said. "You can't continue."

"But we're just crossing the country to get to Paris and Hamburg," I said. "Our tickets are in order, and no one told us we needed visas!"

Without a word he opened his leather bag and dropped in our passports. "Get your luggage," he said. "You must get off the train."

He turned on his heel and went on to the next compartment.

The station was small and dirty. When the train left a few minutes later I felt it was taking my heart away.

It was about eight o'clock when they called Sa'id and me and two other travelers who were waiting for visas. Then, as though changing his mind, the frontier guard told me to wait.

When Sa'id came out of the office, visa in hand, he asked, "Shahzdeh, would you like me to wait?"

I looked at him feeling completely wretched, but the frontier guard behind him ordered him on.

"We are together," he protested, to no avail.

"We may never see each other again," he said, looking suddenly stricken. "I will never forget you. You are a true aristocrat."

I was deeply moved, despite my fear and misery. Digging into my pocket, I withdrew $300 and insisted that he take it for all his valuable services. At first he refused, but at last, with great humility, he said, "Whenever I earn some honest money I always put it aside for a lady friend."

"Really?" I said. "That's very decent of you. Where is she? Why don't you go and live with her?"

"No," he said. "I can't explain. You wouldn't understand."

"Why, is it a secret?" I asked.

"No," he said softly. "She works in a Hamburg brothel. But I will tell her an aristocrat gave this to me—the only aristocrat I have ever met—and probably the last."

I pulled out another $200. "This is for you," I said. "Buy yourself a watch, and every time you look at it you will think of me and our friendship. I wish you every happiness with your lady friend, and I hope one day you will marry or live together."

"How could I marry her?" he said with his whimsical smile. "If ever I quarrel with my associates, they will mock me and describe the way she makes love. I could not stand that and would want to kill them—even though it would mean my own death. No, Shahzdeh, it is better this way."

Poor Sa'id. He had traveled all over the world, crossing national borders without passport or visas. He could outwit any government, but he could never escape his own sordid colleagues.

He stretched out his arms, and we hugged each other. I have never felt such a lump in my throat.

Sa'id ran toward the train. On the step he turned, and for a second I caught his glance. By the time he had reached the window, however, I could tell his expression had changed. He had retrenched and was setting out on a new phase of his journey. I watched the train pull out of the station, carrying away the only friend I had had for thousands of miles.

I was called upstairs, where two men sat facing each other at a desk. The stout guard who had seized my passport stood nearby. Taking the passport out of his bag, he opened it and in English asked, "Why are you traveling with false documents?"

The question came like a clap of thunder. Yet there was no way to lie myself out of it. My briefcase contained all the evidence they needed, and I hardly remembered my new name. I could see from the guard's face that he was already picturing the promotion he would get out of this and would push me to the bitter end. Nonetheless I decided to try a bluff.

"Why make a trivial affair into such a big deal?" I said quietly. "Of course I'm traveling on a false passport. I'm fleeing my country. My real documents are in this briefcase."

I snapped open my bag and withdrew my diplomatic passport, breathing a sigh of relief that I had not thrown it away.

The two men at the desk examined the passport with great interest. The border guard, feeling his prey slipping from his grasp, intervened.

"This is also obviously a fake," he said. "The seal is so badly done it can easily be detected."

But it was too late. "Enough," said one of the men at the desk. "You have made your report. Now go."

Turning to me he said, "Please sit down. We cannot deal with your case here. You will have to see our chief, who works about an hour away."

Shortly thereafter a car picked me up, and we set off through wooded country, reaching at last a modern office building where someone waited for us outside. He spoke French and introduced himself as Mr. Bekov. He served me a good lunch, with beer and coffee, and then the interrogation began. The laws of Bulgaria allowed me either to be returned to my country or to face prison for three to five years after appearing before a magistrate. The choice was mine.

"Yours is a special case," said Bekov. "I will accompany you to a hotel in Khaskovo. Someone will come down from Sofia, the capital, and make the final decision on your case."

On the way to our new destination I at last had time to think. My family was probably expecting the worst, since I had left Tehran ten days earlier and then disappeared. They would think something dreadful had happened, and they would be right. Late in the evening, under heavy rain, we reached Khaskovo. The hotel was modest but clean, and my room had a bath. Over a small snack in the dining room my "guardian," as I called him, said it would be a day or two before the official from Sofia arrived. He made sure my luggage remained sealed, allowing me only the bare necessities for personal hygiene.

I returned to my room and went to bed. In the morning I read a little, but my concentration was poor and my mind wandered. Already I felt trapped. Communist states were known for their intransigence. What, I wondered, would they do to me?

The day dragged by. I walked a little near the hotel but felt that I was being watched and so did not wander far. It was agonizing just waiting, with nowhere to go and no one to talk to. When evening came I gulped my dinner and escaped to bed, hoping sleep at least would offer me reprieve.

The next morning I was informed that someone was waiting upstairs to see me. I felt quite self-conscious, for I'd torn my jacket at the shoulder sometime in the past few days and had been unable to get another one from my luggage. I was taken to a small apartment on the fifteenth floor, where a tall, good-looking man of about fifty greeted me at the open door. He beckoned me to sit on the sofa beside him but waited until I was served coffee before beginning to speak.

In good English he declared, "My name is Luben Belof. I am with the Ministry of Foreign Affairs. I have looked at your case, and it is clear that you are afraid of your government and so have fled. Unfortunately the fact is that simply possessing a false passport already condemns you, whether you appear before a judge or not."

"Yes," I said, "I'm well aware of this. And I am ready to serve my sentence. But I hope you will assign me some constructive work to do. I could teach oil engineering, chemistry, French, or English. All that I ask is that you permit my family to come and visit me at Christmas. I don't mind working. Put me to work in an oil refinery, since that is my profession, or as a gardener, for I am a lover of plants."

Belof and I talked further, and despite everything we began to establish a rapport. He had a shock of white hair and was nattily dressed, and as the conversation continued I learned that he had traveled abroad several times for his work, going even as far as Mexico. He reviewed Bekov's statement, making sure I agreed with every line of it, then suggested we have lunch.

In the restaurant Belof ordered vodka and offered a toast. "To your case!" he said. Although vodka has never been my drink, I raised my glass.

The lunch was served by a lovely young waitress. When the bill came I said that jail was free and so I would pay. It came to $15 and I gave the girl a $10 tip.

"Mr. Farmanfarmaian, you should not have tipped the girl so much," Belof chided. "Service is included in the bill."

"Please," I said, "let me assuage my sorrows. This girl will never again have the chance to meet someone about to go to jail for five years and therefore with no further need for money."

"All right, all right," said Belof. "Well, are you ready to go?"

"To jail?" I asked.

"No." He smiled. "Pack your bags. We're driving to Sofia—in my car."

"My luggage is ready," I told him. "It's been sealed since I arrived and is there with the concierge."

A man who looked like a hotel policeman produced the bags, which had been all wired up. Belof immediately ordered that the seals be broken. "The frontier guards have no right to seal luggage once it's passed the border," he said. "I am going to order a report. The police have to know the law, not invent it."

Sofia was about a hundred miles away, and we stopped two or three times for coffee. The countryside was beautiful, with cultivated fields and apple orchards. Belof explained that Bulgaria had no natural resources and had only been developed after the war through hard work.

Later on he explained that his surname meant "beautiful face."

"What a remarkable coincidence," I told him. "My name, Manucher, means the same thing in Persian."

By the time we reached Sofia I felt we'd known each other for years. Belof had two sons, both of whom were studying at the university. He had an apartment in Sofia and a house on the outskirts, where his wife grew fruit trees. By the time he dropped me off at the Hotel Balkan in the city center, we were calling each other by our first names.

Luben registered for me, since I had no identity papers. Before leaving he said, "For the next few days you will have complete liberty until we decide on your case. This is not Moscow, where the movements of all foreigners are restricted. There are car rental offices in the lobby, and you can go skiing. There are a couple of resorts nearby. Just stay out of trouble. Here are my telephone numbers. Call me on Monday."

I understood what he was saying: Don't try to escape, don't seek refuge at an embassy, don't do anything that will create a scandal. I gave him my word.

The next day, Sunday, I wandered about town, noticing that all the streets radiating from the Hotel Balkan led to public gardens or squares filled with attractive shops. Although Bulgaria had been under Turkish domination for centuries, there was a distinct European feel about the place. Even so in a big city it's difficult to kill time when you don't know the language or have anyone to talk to. Some people find solace in bars, sitting and drinking until someone turns up for a chat. But I am not one of those. Back at the hotel I felt very much alone. I thought longingly of my family but didn't dare call them, thinking it better to play it cool and not concern them.

On Monday Luben took me to a Japanese hotel for dinner and barraged me with questions about OPEC and my experience as a director of NIOC.

"If it is of any interest," I offered, "I would be happy to give a lecture at the university or address your oil company on the problems of production and marketing."

"No," he said. "But on Wednesday a couple of people want to discuss oil matters with you in your room. After that we will see what happens."

My new interrogators arrived midmorning. We talked at length about the international aspects of the oil industry and particularly OPEC. Luben interpreted, speaking mostly in English but occasionally resorting to French. After half an hour the men said something to Luben and left. We went for a drink and lunch, and Luben said, "Do you know what those two men just told me? They said there's no point in examining this fellow— meaning you—any further. He knows his stuff and is who he says he is."

We laughed. I had just been put through a general knowledge test on the oil industry, and apparently I'd passed.

Walking back to the hotel after lunch, we passed the American Embassy, which was cordoned off along the street. A large Cadillac was parked outside.

"Luben," I whispered. "Let's you and me go in there and seek asylum."

"I might be tempted!" he replied, quick as a flash.

"Not likely." I laughed.

"I know you wouldn't either," he returned. "You've passed in front of this embassy many times, and you always cross over to the other side of the street."

He smiled at the game we were playing, but I could tell he knew I was keeping my end of the bargain. Obviously I was being closely watched, and he was being informed of my every move. That afternoon, as we said our good-byes, he invited me to meet his son later in the week at his house in the country. But then he said, "I will meet you for lunch again the day after tomorrow," and I suddenly felt apprehensive, knowing that by then the decision would be made and I might have to spend the next few years in jail.

Back at the hotel I contemplated writing a letter to Petronella, letting her and the children know I was all right. But I was afraid, not wanting to jeopardize my chances, and so I gave up the idea and went to bed.

I've never in my life suffered insomnia and as a result never felt much sympathy for those who do. But during those few nights in Sofia the minutes passed like hours, and I tossed and turned without being able to close my eyes for a second. I must have looked at my watch every fifteen minutes, wondering why the time passed so slowly when years had passed so fast. For the first time in my life I felt depressed. I could not see a path ahead of me. There was no place for my mind to find repose.

At last Friday came. I got up early, feeling drained and tired. At midday, a good hour before my meeting with Luben, I went down to the bar to wait.

Luben arrived just minutes later. Clearly he had been informed that I had appeared at the bar early.

"I knew you would be here," he said breezily, "and I did not want to make you wait. Let's have a drink, and we can talk before lunch."

We sat down, and vodka was served. I was shivering without being cold. I had lost my composure entirely. How would I react if he told me I was going to prison?

I sipped my vodka silently without any sensation, leaning my head on my left hand, waiting for the ax to fall.

Luben paused in drinking his vodka and said, "How strange. The first time I saw you at the hotel lobby in Khaskovo you were holding your head just like that."

"I was concerned then, just as I am now," I said.

"All right," he said. "Time to celebrate! Everything is settled. Arrangements are being made for you to leave Bulgaria in a week for Paris!"

I thought he was joking.

"There's a midafternoon nonstop flight from Bulgaria to Paris every Friday, and next week you'll be on it," he said, smiling. "You will have to travel on your false passport, which needs Bulgarian entry and exit stamps. This will take a few days, for I will have to send your passport to the frontier and have it stamped by the same guard who arrested you in the first place. What an insult that will be to him! He thought he'd caught a big fish, and now he'll have to let it go and his colleagues will laugh at him."

I was so relieved that I called for champagne.

"No, no," admonished Luben. "That's just sweet soda water. Vodka is our drink. Champagne is for capitalists and feudalists like you!"

Over lunch Luben explained that my presence in Bulgaria had to be justified, and so a formal invitation was being issued, which gave privileges such as half price plane tickets. This was indeed a sea change.

Then, almost as an afterthought, he asked, "How do you know they will let you into France?"

"After lunch we can telephone the Ministry of Foreign Affairs in Paris and see," I suggested. The minister, Jean François-Poncet, had been posted to the French Embassy in Tehran, where I had gotten to know him quite well. It was a gamble to call him directly, but I thought it was worth it. I did not tell Luben about François-Poncet, but he agreed to the call and at the hotel got through to Paris by special order. I picked up the phone, and Luben listened in on an earpiece.

"Please give me the minister's personal office," I said to the operator. When François-Poncet's secretary came on the line I said, "I am the former Iranian ambassador, Manuchei Farmanfarmaian."

"Yes, yes," came the answer from the other end. "We know you, sir. What can we do for you?"

"Please tell the minister that I will be arriving in Paris on Friday on a Bulgarian plane about five in the afternoon."

I did not wait for an answer but hung up immediately in case the operator had hesitated. Luben may have had his doubts, but he wanted to hear something positive, since he was as vested in getting me out as I was. Now, finally I could also call my family. With great emotion I told them I was safe and arriving in Paris under the name Shamzin. I knew they would make all further arrangements.

The next few days passed happily. My passport arrived, and once more I was Sheikh Shamzin. Luben came with me to buy my half-price ticket. The last few nights I spent with his family.

Finally it was Friday. Luben brought me to the airport in an official car that dropped us right on the tarmac. He told the captain to watch out for me. "If at the last moment he encounters any problems in Paris," he said, "reserve a seat for him so that he can return to Sofia with you."

He then turned to me. "Don't hesitate to come back. From here I can easily send you to Venezuela, where I know you eventually want to go. You will always be my friend."

Genuine friendship is difficult to find, and yet rare though it is, I had found it once again. Luben Belof had truly saved me—and simply out of the goodness of his heart. It was sobering to think that had I been assigned a different official, I would be wallowing in prison rather than boarding a plane.*

As the plane rose in the sky I looked fondly out over Sofia. It had been a pleasant stay, but it had also been a nightmare, and it was only now, as the city faded into the distance, that I began to believe that I'd really escaped. Yet I also felt a renewed sense of apprehension. What if, at this late stage, I encountered new problems with the French police?

I need not have worried. At the main building I spotted a man who stood near the gate, scrutinizing the new arrivals. By now I knew his kind and felt no surprise when he gestured for me to follow him.

He led me to an office where a French official sat behind a desk. "Your passport," he demanded.

I gave him the passport and started to explain.

"Monsieur, no comments!" he shouted.

Again I tried to speak. This time he banged his fist on the table. Admitting I had a false passport would force him to send me to prison, I suddenly realized, and held my tongue.

He stamped my entry visa and informed me that my residence permit was waiting at the central police station. We shook hands. "Take him to his relatives waiting to the left of the building, not out front where Khomeini's spies usually keep watch," he said to the man escorting me.

Minutes later brothers, sisters, and nephews swarmed around me. At last I was a free man.

*It took me twelve years to find Luben again. With the help of the Bulgarian ambassador to Caracas, I discovered that because he had been with the secret service, he had assumed a new name after the fall of the communist regime. As Lambo Popov, he is still living in Bulgaria and recently sent me a letter reestablishing contact.

EPILOGUE

Each time the devil departs, he is replaced by the angel.
—HAFEZ

Caracas 1995
I was lucky. About a year after I got to Caracas my lost belongings suddenly showed up. They had never even made it onto the boat and had been left standing on the quay for two years. Vandalism and rain had decimated a good portion, and yet had they reached Tehran, I would not have anything at all. As it is, the few prints and books and pieces of pottery that survived are all I have left.

My house in Farmanieh, my property at Vardavard, and my apartment in Saman were all taken over by the government. Eight families were moved into my house, and part of it was turned into a grocery store. The open spaces that once surrounded the house have been filled with highrises. Tehran, with a population of more than 10 million people, has become one of the biggest cities in the world.

My mother's house, located in what is now the center of town, is one of the last freestanding homes in the city. Several times the authorities have asked for permission to turn it into a mosque. There is a Persian phrase that perfectly sums up how I feel: *Cheraghi keh beh khaneh ravast beh masjed haramast*—it is a sin to use a lamp for a mosque when it is needed for the home. My brothers and I, who inherited the house, have so far withheld our agreement. The authorities have confiscated so much of our property that it is a wonder they bother to ask for our permission. But Moslem law recognizes that prayers can be said only with the owner's approbation, so the house remains untouched.

It has been more than fifteen years since the institution of the Islamic Republic, and I believe it will survive. Its roots are deep and growing deeper. In the West we often talk about social and religious restrictions in Iran, but we fail to recognize that these are what the people want. Many women want to wear the black veil and hide their legs; many young men wanted to go to war with Iraq and face death with pride. A tacit moral agreement exists between the government and the people. And the regime of the ayatollahs will adapt—just as all revolutionary governments eventually adapt to the needs of ordinary life.

After fifteen years of the Islamic Republic, the authorities have finally released the various members of my family from prison, and all now live in liberty. The last to be set free was Maryam, who could not believe that the world she rejoined had lost the Soviet Union. She and a few of my brothers and sisters still live in Iran. Rashid and my nephew Eskandar now live abroad. Yet as the years have passed, the Iranian communities in Europe and the United States have dissolved and lost their unity. Even my family is no longer the clan it once was or could have been had we stayed in Iran. Still assimilation has its rewards. Eleven of my nephews and nieces and all three of my own children have gone to Ivy League universities. Four of my nieces obtained degrees from Oxford and Cambridge. The light of education my father believed in so strongly lives on in the next generation.

It is also easy, in these post-Pahlavi days, to be criticized for believing in the Shah. I took great pride in being his ambassador. I thought he was guiding us into the right port. He committed himself to the direction in which the world was moving. Like many other third-world leaders he dove into the stream of progress, even though he lacked the technical expertise or infrastructure necessary to navigate its turbulent waters.

Mossadeq wanted a republic in which the sovereign would reign but not rule. The Shah wanted full freedom of action and therefore separation of church and state. In both cases the state proved too weak to stand on its own. It required monarchy or religion, respectively, to prop it up, and neither nationalism nor capitalism was at last enough.

The Shah made many mistakes, but he is also blamed for many things he did not do. I remember when the picture of the two of us was taken at the oil fields. Afterward I was sharply admonished by SAVAK not to be so familiar with the king.

"Who are you to tell me this?" I asked. "If the Shah mentions something, I will act accordingly. But until then I can't believe that your judgment could be any better than mine."

So much was done in the Shah's name over which he had no control. He didn't even know about many of these things. This is true of most leaders today, and few leave office untarnished.

Among the Shah's greatest achievements (and one that still remains underappreciated) was his strong leadership of OPEC. During his rule the oil market remained stable, and the price of oil gradually increased in tandem with the price of manufactured goods. This abruptly changed with his fall. The ramifications were enormous. During the revolution Iran's production dropped from 6 million to less than 2 million barrels a day. This set off a panic in the United States and other industrialized nations—even though other members of OPEC quite easily made up for the shortfall. The hysteria exceeded even that which prevailed during the Arab oil embargo of 1973 and can only be credited to the developed world's fear that without the Shah, OPEC would come unhinged. In fact the ensuing buying spree by the industrialized nations created the very nightmare they were so terrified of.

By January 1980 the price of oil had jumped from $12 per barrel to $22.50, and by June to $41. OPEC revenues once again skyrocketed, reaching by 1980 the extraordinary sum of $300 billion—constituting, according to economists, the largest transfer of wealth in the history of mankind. The money, most of which was deposited in Western banks, came to be known as petrodollars and led to a rapid upward spiral in interest rates and third-world debt, as well as galloping inflation. In 1982 international trade contracted for the first time since World War II, plunging the world into a recession the likes of which economists had never seen and which came to be called stagflation. The American government, battling 15 percent inflation, went into debt to the tune of $460 billion—more than the entire third world combined.

This string of disasters—all triggered by the Shah's fall and the Iranian revolution—at last led the industrialized nations to adopt a new solution: energy conservation and production of their own resources. By 1988 OPEC's slice of the world oil market had dropped to 44 percent from 74 percent fifteen years earlier. Today the price of oil has leveled off at $12 to $16 a barrel, about what it was the day the Shah left Iran. New discoveries of oil in the Caspian and Orinoco Belt, and new assessments of supply in existing fields, point to another hundred years of exploitation. The fear that oil will run out has all but disappeared.

Today Iran, with its more stable government and its willingness to offer a haven to refugees from Afghanistan, Kurdistan, Azerbaijan, and Chechnya, is becoming once again increasingly important as a regional power. As at the time of World War I, it is surrounded on all sides by turmoil and bloodshed: the Kurds to the west, the Armenians and Chechens to the north, the Afghanis and Pakistanis to the east. It, alone, is peaceful. What's happening today on Iran's western flank—the conflict among the Kurds, the Iraqis, the Turks, and the Americans—is strangely reminiscent of the days when England dismantled the Ottoman Empire and changed the entire map of the region, leading to a chain of discord and war among all the affected peoples. Saddam Hussein's Iraq has become the focus of international power-brokering, and should it too be dismantled, the map of the region will once again be redrawn and the conflicts in the region will only intensify.

Ever since I was a student I've wanted to publish my memoirs. As an ambassador I took copious notes. Today most of those notes are gone, a casualty of the revolution. These words, therefore, have mostly been the product of memory, perhaps faulty at times but based on life as I lived it.

If I had my life to live over, I would change very little. I have lived well and made my mark on the world by germinating OPEC with the great Venezuelan oil minister Juan Pérez Alfonzo. Today I have my potato chip factory—much more automated than the oil refineries were in my day.

Sometimes I think of my father, who when he was sick would take a spoon of cognac in a large glass of water as medicine. Since he'd heard that alcohol made one drunk and that those who were drunk laughed, he would always begin to giggle afterward—and then laugh louder and louder.

Well, that's me too. I have seen much and lost much, but still a spoonful of cognac can make me laugh, for life is good.

APPENDIX

British Foreign Office Internal Memo Reporting the
Death of Prince Abdol Hossein Mirza Farman Farma

British Legation, Tehran
25th November 1939,

My Lord,

I have the honour to report that His Highness Abdul Hussein Farman-Farmayan, G.C.M.G., better known by his former title of Farman Farma, died in Tehran on the 22nd November.

2. On the death of the Farman Farma's son, Prince Firuz, which was reported in my despatch No. 13 of the 15th January 1938, no public announcement whatever was allowed to appear. Prince Firuz had long been under a cloud, and his death was allowed to transpire by way of rumour, inevitably accompanied by hints of foul play. The age of the Farman Farma (over 80), and the fact that he spent his latter years in free and quiet residence in Tehran, in undisturbed enjoyment of his astonishing powers of procreation, have disposed of any such suggestion in his case. Nevertheless, the fact that he was the most eminent surviving Qajar prince (please see No. 77 in Personalities), and that he was a well known public figure of an age that is now officially disparaged, caused the President of the Majlis, Monsieur Hassan Esfandiary, who is connected with him by marriage, to make enquiries of the Shah when it was seen that the old man was ailing and likely to die. Evidently the answer was reassuring, for the death and the holding of two memorial services, one in a mosque and the other at the deceased's residence, have been announced in the press over Monsieur Hassan Esfandiary's signature.

3. In view of the Farman Farma's close association with British authorities in the past, and since he held the honour of Knight Grand Cross of the Order of St. Michael and St. George, I sent my condolences, and the senior Iranian member of the Legation staff attended one of the memorial services. The Protocol Department of the Ministry of Foreign Affairs will be approached in order to recover the insignia of the G.C.M.G.

4. The death of the Farman Farma severs a most outstanding link with the period of the Qajar dynasty, and in particular with that of British intervention in South Persia at the time of the War of 1914–18. Since the establishment of the Pahlavi régime he has lived in retirement, but not in oblivion. For the family life of this remarkable old man has never ceased to be a subject of reverent comment. Until almost the end of his days he was mating and breeding, and though the birth rate in the later stages fell to less than three per annum, the aged father yielded to none in the assiduous care with which he kept track of all his numerous progeny, and it is a fact that he has been known, when an acquaintance made reference to one of the younger ones, to bring out a well thumbed little pocket-book in which particulars were entered, and turn up the relevant page. He is the type of Persian grandee that was once common, but under modern conditions is fast disappearing.

5. Copies of this despatch are being sent to the Secretary to the Government of India in the External Affairs Department, and His Majesty's Consular officers at Ahwaz, Kermanshah, Shiraz and Tabriz.

I have the honour to be with the highest respect,
My Lord,
Your Lordship's most obedient, humble Servant,

[signed] For H.M. Minister
Walter Roberts
The Right Honourable,
The Viscount Halifax,
K.G., G.C.S.I., G.C.I.E.,
etc., etc.

NOTES

Citations preceded by "FO" refer to Foreign Office documents at the British Public Records Office in London, England.

CHAPTER II: THE BLOOD OF THE QAJARS

1. Nasser-edin Shah, *The Diary of H. M. the Shah of Persia During His Tour Through Europe in A.D. 1873*, trans. J. W. Redhouse (London: John Murray, 1874), 142.
2. R. W. Ferrier, *The History of the British Petroleum Company*, vol. 1, *The Developing Years, 1901–1932* (Cambridge: Cambridge University Press, 1982), 589.
3. *The Correspondence of Abdol Hossein Mirza Farman Farma* (in Farsi) (Tehran: Iranian History Publications, 1990).
4. Ella C. Sykes, *Through Persia on a Side-Saddle* (London: John MacQueen, 1901), 149.
5. Sir Percy Sykes, *A History of Persia*, vol. 2 (London: Macmillan & Co., 1921), 503.
6. Private papers of Ahmad Shah shared with the authors by members of the family.

CHAPTER IV: THE DANGEROUS GAME OF OIL

1. John Arbuthnot Fisher, *Fear God and Dread Nought: The Correspondence of Admiral of the Fleet Lord Fisher of Kilverstone*, 2 vols., ed. Arthur Marder (Cambridge, Mass.: Harvard University Press, 1952), 438.
2. Daniel Yergin, *The Prize: The Epic Quest for Oil, Money & Power* (New York: Simon & Schuster, 1991), 172.
3. Lord Curzon to Sir Percy Cox, December 6, 1919, FO 70248/1257, dispatch #264.
4. Ibid.

5. For a complete review of the accounting irregularities, see Mostafa Elm, *Oil, Power and Principle: Iran's Oil Nationalization and Its Aftermath* (Syracuse, N.Y.: Syracuse University Press, 1992), 20–21.

6. Ferrier, *The History of the British Petroleum Company*, vol. 1, *The Developing Years 1901–1932*, op. cit., 603.

7. Yergin, op. cit., 271.

CHAPTER V: UNDER THE HAND OF REZA SHAH

1. See Roman Ghirshman, *Iran* (London: Pelican Books, 1961).

2. Rafael de Nogales, *Four Years Under the Half Moon* (Caracas: Biblioteca de Autores y Temas Tachirenses, 1991), 54.

3. V. Sackville-West, *Passenger to Tehran* (London: Hogarth Press, 1926), 142.

4. Report, 1937; FO 371/20837/16528.

5. Herman Norman to Lord Curzon, October 28, 1920, FO 371/4914/9573, 9600. Quoted in Houshang Sabahi, *British Policy in Persia, 1918–1925* (London: Frank Cass & Co., 1990), 52.

6. H. M. Knatchbull-Hugessen to A. Eden, January 27, 1936, FO 371/20048/16615.

7. *Setareh-ye Jehan*, January 20, 1936, FO 371/20048/16615, 80.

CHAPTER VI: THE OCCUPATION

1. William Fraser, "Anglo-Iranian Oil Company's Concession in Iran," FO 371/24572, 178.

2. "The Oil Revenues of Iran, Enclosure 2 to Annex," FO 371/24570, 195.

3. March 7, 1940, FO 371/24570, 188.

4. Ali Mansur, the prime minister who received the check, was a cousin of my brother-in-law Mohsen Khan's and described the incident to me himself.

5. Esther 2:8–9.

6. "Memorandum, BBC Broadcasts in Persian," August 14, 1940, FO 371/24570, 118–119.

7. W. Averell Harriman and Elie Abel, *Special Envoy to Churchill and Stalin 1941–1946* (London: Hutchinson, 1975), 90.

8. Yergin, *The Prize*, op. cit., 338.

9. Sir Winston Churchill, *The Second World War*, vol. 3, *The Grand Alliance* (Boston: Houghton Mifflin, 1948–53), 477.

10. Sir Reader Bullard to Foreign Office, September 15, 1941, FO 371/27216, 59.

11. Sir Reader Bullard to War Cabinet, September 16, 1941, FO 371/27216, 47e.

12. Masoud Behnoud, *From Seyyed Zia to Bakhtiar: The Governments of Iran for 60 Years* (in Farsi) (Tehran: Javidan Publishing Co., 1990), 146–147.

13. Laslo Havas, *Assassination at the Summit, Tehran 1943* (Paris: Editions J'ai Lu, 1968), 121.

CHAPTER VII: BEARS AND LIONS AT THE DOOR

1. Harriman and Abel, *Special Envoy to Churchill and Stalin,* op. cit., 282.
2. *Mozakerat Majles* (Majles Debates) (in Farsi), Tehran, December 12, 1925.
3. Faramarz S. Fatemi, *The USSR in Iran* (Cranberry, N.J.: A. S. Barnes & Co., 1980), 89–90.
4. Nader Ahari, "Portrait of a Political Enigma: The Life of Mirza Ahmad Khan Qavam al-Saltaneh and His Role in the Azerbaijan Crisis of 1946" (Senior thesis, Brown University, 1984), passim.
5. "Russia: Inside Story of the Squeeze on Iran," *Newsweek,* March 25, 1946, 42.
6. Fatemi, op. cit., 121.

CHAPTER VIII: A HOUSE DIVIDED

1. Ernest Bevin, July 20, 1946, FO 371/52735.
2. Letter in my files at the Ministry of Finance.
3. Fatemi, *The USSR in Iran,* op. cit., 141–142.
4. Ashraf Pahlavi, *Faces in a Mirror: Memoirs from Exile* (Englewood Cliffs, N.J.: Prentice-Hall, 1980), 89.
5. Ibid., 19.
6. Department of State, *Foreign Relations of the United States, the Near East and Africa, 1946,* vol. 7 (Washington, D.C.: Government Printing Office, 1969), 524.
7. Ibid., 524–527.

CHAPTER IX: REHEARSAL FOR A BREAKUP

1. A copy of the letter is in my collection.
2. Manucher Farmanfarmaian, *Considerations on the Problems of Oil* (in Farsi) (Tehran: Masoud Sad, 1953).
3. Anthony Sampson, *The Seven Sisters: The Great Oil Companies and the World They Made* (London: Hodder & Stoughton, 1975), 114.
4. Ernest Bevin to Sir Stafford Cripps, FO 371/75495, March 29, 1949; and Minute, Eastern Department, FO 371/75495, March 24, 1949.
5. Yergin, *The Prize,* op. cit., 427.
6. Sampson, *The Seven Sisters,* op. cit., 114.
7. Anibal R. Martinez, *Our Gift, Our Oil* (Dordrecht, Netherlands: Drukkerij D. Reidel, 1966), 86.
8. Quoted in Yergin, op. cit., 427.
9. Dean Acheson, *Present at the Creation* (New York: Signet, 1974), 650.
10. Foreign Office Meeting, January 16, 1951, FO 371/91524.
11. Ibid.
12. Ibid.

CHAPTER X: NATIONALIZATION

1. George McGhee, *Envoy to the Middle World: Adventures in Diplomacy* (New York: Harper & Row, 1983), 73.

2. William O. Douglas, *Strange Lands and Friendly People* (New York: Harper & Brothers, 1951), 117, 157, 166.

3. Henry Grady to Dean Acheson, October 31, 1950, in Department of State, *Foreign Relations of the United States, 1950,* vol. 5 (Washington, D.C.: Government Printing Office, 1950), 612–613.

4. Sir Oliver Franks to Foreign Office, April 29, 1951, FO 371/91528.

5. Sir Oliver Franks to Foreign Office, May 12, 1951, FO 371/91533.

CHAPTER XI: A LOSING BATTLE

1. UN Security Council Official Records, 560th through 565th Meetings, October 15–19, 1951.

2. Ibid.

3. *Financial Times,* October 22, 1951.

4. International Court of Justice, The Hague, *IJC Reports of Judgements, Advisory Opinions and Orders,* 1952, 94–114.

5. *Etela'at,* June 30, 1952.

6. Minute by Berthoud, June 21, 1951, FO 371/91550.

7. Kermit Roosevelt, *Countercoup: The Struggle for the Control of Iran* (New York: McGraw-Hill, 1979), flyleaf.

8. *Congressional Record,* June 29, 1953, 83rd Congress, 2nd session, 7647–7653.

CHAPTER XII: THE EAGLE LANDS

1. Minute by Fergusson, July 18, 1951, with notes by Eden in the margin, FO 371/98691.

CHAPTER XIII: THE NEW DESERT MASTERS

1. His Imperial Majesty Mohammad Reza Shah Pahlavi Shahanshah of Iran, *Mission for My Country* (London: Hutchinson, 1961), 142.

CHAPTER XIV: A PALACE REVOLUTION

1. Behnoud, *From Seyyed Zia to Bakhtiar,* op. cit., 163.

2. Ibid., 186. See also Marvin Zonis, *The Political Elite of Iran* (Princeton, N.J.: Princeton University Press, 1971), 45–47.

3. Behnoud, op. cit., 195.

CHAPTER XV: THE EMPEROR AND THE AMERICAN DREAM

1. Assadollah Alam, *The Shah and I: The Confidential Diary of Iran's Royal Court, 1969–1977* (London: I. B. Taurus, 1991).

CHAPTER XVI: IN THE KING'S SERVICE

1. Borzou Faramarz, *Towards the Great Civilization* (Tehran: Ministry of Information, 1974), 21–30.

CHAPTER XVII: REVOLUTION

1. Michael Ledeen and William Lewis, "Carter and the Fall of the Shah: The Inside Story," *The Washington Quarterly,* vol. 3, no. 2 (Spring 1980), 34, 36.
2. Conversation reported to the author by King Hussein's brother.

ACKNOWLEDGMENTS

Ye, with good spirit and fine looks I shall love alive or dead
I am the one to whom you always gave
Never allowing a moment to pass without responding,
Dead, I shall take you on my eyelids to the grave.
                                                    —IRAJ MIRZA

As we say in Farsi, *yek dast sedah nadareh*—one hand makes no noise. This has been a collaboration on many fronts, and I want to thank my family in general for their patience and my many friends for their support.

In particular, I wish to acknowledge my debt of inspiration to my brother Abol Bashar, who passed away some years ago with his own hope of writing a memoir unfulfilled. I also owe great thanks to my brother Hafez, who as a historian provided his own writings and research and helped me finalize the family tree. My sincere appreciation goes also to my brother Alaverdi, who as a scientist helped ensure accuracy by providing important backup documentation, as well as offering his lovely cabin in Woods Hole as an emergency office, just one of many ways he expressed his continual interest and support in the project. My nephew Sharogh Firouz has been invaluable in his sharing of photographs and other background material. Thanks also to my nephew and the artist among us, Nasser Ahari, who beautifully designed the family tree, a crutch without which even we would not have been able to keep everyone in the family correctly aged and related. Then there is my sincere thanks to my two sisters Leila Majd and Haideh Hakimi, and to my brother-in-law Ali Mahlouji and his wife, my sister Homi, who all advised me so wisely to leave my feuds aside. I also extend my thanks to Haleh Esfandiari, who helped in the transliteration of all the Farsi into English. Finally there is my dear friend and partner in my potato-chip factory (and previous diplomat in my embassy), Abbas Rostamizadeh, who encouraged me through thick and thin to write both my book in Farsi as well as this one.

And then there is my daughter and collaborator, Roxane, without whom this book would never have become a reality. Together we send this to our publisher as a labor of love.

— M. F.F.

INDEX

ABOUT THE AUTHORS

PRINCE MANUCHER FARMANFARMAIAN was born in Tehran in 1917, the thirteenth child in the vast harem of a Qajar patriarch. He studied petroleum engineering at Birmingham University in England before returning to Iran to become director general of petroleum, concessions, and mines after World War II. In 1958 he became director of sales for the National Iranian Oil Company. He also served on the board of the Consortium, the international oil conglomerate responsible for all of Iran's export sales. A key signatory of the 1959 Cairo agreement that resulted in OPEC, he was Iran's first ambassador to Venezuela.

An avid collector of carpets, ancient Persian pottery, and travelogues by European adventurers to the Middle East, Manucher Farmanfarmaian was a frequent guest at the Shah's court. After the Iranian Revolution, he became a citizen of Venezuela, where he lectured frequently on oil affairs at the Central University. He died in 2003 in Caracas. He was the father of two sons, Alexander and Teymour, and one daughter, Roxane.

ROXANE FARMANFARMAIAN was born in Salt Lake City, grew up in Holland, and graduated from Princeton University with a degree in Middle East studies. She returned to Iran just as the Iranian revolution erupted. During the turmoil, she founded *The Iranian,* an independent weekly newsmagazine. She then moved to Moscow, where she worked as both a reporter and a photographer, publishing pieces in *Time* and *The Christian Science Monitor* on early signs of the collapse of the Communist system. Upon her return to the United States in 1983, she worked for a series of magazines, including *Interview, Working Woman,* and *McCall's.*

In 1992 she moved to Caracas to write her father's autobiography. Upon its publication, she became the West Coast editor of *Publishers Weekly.* Roxane Farmanfarmaian is a Donner Atlantic Studies Scholar at the Centre of International Studies at Cambridge University, where she obtained her M.Phil. in international relations in 2002. She is the editor of the *Cambridge Review of International Affairs* and is finishing a doctoral dissertation on Democracy and Islam. She has one son, Kian.

ABOUT THE TYPE

This book was set in Garamond No. 3, a variation of the classic Garamond typeface originally designed by the Parisian type cutter Claude Garamond (1480–1561).

Claude Garamond's distinguished romans and italics first appeared in *Opera Ciceronis* in 1543–44. The Garamond types are clear, open, and elegant.